INTRODUCTION TO ECONOMICS

Also available from Glengarry Publishing
for use with *Introduction to Economics.*

Study Guide

by Dale M. Sievert

ISBN 0-9621796-1-2

For a description of the study guide, see
page viii in the Preface.

If your bookstore does not have the study
guide in stock, please ask the manager
to order copies for you and your fellow
students.

INTRODUCTION
TO
ECONOMICS

SECOND EDITION

DALE M. SIEVERT
Milwaukee Area Technical College

JOHN W. DODGE Jr.
Indiana Wesleyan University

GLENGARRY PUBLISHING

Cover Design: Robert Hanson
Cover Graphics: Pro Graphics, Inc.
Typesetting: Type Factory
Printer: R. R. Donnelley and Sons, Inc.
Copy Editor: Mary Ann Gross
Typist: Patricia Horschak
Indexer: Marilyn Flaig

Printed in the United States of America.

2 3 4 5 6 7 8 9 10 - 02

ISBN 0-9621796-0-4

Library of Congress Catalog Card Number 00-132316

Glengarry Publishing
W231 S5977 Molla Drive
Waukesha, Wisconsin 53189
Telephone: 262-542-3170
Fax: 262-542-5579
e-mail: glengarry@execpc.com
website: www.glenpub.com

U.S. Currency on Back Cover

1861 $5 Demand Note	1862 $2 Legal Tender Note
1879 $10 Refunding Certificate	1880 $5 United States Note
1891 $2 Treasury Note	1891 $10 Silver Certificate
1896 $1 Silver Certificate	1896 $2 Silver Certificate
1901 $5 Silver Certificate	1901 $10 United States Note

A New Name — A New Approach

In this second edition, John W. Dodge Jr. joins in our effort in making this textbook an even better vehicle for learning economics. He is a professor of economics at Indiana Wesleyan University.

In this edition, his efforts will involve developing a PowerPoint program and a website. Both will be of great benefit to students. PowerPoint is a computer program composed of several hundred "slides," each appearing on the screen separately. They contain written material, such as lecture-type notes, as well as charts and graphs. This material is available in several forms: on a computer disk or a CD-ROM; on our website; or in "hard-copy" form, either paper or transparencies.

Our website will contain an ever-growing array of materials to aid the students: photographs to illustrate concepts, frequently-updated reading lists, and student self-tests.

These materials will never be completed in any real sense. They will constantly be updated and enhanced. Contact us for what is currently available.

e-mail address: glengarry@execpc.com

website: www.glenpub.com

Preface

Introduction to Economics was written for a one-term introductory course in economics. Usually these courses are taken by students who are not majoring in economics or business and who do not intend to take another course in economics. This book could also be used in an introductory course to an MBA program or other graduate programs for students who have not had a course in economics.

To the Student

It would not be surprising if you were to ask why you should spend time taking an economics course and reading an economics book. After all, your time is limited and valuable. But that's precisely the reason for taking the course: your time is limited and valuable—as is the money you spend for tuition and books.

Studying economics involves learning how scarce resources, including such things as your time and money, can be used more wisely. Specifically, there are four main reasons why you will find it beneficial to study economics.

First, the terms and concepts you will learn will make it clearer to you what people are talking about when you are at your job.

Second, it will be clearer how your employer fits into the scheme of the entire economy and its relationships to other elements of the economy. In turn, that will help you to operate more effectively on the job in a market economy.

Third, you will be better able to understand the news and the discussion of public issues. Consequently, you'll feel better about yourself, and you'll be able to make better decisions that affect all of us, such as voting decisions.

Fourth, you'll be able to make better decisions as a consumer and as a manager of your own household, thereby raising your well-being.

To the Instructor

All introductory books do a fairly good, if not an excellent, job of presenting economic concepts. So, how is this book different?

First, less is taken for granted with respect to student understanding than most books. With many books, students miss many concepts or do not completely understand them because a proper groundwork had not been laid out. For example, compare how supply and demand is treated in most books to how it is done in *Introduction to Economics*. Most books jump right into demand, explaining how buyers act, followed by supply, and finish with price determination. In *Introduction to Economics*, the student is asked to consider why there are concepts like demand and supply in the first place. Of course, it is because there are markets. And why are there markets? Because we need places to make exchanges. Why make exchanges? Because specialization forces specialists to do so. Why specialize? To increase resource efficiency. Why do that? Because resources are scarce. Thus, we study price determination because of resource scarcity—the reason for studying economics in the first place. Used throughout the text, this more thorough approach gives the student a better and a more intuitive grasp of the concepts.

Second, the book has many unusual charts and graphs that are designed to present concepts that sometimes are difficult to grasp. For some examples, see Figure 2-7 on page 54 on price determination, Figure 3-2 on page 81 on the effects of innovation, Figure 6-1 on page 179 on the effects of imports and exports, and Figure 8-6 on page 251 on taxing equity.

Third, macroeconomics is presented on two distinct levels of rigor and thoroughness. The first approach uses more elementary flow charts and box diagrams that go a long way in giving students a solid understanding of the concepts and problems in macroeconomics. Some instructors will choose to stop at that level of presentation, either because of time constraints or to avoid a level of rigor better reserved for regular introductory courses. The second level of presentation uses the aggregate-demand/aggregate-supply approach. Of course, this approach allows the price level to change, thereby bringing in a greater deal of reality.

Ancillaries

The back of the book contains the answers to the critical-thinking questions in the text, as well as the answers to the problems at the back of each chapter. It also has a section on some mathematics that is useful in economics.

The student Study Guide, purchased separately, contains several study tips on the more difficult material in each chapter. Each chapter also has a fill-in-the-blanks section, a matching section on the terms, and some questions, both true-false and multiple-choice. Finally, each chapter has several exercises, most requiring some calculation. These exercises often require the pulling together of several concepts to generate the answers. Thus, they are very effective in both testing a student's understanding and in engendering it.

Instructor's Manual

Upon adoption, each instructor will receive a copy of the instructor's manual. It contains very detailed outlines of each chapter. The test bank appears next, and it contains over 2,000 multiple-choice and true-false questions. The bank is also available on computer disk. The program allows the teacher to edit question, add questions, and save tests.

There are over 50 exercises in the manual, identical in format to those in the student study guide. Only the numbers and other related information is different. The instructor can either use these as class work or home work. Also, they can be used as part of an exam or quiz.

Finally, the manual contains all the masters needed to make transparencies for the chart, graphs, and tables.

CONTENTS IN BRIEF

TABLE OF CONTENTS

You are about to begin your study of economics. Economics can be many things to people, including logical, illuminating, frustrating, confusing, boring, exciting, and fun. Some of the following quotes will give you a sample of the subject.

The ideas of economists and political philosophers, both when they are right and when they are wrong, are more powerful than is commonly understood. Indeed, the world is ruled by little else. Practical men, who believe themselves to be quite exempt from any intellectual influences, are usually slaves of some defunct economist.
– John Maynard Keynes

Studying economics won't make you a millionaire nor will it keep you out of the soup line. But it will give you a better understanding of how you got there.   – Anonymous

Every short sentence about economics is misleading (with the possible exception of this one).   – Alfred Marshall, English economist

Take care to be an economist is prosperity; there is no fear of you not being one in adversity.   – T. Zimmerman

In all of human misery, only the free market has come to bear on the age-old problem of scarcity.   – Benjamin Franklin

Remember that time is money. Waste neither time nor money, but make the best use of both.   – Benjamin Franklin

The riches of a country are to be valued by the quantity of labor its inhabitants are able to purchase, and not by the quantity of gold or silver they possess. Trade, in general, is nothing else but the exchange of labor for labor.   – Benjamin Franklin

People of the same trade seldom meet together, even for merriment and diversion, but the conversation ends in a conspiracy against the public, or in some contrivance to raise prices.   – Adam Smith

A national debt, if it is not excessive, will be to us a national blessing.
– Alexander Hamilton, Secretary of the Treasury for George Washington

Work spares us from three great evils: boredom, vice, and want.   – Voltaire

When it come to a question of money, everybody's of the same religion.   – Voltaire

Few of us can stand prosperity. Another man's I mean.   – Mark Twain

Government, like dress, is the badge of lost innocence.
– Tom Paine, 1770s American Revolutionist

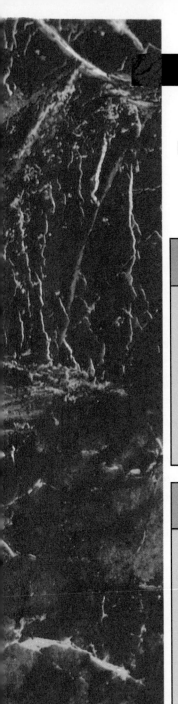

1

INTRODUCTION TO ECONOMICS

CHAPTER PREVIEW

We need resources to produce goods and services, but they are limited in amounts and qualities. That creates the economic problem, meaning we can't get all the goods and services we'd like.

Economics is the study of how we deal with that problem. Decision makers, from consumers to firms to government agencies, use cost-benefit analysis to ensure that resources are used in ways that maximize their economic welfare.

Societies have developed different systems to deal with the economic problem. Our society primarily uses the system called capitalism, whereas others use various types of socialist systems.

CHAPTER OBJECTIVES

After completing this chapter, you should be able to:

◆ Explain the reasons for studying economics.

◆ Explain the relationship between the efficiency of resource use and the economic problem.

◆ Describe a production possibilities curve and what it shows.

◆ Explain how to make decisions by using marginal analysis.

◆ Explain the purpose of asking each of the three Basic Economic Questions.

◆ Explain how each of the Basic Economic Systems answers the three Basic Economic Questions.

◆ Describe the two major characteristics of capitalism.

◆ Compare and contrast the various economic systems.

Decisions, decisions! You need to make them every day, deciding between alternatives. Should you buy a car or a motorcycle—or take the bus? Go to a movie or a concert? Buy steak or ham? Work overtime or stay home? Become a teacher or a computer programmer?

Making decisions or choices, which is necessary when there are limited resources, is often more difficult to do right than we think. It helps to have knowledge of certain basic economic concepts, which lead to certain behaviors. Once you've got the procedure down pat, making wise decisions can often be done quickly, seemingly without any forethought. However, failure to "get it right" to begin with, often in childhood, can doom one to a life of poor decisions. It's a bit like playing baseball without ever having been taught the right techniques. The bad habits that were learned during youth are never lost.

After a course in economics, your view of the world will be different. It's like a child who was discovered to have needed glasses. Up until that point, the child thought that everybody saw things with fuzzy edges and blurry centers. The child quickly appreciates the value of the glasses. Here's hoping that you appreciate your soon-to-be-found "clearer view" of the economic world.

THE BASIC FRAMEWORK OF AN ECONOMY

The subject matter of economics makes a lot of common sense. Essentially, common sense means doing things that are in our best interests. That is, doing things that make us better off after we do them. Also, it means *avoiding* doing things that would make us worse off after we do them.

Economists often say such common sense behavior means that people are rational. All the economic principles you will study in this book assume such rationality. Conversely, deliberate action to make oneself worse off is called irrational behavior.

Although all economic principles and subject matter can ultimately be reduced to common sense behavior, such principles don't always seem so simple or sensible. Why would farmers burn their wheat rather than take it to market? How is it that some benefit from inflation and others lose? Economics is filled with terms and jargon. It has many variables, or items that can change in magnitude, such as prices that can rise and fall. Similarly, interest rates, wage levels, and production costs can rise and fall. Furthermore, many of these variables depend upon or are affected by other variables. That is, there are relationships between such variables. For example, the amount of work you are willing to do partly depends upon the

Figure 1-1

Resources, Goals, and Welfare

People receive satisfaction when they achieve their goals, either materialistic or nonmaterialistic goals.

Materialistic goals, or goods and services, are produced with the resources of labor, capital, natural resources, and entrepreneurship.

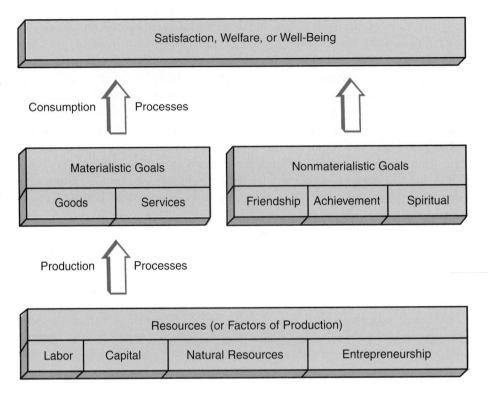

wage you would earn. Thus, there is a relationship between hours of work and wages.

In order to reduce the complexity of situations and relationships that contain many variables, economists make simplifying assumptions. With these assumptions and relationships, they build economic models that give a clearer view of the primary relationships in the economy. A model is an abstraction or simplification of the real world. This is necessary because the real world is too messy. We put on the sidelines issues or variables that seem less important for the issue at hand.

One economic model, shown in Figure 1-1, shows how human goals and objectives relate to satisfaction derived from them. When people achieve a goal or objective, they feel satisfaction. The word "welfare" could be used as a substitute for satisfaction. It refers to the well-being of a person. That is what the writers of the Constitution had in mind when they included "to promote the general welfare" in the preamble. This meaning of welfare is unrelated to public welfare programs.

Goals are arbitrarily split into two categories: materialistic goals and nonmaterialistic goals. A materialistic goal must be produced through the use of resources. Materialistic goals include both **goods**, which have physical substance, and **services**, which are intangible or have no physical substance. Examples of goods include pencils, farm tractors, suits, highways, and compressed gas. Examples of services include auto repair, police protection, education, and house painting.

> A **good** is anything that has physical substance that is produced by humans with resources.

Whereas welfare is the satisfaction enjoyed from all activities combined, *economic* welfare refers to the satisfaction derived from achieving materialistic goals. People get this satisfaction in the consumption process. An example of the consumption process is wearing a coat to keep warm or to be fashionable.

> A **service** is anything that has no physical substance that is produced by humans with resources.

Nonmaterialistic goals include the love of others, a walk in the woods, good grades, prestige, and spiritual well-being. These are the concepts people have in mind when they say, "The best things in life are free." They're not. Although they require few if any resources of the type covered in the following section, they do require time and effort. Economics deals almost exclusively with materialistic goals, although some economists use economic concepts to explain behavior such as religious acts and beliefs and other "nonmaterialistic activity."

RESOURCES AND THE PRODUCTION PROCESS

All individuals and societies must decide how best to allocate their resources in an effort to maximize economic welfare. A **resource** is anything necessary to produce a good or service. This occurs in a production process, where resources are converted into goods and services. A common synonym for resource is "factor of production." There are thousands of different resources that generally fit into one of four classes: labor, capital, natural resources, and entrepreneurship.

> A **resource** is anything necessary to produce a good or service.

■ **Labor** is any human effort to produce a good or service. Laborers not only include factory workers, but also teachers and computer programmers. Usually each laborer is concerned with only a part of the production process. Laborers do not organize the entire production process, leaving that to others.

> **Labor** refers to nonorganizational human effort needed to produce a good or service.

■ **Capital** is any good used to produce another good or service in a business or government enterprise. Examples of capital include lathes, robots, buses, office buildings, roads, computers, schools, and carpenters' saws. However, money is *not* capital because money doesn't directly produce anything. (Money is considered "financial capital," and capital goods are "physical capital." Thus, money can be used to obtain capital. Sometimes economists refer to another form of capital, "human capital," involving the education and training of workers.)

> **Capital** refers to any good used to produce another good or service.

4	*Chapter 1*

A **natural resource** is anything necessary in a production process that appears in nature.

Entrepreneurship refers to the characteristics of an enterprising person, one who provides financial backing and management for a business and who often has an innovative idea.

■ **Natural resources** appear in nature without human help. A synonym for natural resources is land. But land means more than just land used for farming, stores, or factory sites. Natural resources or land is a broad category that includes land and everything on it or in it that we can use, including iron ore, petroleum, limestone, fish, trees, animals, and the like.

■ **Entrepreneurship** refers to the enterprising nature of people. An entrepreneur oversees the entire production process, as distinct from the partial view of the laborer. Thus, an entrepreneur provides the organizational skills required for the success of an enterprise (or business). Besides that, an entrepreneur takes financial risks when entering a business. Although many people consider all business owners as entrepreneurs, this is not entirely true because entrepreneurs also possess a third characteristic. They introduce a new or improved good or service, or they might significantly improve the production processes of existing goods and services. However defined, entrepreneurs go into business to profit from their ideas. Some well-known entrepreneurs include Bill Gates (Microsoft), Henry Ford, Thomas Edison, and Ted Turner (Turner Broadcasting and CNN).

WHY WE STUDY ECONOMICS

Two facts of life lead us to study economics: 1) people have unlimited materialistic goals; and 2) resources are limited.

■ The first condition, people having unlimited numbers of materialistic goals, means there will never be a day when all people have everything they want. Most people will always be able to find use for another room in the house, another shirt, another vacation, another beer, another concert, and so on.

■ The second condition means that such resources as iron ore, water, grinding machines, computers, machinists, and electricians are not in inexhaustible supply. Therefore, we can only produce limited amounts of goods and services. Although people often say resources are scarce, limited and scarce are not the same. Something that is **scarce** is always limited, but it is also something that will increase economic welfare if more of it becomes available. You could also consider an item to be scarce if the amount available is less than the amount people would want if it were free.

Something is **scarce** if it is available in limited amounts and provides utility or benefit.

The economic problem refers to the difficulty caused by the combination of an unlimited desire for goods and services and limited resources.

When considered simultaneously, these two conditions create **the economic problem**. The "problem" is that because resources are scarce, people can get only a fraction of the goods and services they want.

Faced with the economic problem, people have two alternatives: 1) do nothing; or 2) make the best of a bad situation. Economics is the practice of making the best of a bad situation—that is, finding ways to get more satisfaction by using (or allocating) resources more wisely (or efficiently).

Because we want more things than we can produce with our scarce resources, we must choose which things get produced—and do without the rest. Rational people make such choices to maximize their economic welfare. **Economics** studies how members of society choose to use scarce resources in order to maximize economic welfare.

Economics is the study of how members of society choose to use scarce resources in order to maximize economic welfare.

You have similar problems in your own life. You probably want far more things than your money will buy. And you have more things to do than your time allows. Everyone faces this problem of scarce time and money (personal "resources"). Economic principles can help you use your time and money more wisely to increase your economic welfare.

RESOURCE ALLOCATION AND OPPORTUNITY COST

Because different ways to use resources result in different levels of welfare, we need a framework to decide how to use them. This section considers decision making in resource use. **Resource allocation** refers to the directing of scarce resources to specific uses. If decision makers are rational, resources should be allocated so they will maximize economic welfare. On the other hand, resource *misallocation* occurs if resources are used unwisely, leading to achieving less than our potential economic welfare.

Resource allocation refers to how resources are directed to specific uses.

Efficiency means using resources in a way that maximizes economic welfare. More explicitly, efficiency means producing a large amount of output with a given amount of resources. For example, an efficient secretary (the labor resource or input) can type 80 or 90 words (the output) per minute, whereas the average person can type about 50. Alternatively, efficiency means that just a few resources are needed to produce a given level of output. For example, an efficient carpet installer might be able to lay a 14-foot-square room in one hour. The average installer might take two hours. In these examples, efficiency refers to the ratio of inputs to outputs of a specific production process. However, the concept can be extended to mean the input-to-output ratio of a particular firm, a whole industry, or even an entire economy.

Efficiency refers to the ratio of inputs to outputs, or how well resources are used, either in a specific production process or in an entire nation.

How can it be assured that decisions will be made so that efficiency is achieved? Businesses, government agencies, and consumers all make such decisions, but consumers will be used as a model in the example below.

Rational consumers make decisions about the use of their scarce resources of time and money by using **cost-benefit analysis**. This means

Cost-benefit analysis refers to a method of comparing costs and benefits to determine whether resources should be used in a certain way.

Benefit refers to any satisfaction received from an economic activity.

they compare the benefits of spending time or money with the cost. The **benefit** is the amount of satisfaction derived from using resources. Let's assume you can measure the benefit you get from a product. After all, you probably often say that you like one product more than another. *How much more* is impossible to say or measure, but let's assume benefits can be "packaged" into "satisfaction units." (Some economists refer to them as "utils," from the word utility, in the sense that something is useful.) Each "unit" reflects a given amount of satisfaction received when consuming a good or service. Because each good or service provides different amounts of benefits, each yields different amounts of "satisfaction units" to the consumer.

For example, suppose Becky is thinking of buying a calculator for $60, which she values at 640 "satisfaction units" (or "units" for short). Should Becky buy the calculator? There's no doubt she likes it—640 "units" worth. Yet efficient use of Becky's resources requires that the calculator "pass" cost-benefit analysis. Specifically, the calculator must provide more benefits than costs. The benefit of the calculator is 640 "units." And the cost is $60, right? Not really. That's the *price,* the amount of money needed to buy one unit of something. People often mistakenly equate cost and price. Cost is what you give up when doing something. You might think that because Becky gives up $60 if she buys the calculator, $60 is the cost. That's not true. More correctly, cost is *the benefit or satisfaction* given up when doing something—not the money. Thus, if she parts with the $60 for the calculator, she gives up the satisfaction she *could* have had from something else selling for $60.

But *what* else? Suppose Becky can think of three other ways to use the $60. She could use the money to buy a painting (which would provide 475 "units"), a subscription to *Newsweek* (360 "units"), or running shoes (810 "units"). If the cost of the calculator is the benefit given up, is it 475, 360, or 810 "units"? Introducing a new term will help to answer the question. The **opportunity cost** of doing something, such as using resources, is the benefit given up from the *best* of the remaining alternative ways to use the resources. Becky's alternatives to the calculator are the painting, the *Newsweek* subscription, and the running shoes. The pair of shoes, at 810 "units," is the most beneficial. If Becky buys the calculator, she'll give up the satisfaction from the shoes. She'll get 640 "units"—but give up 810. It might be satisfying to buy the calculator, but it would be a foolish buy because the shoes would be even more satisfying. Because Becky wants to *maximize* her welfare, she will not buy the calculator.

Opportunity cost is the benefit given up from the best of the remaining alternative ways of using resources when they are used in a specific way.

This procedure is the same for any person, business, or government buying something that is scarce. What is received (the benefit) should exceed what is given up (the opportunity cost).

MARGINAL ANALYSIS

Economists rely on a concept called marginal analysis to make decision making easier. "Marginal" as economists use it means extra, additional, or the last of some action. The context usually helps explain what is meant by "marginal."

The purpose of marginal analysis is to help us decide how to limit the amount of any activity—that is, how to know when to stop it. Since scarcity means we cannot have everything we wish, we need some way to allocate our time, money, and efforts. Marginal analysis performs this function. For example, how do you decide to order a small, medium, or large pizza or soda? Or how do you decide to get a three-, four-, or five-bedroom house?

On a larger scale and from the standpoint of a business firm, an automobile producer currently making 2,000 cars will weigh the marginal costs and marginal benefits from producing the 2,001st car. If the benefits are

THINKING CRITICALLY ABOUT ECONOMIC QUESTIONS IN OUR LIVES

How Much Does It Cost You to See a Concert for Which You Purchased a $20 Ticket—If Tickets Are Being Scalped for $80?

Things to Consider

1. Beware of equating cost and price.

2. What was your opportunity cost of buying a ticket when they were available at the posted price of $20—and you did not expect them to be scalped later on?

3. What is your opportunity cost of going to the concert, using the ticket for which you paid $20—if there were no scalping activity? Is it the same as in Number 2, or is it different?

4. What would your opportunity cost have been of buying a scalped ticket for $80?

5. What would your opportunity cost be of using that "scalped" $80 ticket to see the concert—the same as in Number 4, or a different amount?

See page 448 for the "answer."

higher than the costs, the producer can make more profit by producing the extra car. But if marginal costs are higher than the marginal benefits, profit would be lost by making the car. Because the marginal benefits and marginal costs change as we consume or produce more, eventually we stop eating pizza, drinking soda, or producing more cars when the marginal costs exceed the marginal benefits. (See Chapter 14 for more detail.)

Following are some situations in which you may find yourself. In some, your actions may not be completely understandable unless you use marginal analysis. You enjoy a very good meal—but you leave some of it on the table. The rest (even an extra helping) would still taste good, and perhaps you are not even full. However, those extra mouthfuls involve increasingly large opportunity costs. The cost of extra bites rises partly because you may not wish to gain weight. Your first few bites will not add much or any weight to your body, for you need some energy to live. Beyond that you will gain somewhat with each bite. You may even be willing to gain a little if you can eat a great meal. But each *additional* bite is *increasingly* "costly" (in terms of weight gain). Eventually, the extra benefit from another bite is less than the extra cost, so you stop eating.

You invariably use every facial tissue in the box and every piece of tape of the roll. But you always toss out a jar of jam with a little left in the bottom. Your inconsistent and *seemingly* wasteful behavior is explained by the facts that: 1) each additional tissue you remove from a box or each additional piece of tape costs you the same effort as previous ones had; but 2) each additional spoon of jam costs you *more* effort—eventually so much that you leave some in the jar. With a new jar of jam, a quick flick of your wrist gets you a spoonful. With a half-empty jar you may need a *slower*, careful move to get the jam without getting your hand sticky. With a nearly empty jar, you *will* get sticky. Thus, you have an extra cost of time to wipe off your hand. Finally, those last traces of jam are so hard to get out (that is, they involve so much time—or cost) that you toss out the jar. (However, would you do the same if you were starving? If not, why not? What changed to explain your change in behavior—the benefit or the cost?)

Do you always finish what you start, such as projects around the house, hobby projects, or even college courses? If you don't, someone might criticize you for throwing away the time or money you have already invested in the activity. However, a good marginal analyst knows that the past is not important when deciding whether to go forward. The past (and all its costs, often called sunk costs) is "water over the dam" and must be ignored. The only things that count are the *extra* benefits and *extra* costs of continuing. If those extra costs exceed the extra benefits—stop what you've been doing. Or as the saying goes, "Don't throw good money after bad."

THINKING CRITICALLY ABOUT ECONOMIC QUESTIONS IN OUR LIVES

Why Do You Follow Other Cars as Closely as You Do?

Things to Consider

1. Assume that there are no other cars on the road near you except the car ahead of you, so you have no worry of anyone cutting in between you and the car ahead. Also, assume that you are either content to remain behind the car in front or that you are not able to pass for some reason.

2. What are your benefits of being one car length ahead of a particular position (such as moving from six car lengths behind the car ahead of you to five lengths)? What are your costs of moving up that one car length? These are known as your marginal benefit and your marginal cost.

3. Will the marginal benefit and the marginal cost of moving a second car length be the same as it was for the first? Or will they change?

4. What will be the marginal benefits and marginal costs of every other car length, right up to where you would be bumper to bumper?

See page 448 for the "answer."

PRODUCTION POSSIBILITIES CURVES

Saying that resources are scarce means that society doesn't have enough of them to make everything it wants or that we can make only so many things with our available resources. That is the economic problem.

Perhaps a graph can help explain the economic problem and the necessity of careful choice of resource use. Figure 1-2 shows a **production possibilities curve.** It shows all the possible combinations of two goods that can be produced with a given amount of resources.

A **production possibilities curve** is a graph showing all possible combinations of two goods that it is possible to produce with a set of resources.

Figure 1-2

Production
Possibilities Curve

Line ABCD, called a
production possibilities
curve, shows all the
combinations of two
goods, X and Y, it is
possible to produce with a
set of resources. It
assumes resources are
used as efficiently as
possible. The Zone of
Inefficiency shows output
combinations where
resources are not used
efficiently. The Zone of
Impossibility shows output
combinations that are
impossible to produce,
either because there are
not enough resources or
because they aren't
efficient enough.

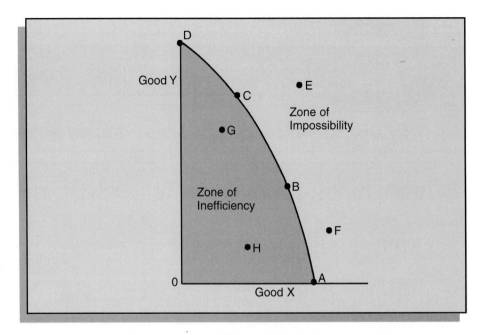

Imagine a simple economy that could produce only two goods, Good X and Good Y. Even if all this economy's resources produced only Good X, it could not produce an infinite amount of it. Rather, it could produce an amount represented by the distance between 0 and point A. Alternatively, if all the economy's resources were used to make only Good Y, an amount represented by the distance between 0 and point D would be produced. Points A and D show two of the possibilities of production of Goods X and Y. There are more possibilities, such as B and C—an infinite number, in fact. And each of these combinations would be represented by a point. This infinite number of points traces out a line, and this line is the production possibilities curve.

Any point "outside" the curve (such as E and F) represents combinations of Good X and Good Y that cannot be obtained because there are not enough resources or technical knowhow to produce them. This area is known as the zone of impossibility. Points "inside" the curve (such as G and H) represent levels of output that are less than what the economy is capable of producing. Thus, the area inside the curve is called the zone of inefficiency. Finally, notice that the curve is bowed out. This is because all resources are not equally suited to produce Good X and Good Y. It is one of the reasons why a nation that wishes to maximize its economic welfare will specialize in the use of its resources. (For a more detailed analysis of this concept, see the appendix on pages 33-35.)

BASIC ECONOMIC QUESTIONS

Virtually all decisions about resource use fit into three sets of questions, called **Basic Economic Questions**. If people are to maximize their economic welfare, they need to answer these correctly. They do so when they practice cost-benefit analysis. These questions are not answered in any special sequence. Rather, decision makers (consumers, firms, and government authorities) answer all of them simultaneously.

Basic Economic Questions are sets of questions to be considered in allocating resources, including What to Produce? How to Produce? and For Whom to Produce?

What to Produce?

So far, this book has concentrated on this first question (What to Produce?). Literally tens of millions of things could be useful or beneficial to us. Yet, because there are not enough resources to make them all, only relatively few are made. You might think most things that could be made *are* made. That isn't true because it's hard to visualize what *isn't* there— but could be. For example, cardboard sofas, passenger trips to the moon, and wine made from chokecherries could be produced. But society has answered the question of whether to produce cardboard sofas, for example, with a "no." Alternatively, it says "yes" to the question of whether to produce sofas made of wood and polyester fabric.

How do we know whether to say no or yes in each case? We simply ask if the resources needed to make each item give the most satisfaction as compared with their use in making any other item. If they do, the item is made. If not, it is not made. Of course, such decision making is difficult because it is hard to accurately measure the cost and benefit of each alternative use of our resources.

What-to-Produce questions often mean we must choose what to consume or buy. For example, decisions to order the steak or the pork on the menu ultimately lead farmers to raise more steers or, alternatively, more hogs. So, What-to-Produce questions might be thought of as What-to-Consume questions instead. We might also consider them as How-Much-to-Consume (or Produce)? because we often choose between larger and smaller quantities of items, such as steak.

How to Produce?

After a decision is made to produce something, selection must be made from among several possible production processes. Consider paper production. Paper comes from wood that is broken into tiny particles. That process could start either with: 1) people who cut off chunks of wood with knives; or 2) machines that lop off chunks. Next, the chunks are made into smaller bits until they look like oatmeal. Various machines or chemicals could do this job. Next, most of the water is extracted so the particles bind together to make sheets of damp paper. It is possible to hand-squeeze single sheets and air-dry them, as was done many years ago. But it is also possible to roll the sheets through a machine. Finally, cutting the paper into small sheets could be done with choppers, sharp rollers, or even lasers. Thus, there are many possible ways of making even simple things.

How-to-Produce questions are correctly answered by selecting production methods that use the least amount of all resources combined (labor, capital, entrepreneurship, and natural resources). In the case of paper, this ensures there will be as many resources as possible left over for making other things. In turn, that maximizes the output of goods and services and, therefore, economic welfare. Of course, minimizing resource use in production also ensures the lowest possible production cost.

For Whom to Produce?

Once goods and services are made, who will get them? Should everyone share equally in everything produced? Or should people who have hard, dangerous, or skilled jobs get more of everything—or less? In the United States, the distribution of goods and services is determined largely by income levels. Those with more income get to buy more goods and services. An individual's income depends mainly upon what price can be "commanded" in the marketplace for the resources that individual sells.

Many Americans believe this system gives the closest approximation to the "right" distribution of goods and services, the one maximizing society's economic welfare. Yet, alternatives are sought when government leaders make changes in tax laws, welfare programs, minimum wage levels, and immigration practices. Such changes result in some people becoming worse off, while others become better off.

The Basic Economic Questions are often interrelated, so that the answer to one affects the answer to another. The answers to What to Produce? determine the income levels of various individuals (thus, the answer to For Whom to Produce?). For example, more people wish to see Jim Carrey act in movies than hear your economics teacher lecture on the laws of supply and demand. So, Carrey gets the big bucks–and your teacher gets peanuts (comparatively speaking). Also, the answers to How to Produce? determine what types of tools, equipment, or other resources will get produced (What to Produce?). Again, that affects income levels of resource providers (For Whom to Produce?).

THE STRUCTURE OF ECONOMIC SYSTEMS

Members of different societies answer the Basic Economic Questions with their own unique **economic system**—an array of institutions, concepts, and procedures that address the economic problem. Each country's economic system has two major characteristics. The first is the method the country uses to answer the Basic Economic Questions. The second involves the people who own the resources and produce the goods and services.

There are three fundamental methods to answer the What, How, and For-Whom-to-Produce questions. These are the three **Basic Economic Systems**: the traditional, the command, and the market systems. All economies use each of these to a certain extent, but usually one system dominates in a country.

> An **economic system** refers to the institutions, concepts, and procedures a society uses to deal with the problem created by a scarcity of resources.

> **Basic Economic Systems** are the systems upon which the structures of all economies are based, including the traditional, the command, and the market systems.

The Traditional Economic System

A nation using the **traditional economic system** answers the Basic Economic Questions the same way each year. The same kinds of goods and services are made (exactly the same style, color, and so on); the same production techniques are used (therefore, there is no innovation); and the same income (and, therefore, the amount of goods and services) goes to each person. Whenever things are done today as before, *specifically because* that is the way they were done before, the traditional economic system is in use.

> The **traditional economic system** is a Basic Economic System where all economic decisions are made the way they were made in the past.

Although it seems foolish to use a system that guarantees stagnation, it does have a powerful advantage. It guarantees that a society will be safe from failures that might result from unwise innovation. An example could be a lethal buildup of salts in the soil following the introduction of irrigation from a river in a subsistence agricultural society in an arid region. (Rivers often carry dissolved salts from the lands their watersheds drain.) Thus, a decision to follow tradition could be a rational decision to avoid risk in a world of uncertainty and where vital knowledge is lacking.

Modern industrial societies don't use the traditional system often. Yet, it is (usually) used whenever people buy things (that is, decide What to Produce?) out of habit, such as always going to the same restaurants (and avoiding new ones) or always buying the same make of car. It is also used when production techniques (How to Produce?) do not change, even though better techniques exist. Finally, the traditional system is often used when people follow their parents' careers.

The Command Economic System

The **command economic system** is a Basic Economic System in which economic decisions are made by government authorities.

In a **command economic system**, some individual or group in authority decides what goods and services will be made, how they will be made, and who will get how much of each (their income). These decision makers could be: the whole of society acting by majority rule, appointed or elected officials, or dictators. An ordinary individual has little or no influence in such decisions. In extreme cases, the authority even decides: what people will eat and wear; where they will work, travel, and go to school; and how much they will earn. Examples in our society include compulsory education and inoculations, OSHA safety standards in workplaces, and minimum wage laws.

Every country has at least some elements of a command system. A synonym for a command economy is a central-directed economy because leaders in the (central) government make economic decisions directing or allocating the use of resources. A command economy is also sometimes called a planned economy because leaders can plan the use of resources well into the future.

The Market Economic System

A **market** is a place where people meet to exchange things of value.

A **market** is where people meet to exchange things of value. These include goods, services, resources (such as land or labor), and financial instruments (such as stocks, bonds, and credit).

In a barter system, two things of value are exchanged for each other, such as one good for another good. In modern societies, where barter is rare, usually only one thing of value is exchanged for something that *represents* value or, more accurately, represents *the power to purchase* something of value. That something is money. But money, in and of itself, has no value. People lost in the desert carrying lots of money soon discover that.

A market consists of: 1) a demand side, composed of buyers; and 2) a supply side, composed of sellers. Buyers and sellers voluntarily come to markets to improve their individual economic welfare. Because buyers and sellers seek to improve satisfaction from materialistic goals, they might be considered selfish people. But because such "selfish" moves usually are not designed to hurt others, we might consider most market transactions to be moral. However, although no one is forced to buy or sell anything, well-functioning markets require a certain level of honesty in sellers and buyers.

In a *free* market, buyers and sellers make exchanges voluntarily because exchanges increase the economic welfare of each. Occasionally markets that are *not* free are encountered, where exchanges occur *involuntarily* in "compulsory markets," such as forced labor in a military draft or compulsory community service (or "national service," as is sometimes proposed). Another example is being forced to wear clothes in public (that is, you must purchase clothes in the clothing market and wear them).

Before exchange voluntarily occurs in free markets, not only must there be buyers and sellers, but there also must be agreement on the rate of exchange—that is, how much of one thing of value trades for the other thing of value. In modern societies, where market participants rarely barter, this rate is known as the price, or the amount of money to be traded for one unit of a good, service, or resource.

Thus, a market exists for an item when there are buyers, sellers, and agreement on a price. If all three of these do not exist for, say, typewriters, then the question, "Shall we produce typewriters?" (a What-to-Produce question) is answered no. If all three do exist, the answer is yes. There is no need to look to the past or to ask the government if it is all right to make or buy typewriters. (Incidentally, in the United States, the question to produce typewriters or not was answered yes only until 1995, when the last U.S. maker of them, Smith-Corona, closed down.)

How-to-Produce questions use resource markets for answers. Producers often can make things in different ways by using different resources. For example, manufacturers can stitch coats by hand or with sewing machines. In a market system, the owner or manager of a manufacturing firm examines the price of each resource it could use in making an item. The item is then made in the way that minimizes the cost, which depends upon resource prices. Owners make such decisions in their own self-interest. But this also saves their customers' money because lower costs can lead to lower prices. Everyone can win.

The market system answers For Whom to Produce? in a roundabout way. "For Whom" really means who will receive the goods and services, which is determined by income levels. Those having higher incomes will receive more goods and services than others. People, of course, own resources such as labor, land, and capital. These people earn income by selling resources. Thus, in a market system, your income depends upon how many resources you sell as well as the prices of those resources.

This concludes the analysis of the first characteristic of a country's economic system. Next examined is the second characteristic—who owns the resources and does the production. In a modern economy, unlike an economy of self-sufficient individuals, there are two fundamental types of resource ownership: 1) resources can be privately owned; or 2) they can be publicly owned.

THINKING CRITICALLY ABOUT ECONOMIC QUESTIONS IN OUR LIVES

Do You Eat the Right Animals?

Things to Consider

1. "Eating the right animals" refers to "eating the right kinds of meat," such as pork, beef, or poultry. If you are a vegetarian, rephrase the question, "Should You Eat Meat?"

2. Would you ever consider eating horses, giraffes, porcupines, lizards, or pandas on a regular basis? If not, why not?

3. Think of how What to Produce? *should* be answered to maximize your economic well-being.

4. How *do* you answer What to Produce? Is it the same as your answer in Number 3?

   See page 449 for the "answer."

Resources That Are Privately Owned

Privately owned resources refer only to capital and natural resources because labor and entrepreneurship always belong to the individual. (Do not equate private resources with "private property," which includes consumer goods owned by individuals, such as your clothes and car.) When there is private ownership of resources—that is, in a system that allows **private property**—only some people own capital equipment or natural resources. Capital equipment could be owned by one person or a group. A group could include several people or thousands, as with ownership of General Motors (actually, the equipment and other assets of GM). Another example of private property is the land of David King, an Ohio farmer.

An economy with private property uses the private enterprise system. A **private enterprise** is an organization that produces goods and services with privately owned resources in order to improve the economic welfare of the owners. Examples of private enterprises include Ford Motor Company, Bob's Auto Repair, and David King Farms, Inc.

Private property refers to resources owned by one or more individuals.

A **private enterprise** is an organization that produces a good or service and is owned by one or more individuals.

Publicly Owned Resources

Public property refers to capital and natural resources that belong to everyone in the society. Public parks, national forests, most highways, and public schools are all examples. Individuals cannot sell their share of these resources, possess more than anyone else, or exclude anyone else from using them.

Public property refers to resources owned by all the citizens of a government.

Nationalization refers to the takeover of privately owned resources by the public, generally at the central (national) government level. The takeover can be involuntary or voluntary, and the former owners usually receive some payment.

The opposite of nationalization is privatization, which occurs when publicly owned resources are sold to private individuals. For example, a city-owned airport such as New York's Kennedy airport could be sold to private investors. Privatization also can mean contracting out to private businesses for government services that were previously performed by government enterprises. Examples include garbage pickup, fire protection, and prison operations. Finally, privatization occasionally refers to situations where the government provides a voucher that can be used to buy a good or service at a privately owned business. An example is a school voucher, which is paid for with public tax dollars but can be used to obtain an education in a private school as well as a public one.

When the public owns resources, **public enterprises** (or government enterprises) produce goods and services with them. The intent is not to improve the economic welfare of specific individuals through profits as in the private enterprise system, but rather to benefit the entire society. The U.S. Postal Service, public schools, and the U.S. Army are examples of public enterprises.

A **public enterprise** is a government enterprise that produces a good or service.

MAJOR ECONOMIC SYSTEMS

You just learned the two primary characteristics of any society's economy: 1) which Basic Economic System dominates (command or market); and 2) who owns the resources (private individuals or the public). Each characteristic involves an extreme position that a nation can choose. That is, a nation can choose to have either a complete command economy or a complete market economy. Likewise, its resources either can be completely publicly owned, with government enterprises producing all the goods and services, or they all can be owned by private enterprises. More realistically, a nation can choose to have any combination of: 1) the command or the market system; and 2) private or public ownership of resources.

In this section, both of these characteristics are combined, allowing the placement of all economies into four categories of economic systems: capitalism, authoritarian capitalism, market socialism, and authoritarian socialism. However, no country fits perfectly into any of these categories. These labels merely mean a country is generally *closest to* one of these models of economic systems.

Capitalism

Capitalism is an economic system whose main characteristics include individuals making decisions about their privately owned resources in a system of competitive, free markets.

Competition refers to the struggles of market participants for the purpose of maximizing their economic welfare.

The economic system of **capitalism** has two major characteristics: 1) decisions about resource use are made in a system of free markets; and 2) privately owned resources are used to produce goods and services by private enterprises. Commonly used synonyms for capitalism are a free enterprise system and a market economy.

All people, including owners of firms, face a personal scarcity of time and money. Buyers and sellers alike deal with this problem in market exchanges. Individuals try to maximize their economic welfare by acting in their own self-interest. **Competition** refers to the struggles of the market participants for the purpose of maximizing their economic welfare. Competition is not limited to struggles between sellers. Buyers often compete with other buyers for scarce items. Recall that in a *free* market no one has any control over any other market participant or over the price. However, consumers essentially control producers. Producers who don't realize the consumer is king (or "sovereign") in free markets soon become paupers.

It might seem that millions of people, who are all trying to act in their own self-interest, would lead to a destructive free-for-all. In *The Wealth of Nations* in 1776, Adam Smith argued differently. In acting selfishly, he said, each person:

> intends only his own gain, and he is . . . led by an *invisible hand* to promote an end which was no part of his intention. By pursuing his own interest, he frequently promotes that of the whole society more effectually than when he really intends to promote it.

Thus, selfish people who try to sell things help others, though unintentionally. The reason is that for sellers to become rich, they must be successful at selling. And what sells the best is what buyers want the most—that is, what satisfies them the most. Adam Smith put this very well with this famous passage:

It is not from the benevolence of the butcher, the brewer, or the baker, that we expect our dinner, but from their regard to their own interest. We address ourselves, not to their humanity but to their self-love, and never talk to them of our own necessities but of their advantages. Nobody but a beggar chooses to depend chiefly upon the benevolence of his fellow citizens.

In pure capitalism, there would be no use made of the traditional or command economic system and there would be *no* publicly owned resources. The government neither would produce any good or service nor try to regulate any economic activity. All goods and services—cars, food, education, security (police, etc.), mail delivery, roads, insurance, and so on—would be provided by privately owned firms. Also, individuals would make economic decisions with no interference by any person or government. People could buy any clothes, drugs, and reading material they wanted, and they could travel anywhere. A government policy that favors such an economy is called **laissez faire**, which means "let the individual be." (Take care not to confuse this use of the term with its more common use in American history, most notably in the late 1800s, the "laissez-faire period." That period had anything *but* free markets, when business owners commonly sought to restrict competition, often with the help of government.)

A **laissez faire** policy is a government policy of minimum interference with the economic affairs of businesses and into all markets.

No country has ever had an economy in which all persons could do everything they pleased. That would lead to socially unacceptable problems, including pollution, widespread use of automatic weapons in public, and other offensive economic activity (far worse than we already have), such as bizarre house colors, rampant cocaine consumption, and lewd entertainment. In pure capitalism, there also would be no public police protection, public highways, or public parks. Because such a society is generally unacceptable, people, through government, *do* interfere with the economic decisions of others and *do* insist upon some public provision of goods and services.

Authoritarian Capitalism

Many nations are called capitalist simply because they have private enterprise systems. But capitalism is not synonymous with private enterprise. Capitalism uses the private enterprise approach to production, along with the *free* market system. Many nations, incorrectly referred to as having capitalist economies, allow private enterprises but have relatively few free markets.

Authoritarian capitalism is an economic system where most resources are privately owned and where heavy use is made of the command economic system.

Many of these "capitalist" nations actually have an economic system we might call **authoritarian capitalism**. Such a system has two major characteristics. First, a nation with such a system has a private enterprise system, as in ordinary capitalism. Second, and in contrast to capitalism, such a nation makes heavy use of the command system to answer the Basic Economic Questions.

As with pure capitalism, no such *purely* authoritarian capitalistic economy exists. Nations lie somewhere between the two extremes. Yet there are many examples of nations with *largely* authoritarian or restricted capitalistic systems. National socialism or fascism—of which Nazi Germany was an example—is such a system. Once Hitler came to power, his government dictated much of the production of goods and services, especially those related to the military, even though the firms were in private hands.

Many countries today, although called capitalist, are really authoritarian capitalistic. Virtually all of Latin America uses the private enterprise system. However, it is difficult if not impossible for many Latin Americans to enter business or certain occupations. Often restrictions take the form of government red tape, bribery, and the like. In other cases, a rigid class structure prevents upward economic mobility. Equally restrictive is a lopsided political system that denies political power to people with little economic power. As a consequence, a sizable percentage of economic activity is done illegally on the black market. However, in the last 10 years or so, many of these nations have been freeing up their economies and are selling off many public enterprises as well.

South Korea, Taiwan, and Singapore are examples of Pacific Rim nations with authoritarian capitalism that have been more successful economically. An important difference in these countries compared with Latin American countries is the greater ease of entering business.

Another Pacific Rim nation, Japan, is fundamentally capitalistic. But it also has much government involvement, though it is less authoritarian than its neighbors. The government's most significant effect is through its industrial policy, where certain industries are targeted for expansion and development. The government provides money and other assistance to these industries through various agencies.

Finally, a form of authoritarian capitalism that might be called amended capitalism should be noted. Here, although free markets generally are used to answer the Basic Economic Questions, these answers are changed or amended by the government *after* free markets were used. For example, the income of many people is determined by what they earn in the marketplace *plus* what the government grants them in the form of welfare, subsidies, or tax breaks. Governments also help certain people to increase their incomes by granting privileges that reduce competition between those in particular markets. This includes granting power to form labor unions or requiring licenses to enter a profession or business. In such cases, justification for such intervention usually centers on the alleged failure of capitalism to provide equity or fairness to people in those markets.

Authoritarian Socialism

There are several forms of socialism, and this section and the next will divide them into two major groups. The first is **authoritarian socialism** (or **communism**). Its first characteristic is the public ownership of resources. In this system, government or public enterprises produce goods and services. The second characteristic is that government authorities make all major economic decisions and many minor ones as well.

Socialists believe that private property contributes to large and inequitable income differences and, consequently, to conflict between the upper and lower classes. Karl Marx and Friedrich Engels wrote of this class struggle in their *Communist Manifesto* in 1848. They wrote of the struggle between the workers (the proletariat) and the business owners (the capitalists). The *Manifesto* ended with:

> The proletarians have nothing to lose but their chains. They have a world to win. Workingmen of all countries, unite!

In his book *Das Kapital,* Marx argued that capitalists robbed laborers of their output. He maintained that all economic value embodied in products came from the efforts of laborers and that the owners of capital paid workers only a fraction of their value. Thus, he believed that laborers were exploited and would face increasing misery as capitalism developed. Eventually, workers would tolerate their miserable condition no longer and would revolt.

In Marx's vision, after the revolution a "dictatorship of the proletariat" would emerge, in which the workers would exercise control through the state. After all elements of capitalism were wiped out, the state would "wither away," leaving a classless and communistic (communal) society. Once the concept of profit was gone, all economic decisions (including decisions by individuals) would be made for the benefit of the *community*, not necessarily for the individual. In such a society, workers would produce as much as they could but would consume only what they needed. Thus, the communist doctrine: "*From* each according to his ability, *to* each according to his needs."

Authoritarian socialism is an economic system where most resources are publicly owned and where government authorities answer most economic questions.

Communism is a form of authoritarian socialism popularized by Marx and Engels, where eventually the state would disappear, with all production carried out in the best interest of the community.

This brings up the second characteristic of authoritarian socialism: the Basic Economic Questions are answered collectively by a government body that acts for all the members of society. Decisions regarding resource use (What?, How?) and income distribution (For Whom?) are centrally directed (answered) rather than individually directed as in a system of free markets. Theoretically, because decision making and property ownership are communal, the best interests of all are met.

Until the 1989-1992 period, many countries were labeled Marxist (or communist), including the Soviet Union, East Germany and all the other East European countries, Mongolia, Nicaragua, Angola, and a few others. Today, Cuba, China, North Korea, and Vietnam still call themselves Marxist. However, none of these nations had (or have, in the case of Cuba, China, North Korea, and Vietnam) much resemblance to the plan of Marx. Workers, whether on farms, in offices, in factories, or in mines, have had little voice in economic decision making. Instead, nondemocratically elected officials decided the answers to the major economic questions, such as the output levels of food, steel, autos, and coal, as well as income levels of all citizens, and sometimes where people worked. China and Vietnam have allowed significant numbers of private enterprises to become established, especially since the early 1980s (of course, this contradiction to socialism assumes that people have not been convinced to put the interests of society ahead of their own—which *has* been a good assumption for all communist nations).

Market Socialism

Purely authoritarian socialist economies have some severe problems. For one, because individuals are not rewarded for being exceptionally innovative or productive, such economies do not have high economic growth rates. People with good ideas, which may take great effort to implement, often don't bother with the effort. They also are likely to resent sharing the benefits of their ideas with others, or not being allowed to make many economic decisions for themselves.

Market socialism is an economic system that combines the public ownership of resources with a system of markets that largely directs resource use.

However, because many people do prefer the public ownership of resources, a hybrid of capitalism and communism, called **market socialism**, appeals to them. In this system, the public owns the resources (and government enterprises produce things), but the What, How, and For Whom questions rely upon the market system for answers.

Although firms are government (publicly) owned, government authorities do not decide what goods and services to make. Individual buyers do, acting in their self-interest in markets where the sellers happen to be public enterprises. Yet, although different from capitalistic sellers who own their businesses, the sellers act like capitalists in promoting their self-interest. That is because *several* government enterprises make each kind of good or service. The more successful a particular enterprise is, the higher the incomes for its managers and workers. For example, 20 elementary schools in a city could accept students from anywhere in the city. The better schools would tend to get more students, and the poorer schools would get fewer students, perhaps even having to close.

As with capitalism, there is little role for government central control in the pure form of market socialism. Even prices are determined without government intervention. There also is much personal economic freedom, which satisfies those who value such freedom.

MICROECONOMICS AND MACROECONOMICS

Economic subjects and concepts can usually be split into two categories, microeconomics and macroeconomics.

Microeconomics deals with the economic behavior of individual units in the economy. Examples of microeconomic units include a consumer, a firm, an industry, a laborer, a saver, and an investor. Microeconomic concepts cover such topics as: what affects the price of an individual good or service; what determines the output level of a firm; how tax rates affect the typical investor in stocks; and how increased competition affects prices in the airline industry. Chapters 1-7 and 14 deal with microeconomic concepts.

Microeconomics is the branch of economics that studies the economic behavior of individuals, including consumers, firms, and resource sellers, and the variables and relationships relating to them.

Macroeconomics deals with the behavior of larger or aggregated sectors of the economy. These include all consumers combined, all manufacturing firms combined, the labor force, and the like. Macroeconomic concepts cover such topics as: the price level and how much it changes (the inflation rate), total output of the nation (measured by the gross domestic product), the unemployment rate, and the effect of changes in the tax rate on savings or interest rates. Chapters 9-13 deal with macroeconomics.

Macroeconomics is the branch of economics that studies the behavior of large sectors of the economy and their related variables and relationships.

A BRIEF SURVEY OF ECONOMIC THOUGHT

This final section of the chapter gives a brief introduction to major economic ideas and beliefs from ancient times to the present. This survey of economic thinkers is essentially Western in nature. Other societies would have quite a different list.

Economic Thought From Ancient to Medieval Times

In 400 B.C., the ancient Greeks produced the first significant writings on economics. In fact, the word economics has its base in a Greek word, *oikonomos*. Essentially, it means household management, referring to the management of resources of a community as well as a "house." Plato wrote in *The Republic* that there should be public or common ownership of property. He also saw the wisdom of specialization and the division of labor. His follower, Aristotle, defined wealth as the necessities of life that people possessed. He objected to the use of currency, lending for interest (usury), and commerce for personal gain. Like the Greeks before them, the Romans did not place a high regard on the accumulation of power and wealth through commerce.

After the Roman Empire fell in the fifth century, the lack of political order led to the development of feudalism in Europe. The Middle Ages feudal estate, led by the lord, directed production and determined consumption patterns of the serfs. Each estate was almost completely self-sufficient and self-governed in a nearly complete economy. There was very little trading or market activity as we know it. St. Thomas Aquinas, a prominent philosopher of the Middle Ages, proposed a system of "distributive and compensatory justice." Distributive justice focused on who should receive how many goods and services. Compensatory justice aimed at finding a fair or "just price" for whatever exchanges occurred. To this day people use the term "fair price" for an item, such as a used car. Many beliefs about economics in the Middle Ages stemmed from church doctrine. For example, the church condemned lending for interest and noted that the Bible says, "Love of money is the root of all evil."

Mercantilism and the Enlightenment

Mercantilism was a system where governmental policies were established to promote exports and discourage imports for the purpose of accumulating gold and silver.

Feudalism declined significantly by the thirteenth and fourteenth centuries, accompanied by the formation of stronger nations. Throughout this period and later, people gradually gained the freedom to enter into market contracts, giving them the opportunity to accumulate material wealth. In the economic sense, a contract is an agreement between a buyer and a seller to exchange a given amount of some item for a specified amount of money or other thing of value (usually called the price). By about 1500, a philosophy had developed that a nation also could improve its lot by accumulating wealth in the form of gold and silver. Called **mercantilism,** it promoted exports, paid for in gold and silver. It also discouraged imports because they would drain gold and silver from the country. The plundering of New World gold and silver by the Spanish in the 1500s was partly a result of this philosophy. Mercantilist policy also included the granting of monopolies, regulation of wages and prices, and the exploitation of colonies by the government—all designed to boost output to be sold abroad for gold and silver.

The eighteenth century, the century of the Enlightenment, was a period of discovery in all areas, starting with many scientific discoveries, such as Newton's laws. Then, because the church and the ancients were generally judged to be wrong in scientific areas, people began to question the church's views on materialistic matters. Newly aware that natural subjects such as rock and air obeyed natural laws, philosophers proposed that there were similar "natural laws" for humanity to obey in economic life. Therefore, it was believed that human misery occurred because such laws were violated.

Much of the impetus of the American Revolution stemmed from such ideas. In 1625, Hugo Grotius (1583-1645) spoke of the "inalienable and indestructible rights of the individual" in such a "state of nature." John Locke (1632-1704) emphasized the "natural rights" of life, liberty, and property and said that all people had a right to the fruits of their individual labor. In 1762, Jean Jacques Rousseau (1712-1788) wrote the key phrase used in the Declaration of Independence 12 years later—the "inalienable rights of life, liberty, and the pursuit of happiness."

The first group of true economists, called the **Physiocrats,** appeared during this period. The term comes from the Greek word *physiocracy*, which means "the rule of nature." They believed in natural law and that all wealth comes from the land. Thus, the "husbandmen" (farmers, fishermen, and miners) were the only true producers. The Physiocrats regarded industrialists, craftsmen, and tradesmen as "sterile" or unproductive. They wanted little government involvement in economic affairs, believing in *laissez faire et laissez passer*—that is, "don't interfere, for the world will take care of itself." Because "true" nature did not require government interference, the Physiocrats believed the economy didn't either.

Physiocrats were the first true economists, who believed in natural law and that all wealth came from the land or working it.

Thomas Jefferson and many of the other Founding Fathers were strongly influenced by the concept of natural rights and the Physiocrats. Many were farmers (or "planters") and felt strongly that the success of democracy depended upon the ownership of land and farming of it by citizens. The Northwest Ordinance of 1787 and various land acts extending to the Morrill Act of 1862 aided the establishment of "smallholder agriculture" (small farms). These acts led to the establishment of "the family farm," which we still seek to maintain, and something like a purely competitive market structure (covered in more detail in Chapters 4 and 5).

The Classical Economists

The Physiocrats set the stage for the most influential writer in economics, Adam Smith (1723-1790). In 1776, he wrote *The Wealth of Nations,* in which he supported a new economic system based upon free markets with little government intervention. The book serves as the basis for capitalism, a system most Western nations generally use today. Smith fought for an end to government promotion of mercantilist policies, the granting of monopolies, and subsidies (money grants to businesses).

In 1798, another Classical economist, Thomas Malthus (1766-1834), predicted perpetual misery in his *Essay on the Principles of Population.* He believed population would increase at a geometric rate while food output would increase at only an arithmetic rate, leading to mass starvation. The English essayist Thomas Carlyle branded economics "the dismal science" largely because of this pessimistic outlook, and economics never lost the name.

David Ricardo (1772-1823) extended and clarified Smith's work by explaining that rent on farmland was high as a consequence of high grain prices. This idea was revolutionary because people previously believed grain prices were high because land rents were high. Ricardo also explained how trade or exchange occurs by introducing the concept of the "law of comparative advantage" (covered in Chapter 3). Finally, he refined Malthus's "iron law of wages," which held that workers' wages would gravitate toward subsistence levels in a period of no economic growth.

Leon Walras (1834-1910) founded the Lausanne School of economic thought. He believed that economics could become more precise and useful if it used mathematics. In this he actually followed the father of mathematical economics, Antoine Augustin Cournot (1801-1877), who introduced supply and demand curves into economics. Walras is best known for developing general equilibrium analysis, in which he showed how each individual market is connected to all other markets. He also explained how prices can be determined in competitive markets through *tatonement* (a French word meaning groping, likened to people trying to find their way in the dark). Walras wrote *Elements* (Volumes I and II) in 1874 and 1877. Alfredo Pareto (1848-1923) elaborated on Walras's work. He made general equilibrium analysis easier to understand and established the conditions necessary for maximizing welfare in society.

Alfred Marshall (1842-1924) wrote *Principles of Economics* in 1890. Extremely respected, he is especially known for his theory of consumer behavior, for his connection of supply and demand, and for his insistence on precise analysis, especially in his use of mathematics.

Socialist Writers and Thought

Although many people believe that Karl Marx (1818-1883) was the father of socialism, some basic premises of this theory appeared in the Bible and other theological works. Marx was only one of many socialists. The **French Utopians** were the first modern proponents of socialism. A prominent Utopian was Francois Emile Babeuf (1760-1797), guillotined during the French Revolution for promoting a French socialist state. Other early framers of socialist thought include Louis Blanc (1811-1882), who coined "from each according to his ability, to each according to his needs." Another was Jeremy Bentham (1748-1832), who sought an economy that would provide the "greatest good to the greatest number." The more famous socialists Karl Marx and Friederich Engels (1820-1895) had their influence 50 to 100 years after these early socialist thinkers. It was their writings, including *The Communist Manifesto* and *Das Kapital* (Vol. I, 1867; Vol. II, 1886; Vol. III, 1895), that aided the development of communist movements.

French Utopians were a group of early socialists of the 1700s who were concentrated in France.

Although not classified as a socialist, John Stuart Mill (1806-1873) influenced socialist thought profoundly when he criticized the distribution of income and wealth in capitalist systems. His criticism also opened the door to government intervention in the economy, especially with respect to income distribution (the For-Whom-to-Produce question). He wrote *Principles of Political Economy* in 1848.

The Austrian School of Economics

The Austrian School of Economics consisted of several prominent economists, including the founder, Carl Menger (1840-1921). He was one of three economists who introduced the marginal utility theory, along with Walras and William Stanley Jevons (1835-1882). Menger and his students, including Eugen Bohm-Bawerk (1851-1914), developed models of capitalist economies. Bohm-Bawerk's student, Joseph Schumpeter (1883-1950), wrote *The Theory of Economic Development* in 1912. He showed how entrepreneurs promote change through "creative destruction" of the existing economic order.

Ludwig Von Mises (1881-1973) founded the Modern School of Austrian Economics. Two of his books, *Socialism* (1922) and *Human Action* (1949), established his stature as a champion of freedom of the individual and the capitalist model. His student and like-minded follower, Friederich Hayek (1899-1992), gained fame with his own book, *The Road to Serfdom,* in 1944 in which he attacked government intervention in the economy as a destroyer of individual liberty.

20th Century Economic Thought

Several economists in the early 1900s rocked the boat of "laissez faire capitalism" (an economy free of government intervention). They are called **institutionalists** because they often attacked various economic and social institutions as roadblocks to higher economic welfare. They believed that institutions, customs, and social mores and values were as important in explaining economic behavior as the traditional economic concepts such as supply and demand. Some prominent institutionalists include: Thorstein Veblen (1857-1929), author of *The Theory of the Leisure Class* (1899); John R. Commons (1862-1945), who provided the political Progressives with ideas on tax reform, public utility regulation, and labor legislation; and Wesley C. Mitchell (1874-1948), who co-founded the National Bureau of Economic Research.

Irving Fisher (1867-1947) was the most famous American monetary economist of the early 20th century. He established the connection between the nominal rate of interest and the real rate of interest and did work on the equation of exchange (see pages 365 and 366).

Usually considered the most influential economist of the century, John Maynard Keynes (1883-1946) attacked the Classical belief that government should not interfere with an economy in the midst of a recession. He wrote *The General Theory of Employment, Interest, and Money* in 1936. His theories led to an active role for government in regulating national output, employment, price levels, and interest rates. To this day economists argue about the wisdom of such intervention.

Joan Robinson (1903-1983) and Edward Chamberlin (1899-1967) both did work on monopolistic competition (see Chapter 4), which made it easier to understand how firms that are not purely competitive determine their prices and output levels.

SUMMARY

Economics studies how people think, as well as how they act, especially in their relations with others. We assume people are rational in their behavior, which means they seek to maximize satisfaction by attaining goals and objectives.

Economics deals for the most part with the materialistic goals of goods and services. They are produced with the resources of labor, capital, natural resources, and entrepreneurship. Desires for goods and services are unlimited, while resources are limited. Thus, resources are scarce, and the intent of studying economics is to help society deal with this scarcity.

People maximize their economic well-being by allocating or using resources efficiently. This is accomplished by using cost-benefit analysis, ensuring that resource users have more to gain (benefit) than they have to lose or give up (opportunity cost).

A production possibilities curve exhibits the economic problem graphically. It shows how the output of two goods is limited by the amount of resources available. It also shows that resources are not equally suited to producing all goods.

Marginal analysis shows that good decision making involves looking at just the extra benefits and extra costs one incurs. This means the benefits and costs of past actions are irrelevant for future decisions.

Cost-benefit analysis is properly carried out in a society when the three Basic Economic Questions are properly answered. What to Produce? is asked so that the most beneficial goods and services are made. How to Produce? is asked so that the most efficient production processes are used. For Whom to Produce? is asked to ensure that the goods and services provide the maximum economic well-being for all members of society combined.

The purpose of economic systems is to help societies deal with the problem of resource scarcity. All economic systems are based on one of or a combination of the three Basic Economic Systems: the traditional, the command, and the market systems.

The economies of nations differ in two primary ways: 1) the degree to which their resources are privately or publicly owned; and 2) the degree to which they use the command and the market economic systems.

Capitalism is an economic system that combines the private ownership of resources with the use of the market system to answer the Basic Economic Questions. It is based upon a society of individuals, all seeking to maximize their own economic welfare in a competitive framework. All capitalist societies modify the capitalist model to varying degrees through government intervention.

There are several variants of socialism, though all have resources largely owned by the public. Communism or authoritarian socialism makes heavy use of the command system to make economic decisions. Alternatively, market socialism allows the market system to direct resource allocation in most areas, which gives people more freedom in the economy.

Economics is split into microeconomics, the study of small elements of the economy, and macroeconomics, the study of large sections.

Over the centuries, there have been many schools of thought on economic concepts. These largely reflect the different views regarding the mechanisms at work in a capitalist system. This largely explains why economists disagree as much as they do.

QUESTIONS FOR DISCUSSION AND THOUGHT

1. Can you "overeat"? Can you be "overweight"? Use economic concepts to answer the questions.

2. In many cases (perhaps most), using a snowblower to remove snow from sidewalks and driveways takes more time than using a shovel. This is especially true when including the time to maintain and store the snowblower. Other than the case where someone is too old or weak to use a shovel, why do people buy snowblowers when they "waste" time and money? What "resource" are owners conserving?

3. How long should you stay at a party? How should you decide?

4. Should you eat candy just because it is in front of you? Does it matter if you bought it or if someone else did?

5. Why don't you always walk as fast as you can, which would save time? Why don't you walk as slowly as you can, which would save energy and minimize the danger of an accident or wear and tear on your joints? Thus, how fast should you walk?

6. How often do you walk out of a movie in a theater? How often do you shut off the TV while watching a program? If your "walkouts" are at different rates, why is this? If you got "free" movie tickets, would you be less or more likely to walk out? Why?

7. Suppose you buy a hamburger today costing one dollar. Fast forward to a year from now. Will that same hamburger (the one you actually ate) cost you anything next year? Think of what opportunities you will be forced to give up next year because you ate the hamburger this year. Finally, if you are 20 years old today, what will eating the hamburger have cost you over your lifetime by the time you reach 70?

8. Which class of resources (labor, capital, entrepreneurship, or natural resources) seems most important in producing all goods and services combined? In answering, consider which resource you would do without if you were forced to? Is the question similar to the questions: Which is more important to you, your heart or your lungs? and Which would you choose to do without if you were forced to, your heart or your lungs?

9. If resources would cease being scarce, how would the economy change?

10. Think of how you used the traditional economic system recently as a consumer. Were you rational in doing so? How might actually using the market system have been misconstrued as using the traditional system by someone observing your actions?

11. Is the United States becoming more socialistic? What evidence can you offer to substantiate your belief?

12. The main benefit of regulating the production and sale of toxic materials is to avoid accidental deaths. However, such regulation costs money. So, if a certain program costs X dollars and saves Y lives, a good decision requires knowing the value of these lives. But how much is a life worth? Government officials need to know this to make a good judgment on spending programs and regulation of the economy. We often hear that a life is "priceless"—supposedly worth an infinite amount (or at least a huge amount) of money. Is that true? The Save the Children Fund, Care International, and other agencies regularly keep many people from starving to death. How much does the average American contribute to these agencies to save lives? Does that tell you anything about how much the average American values a life? Or is there some other explanation for people's limited contributions to charity?

PROBLEMS See pages 478-479 for the answers.

1. Who is more efficient in the following cases?
    a) Jason cut grass for several neighbors from eight in the morning until noon. Their lawns had the following square footages: 8,000 ft., 4,000 ft., 12,000 ft., and 10,000 ft. Bob also cut grass, working from seven until ten thirty in the morning. His lawns, similar in pattern and difficulty to Jason's, had the following areas: 9,000 ft., 5,000 ft., 12,000 ft., and 11,000 ft.
    b) Julie can make 90 pizza crusts if she works from 1:00 p.m. until 7:30 p.m., with two 15-minute breaks. Sara can make 85 pizza crusts if she works from noon until 6:00 p.m., with a half-hour break. How many crusts per hour can each make? How long does it take each to make one crust?
    c) Kristin washed the following two-square-foot windows in her last five eight-hour shifts: 700, 660, 820, 740, and 680. Ken washed the following four-square-foot windows in his last four eight-hour shifts: 300, 400, 360, and 380.

2. Tricia has $150 to spend, allowing her to buy the following items that provide her with the "satisfaction units" listed: two dresses, 652 units; a CD player, 815 units; a kitchen chair, 466 units; and a tuneup of her car, 720 units.
    a) What is her opportunity cost if she buys the:
        i. two dresses?
        ii. CD player?
        iii. chair?
        iv. tuneup?
    b) If she uses cost-benefit analysis, how will Tricia spend her $150?
    c) If her car "needs" a tuneup (it is in danger of stalling at any point) and Tricia knows this, what should she buy? Why?
3. The following gives the production possibilities for a country.

Combination	Houses (thousands)	Wheat (millions of bushels)
A	0	90
B	30	80
C	60	60
D	90	35
E	120	0

    a) Make a graph of these production possibilities.
    b) What is the opportunity cost of the first 30,000 houses? The second 30,000? The third? The fourth?
    c) Why did the opportunity cost change the way it did as additional houses were built? What economic law does it reflect?
    d) Let point F on your graph represent the output of 40,000 houses and 60 million bushels of wheat. Is it in the zone of inefficiency or the zone of impossibility? Why?
    e) Let point G on your graph represent the output of 40,000 houses and 80 million bushels of wheat. Which zone is it in? Why?

APPENDIX: PRODUCTION POSSIBILITIES CURVES

Suppose a farmer would like to grow as much corn and potatoes as possible. However, there is only a limited amount of resources with which to produce them—100 acres of land, 90 hours of labor, 70 hours of tractor time, and so on. The question then is: How much corn and potatoes *can* be produced with these scarce resources? The answer partly depends upon how the resources are distributed between the corn and potato enterprises.

The points along the bowed curve in Figure A1-4 show the *maximum possible* outputs of corn and potatoes. If the farmer makes any mistake in using the resources, such as driving over a row of corn while cultivating, the actual yield will be less than the curve indicates. Such situations are represented by points within the curve.

Point A in Figure A1-1 shows that if the farmer uses all the resources to grow corn, 16,000 bushels of corn will be produced, but no potatoes. Alternatively, point B shows that the resources could produce 10,000 bushels of potatoes if no corn is grown. But suppose the farmer devotes half of the resources to each crop. You might expect the farmer to get half the yield of corn that was produced at point A and half the potatoes that were produced at point B—that is, 8,000 bushels of corn and 5,000 bushels of potatoes, shown as point C. You might further expect the farm to yield other combinations of corn and potatoes if the resources were divided differently, but you might also expect that all combinations would appear along the line connecting points A, C, and B.

In reality, such output combinations would appear along the curved line connecting points A, D, E, F, and B. The curve is called a production possibilities curve because it shows what it is possible to produce of both crops, given a set of resources. The farmer thus gets a "bonus" (that is, a bigger yield than expected) if the resources are split between two crops, as the graph shows. For instance, note point C again, indicating the initial *expected* output of 8,000 bushels of corn and 5,000 bushels of potatoes. In reality, the farmer can produce 13,000 bushels of corn if 5,000 bushels of potatoes are grown, shown at point D—a 5,000 bushel "bonus" of corn. Alternatively, point F represents another possible production situation, where producing 8,000 bushels of corn is associated with a "bonus" of 3,700 bushels of potatoes over point C. Finally, the farmer could split these bonuses at point E, getting a 3,000-bushel corn bonus (= 11,000 - 8,000) and a 1,800-bushel potato bonus (= 6,800 - 5,000).

Such unexpected increases arise because many resources are not equally suited to produce different goods and services. The 100-acre field might have widely varying soil conditions, from sand to clay. Potatoes will tolerate sand better than corn, and vice versa for clay. But when *all* the land is either in corn or potatoes, then *some* of the land is used to grow a crop ill-suited for the soil. However, if the farmer splits up the land, it is possible to match each crop with its "favorite" soil, thereby boosting yields, the source of the "bonuses."

Such relationships between resources and the outputs of two goods and services are almost universal. It is a main reason for the law of increasing costs, which states that higher levels of output of a particular good or service are increasingly costly. This is because increasingly ill-suited resources are used to make the extra output. Consequently, it takes more resources (thus, more costs) to make each additional unit of output. It's a bit like choosing players for a pickup basketball game. The best player is chosen first, then the next best, and so on until the poorest players get picked. It might take the last three players picked to score as many points as the first player.

Figure A1-1

Production Possibilities of Corn and Potatoes

A 100-acre farm can be planted in corn or potatoes. Line ACB shows all the production possibilities if all the land is homogeneous. That is, each acre will yield as much corn or potatoes as any other acre.

Line ADEFB shows the production possibilities if the land varies in productivity. This leads the farmer to grow corn and potatoes only on the land best suited for each. Consequently, the farmer gets a "bonus" in output of both crops. To illustrate, point C shows the yield of corn and potatoes if 50 acres of each are grown on homogeneous land. Point E shows the increased yields if the land is not homogeneous.

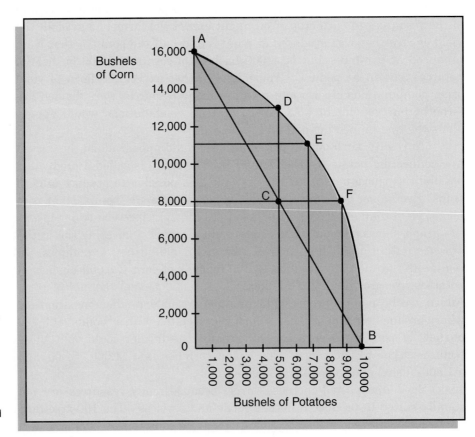

Production possibilities curves also can be used to show opportunity costs. Suppose the farmer was at point F and wanted to shift to point D by growing more corn—5,000 bushels more. It cost the opportunity of having 3,700 bushels of potatoes because potato output fell from 8,700 to 5,000 bushels. Conversely, moving from point D to point F means the opportunity cost of growing an extra 3,700 bushels of potatoes is 5,000 bushels of corn. Finally, if the move was from point D to point E, the cost of growing an extra 1,800 bushels of potatoes is 2,000 bushels of corn.

2

DEMAND, SUPPLY, AND MARKET PRICES

CHAPTER PREVIEW

In modern economies, individuals specialize in order to be more efficient. But this forces them to trade with each other. In a market or capitalist economy, such trades are voluntary.

The "rates of exchange," or prices, are determined in a complex system of concepts and relationships. One is called demand, describing how buyers respond in a market. Another is called supply, describing how sellers respond in a market.

Changes in demand can occur for an item, and they are caused by several factors. Similarly, changes in supply can occur for an item for several reasons. These changes in demand or supply can affect the market price for that item.

Thus, this chapter introduces you to how prices are determined in a competitive market setting and why they are likely to change.

CHAPTER OBJECTIVES

After completing this chapter, you should be able to:

◆ *Explain why the law of demand is followed by buyers.*

◆ *Compare and contrast elastic and inelastic demand.*

◆ *Describe what happens when there is a change in demand and why it occurs.*

◆ *Explain why the law of supply is followed by sellers.*

◆ *Describe what happens when there is a change in supply and why it occurs.*

◆ *Explain why prices tend to change when there are shortages and surpluses.*

◆ *Determine how equilibrium price and quantity will change if there is a change in demand or supply.*

In this chapter, you will learn how the market system determines prices. You also will learn why prices change. After introducing the purpose of markets, the buyers' side of the market, known as demand, will be explored, followed by the sellers' side, known as supply. Last, you will learn how the interactions of demand and supply determine price.

The price system provides signals to all participants in a market economy. Such signals direct economic activity, so the price system is at the core of wise decision making in economic affairs.

THE PURPOSE OF MARKETS

The Basic Economic Questions can be answered with a system of markets, where buyers and sellers of goods, services, and resources come to make exchanges with money in order to increase their economic welfare. The **price** is the rate of exchange of money for one unit of what is sold. For a market to exist for anything, there must be buyers, sellers, and agreement on a price.

A **price** is the rate of exchange of money for one unit of what is sold.

To completely understand how the price system does all this, you must thoroughly understand what a price is—and why prices even exist. A price is the amount of money that is exchanged for one unit of something. Simple enough, you say. But what is this "something"? It could be a good, a service, a resource (a machine, coal, or an hour of labor), or a financial instrument (a stock or bond). Each of these "somethings" have one thing in common. They are all available in limited amounts, and they are all useful or have value. That is, they are scarce. Thus, only scarce items have prices. (To prove this, try to sell a piece of broken glass to somebody. If you can't even get a penny, then broken glass has no price.)

Let's go further and explore why we make such exchanges in the first place. We wouldn't have to. We could live like our caveman ancestors who produced all their own needs. Each of us could live alone or independently of others. However, Chapter 3 shows that such behavior would be very inefficient, dooming us to grinding poverty. Instead, we specialize—in production, that is. However, each of us makes only a few things, at the most. That means we must get everything else we want from others—other specialists. We get these things in markets, places where things of value are exchanged.

This may not be clear in modern societies because we rarely exchange *things* of value in a market. Rather, we exchange *one* thing of value. Specifically, a seller passes a thing of value (such as a good or service) to a buyer. The buyer passes money to the seller, which has no *intrinsic* value. It only has value in the sense that it can be exchanged for another thing of real value (a good or service). In simpler economies, where barter was used, one unit of Good X might have traded for three units of Good Y. So the "price" of Good X was three units of Good Y. For example, one bushel of wheat could have traded for three drinking glasses.

Today, a wheat farmer who wants some glasses doesn't try to find a glass maker who wants some wheat, nor does a glass maker seek out a wheat farmer who wants glasses. Wheat farmers exchange their wheat for money, say, for three dollars a bushel. Glass makers also exchange their glasses for money, say, for one dollar a glass. Thus, in effect, wheat still exchanges for three glasses today. However, we don't say that. Instead, we say that the price of a bushel of wheat is three dollars and the price of a glass is one dollar.

Thus, markets are the result of specialization of production. Specialists must exchange what they have for what they want. In some markets they are buyers (or demanders), where they are called consumers. In other markets they are sellers (or suppliers), where they either "sell" time if they are laborers or goods or services if they are business owners. That is, they are either on the demand side or the supply side of any market they enter. Next, detailed examination of both sides of such markets will be undertaken.

DEMAND

All consumers have limited or scarce income, so they need to get all they can from each dollar. To do so, they bargain with sellers and often compete against other buyers, who also face a scarcity of income.

How much consumers wish to buy of some item depends upon several factors, including: 1) the price of the item; 2) the benefit it provides; 3) the size of the population; 4) the level of consumers' incomes; 5) the prices of substitute goods; 6) the prices of complementary goods (goods used together, like VCRs and videotapes); and 7) the future expectations of price and availability of the item. The factors can vary in level or magnitude (such as the size of the population), and when they do, people wish to buy more or less of the item. Economists built a model of a market in which they assume that only one of these factors can vary—the price of the item. They assume that all the other factors will have a certain "level"—a certain income level, prices of substitute goods, and so on. Then only changes in the item's price will cause a change in the amount consumers wish to purchase. (The term *ceteris paribus*, meaning all things being equal, refers to this condition.)

Demand refers to the relationship between an item's price and the amount consumers wish to purchase. (Here, "wish" means they want the item *and* have the money to buy it, but it doesn't necessarily mean they are

Demand refers to the relationship between the various amounts that buyers are willing to purchase of some item and all possible prices of that item.

able to find that much to buy.) This amount is termed **quantity demand- ed**. Be careful not to mix up these two terms. Demand is a *relationship* (it is not an *amount*) between price and the quantity demanded (which *is* an amount). This demand relationship refers to the *various* amounts consumers wish to buy at *all possible* prices.

> **Quantity demanded** is the amount of an item buyers wish to purchase at a specific price.

For virtually all goods and services, the demand relationship is an inverse one. That is, at higher prices, consumers wish to buy less of an item than at lower prices. (The only major exceptions are items that provide "show-off " or snob-appeal satisfaction as they become more expensive.) Because this concept is so universal, we say people follow the **law of demand**, stated as follows: At higher prices, consumers wish to buy less of an item; at lower prices, consumers wish to purchase more of an item.

> The **law of demand** states that at higher prices for an item, buyers want to purchase less of it, and at lower prices, they want to purchase more of it.

For example, consider the market for steak in a city where the population is 50,000, where the price of pork (a substitute) is $3 a pound, and so on (for other factors that influence purchases). Now suppose that steak sells for $2 a pound and that consumers want 700 pounds. However, if the price is $3 rather than $2 and all other influences on purchases remain the same, consumers will ask for less, perhaps only 600 pounds. Further, at $4 they want 500 pounds; at $5 they want 400 pounds; at $6 they want 300 pounds; and so on. Remember, economists call each of these quantities the quantity demanded at those specific prices.

Consumers follow or obey the law of demand for two reasons: 1) the substitution effect; and 2) the income effect.

■ The **substitution effect** reflects the fact that rational consumers seek to maximize economic welfare by getting as much satisfaction as possible from each dollar spent. Because there are alternative ways to spend each dollar, consumers need to find the *best* combination of purchases in order to maximize economic welfare. In other words, if a consumer buys something, the benefit must exceed the opportunity cost. Suppose this is true for each of the consumers who want the 700 pounds of steak at $2. Each dollar of the 1,400 dollars spent buys half a pound of steak, providing a certain level of satisfaction (benefit). Buying pork instead with any of those dollars would provide somewhat *less* benefit. Otherwise consumers would buy pork. However, what if steak rises in price to $3 a pound and nothing else changes, including the price of pork? Then a dollar buys only a *third* of a pound of steak, so consumers now get less satisfaction from a dollar spent on steak. Since the price of pork does not change, neither does the benefit from spending a dollar on pork. *Some* of the consumers who wanted steak at $2 a pound now find that a dollar spent on steak brings *less* satisfaction than a dollar spent on pork. Such consumers then switch from steak to pork, a substitute good.

> The **substitution effect** refers to the act of buyers purchasing less of an item whose price rises because a substitute good becomes a better purchase, and vice versa.

The **income effect** refers to the decrease in purchases as the result of an increase in an item's price, as one's income can buy fewer items, and vice versa.

■ Consumers also obey the law of demand because of the **income effect**. This means that if the price of a good increases, consumers cannot buy as many goods and services in total. This is a consequence of limited incomes not going as far. The effect of an increase in prices is the same as if consumers suffered a cut in income. They could buy fewer things. For example, when the price of steak rises from $2 to $6 a pound, consumers, facing a scarcity of money, can buy fewer things, including steak.

Figure 2-1 shows the demand relationship in two different ways. The first way is the demand schedule, where a list of prices appears with a list of consumers' wishes to buy, or quantity demanded. In the steak example, you see the price and pound amounts mentioned earlier. These amounts consumers wish to buy depend not only upon the price of steak, but also upon consumers' incomes, the benefits of steak, the price of complementary goods, and so on. Each influence on the desire to buy (other than the price) *could* change but *doesn't* in Figure 2-1. Each has a specific level or magnitude (for example, the population of the market area being 50,000). Because the magnitude of each influence can vary, the relationship in the demand schedule is only one of many possible relationships.

The second way to show the demand relationship uses a graph. The price is measured on the vertical axis and the quantity (demanded) on the horizontal axis. Notice the five dots on the line labeled D, which graphically represents the demand relationship. Each dot represents two pieces of information, one about the price and the other about the quantity demanded. There are thousands of potential points in addition to the five shown. Connecting all these points gives what is called the demand curve.

Figure 2-1

The Demand for Steak

The demand schedule at left shows some of the combinations of prices and quantities of steak that buyers wish to purchase. The demand curve at right shows *all* such combinations of prices and quantities demanded. Its downward slope shows that demand is an inverse relationship between price and quantity demanded.

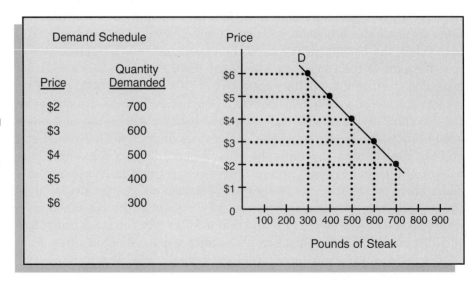

Demand Schedule	
Price	Quantity Demanded
$2	700
$3	600
$4	500
$5	400
$6	300

Elasticity of Demand

If firms know the demand relationship, they can predict changes in sales if they charge different prices. The **elasticity of demand** refers to the extent consumers change their purchases as price varies. Suppose the price for some good increases. If consumers cut their purchases at a greater rate than the price rises, the demand is **elastic**. However, if consumers cut purchases by a smaller rate than the price increases, the demand is **inelastic**. For example, if the price of sofas rises by 40 percent and consumers buy 60 percent fewer sofas, the demand for sofas is elastic. But if the number of sofas sold falls by only 30 percent, the demand is inelastic.

Businesses need to know the elasticity of demand because their sales or **total revenue** (TR) equals the price multiplied by the amount sold. Figure 2-2 shows four possible scenarios with price changes and differing elasticities. In the first case (top left), price rises when the demand is elastic. Because the gain in sales from the price increase is less than the loss in sales from the reduced purchases, the net effect is a decrease in sales. However, with an inelastic demand, total revenue rises as price rises, since consumers don't reduce purchases significantly (top right). The situation reverses for price decreases, shown in the bottom two cases. Obviously, a business owner would like to face an inelastic demand. Then when the price is increased, there will still be lots of buyers. (There is an appendix on elasticity on pages 65-67 providing considerable elaboration.)

The **elasticity of demand** refers to the responsiveness of buyers to changes in price with respect to the amount purchased.

An item's demand is **elastic** when a given price change results in a proportionately greater change in purchases.

An item's demand is **inelastic** when a given price change results in a proportionately smaller change in purchases.

A firm's **total revenue** equals its total sales received from producing and selling a specific amount of output of a good or service. It is found by multiplying the price by the amount sold.

Figure 2-2

Price Changes	Type of Demand Elasticity	
	Elastic Demand	Inelastic Demand
If the Price Rises by x Percent	1) Consumers Reduce Purchases by More Than x Percent 2) Total Revenue Falls	1) Consumers Redu Purchases by Le Than x Percent 2) Total Revenue
If the Price Falls by x Percent	1) Consumers Increase Purchases by More Than x Percent 2) Total Revenue Rises	1) Consumers In Purchases by Than x Perce 2) Total Rever

Changes in Demand

Because the other influences on how much consumers wish to purchase (besides price) can vary in magnitude, there are many possible demand relationships. Take the numbers used in the steak example as the initial relationship. They show that at different prices, consumers want different amounts of steak. Yet remember that a certain level of income, prices of substitutes, and so on are assumed. Now the magnitude of one of these factors will change—the benefits that consumers get from steak.

Suppose the initial demand stems only from the knowledge that steak tastes good and provides food value. But if researchers find that steak delays the onset of old-age symptoms, the perceived benefit from steak is higher, and consumers will want to eat more steak. Assume that steak is $3 a pound. Initially, consumers wanted 600 pounds. (Or, in economists' language, the quantity demanded at $3 a pound was 600 pounds.) Now, buyers request 700 pounds at $3 a pound, or 100 pounds more than before. Similar increases of 100 pounds are made for whatever price steak sells for and appear in the demand schedules and graphs in Figure 2-3.

A **change in demand** is a change in the amount buyers wish to purchase at each price, even though there is no change in price.

What was just illustrated is a **change in demand**, which occurs when consumers wish to buy a different amount of a good or service *at each price*. Take care to distinguish a change in demand from a change in the amount consumers want *because of a change in the price,* known as a change in quantity demanded. A change in demand means consumers want a different amount because some influence *other than the price* changed.

An **increase in demand** is an increase in the amount buyers wish to purchase at each price.

The example above, which links eating steak to a delay in aging, involves an **increase in demand**. It means consumers want more at each price than before. Demand increases if: 1) the perceived usefulness of the item rises; 2) prices of substitutes rise; 3) prices of complements fall; 4) consumers' incomes increase; 5) consumers expect prices to be higher in the future or that the product will be less available; or 6) population increases.

A **decrease in demand** is a decrease in the amount buyers wish to purchase at each price.

A **decrease in demand** means consumers want less of an item at each price. This results from fewer benefits from the item, lower prices of substitutes, higher prices of complements, lower incomes, expectation of lower future prices, or a lower population.

SUPPLY

The English economist Alfred Marshall compared supply and demand to a scissors, which requires two blades to cut. To find how the market system establishes prices for goods and services, you also need two "blades" because every purchase (demand) is also a sale (supply). Attention is now turned to an examination of supply, or the sellers' side of a market.

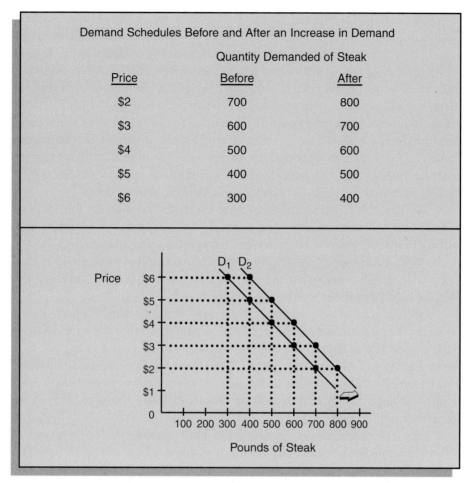

Demand Schedules Before and After an Increase in Demand

Quantity Demanded of Steak

Price	Before	After
$2	700	800
$3	600	700
$4	500	600
$5	400	500
$6	300	400

Figure 2-3

An Increase in the Demand for Steak

At each price, consumers wish to purchase 100 more pounds of steak than earlier. This can be shown with either a new demand schedule, shown at top, or a new demand curve, D_2 shown at bottom.

The Law of Supply

Sellers, like buyers, are people who face a personal scarcity of time and money. Thus, their selling decisions should reflect cost-benefit analysis designed to maximize their welfare. Several factors influence how much of some good or service sellers offer for sale, including: 1) price; 2) cost of production; 3) expectations of future prices; 4) number of sellers; and 5) the prices of related goods.

■ Because price is the prime factor determining the benefits of selling, price is the first factor determining how much of a good or service firms wish to sell. The higher the price, the more that firms wish to sell (more about this below).

■ Cost is the second influence on how much firms wish to sell. Rational people sell things only when the benefits exceed the costs. However, a firm's production cost is not always easy to determine. It generally includes the amounts firms pay for resources, such as labor, supplies, and machinery. (In addition, it includes the costs of complying with government regulations, as well as taxes.) However, when *opportunity* cost is taken into account, a firm's cost also includes the profits it does *not* receive from producing some other product. For example, a window shade manufacturer gives up the opportunity to profit from manufacturing canvas tents. Consequently, the manufacturer will produce window shades only if profits from making them exceed the profits from making tents.

■ The third factor affecting how much firms wish to sell is their expectation of future prices. For example, an oil producer would be less willing to sell oil today if oil prices are expected to soar next month.

■ The number of sellers, the fourth factor, affects the amount that firms wish to sell because the more firms that are trying to sell an item, the more of that item there will be "on the market."

■ The price of related goods is the last item affecting what is offered for sale. For example, the amount of pine boards offered for sale depends partly upon the price of plywood sheets. If plywood prices suddenly rise, fewer boards will be sent to market. Some pine logs will be made into plywood instead. (This concept is actually another case of opportunity cost, where the opportunity cost of making boards includes the profits given up from making plywood.)

As with demand, economists have built a model of the behavior of sellers in a market by assuming that only variances in prices of an item can cause sellers to offer more or less of it for sale. Thus, production costs, the number of sellers, and so on are fixed at given levels (*ceteris paribus* again). The amount that sellers wish to sell at any particular price is called the **quantity supplied. Supply** refers to the relationship between the price of an item and the quantity supplied of it by sellers.

Sellers act the opposite of consumers (who follow the law of demand when they buy *less* as prices rise). For sellers, the **law of supply** means they will offer more for sale at higher prices than at lower prices. Thus, supply is a direct relationship between price and quantity supplied.

Consider again steak as an example. Suppose that if steak sells for a retail price of $2 per pound, beef producers (including ranchers, feedlot operators, butchers, and store operators) wish to sell 300 pounds in our town of 50,000. However, if the price is $3 instead, they wish to sell 400 pounds. At $4, they wish to sell 500 pounds. At $5, they wish to sell 600 pounds. At $6, they wish to sell 700 pounds, and so on. "Wish to sell" is

Quantity supplied is the amount of an item sellers wish to sell at a particular price.

Supply refers to the relationship between the amounts that sellers offer for sale of some item and all possible prices of that item.

The **law of supply** states that at higher prices for an item, sellers will offer more of it for sale, and at lower prices, they will offer less for sale.

used because, although those are the amounts that are in the best interests of producers to sell, buyers might not be willing to purchase those amounts. The wishes of sellers and buyers are independent of each other, with each having separate foundations.

The law of supply is followed because different units of a good or service cost different amounts to produce. To understand this, suppose that each tire that could be produced in a certain factory costs the *same* to produce as all others, say $20. If the price of the first tire is $23, the firm wants to sell it, for the benefit (price) exceeds the cost of $20. The same holds true for every other tire that can be made. In fact, this firm would wish to expand its factory to an *infinite* size because each tire makes a profit.

However, such a scenario would rarely happen. In actual economies, firms are willing to sell just so much at any given price. Most McDonald's outlets, for example, do not even try to sell hamburgers for 59¢ at 4:00 a.m. They *could* sell some at that hour, but such sales wouldn't be profitable. Otherwise McDonald's would be open. A hamburger made at that time looks and tastes the same as one made at noon, yet it costs more to make. That's because firms can usually produce at low cost only in large volume. But since the demand for hamburgers is low at 4:00 a.m., the cost is high— so high that the benefit is below the cost.

For a given firm size (that is, the amount of capital it has), additional outputs of an item become increasingly costly. The average cost rises so that beyond some level of output, it exceeds the price. Therefore, firms wish to sell no more than that amount of output.

What happens if the price is higher? Then firms can afford to produce (that is, produce at a profit) the more costly, larger amounts of output. This explains why there is a law of supply, for at higher prices, the amount offered for sale is higher. In summary, *firms obey the law of supply because, at higher prices, they can afford the more costly production techniques of the higher levels of output.*

In short, as the old saying goes, "Money talks." Individuals follow the law of supply as well as firms. You would not sell your favorite tape for $5 if you would give up more satisfaction from the tape than you would gain from whatever else you bought for the $5. But when offered $40, you would probably sell the tape because you "can afford it" (the "it" being the satisfaction you lose from not hearing the music).

To review and emphasize, supply is the relationship between price and the amounts of a good or service all firms combined wish to sell. Thus, supply refers to the relationship between the *various* quantities sellers offer and the *various* prices at which the items could sell. (Or, in economists' terminology, supply is the relationship between price and quantity supplied.

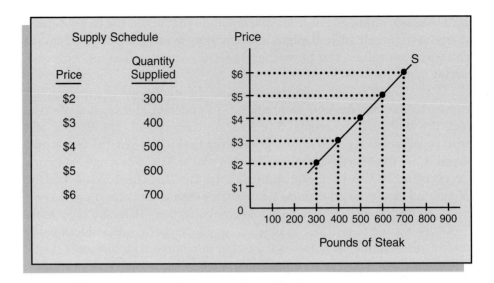

Figure 2-4

The Supply of Steak

The information in the supply schedule on the left also appears in the supply graph. Each point on the graph shows a combination of price and quantity supplied.

Supply does not refer to any *specific* quantity.) As with demand, this relationship holds when it is assumed that all other influences on selling remain unchanged.

Consider the market for steak again, but this time from the sellers' viewpoint. Figure 2-4 shows the supply relationship in two different ways, with a supply schedule and a supply curve. Notice that steak producers can provide at least 700 pounds of steak, for they are willing to do so at $6 a pound. However, why do they wish to sell only 300 pounds at $2? They could provide 400 pounds more but don't want to because each of these 400 pounds of steak costs more to produce than the first 300 pounds (and more than $4 a pound). This is because steers differ in how rapidly they gain weight, how large they get (and how much steak they provide), and so on. If the price were high enough, beef producers would even find it profitable to raise steers that were very costly to produce (very slow weight gainers or smaller steers).

The supply relationship assumes: 1) a certain level of costs for each unit of output; 2) given expectations of the future; 3) a given number of sellers; and 4) a given level of prices of related goods. Thus, the relationship is merely one of many that are possible.

Changes in Supply

Now suppose one of these other influences on the amount produced changes—the cost of production, for example. Suppose a highly mechanized feeding system is introduced in beef feedlot operations. This reduces the cost of raising steers, both low-cost steers (the fast gainers) and high-cost steers (the slow gainers). Some steers previously *possible* to raise at, say, $4 a pound, but *unprofitable*, now *are* profitable. Before this cost reduction, only 500 pounds of steak were profitable to produce at $4 a pound. But now producers can profitably offer up for sale the 501st, 502nd, and all the way up to the 600th pound of steak. Because the remaining pounds of steak (numbers 601 and above) are so *very* costly (in excess of $4 of pound), they remain unprofitable, so they are not offered for sale. A similar increase in output occurs at every other price.

Figure 2-5 shows a change in supply in two ways. In each case an "old" or original relationship and a "new" one appear.

Supply Schedules Before and After an Increase in Supply

	Quantity Supplied of Steak	
Price	Before	After
$2	300	400
$3	400	500
$4	500	600
$5	600	700
$6	700	800

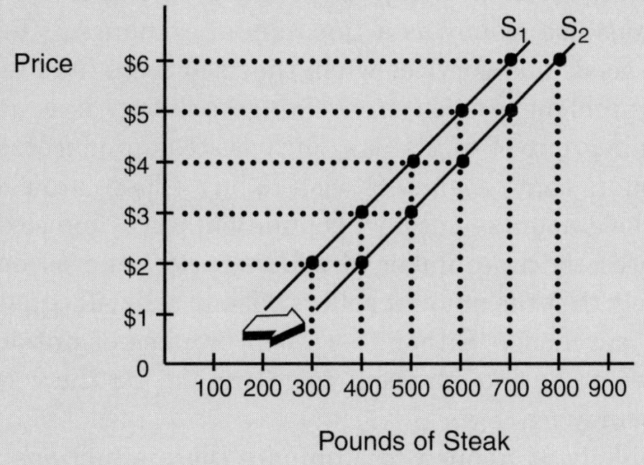

Figure 2-5

An Increase in the Supply of Steak

At each price, producers offer 100 more pounds of steak for sale than earlier. This is shown in the two supply schedules above. It is also shown as a shift in the supply curve below from S_1 to S_2.

A **change in supply** is a change in the amount sellers wish to sell at each price.

An **increase in supply** is an increase in the amount sellers offer for sale at each price.

A **decrease in supply** is a decrease in the amount sellers offer for sale at each price.

A **change in supply** occurs when producers want to sell a different amount at each price. This must be distinguished from a change in desired output *that results from a change in price,* known as a change in quantity supplied. A change in supply occurs when there is a change in any of the influences on desired output *other than the price.* When producers want to sell *more* at each price, there is an **increase in supply**. This occurs if: 1) production costs decrease; 2) producers expect lower prices in the future; 3) the number of sellers increases; or 4) other goods that producers were making with their resources decrease in price. The opposite, called a **decrease in supply**, occurs when producers want to sell *less* at each price. This happens when production costs rise, producers expect higher prices in the future, the number of sellers decreases, or other goods that producers were making with their resources increase in price.

HOW MARKET PRICES ARE ESTABLISHED

So far, several possible prices were considered for both the demand and supply situations. But any exchange between a buyer and a seller occurs in a market at *just one* price. This section explains how that price is determined under free-market, competitive conditions.

The Rationing Role of Prices

In a modern industrial economy, people are specialists, whether specialized laborers (clerks, pilots, machinists) or producers of certain products (bakers, potato farmers, jewelers). Specialists need to exchange their goods and services for other goods and services they need but do not produce. This could be done in a barter system, where one good trades for another, but modern economies use money as a "medium of exchange." Today, specialists trade their goods and services when they sell them (and buy others).

A major problem in such an exchange economy is equating: 1) the amounts a certain group of specialists (such as steak producers) wish to sell; and 2) the amounts that consumers wish to buy. There are several factors affecting both the amounts—income, population, price, and so on for buyers and production costs, the number of sellers, price, and so on for sellers. Thus, it's unlikely that the amount sellers wish to sell will equal the amount buyers wish to purchase. Either there will be piles of unsold (untraded) goods or there won't be enough goods to go around. At the very least, both situations are annoying.

What is likely to happen to eliminate these situations in a market economy? Consider the case of a pile of unsold steak in supermarket meat

THINKING CRITICALLY ABOUT ECONOMIC QUESTIONS IN OUR LIVES

If You Had to Set the Price of Everything, How Would You Do It?

Things to Consider

1. Consider why there are prices in the first place. What does the price of an item indicate about it?

2. What if a particular item had an extremely high price? How would buyers respond? How would sellers respond? Conversely, what if it had an extremely low price?

3. Consider what markets are and why we have them.

4. Bear in mind that What to Produce? must be answered correctly if society is to maximize its economic welfare. Also, remember that resources (or the goods and services they produce) should not be wasted or go unused, as they are scarce.

5. Thus, if there were 10 million items made and sold and you had to set the prices for all of them, how would you do it so there would be well-functioning markets that result in the maximum economic welfare for society?

   See page 450 for the answer.

cases or slaughterhouses. Each of the following will make such a pile disappear: 1) production costs of steak could rise; 2) some sellers could go out of the beef business; 3) the price and profitability of a similar product that could be produced with the same resources (sheep or hogs) could rise; 4) people could increase their desire to eat steak; 5) the population could increase; 6) incomes of the buyers could rise; 7) the price of a substitute for steak (like pork) could rise; 8) the price of a complement of steak could fall; and 9) the price of the traded good (steak) could fall.

Perhaps you noticed that each of the possible changes was a factor affecting either the amount sellers wish to sell or that consumers wish to purchase. The next question is: Which of these possibilities is likely to happen *because there is* a pile of unsold steak? Will the cost of producing steak rise? No. Will people move to town because the pile attracted them? No.

Will *any* of the nine possibilities result because of the pile? Yes, but just one. The price will change. In fact, it will change as much as is necessary to bring the amounts that buyers and sellers wish to trade to the same level.

The opposite situation, where people want more steaks than are being sold, also has at least nine solutions that would make that shortfall disappear. For example, if enough people left town, it would disappear—but they won't just because they can't always find steak. Nor will any of the other eight be our salvation except one. The price will change.

Therefore, prices serve a rationing role in markets. That is, they ration (or "spread out") the available goods and services that people want. The next section will show that prices will vary to carry out this rationing role—not only when people want more of something that is available, but also when there is more available than they want.

Low Prices, High Prices—and Those in Between

In a competitive market, who sets the price? Actually, no one does—at least not alone—because the price is the collective result of many people's actions. Sellers can't set or dictate prices. Otherwise prices would be much higher than they are. Buyers don't set them either. Otherwise prices would drop to near zero. Essentially, prices are set in an economic tug-of-war, with buyers and sellers alike seeking to gain an economic advantage. Thus, as in a real tug-of-war (when two teams pull on a rope), where the final position of the rope is the collective effect of everyone's actions, so, too, a price is the collective effect of all buyers and sellers.

If a good or service sells at only one of many possible prices, why that *particular* price? To see why, return to the steak example and consider several different prices. Figure 2-6 brings together the demand for steak from Figure 2-1 and the steak supply from Figure 2-4.

Suppose steak sells for $2 a pound. Is everyone content with that price? Well, at $2 consumers want 700 pounds. But they can only buy what steak producers wish to sell—300 pounds, so there are a lot of unhappy people who won't get the 400 pounds of steak they want. There is a **shortage**, which occurs when buyers want to purchase more than sellers offer to sell at a certain price. Thus, a shortage is the excess of the quantity demanded over the quantity supplied. Shortages create price instability because of two groups: sellers and buyers.

A **shortage** is the excess of what buyers wish to purchase over what sellers offer for sale at some given price. It is found as the excess of the quantity demanded over the quantity supplied.

■ First, individual producers of steak notice they are selling all they wish to sell but still have extra customers who don't get any steak. Perhaps, a producer thinks, *some* people who did not get steak might be willing to pay *more* than $2. Some might crave steak so much they would pay $20 a

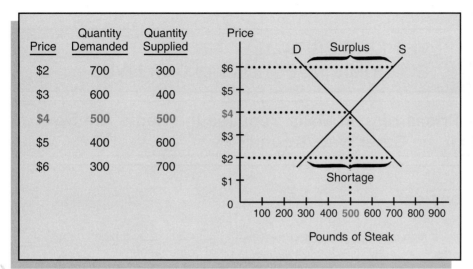

Figure 2-6

Determination of Price in the Market for Steak

Prices lower than $4 lead to shortages. Prices higher than $4 lead to surpluses. Only at $4 a pound do buyers wish to purchase the same amount that producers offer for sale (500 pounds).

Thus, the equilibrium price is $4 and the equilibrium quantity is 500 pounds.

Price	Quantity Demanded	Quantity Supplied
$2	700	300
$3	600	400
$4	500	500
$5	400	600
$6	300	700

pound, or some might be "fat cats" with so much money that price doesn't matter much to them. On the other hand, some who *did* get steak at $2 are "cheapskates" who would only buy steak if it was $2 a pound or less. What if that producer increases the price to $3? Some people (the "cheapskates") who would buy steak at $2 would not buy any at $3, but perhaps most people would pay the price. Anyway, the seller of steak can afford to lose some customers because there is an excess of them at $2. Essentially, the seller replaces "cheapskates" with "fat cats"—and still sells out of steak, thereby getting more revenue.

If all steak producers increase their prices to $3, Figure 2-6 shows that consumers now want only 600 pounds, 100 pounds less. Note also that producers now wish to sell 100 pounds more, or 400 pounds. These changes, dictated by the law of demand and the law of supply, reduce the shortage to 200 pounds of steak.

■ Customers who could *not* buy steak at $2 make up the second group that forces a price increase when there is a shortage. Not being able to spend $2 in the best way frustrates them. Such a customer might complain to a steak producer, "Why sell steak to someone else for $2 but none to me when I am willing to pay you *more*—shall we say $3?" It might seem foolish for a buyer to offer more than the going price. Yet, often *some* steak at $3 is better than *no* steak at $2. This is what happens at an auction. The auctioneer never raises the price, but only asks if a *buyer* will raise it.

THINKING CRITICALLY ABOUT ECONOMIC QUESTIONS IN OUR LIVES

Are Cookie Prices High in Malls Because the Rents Are So High—Or Is It the Other Way Around?

Things to Consider

1. If something has a high price, people generally say that it is caused by a high cost of production. Perhaps, they say, it is due to the high price of some resource.

2. It is well known that fresh-baked cookies (and many other products) in shopping malls are generally significantly higher in price than in other locations. It is also known that mall stores usually pay steeper rents than other locations. Therefore, it is reasonable to believe that the store owners have to charge high prices to pay their high rents.

3. Before you accept this argument, consider what rent is. It is a price. Think of why anyone would even pay a dollar to rent a retail space. Also, think of why anyone would pay more to rent one place than another. Finally, think of how you act in the market for cookies. Does location have anything to do with how you act as a cookie buyer—such as how much you are willing to pay?

See page 451 for the answer.

Equilibrium price is the price where the amount buyers are willing to purchase equals the amount sellers offer for sale.

Equilibrium quantity is the amount of an item that is exchanged (sold or purchased) at the equilibrium price.

There is still market instability at $3, for a shortage still exists, though it is smaller. (In general, the lower the price for anything, the greater the shortage will be.) Thus, the price continues to rise until the shortage disappears. This happens at $4 a pound, when consumers wish to buy 500 pounds and steak sellers wish to sell the same amount. With the shortage gone, there is no force tending to raise the price. The market is at the equilibrium position, which means nothing will change, neither the price nor the amount sold. The **equilibrium price** is the price where buyers want to buy the same amount that firms want to sell (where the quantity demanded equals the quantity supplied). The **equilibrium quantity** is the amount exchanged (sold or purchased) at the equilibrium price. Thus, in the steak market, the equilibrium price is $4 and the equilibrium quantity is 500 pounds.

Now suppose the price of steak is *higher*, not lower, than the equilibrium price—say, $6 a pound. Although this sounds great for the steak sellers, they are not completely content. They want to sell 700 pounds, but customers buy only 300 pounds. There is a **surplus**, which means sellers want to sell more than buyers want to purchase at a certain price. Thus, a surplus is the excess of the quantity supplied over the quantity demanded. Generally, the higher the price for something, the larger the surplus. At $6 the surplus is 400 pounds. As with a shortage, a surplus leads to price changes because of the actions of two groups.

> A **surplus** is the excess of how much sellers offer for sale over what buyers are willing to purchase. It is equal to the excess of the quantity supplied over the quantity demanded.

■ First, individual sellers of steak sell only part of what they want to sell and see that other sellers have customers who *could* be theirs. One seller might say, "How can I get some of my competitors' customers so I can sell *all* that I wish? Perhaps if I reduce my price, steak buyers will abandon my competitors and come running to me." So that seller does just that, and it works—for a while. However, before long other sellers play the same game. It's called competition, and it soon drives the price down to $5, where the surplus is only 200 pounds. The surplus shrinks from 400 pounds for two reasons. First, buyers want more steak at the lower price. Second, sellers offer less steak for sale—steak that is no longer profitable to produce. This process continues until the equilibrium price eventually is established, in this case at $4 a pound.

■ The second group that forces the price down consists of buyers aware of the surplus facing the steak producers or sellers. Such a buyer takes advantage of this "buyers' market" by saying to a seller, "Look, if you don't sell me steak at less than $6 a pound, I'll find a seller who will." Sooner or later, this forces sellers to grudgingly accept lower prices, for the old "half a loaf is better than none" adage is at work. Prices continue to fall so long as there is a surplus, in this case to $4. Now consumers buy all that producers wish to sell. Again the market experiences equilibrium.

Figure 2-7 summarizes this entire competitive market price-setting mechanism. Whether the market starts at prices that are "too low" or "too high," it ends up at the equilibrium position.

Reasons Why Equilibrium Is Not Always Reached

Theoretically, all markets are *supposed* to work the way this market for steak works. Because of competition, shortages and surpluses force prices to the point that "clears the market"—that is, "clear" of shortages and surpluses. However, it doesn't always work like that. Often, the actual market price is either lower or higher than the equilibrium price. Consequently, shortages or surpluses persist for long periods—sometimes forever.

Figure 2-7

How Buyers and
Sellers Agree on
a Price in a Market

A "low price" (one below
the equilibrium price)
encourages much buying
but little output. Thus,
there are shortages. This
leads to auction-like
activity, where buyers
outbid each other. It also
leads sellers to raise
prices, as they are willing
to lose some customers,
so long as new ones who
are willing to pay higher
prices replace them. This
is shown on the left side of
the figure.

Alternatively, a "high price"
(one above the equilibrium
price) causes a surplus. In
response, either buyers
demand a "better deal" or
sellers undercut each
others' prices to rid
themselves of their
surpluses by "stealing"
each others' customers.
This is shown on the right
side of the figure.

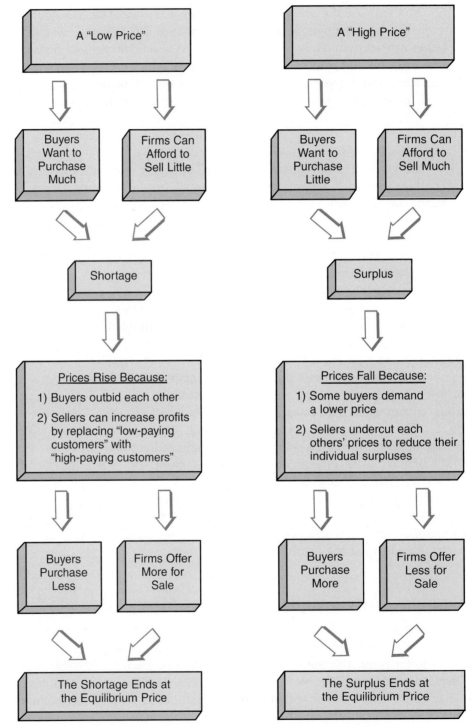

Markets may not clear like the market for steak in the example for four main reasons: 1) ignorance of the equilibrium price; 2) collusion; 3) sellers refuse to raise prices; and 4) government price controls.

■ The first reason markets fail to clear is that sometimes no one knows what the equilibrium price is. No one actually has convenient tables like those in our steak example in order to pinpoint the equilibrium price. Many markets have small surpluses or shortages, caused by prices slightly higher or lower than the equilibrium price. Such situations persist mainly because firms will not change prices, often because changing prices takes time that is too costly to be worthwhile. Also, problems for sellers and buyers caused by the small surpluses and shortages are so slight that no one feels compelled to change prices. An example is a popular sweatshirt that is occasionally out of stock. Another is a long line (the shortage) at a restaurant on a Saturday night. Finally, often buyers or sellers are not aware of such surpluses or shortages. One such example is a surplus of motel rooms in the form of slightly more unrented rooms than normal. Given enough time, however, many of these problems disappear as market knowledge becomes available.

■ The second reason markets fail to clear involves an agreement between sellers to fix prices, setting them above the equilibrium price. A **cartel** is an organization of such sellers. Because the fixed price is above the equilibrium, the cartel members face a surplus that cannot be sold. To deal with this surplus, each cartel member, though wishing to sell more than it can, agrees to limit its production, usually called a quota. Consequently, the total output of the cartel shrinks to meet the lower amount that consumers are willing to buy.

The best-known cartel is OPEC, the Organization of Petroleum Exporting Countries. Cartels usually collapse at some point because individual cartel members have an incentive to cheat on the agreements. For example, a member might secretly offer a lower price through a rebate plan to some favored buyer. Eventually, other cartel members will find out and retaliate, and the cartel will either collapse or become less effective. A main reason for Iraq's invasion of Kuwait in 1990 was that Kuwait often produced and sold in excess of its agreed-upon quota, thereby angering Iraq (and other OPEC members). Saddam Hussein put a stop to that.

Collusion refers to price-fixing agreements between sellers that are prohibited by law. Although cartels are generally illegal in the United States, farmers and fisheries are exempt. Also exempt are laborers, who form unions that operate like a cartel.

■ The third reason markets don't clear is because sellers sometimes don't take advantage of an opportunity to raise prices when there is a short-

A **cartel** is an organization of sellers that seek to control a market, which usually involves raising the price in that market above equilibrium, accompanied by a restriction in output to avoid an unsold surplus.

age. You probably faced some of the following situations: you couldn't find a popular item at a store; you couldn't buy a ticket to the World Series or a concert; or you couldn't find a parking space. In some cases, the price might have to increase tremendously to match the amount consumers want to buy with the amount sellers want to sell. But it could be done. The most common reason it isn't done is that firms will not risk losing consumer good will. For example, if a hardware store sharply increases the price of chain saws following a hurricane, consumers might pay the extra amount because they need the saws so urgently. However, they might never return when they need to buy other things in the future.

Another explanation of why some sellers do not raise prices when there are shortages is that maximum monetary gain may not be their primary goal. Some examples: cities do not charge all they could for parking because they also want people to shop downtown; you might not charge a friend as much for something as you would a stranger, in order to maintain

if the prices are stabilized

??? THINKING CRITICALLY ABOUT ECONOMIC QUESTIONS IN OUR LIVES

Disasters: Do They Cause Disastrous Prices?

Things to Consider

1. Hurricanes, earthquakes, and other natural disasters are usually followed by skyrocketing prices for relief supplies and building materials. Irate buyers often demand price ceilings to keep prices from rising.

2. Overall, are such price controls good or bad for the stricken communities?

3. To help you gauge the effects of such controls, consider the rationing role played by prices. Also, consider why some prices are higher than others. ✐

4. Finally, consider how both buyers and sellers respond to changes in prices and why they do so. Now, if prices were not allowed to change (rise), will the effects be good or bad for the communities? *yes,*

See page 452 for the answer.

your friendship; and some people feel guilty about charging "whatever the market can bear."

The last reason markets fail to clear involves government intervention to help either buyers or sellers. Buyers would like to pay less for things, and sellers would like to get higher prices. If buyers or sellers cannot change the price themselves, they occasionally ask the government for help. Price controls are government laws to establish the market price either below or above the equilibrium price. Such controls fall into two classes: price ceilings and price floors. A **price ceiling** is the maximum legal price for something. Because the government's intent is to aid buyers, it sets the price *below* the equilibrium price.

A **price ceiling** is the maximum price allowed by law in some market.

Consider the market for audiotapes. Suppose the government does not want people to have to pay the equilibrium price of $8 for tapes. Thus, it passes a law that tapes cannot be sold for more than $4. Figure 2-8 shows this situation. Any price equal to or below the price ceiling limit of $4 is legal. Now suppose tape sellers charge the legal maximum of $4. The graph indicates a shortage as the horizontal distance between the demand and supply graphs at $4. The shortage occurs because many people want the relatively cheap tapes, while producers can profitably offer only a small amount.

Some examples of goods or services with current or recent price ceilings include: oil, natural gas, and gasoline (until 1981); rent in over 200 U.S. cities; and interest rates for credit (called usury laws). Shortages accompany or accompanied each of these market interventions, and the "energy crisis" of the 1970s was the most dramatic.

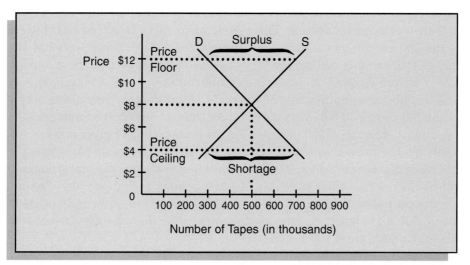

Figure 2-8

Price Ceilings and Price Floors

A price ceiling, if set below the equilibrium price, will cause shortages.

A price floor, if set above the equilibrium price, will cause surpluses.

A **price floor** is the minimum price allowed by law in some market.

A **price floor** is the minimum legal price for something. In some cases it is called a price support because its intent is to "support" prices and prevent them from falling to the equilibrium.

Suppose the government wants to help tape producers by setting a legal minimum of $12 per tape, well above the competitive equilibrium of $8. The producers' gain in price comes at the expense of the buyers. Figure 2-8 shows a surplus of 400 as the horizontal distance between the supply and demand graphs at $12. Tape producers would love to sell many of these high-priced tapes, but consumers refuse to buy many.

Examples of price floors include price supports on many agricultural products (such as wheat, corn, cotton, honey, and milk) that American farmers produce in surplus. There is also a floor for the "price" of labor, known as the minimum wage. Many economists believe that one consequence is a surplus of labor—or unemployment.

Why There Are Changes in Equilibrium Prices

Some prices—as for salt, pencils, and film—never seem to change much. Other prices fluctuate, often wildly, as for lettuce, gasoline, and corporate stocks. This section explains why equilibrium prices change.

In Figure 2-6, note that $4 a pound is the price where buyers want the same amount as steak producers wish to sell (500 pounds). This equilibrium condition will remain so long as there is no change in demand or supply. Now let's consider such changes and observe the effects on the equilibrium price and quantity.

■ Consider an increase in the demand for steak, which means consumers wish to buy more steak *even if there is no change in the price.* Figure 2-9 shows the consequences. The new demand curve D_2 shows that buyers want 200 pounds more than with the old curve D_1, no matter what the price. There is only one supply curve because there is no change in supply.

Before demand changed, the equilibrium price was $4 a pound, and the equilibrium quantity was 500 pounds. After demand increases, people want 700 pounds at $4—yet producers continue to offer 500 pounds for sale, creating a shortage of 200 pounds. The $4 price no longer gives market stability, so the price climbs to a *new* market-clearing level at $5, where the shortage disappears for two reasons. First, buyers follow the law of demand when they reduce their purchases by 100 pounds to 600 pounds. Second, producers follow the law of supply by offering 100 more pounds of steak (from 500 up to 600). So long as there are no further changes in demand, the new equilibrium will remain.

■ The equilibrium price could also increase if the supply decreases.

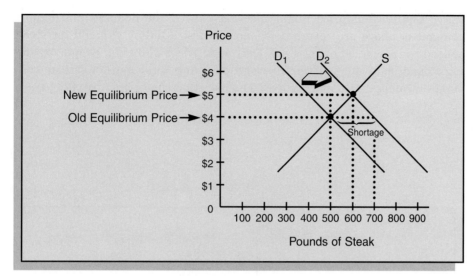

Figure 2-9

An Increase in Demand

An increase in demand for steak creates a shortage of 200 pounds at $4, the old equilibrium price. This shortage forces the price up to a new equilibrium price at $5. Thus, this shortage is only temporary.

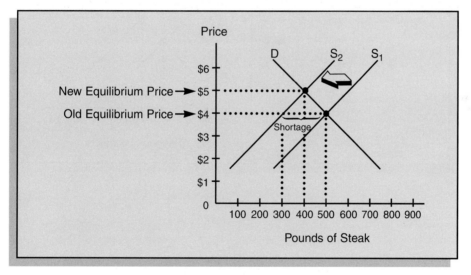

Figure 2-10

A Decrease in Supply

A decrease in supply of steak creates a shortage of 200 pounds at $4, the old equilibrium price. This shortage forces the price up to a new equilibrium price at $5. Again, this shortage is only temporary.

Figure 2-10 shows the effect of such a cutback in supply. The initial equilibrium price is $4 a pound, and the equilibrium quantity is 500 pounds. After supply falls, steak producers offer 200 pounds less for sale at each price. The market no longer clears at $4 because there is a shortage of 200 pounds. This is because consumers continue to ask for 500 pounds. Their buying decisions are unrelated to the producers' problems, such as increased costs. This shortage leads to a new equilibrium price and quantity of $5 a pound and 400 pounds.

Equilibrium price might also *decrease* if the demand and supply changes of above are reversed. Consider first a falling demand for steak caused by: people enjoying steak less; pork prices plunging; people expecting a big drop in steak prices; fewer people living in the market area; or consumer incomes dropping. Figure 2-11 shows that condition. Any of these sit-

Figure 2-11

A Decrease in Demand

A decrease in demand of steak creates a surplus of 200 pounds at $4, the old equilibrium price. This surplus forces the price down to a new equilibrium price at $3. Thus, this surplus is only temporary.

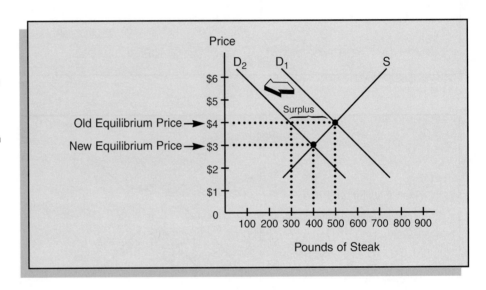

uations would force consumers to buy less than the 500 pounds they bought at $4 a pound. Suppose they only wish to buy 300 pounds at $4 a pound (actually, they would buy 200 pounds less at *any* price). Because steak producers have no reason to sell less, a surplus of 200 pounds appears at $4 a pound. Consequently, prices fall until this surplus disappears at a new, lower equilibrium price of $3 a pound, which corresponds to a lower equilibrium quantity of 400 pounds. Such a situation occurs with sale-priced merchandise at the end of a season or when something goes out of style.

Price can also decline in a market because of a surplus caused by an increase in supply. Figure 2-12 shows that situation. This could occur in the steak market example if: production costs decline; the profitability of other animal enterprises (such as hogs or sheep) declines; or growers expect the future price of steak to be lower. Such circumstances will *not* affect the steak buyers. They still want only 500 pounds at $4 a pound. The extra steak output becomes a surplus. Consequently, the equilibrium price falls to $3, but in this case the equilibrium quantity is higher (600 pounds) than it was originally. The computer industry offers one of the best examples of an increase in supply. Dramatic reductions in manufacturing costs due to innovations led to increases in the supply of computers, thereby decreasing their prices and increasing the amount sold.

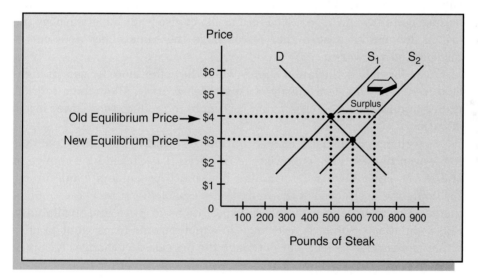

Figure 2-12

An Increase in Supply

An increase in the supply of steak creates a surplus of 200 pounds at $4, the old equilibrium price. This surplus forces the price down to a new equilibrium at $3. Again, the surplus is only temporary.

These and countless other examples of changing prices illustrate the vital role played by the concepts of supply and demand in understanding the world around you—and why that world is changing. You will often be in a stronger economic position if you can predict such price changes *before* they occur.

SUMMARY

The purpose of markets is to facilitate exchanges between specialists. In modern markets, a single good, service, or resource is exchanged for money. The price is the amount of money exchanged for a single unit of the item exchanged.

The amount of a good or service traded between buyers and sellers depends upon several things. One of these factors, price, merits special attention. If the amounts that buyers and sellers want to exchange at a given price are not alike, the price will change. In turn, changes in the wishes of buyers and sellers will make these two amounts alike. Once that point of balance, called equilibrium, is reached, there are no further changes in price and the amount traded, so long as demand and supply remain constant.

Buyers follow the law of demand when they buy less of a good or service at higher prices, and vice versa. They do so primarily because of the substitution effect. When an item becomes more costly, substitutes often become better things to buy. The income effect also leads buyers to obey the law of demand because higher prices have the same effect as a cut in income, and vice versa.

Sellers follow the law of supply when they offer more for sale at higher prices. They do so primarily because higher prices allow them to profitably produce levels of output that cost more to produce than lower levels of output.

A change in demand means that buyers want to buy either more or less—even though there is no change in price. It is caused by a change in one of the other factors determining how much consumers want to buy, including the usefulness of the item, the prices of substitutes and complements, consumers' incomes, future expectations of price and availability, and population. Similarly, a change in supply means firms want to offer either more or less for sale—even though the price doesn't change. A change in supply will occur following a change in any of the other factors determining how much firms wish to offer for sale, including production costs, expected future prices, the number of sellers, and the prices of other things it is possible to make with the same resources.

Low prices tend to create shortages because buyers want a lot of a low-priced item and sellers can't afford to offer much for sale. Customers who can't buy all they want, along with sellers seeking to increase profits, raise the price up to the equilibrium price. High prices do the opposite because low purchases and high availability create surpluses. Firms undercutting each others' prices plus bargain-demanding buyers force the price down to the equilibrium price.

Several things can prevent the price from moving to the equilibrium level, including government price controls, collusion, ignorance of the equilibrium price, and a reluctance to take advantage of market conditions.

The equilibrium price will rise if demand increases or supply decreases because either of these causes a shortage. The equilibrium price will fall if demand decreases or supply increases because either of these will cause a surplus.

QUESTIONS FOR DISCUSSION AND THOUGHT

1. If something has a "negative price," what does that suggest about the item? For example, a ticket to see your neighbor, a beginner, play a violin might be *minus* $20, meaning you'd go if you were *paid* $20. What is it about the demand for this concert that is different from other musical concerts that explains the price?

2. How much is your right arm worth? That is, what if you only had a left arm and could buy a right arm and have it attached (and have it work as well as your actual right one currently does)? How much would you pay? What about buying a left arm (assuming you now have a right one)? Suppose that you could do as much with either one of your purchased arms as you now can with your actual right and left arms (which would be different, as you are either right- or left-handed). If you are willing to pay more for one than the other, why are you so willing? What does that suggest about the relative strengths of demands for right arms vs. left arms? What is the basis of these strengths?

3. Does "price gouging" anger you? An example is when an item that everyone wants but which is extremely limited in quantity sells for a steep price. Suppose you discover a rare coin, stamp, or baseball card in some attic. If lots of people collect such items, that item could perhaps command a high price. If you don't particularly like the item and are not a collector, would you throw it away or give it away? After all, it's not worth anything to you. Or will you sell it? If you sell it, at what price will you sell it for? A low price? Or a very high price you *can* get? If you choose the high price, isn't that "price gouging"? If you answered yes to the first question above about price gouging, how can you explain yourself out of your inconsistent attitudes toward prices?

4. Very often you see an item selling for the same price at many different businesses. Does this suggest that there is collusive price fixing going on? What else could explain it?

5. Determine if your personal demand for hamburgers, movies, and college tuition would be elastic or inelastic if their prices would increase by 50 percent. Why do these demands have such elasticity?

6. What are some factors that would lead to a decrease in demand for swimsuits? Would they also affect supply? Why or why not?

7. Find three examples each of shortages and surpluses. Why doesn't the price change to clear the market in each case?

8. Winning bidders at auctions often do not pay as much for the item as they are willing to pay. Why not? In such cases, does the value of the item equal the price, or is one larger than the other—both for the winning bidder and the other bidders?

9. Should there be a ceiling on college textbook prices? Why or why not? What would be the consequences, if any?

10. If you lived in a house that had a yard when you were growing up, was the entire yard filled with sweet corn? If not, why not? (Answer the question using economic analysis.) What *might have* induced your parents to fill it with sweet corn?

PROBLEMS   See pages 479-480 for the answers.

1. Following are some changes that will affect the market for oranges. You are to determine what the effect will be (if any) on the demand, the supply, the equilibrium price, and the equilibrium quantity of oranges.
   a) the price of grapefruit juice falls
   b) orange juice has been found to combat certain types of cancer
   c) pickers of oranges get a raise
   d) the price of vodka falls
   e) genetic engineering results in all the oranges on a tree ripening at the same time (now they ripen over a several week period)
   f) the price of oranges is expected to fall sharply one month from now

2. Suppose that at $18 firms jointly supply 22 million compact discs (CDs), and consumers wish to buy 18 million. For each one dollar change in price, firms wish to sell one million more or less; consumers wish to buy one million more or less.

   What is the equilibrium price for CDs? The equilibrium quantity? If the government sets a price ceiling of $14, will there be a shortage or a surplus of CDs and, if so, how large will it be? If it sets a price floor of $21, will there be a shortage or surplus? If so, how large will it be?

APPENDIX: THE ELASTICITY OF DEMAND

The elasticity of demand refers to buyer response to changes in price. If demand is elastic, a given percentage price change will result in a greater percentage change in purchases. Alternatively, if demand is inelastic, a given percentage change in price will result in a smaller percentage change in purchases.

The Coefficient of Elasticity

The coefficient of elasticity indicates just how elastic or inelastic the demand for a good or service is. It is found by dividing the percentage change in quantity purchased by the percentage change in price, or:

$$e = \frac{\textbf{Percentage Change in Quantity}}{\textbf{Percentage Change in Price}}$$

If these percentages are not known, the coefficient can be calculated by the formula:

$$e = \frac{(Q_2 - Q_1)}{Q_1} \div \frac{(P_2 - P_1)}{P_1}$$

P_1 refers to the initial price and P_2 to the new price. Q_1 is the initial amount consumers want and Q_2 the amount purchased after the price change. Because demand is an inverse relationship, the coefficient is always negative. However, it is always stated in absolute value form (meaning the minus sign is dropped). If the coefficient is: 1) greater than one, the demand is elastic; 2) equal to one, the demand is unitary elastic; or 3) less than one, the demand is inelastic. (There is a more complex, but also more accurate, version of the formula. The single Q_1 in the numerator is replaced by $(Q_1 + Q_2) \div 2$. The single P_1 in the denominator is replaced by $(P_1 + P_2) \div 2$.)

Suppose consumers want to buy 600 sweatshirts if the price is $12. If the price rises to $15, they want fewer shirts—say only 500. Figure A2-1 shows a demand curve reflecting such desired purchases. The coefficient of elasticity is 0.67, found in either of two ways. First, as the price rose 25 percent ($12 to $15) and the quantity fell by 16.67 percent (600 down to 500), then $e = 16.67\% \div 25.0\% = 0.67$.

Second, the formula given above can be used to calculate e as follows:

$$e = \frac{(500 - 600)}{600} \div \frac{(15 - 12)}{12} = \frac{100}{600} \div \frac{3}{12} = \frac{1}{6} \div \frac{1}{4} = 0.67$$

Thus, between $12 and $15, demand is inelastic.

On the other hand, the demand curve in Figure A2-2 is elastic between these prices. For the same 25 percent increase in price, quantity purchased fell 50 percent (600 down to 300), so that e = 50% ÷ 25% = 2.0

Essentially, e = 2.0 means the response in purchases to the price change is twice as large as the price change itself.

Notice that the demand curve is steeper for the inelastic case than the elastic case. In general, you can say that steeper demand curves imply more inelasticity.

If the demand line is horizontal, the demand relationship is called perfectly elastic. Alternatively, a demand line that is vertical means the demand is perfectly inelastic. That means any change in price has no effect on consumer purchases. You may have experienced this situation when you buy a replacement part for your car. If the manufacturer is the only firm selling the product (it is then a monopolist), the price tends to be sky high. For what else will you do—junk the car? Hardly.

Figure A2-1   An Inelastic Demand

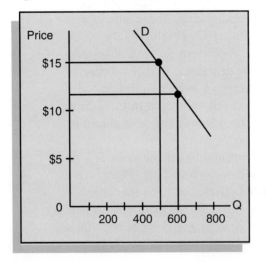

Figure A2-2   An Elastic Demand

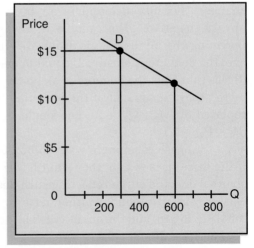

Determinants of Elasticity

Four major factors determine the degree of elasticity of demand for a good or service: 1) the number of substitutes; 2) the share of income spent on an item; 3) how necessary the item is; and 4) the length of the market period.

■ The first determinant of demand elasticity is the number of substitutes. The more substitutes a product has, the more elastic the demand tends to be. For example, a certain theater might face competition from a dozen other theaters. A dollar increase in price at the first theater would drive many people to competing theaters. On the other hand, in a small town with a single theater and little other entertainment, the theater probably wouldn't lose many patrons after a similar price increase. In the extreme, this leads to the case above of expensive replacement parts.

■ Second, the share of a person's income spent on a product influences elasticity. An item that takes a tiny share of a budget, such as a box of matches, tends to have a very inelastic demand. However, sellers of items such as sailboats and luxury cruises generally find that customers are very price conscious (as was discovered with the imposition of the 10 percent excise tax on luxury boats in 1991).

■ Third, necessary items such as insulin and work uniforms tend to have extremely inelastic (or even perfectly inelastic) demands. People must pay whatever price is asked. However, when things that people can easily do without, such as hot tubs, go up in price, their sales drop sharply.

■ Finally, the length of the market period influences price elasticity. Generally, the longer the period of time following a price increase, the more that consumers will reduce their purchases. A good example was gasoline in the 1970s. Prices tripled in a three-year period, but it took at least 10 years before the full response was felt. That was largely because cars generally last 10 years or more. So a new gas guzzler purchased in the early 1970s would not have been replaced by a more fuel-efficient car until the early 1980s or so.

3

ECONOMIC GROWTH AND PRODUCTIVITY

CHAPTER PREVIEW

The economic problem, caused by resource scarcity, limits the level of our economic welfare. We seek to raise economic welfare by increasing either the quantity of resources or how efficiently these resources are used.

We can increase resource efficiency by reducing resource waste, specializing in their use, or innovating. These all affect production costs, profits, and prices, ultimately leading to higher living standards.

Centuries of innovations have resulted in the mass production of many of the goods and services we use. This has shaped our lifestyles, affected our labor markets, and made us interdependent. In essence, this chapter shows why our economy has changed so much in the last few centuries and why it will keep changing.

CHAPTER OBJECTIVES

After completing this chapter, you should be able to:

◆ List the primary ways to increase living standards.

◆ Explain how specialization increases the efficiency of resource use.

◆ Explain how to determine the comparative advantage of a resource.

◆ Explain how innovation influences efficiency, production costs, prices, and living standards.

◆ Explain the relationship between returns to scale and production costs.

◆ Explain the influence that mechanization has on relative prices, average firm size, and the number of firms in an industry.

◆ Explain how innovations that lead to mass production create new jobs.

Because resources are scarce, there will be a limited amount of goods and services produced. As that limits our economic welfare, we all have a vital interest in how our resources are used.

This chapter will introduce various ways of achieving **economic growth**, which is an increase in the output of goods and services. This, in turn, can increase economic welfare. You will learn how society can achieve economic growth by raising the amount of resources as well as by more efficient use of existing resources, mainly through specialization and innovation. Finally, you will learn how the economy and society have changed over the centuries as a consequence of economic growth.

> **Economic growth** is an increase in the output of goods and services.

INTRODUCTION TO ECONOMIC WELFARE

Before exploring how economic welfare is raised, it is useful to discuss a way to measure it. This section introduces a measure of economic welfare and takes a broad look at how to raise its level.

How Economic Welfare Can Be Measured

Economic welfare refers to satisfaction achieved when consuming goods and services. Measuring satisfaction is difficult, at least objectively. Instead, your best available measure of economic welfare might be subjective. You could observe how often someone smiles, laughs, or makes cheerful remarks. However, this wouldn't work because happiness comes from many sources besides materialistic ones.

However, economic welfare can be measured indirectly by measuring the output of goods and services. Not only do Americans surpass most foreigners in personal possessions, but today's Americans easily surpass earlier Americans in their possessions. For example, in 1910 *no* family had a vacuum cleaner, washing machine, refrigerator, dishwasher, toaster, coffee maker, or television set—all items many people today call "necessities." In homes in 1900, only 24 percent had running water, 15 percent had flush toilets, and three percent had electricity. Today most people take out-of-state vacations, often yearly. In the 1950s, only a small minority did. Further, foreign travel is getting fairly common, but it was extremely rare in the 1950s.

In a broader and more accurate sense, *total* output for the nation is measured in an entire year. This is a measure of the *collective* economic welfare of all the 265 million Americans combined. Similarly, the 28 million Canadians can add up their output. Nations measure their total output with the gross domestic product (GDP), or the total value of output in a year (presented in more detail in Chapter 9).

However, those figures don't indicate whether the *average* American has more goods and services than the *average* Canadian. To find that amount—the amount of *individual* economic welfare—you must divide total output by the population. This amount is called the **living standard** or standard of living. It refers to the amount of goods and services produced in a year for each person, on average, or per capita output.

The **living standard** is the amount of goods and services produced in a nation in a year for each person, on average.

$$\text{Living Standard} = \frac{\text{Total Output of Goods and Services}}{\text{Population}}$$

Of course, few people actually receive that exact amount of goods and services. They get either more or less than that. Historically, each generation has seen a significant increase in living standards, though they have not risen every year.

THINKING CRITICALLY ABOUT ECONOMIC QUESTIONS IN OUR LIVES

Why Aren't We Happier Than Our Great-Grandparents Were?

Things to Consider

1. Look at a number of photos from the 1800s of people in everyday life. You will often see them smiling, laughing, and having fun—just as you'd see in photos of today. If you read diaries or other first-person accounts of the period, you'd get the sense that people were just as happy (or nearly so) then as we are today. Some empirical research also suggests that this is true.

2. Wouldn't you expect our level of happiness to be much higher, in light of our much higher living standards? We buy goods and services because they provide us satisfaction (or happiness). Thus, as we have far more goods and services than our great grandparents did, we should be far happier.

3. If we, indeed, are not any happier (or much happier), how can you explain it?

See page 453 for the answer.

There are two major objections to the use of the living standard to measure economic welfare: 1) the problem of varying income distributions is not addressed; and 2) other goals and values are not considered.

■ First, the living standard ignores the effect that varying income distributions have on the "collective satisfaction" of the society. In one possible income distribution, everyone would have an equal income. In another, 90 percent of the income would go to five percent of the population, with the remainder barely surviving on 10 percent of the income. Although "collective satisfaction" cannot be measured, perhaps the equal distribution would yield a happier society.

A greater "collective" economic welfare is the goal of legislatures, courts, and other government agencies when they make changes in taxes, earning power, and the public welfare system.

■ The second objection to using the standard of living to measure economic welfare is based on the criticism of our "quality of life." We have an economically rich society, but at what cost? Our air, rivers, and lakes are often fouled; the stress of the "rat race" leads to phenomenal use of tranquilizers, alcohol, and psychotherapy; the crime rate is high; and institutions—the family, schools, churches—are withering. Thus, a higher living standard for a society doesn't necessarily mean it will enjoy a higher "quality of life"—or more happiness for that matter.

Some First Steps in Raising Living Standards

Some clues to raising the living standard are found in the formula on page 70. A nation can raise its living standard either by: 1) decreasing the denominator (the population); or 2) increasing the numerator (the output of goods and services).

■ Reducing the population obviously is not the answer. Yet controlling population *growth* does deserve attention. America's population grows around one percent per year, whereas that of many less-developed nations climbs between two and three percent per year. A higher growth rate results in a higher percentage of the population that is young—and not yet producing goods and services. Because these young people need food, clothing, and the like, the available output spreads more thinly in such nations.

■ The primary way to increase the living standard is to produce more goods and services. Nations do this: 1) by finding or developing more resources; and 2) by becoming more efficient in using existing resources.

Before examining how this is done in the economy, consider how it might have worked in a self-sufficient, pioneer farm family. A family that lived at a subsistence level may have wished to increase its welfare. First, it could have done so by adding to the stock of resources it already had. Labor resources could have been increased by working longer hours and by having larger families. More farmland could have been produced by clearing woodlands, draining swamps, and plowing virgin land. More capital would have been available after new tools were made, buildings were constructed, and dams were built as power sources and reservoirs.

Second, the family could have been more efficient in using its resources. Trial and error in new production techniques would have improved crop yields and the productivity of other outputs over time. Specialization would have raised productivity significantly. Men would have learned what tasks they were best at—probably those requiring strength and endurance, such as field work. So would women—probably the lighter farm work, such as milking and tending chickens, as well as the household work of cooking, clothes-making, candle-making, and so on.

In a modern economy, such increases in the living standard come in the same two ways. Yet, the process is less obvious because it is harder to observe an entire economy than a single farm family. Nevertheless, consider how it is possible to have an increase in the available resources in an entire economy.

Consider natural resources. Although the amount of natural resources can't be increased, the amount of *practically available* natural resources is increased when people: find and develop a new oil field; develop a mining process to extract a previously useless low-grade metal ore; drain wetlands for farm use; and build roads into remote forests.

The labor resource can increase in several ways. Population can increase through normal excesses of births over deaths or by immigration. Often nations try to encourage the "right" people to immigrate and enter the labor force. U.S. immigration laws in the past limited immigration from various "undesirable nations," usually where people had few skills.

Labor availability could also be increased by: increasing the workweek from 40 to 50 or 60 hours; extending the retirement age and encouraging retired people to go back to work; setting up more workshops for the one million Americans in prisons; encouraging more homemakers to get jobs outside the home; and relaxing child labor laws.

Last, labor resources increase when otherwise "useless" raw human talent becomes educated. School "socializes" people so they can work cooperatively with others and handle work discipline. It also provides them with complex mental and physical skills to be highly productive. Educated people are "human capital," for labor resources are created in schools, just like any tool or machine is created.

The amount of capital resources (or capital stock) of the economy increases when, for example: Caterpillar builds a bulldozer for a contractor, Apple makes a computer for an office at General Motors, and Stanley produces another hammer for a carpenter; the Army Corps of Engineers builds a dam to improve navigation, control floods, and supply irrigation water; a developer erects an office building in Los Angeles; and government expands the interstate highway system or builds new schools.

Finally, where do entrepreneurs come from? Some ways that government and private enterprise can encourage people to become entrepreneurs are: change tax laws to allow rich people to keep more of their income; develop sources of financial backing for entrepreneurs; stimulate original thinking and independence in schools; and expand Junior Achievement and similar programs.

HOW TO RAISE THE EFFICIENCY OF RESOURCES

Efficiency refers to how well resources are used. That is, it refers to how much output of a good or service is produced from a given amount of resources. This concept of efficiency has to do with producing things. Somewhat apart from that, economists refer to **allocative efficiency**, which means firms produce the goods and services most preferred by consumers. Thus, the What-to-Produce question is answered so that any other way of answering it (that is, changing what is made) will reduce economic welfare. Another aspect of efficiency refers to how well the nation's total output is distributed. This is called distributive efficiency.

Allocative efficiency means firms produce the goods and services most preferred by consumers.

One often hears of another concept, called productivity, that seems identical to efficiency. Economists generally use the term efficiency when speaking of many resources being used in conjunction with each other. But productivity refers to the productiveness of a specific resource (even though that resource is usually used in conjunction with other resources). Most commonly, people refer to **labor productivity**, or output per hour. It includes the hours worked by all laborers: assemblers, shipping clerks, secretaries, janitors, and so on. It is calculated for a particular production process in some given period with the formula:

Labor productivity is the output produced by a laborer working one hour.

$$\text{Labor Productivity} = \frac{\text{Total Output}}{\text{Total Hours Worked}}$$

For example, a window manufacturer makes 90,000 windows in a year with 30 employees working a 40-hour-week shift, 50 weeks per year. Total hours worked is then 60,000 hours (= 30 x 40 x 50), and labor productivity is 1.5 windows per hour (= 90,000 windows ÷ 60,000 hours). Thus, for each hour of every laborer's time, on average, the firm makes 1.5 windows. (Bear in mind that it isn't only labor that produces the windows, but machines, buildings, and other capital resources as well, plus all other resources.)

In addition, occasionally one hears of capital productivity (the amount of product produced by one hour of machine time) and land productivity (the yield of a crop per acre of land).

This section introduces the three primary ways of increasing efficiency: 1) eliminating waste in existing production processes; 2) increasing the specialization of resource use; and 3) innovation.

Eliminating Waste in Existing Production Processes

Few resources achieve their potential, even when producers use them in the best available production process. Here are a few of the millions of ways to cut the waste of resource use *without* changing the production process itself. Office workers could produce more by stopping idle chatter, eliminating personal phone calls, and not calling in "sick" when they are not. Assembly line workers can boost their productivity by speeding up the line, keeping parts handy, and reducing breakage by being more careful. Managers can be more effective by becoming more skillful in dealing with subordinates.

Besides the waste of labor, often firms don't use their capital equipment to its potential. Better maintenance would reduce breakdowns. Improved scheduling of supplies and production would reduce idle machine operation time. Adding second and third shifts is another way to increase capital productivity.

Natural resources also are often squandered. The loss of U.S. soil through wind and water erosion in the last hundred years or so is a national scandal. Wiser selection of crops and tillage practices would sharply reduce erosion. Our forest resources also suffered from mismanagement, especially in the upper Midwest in the late 1800s and early 1900s.

Increasing the Specialization of Resource Use

The second way to raise the efficiency of resource use is by increasing the degree of **specialization**. (We assume specialization has already been introduced into the economy. But many thousands of years ago, we might speculate that each person was a "Robinson Crusoe type" that didn't specialize at all. Everyone was completely independent, which meant that

Specialization refers to the use of a resource to produce only one item, or perhaps to produce only part of an item.

everyone was very poor—in terms of the amount of goods available.) When a resource's use is specialized (such as laborer's time), it produces only a few goods or services—or even one. This is often called the division of labor by product. Bakers, auto workers, bus drivers, and telephone operators all produce one thing, or, at the most, several closely related items.

Specialization can go a step further when a laborer doesn't make the whole good or service. Because the laborer participates in only one part of the production process, economists call this the division of labor by process. It's what usually is meant by the **division of labor**. In auto manufacture, for example, someone might work only on the engine, and just on the camshaft.

The **division of labor** refers to each laborer carrying out only one task in the production process of a single product.

The use of resources other than labor can also be specialized. The value of specializing the use of land and natural resources is fairly obvious if we suppose that the only crops we can produce are wheat and rice. Since rice requires a lot of water and wheat only moderate amounts, land in Arkansas is ideal for growing rice. On the other hand, Kansas receives little rain and is a poor region for growing rice, but it has adequate rainfall for wheat.

The case for specializing capital is a little less obvious because some forms of capital, like trucks and buildings, can serve many functions. Even here, however, specialization can improve efficiency. For example, a general purpose truck could not carry much oil compared with a tanker truck that is designed for that purpose.

Specialization in the use of labor, or the division of labor, increases labor efficiency for three main reasons: 1) many jobs take a long time to master; 2) people differ in their capabilities at different tasks; and 3) time between steps of a production process is saved.

■ First, many jobs take a long time to master. Thus, if a worker does only one task, this minimizes the learning time for the worker, and learners produce less than masters. Alternatively, a worker with many tasks spends a longer time learning them and, consequently, produces less than top output during that learning period.

■ Second, the division of labor increases efficiency because people differ in their capabilities at different tasks. It's foolish for every worker at a firm to share all the jobs because output wouldn't be as high as with specialization. Similarly, farmers use the land in different parts of the country for different crops—corn and soybeans in the Midwest, pecans and peanuts in the Southeast, and wheat in the Great Plains.

■ Third, the division of labor increases efficiency because it eliminates time that would otherwise be spent between the steps of a production process. For example, suppose six people are to make 500 pizzas for a club project. Each could make a complete pizza by following these steps: 1) put down the cardboard; 2) get a crust and set it on the cardboard; 3) get a ladle and spread some sauce on the crust; 4) get some cheese and put it on top of the sauce; 5) get some sausage and put it on the cheese; 6) package the pizza. Because so much time would be lost *between* steps, it would save time if each of the six people would do only one job.

Once it is decided to specialize in the use of a resource, how should the resource be used? That seems easy. Shouldn't, for example, Michael, a laborer, do what he does well? Not always, for it's not that simple. When a resource is the most productive of all such resources in making something, it has an **absolute advantage** in that production process. But having an absolute advantage doesn't dictate how a resource should be used. A real example might help.

An **absolute advantage** occurs when a particular resource of a class of resources is the most efficient or productive at a task of all resources of that class.

Once there was a very good baseball pitcher, possibly the best in the league. But after he was traded, his new manager refused to let him pitch. He was sent to the outfield so he could play more often. The player's name was Babe Ruth. Did the manager make the right move? Obviously yes, most would say. But we'll never know. Although Ruth was a phenomenal home run hitter, maybe he would have done *even better* as a pitcher. Consequently, perhaps our best pitcher award would be the Babe Ruth Award—not the Cy Young Award.

Many business managers face similar situations. If a particular employee is the best of all employees at two or more jobs, which job should be assigned to that employee? It's equally hard when a resource isn't very good at producing *anything*. In either case, deciding how a resource should be used requires finding its **comparative advantage**. A resource has a comparative advantage when it can produce something with a lower opportunity cost than any similar resource.

A **comparative advantage** occurs when a particular resource has the lowest opportunity cost in producing something of all resources of that type.

Table 3-1 gives an example of finding comparative advantage. John and Bob are to split the production of bread and coats. Notice from the production figures that Bob can't brag about any of his talents. But John can,

Table 3-1

Finding Comparative Advantages

John has a comparative advantage in making coats, and Bob has one in making bread.

| Person | Production per Week of: | | Opportunity Cost of Producing: | |
	Bread	Coats	1 Loaf of Bread	1 Coat
John	1,000 Loaves	100 Coats	$0.100 \text{ Coat} = \dfrac{100 \text{ Coats}}{1,000 \text{ Loaves}}$	$\mathbf{10.0 \text{ Loaves}} = \dfrac{1,000 \text{ Loaves}}{100 \text{ Coats}}$
Bob	800 Loaves	60 Coats	$\mathbf{0.075 \text{ Coat}} = \dfrac{60 \text{ Coats}}{800 \text{ Loaves}}$	$13.3 \text{ Loaves} = \dfrac{800 \text{ Loaves}}{60 \text{ Coats}}$

for he has an absolute advantage in both products. When asked what Bob should do, some people would say, "Just stay out of the way!" But remember that resources are scarce. So long as Bob can make *something,* that's better than producing nothing.

In Chapter 1 you learned that the purpose of economics is to find ways to get the most from our scarce resources. That is, we wish to maximize the output of all goods and services combined. Similarly here, the goal is to maximize the production of coats plus bread. Think of Bob and John as a team, each making one item, putting their products on a common pile of bread mixed with coats (figuratively speaking, of course). When John (or Bob) makes the pile grow by adding a coat, he *keeps it* from growing by *not* adding bread. Simply put, the benefit (the coat) is offset by the opportunity cost (the bread). Because the coat is the same whether Bob or John makes it, the only decision is to find how to minimize the opportunity cost—the bread given up. The table shows that John gives up 10.0 loaves when he makes a coat, and Bob gives up 13.3. Because John gives up less, he has the lowest opportunity cost and a comparative advantage in making coats.

Alternatively, Bob has a comparative advantage in bread making. He only gives up the opportunity to make 0.075 coats when he makes a loaf of bread. But John, when making an identical loaf of bread, gives up more of a coat—0.100 of one. So Bob, though lacking an *absolute* advantage, has a *comparative* advantage and should make bread. He won't make bread because he is *good* at it, but because he is better at bread making *as compared with* coat making.

Consider this in another way. Bob can make bread at 80 percent of John's rate (800 ÷ 1,000), but coats at only 60 percent of John's rate (60 ÷ 100). Thus, Bob is *closest to* John in bread making. So Bob should make bread. Similarly, comparative advantage explains why parents assign young children to relatively simple chores, such as trash removal, vacuuming, and garden watering. Children are almost as fast as parents at these tasks, but nowhere close when it comes to mending clothes, cooking, or painting.

In conclusion, just because a resource *can* do something doesn't mean it *should* do it. You must consider what else it could do as well.

This brings up the next point—trade, or exchange. Whenever you specialize in producing a certain good, you produce far more output of that good than you need personally. You have a "surplus." However, you will not have any of the other goods and services needed for survival. You have personal "shortages." Because all specialists face this predicament, they must exchange their respective surpluses for the surpluses of other specialists. Figure 3-1 illustrates all these relationships about specialization.

Figure 3-1

How Specialization, Living Standards, and Exchange Are Related

Resources usually become more efficient when they are specialized. That allows more goods and services to be produced from our scarce resources. That is, living standards are higher.

When people (laborers and entrepreneurs) specialize, they produce more than they can consume themselves. But they have little time to make the other goods and services they need. Consequently, specialists trade or exchange with each other. That is why we have a complex, interdependent economy today, rather than a self-sufficient, subsistence economy as in the past.

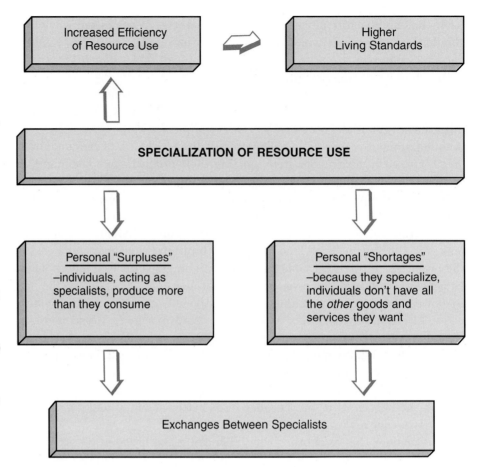

Innovation

An **innovation** is a change in the way resources are used.

The last way to increase efficiency is through **innovation**, which is a change in the way resources are used. In a broad sense, innovation includes the elimination of waste in production processes, along with increased specialization. But in this section you will learn that innovation generally occurs when there is a change in the answers to What to Produce? and How to Produce? so that there is an increase in the efficiency of resource use.

Most innovations fit into one of four classes: 1) mechanization of the production process; 2) reorganization of the production process; 3) alteration in energy sources; and 4) product innovations involving new consumer goods and services. The first three innovations increase the efficiency of production itself and reduce production costs. The last innovation leads to

**THINKING CRITICALLY ABOUT
ECONOMIC QUESTIONS IN OUR LIVES**

**Would Your Great-Great-Great-Great-Grandparents Have
Expected You to Have a Job?**

Things to Consider

1. Suppose you could go back in time and visit your distant ancestors. They'd likely be living in a subsistence, rural economy. They would make virtually all the goods they use—their clothes, food, housing, and so on.

2. The tasks of making all these items would keep them busy from dawn till dusk (and beyond). That is, they would be "fully employed" or have plenty of jobs (work).

3. How do you suppose they would react if you told them that you make only one good—say, chairs? Would they feel sorry for you, knowing you must be hungry without eating or cold without clothes? Would they think you are bored, with so little to do but make yourself a chair every now and then?

4. How would you explain that you (and others you live with) could possibly be "fully employed"? How would you make it clear to them how such a transition could have occurred?

See page 454 for the answer.

more consumer satisfaction and welfare from the same resources when a new and better product is made.

■ The first class of innovations involves mechanization. Essentially, mechanization means replacing some labor resource with some capital resource or, more plainly, replacing people with machines. Thus, What to Produce? is answered differently when a new machine is made. In turn, this leads to How to Produce? being answered differently.

■ The second class of innovations involves a change in the organization of the production process or a fundamental change in production methods without any significant increase in mechanization. One example is tilting a product so workers don't have to bend over to assemble it. Often such innovations are small and seemingly trivial. Yet because there are so many of them, they add up to major productivity improvements in the long run.

■ The third class of innovations involves changing the energy sources needed to accomplish work. Early humans used raw muscle power to produce everything, but eventually animals provided much of the power. Natural resources eventually replaced animal and human power. Early dependence upon water and wind power switched to fossil fuel (coal, gas, and oil) power in the 1800s. Finally, nuclear power and solar energy emerged in the 1900s and may become the dominant energy sources in the 21st century.

■ The last class of innovations involves new products for consumers that are enjoyed more than older ones and require similar amounts of resources. Compact discs that replaced records, video cameras with sound that replaced silent film cameras, interstate highways that replaced two-lane highways, and airplanes that replaced trains, buses, and ships are all examples.

In a capitalist economy, most innovations occur in existing businesses or come from people who begin businesses to take advantage of their ideas. The incentive, of course, is profit. Also, if the competition between firms is strong enough, a firm must innovate just to stay in business.

Figure 3-2 shows the sequence of events that follows an innovation in the manufacture of a good, called Good A. (This illustrates an innovation in the *production process* of a good and is distinct from a *product* innovation, such as the introduction of electric cars.) It initially takes X amount of resources to make one unit of Good A. The upper set of boxes represents the situation before the innovation, and the lower set represents the situation after the innovation. The blue box on the right represents the *physical* amount of resources needed to make just one unit of Good A. For example, if Good A is a house, the box would represent all the laborers, the wood, the tools, and whatever else it takes to build a house. The middle blue box represents the *dollar* amount of those resources, or the average cost of producing Good A (the house). The blue box on the left represents the price of Good A (the house), for price equals average cost plus the profit margin.

Innovations of the first three types covered reduce the resources needed to make something. Look at the lower set of blue boxes in Figure 3-2. The area on the right box labeled "Saved Resources" represents the resources saved in making one unit of Good A. In the house example, it might represent laid-off workers, leftover wood, and other resources after the innovation. Those resources are now "freed up" or available to produce something the economy previously never had the resources to make. Thus, the living standard increases when the resources are used elsewhere.

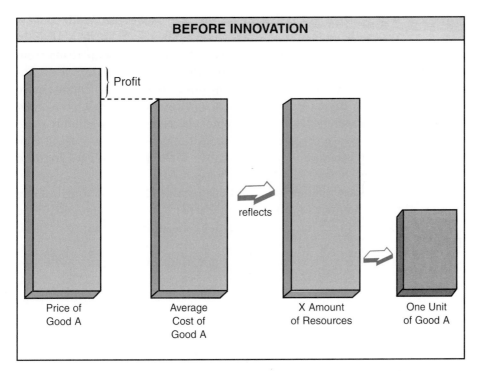

BEFORE INNOVATION

Profit

Price of
Good A

Average
Cost of
Good A

reflects

X Amount
of Resources

One Unit
of Good A

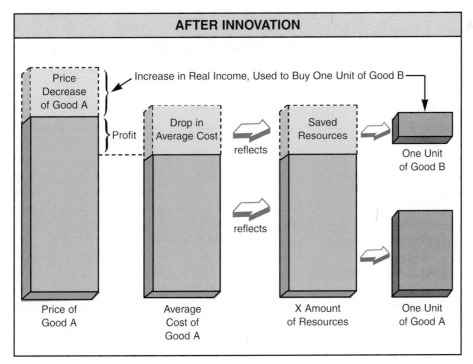

AFTER INNOVATION

Price
Decrease
of Good A

Increase in Real Income, Used to Buy One Unit of Good B

Profit

Drop in
Average Cost

reflects

Saved
Resources

reflects

One Unit
of Good B

Price of
Good A

Average
Cost of
Good A

reflects

X Amount
of Resources

One Unit
of Good A

Figure 3-2

The Effect of Innovation on Production Costs, Prices, and Real Income

Before a firm innovates the production of Good A, it takes X amount of resources to make one unit of it. The average cost is the dollar value of these resources. The price of Good A equals this cost plus the profit margin.

An innovation allows the firm to reduce the resources in making one unit of Good A. This innovation allows it to cut its average cost, as well as the price of Good A.

Consequently, consumers can now buy one unit of Good A plus a unit of Good B for the same amount of money as Good A used to take. That is, their real incomes rise.

As more people are now needed to make Good B, the new jobs created offset the jobs lost when Good A was innovated. This explains why the unemployment rate hasn't changed much since the Industrial Revolution, on a long-term average.

Because average cost reflects the resources used in production, average cost drops with innovation, as indicated by the area labeled "Drop in Average Cost" in the middle box. Finally, when there is competition from other firms, this innovative firm will reduce the price of Good A. Even without much competition, a firm might drop prices if it can sell many more products at a lower price. Finally, when the price of Good A falls, the effect on consumers is the same as if their incomes increased. They can buy more goods and services with the same amount of income—one unit of Good B in this case. Although their *money* income does not change, their **real income** (what their money income can buy) increases. Taking the house example, what other things would people buy if house prices fell? Anything, but one thing could be a product requiring wood, carpenters, and so on, such as a cabinet for the stereo equipment that earlier generations could never afford. Thus, the laid-off ("freed-up") resources find new uses.

Real income is the amount of goods and services that can be purchased with a given money income.

Some examples of the millions of innovations in the last few centuries will help you see their effects. Eli Whitney's cotton gin of 1793, which

THINKING CRITICALLY ABOUT ECONOMIC QUESTIONS IN OUR LIVES

Are You Rich? Why—or Why Not?

Things to Consider

1. Bill Gates (founder of Microsoft) is the richest man in America. Sam Walton (founder of Wal-Mart) also became one of the richest men in America. They, like so many other rich people, did not inherit their wealth.

2. Why are you rich—or not rich? Other than inheritance, lottery winnings, or others miscellaneous sources of wealth, how do people become rich? Consider what that process has to do with resource scarcity and the economic problem.

See page 455 for the answer.

picked the seeds out of the cotton, increased the output of laborers from three pounds of cotton per day to 17 pounds per day. It led to a sharp reduction in the price of cotton, transforming it from a luxury cloth to a cheap fabric. The Erie Canal, completed in 1825, allowed two mules pulling a boat to move 1,000 bushels of grain, instead of the six bushels they could carry on their backs. Consequently, prices for shipping dropped 90 percent. The introduction of the transistor (1948) and the integrated circuit (1969) led to falling prices for electronic goods. Calculators, introduced in the early 1970s and which sold for over $200, sell for less than $10 today.

One last point about innovation is the extent of unemployment caused by mechanization and other innovations. Many people fear it. People always did. In the 1600s and 1700s, people worried that the steam engine, first used in pumping water out of mines, would throw water haulers out of work. Then in the late 1700s, a group of English weavers, called the Luddites, smashed new weaving machines which they feared would replace them. By the late 1800s and early 1900s, mechanization was throwing millions out of work, including glass blowers, barrel makers, and cigar makers. Such mechanization continues to reduce labor needs today.

Thus, the only thing new about jobs being lost are the *kinds* of jobs and the *reasons* for their losses. Throughout most of our history, including today, only from three to eight percent of workers could not find jobs. If mechanization does create widespread unemployment, it surely would have appeared by now. Of course, some people will say today is different. But it is likely that the people of the 1800s were as fearful of McCormick's reaper and Duke's cigarette-making machine as some people today are of computers and *maquiladoras* (Mexican factories along the U.S. border).

Why *doesn't* mechanization cause unemployment? Actually, it can cause some *types* of unemployment, but the *overall* unemployment rate changes only slightly as new types of jobs appear. Glass blowers, teamsters (horse drivers), and ice deliverymen are gone. New large labor groups of the 1900s include auto workers, restaurant workers, electronics workers, and workers in recreation and entertainment industries. Most of them don't make things we need to survive, but things we like to have anyway. That is, they make luxuries. How can people today afford so many more things than their ancestors could? Because resources were saved through millions of innovations, which raised real incomes that were used to purchase compact discs, microwaves, airplane trips, and the like.

For the same reason, will the 2090s be as different from the 1990s as the 1990s are from the 1890s? Why not? We still have not found all the best production processes, and we have not eliminated all the waste in using our resources.

MARGINAL PRODUCTIVITY

Every good or service needs several resources for production, including various types of laborers, capital equipment, and raw materials. A firm can boost its output by increasing just one of its resources. The extra output from adding just one unit of a resource to a production process is the **marginal product**.

The **marginal product** is the additional output of a good or service that results from the addition of one more unit of a particular resource to a production process.

Consider a farmer's corn field as an example of increasing a single resource. Suppose the farmer wants to find what happens to corn yield (production) as extra tons of fertilizer resources are added to each acre of a field. Like many of the resources used to grow corn, including seeds and labor, fertilizer is a "variable resource." When variable resources change in quantity, the output also will change. Other resources are considered to be fixed or given in quantity, at least in the short run. Examples include the available amount of land and machines.

Examples of increasing a single resource in other production processes include: a tavern owner hiring extra bartenders, an electric power plant burning more coal, and a store hiring additional salesclerks.

Table 3-2

Marginal Products of Fertilizer

Using no fertilizer, one acre of land grows 100 bushels of corn. The *increases* in yield (or marginal products) result from applying the stated tons of fertilizer. The point of diminishing returns occurs with the third ton.

	Tons of Fertilizer Applied							
	0	1	2	3	4	5	6	7
Yield (Total Product)	100	120	150	175	195	210	210	190
Marginal Product	–	20	30	25	20	15	0	-20

For the corn example, Table 3-2 shows the input and output data up to the seventh ton of fertilizer. The marginal product is the difference in yield between successive tons of fertilizer used. The data show a common pattern in the production processes of most goods and services when firms increase a single resource. The marginal product increases initially, but it eventually declines (diminishes) beyond a certain point—in this case with the third ton of fertilizer. Because this occurs so commonly, economists say there is a **law of diminishing marginal returns** that seems to hold in production processes. Notice further that marginal product becomes negative after the sixth ton of fertilizer.

 In the other examples given above, diminishing marginal product exhibits itself as: additional bartenders selling fewer drinks than bartenders hired earlier; extra tons of coal producing fewer kilowatts of power than the first few tons; and the last-hired salesclerks selling less than those hired first. Observing such production data, you might think something is wrong with the last resources used. Perhaps the fertilizer or coal are of poor quality. Maybe the last bartenders and salesclerks are lazy or poorly trained. But marginal product falls even if all units of resources in each of these cases are identical. It falls primarily because the other resources in the production processes remain unchanged in quantity. This creates an imbalance of resources, in which the resources in constant supply become increasingly scarce compared with the resource being increased.

 To elaborate, in corn production the extra fertilizer increases the nutrients available to the corn plants—but does nothing about the water needed. Because the same amount of ground water must support more vegetative matter, corn plants become increasingly "thirsty" as fertilizer is added. Consequently, water becomes a critically limiting resource, which holds down the gains expected from more fertilizer. Eventually, additional fertilizer *reduces* output because fertilizer is a salt that can "burn" plants if it is too abundant.

 Why does the marginal product first *increase* before it eventually decreases? The initial increase in the marginal product generally stems from the gains in efficiency due to specialization. In the case of labor resources, workers divide the tasks of the production process. The marginal product figures suggest that each additional worker is more productive than those already working, until the point of diminishing returns is reached. That is misleading because *everyone* becomes more productive when specialization increases. (The first worker or two used to be inefficient because they did some jobs they weren't good at. Following specialization, they only do jobs they can do well.) However, everyone's *increased* output is reflected in the output of the last worker hired. These gains from specialization end when there are no more ways to specialize. Then resources become so imbalanced that the marginal product falls.

 In actual businesses, such data on the marginal product often are extremely difficult to obtain. Also, in many cases, such as retail stores, finding "identical" workers is impossible.

The **law of diminishing marginal returns** states that as additional amounts of a single resource are added to a production process, the marginal product eventually declines.

INCREASING THE SCALE OF PRODUCTION OPERATIONS

Another way a firm can increase its output is to increase all resources at an equal rate. For instance, the corn farmer could increase all resources by 30 percent—the land area, the amount of seed planted, tillage implements, and cultivation labor. Economists call such expansion an "increase in scale," as all resources expand proportionately or at the same percentage rate.

Production processes fit into three categories, depending upon how much production increases in relation to proportionate increases in resources: 1) increasing returns to scale; 2) constant returns to scale; and 3) decreasing returns to scale.

Increasing Returns to Scale

Increasing returns to scale describes a production process in which an increase in inputs of x percent results in output increasing by more than x percent.

A production process experiences **increasing returns to scale** if the total output increases at a faster rate than resources are increased. (A common synonym is economies of scale, as average costs of production fall following expansion.)

The example of a shipyard in Figure 3-3 illustrates this case. Suppose the shipyard owner wants to expand from the present four-ships-per-year capacity, perhaps because the firm has many waiting customers. The yard now needs $40 million in resources to produce four ships, giving an average cost per ship of $10 million.

Suppose the shipyard owner decides to double the amount of each resource used—yard space, buildings, labor, fabricating steel, and derricks. Consequently, total cost per year doubles to $80 million. Note that the middle diagram, which represents total costs, doubles in size. Next, note that output increases to 12 ships per year—triple the original amount, or a 200 percent increase. Because resources increase by 100 percent and output by 200 percent, the production process experiences increasing returns to scale. The words "increasing returns" imply that each resource now "returns" or produces more of a ship than in the smaller operation. For example, if two derricks are used in producing four ships in the smaller operation, then each derrick (helps to) produces two ships. But after the expansion, each derrick produces *three* ships (= 12 ÷ 4). Thus, the "returns" to derricks climb from two to three, a 50 percent rise. The same thing holds for the other resources.

Finally, note that when dividing the $80 million total cost by 12 ships, the average cost of each ship is now $6.7 million (= $80 million ÷ 12 ships), down from $10 million. That is why a synonym for increasing

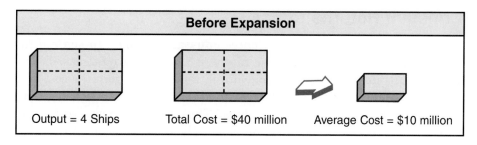

Before Expansion

Output = 4 Ships   Total Cost = $40 million   Average Cost = $10 million

Figure 3-3

Increasing Returns to Scale

A shipyard builds four ships a year for $40 million, or $10 million each.

If it doubles its resources (or costs, to $80 million), it triples its output to 12 ships, allowing the average cost to fall to $6.7 million.

This is made possible by the increased productivity (or "returns") from the resources.

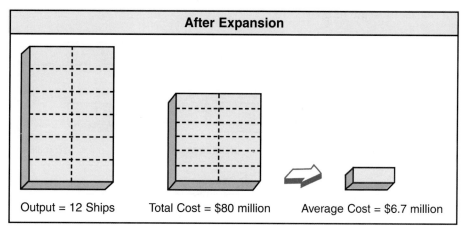

After Expansion

Output = 12 Ships   Total Cost = $80 million   Average Cost = $6.7 million

returns to scale is economies of scale, for firms gain "economies" or cost savings by "scaling up" their size of operations (that is, going from a "small scale" to a "large scale").

There are several reasons why expanding firms experience increasing returns to scale. One is that expansion allows for an increasing degree of specialization. A large factory has dozens of job classifications to reap the benefits of the division of labor. A second reason is that many machines need to attain a certain size before they can be efficient. Some examples are metal stamping machines, bottle fillers in beverage plants, mechanical bean pickers, auto assembly lines, blast furnances in steel plants, and the "cracking towers" in oil refineries.

Constant Returns to Scale

Constant returns to scale describes a production process in which an increase in inputs of x percent results in output increasing by x percent.

A production process experiences **constant returns to scale** if the total output increases at the same rate that resources are increased. This case is illustrated for the same shipyard in Figure 3-4. Again the cost doubles because the amount of resources used doubles. But now the output doubles as well, from four to eight ships. Thus, each ship has a cost of $10 million (= $80 million ÷ 8 ships), the same as before expansion. A firm that experiences constant returns to scale has the same average cost as it increases its scale of operation.

Figure 3-4

Constant Returns to Scale

In this case, the firm doubles its output following the doubling of its resources (from $40 million to $80 million).

This is made possible when resources have the same productivity following the expansion.

Consequently, each ship costs the same to produce before and after the expansion, or $10 million.

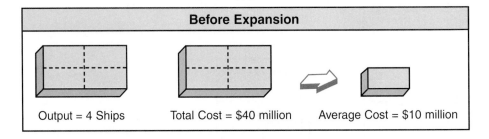

Output = 4 Ships   Total Cost = $40 million   Average Cost = $10 million

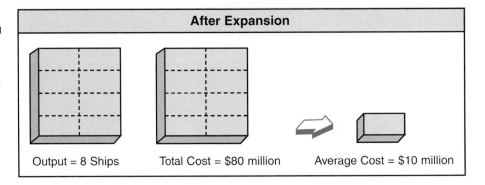

Output = 8 Ships   Total Cost = $80 million   Average Cost = $10 million

Constant returns to scale occur because each resource is just as productive after the expansion as before (thus, the term "constant returns"). The flip side of that is that it takes the same amount of resources to produce one unit of output, which is why the average cost remains constant during expansion.

Decreasing returns to scale describes a production process in which an increase in inputs of x percent results in output increasing by less than x percent.

Decreasing Returns to Scale

Finally, a production process experiences **decreasing returns to scale** if the total output increases at a slower rate than resources are increased. (A common synonym is diseconomies of scale. This case is illustrated for the shipyard in Figure 3-5, where output merely increases to six ships, a 50 percent increase. Because resources increase by 100 percent and costs also increase by 100 percent to $80 million, the average cost of each ship *rises* to $13.3 million (= $80 million ÷ 6 ships). Thus, a firm experiencing decreasing returns to scale experiences higher average costs as it expands. That is why we say it faces *dis*economies of scale.

This situation occurs because resources are less productive following expansion (thus, there are "decreasing returns"). This forces firms to purchase more resources to make one unit of their product, reflected in a higher average cost. Take the capital resource, for example. No machine can continually expand to gargantuan size and continue to increase its efficien-

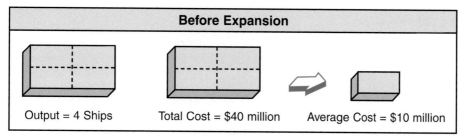

Before Expansion		
Output = 4 Ships	Total Cost = $40 million	Average Cost = $10 million

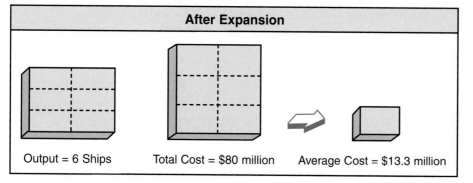

After Expansion		
Output = 6 Ships	Total Cost = $80 million	Average Cost = $13.3 million

Figure 3-5

Decreasing Returns to Scale

In this case, the firm only increases its output by 50 percent (from four to six ships) as it increases its resources by 100 percent.

This is because resources are less productive (provide lower "returns") after expanding. Therefore, each ship takes more resources to produce.

Consequently, each ship costs more to produce, $13.3 million vs. $10 million earlier.

cy. Thus, sooner or later firms experience decreasing returns to scale—partly because of the limits on capital size. Often a more important reason is that managers find extremely large businesses difficult to manage. One problem is that very large firms have several "layers" of managers, so top managers often lose sight of what happens in each part of the production process. This is usually the primary cause of diseconomies of scale.

THINKING CRITICALLY ABOUT ECONOMIC QUESTIONS IN OUR LIVES

Why Don't They Build Bigger Train Locomotives?

Things to Consider

1. Observe several freight trains. Notice that they are usually pulled by several locomotives—not just one. Next, observe several semi-trailer trucks. You only see one tractor pulling a trailer in all cases.

2. Wouldn't you think it would be wasteful to build multiple locomotives to pull a train, when one larger and more powerful one could be built to do the same job—as is done with trucks?

3. How can you explain why General Electric (a locomotive maker) doesn't make such larger locomotives? (It is not because they would be used so infrequently, as multiple locomotives are often being used. Also, it is not due to size restriction, as the locomotives could be longer, with more cylinders in the engine. They would not have to be made wider. Thus, the locomotives would still fit through tunnels and other tight spots.)

See page 456 for the answer.

THE MODERN MASS-PRODUCTION ECONOMY

Hundreds of years ago, all firms were very small and produced small amounts of the items they made. This was not only true for farms, but for makers of wagons, tools, clothes, and every other good or service. Today, each firm in almost all industries produces far more output than their counterparts of the past. That is, many firms today engage in mass production, where they produce a large amount of a good or service in a certain period. Contrast this with a custom-made production process, in which each customer's good or service is unique. Another type of production process is the batch process, in which a limited number of identical products are made. Mass-produced products include steel, ball-point pens, canned peaches, television sets, and most baseball bats. Batch-process items include baseball bats made for professional ballplayers and jetliners. Custom-made items or services include haircuts, portraits, and tailor-made suits.

It is important not to equate mass production with "factory-made." Mass-production techniques indeed include most large factory operations, but they also include commercial farms, mines, timbering operations, transportation operations, and electric power production.

This section examines two major aspects of the modern mass-production economy, which explain why it didn't exist prior to the 1800s. First, you'll learn about the characteristics of mass production, and then about the role played by mass markets in a mass-production economy.

Some Characteristics of a Mass-Production Economy

Most mass-production processes possess four major characteristics: 1) specialized, high-volume capital equipment; 2) standardization and interchangeable parts; 3) continuous production processes; and 4) a specialized labor force. These are not completely independent of each other. Rather, they often complement or depend upon each other. This is indicated by the dotted lines connecting the boxes in the top row of Figure 3-6 on page 100.

■ The first characteristic of mass production reflects the role played by capital. Virtually all large-scale operations use a sizable amount of high-volume capital equipment, which is generally very specialized to fit a particular production process. Some examples include: draglines that excavate coal or metal ores, assembly lines that turn out cars, oil tankers that transport petroleum, and blast furnaces that produce steel. Each machine is useless for almost anything besides its intended purpose. Also, today's machines generally produce goods in larger amounts and in less time than the smaller, simpler machines of the past.

■ The second characteristic of mass production involves the related concepts of standardization and interchangeable parts. Although often used as synonyms, these words have somewhat different meanings. **Standardization** refers to the matching size, shape, and pattern of *parts of products of different firms*. Some examples: all 60-watt light bulbs made by all bulb manufacturers have bases that fit in every table lamp made by any lamp maker; all typing paper in the United States is 8.5 by 11 inches; and all film companies make film that fits in all 35-millimeter cameras. Without standardization, firms would make much smaller amounts of many products. For example, Sylvania would make 60-watt bulbs with bases of many different sizes—one for each lamp manufacturer. Also, Kodak would

Standardization refers to the matching size, shape, and pattern of parts of products of different firms.

have to make dozens of film sizes to fit the varying film sizes each camera maker used. Thus, without standardization there would be much less mass production (and more batch-process production). Consequently, production costs and prices would be higher.

Interchangeable parts means *each part of one unit of one firm's product* is identical to the respective parts of all other such units produced by that firm. This concept was conceived in France by Honrere Blanc, promoted by Thomas Jefferson, and introduced around 1800 by Eli Whitney in musket manufacture and Simeon North in pistol manufacture. For example, each flintlock (which held a piece of flint used to fire the powder) Whitney made fit in any of his muskets. Previously, because each barrel, stock, trigger, breech, and every other part of the musket had a unique size and shape, each flintlock had to vary in size to match the varying sizes of the other parts before it would fit perfectly. To make these parts identical (thus, interchangeable), Whitney and North needed machine tools, machines (such as a lathe or a drillpress) that cut or shape metal or other materials. They made most of these machine tools themselves.

Interchangeable parts make possible the production and assembly of products with the aid of machines. Machines depend upon sameness, whether they're machines that make parts or machines that help assemble parts into finished products. Imagine the mess a machine would make if it had to grab and bottle pickles of widely varying sizes (which is why they are still packed by hand). When products are uniform, as in cigarette manufacture, the packing process is a breeze. Consequently, interchangeable parts vastly increased the potential output possible at individual firms making guns, stoves, pumps, and thousands of other items.

■ The third characteristic of mass production is the **continuous production process**, where production is broken into several steps, with the steps usually taking place in different locations. In addition, raw materials continually flow into the production process while finished products continually exit the process. For example, in grain milling, the cleaning, grinding, and separation of the starchy center of the kernels (the flour) from the outer hulls occur in sequence at different locations in the mill. Grain continually flows into the mill, and flour continually leaves the mill. Indeed, it was in corn milling that Oliver Evans first applied this concept in 1785.

The continuous production process makes mass production possible primarily because it allows high-volume, specialized machines to aid production. With most products, there are so many steps in production that a single machine could not do all of them simultaneously. Yet several machines, each doing one task and working in sequence, can greatly

---

Interchangeable parts refers to a situation where each part of one unit of a firm's product is identical to the respective parts of all other units.

The continuous production process refers to the breakdown of a product's manufacture into a series of steps, where specialized machines do a large share of the production, and where raw materials continually enter the production process and finished products continually exit the process.

increase output. (However, the continuous production process is not used in all industries. In rice growing, for example, seed is planted once a year, so the planter is used only a fraction of the time.) A continuous production process also makes mass production efficient by allowing for the division of labor. Laborers differ in their aptitude for the various steps in the production process. The continuous production process allows all laborers to specialize in jobs in which they have a comparative advantage.

The combination of interchangeable parts, the continuous production process, and specialized capital equipment led to one of the greatest innovations of all time, the moving assembly line. Here, partly finished products are brought to the workers—rather than the workers coming to the product—and a worker assembles only one part of the product. Henry Ford usually gets the credit for adopting this concept in auto production in 1913. It allowed him to slash the assembly time of the Model T from 12.5 hours to one hour and 33 minutes.

■ The last characteristic of a mass-production economy is a force of specialized laborers, some requiring a high degree of skills. Examples include machining center operators (who need complex math and computer skills), electronic technicians, and laser operators. However, skilled laborers sometimes are replaced by unskilled laborers following mechanization (as in Ford's plant).

The Role Played by Mass Markets

The four characteristics of a mass-production economy refer only to the production side of the picture. That is, they result in low production costs because of the large volume of output. However, of what value is the capacity to make vast quantities of a good or service if all the output can't be sold? A mass-production economy also depends upon the existence of **mass markets**, where large numbers of buyers are willing and able to buy a product.

Mass markets are markets for goods and services where there are very many buyers, made possible by a large population and efficient transportation and communication systems.

There are two requirements for mass markets. The first is a large number of potential buyers, either in a large domestic population or in a large foreign population. The second is a low product price compared with the average income, so people who want the item can afford to buy it. This is the same as saying that people have high real incomes. In turn, four major requirements must be met before a product's price is low relative to income: 1) low production cost; 2) low transport cost; 3) low communication cost; and 4) low marketing cost.

■ First is a low production cost, which essentially requires efficient production as explored so far in this chapter.

■ Second, transportation costs of the product from the factory to the buyer must be low. Otherwise, the buyer will purchase a locally made product with little shipping cost. Local buying is a problem for two reasons. First, the buyer of a local product cannot benefit from any lower *production* costs of a distant manufacturer, who may be more efficient because of better raw materials, more skilled workers, and more know-how. Second, if everyone in the nation bought from local producers, each producer would have a small operation because of the small local market. Then we would not receive the benefits of mass production—high living standards. The primary value of interstate highways, railroads, dock facilities, and trucks and other transportation equipment is that they all reduce transportation costs so that manufacturers can achieve mass markets.

■ The third requirement for low price relative to income is low communication cost. Communication is not difficult or costly for buyers and sellers who live near each other. But mass markets require *distant* markets, requiring long-distance communication. As with transportation, the cost of communicating between buyers and sellers must not raise the price so high that only *local* production occurs. Central to a mass-production economy are the telephone, airmail, satellite communication, and electronic mail (including fax machines).

■ The final requirement for low price relative to income is a low marketing cost. A low marketing cost often is difficult to achieve in retailing because products usually are sold one unit at a time, with few economies of scale. Consequently, retailers often need to sell items for twice the wholesale price to cover the selling costs. There are several ways to overcome some of these costs, including self-service stores, "superstores," and bar-code scanners.

CONSEQUENCES OF A MASS-PRODUCTION ECONOMY

The 200-plus years since the Industrial Revolution have brought great changes to the economy. Consider some of the major ways our economy differs from that of our ancestors and how it is still changing: 1) higher living standards; 2) a shift from labor to capital; 3) changing relative prices; 4) the appearance of large firms in some industries; and 5) changes in labor markets. Virtually all of these changes stem from the shift to a mass-production economy.

Living Standards Are Higher

The continuing Industrial Revolution provides benefits that past generations never dreamed possible. What is available now that was not available to our ancestors? Refrigerators and other kitchen appliances, furnaces and air conditioners, TV sets and radios, stereo equipment, paved streets, vacations to Disney World, higher education, cars, indoor plumbing, carpeting, and hundreds of other things.

Our ancestors could not have afforded such luxuries even if they had known how to produce them. They *had to* concentrate on essentials because just providing their basic needs of food, shelter, and clothing took most of their resources. In 1800, seventy two percent of the workforce grew food for the population, compared with three percent today. Thus, few resources were left to make luxuries.

Material abundance resulted from economic changes, including increased specialization and the innovations of interchangeable parts, computerization, and mechanization. These increased the efficiency of resource use, essentially making resources less scarce. Now people can make *more* of the unlimited things they want than with previous production methods. Not all they want—just more.

Will living standards continue to grow? Will hot tubs, swanky five-bedroom homes, eating out every week in gourmet restaurants, facelifts, four-car garages filled with luxury cars, yearly trips abroad be available to most people in the future? Why not? How can it be done? By doing more of the same—more specialization, more innovation, and more elimination of resource waste.

A Shift in Resource Use

All goods and services require labor, capital, natural resources, and entrepreneurship to be produced. In the distant past, labor was the dominant resource used in virtually all production processes, which meant things were usually handmade. Thus, the largest share of the average cost was used to pay the owners of the labor resources—the workers. When producers use such a production process to make a good or service today, economists say the production process is **labor-intensive**.

Because of the countless number of innovations involving mechanization, production processes of many goods and services today are **capital-intensive**. This means capital is the dominant resource used in production, so that much of the average cost involves paying for capital. Our mass-production economy means that machine-made, rather than hand-made, processes dominate the production scene.

A **labor-intensive** production process is one where the largest share of the costs involves labor resources.

A **capital-intensive** production process is one where the largest share of the costs involves capital resources.

Relative Prices Change

During inflation most prices increase, but some prices increase more than others. Consequently, economists distinguish between two concepts of prices.

The **absolute price** is the amount of money that is paid for one unit of an item.

The **relative price** is the amount of some other good or service that can be exchanged for one unit of some particular good.

Absolute price refers to the normal concept of price, or the number of dollars it takes to buy something. **Relative price** refers to the amount of some other good or service you could have bought with the money it took to buy item x. Suppose a melon sells for 60¢ and a peach for 30¢. Then a melon costs (or has a relative price of) two peaches, and a peach costs half a melon.

Suppose the price of a melon increases to $1.20 and the price of a peach increases to 40¢. Now a melon trades for three peaches, so the relative price of melons rose from two to three peaches. In contrast, the relative price of peaches fell from a half to a third of a melon.

The primary reason that the relative price for an item falls is because its production process is more subject to innovation than most other processes. This generally occurs because it is easier to innovate (generally, to mechanize) its production. A firm will innovate only if it expects lower average costs. Thus, the more some item's manufacture is subject to innovation compared with all other things, the less costly it will be to make compared with all other goods and services. Consequently, its (absolute) price

Table 3-3   Changes in Relative Prices

In general, over long periods of time, the manufacture of goods is subject to innovation. However, the production of services generally is less subject to innovation. Listed below are the average costs, profit margins, and absolute prices of a good (air conditioner) and a service (engine overhaul). The average cost for the overhaul rose the fastest over time, as it is less subject to innovation. Consequently, the relative price of the engine overhaul rose 10 percent. However, the relative price of the air conditioner *fell* 10 percent, as its absolute price rose more slowly than did the overhaul. (Note: The abbreviation E.O. stands for engine overhaul and A.C. stands for air conditioner.)

Time Period	Average Cost		Profit Margin		Absolute Price		Relative Price	
	Air Conditioner	Engine Overhaul	Air Conditioner	Engine Overhaul	Air Conditioner	Engine Overhaul	Air Conditioner	Engine Overhaul
1	$900	$1,800	$100	$200	$1,000	$2,000	0.50 E.O.	2.0 A.C.
2	$1,200	$2,700	$100	$200	$1,300	$2,900	0.45 E.O.	2.2 A.C.
Percent Change	33%	50%	—	—	30%	45%	(−) 10%	(+) 10%

will be lower than if its production process was not mechanized. That is, its relative price will fall.

Conversely, when the relative price for a good or service rises, generally this is because it is difficult or impossible to mechanize or otherwise innovate its manufacturing process. Because costs cannot be cut, its (absolute) price becomes higher relative to more mechanized items. That is, its relative price rises.

Table 3-3 shows an example of both cases occurring between two time periods. It shows the relative price of an air conditioner falling (from 0.50 to 0.45 engine overhauls) and the relative price of an engine overhaul rising (from 2.0 to 2.2 air conditioners). The average cost plus the profit margin (assumed to remain unchanged) equals the price. Note that the average cost of the air conditioner rose less rapidly than for an engine overhaul (33 percent compared to 50 percent). This could have been the result of innovation in manufacturing air conditioners, which kept the costs from rising even faster (perhaps as high as 50 percent, as in the case of the overhaul). Consequently, the relative price of an air conditioner *fell* 10 percent, while the relative price of an engine overhaul *rose* 10 percent.

Using machines to produce an item requires product uniformity. Machines that help assemble products cannot deal with constantly changing sizes and shapes of parts. In general, goods possess such uniformity but services do not.

Services (such as overhauling an engine) generally cannot be mechanized very well. This is primarily because the services each person requires are unique, such as with medical care, product repair, and haircuts. Consequently, absolute prices of services generally increase faster than prices of goods. Therefore, relative prices of services generally increase over time while relative prices of goods decrease. To a large extent, that explains why medical and education costs (and tuition) rise faster than costs of most items. However, an increasing number of services are being provided more efficiently through the use of wireless data networks, which are directed by powerful computers and various "smart machines." This allows for such things as reading electrical and gas meters, monitoring vending machines, and processing insurance claims with far less labor than before.

Other problems prevent the mechanization of some production processes. Some processes (such as litter pickup) cannot be centralized. Some, such as restaurant services, require significant human involvement. Others involve limited or unique production, such as art and personal medical equipment (prosthetics, hearing aids).

Many changes in our lifestyle over the years are rooted in changes in relative prices. As already noted, we became a "throwaway society" because of escalating repair costs. Synthetic fibers replaced wool, linen, and cotton in many fabrics. The fax machine is rapidly replacing the hand-delivered message (the mail). Mail delivery defies innovation because mailbox sizes and locations are so variable, forcing stamp prices to skyrocket. Years ago, even men of modest means commonly got shaves in barbershops—an extravagance today.

We can, in effect, go back in time to before when our lifestyles changed by traveling to third-world nations. There, things we commonly throw away are repaired (in Africa, some people make a living repairing cigarette lighters). Men commonly get shaves in barbershops, and middle-class people often have maids (especially in South America).

Firms Get Very Large in Some Industries

Until the early 1800s, many competing small firms made goods and services. In the 1800s, each town of any size had several wagon makers, the forerunner of semi-trailer manufacturers. Today there are only 12 semi-trailer makers in the whole country. In the 1800s, each town usually had a brewery, producing only several hundred barrels per year, compared with a handful of breweries today that brew millions of barrels per year. Finally, with massive packing plants now slaughtering millions of hogs a year, few are needed to provide our pork and ham. In the 1800s and early 1900s, even small towns had several butcher shops.

Some industries today still have the characteristics of these industries of the 1800s. Restaurants, jewelry makers, repair shops, and dental offices are all small and numerous. Other industries, such as the auto, coal, and appliance industries, have only a handful of firms, with giant operations. This is because only a few of these large firms are needed to supply the needs of the buyers.

When firms are large but few, it is usually because it is possible to reduce costs by mass producing, generally with a capital-intensive process. In other words, sometimes firms must be very large in order to reach maximum efficiency.

In contrast, if an industry is composed of firms that are small but numerous, it is because this small size is the cheapest way to produce. It makes no sense to get larger, for mechanization is either not possible or will not reduce costs. Firms still can increase production, but they do so by building multiple production facilities, each small in size (like fast-food chain restaurants).

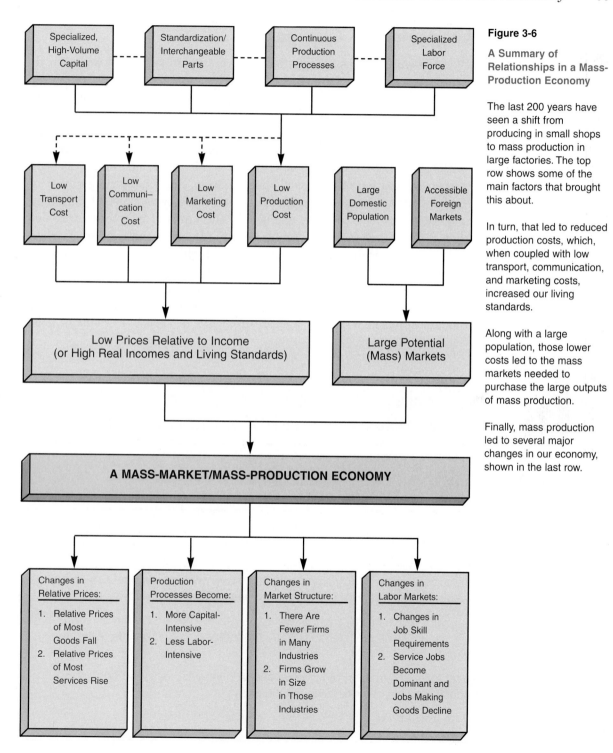

Figure 3-6

A Summary of Relationships in a Mass-Production Economy

The last 200 years have seen a shift from producing in small shops to mass production in large factories. The top row shows some of the main factors that brought this about.

In turn, that led to reduced production costs, which, when coupled with low transport, communication, and marketing costs, increased our living standards.

Along with a large population, those lower costs led to the mass markets needed to purchase the large outputs of mass production.

Finally, mass production led to several major changes in our economy, shown in the last row.

Labor Markets Change

Because of mass production, laborers today work in a world far different from the past. Three major differences between the past and present centuries include: 1) changes in skill requirements; 2) a shift from producing goods to producing services; and 3) the creation of new jobs.

■ First, a vast change occurred in skill requirements. Some products that once required great labor skills to make (barrels, wheels, wagons, glass bottles) are made today with unskilled or semi-skilled laborers. This is due to the combination of increased specialization, interchangeable parts, and mechanization. As noted earlier, changes in lifestyles caused by changing relative prices lead to many changes in the kinds of jobs there are. Jobs have disappeared for many repairmen, mail clerks and carriers, barbers, and engine overhaulers. Yet today, many highly skilled people have jobs that didn't exist in the 1800s, including flying aircraft, programming computers, administering x-rays, and operating lasers.

■ Second, jobs producing services dominate today's labor market. In 1800, most people worked in agriculture, while in 1900 jobs producing goods

THINKING CRITICALLY ABOUT ECONOMIC QUESTIONS IN OUR LIVES

Will We All End Up Taking in Each Other's Laundry?

Things to Consider

1. Innovations, from mechanization to computerization, have eliminated countless jobs, usually in producing goods. Service jobs tend to be less affected by innovation.

2. A common complaint of this process is that we appear to be moving toward an economy where only services will provide jobs. Thus, the lament, "We all will be taking in each other's laundry."

3. Is this a reasonable fear? Are all or most service jobs low-paying or "dead-end" jobs? Or will the process lead to yet higher living standards?

See page 457 for the answer.

were dominant. The inability to mechanize the production of services, while food production on farms and goods production in factories were rapidly mechanized, forced such shifts. Thus, jobs were "lost" in agriculture and factories at a greater rate than in the service sector. Consequently, by the latter half of the 1900s, service jobs dominated the job scene.

■ The third effect of mass production is the creation of many new jobs, approximately equal to those destroyed by the innovations that led to mass production. How did these new jobs come about? Suppose a labor-saving innovation (one creating some initial unemployment) reduces a firm's average cost of production. The firm can then reduce its price while maintaining its profit margin. Buyers can purchase this firm's product and have money left over, which wasn't possible in earlier periods of higher prices. They use this money to buy goods and services they could not afford previously. Many of the people who lost their jobs because of such innovative ideas now make these items.

But what if the firm does not reduce prices, letting its profit margin grow instead? How will unemployment be avoided then? The answer is that now the firm's owners, rather than its customers, get to buy more goods and services than previously, again putting more people to work.

Incidentally, another reason for today's dominance of service jobs is that we are rapidly increasing our purchases of personal services because we can finally afford them. These are things we often find to be a nuisance, such as lawn mowing, house cleaning, and food preparation.

The growth of mass production made us richer than our ancestors—but also more dependent upon others in this economy of specialists.

A HISTORICAL SKETCH OF AMERICAN BUSINESS

People who lived in the 1800s wouldn't recognize our economy. This section describes some major differences in the production processes of the economy and some of their consequences in different time periods.

Eras of American Business

We can trace the transition of the American economy from a subsistence, agrarian state to a modern, mass-production economy by dividing the last 400 years into four eras: 1) the Pre-Industrial Revolution Era; 2) the Early Industrial Era; 3) the Emergence of Big Business Era; and 4) the Modern Business Era.

■ The Pre-Industrial Revolution Era stretched from the earliest settlement in North America until the late 1700s. This period had largely a subsistence economy, with little specialization and, thus, little trade between people. When someone did buy a good or service from someone else, it was generally made to order. Wagons, shoes, and tools were "tailor-made" in small shops. Firms usually did not make products and store them in warehouses in anticipation of selling them in the future. There was no mass production. Consequently, resource use was inefficient, which meant that living standards were low.

■ The Early Industrial Era spanned the years from the American Revolution to the Civil War. Interchangeable parts, continuous production processes, early wide-scale mechanization, and increased use of water and animal power led to the beginning of the factory system of production. Firms began to make large amounts of products in anticipation of future sales. They hired large numbers of workers, creating a labor class. This production change also led to the growth of cities, making exchanges between specialists easier. During this period, early transportation systems began to develop, with improved roads beginning in the 1810s, canals in the 1820s, and railroads in the 1830s. To gain economies of scale, firms began to grow in size.

■ However, only a few industries experienced such a transition before the Civil War. Such changes became widespread later on in the Emergence of Big Business Era, extending from the Civil War to the early 1900s. Giant firms appeared for the first time, especially in steel production. Consequently, oligopolies (industries with only a few firms) began to appear. Further consolidation into virtual monopolies through the formation of trusts occurred from the 1870s until the end of the century.

■ The last era is the Modern Business Era, extending to the present. In this era, businesses developed modern practices of accounting, management, marketing, and advertising. Economies of scale continued to grow in many industries, leading to further business concentration and lessened competition. Small businesses, however, still dominate those goods and services in which mechanization is difficult. Throughout this era, innovations created fears about employment, labor unrest, class conflict, and reduced competition, along with the growth of monopoly power of big businesses. During the last hundred years, such concerns led to legislation regulating business, putting an end to the laissez-faire philosophy of the 1800s.

Paving streets with bricks in the early 1900s was very labor-intensive. Modern, capital-intensive concrete paving has made brick streets prohibitively expensive. Consequently, jobs were lost in the brick industry and in laying bricks but were replaced with jobs making cement, concrete mixers, and paving equipment (and in operating such equipment).

Blacksmithing in Pakistan. Where labor is cheap, it often costs less to employ lots of labor to repair products rather than to produce new ones. In high-wage economies, the opposite is often true. As Pakistan modernizes its economy and becomes more productive, in general, handcrafts such as blacksmithing will become uneconomical as people will have higher-income opportunities elsewhere.

Using a wooden plow in Peru. The plow, more like a stick, does not allow the farmer to till much area in a day.

A water-powered rice mill in Sumatra, Indonesia. A water wheel turns the large horizontal shaft, which has cams that lift seven vertical poles. The poles then drop into depressions that hold several quarts of rice, which takes two hours to turn to flour. A family of four working in the mill earns the equivalent of $10-$12 a day. As in the case of Pakistan above, such mills and their workers will be replaced by more efficient large-scale operations as Indonesia modernizes.

Spinning wool in Peru. While walking or just standing, women turn bundles of wool into yarn. Thus, otherwise idle time is used productively. This is significant, as walking is the main mode of transportation.

Transplanting rice in Sumatra. Plants are pulled from a seeding bed and stuck into the mud. This labor-intensive process in avoided in the United States when either a machine plants seeds in rows or seeds are dropped from an airplane.

Harvesting rice with a knife in Sumatra. Two improvements in cutting grains were the sickle (a curved knife) and the scythe. Neither is used very often in Sumatra.

Threshing rice in Sumatra by beating the plants over boards above a bin.

Cutting wheat in the Midwest in the 1880s. Cyrus McCormick produced the first reaper (mechanical cutter) in 1835. Later, machines called binders also tied the grain into bundles or sheaves with twine. After drying, the bundles were fed into a threshing machine to separate the grain from the staw. By the mid-20th century, the combine (shown below) combined these two machines into one.

Threshing wheat in Peru by walking cattle over the grain.

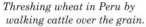

(Courtesy of J.I. Case Company)

SUMMARY

Economic well-being, or economic welfare, has been increased primarily by increasing the amount of goods and services produced, known as economic growth. Economic welfare is measured by the standard of living.

Economic growth results from: 1) having more resources available; and 2) increasing the efficiency of the existing resources, also known as increasing productivity. Productivity is raised by: 1) eliminating waste in the current production processes; 2) increasing the specialization of resource use; and 3) innovation.

A resource's use should be specialized in an area where it has a comparative advantage, meaning this resource will have the lowest opportunity cost of all resources. Because people specialize, they must trade with each other.

An increased productivity of resource use reduces the amount of resources needed to produce a good or service. As this reduces the cost of production, producers of such items in a competitive marketplace reduce prices. Therefore, out of their given incomes, consumers are able to buy more goods and services—which means that living standards are higher and that real income increased.

Firms could increase their outputs to larger levels in two ways. First, they can increase a single resource, leaving other resources unchanged. Second, firms can increase all resources at the same rate. If production costs decline with such expansion, firms experience increasing returns to scale. Because of lower production costs, firms tend to become large and engage in mass production. Alternatively, if costs decline with such expansion, firms experience decreasing returns to scale. Such firms tend to have multiple, small operations.

In addition to producing large amounts of output, firms that mass produce also use large-capacity, specialized capital equipment. Mass-production processes depend upon standardization, interchangeable parts, the continuous production process, and specialized laborers. Finally, mass production depends upon the existence of mass markets. In turn, such mass markets depend upon efficient transportation and communication systems, low production costs, and low marketing costs.

Besides raising living standards, a shift to a mass-production economy leads to more capital-intensive production techniques, decreases in relative prices of items whose production processes can be innovated, industries dominated by a few large firms, and a labor market increasingly dominated by service jobs.

QUESTIONS FOR DISCUSSION AND THOUGHT

1. How many people should be employed making cars in the country (or even the world)? Making computers? Or brooms, bologna, or anything else? If someone told you the answer is one person for each item, can you explain the reasoning behind such an answer?

2. Try to estimate the economic welfare as well as the happiness of some people you know. Do you find any connection between their welfare and happiness? If living standards were to be raised by having certain segments of the population "disappear," which segments should go?

3. Make a list of 10 jobs making convenient-but-not-necessary items (i.e., luxuries) that were not made in 1900. Which of the jobs do you think will still exist in the year 2050?

4. Do "quick oil and lube" shops have large increasing returns to scale? If they do, what makes this possible? If they don't, what prevents it?

5. Think of five items that are not mass produced and explain why they are not. Find three examples each of standardization and interchangeable parts in your classroom.

6. Why do producers of potatoes find it more difficult to sell at a great distance from where they are located than battery producers?

7. Calculate the relative prices of your school's tuition and one of your favorite foods for today and for 10 years ago. Did they change? If so, why do you think they changed in the way they did?

PROBLEMS   See pages 480-481 for the answers.

1. The manager of a shirt factory wants to know the effect on labor productivity after adding a second shift. Before adding it, there were 260 production workers and 16 machine-maintenance and other support workers, each group working a 40-hour week. There were also 12 office workers, each working 50 hours a week. After the additional shift, there are an additional 240 production workers and 14 support workers, both working 40 hours a week. There are four office staff on the second shift, working 40 hours a week.

   The weekly output of shirts rose from 48,620 to 95,460. Calculate the labor productivity with a single shift and with two shifts. Also, calculate how many minutes it takes to make just one shirt, on average, both with a single shift and with two shifts. What clue does that give you about the change in average cost as the firm moves from a single shift to a double shift?

2. Debra and Jim work in a grocery store. The manager needs to assign one person to bag groceries and one to empty food cartons and stack shelves. Debra can bag groceries for 12 customers per hour, and Jim can do it for 14 customers. Debra can stack 36 cartons of food per hour, while Jim can stack 31 cartons. Who has an absolute advantage in bagging groceries? In stacking shelves? Who has a comparative advantage in bagging groceries? In stacking shelves?

3. The clothing department of a store has the following average daily sales of clothes when hiring various numbers of clerks: 1 clerk-$1,200; 2 clerks-$2,600; 3 clerks-$3,800; 4 clerks-$4,800; and 5 clerks-$5,600. What is the marginal productivity, expressed in dollar sales, for each of the five clerks? After which clerk is the point of diminishing marginal returns reached?

4. The ABC Storage Company stores files for other businesses. It currently has a square building 100 feet on a side and 10 feet high, allowing it to store 100,000 boxes that are one foot on each side. It wants to expand its facilities and is trying to decide what size of structure to build. It needs to store an additional 200,000 boxes (requiring 200,000 cubic feet of space). (Assume that there are no aisles and that the building is filled to capacity.) It is considering: a) two more buildings like it already has, 100 feet x 100 feet and 10 feet high; or b) a building 100 feet x 100 feet, but 20 feet high. Suppose all building materials cost $5 per square foot, whether for floors, walls, or ceilings. What will the material cost be per box stored if it builds two smaller buildings? If it builds the single, larger one? As this material cost is part of the average cost of storing boxes, what do your answers tell you about the efficiency of storing boxes in the two buildings? If you note any difference in efficiency, what is its source? If cost was the only factor, which building would you advise the company to build? In going from a smaller building to the larger one, does the firm experience increasing, constant, or decreasing returns to scale?

5. In Year 1, it takes $400 to purchase a refrigerator and $2,000 to have an appendix removed. By Year 2, it takes $600 to purchase the refrigerator and $4,000 to have an appendectomy. Calculate the relative prices for both items for Year 1 and Year 2. Note how the relative prices changed and explain the reasons why this change might have occurred.

4

INTRODUCTION TO BUSINESS OPERATION

CHAPTER PREVIEW

In a capitalist economy, privately owned business firms serve a vital role in helping to solve the economic problem caused by resource scarcity. There are several types of business firms that are described in this chapter.

You will be introduced to some of the costs faced by business firms and how these costs affect their behavior. These costs affect us all, initially on the prices we pay for goods and services, but ultimately on our living standards.

Costs, when combined with prices, also affect profit levels. In turn, profit levels determine business behavior regarding resource use. Ultimately, then, profits (or losses) help determine how efficiently a society uses its resources.

CHAPTER OBJECTIVES

After completing this chapter, you should be able to:

◆ *Compare and contrast the four forms of business organization.*

◆ *Explain how to calculate the costs of business operation by using the various methods of measuring costs.*

◆ *Explain the difference between an accountant's and an economist's approach to costs.*

◆ *Compare and contrast the effects of profits and losses on resource allocation in an industry.*

◆ *Compare and contrast the four market structures.*

◆ *Describe how a firm determines its maximum profit level of output.*

We in the United States choose to have most of our goods and services produced by privately owned business firms. These firms compete against each other in the marketplace, ideally in as competitive a manner as possible. Thus, we choose to use the capitalist system to deal with the economic problem of a scarcity of resources.

THE ORGANIZATION OF BUSINESS FIRMS

Newspapers, magazines, and books are filled with references to business firms, from how they are organized to how they operate. To understand how the world of business operates, then, you must be aware of the many terms and concepts related to business.

Types of Business Firms

Depending upon how business is defined, America has between 15 and 20 million firms. Businesses generally fall into one of four categories: 1) single proprietorship; 2) partnership; 3) corporation; or 4) cooperative.

■ The first type of firm is the **single proprietorship** (also called the sole proprietorship) which has a single owner. Three of every four firms are proprietorships, but their combined sales account for only 10 percent of the nation's total sales because these firms are usually small (the most numerous being farms and small retailers).

The proprietor owns the business and in a legal sense *is* the business, keeping all the profits and being liable for its activities. Probably the major reason there are so many proprietorships is that owners get to be their own bosses. A major disadvantage is that the owner faces **unlimited liability** because there is no limit to the amount for which the owner can be sued (including personal assets, such as cars, homes, and retirement accounts). Also, proprietorships die with their owners. Another disadvantage is the inability to raise any money beyond the personal credit of the proprietor, thereby limiting the firm's size and its efficiency of operation. Some advantages of the single proprietorship are its ease of formation, flexibility, and being able to avoid the corporate income tax (although the proprietor must pay personal income taxes on the profits). In addition, government requirements (paperwork and regulations) for single proprietorships are generally lower. Proprietorships also experience the smallest risk of an income tax audit, as the government finds it more efficient to focus on larger firms.

A **single proprietorship** is a type of business where there is only one owner, who faces unlimited liability and earns all the profits.

Unlimited liability is the condition where an individual is responsible for all the debts incurred by a business.

A **partnership** is a type of business structure with more than one owner, each sharing responsibilities and being liable for the debts of the firm.

■ The second business type is the **partnership**, which has two or more owners. Two of its advantages are the ability to raise more funds (because of multiple investors) and to attract a wider range of talents. One disadvantage is that each partner usually faces unlimited liability. Another problem is possible friction between partners, which is the main reason why fewer than one firm in ten is a partnership. Partnerships are most frequent in professions (law firms, accounting firms) and farming.

A **corporation** is a form of business owned by stockholders, each having limited liability, and where the business is considered to be a person in legal matters.

■ The third form of business is the **corporation**. Although only one in six firms is a corporation, five out of every six dollars spent in this nation go to corporations. Most big firms are corporations. Technically, a corporation is a "legal person" because, just like a real person, a corporation earns income, pays taxes, can sue and be sued, can own property, and can make contracts, all in the name of the corporation.

Whoever owns a share of corporate stock owns part of the corporation. Most often, there is just one stockholder (usually these firms are small), but large corporations usually have thousands. One advantage of the corporate form is **limited liability**, which means stockholders cannot lose more than the amount of money they invested in the firm. Another is the ability to raise large amounts of money to finance the enormous capital purchases of large firms by selling stocks and bonds. Corporations also raise money by selling bonds. A bond is a promissory note, so a bondholder is a lender to or a creditor of a corporation. A last advantage of corporations is the possibility of perpetual life, as the stock of deceased stockholders passes or is sold to others.

Limited liability is the condition where stockholders in corporations are only liable for the firm's debts to the extent of their investment in the firm.

The corporate form also has disadvantages. Owners suffer "double taxation," for after the corporation itself pays income taxes, the owners also pay taxes on any dividends the corporation distributes. Corporations require more paperwork, from getting the charter to routine forms and more complex tax returns.

A **cooperative** is a form of business where those who are served by the business are the owners and where control of the business is shared by all equally.

■ The final form of business is the **cooperative** (or co-op), in which the owners are the people who use the services of the business. The owners, or stockholders, receive dividends in proportion to the amount of business transacted. However, since each owner usually has one vote in a democratic process, there is equal control of the operation of the business.

You might know of a food co-op, where members purchase food, often contributing unpaid labor to the business. Co-ops are common in agriculture, where farmers establish marketing cooperatives to sell (and often process) their products. Ocean Spray (cranberries), Sunkist (citrus fruits), and Blue Diamond (almonds) are some examples. Farmers commonly use service cooperatives from which they buy supplies and services. Credit unions are also cooperatives, where the depositors are the owners.

Terms That Are Unique to Corporations

The terminology common to corporations is widely used. While holders of corporate stocks (or shares) are legal owners of that corporation, there are generally two broad categories of stock, common and preferred. Both allow the holders of them to share in the rewards (or suffer the losses) of the corporation. Common stock gives the stockholder the right to vote at stockholders' meetings. Each stockholder has as many votes as shares held. Preferred stock, on the other hand, gives no voting rights to stockholders. However, they have the first claim on profits, which is important in years when profits are low. (Holders of corporate *bonds*, on the other hand, do not own the corporation. They are creditors of the corporation, as a bond is a promissary note.)

A firm known as a private corporation (or a closely held corporation) is one in which all or virtually all the stock belongs to a few people, and no one else can buy it. Alternatively, a firm known as a public corporation has many stockholders, and anyone can buy the stock. These are the shares generally bought and sold at stock market exchanges, such as Wall Street. (See the appendix in Chapter 14 for more detail on the stock market.)

Stockholders elect directors, who make up the board of directors. The directors' function is to ensure that the returns to the stockholders' investments are maximized. Stockholders hire directors as "watchdogs" because the stockholders might be far away from the firm's operations, ignorant of business operations, or occupied elsewhere. The board, in turn, selects the president, secretary, and other officers who actually operate the firm.

A **merger** combines two or more corporations into one corporation. Generally mergers fit into one of three categories: horizontal, vertical, or conglomerate.

> A **merger** is a combination of two or more corporations into one.

■ A horizontal merger combines firms that do much the same thing. An example is the 1996 merger of Scott Paper Company and Kimberly-Clark Corporation, both paper makers. Another is the 1995 merger of Burlington Northern, Inc. and Santa Fe Pacific Corporation, both railroads.

■ A vertical merger combines firms that are involved in different stages of the production process or the marketing of an item. An example is General Motors' purchase of AC Spark Plug Corporation. A special type of vertical merger involves the marketing of a firm's product. Ford Motor Company's 1996 purchase of Budget Rent A Car Corporation is an example.

■ The third type is the conglomerate merger, a combination of unrelated firms. Often called diversified companies, they include LTV, Tenneco, Gulf + Western, and ITT. The reverse of diversification, called divestiture, became common in the 1980s after many conglomerates fared poorly.

A **subsidiary** is a corporation that is owned by another corporation.

A **subsidiary** is a corporation owned by another corporation, either partly or completely. Miller Brewing Corporation, for example, is a subsidiary of Philip Morris Companies, Inc. The subsidiary retains its identity as a corporation, which is not true in most mergers. In the future, the subsidiary could again become completely independent.

A franchiser is a firm that gives another firm, the franchisee, the right to do business in a specified way and area. The franchisee receives guidance, financing, advertising, and other assistance. It pays the franchiser a franchise fee for this plus a share of the sales or profit. Franchises are most common in the fast-food restaurant industry and other small retail operations.

Venture capital is money provided to a new firm that needs it to start operations. Usually the firms are innovators, not copies of existing firms. Among many sources of venture capital is the so-called venture-capital firm. Usually someone in the venture-capital firm obtains a position on the board of directors of the new firm.

BUSINESS ACCOUNTING—REVENUES, COSTS, AND PROFITS

In the careful record-keeping that sound business operation requires, two business statements are most critical: 1) the balance sheet or net worth statement; and 2) the income statement.

A **balance sheet** is a business statement showing the condition of a business at a point in time, listing the firm's assets and liabilities.

On the **balance sheet**, the firm first lists all its assets (what it owns plus other "positives"), including cash, accounts receivable, land and buildings, its inventory of supplies and finished goods, stock owned in other firms, and so on. Next, the firm lists its liabilities (or what it owes plus other "negatives"). These include accounts payable (bills), accrued (unpaid) wages, loans, and accrued taxes. The difference between assets and liabilities is the net worth or owner's equity. Only "stock variables" appear on a balance sheet. Like the number of gallons of water in a tank, stock variables are always measured at a *point* in time.

An **income statement** is a business statement showing the condition of the business over a period of time, containing information on revenues, costs, and profits or losses.

The **income statement**, or the profit and loss (P&L) statement, has three broad sections: 1) revenue; 2) costs; and 3) profit or loss. The P&L statement shows how well the firm did financially for a given period of time. Revenue, cost, and profit or loss are all examples of "flow variables." Like water flowing into a tank that is measured in gallons per minute (a *period* of time), they are measured over a period, such as a month, quarter, or year.

Because flow variables and stock variables are measured on a different basis, they cannot be compared meaningfully. Thus, a business needs the two accounting statements to gauge its degree of success.

■ First, the income statement shows the firm's revenues, or sales, known as total revenue (TR), or total sales. TR equals the price (P) times the quantity sold (Q)—or, TR = P x Q.

■ Second, this statement shows production expenses or costs. A firm expresses its costs or expenses in two primary ways, by using the total cost concept or the average cost concept. A firm's total expenses, or its **total cost** (TC), equals the sum of all the money it spends for all the resources needed to produce a given level of its product. The **average cost** (AC) is the cost of producing just one unit of output, on average, calculated with the formula: AC = TC ÷ Q, where Q stands for the quantity of output that the business produces.

Total cost includes all the costs of producing a specific amount of output of a good or service.

Average cost refers to the amount of expenses in producing one unit of a good or service, on average.

Often a firm splits its total cost into two categories, fixed and variable. Its fixed costs, which include such things as property taxes, license fees, and rent, do not change if the firm changes its output. The fixed costs are a reflection of the resources a firm needs to get established but does *not* need more of to *increase* its output. Such resources are called fixed resources, meaning they are fixed at some level, no matter how much a firm produces. For example, a map maker needs to spend money to design its map. However, if it wants to increase its output from 200 maps per day to 210, it wouldn't have to spend any more money to design the map. Adding up the various fixed costs gives the **total fixed cost** (TFC), commonly known as overhead.

Total fixed cost includes all the overhead or fixed costs of producing a specific amount of output of a good or service.

If a firm spreads its overhead evenly over each unit of output, each unit's share of the overhead is the **average fixed cost** (AFC). Average fixed cost is found by the formula: AFC = TFC ÷ Q. Suppose a lamp maker makes 20,000 lamps a year and has total fixed costs of $800,000. Thus, its AFC = $800,000 ÷ 20,000, or $40. This means the firm pays $40 per lamp for fixed resources, like its design costs or its rented factory. Now suppose the firm adds a second shift in this same factory, boosting output to 40,000 lamps per year. Then the AFC falls to $20 per lamp, as AFC = $800,000 ÷ 40,000, or $20. For a given business size (its capital stock), the larger the output, the lower the average fixed cost.

Average fixed cost refers to the amount of overhead or fixed expenses in producing one unit of a good or service, on average.

The second category of costs that make up total cost is variable costs. Such costs vary as a firm's output varies. They are a reflection of the resources a firm needs more of to increase its output. They are called variable resources, and they include raw materials, labor, and fuel for machines and vehicles. (For the map maker referred to earlier, the paper it uses to print the maps would be a variable resource, as it needs more paper to increase output from 200 to 210 maps.) **Total variable cost** (TVC) is the sum of all such variable costs, commonly called operating costs or production costs. If these are spread evenly over all units of output, the result is

Total variable cost is the sum of all the operating or variable costs of producing a specific amount of output of a good or service.

average variable cost (AVC). You find AVC by dividing the total variable cost by the level of production—or, AVC = TVC ÷ Q. Suppose the lamp maker has $1,200,000 in variable expenses when it makes 20,000 lamps a year. Then the AVC is $60, for $60 = $1,200,000 ÷ 20,000. This tells the firm that each lamp cost $60 for operating or variable expenses.

Total cost is found by adding TFC and TVC. The firm now knows its total cost of producing x number of lamps. Dividing total costs by output gives the average cost—or, AC = TC ÷ Q. You can also find average cost by adding the average fixed cost and the average variable cost—or, AC = AFC + AVC. The average cost of making lamps reflects payment for all the resources needed to make one lamp, on average. Thus, it reflects the efficiency of resource use in making lamps.

One more useful cost concept is **marginal cost** (MC), or the *extra* cost to make one *extra* unit of output. Consider again the lamp maker. At an output of 20,000 lamps, its total cost is $2,000,000 (as TFC = $800,000 and TVC = $1,200,000). If it makes lamp number 20,001, any addition to that $2,000,000 is the marginal cost. Suppose the total cost for 20,001 lamps is $2,000,070. Then the marginal cost is $70 (= $2,000,070 − $2,000,000). So the MC is the difference in the total cost between successive levels of output. However, because fixed costs do not increase as output increases, MC is also the difference in the total variable cost between successive levels of output.

A related concept is **marginal revenue** (MR), the *extra* revenue a firm makes by selling an extra unit of output. If the firm has a total revenue of $2,400,000 when selling 20,000 lamps and $2,400,090 when selling 20,001 lamps, then its marginal revenue for lamp number 20,001 is $90 (= $2,400,090 − $2,400,000).

Table 4-1 lists all the cost formulas covered thus far. Table 4-2 presents another example of a producer, which shows a table manufacturer's costs at various daily output levels.

Table 4-1

Cost Formulas

$$TC = TFC + TVC \qquad AC = AFC + AVC$$

$$AC = \frac{TC}{Q} \qquad AFC = \frac{TFC}{Q} \qquad AVC = \frac{TVC}{Q}$$

Looking at the average cost column in Table 4-2, notice that AC is lowest at an output of 10 tables, or $150 per table. Therefore, that is the most efficient level of production because the firm is using the least amount of resources per table to make tables. (Incidentally, the most efficient level of output is not necessarily the most profitable level of output.)

Q	TC	TFC	TVC	AC	AFC	AVC	MC
0	$ 320	$320	$ 0	—	—	—	—
1	600	320	280	$600.00	$320.00	$280.00	$ 280
2	800	320	480	400.00	160.00	240.00	200
3	920	320	600	306.67	106.67	200.00	120
4	1000	320	680	250.00	80.00	170.00	80
5	1050	320	730	210.00	64.00	146.00	50
6	1110	320	790	185.00	53.33	137.67	60
7	1180	320	860	168.57	45.71	122.86	70
8	1260	320	940	157.50	40.00	117.50	80
9	1370	320	1050	152.23	35.56	116.67	110
10	1500	320	1180	150.00	32.00	118.00	150
11	1720	320	1400	156.36	29.09	127.27	220
12	2000	320	1680	166.67	26.67	140.00	280
13	2320	320	2000	178.47	24.62	153.85	320
14	2700	320	2380	192.86	22.86	170.00	380
15	3250	320	2930	216.67	21.33	195.33	550
16	4800	320	4480	300.00	20.00	280.00	1550

Table 4-2

The Various Categories of Costs of a Firm That Manufactures Tables

■ The third and last section of the income statement shows whether the firm made a profit or had a loss. That figure appears on the last or bottom line of the statement and is the source of the phrase "the bottom line."

Profit can be measured in a number of ways. First, the bottom of an income statement gives the gross income. Gross income (or profit before income taxes) equals total sales minus total expenses. If the firm is a corporation, it must pay income taxes on this gross income. The remainder is the firm's net income or net profit.

Second, the net margin method of measuring profit shows what percent of a firm's sales (TR) it earns as net income. The remainder goes to cover its expenses and income taxes. Net margin is found by dividing net income by sales.

Third, the rate of return on equity shows what percent of a firm's equity it earns in net income. (Equity equals assets minus liabilities.) It is found by dividing net income by its equity. This method can be likened to the rate of interest on a savings account in a bank.

Fourth, the net income per share shows how much net income a corporation earns for each share of stock. It is found by dividing the net income by the total number of shares held by the stockholders.

Table 4-3

Formulas Used to Determine Profit

Firms report their profits in various ways, noted in bold. These formulas show how they are calcutated.

Total Revenue = Price x Quantity Sold or TR = PxQ

Gross Income = Total Revenue − Total Costs

Net Income = Gross Income − Income Taxes

$$\textbf{Net Margin} = \frac{\text{Net Income}}{\text{Total Revenue}} \times 100$$

$$\textbf{Rate of Return on Equity} = \frac{\text{Net Income}}{\text{Owner's Equity}} \times 100$$

$$\textbf{Profit per Share} = \frac{\text{Net Income}}{\text{Number of Shares}}$$

Table 4-3 summarizes all the formulas relating to the measure of profit. Table 4-4 presents an income statement for a firm with the various measures of profit shown at the bottom. Distributions of dividends to stockholders (not shown in Table 4-4) are usually drawn from net income.

Total Sales..**$500,000**

Expenses
  Supplies $170,000
  Wages and Salaries $148,000
  Depreciation.....................................$ 40,000
  Utilities ....$ 11,000
  Legal and Other Professional Fees.........$ 3,000
  Rent ....$ 2,000
  Other Expenses ....$ 26,000

Total Costs **$400,000**

Gross Income...................................**$100,000**

  Income Taxes ....$ 20,000

Net Income ....**$ 80,000**

Net Margin $= \dfrac{\$80,000}{\$500,000} \times 100 = 16.0\%$ Note: Equity = $600,000
                                                                    Number of Shares = 50,000

Rate of Return on Equity $= \dfrac{\$80,000}{\$600,000} \times 100 = 13.3\%$

Net Income per Share $= \dfrac{\$80,000}{50,000} = \$1.60$ per Share

Table 4-4

An Income Statement

An income statement shows the position of a hypothetical firm over a period of time. It shows its sales or revenues, its costs or expenses, and its profit (or loss).

The lower part of the table calculates the various measures of profit for this firm.

THE ROLE OF PROFIT IN THE ALLOCATION OF RESOURCES

Recall that the purpose of studying economics is to reduce the problem caused by resource scarcity. This occurs when resources are used more efficiently so there are better answers to the Basic Economic Questions. Now you will learn how profits (or sometimes the *lack* of them) help maximize efficiency and our economic welfare.

Economic vs. Accounting Profit

Until now it was implied that all costs or expenses require a business to pay money to owners of resources, such as laborers and suppliers. Such

An **explicit cost** is a business cost that involves payment of money to a seller of a resource.

An **implicit cost** is a business cost that does not involve payment of money to a seller of a resource.

Normal profit equals the total of a typical firm's implicit costs in an industry.

Economic profit equals the excess of a firm's total revenue over its explicit plus implicit costs.

Economic loss equals the shortfall of a firm's total revenue compared with the sum of its explicit plus implicit costs.

costs are known as **explicit costs** because paying money makes it explicit or obvious that the firm gives up something of value. These are the only costs that appear on an income statement.

Yet every business—or rather its owner—gives up other things of value besides money when operating the business. These are called **implicit costs**. Remember, a cost is anything of value that is given up to gain something else. Suppose that Mr. Edwards, the owner of a radio manufacturing firm, gave up a $300,000-a-year job managing another firm so he could be his own boss. Since he no longer has that $300,000, it is a real cost for him of making radios. This cost is called implicit wages and is one of the implicit costs of doing business. Another is implicit interest, which is interest given up when money is drawn out of a bank or an investment to be used in a business. Many of these costs can be expressed in money terms, but it's harder to quantify others. They include time given up from leisure activities and family (especially by entrepreneurs who work long hours), as well as the stress caused by competition, fear of failure, and responsibility.

Implicit costs are nothing more than opportunity costs. Economists term the combination of all a firm's implicit costs its **normal profit** (the reason it's called "normal" will be explained shortly). If a firm has enough sales to pay its explicit costs *and* its implicit costs or normal profit, any money left over is called **economic profit**. This situation is shown in the bottom part of Figure 4-1. Note that the economist's explicit costs are identical to the accountant's view of costs in the upper part of the figure.

Alternatively, if there are *not enough* revenues to cover the explicit costs plus the implicit costs, this shortfall is called an **economic loss**. This *economic* profit and loss is different from a profit or loss that appears on the income statement, (here called an accounting profit or accounting loss).

Figure 4-2 shows a firm's five possibilities for accounting and economic profit. Each case represents an increasingly less desirable position, and its position determines whether it will: 1) continue making the item it does; or 2) make some other item or completely close down its operations. The next section on the role of profit explains these decisions in more detail.

■ In the first case, the firm has sufficient revenues to pay all its explicit and implicit costs. Any money left over is its economic profit. This situation means the owners get more benefits from their resources than they could from any other way of using them. Thus, such a firm will keep making whatever it makes so long as it earns this profit. Also, new firms will enter such an industry in order to earn these unusually high profits.

■ In the second case, there are no such "excess" funds, only enough to pay all costs, explicit plus implicit. There is no economic profit, yet no economic loss either. Occasionally a business owner who faces such a situ-

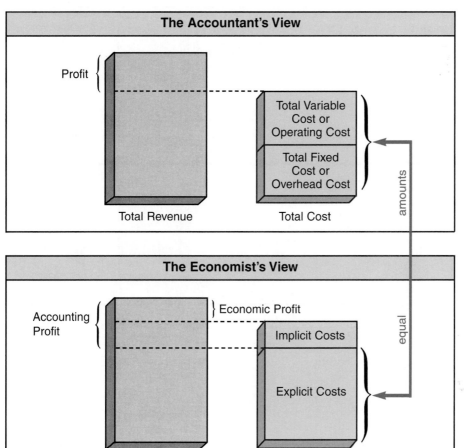

Figure 4-1

Revenues, Costs, and Profits – Viewpoints of Accountants and Economists

Traditional accounting considers a cost as something requiring the owner to pay money to a resource owner. This view is reflected in the top diagram. Economists call these a firm's explicit costs. In addition, economists consider the implicit costs of the owner of a firm. These are forgone opportunities that do not involve the payment of money.

Subtracting explicit costs from revenues equals accounting profit. To the economist, profit is found by subtracting the explicit plus the implicit costs from revenues. In the long run, firms in competitive industries generally earn accounting profits equal to their implicit costs.

ation says, "I'm not making any profit." This can confuse many people, for any accountant or IRS agent will swear that profits are indeed being earned. But these are accounting profits, and in this case they equal the amount of implicit costs. And because business owners consider implicit costs to be just as real as explicit (cash) costs, owners in this situation say they are just breaking even—or are making no profit. But the profit the *owners* are speaking about is *economic* profit.

As you saw a few paragraphs above, a firm in this situation is said to be earning only normal profit. The word normal indicates that this is the amount most firms in a competitive industry generally (or normally) earn. The reason they only earn this amount will be explained in the next section. An industry whose firms earn only normal profits and have no economic profits or losses will not attract new firms nor will it lose any.

Figure 4-2

**Accounting and
Economic Profit
or Loss Possibilities**

In Case 1, firms earn
economic profits, which
draw in new firms into the
industry.

In Case 2, all costs are
just covered, so no firms
enter the industry nor
leave it.

In Cases 3 through 5,
there are economic
losses, so firms leave the
industry in all cases.
However, firms still earn
accounting profits in
Case 3.

In Case 4, firms have
enough revenue to pay
their explicit costs – a
"break-even point" in
common business terms.

In Case 5, firms face
accounting losses.

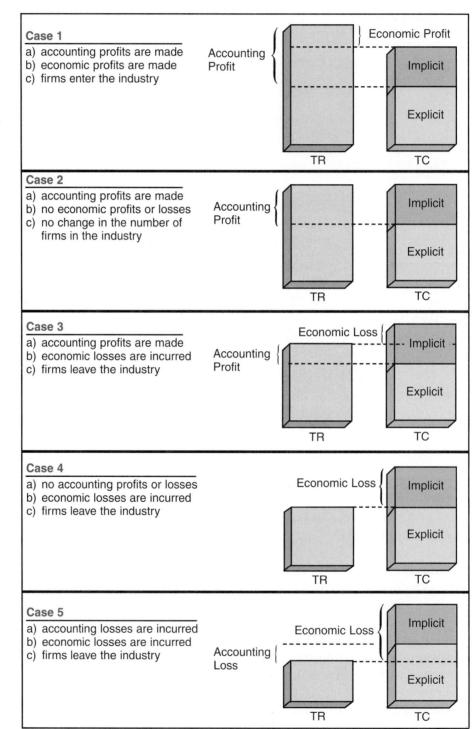

Case 1

a) accounting profits are made
b) economic profits are made
c) firms enter the industry

Accounting Profit — Economic Profit — Implicit — Explicit — TR — TC

Case 2

a) accounting profits are made
b) no economic profits or losses
c) no change in the number of firms in the industry

Accounting Profit — Implicit — Explicit — TR — TC

Case 3

a) accounting profits are made
b) economic losses are incurred
c) firms leave the industry

Accounting Profit — Economic Loss — Implicit — Explicit — TR — TC

Case 4

a) no accounting profits or losses
b) economic losses are incurred
c) firms leave the industry

Economic Loss — Implicit — Explicit — TR — TC

Case 5

a) accounting losses are incurred
b) economic losses are incurred
c) firms leave the industry

Accounting Loss — Economic Loss — Implicit — Explicit — TR — TC

THINKING CRITICALLY ABOUT ECONOMIC QUESTIONS IN OUR LIVES

Should There Be Stores Downtown?

Things to Consider

1. The downtown shopping areas of very many towns and cities are suffering financially. The advent of large malls and strip malls on the outskirts of towns or in the suburbs in the last 30-40 years have changed how people shop.

2. Many cities are spending large amounts of tax money to revitalize their downtowns to attract shoppers and keep them alive.

3. Consider the effect of such efforts on the economic welfare of society as a whole— not just the downtown merchants. Is this a wise policy? Consider why people changed how they shop and what effect that change had on their welfare.

See page 458 for the answer.

■ In the third case, there is enough revenue to pay all *cash* (explicit) expenses, plus there is some revenue left over to cover *some* implicit costs. However, the remainder of those implicit costs are *not* covered. That is the *economic* loss the owner incurs. Owners of firms with economic losses could earn more if their resources were employed elsewhere. An owner of a business with economic losses might go into another business or line of work.

■ In the fourth possibility, the firm has only enough sales to pay its cash expenses or its explicit costs. It is at its break-even point in the accounting sense. There is not even any accounting profit, and the firm has a big economic loss, equal to the full amount of its implicit costs. Owners of such firms are not able to pay themselves any money for their time spent in the business and will eventually close down.

■ In the fifth case, there is not even enough money to pay for all the explicit costs. As the firm can't pay all its bills, it faces both an economic loss *and* an accounting loss. In this case, the economic loss equals the accounting loss plus the implicit costs. Such a firm will quickly leave this industry.

The Role of Profit

Profit often has received a bad name. Perhaps that is because some people believe that profit is merely something businesses try to earn at the consumer's expense. Like it or not, profit greatly affects everyone's economic welfare in two primary ways: 1) it is an incentive for entrepreneurs; and 2) it redirects resource use, thereby affecting efficiency.

■ First, profit serves as an incentive to bring the extremely scarce resource of entrepreneurship to production processes. (The "profit" here is *economic* profit.) Entrepreneurs organize such processes, and good ones do it better than others. Better organization increases the efficiency of resource use, which increases economic welfare. When entrepreneurs are successful, their reward is high income (profits), which is the consequence of the lower production costs in more efficient production processes. In a free market economy with strong competition, the efficient entrepreneur usually is forced to pass on much of these cost savings to consumers. Therefore, *everyone* gains when an entrepreneur can rise above the rest.

■ The second role of profit is to redirect resource use in order to answer What to Produce? or How to Produce? differently. Suppose that too little of a product (say, auto mufflers) is produced. "Too little" means not enough mufflers are produced to maximize economic welfare from society's scarce resources. Some resources currently used to make something else (such as shovels) should be used to make mufflers instead. Economists call such a redirection of resource use a reallocation of resources.

In a command economy, the reallocation of resources is the job of government. With capitalism, the profit levels in different industries bring about such reallocation. If firms produce too few mufflers, muffler prices are likely to be quite high, probably higher than the average cost of producing them, including the implicit costs. Consequently, firms that make mufflers will have economic profits, which will attract additional manufacturers. The production of the new firms amounts to an increase in the supply of mufflers. Now all sellers combined offer more mufflers at the original price than previously. The higher supply creates a surplus, and the surplus forces the price down. This process of firms entering the industry, increasing supply, and price decline continues until the price equals the average cost. That is because economic profits disappear at that point, as does the incentive for firms to enter the industry. Case A in Figure 4-3 provides a summary of this sequence of events.

Examples of products that have gone through this process are: cotton after Whitney's invention of the cotton gin in 1793; steel after the invention of the Kelly-Bessemer process in the mid-1800s; oil in the 1860s and

Case A: When There Is "Too Little" Made of Good X	Case B: When There Is "Too Much" Made of Good X
Economic Profits Are Made (P>AC)	Economic Losses Occur (P<AC)
New Firms Enter the Industry (more resources are used to make Good X)	Firms Leave the Industry (fewer resources are used to make Good X)
The Supply of Good X Increases (more of Good X is offered for sale at the equilibrium price)	The Supply of Good X Decreases (less of Good X is offered for sale at the equilibrium price)
A Surplus of Good X Develops (because the *extra* supply is not matched by any *extra* demand)	A Shortage of Good X Develops (because the *reduced* supply is not matched by any *reduced* demand)
The Price of Good X Decreases (consequently, the surplus disappears)	The Price of Good X Increases (consequently, the shortage disappears)
Economic Profits Disappear (when price falls enough so P=AC)	Economic Losses Disappear (when price rises enough so P=AC)
Firms Stop Entering the Industry	Firms Stop Leaving the Industry
Prices Stabilize	**Prices Stabilize**

Figure 4-3

How Economic Profits and Losses Redirect Resource Use

In Case A, an industry has insufficient resources, meaning that it produces "too little" of Good X. That causes economic profits, leading to firms entering the industry and more resources with which to produce Good X.

In Case B, there are excess resources and amounts of Good X made, creating economic losses that force firms to leave the industry.

In both cases, the indusry ends up with a stable number of firms, stable prices, and neither economic losses nor profits.

1870s; autos from 1900 to the 1920s; refrigerators in the 1930s and 1940s; televisions in the 1940s and 1950s; snowmobiles in the 1960s; fast-food restaurants in the 1960s and 1970s; personal computers in the 1970s and 1980s; and cellular phones in the 1990s.

Alternatively, firms might produce too *much* of something, which indicates that the resources used should produce something else instead. Suppose again that the good in question is a muffler. When too many mufflers are produced, muffler firms are unable to sell anywhere near their capacities. This leads to low prices and economic losses—even *accounting* losses in severe cases. The average cost of production exceeds the price. No firm will keep producing mufflers if economic losses are expected to continue indefinitely. There are better opportunities elsewhere. Thus, firms leave the muffler industry, reducing the supply of mufflers. Because people still want to buy the same number of mufflers as before, a shortage occurs, forcing muffler prices up. This sequence continues so long as there are economic losses, which finally stop when the price goes up high enough to equal the average cost. This sequence appears in Case B in Figure 4-3.

Sometimes an industry's low profits (or losses) are caused by a sharp drop in demand for its product because some alternative product became available that consumers preferred. Ultimately, the first product will disappear from the scene, and that industry will cease to exist. History presents noteworthy examples of firms in various industries that disappeared this way: canal companies replaced by railroads in the 1840s and 1850s; cooper shops, which made wooden barrels; corsetmakers; manufacturers of harnesses, horseshoes, and other horse-related goods; carriage manufacturers replaced by auto manufacturers; firms that cut ice from lakes and rivers for iceboxes in prerefrigerator days; manufacturers of film movie cameras replaced by video camera manufacturers; and carburetor manufacturers replaced by fuel injector manufacturers.

However popular these items had been, people decided (with their spending shifts) that their production should end. Were those good decisions? Would you want to buy those goods today—corsets, carriages, iceboxes, and movie cameras that use film? If not, then society decided wisely when it reallocated its resources to make what we do want today instead. Clearly, the people who made those decisions (and everyone else) benefited by such reallocation and modernization, even though the adjustment was painful. Did the coopers, the harness and corset makers, and the ice cutters *want* to go out of business? Of course not. They all suffered, as did owners and employees of firms in hundreds of other industries. That is one cost of progress. However, many people have the misconception that such dislocation and its costs are unique to the late 20th century.

This process still occurs. Think how life today differs from the early 1980s or the 1970s following sharp increases in the price of gasoline. For example, a lot of gas stations closed in the 1970s during the energy crisis and were turned into convenience stores, hair salons, and muffler shops.

Those affected by resource reallocation sometimes try to stop the process either because they can't make such transitions or are not innovative enough. Competition is often painful for firms, but it is the most important factor in forcing firms to improve themselves.

MARKET STRUCTURE

An **industry** includes all the firms that produce a particular (or closely related) good. There's the auto industry, the garment industry, the beef industry, and so on. (Be careful not to refer to a particular *firm* as an industry, as many people incorrectly do.) Market structure refers to the characteristics of an industry: the number and size of firms; the degree of competition and price-setting power of the firms; the similarity of competitors' products; and the ease of entering and leaving that industry. Economists place all industries into one of four major categories: 1) pure competition; 2) monopolistic competition; 3) oligopoly; and 4) monopoly.

■ **Pure competition** is the market structure many economists believe is ideal because, theoretically: 1) buyers can be expected to get the lowest price; and 2) the efficiency of resource use is maximized. An industry in pure competition has many small firms, often hundreds or even thousands. With so much competition, no firm can command a price higher than the rest. Each firm is a "price taker," which means it must accept the "going price." The firms' products are identical, and no firm has more production knowledge than any other. Finally, firms can easily enter and exit the industry because no law, cartel, or other barrier prevents such movement. Consequently, in the long run, there are neither economic profits nor economic losses. Few industries meet these standards, but producers of most agricultural commodities do face pure competition.

■ **Monopolistic competition** is a market structure characterized by many firms, usually of small size. Their products are somewhat different from their competitors'. Each firm has some ability to raise its price above its competitors' prices without losing all its customers. Entry into the industry is sometimes difficult because of a **barrier to entry**, such as licenses, permits, franchises, patents, copyrights, and high capital costs. The fast-food industry is a good example of monopolistic competition, for hamburgers and fries of different restaurant chains are not significantly different and prices do vary slightly.

An **industry** includes all the firms that produce a particular good or service.

Pure competition is a market structure characterized by many small firms, each having identical products sold at a single market price, and where there is easy entry into and exit from the industry.

Monopolistic competition is a market structure of many firms, each having a slightly different product sold at slightly different prices and where there usually is easy entry into and exit from the industry.

A **barrier to entry** prevents a new firm from entering an industry, including patents, copyrights, licenses, permits, franchising requirements, and high capital costs.

An **oligopoly** is a market structure characterized by a few large firms with significant price-setting power and unique or homogeneous products and where there are significant barriers to entry.

■ **Oligopoly** is the structure of most "big businesses" (firms that produce a lot of output, such as Westinghouse, IBM, and Kellogg). Firms are generally large and few in number. Products are often distinctive (autos, for example), usually identified by a brand. In other cases, such as steel, products are homogeneous. Although each firm has much power to manipulate price, competition is occasionally very strong. Sometimes competition exhibits itself in product design. Often there are heavy financial requirements or other barriers to entry. The auto, steel, breakfast cereal, large appliance, and tire industries are all oligopolies.

THINKING CRITICALLY ABOUT ECONOMIC QUESTIONS IN OUR LIVES

Should Some Towns in the Great Plains Become Ghost Towns?

Things to Consider

1. If you'd note the population of 10 randomly selected towns of western Nebraska today, you'd see that it dropped from decades ago. Why did their populations drop?

2. Suppose you had the job of deciding where towns should be today in western Nebraska. The economy in that area is almost completely agricultural. (Imagine that no one lived there until right now, so towns need to be built to support the farmers.) You must ensure that there are business and other services within reasonable distances of all the farmers. Further, you must take care not to waste resources by building so many stores and other businesses that many of them cannot survive. Also, school buildings, city offices, and police/fire stations are resources that should not be wasted (that is, they should be in full use much of the time).

3. In light of the shrinking population over the last few decades, how fully do you think the resources currently in place are used? Thus, would you choose to build as many towns (buildings, streets, and such) as exist now? If not, what should be done with the "excess towns" and their "excess resources" in western Nebraska today? Perhaps move everyone out of selected towns and have them become ghost towns?

See page 458 for the answer.

■ The last structure, **monopoly**, is rarer than people think. In monopoly there is only one firm supplying the output. Thus, it can set price wherever it likes, but its power to do so is limited because people usually don't *have* to buy the product—and don't if the price is too high.

A **monopoly** is a market structure where there is only one firm and where there is a barrier to entering the industry.

Technically, a single grocery store in a small town is a monopoly, but this doesn't convey the concept adequately. A true monopolist faces no competitors because of some barrier to entry. Polaroid Corporation is a monopoly producer of instant cameras because of the patents it holds. A public utility, such as a gas or electric company, is called a natural monopoly because certain characteristics of the service make multiple production facilities extremely wasteful. Five electric companies would require five sets of wires all over town, creating a costly mess and no extra benefit. States grant franchise rights in specified areas to natural monopolies and establish price-setting power in public service commissions.

Figure 4-4 summarizes the major characteristics of each of the four market structures.

Figure 4-4   **Market Structures and Their Characteristics**

Generally, firms that make up an industry to produce a good or service can be categorized into one of four market structures. Some of the characteristics of the markets for the products of the firms in these market structures are given in the chart.

MARKET CHARACTERISTIC	MARKET STRUCTURE			
	PURE COMPETITION	MONOPOLISTIC COMPETITION	OLIGOPOLY	MONOPOLY
Degree of Product Differentiation	Homogeneous	Differentiated	Homogeneous or Differentiated	Unique
Number of Firms	Very Many	Many	Few	One
Barriers to Entry	None	Few	Many	Very Many
Control Over Price by Firms (or market power)	None	Some	Much	Complete
Ability to Earn Economic Profit	None	None	Some	Much

BUSINESS OPERATION

This section is a brief introduction to business operations. It covers business goals, determination of firm size, and determination of a purely competitive firm's maximum profit point.

Goals of Business

One might find it difficult to determine the goals of different businesses. One firm might seem to be seeking to maximize sales; another, the growth of its scale of operations; and another, the returns to its investors or owners. Actually, many firms have a complex mix of goals, some of which may actually conflict. However, profit maximization is usually a major goal for most firms.

Another important and related goal of businesses, especially oligopolies, is market share, a firm's percentage of total sales in the entire industry. Jif peanut butter, for example, accounts for 33 percent of all peanut butter sold. The managers at Jif might, however, believe they need 40 percent to ensure brand loyalty. To achieve that, they might cut price—and sacrifice some short-run profit. Other firms gain market share by stressing quality.

A final major goal of some businesses is community good will. A business, wanting to be a "good neighbor," might contribute to local fund drives. Critics of such gifts complain that managers, who often are *not* the owners, give away money that belongs to the stockholders (who *are* the owners) in order to get a "pat on the back" from the community. Good will may be the goal of managers, but usually the firm's owners will support it only if it is profitable. This is possible if the good will serves as a form of advertising or helps establish consumer loyalty to the firm's product.

How a Firm Decides How Large to Become

It isn't by accident that firms become large, small, or middle size. This section briefly explains the main reason for size differences among firms in different industries. In some industries, such as appliance repair and raspberry production, most firms are small. In other industries, such as pencil production, most firms are large.

To begin, the concept of returns to scale, first covered in Chapter 3, will be briefly reviewed. Returns to scale refer to how the level of output changes as a firm increases all of its resources at the same rate. If a firm doubles its resources and consequently *more* than doubles its output, the firm experiences increasing returns to scale (economies of scale), and average cost falls. However, if doubling resources results in an increase in output that is *less than* double, the firm experiences decreasing returns to scale (diseconomies of scale). Now average cost increases with scale increases.

The question facing any business firm is: What size operation should it have? It could be large or small, but the firm needs to find its **optimum scale of plant**. This is the plant with the lowest average cost of production, given some particular demand for its output. Because average cost reflects efficiency, this is the most efficient plant.

> The **optimum scale of plant** is the size of a firm's capital stock associated with the lowest average cost.

But what if a firm can sell much *more* than its optimum size plant can produce? Should it limit its sales to the output level of that plant? Or should it build a bigger plant than the optimum size? The answer is neither. Rather, it should build *multiple* operations of the same optimum size plant. That is the primary reason for the large number of fast-food restaurants. Similarly, most electric power companies have several generating plants rather than a single plant because the *generation* of electricity does not involve economies of scale beyond a certain size of generating plant. However, the *transmission* of electricity through wires does, which explains why it is a (natural) monopoly.

For a similar reason, some industries have many firms. Suppose the optimum size operation for some industry can produce only a thousandth of the demand for the good. Will one firm—a monopoly—have 1,000 plants? Hardly. Rather, there could be as many as a thousand competing firms, each very small. That's how pure competition arises, such as in wheat and corn farming, where there are hundreds of thousands of farms (firms).

Alternatively, suppose the optimum size operation for another industry produces a fourth of the product's demand. Then this industry will have a handful of firms, each probably of large size. This is how economists explain the presence of most oligopolies, such as in auto or refrigerator manufacture.

Finding the Point of Maximum Profit

Consider a firm in a purely competitive industry, whose sole goal is to maximize profit. After the firm determines the size of its operation, it must decide how much output to produce to maximize its profit. Should it operate at its full capacity or at only a fraction of capacity? You might wonder why a firm would use less than its full capacity. This happens because

The **short run** is a period of time when a business is not able to change the amount of its capital stock.

The **long run** is a period of time long enough for a firm to increase or decrease its capital stock.

firms operate both in the short run and the long run. In the **short run**, some of the firm's resources, usually its capital stock, cannot vary in quantity. Obviously such factors as plant or store size and the amount of machinery are relatively inflexible. These take months or years to expand. However, the firm usually *can* quickly increase its work force, supplies, and the like—which is how it can vary output in the short run. In the **long run**, all resources are variable, so output can be increased by adding capital stock.

How does one firm in a purely competitive industry decide how much to produce in the short run? The answer is determined by the amount that maximizes its profit. Two ways to locate that maximum profit amount will be presented: 1) the total-revenue/total-cost approach; and 2) the marginal-revenue/marginal-cost approach.

■ With the first method, it is important to know that a purely competitive firm faces a perfectly elastic demand. This means it can sell as much as it wants at the market price, even without advertising. (This actually occurs with many agricultural commodities. Farmers can sell all the produce they wish at the market price.) Suppose a potato farm is capable of producing about a million pounds of potatoes a year if all the land is used. However, the farmer doesn't *have* to use all the land, so how many bushels *should* be produced? That is, how much of the available land should be planted? Figure 4-5 clearly shows the answer.

In Figure 4-5, look at the line labeled Total Revenue. The starting point at the lower left corner indicates zero production and sales, where no land would be planted. As the line rises to the right, it indicates that there is an increasingly larger amount of potatoes grown, as measured on the horizontal axis. Suppose the farmer sells potatoes for 10 cents a pound. As total revenue equals price times quantity sold, one can now calculate the total revenue for the farm. The vertical axis is measured in dollars. Thus, the total revenue line shows the relationship between output and total revenue. For instance, when the farmer sells 200,000 pounds of potatoes, total revenue will be $20,000 (= 10¢ x 200,000). At 400,000 pounds, total revenue will be $40,000 (= 10¢ x 400,000).

The line labeled Total Cost shows the relationship between the output of potatoes and the farm's total expenses, including both fixed costs and variable costs. The level of fixed costs can be seen as the level of total costs when there is zero output, or $18,000. The continual rise in the total cost line as output increases is attributable to the variable costs that are incurred in producing ever increasing amounts of potatoes. The uneven rise in the total cost line reflects varying levels of efficiency of resource use as output rises.

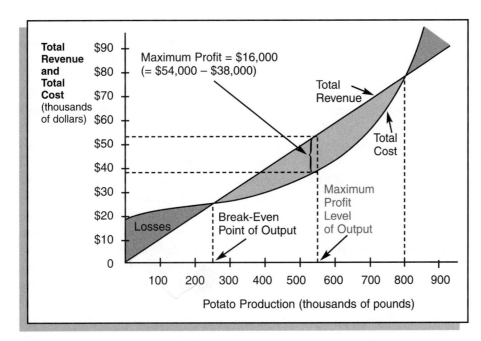

Figure 4-5

Profit Maximization
Using the
Total-Revenue / Total-Cost
Approach

The potato farmer faces losses on outputs up to 240 thousand pounds (as well as beyond 800 thousand pounds). Profits are earned between those levels, and the most profit is earned at 550 thousand pounds.

The farmer "breaks even" (has costs equal to revenues) or has zero profits or losses at 240 and 800 thousand pounds. The price is 10¢ a pound.

Note: Remember, the profits and losses referred to in this chart are *economic* profits and losses.

Comparing the total cost and total revenue graphs allows you to see the farmer's profits or losses. Any variable measured in dollar amounts, such as revenue and cost, is measured on the vertical axis. Because profit (or loss) is the difference between total revenue and total cost, profit is also measured on the vertical axis. For any particular level of output, profit (or loss) equals the vertical distance between the total revenue curve and the total cost curve. For output below 240,000 pounds, the farmer incurs a loss, for the total cost line exceeds (lies above) the total revenue line. At 240,000 pounds, the farmer breaks even—no loss or profit—for there is just enough revenue to cover costs. Between 240,000 and 800,000 pounds, the farmer makes a profit, for now total revenue exceeds (lies above) total cost. But the *amount* of profit varies. It's a small amount near 240,000 pounds and 800,000 pounds and a large amount near 550,000 pounds. In fact, the 550,000-pound level is the *most* profitable level of output because the vertical distance between the total revenue and total cost lines is the largest. Finally, producing amounts beyond 800,000 pounds again creates losses. (Incidentally, this could be because the last few acres of land available are of low quality. Thus, the yield is low, forcing costs up. But many other factors could also cause lower efficiency and higher costs.)

■ The second way to find the maximum profit point uses marginal analysis. Suppose you are in a purely competitive business such as cleaning carpets or painting houses and produce a certain level of output. If you could produce and sell one more unit, *should* you? Only if the *extra* revenue from the sale of that unit (the marginal revenue) exceeds the *extra* cost (the marginal cost). The difference between the two is added to any profit made from the earlier outputs.

Returning to our potato farmer, Figure 4-6 shows the marginal revenue and marginal cost at each level of output. The marginal revenue is shown as a horizontal line at 10 cents a pound. Thus, the price equals the marginal revenue. This means the farmer gets an additional 10 cents of total revenue for each additional pound of potatoes grown and sold. As potato farmers are in a purely competitive industry, farmers can sell all they want at the "going price" without having to cut their prices.

The marginal cost, however, changes as output increases. It first falls, reflecting an increase in the efficiency of resource use as the farm makes better use of its equipment and other resources. One source of increasing efficiency is an increase in the marginal productivity of resources (see Chapter 3 for review). Eventually, however, higher levels of output have higher marginal costs, shown as an upward sloping curve. This reflects a decrease in the efficiency of resource use. This could be caused by a fall in marginal productivity, perhaps due to some "resource imbalance." An example could be the potato storage shed that gets very full at higher levels of output. To fit in the higher levels of output, the farmer must spend time

Figure 4-6

Profit Maximization
Using the Marginal -
Revenue / Marginal-Cost
Approach

A firm maximizes its profit
where its marginal
revenue equals its
marginal cost. This occurs
at 550 thousand pounds,
where the marginal
revenue and the marginal
cost are both 10 cents.

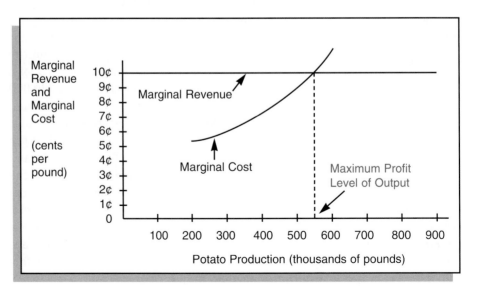

pushing the potatoes around to fill the building to the ceiling. This extra time to produce higher levels of output is reflected in higher marginal costs. Notice that for all output levels below 550,000 pounds that the marginal revenue exceeds the marginal cost. For example, say the farmer has been producing 399,999 pounds of potatoes. Should one more pound be produced? The marginal revenue from the 400 thousandth pound is shown to be 10 cents. The marginal cost is around 8 cents. Thus, the farmer has more to gain than to lose by two cents (10 cents minus 8 cents). This two cents is added to the farm's total profit. That explains why the profit grows in Figure 4-5 for all levels of output below 550,000 pounds. Thus, so long as the marginal revenue exceeds the marginal cost, the farmer should increase output. Eventually, the marginal revenue equals the marginal cost at 550,000 pounds. That last pound of potatoes, then, does not change the level of total profit. However, if any potatoes are produced beyond that point, they will have marginal costs in excess of marginal revenue. Thus, each of these pounds of potatoes will be produced at a loss, forcing total profit to fall. That is shown as a shrinking profit in Figure 4-5 beyond 550,000 pounds. In fact, profits would fall to zero if 800,000 pounds would be produced, and losses would be incurred beyond that point. Therefore, the rule for maximizing profit is to produce the level of output where marginal revenue equals marginal cost.

With such data and graphs, it is easy to find such maximum profit points as well as the optimum size of operation. However, owners of farms, furniture firms, steel firms, and other firms don't have it so easy. They must *find* such information, but it is hard to find, requiring searches and calculations by engineers, accountants, and managers. Perhaps more often than not, they guess what that information is. Their guesses might be educated ones based on years of training and experience, but they are, nonetheless, guesses. Successful business owners generally make the best guesses.

SUMMARY

Private business firms fit into four categories: single proprietorships, partnerships, corporations, and cooperatives. Most firms are proprietorships. Corporations have the advantages of limited liability and the ability to raise large amounts of money by selling stock.

A balance sheet indicates a firm's financial position at a given moment, and the income statement indicates its position over a period of time. Only cash or explicit expenses appear on an income statement, but economists also consider implicit expenses as costs. A firm can view its expenses from the standpoint of either total cost or average cost. Also, it can split expenses into fixed costs and variable costs.

Profit is the difference between total revenue (sales) and total cost. It can be viewed in several ways, including total profit, net margin, rate of return on equity, and net income per share. Accounting profit considers only the difference between sales and explicit costs. Economic profit is the difference between sales and all costs, including implicit costs.

Profit serves to attract entrepreneurs to the production process and to redirect resources away from or into specific industries. Economic profits from producing a good or service will attract resources to that industry, leading to more firms producing that good or service. Conversely, economic losses will drive firms and resources out of the industry.

Industries and their firms are categorized in one of four market structures in decreasing order of competitiveness: pure competition, monopolistic competition, oligopoly, or monopoly. Firms find their optimum scale of plant by considering the size of demand as well as the existence of increasing, constant, or decreasing returns to scale.

The short run is a period in which the firm cannot change its capital stock. Its maximum profit point in the short run is where total revenue exceeds total cost by the largest amount. That is also the point where the marginal revenue equals the marginal cost.

The long run is a period in which firms can change to any size operation or even go out of business. Also, new firms can enter the industry in the long run. In a purely competitive industry, no economic profits are earned in the long run. Any economic profit draws in new firms, leading to increases in supply, surpluses, and price decreases until all profits are gone. Monopolistically competitive firms cannot earn economic profits in the long run because there is still a high degree of competition and easy entry into and exit from the industry. Because of the less than perfectly competitive nature of oligopoly and monopoly, economic profit can exist in the long run.

QUESTIONS FOR DISCUSSION AND THOUGHT

1. Consider a small business and a big business in your community. Why do you think these firms are of such size?

2. The Burlington Northern Railroad and the Santa Fe Railroad merged in 1995. What might be some reasons for these railroad companies to have merged? What might happen to their (combined) revenues and costs?

3. Many retail shops close at five o'clock. Why not at six? Or seven? How does the owner decide when to close? What are the costs and benefits of operating from four to five vs. five to six? Five to six vs. six to seven? If you think either costs or benefits are different in each hour, what do you think makes them different and how might that help to explain closing times? A related question is: Why do most stores in Switzerland close from noon until two o'clock for lunch, but not American shops?

4. At times, only one firm sells a product in a certain geographic area. Examples are tire stores or bookshops in small towns, the maker of cedar chests (Lane Corporation), and Polaroid Corporation. Would you expect their prices to be "high" or "low" (compared with what you'd expect in more competitive marketplaces)?

5. Al Thompson used to earn $65,000 a year managing a large hardware store for a national chain. He now earns (or has an accounting profit of) $45,000. But he never thinks twice about working for someone else again. Can you explain his behavior? Could you conceive of a concept (and coin a name for it) similar to one introduced in the chapter that would explain his behavior?

6. Mary Collins recently purchased a music store for $120,000 in the center of a small town. The downtown is "dying," as many businesses are losing out to the new firms on the outskirts of town. To prevent further losses, city officials decided that firms which stay downtown will have their property taxes cut $1,000 per year. Mary had been clearing $3,000 per month (including the payments on her mortgage). She was content to stay, but a medical problem forced her to sell. She was able to sell out for $130,000. What might her "profit" (capital gains) of $10,000 suggest about the profit picture of the music store business in her town before and after the property tax relief? What was Mary's profit situation? That of the new owner (which started *after* the property tax relief)?

7. Firms in pure competition don't have to advertise, as they can sell all they wish at the "going" or market price. Does this give them the opportunity to earn higher profit rates than firms in industries that do advertise?

8. Suppose that, on average, retail shops have two percent "shrinkage" (losses from shoplifting and employee theft) per year. How does that affect profit levels in the long run? Does your answer suggest something else that happens in the economy?

9. If you were constructing an office building, one important criterion of financial success is to have a low per-square-foot cost (= Total Cost ÷ Total Square Footage). The more stories you add to a building, the more difficulty (thus, cost) you encounter. The greater height adds weight on the lower floors, which requires stronger wall supports and foundations. So, why would you ever construct a building that is 10 or 15 stories? A related question is: Why are office buildings taller in major cities than in smaller ones?

PROBLEMS   See page 482 for the answers.

1. Suppose that it cost General Motors Corporation $80 million to design and build a prototype of the body of a new Cadillac, of which GM expects to sell 100,000. Also, suppose that it cost them $70 million for similar work on a Chevrolet, of which GM expects to sell 700,000. With very nearly the same costs, why do Cadillacs sell for so much more than Chevrolets?

2. You are given the revenues, costs, assets, and liabilities for two corporations, A and B. Fill in the blanks regarding the profit picture of the two firms. Assume that the corporations pay an income tax of 20 percent. Which corporation is more profitable? Why did you choose that one? Could you make a case for choosing the other one?

Firm	Total Revenue	Total Cost	Gross Profit	Net Income	Assets	Liabilities	Net Worth	Net Margin	Rate of Return on Equity
A	$800,000	$600,000	$____	$____	$4.0 million	$2.4 million	$____	____%	____%
B	$40 million	$38 million	$____	$____	$60 million	$40 million	$____	____%	____%

3. Find the net worth of Ace Corporation if it had the following financial picture: loans–$44,000; accounts receivable–$16,000; Chrysler Corporation bonds held by Ace–$3,000; cash on hand–$11,000; accrued wages–$2,000; capital equipment–$15,000; accounts payable–$2,000; land and buildings–$210,000; and accrued taxes–$8,000.

Output	Total Fixed Cost	Total Variable Cost	Total Cost	Total Revenue	Profit (Loss)
0	$100	$0	$ 100	$ 0	$ (100)
1	$100	$220	$ 320	$ 220	$ (100)
2	$100	$300	$ 400	$ 440	$ 40
3	$100	$390	$ 490	$ 660	$ 170
4	$100	$530	$ 630	$ 880	$ 250
5	$100	$690	$ 790	$ 1100	$ 310
6	$100	$910	$ 1010	$ 1320	$ 310
7	$100	$1160	$ 1260	$ 1540	$ 280

4. A perfectly competitive firm faces the costs shown above in the short run. If the market price is $220, what level of output will the firm produce in order to maximize profit in the short run? What will be its profit or loss? At what level (or levels) of output does the firm break even?

APPENDIX A:
A GRAPHIC APPROACH TO COSTS AND PROFITS

Table A4-1 repeats the information given in Table 4-2 for a table manufacturer. In addition, there are columns for price, total revenue, and profit. These extra columns will be examined shortly, but first consider how Figure A4-1 is related to the cost information in the table. The vertical axis measures dollars per unit of output. Thus, the axis could be used to measure AC, AVC, AFC, MC, MR, or price, for these are all stated in terms of one unit of output. First, note that AFC starts out very high because the first few tables have to absorb all the fixed costs. As output (Q) increases, AFC continually falls, but never to zero.

The AC and AVC curves are both U-shaped, which means these measures are higher for both low and high levels of output. The MC curve also follows this pattern, but it starts rising before both AVC and AC rise. Note that as soon as MC crosses the AVC curve, AVC starts upward. The same thing happens to the AC curve. This is similar to the effect increasingly heavy students would have on the average weight in your classroom. If there are 20 students with an average weight of 120 pounds, then if a 21st student who weighs 105 pounds walks in, the average would drop. The same holds if the 22nd student weighs 107 pounds, the 23rd weighs 109 pounds, and so on. Now suppose the 29th student weighs 115 pounds and

Table A4-1

Costs, Revenues, and
Profits of a Table
Manufacturer

Q	TC	AFC	AVC	AC	MC	P=MR	TR	Profit
1	$ 600	$320.00	$280.00	$600.00	$ 280	$220	$220	-$380
2	800	160.00	240.00	400.00	200	220	440	-360
3	920	106.67	200.00	306.67	120	220	660	-260
4	1000	80.00	170.00	250.00	80	220	880	-120
5	1050	64.00	146.00	210.00	50	220	1100	-50
6	1110	53.33	137.67	185.00	60	220	1320	210
7	1180	45.71	122.86	168.57	70	220	1540	360
8	1260	40.00	117.50	157.50	80	220	1760	500
9	1370	35.56	116.67	152.23	110	220	1980	610
10	1500	32.00	118.00	150.00	150	220	2200	700
11	1720	29.09	127.27	156.36	**220**	**220**	2420	**700**
12	2000	26.67	140.00	166.67	280	220	2640	640
13	2320	24.62	153.85	178.47	320	220	2860	560
14	2700	22.86	170.00	192.86	380	220	3080	380
15	3250	21.33	195.33	216.67	550	220	3300	50
16	4800	20.00	280.00	300.00	1550	220	3520	-1280

that the class average is also 115 pounds when (and after) that student enters. If the 30th student weighs *more than* 115 pounds—say 118 pounds—the average would climb. Finally, if each new student after the 30th one weighs more than the average, the class average would continue to climb.

Now consider prices to see how profits are measured. Figure A4-2 is simplified from Figure A4-1 in that the AVC and AFC curves are gone (the horizontal axis in also compressed, which alters the curves). Because it is assumed that the table manufacturer described here is in pure competition, price and marginal revenue are identical. This means the firm can sell as many tables as it wants at the market price. In effect, the line labeled P = MR is the demand curve *for the firm* because it shows all the combinations of price and quantity buyers will take from this firm.

Table A4-1 also has a column labeled P = MR. If the price is assumed to be $220 per table, the next column, which measures total revenue (TR), reflects the formula TR = P x Q. Finally, as profit = TR – TC, the last column shows the profits for different levels of table output and sales. Note that the firm loses money at low levels of output and at the highest level. Although it makes profit at several different middle levels, it *maximizes* profit if it produces 11 tables. (The firm does equally well at 10 tables, so whether it produces 10 or 11 tables is a matter of indifference.) Finally, notice that MC equals MR ($220) at 11 tables. Recall that this is an alternative way to find the maximum profit point. In Figure A4-2 the MC line crosses the MR line at exactly 11 tables.

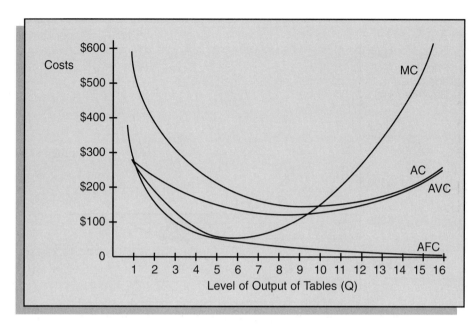

Figure A4-1

Average Costs and
Marginal Cost

Average costs and
average variable costs
initially decline as output
increases, but eventually
rise, as shown by their
U-shaped curves. The
marginal cost curve also
follows that pattern and
can actually be
considered to "drive" or
determine those two
average cost curves.

The height of the AC
curve equals the added
heights of the AFC and
AVC curves.

Because it is not stated in a per-unit-of-output form as are some cost concepts, profit cannot be measured on the vertical axis. However, it is shown as the rectangular, shaded area. The area of that rectangle (and the amount of profit) is given by the formula: Profit = (P – AC) x Q as well as by Profit = TR – TC.

That is because TR = P x Q and TC = AC x Q, so: Profit = TR – TC = (P x Q) – (AC x Q) = (P – AC) x Q. Because (P – AC) is measured on the y-axis and Q on the x-axis, the profit is measured by (P – AC) times Q—or the length times the width of the shaded rectangle in Figure A4-2. The AC is shown to be $156.36 if Q equals 11 tables, so the profit margin of $63.64 (= $220.00 – $156.36) multiplied by 11 gives a total profit of $700.

Figure A4-2 shows what can happen in a purely competitive industry in a short-run situation, before new firms have a chance to enter the industry and earn some of these economic profits. Figure A4-3, however, shows the long-run equilibrium situation for the competitive industry. The economic profits in Figure A4-2 draw in new table manufacturers, the price falls to $150, and the typical firm makes no economic profit at all. The firm operates where average cost is at a minimum, corresponding to the point of maximum efficiency of resource use.

Figure A4-2

Costs, Price, and Marginal Revenue

A firm maximizes profit at the output level where marginal revenue equals marginal cost. Profit equals the difference between total revenue and total cost. Profit is found by multiplying the quantity produced times the difference between the price and the average cost.

The table manufacturer maximizes profits when it makes 11 tables.

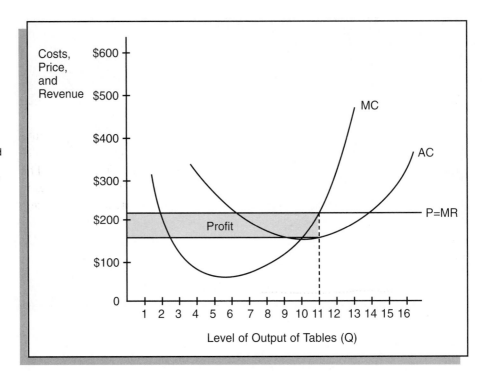

Figure A4-3

Long-Run Equilibrium in Pure Competition

In the long run, firms enter or leave an industry until no (economic) profits are earned or losses are incurred. This occurs at the output level where price equals average cost.

In the graph, an output of 10 tables results in an average cost of $150. As the price is also $150, there are no profits or losses, so the industry is in equilibrium.

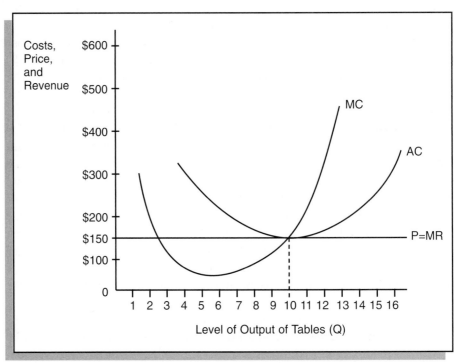

APPENDIX B: MONOPOLISTIC COMPETITION

There are four primary economic differences between pure competition and imperfect competition. In an industry where there is imperfect competition: 1) prices are higher; 2) production costs are higher; 3) firms operate at less than the optimum output level; and 4) there are excess resources in the industry. The first three can be seen graphically in Figure A4-4. The graphs depict the situation for a typical firm in an industry in monopolistic competition. The first figure shows the short-run situation, where economic profits are made. The second shows the long-run situation, where no economic profits are made—only normal profits. (In the cases of oligopoly and monopoly, economic profits often *are* made in the long run.)

There are no differences in the AC (average cost) and MC (marginal cost) curves for purely competitive firms and imperfectly competitive ones. But notice in Figure A4-4 how the demand curve for the monopolistically competitive firm slopes downward. Imperfectly competitive firms must lower their prices if they want to sell more. Thus, their demand curves slope downward, showing an inverse relationship between quantity sold and prices.

Another distinction is the MR (marginal revenue) function. For a purely competitive firm, it is horizontal, and the MR is always equal to the price, which means one extra unit of output sold brings in an amount of extra or marginal revenue equal to the price. But an imperfectly competitive firm that sells an extra unit brings in an amount of MR that is *less* than the price. This might seem puzzling, for if a product sells for $8, shouldn't an extra unit sold yield marginal revenue of $8? No, for the firm must reduce the price on *all* units sold. Because it could have sold all the units except the last one at a price *greater* than $8, the firm loses some revenue on each unit previously sold at the higher price. This loss somewhat offsets the *gain* in revenue made by selling the extra unit at $8. The MR line depicts the net effect of this gain and loss for each unit of output.

The firm in Panel (a) maximizes profit where its MC equals its MR—that is, at level of output Q_{SR}. It is able to sell this amount at a price of P_{SR}. This price is found by moving straight up to the firm's demand curve from output level Q_{SR}, then moving horizontally to the vertical axis.

This firm has an average cost of AC_{SR} for Q_{SR} of output, which is lower than P_{SR}. Therefore, the firm makes a profit shown by the shaded rectangle—that is, equal to an amount given by multiplying $(P_{SR}-AC_{SR})$ by Q_{SR}. (Recall that profit = (P − AC) x Q.)

These (economic) profits attract new firms because there is freedom of entry into industries that are monopolistically competitive. However, unlike pure competition, these new firms sell their output at the expense of the original firms. In short, the new firms "steal" customers from the old firms. This is depicted by a demand curve in Panel (b) that is farther to the left (or "smaller") than the one in Panel (a).

Such shifts occur in the typical firm's demand curve so long as new firms enter the industry. When there are no longer any economic profits to be made, no new firms will enter the industry and the demand curve will stabilize. Panel (b) shows this final, or long-run, situation of monopolistically competitive industries.

Again, the typical firm produces an output where MC equals MR—this time Q_{LR}. It can sell this amount at a price of P_{LR}, and it faces an equivalent amount of costs of AC_{LR}. Thus, the firm makes no (economic) profit—only normal profit.

Now you can see the three economic differences from the purely competitive model. First, the price is higher for the firm in monopolistic competition. Remember that in pure competition the price is equal to the AC at the level of output where AC is at a minimum. Second, the AC is higher for the firm in monopolistic competition, for its AC at the point of maximum profit is not at the lowest possible amount—as it is for purely competitive firms. Third, because the output level for the monopolistically competitive firm is not where resources are used most efficiently—that is, where AC is the lowest—the firms operate at less than the optimum level of output.

Figure A4-4

A Firm in Monopolistic Competition

In the short run, it is possible to earn profits in a firm that is in monopolistic competition, shown in Panel a.

However, as new firms enter the industry, a typical firm faces a falling demand. This leads to lower prices, where profits shrink to zero, shown in Panel b.

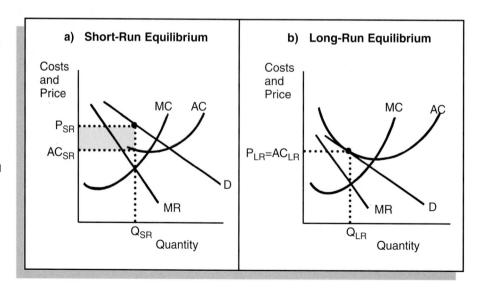

Consequently, more firms are needed to produce the output that is demanded. Thus, the resources used by these additional firms are wasted, adding to the scarcity problem that already exists in the economy.

The first factory in America (on the right), a cotton-spinning mill, built by Samuel Slater in 1790 in Pawtucket, Rhode Island. This water-powered mill employed many single women who lived in the dormitory to the left of the mill.

5

THE MARKETS FOR RESOURCES

CHAPTER PREVIEW

In a capitalist economy, privately owned resources are voluntarily sold in markets. This chapter introduces those markets, explaining the major factors in the supply and demand for resources.

Prices of resources are determined in much the same way that prices are determined in the markets for goods and services. However, it appears to work much differently, especially for the labor resource.

Besides labor, the chapter examines the vital roles played in the determination of living standards by natural resources, capital, and entrepreneurs.

CHAPTER OBJECTIVES

After completing this chapter, you should be able to:

◆ *Explain what influences the demand for labor for an occupation.*

◆ *Explain what influences the supply of labor for an occupation.*

◆ *Explain how wages are determined in a competitive labor market.*

◆ *Compare and contrast the three ways the market wage can be made to exceed the competitive equilibrium wage.*

◆ *Compare and contrast the two primary types of capital.*

◆ *Describe the relationships between economic growth, capital, the interest rate, and the savings rate.*

We say that resources are scarce because there aren't enough to produce all the goods and services that people want. This problem is partly solved when people make more efficient use of resources, primarily by increasing resource specialization and by innovation. This, in turn, requires exchanges between specialists.

This chapter describes the markets for labor, entrepreneurship, capital, and natural resources. The first section connects the product and factor markets in the "circular flow." The next two sections examine how workers "sell" labor and employers "buy" labor in both competitive and noncompetitive markets. Next is a glimpse of labor unions. The remainder of the chapter covers the markets for entrepreneurs, capital, and natural resources.

THE CIRCULAR FLOW OF ECONOMIC ACTIVITY

Figure 5-1 presents a simplified model of the microeconomy, showing the relationships between small or "micro" parts of the economy, such as laborers, business firms, and consumers. "Circular" refers partly to money, which flows continually between owners (sellers) of resources and the buyers of resources. Owners include: individuals, such as laborers and landowners; businesses, such as producers of textile machinery; and governments and their agencies, such as the Department of the Interior, which sells off-shore oil leases. Resources "flow to" or are sold to businesses and government enterprises, which convert them into goods and services. The exchange of money for these resources occurs in **factor markets**. The prices in these markets often have special names, such as wage, salary, commission, rent, or the interest rate.

A **factor market** is a market in which a resource is traded or exchanged.

These special prices reflect the income of resource owners, who spend this income on finished goods and services in **product markets**. The money paid for such products becomes income to sellers of these goods and services and is called sales or total revenue. In turn, this revenue provides firms with the ability to buy resources in factor markets. This maintains the continual and simultaneous "flow" of money and goods and services between market participants.

A **product market** is a market in which a good or service is exchanged.

These "flows" of money, resources, and products do not occur at constant rates over time. When they are increasing to particularly high levels, we say we are experiencing prosperity. Declines in the flows mean we are experiencing recession. Finally, activities in any specific market, whether product or resource, can have effects in a multitude of other markets. Thus, a system of markets is a very complex array of interrelationships between individuals.

Figure 5-1

The Circular Flow of Economic Activity

In factor markets, resource owners provide resources to producers in exchange for money.

In product markets, buyers obtain goods and services in exchange for money.

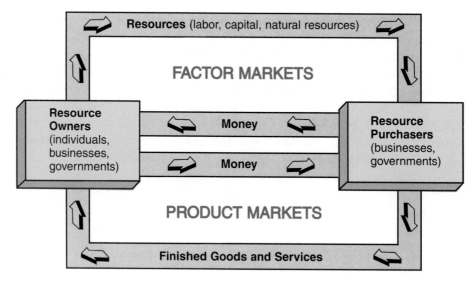

THE MARKET FOR LABOR UNDER COMPETITIVE CONDITIONS

The third Basic Economic Question is For Whom to Produce? It really pertains to income distribution, for our society produces more goods and services for those who have more income. But why do incomes differ, and differ so much, in our society? Explaining these differences is the primary intent of this section.

Some people have a poor grasp of how incomes are determined in a capitalist system. More specifically, they don't know what it is that determines their incomes. People often believe they deserve higher wages than they earn, and many are resentful because of their "low pay." Part of this poor understanding of income distribution in capitalism is because most of us were raised in "socialist" homes. That is, until adolescence or even beyond, we were given all our basic needs plus many extras—often without being expected to contribute much in return. Although we were constantly told of scarcity of resources (income) by our parents, this is not the same as truly experiencing it as an adult. We seldom associated our parents' income with their productiveness. So it is not surprising that some new employees tell their employers they need x number of dollars per hour because that's what they "need to live." Wages are not determined that way. Let's see how they really are.

In this section it will be assumed that competitive conditions exist in labor markets. Such conditions mean that: 1) no one prevents anyone else from buying or selling labor; 2) no individual buyer or seller can control the price of labor (the wage); and 3) the government is not involved in labor markets. Except in rare cases, these conditions do not exist. However, assuming that they do allows us to understand what the main factors are that determine incomes.

The Demand for Labor

Employers are as interested in their self-interest as you are in yours because they face scarcity just as you do. An employer evaluates a particular laborer who applies for a job in much the same way you evaluate a particular shirt you consider buying. A shirt provides you benefits by keeping you warm. A laborer provides an employer benefits by making products that can be sold (provide revenue). The employer wonders if a particular laborer will provide more revenue than any other laborer—or any other resource, such as a machine. This is like you deciding if one particular shirt is as enjoyable (beneficial) as another—or as another article of clothing.

Several factors determine how many workers with a particular skill an employer wants to hire. Major factors include the wage, the productivity of the laborers, and the price of the firm's good or service. Because the price of the good or service depends in part upon the demand for that good or service, the demand for labor is called a **derived demand**. For example, the demand for glass workers depends upon the demand for glass. If people stop buying glass, replacing it with plastic, the demand for glass workers will fall to zero and the demand for plastics workers will rise.

> **Derived demand** refers to the demand for a resource which stems from the demand for the good or service which that resource produces.

Profit-maximizing firms will hire workers so long as the *extra* revenue each worker contributes, called the **marginal revenue product** (MRP), exceeds the cost of hiring such workers, measured by the wage rate. Essentially, this means they will hire workers so long as workers provide more benefits than costs (MRP>wage). This is the same concept used when you decide how many shirts to buy—namely, cost-benefit analysis. The formula for the MRP is:

> The **marginal revenue product** is the value of the output of a good or service produced by adding one additional unit of a resource, such as a laborer.

Marginal Revenue Product = Price x Marginal Product

Remember from Chapter 3 that, because of the law of diminishing marginal returns, marginal product declines as firms hire additional workers. Sooner or later firms will stop hiring workers, for eventually the MRP (the benefit) will be less than the factor cost of hiring workers (the wage).

Therefore, the number of jobs of one type in an industry depends upon three major factors: 1) the wage; 2) the price of the good or service produced; and 3) the productivity of the workers. Remember from Chapter 2 that the demand for a product is the relationship between price and how much people are willing to buy. Similarly, **labor demand** is the relationship between the wage and the number of workers all employers combined wish to hire. (Beware of equating labor demand with the number of employees firms wish to hire. Labor demand is the *relationship* between the wage and that number, not the number hired itself.)

Labor demand refers to the relationship between wages and the number of people employers wish to hire.

Each labor market has many possible demands. Table 5-1 illustrates labor demand for a hypothetical market—that of accountants. The table shows the different number of jobs offered (or job openings) by employers at three different wages under three different "strengths" of demand—weak, average, and strong. An average demand for accountants means all occupations, on average, have these numbers of jobs. For example, at $10 per hour, firms wish to hire 900 accountants—the average number of job openings expected for all other occupations. (To clarify, suppose there are 90 million jobs in an economy if each and every one paid $10 per hour. If there were 100,000 occupations, then each occupation, *on average,* would have 900 jobs, as $90,000,000 \div 100,000 = 900$. However, each occupation would likely have either more or less than 900 jobs.)

A strong demand for accountants means more jobs are open than in most other occupations. In this case 1,300 accountant jobs are open at $10 per hour, compared with 900 for other occupations, on average. A strong demand for labor is created by two main conditions: 1) a high price for the product produced; and 2) high labor productivity. Both lead to a high MRP, and a high MRP means firms can profit by hiring many workers.

In turn, what causes high prices and high productivity? A high price is caused by either a strong demand for the product or a small supply of it. Generally, a product with a strong demand is very useful (beneficial) to consumers.

Table 5-1

The Demand for Labor Under Varying Conditions

For any given wage, different occupations have different numbers of jobs available.

	Number of Jobs Provided by Employers When There Is a:		
Wage	Weak Demand	Average Demand	Strong Demand
$20	100	500	900
$15	300	700	1100
$10	500	900	1300

High productivity can result from: good education and training; good physical and mental skills; good work attitudes; a high quantity and quality of capital equipment used by the workers; and a good work environment, such as clean, well-lighted, and pleasant surroundings.

In Table 5-1, a weak labor demand means firms want to hire only 500 accountants at $10, compared with 900 in other occupations, on average. A weak labor demand is caused by: 1) low product prices; and 2) low productivity. A low price is caused by either a weak demand for the product or a large supply of it. In turn, a product could have a weak demand if it provides little satisfaction to consumers. Low productivity could result from poor education, low worker skills, poor work attitudes, a low quantity or quality of capital, and a poor work environment.

THINKING CRITICALLY ABOUT ECONOMIC QUESTIONS IN OUR LIVES

Should You Have the Right to Quit Your Job?

Things to Consider

1. Think of what a job really is—a trade (of your time). Think what the "terms of trade" are for the job. These are all stated in the contract. You may not even think you've made a contract when you take a job. But all the job responsibilities you have and all the benefits promised you are part of the contract. Think of why you and your employer agreed to those terms.

2. How is that contract similar to virtually all the other contracts you make—that is, every time you buy something? Are you on the same "side" of the trade or exchange in those contracts? That is, are you sometimes a buyer and sometimes a seller? If so, does your view of the seller's position in a trade change when you are the seller from when you are a buyer?

3. If your answer to the last point in Number 2 is yes, why are you inconsistent? How do you justify it—if you can?

See page 459 for the answer.

At a higher wage in Table 5-1, firms want to hire fewer accountants, whether the demand is weak, average, or strong. These inverse relationships between wages and the number of job offerings show that the law of demand applies to labor resources just as it does to consumer goods. Higher wages lead employers to "buy" (hire) less labor for two reasons: 1) the substitution effect; and 2) an effect similar to the income effect.

■ The substitution effect occurs when escalating wages prompt firms to replace workers with cheaper alternatives. These include: 1) capital equipment, such as high-speed drills, computers, and conveyer belts; 2) natural resources, such as oil, which generates electricity used by labor-replacing machines; and 3) cheaper laborers. Cheaper laborers can be found in various places, such as foreign countries or other parts of the United States where wages are lower. A firm can also find cheaper laborers by subcontracting or "outsourcing" part of its work to firms that hire nonunion, lower-paid workers or that have lower costs for other reasons.

■ The second reason firms follow the law of demand is similar to the income effect with demand for a good. (See page 40 for review.) At higher wages, production costs are higher. In turn, prices will be higher. Since consumers buy fewer products at higher prices, firms need fewer employees.

Figure 5-2 provides an alternative way to view these three labor demand relationships. The three demand graphs show the inverse relationship between wages and job openings.

Figure 5-2

Different Strengths of Labor Demand

A weak demand for labor means that, for any given wage, firms wish to hire relatively few workers. The opposite holds for a strong demand.

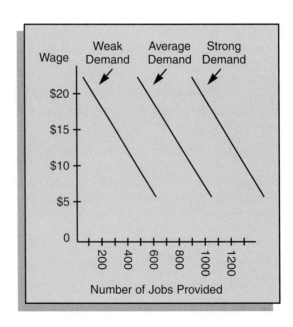

The Supply of Labor

People will work only if the benefits they receive (wages and any nonmonetary satisfaction from the job) exceed the cost. The cost of working at a job for a given period includes the satisfaction that could have been received from the best alternative use of that time—perhaps the benefits from an alternative job or a leisure activity.

Several factors determine how many people want to work and are qualified to work in any given occupation. These include: the wage of the occupation, the wages of other occupations, the skills required for the occupation, any enjoyment workers get from the job, any negative aspects of the work, the population of the market area, and the ability of qualified workers from elsewhere to move to the market area.

Earlier you learned that supply is the relationship between the price of an item and how much is offered for sale. Similarly, **labor supply** for an occupation is the relationship between the wage and the number of people who are willing and qualified to work in that occupation.

Consider again the job market for accountants. Table 5-2 presents three possible supply relationships for these accountants. Each relationship shows the numbers of qualified people who wish to work as accountants at three different wages: $10, $15, and $20 per hour. The average supply relationship means the number of people who wish to work in any other occupation, on average, equals the number who choose to work as accountants. (To clarify, just as with labor demand, the number of jobs at, say, $10 per hour, is found by dividing total employment in all occupations combined by the number of occupations. For example, that could mean there are 500 jobs for each occupation, on average. However, each specific occupation would likely have more or less than 500 jobs.)

Three factors explain most of this variance in labor supplies: 1) the degree of skills required; 2) job satisfaction; and 3) unpleasant aspects of the job.

Labor supply refers to the relationship between the wage and the number of people willing and qualified to work.

	Number of People Offering to Work When There Is a:		
Wage	Weak Supply	Average Supply	Strong Supply
$20	500	900	1300
$15	300	700	1100
$10	100	500	900

Table 5-2

The Supply of Labor Under Varying Conditions

■ The degree of skills required to do a job is usually the most important factor of supply. If a job is very difficult to learn, many people may be *willing* to do it for $12 per hour. However, perhaps few can qualify, either because few people are: 1) capable of acquiring the skills; or 2) willing or financially able to acquire the skills. Jobs that are difficult to learn (programming computers or piloting airplanes) or have high learning costs (long and/or expensive training, as for physicians) tend to have a weak labor supply. Conversely, jobs that are easy to learn (flipping hamburgers or collecting trash) or have low learning costs (perhaps only an elementary school education) tend to have a strong labor supply.

■ Job satisfaction is the second major factor of labor supply. An enjoyable job tends to draw many people into that occupation. Benefits people derive from the job itself, often called psychic income, include good working conditions, interesting and challenging work, a good work schedule, and prestige and other personal rewards.

■ Unpleasant aspects of an occupation tend to lead to a weak (small) supply of labor in the field. Such negative factors include boredom, danger, low prestige, a long commute in heavy traffic, stress, job politics, long hours, and hot, smelly, or otherwise undesirable working conditions.

In each of the three labor supply relationships shown in Table 5-2, more people want to be accountants at higher wages than at lower wages. These direct relationships between wages and the number of people who want to work show that the law of supply applies to labor, just as it does to goods and services. The reason people obey the law of supply for labor is also the same. That is, at higher wages (prices) people are more willing to work at a job (sell labor) because they can "afford to." Consider the average supply case. Although at least 900 people are qualified to be accountants (since that's how many seek jobs at $20 per hour), only 500 want jobs at $10 per hour. The other 400 have other things to do, such as other jobs or leisure activities, that provide more benefits. In short, the accountant job costs them too much. However, at a higher benefit of $15 or $20 per hour, more people decide that being an accountant is a good choice.

Incidentally, the law of supply helps explain the concept of overtime pay. Even if not compelled by law, employers often must pay higher wages to get workers to work longer hours because the extra hours are more "costly" to the workers. The first few hours worked each day force workers to give up relatively unimportant activities, such as the tenth hour of sleep or some unimportant leisure activity. But the tenth or eleventh hour of work forces workers to give up very enjoyable (thus, costly) leisure activities. The only way they will work those hours is for a higher benefit (wage).

Figure 5-3 shows there are increasing numbers of workers at any

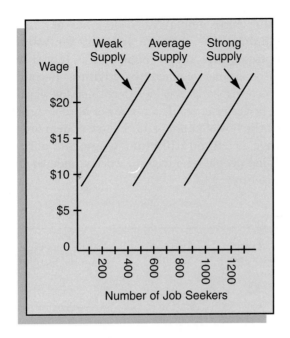

Figure 5-3

Different Strengths of
Labor Supply

A weak supply of labor
means that, for any given
wage, relatively few people
wish to work at that job.
The opposite holds for a
strong supply.

given wage for increasingly strong labor supply relationships. The labor
supply curves for the stronger relationships are farther to the right.

Wage Determination Under Competitive Conditions

Wages in labor markets under competitive conditions are determined
the same way that prices are determined in product markets. Employers
and employees interact in a large "auction" for labor resources. No single
individual or firm determines the wage, yet all participants have an influence on it.

Table 5-3 brings together the demand and supply for accountants
under average conditions, shown in Tables 5-1 and 5-2. The last column
shows that there can be either "too many" job seekers, creating a **labor surplus**, or "too few" workers, creating a **labor shortage**. A labor surplus
occurs when there are more people willing to work at a specific wage than
employers are willing to hire. A labor shortage occurs when employers wish
to hire more people than there are people who wish to work.

If employers pay accountants only $10 per hour, there is a labor
shortage of 400 accountants. To end such a shortage under competitive conditions, a firm may try to hire accountants from other firms by offering more
than $10 per hour. Also, employees demand higher wages in shortage situ-

A **labor surplus** occurs
in a labor market when
there are more people
willing to work at a
specific wage than
employers are willing to
hire.

A **labor shortage** occurs
in a labor market when
employers want to hire
more workers at a specific wage than there are
people willing to work.

ations because they have employers "over a barrel." As wages rise, two developments eliminate the shortage and stop the wage from increasing further (in this case beyond $15 per hour). First, higher wages attract people from other occupations or nonwork activities. Second, employers substitute cheaper resources and also have less need for workers as production (labor) costs and prices rise, resulting in fewer of their products sold. These two events mean the law of supply and the law of demand are at work. The $15-per-hour wage is the **equilibrium wage**, the only wage where the number of qualified people who wish to work equals the number of people employers wish to hire.

The **equilibrium wage** is the wage where the number of workers employers wish to hire equals the number of qualified people looking for work.

Table 5-3

"Average-Wage" Conditions of Labor Demand and Supply

Wage	Average Demand	Average Supply	Labor Shortage or Labor Surplus
$20	500	900	Surplus of 400 Workers
$15	700 ◄equal► 700		No Surplus or Shortage of Workers
$10	900	500	Shortage of 400 Workers

Figure 5-4

"Average-Wage" Conditions of Labor Demand and Supply

In the "average occupation," there are 700 people who work at the equilibrium wage of $15 per hour.

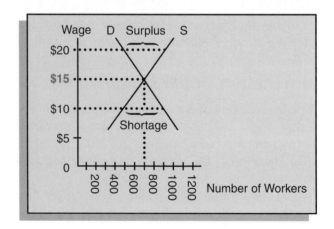

Alternatively, if the wage is $20 per hour, more people want the job than there are jobs open (400 more), so there is a labor surplus. Either employers will refuse to pay such high wages or the people who can't find work will offer to work for less. Again, this process sets the laws of supply and demand in action. At lower wages: 1) more jobs open up; and 2) fewer people want them. Eventually the labor surplus disappears at the equilibrium wage of $15 per hour.

In Figure 5-4, the supply and demand graphs intersect at $15 per hour—the equilibrium wage. At any wage higher than that, such as $20 per hour, there is a surplus of workers. Any wage lower than the equilibrium, such as $10 per hour, leads to a shortage of accountants.

If $15 per hour is the equilibrium wage for the average occupation (at least for jobs above entry-level positions and part-time, low-skill jobs), why do some occupations pay more and some less than that? Because either labor demand or labor supply is different from the average occupation. Figure 5-5 and the left half of Table 5-4 show one reason why an occupation will pay "higher wages" (or higher than most occupations). They show that a weaker labor supply coupled with an average labor demand creates a labor shortage at $15 per hour. The shortage drives up the wage to the equilibrium at $20 per hour. Similarly, the wage is $20 per hour on the right side of Table 5-4, where a strong labor demand is coupled with an average labor supply.

Wage	Average Demand	Weak Supply	Strong Demand	Average Supply
$20	500 ◄equal► 500		900 ◄equal► 900	
$15	700	300	1100	700
$10	900	100	1300	500

Table 5-4

"High-Wage" Conditions of Labor Demand and Supply

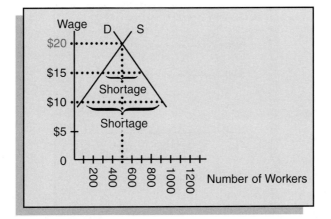

Figure 5-5

"High Wages" Due to an Average Demand and a Weak Supply

Wages lower than $20 lead to labor shortages for this occupation.

Conversely, Table 5-5 shows why the pay in some occupations is low, compared with most other occupations. Such low pay can result from either: 1) a relatively weak labor demand, which means there is little competition between employers for the available workers; or 2) a relatively strong labor supply, which means competition between job seekers for the available jobs is relatively strong. Either case leads to a surplus of workers at the $15-per-hour equilibrium wage paid for the average occupation. Because workers at $15 per hour are "a dime a dozen" for such occupations, the equilibrium wage is much lower. In the example, only at $10 per hour do employers want to hire all the people who want jobs in that occupation. Figure 5-6 also shows this second cause of lower wages.

Table 5-5

"Low-Wage" Conditions of Labor Demand and Supply

Wage	Weak Demand	Average Supply	Average Demand	Strong Supply
$20	100	900	500	1300
$15	300	700	700	1100
$10	500 ◄—equal—► 500		900 ◄—equal—► 900	

Figure 5-6

"Low Wages" Due to an Average Demand and a Strong Supply

Wages higher than $10 lead to labor surpluses for this occupation.

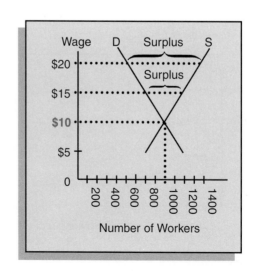

Here are some reasons, along with examples, why an occupation tends to be relatively low paying: 1) it requires relatively few skills (fast-food service, janitorial service); 2) it has very enjoyable aspects (photography, flower arranging, bank teller, teaching nursery school); 3) it has few strongly unfavorable aspects (clerking in stores); 4) demand for the product is relatively low (professional soccer in the United States); or 5) its workers are relatively unproductive (shining shoes).

Alternatively, an occupation will tend to be relatively high paying if: 1) it requires great skills (top entertainers, professional football quarterbacks, corporate executives, physicists); 2) it provides very little psychic income; 3) it has very unfavorable aspects (bomb squad work, skyscraper construction); 4) demand for the product is high (professional football); or 5) the productivity of its workers is high (open-pit coal mining, flying airplanes).

THINKING CRITICALLY ABOUT ECONOMIC QUESTIONS IN OUR LIVES

How Can Shaquille O'Neal Be Worth $17 million a Year?

Things to Consider

1. How much are you "worth" at your job? How did you come up with that figure? Likewise, how much is Shaquille O'Neal (the center for the Los Angeles Lakers) worth, using your concept of valuation?

2. Why does your employer pay you what you get? Why do the Los Angeles Lakers pay O'Neal the $17 million a year that he gets?

3. What is the goal of your employer in hiring you? Of the Los Angeles Lakers in hiring O'Neal? How do they accomplish these goals?

See page 460 for the answer.

INCREASING INCOMES ABOVE COMPETITIVE LEVELS

In the theoretical capitalist or competitive market model, all wages and prices are determined by supply and demand. In real life, however, if people see an opportunity to increase their incomes above competitive levels, they usually take advantage of it. This section outlines three ways of accomplishing that: 1) controlling labor demand; 2) controlling labor supply; and 3) raising the wage above the equilibrium level.

Increasing the Demand for Labor

Increasing the labor demand above the free-market level will increase the equilibrium wage above the *competitive* equilibrium wage. This might be called "controlling demand," as workers manipulate the labor market to their advantage. In essence, workers seek to increase the competition among employers for the same number of available workers.

Figure 5-7(a) shows the initial competitive conditions in a hypothetical labor market, represented by D_1 and S, where the equilibrium wage is $7 per hour and there are 800 jobs. It also shows that a larger, controlled labor demand (D_2) leads to a $9-per-hour wage and 100 more jobs. Workers increase demand for themselves in several ways, including: 1) jurisdiction; 2) work rules; and 3) advertising.

■ First, if workers are in a union, they can demand jurisdiction over certain work, which means only members of that union can do such work. For example, the workers in a school's audiovisual department could insist that only they, not teachers, can operate audiovisual equipment in the classroom.

A **work rule** is a worker-influenced guideline on how to perform a certain job.

■ Second, again with union support, workers can push for **work rules**, which are worker-established or -influenced guidelines on how to perform certain jobs. Although the stated purpose of such rules is usually increased worker safety or increased work quality, often the real purpose is the extra work (or "featherbedding") these rules provide.

■ Last, laborers could increase labor demand through advertising. Electricians, for example, might take out an ad that shows the danger of tinkering with electrical wires, thus increasing demand for professional electrical service. Also, GM's Mr. Goodwrench ads might just as well have been taken out by mechanics at GM garages.

Reducing the Supply of Labor

Workers can also increase their wages by reducing labor supply below the free-market level. Their intent is to eliminate the competition

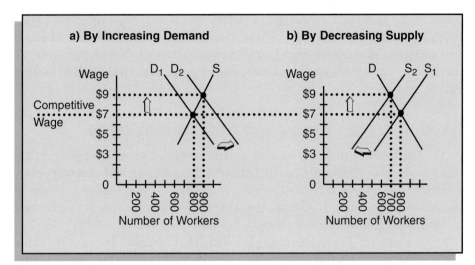

Figure 5-7

Raising the Equilibrium Wage Above Competitive Conditions

The equilibrium wage can be raised above the competitive wage either by increasing the demand for labor or reducing the supply of labor.

between themselves for the available jobs. The reduced competition creates a labor shortage and, in turn, higher wages. This is accomplished by: 1) raising job qualifications; or 2) discrimination.

In Figure 5-7(b), a reduced supply (from S_1 to S_2) raises wages from $7 to $9 per hour, but in this case there will be 100 *fewer* jobs than under competitive conditions.

■ The first way to reduce the supply (from S_1 to S_2) of labor is to prevent potential workers from attaining the minimum job requirements by making them more difficult to obtain. Such increased requirements could include: a college degree; age, height, or strength standards; an apprenticeship period; or a passing score on an entrance exam. If workers who are already employed in an occupation have a voice in job requirements, it is in their best interest to make job requirements difficult for newcomers to attain. Doctors, through the AMA, and CPAs (certified public accountants) are often accused of restricting supply in their fields by various techniques.

■ The second way to reduce labor supply is through discrimination. If, for example, airline pilots could prevent airline companies from hiring non-whites, non-Christians, or women, only a third or so of the potentially qualified people could become pilots. (Discrimination could be considered a special case of the first method of reducing supply.) In the past, workers in many occupations "earned" higher incomes because of discrimination.

The losers from discrimination are not only those discriminated against. Everyone loses because scarce resources (laborers) are *not* used in the best possible way. If our economy operated today as it did in the past, well-qualified women, blacks, Hispanics, and other groups would not be permitted to be productive construction workers, physicians, engineers, corporate executives, and the like. There would be less overall output of goods and services. In effect, discrimination *increases* the scarcity of resources. If the goal in economics is the efficient use of resources, then discrimination makes no sense.

Raising Wages Above the Equilibrium Wage

The last technique for raising incomes works with no change in either labor demand or labor supply. Instead of letting supply and demand determine the wage, some groups of people set the wage above the equilibrium in one of two ways: 1) by establishing minimum wage laws; and 2) by allowing collective bargaining between employers and labor unions.

■ First, the government might decide that an equilibrium wage is too low. So it passes a minimum wage law prohibiting employers from paying workers less than a certain amount. Although there is much disagreement on the subject, many economists believe the law of demand leads to fewer jobs in occupations that pay the minimum wage. Also, at the higher wage, more people now want the job. Thus, some people who want a job won't get one. Figure 5-8 shows the possible effects of minimum wage legislation.

Figure 5-8

The Effects of a Minimum Wage Law

Theoretically, a minimum wage set above the equilibrium reduces the number of job openings and increases the number of people wanting jobs. Consequently, there is a labor surplus, or unemployment.

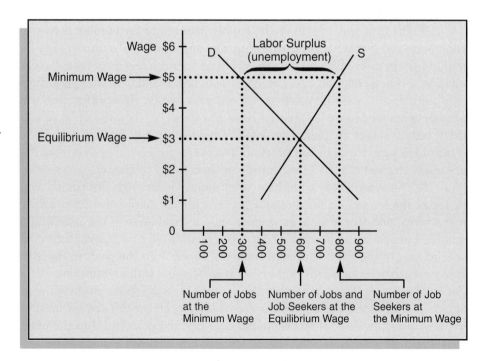

■ The second method of raising wages above equilibrium is to give workers the same power as sellers in a cartel. Members of cartels agree not to undercut each others' prices after raising those prices above the equilibrium level. A labor union uses the same technique as a cartel. But instead of selling a product, the members "sell labor." Instead of bargaining *individually* for their wages, workers use the **collective bargaining** approach. This means all workers bargain as one through a "bargaining unit." If employers refuse to pay the demanded higher wage, workers can strike— which is a refusal to "sell labor."

Collective bargaining refers to the actions of a group of laborers operating in unison to improve their wages, fringe benefits, and working conditions.

THE LABOR UNION MOVEMENT

American labor unions have existed in various forms for over two centuries. In many respects, unions are remnants of medieval guilds, which were associations of individual craftsmen (shoemakers, silversmiths, gunsmiths, etc.). This section gives a cursory view of unions.

Labor Organizations

The first unions appeared in the late 1700s and were organizations of localized workers, with no connection to other unions. These were usually **craft unions**, composed of skilled workers in one occupation. By the 1830s, unions began to combine with other local unions, forming federations to gain strength. In the 1850s, many similar local unions combined to form the first **national union**. The Knights of Labor, formed in 1869, was the first widespread national union. It reached its peak membership in the 1880s, when successful rail strikes made it popular. The Knights accepted workers from all occupations, whether skilled or not. This open membership caused problems with the craft unions, which believed they could do better on their own. There were problems within the Knights, too, because members disagreed on goals. Some only wanted to improve their economic welfare within a capitalistic system, while others wanted to revolutionize the whole economic system and move it toward socialism. Such disagreements and other problems led to the Knights' decline.

A **craft union** is a labor union composed of people working in the same craft or job description.

A **national union** is an organization of all the local unions of one type in the nation.

In 1886, a group of national craft unions founded the American Federation of Labor (AFL). Samuel Gompers was its first president, serving until 1924. He sought immediate gains of better working conditions, higher pay, and shorter hours, but did not get involved in political and economic ideology. Throughout its history, the AFL followed a "conservative" philosophy. That is, it wanted to maintain capitalism, but to get a larger share of the economic pie.

The AFL had little desire to organize unskilled workers. Yet by the 1920s and 1930s, industries that required many unskilled workers, such as steel and rubber, were growing rapidly. Also, mechanization in other industries, such as the auto industry, reduced the need for skilled workers. Eventually, such workers were organized by **industrial unions**, where all workers in one industry, both skilled and unskilled, belonged to the same union. John L. Lewis headed one of these, the United Mine Workers. In 1935, after disagreements with AFL leaders, he and others formed a new federation of industrial unions, the Congress of Industrial Organizations (CIO). After success in the steel and auto industries, the CIO rapidly gained strength. The two federations joined in 1955 to form the AFL-CIO, which has 78 affiliated national unions today.

An **industrial union** is a labor union composed of people who work in the same industry at many different crafts or jobs.

Union membership as a share of the total workforce is declining. For decades it had been a little over a fourth of the workforce. However, it is currently about 15 percent of the work force (11 percent in the private sector and 38 percent in the public sector) and slowly declining.

Labor Legislation

Without government assistance, laborers would have a hard time overcoming their competitive tendencies. Although some court actions and legislation have weakened unions, major legislation over the years has enabled workers to form unions. Following are summaries of some federal laws affecting laborers.

■ The Sherman Antitrust Act of 1890 was designed to end monopolies in markets for goods and services. However, it was used to stop unionization because federal courts considered unions to be illegal "conspiracies in the restraint of trade." To eliminate this unintended effect, the Clayton Antitrust Act of 1914 exempted unions from the Sherman Act.

■ The Davis-Bacon Act of 1931 requires private contractors to pay "prevailing wages" (which is usually whatever unionized workers receive) on all construction projects that are totally or partly financed by the federal government. It was designed to prevent certain construction firms that had lower-paid, nonunionized workers from competing with unionized firms on construction projects.

■ The Norris-LaGuardia Act of 1932 eliminated some of the employers' weapons against organized labor, especially the "yellow-dog contract"— in which a worker agreed not to join a union if hired

■ The National Labor Relations Act (or the Wagner Act) of 1935 gave laborers the legal right to bargain collectively. The act set up the National Labor Relations Board (NLRB), which supervises elections and decides which union will represent the workers. The law prohibits firms from interfering in union organizing activity and union administration and from discriminating against union employees. Such actions are called unfair labor practices. However, the act does not cover government employees.

■ The Taft-Hartley Act of 1947 amended the Wagner Act and reduced union strength. The act: 1) outlaws the **closed shop**, where workers are forced to join a union before being hired; 2) allows *states* to pass **right-to-work laws**, which outlaw the **union shop** (where workers must join a union after working for a short period); 3) outlaws certain labor practices, most notably featherbedding; 4) prohibits secondary boycotts, in which striking workers pressure a third party not to deal with their employer; and 5) allows the government to suspend a strike with an injunction for an 80-day "cooling-off period" if the strike imperils the national security.

■ The Landrum-Griffin Act of 1959 was designed to eliminate corruption in unions and to promote democratic procedures. It placed tight controls on union finances.

A **closed shop** refers to a workplace in which a person must be a member of a labor union before beginning to work.

A **right-to-work law** is a state law, authorized by the Taft-Hartley Act, outlawing union shops in that state.

A **union shop** refers to a workplace in which a person is required to join a union following a brief period.

Collective Bargaining and Union Goals

What do union members want? Obviously, higher wages are important, but closely related are fringe benefits, such as health and life insurance, pensions, and vacations. However, higher wages and fringe benefits could cost the union members jobs (because of the law of demand), so the level of employment is also a goal. Consequently, unions occasionally try to delay the introduction of labor-saving devices. A goal that ties wages and employment is for unions to maximize the wage bill, which is the total income received collectively by the members. Finally, unions want better working conditions, better hours, and job security.

A union achieves its goals through the collective bargaining process, in which negotiations occur between management and the union bargaining team. This team, representing the "rank and file" (union members), either: 1) accepts a tentative agreement and recommends it for ratification (acceptance); or 2) recommends a strike to obtain a better agreement. Both actions are voted on by the membership as a whole. If there is ratification, the entire agreement is written into the contract. If not, a strike occurs and all parties return to the bargaining table.

Strikes make headlines, but they are relatively rare, or are at least rarer than during the 1950s and 1960s. Labor and management usually reach agreement after long negotiations on dozens of issues. If an agreement cannot be reached, a third party often is called in to assist. Such third-party interventions take one of three forms: 1) fact-finding; 2) mediation; or 3) arbitration. Fact-finding involves a government board that studies the issues and makes suggestions, which do not have to be followed. In **mediation**, the third party listens to the arguments of labor and management and offers nonbinding solutions. If all else fails, the bargainers can agree to **arbitration**, after which a jointly selected arbitrator's recommendations must be followed.

Mediation is a process of settling differences between labor and management, where a third party's opinion is requested by both sides but does not have to be accepted.

Arbitration is a process of settling differences between labor and management, where the terms of a third party must be accepted.

ENTREPRENEURSHIP

Entrepreneurs play a vital role in increasing our living standards. This section examines that role and reasons some people want to become entrepreneurs.

The Economic Roles of Entrepreneurs

Entrepreneurs fulfill three main roles in the economy: 1) they organize the production process; 2) they increase resource efficiency; and 3) they redirect resource use.

■ The first role of entrepreneurs is the organization of the production process. Specifically, their intent is to produce a good or service with the smallest amount of resources, given a specific production process. In short, their role is to maximize the efficiency of resource use.

■ Closely related is the second role, increasing the efficiency of resource use through innovation. By changing the production process or how something is produced, firms can often produce more than was possible earlier. Entrepreneurs don't actually sell their resources in any market to someone who turns them into goods or services. They use their resources themselves in their *own* businesses.

■ The last role of entrepreneurs is to redirect resource use into or away from various industries where there are insufficient or excess resources. In other words, their role is to increase allocative efficiency, meaning producing the goods and services most wanted by people.

Some Influences on Entrepreneurs

Many factors determine the number of entrepreneurs—the "supply" of entrepreneurship—in an economy. For example, the education system affects the quantity and quality of entrepreneurs because schools help develop initiative, independence, and organizational skills. Other factors that affect these character traits include parental guidance and peer values.

The number, size, and risk-taking position of financial institutions (banks and the like) also determine how many people take the plunge into business. These institutions control the finances which most entrepreneurs do not possess themselves. Entrepreneurs must borrow.

The government interacts with entrepreneurs in several ways. First, the tax system determines how much profit entrepreneurs can keep. Many argue that taxing rich, successful entrepreneurs at high rates discourages them and other aspiring entrepreneurs from further innovations of the kind that made them rich (and the rest of society better off with higher living standards). Other government influences are bankruptcy laws, government loans to businesses, and technical and other informational assistance to firms.

A relatively new and rapidly growing technique to encourage and assist entrepreneurs is the so-called business incubator. These vary in form, from locations where several tiny businesses share buildings, equipment, and knowledge to where old buildings have been converted to the needs of the new firms and are rented at subsidized rates. Over half of the incubators are sponsored by universities, which use them to make commercial use of what has been learned in their laboratories.

THE MARKET FOR CAPITAL

Capital is defined as any good produced by humans used to produce another good or service. Capital, then, is really capital equipment or capital goods—and not money.

Types of Capital

Capital goods generally can be placed into two categories: 1) social overhead capital; or 2) direct capital.

■ **Social overhead capital**, more commonly called infrastructure, includes capital goods involved in providing such services as transportation, communication, energy, education, and public safety. A modern economy, where specialists exchange goods and services, needs a well-developed infrastructure to function efficiently. Examples of such capital include railroad tracks and roadbeds, power lines, airports, schools, highways, dams, sewer lines, police stations, oil pipelines, dock facilities, and courthouses. Such capital is usually very large and immobile. Often these capital goods do not directly produce other goods or services. A dam, for example, can provide flood control, which in the normal sense is neither a good nor a service. Yet a dam makes possible (or at least facilitates) the production of agricultural

Social overhead capital refers to capital goods which provide the foundation for all production by supplying such services as electricity, transportation, communication, education, and public safety.

crops and improves river navigation by barges and ships. You also learned earlier that some infrastructure, especially when involved with transportation and communication, is essential for mass markets, a vital component of an efficient, mass-production economy.

A relatively new type of infrastructure is the "information highway." Initially begun on a small scale in the 1960s, it now links millions of computer users in over 35 countries. Users are able to pass messages and browse through a multitude of "bulletin boards." The current system is called Internet, but passage of the 1991 High-Performance Computing Act commits $3 billion to build a new system. That system, the National Research and Education Network (NREN), will have fiber optic cables 100 times faster than Internet's. For example, it will allow anyone anywhere to look at any material in the Library of Congress or to access detailed maps made from satellite photos. Countless other databanks will provide the specialized information that is vital for efficient production in our so-called modern postindustrial information age.

■ A metal-stamping machine is an example of the second category of capital goods, by far the most common, numerous, or voluminous of the two types. Such goods vary in size from very small to very large, and they can usually be moved from place to place. Because they produce other goods and services more directly, we might call them direct capital. Other examples of direct capital include train locomotives and boxcars, office computers, chain saws of logging crews, drill presses, taxis, and farm tractors.

Financing of Capital

Many capital goods are expensive, so financing them is a major task. Consider social overhead capital first. This type of capital is owned mainly by the public and includes postal facilities and most roads and dams. Private firms also own some, such as railroad rights-of-way and pipelines.

Governments finance their infrastructure in three primary ways. First, governments tax their citizens. Second, governments charge individuals and firms user fees whenever use is made of the capital. A bridge toll is an example, as are airport takeoff and landing fees paid by airlines, and charges to ships using the St. Lawrence Seaway. Third, governments borrow money to purchase capital goods by selling bonds. Governments then collect user fees and/or taxes to repay the bondholders.

Privately owned firms obtain capital in four primary ways: 1) leasing; 2) retained earnings; 3) equity financing; and 4) debt financing. The first method, leasing, is the only one that doesn't involve ownership of the capital by the user. A lease is a contract giving the firm the right to use capital belonging to someone else for a specified period. The payment for that use appears as an expense on the income statement.

The other three methods of obtaining capital involve ownership. (In these cases, payment for the capital appears as depreciation on the income statement.) The first is financing through retained earnings, which occurs when a firm uses some of its profits to purchase capital. The second method, equity financing, occurs when corporations raise money by selling new corporate stock. Finally, firms obtain funds through debt financing when they borrow money by taking out loans at lending institutions or insurance companies. Corporations also borrow funds by selling corporate bonds and other financial instruments, collectively known as commercial paper.

Capital and Economic Growth

Economic growth is an increase in the amount of goods and services that an economy produces. (It is represented by an outward shift in the production possibilities curve.) One way to achieve it is to increase the amount of resources in an economy, including capital. Increasing the capital stock of a nation is also known as capital formation.

When a nation produces capital goods, it is saving for the future. That is, instead of producing consumer goods to be enjoyed in the present, it produces capital goods that will be used to produce consumer goods *in the future*. Many factors determine how many capital goods are produced, including: the expected level of future business activity; business tax rates; the amount and type of government regulation of business; the inflation rate; the level of interest rates; the savings rate; and the number and creativity of entrepreneurs.

Two of these factors deserve elaboration: the level of interest rates and the savings rate. Spending by private business on capital stock, known as investment, tends to rise when interest rates fall. The various capital projects in which firms can invest have different productivities and rates of return (rates of profitability). A firm will invest in a particular project only if it expects the benefit (the extra profits, excluding borrowing costs) to exceed the interest on the loan. Therefore, when interest rates fall, firms will invest in projects that are less productive and which would not have been carried out at higher rates. Consequently, the capital stock grows. The interest rate, therefore, is a mechanism for dealing with the scarcity of capital. The less scarce these funds are, the lower the interest rate, and the greater the capital stock and economic growth rate.

The savings rate is the other main factor affecting the interest rate. The larger the share of their incomes that people save, the more money there is available for lending. This leads to a lower interest rate because: 1) borrowers have more sources of funds, so they don't have to "bid" as high for credit (pay high interest rates); and 2) lenders, no longer in such a "sellers' market," can't demand such high interest rates.

The United States is notorious for its low savings rate, around four or five percent of after-tax personal income. The Japanese save between 17 and 20 percent of their pay. Consequently, one would expect the Japanese to have a higher rate of capital formation and a higher economic growth rate. This was the conventional wisdom for many years. However, a study published in 1996 by the McKinsey Global Institute shows that the United States fares very favorably in growth rates with Japan, as well as the rest of the West. This is because the productivity of U.S. capital is significantly higher. That is, we get more goods and services from a given set of capital resources. Consequently, Americans have to save less (and can consume more) to generate the same level of growth as other economies.

THE ECONOMICS OF NATURAL RESOURCES

A natural resource is anything found in nature that is necessary to produce certain goods and services.

Nonagricultural Resources

Nonagricultural resources generally fit into four categories: 1) mineral resources; 2) energy resources; 3) forest resources; and 4) waterways. The United States is blessed with an abundance of many of these, providing a primary source of high living standards.

As technology changes, some natural resources become either more or less useful. For example, iron ore is still a vital resource, but less so than formerly because plastics and other materials often substitute for iron and steel. Alternatively, titanium, a very strong and light metal, once considered of little use, is now extremely valuable to the aircraft, aerospace, and golf club industries.

People often worry that the country will run out of this or that natural resource, but the law of demand usually saves the country from such problems. If a resource becomes so scarce that its price climbs sky-high, a substitute resource usually becomes cheaper. A good example was the development of the English coal industry in the 1700s after wood prices rose sharply because the English forests were being cut for fuel. The existence of coal was always known, but wood was always cheaper to use—until then. In turn, the relatively recent development of Britain's North Sea oil fields led to the demise of its coal industry. For the same reason, the British and the rest of the world need not worry about the depletion of oil. When the price of oil rises high enough, another energy source will eventually substitute for it.

The world became painfully aware of the importance of energy resources in the 1970s after Arab members of OPEC refused to sell oil to the United States and other countries that aided Israel in the 1973 Yom Kippur War. (Gasoline prices rose from about 35 cents a gallon to between 60 and 70 cents a gallon from 1972 to 1974. They would have even gone higher if not for U.S. price controls, which were lifted in 1981.) Although the United States is a major oil producer, it has less than five percent of the world's proven reserves of oil. However, the United States is rich in coal deposits, with about a fourth of the world's total. But burning coal causes environmental damage, especially acid rain. Natural gas, available in abundance, is a much cleaner fuel. Nuclear energy lost favor in recent years because of the growing radioactive waste problem and the Chernobyl nuclear power plant explosion in the former Soviet Union in 1986.

The United States has vast forest resources, covering over 31 percent of its landmass, or 731 million areas, of which 483 million acres are suitable for timber. Our forest lands still amount to 75 percent of the area forested in 1600, and there are more trees now than in 1920. Every year more than two billion tree seedlings are planted. This partly explains why the total amount of wood that is grown per year exceeds the country's yearly use of wood by over 35 percent. The public owns 28 percent of American forest land, most of it in national forests. Fifteen percent is owned by forest industry firms, and the remaining 57 percent is in nonindustry private hands.

The United States is rich in waterways. The Mississippi River system allows inexpensive, high-volume shipping from New Orleans to the Great Plains, the upper Midwest, and as far east as Pennsylvania. Ships from around the world reach as far as Duluth and Chicago via the Great Lakes and the St. Lawrence Seaway. Many other river systems and fine harbors allow firms to achieve mass markets, vital for marketing the large outputs of the mass-production system.

Agricultural Resources

No other nation has such an abundance of agricultural resources as the United States. Almost a fourth of its land area grows crops, and another third is grassland for livestock. Much of America has fertile soil, a temperate climate, and adequate rainfall. American farmers possess huge amounts of capital resources (tractors, harvesting equipment, and buildings) and human capital resources in the form of farmer education.

Consequently, one American farmer today can feed over 90 people. More than a third of U.S. farm output is shipped abroad. In 1800, more than 90 percent of the population lived on farms, compared with only two percent today. While it took three hours to produce a bushel of wheat in 1830, it took only seven minutes in 1960 and about four today. Because of such advances, the average American in 1993 spent only 11 percent of after-tax income on food. In 1933, food took 26 percent of the average person's income without the help we get today from commercial food processors, who do everything from preslicing our cheese to making our pancake mixes. Further, today we spend 40 percent of our food dollar away from home in restaurants and on carryouts, up from 15 percent in 1940.

Excess Resources in Agriculture

Unfortunately, this great agricultural resource abundance and productivity is connected to the problems facing farmers today. First, farmers produce more food than they can sell and still earn what they consider adequate incomes. Thus, America has an *excess* of agricultural resources, which could disappear if we ate more, if more food were sold abroad, or if other uses were found for agricultural products. But food consumption may not increase, given low birthrates and the trend to lighter diets. Second, nations such as Canada, Australia, Argentina, and Western European countries face a similar excess agricultural capacity. Also, many nations American farmers once helped to feed, such as India and Bangladesh, have increased their output and no longer need American food. Simply giving food to poor nations would depress farm prices in those nations, reducing their own farm output. Last, it's unlikely that new major uses will be found for crops.

For nearly a century now, these excess resources have led to incomes for farmers that are lower than business ventures that are similar in financial and managerial requirements. Firms usually leave industries in which profits are very low, taking the "excess resources" with them. This leads to shortages, then rising prices, and, finally, to adequate profits for the remaining firms. This does *not* happen in agriculture because: 1) many agricultural resources are immobile; and 2) farming is a "way of life."

■ Many agricultural resources are immobile and can't be shifted into any other industry. What use is a farm silo except for storing animal feed? Barns, plows, and combines have few, if any, uses outside of farming. Most important, land is completely immobile and most of it has few realistic alternative uses.

■ For many people, farming is a "way of life," not just a business. Many families have lived on the same farms for generations. Farmers tend to feel strong bonds to their land. People who don't live on farms may still feel nostalgic about farming because their parents or grandparents were farmers. Such nostalgia leads to attempts to save the "family farm"—a business owned and operated by the whole family. Since the late 1920s, the government has been trying to prevent the market from working its "solutions" in agriculture.

Government Involvement in American Agriculture

The government assists farmers in five primary ways: 1) price supports; 2) target prices; 3) supply-restriction programs; 4) credit; and 5) technological research.

■ A price support is a price floor designed to keep farm prices high enough to provide adequate incomes for farmers. The federal government forces food processors to pay prices higher than equilibrium prices to farmers. Of course, this *encourages* more production and *discourages* consumption—creating crop surpluses. The government then purchases these surpluses and stores them, gives them away to the poor, or sends them abroad under the PL-480 Food for Peace program. At various times since 1928, such programs were in force for milk, corn, wheat, cotton, peanuts, and honey.

■ Another program sets a so-called target price for certain crops. A farmer participating in the program obtains a "loan" from the government equal to the amount of output times the target price. If the price of that crop doesn't rise as high as the target price, the farmer doesn't have to repay the loan, and the government then takes the "collateral" (the crop).

■ Supply-restriction programs are designed to reduce crop supplies. These include: 1) "set-aside" programs, which encourage farmers to reduce acreage of these crops; 2) the Soil Bank of the 1950s and 1960s, which paid farmers *not* to produce anything on some of their land; 3) the Conservation Reserve Program, which is removing up to 45 million acres of land from crop production that is very likely to erode; 4) allotment or quota programs, which require permission from the federal government to grow a crop (peanut, cranberry, and tobacco farmers need such permits); and 5) marketing orders, which restrict the sale of commodities by setting quality standards. The government has 47 marketing orders covering 33 products.

■ The government also assists farmers in the credit markets. For decades the Production Credit Association provided credit at low interest rates to farmers for seed, fertilizer, and other production resources.

Similarly, the Farmers Home Administration provided loans for buying land. By the early 1980s, many farmers were in danger of defaulting on their loans. Congress then provided several billion dollars in new money to Farm Credit Services, a new agency that merged the two previous lending institutions.

■ The last farm-aid program involves technological research. The Morrill Act of 1862 led to the establishment of over 70 land-grant colleges and universities in most states. The federal government gave states 13 million acres (30,000 acres for each congressman) of unsettled land that it owned, which was then sold to farmers. Money from these sales was used to establish agricultural colleges to teach "agriculture and mechanic arts" and to provide agricultural research. During the last 130 years, such efforts have led to a vast array of discoveries, in such areas as crop breeding, disease control, erosion-control techniques—and even rat poison.

THINKING CRITICALLY ABOUT ECONOMIC QUESTIONS IN OUR LIVES

Why Is a Wheat Farmer More Deserving of Help Than a Potato Farmer?

Things to Consider

1. Wheat farmers and a few others (mainly corn, cotton, peanut, dairy, and tobacco farmers) have received substantial government assistance in the last 60 years or so, either in the form of guaranteed (higher) prices and/or cash payments.

2. The justification for such help has been: a) the relatively low incomes for farmers (compared with other business enterprises of similar risk and time requirements); and b) very erratic farm incomes because of wide swings in farm prices, generally due to changes in the weather.

3. However, farmers of virtually all crops face these problems. But growers of most other agricultural commodities, such as potatoes, strawberries, carrots, and peas, receive little or no such help. Why do you think we assist the farmers of only a handful of these crops?

See page 460 for the answer.

SUMMARY

The circular flow model shows the flows of money that occur between buyers and sellers of resources in factor markets, as well as between buyers and sellers of goods and services in goods markets.

The income received in most occupations depends primarily upon the strengths of the demand for labor and the supply of labor. The labor demand for an occupation depends upon the profitability of hiring workers. Firms determine this profitability by comparing the workers' marginal revenue products with their factor costs (wages). In occupations where workers are highly productive and/or the product sells for a high price, labor demand tends to be strong, and vice versa. In occupations where few skills are required and the jobs have many favorable aspects, labor supplies tend to be strong, and vice versa. Occupations tend to have higher incomes when there is a strong demand and/or a weak supply. Lower wages are often caused by weak labor demands and/or strong supplies of labor.

People can increase their incomes in an occupation by: 1) increasing the labor demand; 2) decreasing the labor supply; and 3) establishing an income or wage floor. These techniques often require the government to grant special powers to such groups, including the power to form unions, to establish licensing programs, and to raise job qualifications. Unions allow workers to raise their incomes primarily by bargaining collectively with employers.

Entrepreneurs organize production processes, introduce innovations, and redirect resource use. Credit availability, attitudes toward risk, and tax laws are some of the factors that can influence the number of people who become entrepreneurs.

Capital is divided into: 1) social overhead capital (or infrastructure), usually publicly owned; and 2) direct capital, usually privately owned. Publicly owned social overhead capital is usually financed by taxes, borrowing, or user fees. Privately owned direct capital is financed by selling stock, retained earnings, borrowing, and leasing.

The United States has an abundance of natural resources, including coal, gas, many minerals, forest lands, waterways, and farmland.

QUESTIONS FOR DISCUSSION AND THOUGHT

1. Why should employees be upset or surprised when their hours are cut (or even when they get laid off) when their firm's sales are down? After all, the owners of the firm suffer a drop in income as well. Shouldn't employees prepare for these occasional "sales dropoffs" (reduced or canceled wages) as business owners do?

2. Is there more demand for teachers or for surgeons? How would you prove that? Does that explain the difference in their salaries—or is there some other factor that is equally or more important?

3. In the 1980s, there were two times when there were severe nationwide shortages of nurses. Why do you think the wage didn't rise high enough to eliminate those shortages?

4. Do you prefer capitalism or socialism? If it were possible to control the labor market you are in to your advantage, would you do so? If you preferred capitalism and would control the market, how can you reconcile your inconsistency?

5. Make a list of 10 consumer goods made in your community and another list of 10 capital goods made. Which list was easier to make? What does that tell you about your local economy?

6. Businesses seek to earn profits. What is the counterpart to profit (both accounting and economic) for an employee? How are such "employee profits" calculated?

7. Different cities have widely different numbers of restaurant cooks, machinists, auto mechanics, and other workers. Further, a high percentage of people who wish to be cooks, machinists, and auto mechanics in any city manage to find work in their chosen occupations. Finally, most employers of cooks, machinists, and auto mechanics are almost always able to hire the number of people they want. Is this all an amazing coincidence—that there seems to be just the right number of jobs and employees in each city, no matter the size? Or can it be explained in some other way?

PROBLEMS   See page 483 for the answers.

1. Employers in the city of Madison wish to hire 90 machinists if they have to pay $8 an hour. For every rise of $1 per hour in the wage, employers wish to hire 10 fewer machinists. On the other hand, 110 residents of Madison wish to work as machinists if the wage was $16 an hour. But for each cut in wages of $1 an hour, 10 of them seek work in other fields.
    a) What is the equilibrium wage for machinists?
    b) What is the number of people who will be working as machinists under competitive conditions?
    c) If the wage is $8 an hour, will there be a labor shortage or a labor surplus? How large will it be?
    d) If the wage is $16 an hour, will there be a labor shortage or a labor surplus? How large will it be?

2. Suppose the equilibrium wage for bakers was $9 an hour, where 600 bakers would have jobs. The bakers wish to increase their wages to at least $11 an hour. They consult with four professors at the local college for suggestions. Each offers two suggestions, which follow. Which professor's plan is most likely to succeed, and why do you think so?

    Professor Roberts suggests:
        a) reducing the number of jobs offered to 500
        b) reducing the number of people willing to work to 500
    Professor Green suggests:
        a) reducing the number of jobs offered to 400
        b) increasing the number of people willing to work to 700
    Professor Hanson suggests:
        a) increasing the number of jobs offered to 700
        b) decreasing the number of people willing to work to 500
    Professor Rollins suggests:
        a) increasing the number of jobs offered to 800
        b) increasing the number of people willing to work to 900

6

INTERNATIONAL ECONOMICS

CHAPTER PREVIEW

The concepts of international trade are merely extensions of the concepts involved in solving the economic problem in our own nation.

Trade, whether done between people living next door or across oceans, is the result of specialization. We specialize in order to increase the efficiency of resource use so we can raise our economic welfare.

For various reasons, many people argue for a restriction on international trade. Through their governments, they establish obstacles to free trade.

CHAPTER OBJECTIVES

After completing this chapter, you should be able to:

◆ Outline the purposes of exchange and trade.

◆ Explain how a nation finds the products in which it has a comparative advantage.

◆ Compare and contrast the effects of imports and exports on living standards.

◆ Determine the effects of fluctuating exchange rates on imports and exports.

◆ Differentiate between merchandise trade deficits and surpluses.

◆ List the objections to free trade.

◆ List the obstacles that restrict free trade.

There has been much heard about the global economy in recent years. At times it is accompanied by fear or confusion because people too often do not have an understanding of international economics.

The principles of economics apply beyond a nation's borders as well as within them. Each nation faces its own economic problem brought on by the scarcity of resources. Thus far you have learned that individuals interact with others to solve their personal economic problems by specializing and exchanging. This chapter shows how such interaction extends beyond national borders. It also shows some of the special relationships and problems arising from international economic interaction.

INTRODUCTION TO THE GLOBAL ECONOMY

International economics is easier to understand if one draws parallels between different elements of the world economy. This section lists these elements and illustrates how they interact, especially during exchange or trade.

The Basic Concept of Trade

Elements of the world economy—individuals, consumers, resource sellers, producers, regions of a nation, and nations themselves—all interact because it benefits them. Such interaction usually involves exchange or trade. In a sense, individuals who work at different businesses (as specialists, of course) often trade with one another. For example, while buying doughnuts, a person who makes shoes at the Florsheim Shoe Company might encounter a baker wearing Florsheim shoes. Selling doughnuts gives the baker the ability to buy the shoes, and "selling labor" gives the shoemaker the ability to buy doughnuts.

Trade also is said to occur between regions of a nation, but this actually means that many *individuals* from different regions are making trades. For example, individuals (owners and employees of businesses) in the coastal regions of New England ship lobsters and fish to individuals (wholesalers and, ultimately, consumers) in Virginia, North Carolina, and Kentucky. In return, individuals in these states send or "export" tobacco products, furniture, textiles, and other products to individuals in New England.

Finally, it is commonly stated that trade occurs between nations. Again, it is the individuals of different nations who trade, rather than the nations themselves. Canada and Spain do not trade, but Canadians and Spaniards do.

What Is the Purpose of Trade?

People trade with one another for two main reasons: 1) to obtain certain things that they cannot produce themselves; and 2) to gain the advantages of specialization.

■ First, it is usually impossible to produce all the items you want. You can't make an apple pie *totally* "from scratch." You would have to grow an apple tree *and* a cinnamon tree *and* sugar cane, etc. Also, few people can set their bones if they break them, so they get medical services from others. Finally, residents of Maine can find no natural gas, coal, and petroleum in their state, so they buy energy from elsewhere.

■ The second reason for trade is related to specialization. Resources are more efficient when their uses are specialized. Consequently, the living standard increases. Thus, one could say that we trade in order to gain the advantages of specialization—more efficiency and higher living standards.

Everyone agrees that individuals should specialize in what they produce. If not, each of us would be self-sufficient, making everything we consume. And because we would be so inefficient, we would be poor. None of us minds trading with a specialist in our neighborhood or even across town. We trade when we buy goods and services from our local stores, doctors' offices, or repair shops. Even buying products made in the other side of the state doesn't bother us. Finally, virtually no one objects to buying a good or service produced in an adjoining or even a distant state. For example, someone from East St. Louis, Illinois, would not refuse to buy Budweiser beer made across the Mississippi River in St. Louis, Missouri—or Lone Star beer made in Texas—just because it was brewed in another state.

However, there are a couple of rivers that some Americans do not want to cross in getting their beer—or clothes, cars, televisions, and so on. They are the Rio Grande River and the St. Lawrence River, that is, our Mexican and Canadian borders. Many Americans will refuse to drink Tecate or Corona because Mexicans make it, or Molson or Labatts because Canadians make it. However, the advantage of specialization, increased living standards from increased resource efficiency, does not end at a nation's borders—or any other border. Local specialization within a city, regional specialization within a country, or international specialization are merely different degrees of the same concept.

THE MECHANICS OF INTERNATIONAL TRADE

Certain forces and economic laws direct specialists of the world to trade with one another. How this occurs is the first subject covered in this section, where the consequences of trade, the concept of exchange rates, and the U.S. position in world trade will all be considered.

How Trade Occurs

How do people in a nation decide what their specialties should be and how to trade? The **law of comparative advantage** directs a resource to its proper specialized role. It says a resource has a comparative advantage in producing a good or service when it has the lowest opportunity cost of all other resources.

Opportunity cost refers to the *next best* thing that *could* have been produced with a resource once it is committed to making some good or service. Suppose Americans want some New Year's Eve noisemakers, which American laborers can easily make. However, what if these laborers could also make complex solar equipment? Then the more noisemakers these laborers make, the more solar equipment Americans give up. This forgone solar equipment is the opportunity cost of noisemakers, if one assumes that such equipment is the most valuable alternative product they could make. Now assume that laborers in Pakistan can also make noisemakers but lack the skills to make solar equipment. However, suppose they *can* make toy cars—in fact, suppose that is the most valuable product they can make. Then the opportunity cost of Pakistan laborers making noisemakers is the value of toy cars they *could* have produced. If it is assumed that solar equipment is more valuable than toy cars, then Pakistan laborers have a lower opportunity cost when they make noisemakers. That's because Pakistan-made noisemakers cost Pakistan residents low-valued toy cars, while American-made noisemakers cost Americans valuable solar equipment. Therefore, Americans should buy noisemakers from Pakistan. The owners and laborers at the noisemaker firms in Pakistan can take the money they earn and buy American solar equipment or other American goods.

> The law of comparative advantage states that a resource should specialize in producing a product in which it has the lowest opportunity cost of all other resources.

How Importing and Exporting Affect Living Standards

Many people have misconceptions about how they are affected by imports and exports. Suppose a pollster asked, "Assuming we could increase just one, would you prefer that our nation increase its imports or its exports?" Most respondents probably would choose exports. That's because most people believe exports create jobs for Americans and imports hurt American efforts to maintain high living standards and employment.

Yet, it's the act of *importing*, not exporting, that raises American living standards. Exports are a *cost* to Americans. That's because Americans have to *give the exported goods up* to foreigners to get imports. Thus, the act of exporting *reduces* American living standards. Figure 6-1 illustrates this. Case 1 shows a situation when the United States has no foreign trade at all. All of the output or goods and services available to Americans (represented by the rectangular box in the center) comes from U.S. resources alone. The standard of living equals a share of that output, reflecting the amount of goods and services available for each person, on average.

Suppose the Portuguese and other foreigners use some of their resources to make things for Americans. These things are exports for the foreigners and imports for Americans. Note in Case 2 that this *raises* the output available to Americans—and the American living standard.

Now suppose that some American labor, land, machines, and other resources are used to make things for the Portuguese and others. Who benefits from that? *Foreigners* do because *they* have more goods and services. Americans have *less* available output and *lower* living standards. Case 3 in Figure 6-1 shows the effect in the United States, where the total amount of goods and services available to Americans falls by the amount of exports. (Though not shown, the total amount of goods and services available to the Portuguese would rise, as would their living standard.)

It might seem ideal to import and not export because living standards could rise to phenomenal heights and no one would have to work. But, obviously, no country has people foolish enough to spend much of their time making things for us without getting something in return. Such people would have less time to produce things for themselves. But what if Americans give foreigners green pieces of paper in exchange for their goods? Will foreigners accept this paper for goods? Yes—so long as they can exchange that green paper for things from Americans. Of course, these "things" are imports for foreigners (and exports for Americans)—and the green paper is U.S. currency.

A country *must* export. Otherwise imports that raise living standards and provide unattainable items would not be available. In a similar way, when people work, they "export" labor services to their employers. They generally don't work because they *want* to, but because they *must* in order to get money with which to buy goods and services (their "imports"). How nice it would be if stores gave customers whatever they wanted for nothing in exchange. But store owners are no more foolish than foreigners.

Many people fear that foreigners will want to sell to Americans but not to buy from them. However, a foreign nation is no more likely to accumulate dollars from selling goods and services to Americans than an indi-

Figure 6-1

The Effects of Imports and Exports on Living Standards

The amount of goods and services available to Americans (and the American living standard) is raised by imports into the United States. Conversely, exports reduce American living standards, as they reduce what is available to Americans. As no nation will grant us Case 2, we must export in order to get foreigners to send us products. Case 4 is the result.

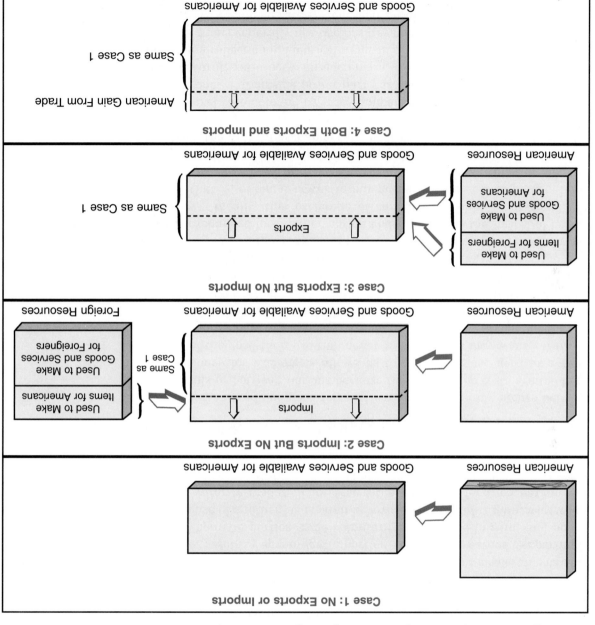

vidual will accumulate dollars from working without intending to spend them. Foreigners will eventually use those dollars to buy goods and services from Americans. In the long run, exports will approximate imports. Similarly, over their lifetimes, the value of what people "sell" (their income) will approximate what they spend (or "import" from others). In the *short run*, however, a nation that exports more than it imports can use the difference to purchase assets abroad, such as land, firms, or financial securities. And this "short run" can extend well beyond a decade in length. Likewise, in the short run, an individual can build up considerable savings and other assets by spending ("importing") less than is earned ("exporting").

When two parties trade voluntarily, *both* stand to gain—not one at the expense of another, as is often believed. If both *didn't* gain, why would both *voluntarily* trade? The same situation exists for each nation with which the United States trades. That is Case 4 in Figure 6-1.

Foreign Exchange Markets and Exchange Rates

Exchange of one good for another, or barter, rarely occurs between individuals or between nations because the transaction costs are too high. Using money for exchanges allows us to trade only one good at a time. Sellers of the good then use the money to buy things they want. *Within a* nation this is no problem, for all individuals use the same "medium of exchange" (money). But the U.S. dollar is *not* money in France—where they use paper notes called francs, and this creates a problem. If Kevin Kostner wants to buy a French-made Citroen car, he cannot use dollars to buy it because the Citroen Corporation will only accept francs.

The **exchange rate** refers to the amount of one nation's currency that is exchanged for another nation's currency. It is the "price" of foreign currency. Ideally, this exchange of currencies should be of equal *real* value—that is, of equal power to buy goods and services in both nations. Suppose a sugar bowl made in France costs six francs, while an identical bowl made in the United States costs one dollar. Because the products are identical, the natural exchange rate, as it is called, is six francs to the dollar. Conversely, one franc equals one-sixth of a dollar, or 16.7¢. Actually, this natural rate is found by price comparisons of large numbers of goods, not just one. Purchasing power parity is another commonly used term for this "natural" ratio between currencies, which mirrors the ratio between prices of a collection of identical items in different countries.

Nations generally use two basic systems to establish exchange rates: 1) the fixed exchange rate system; and 2) the flexible or floating exchange rate system.

An **exchange rate** is the rate of exchange between the currencies of two nations, or the price of one currency in terms of another currency.

■ With a **fixed exchange rate system,** a government decides the rate for which its currency will exchange for other nations' currencies. Governments might try to set these rates at the natural rate, but other objectives could result in a different rate.

■ In a **floating exchange rate system,** rates are determined in the foreign exchange market, where different currencies are traded as in any other market. Before Kevin Kostner can buy a Citroen, he must buy French francs with American dollars. Thus, he supplies dollars and demands francs in the foreign exchange market. (Actually, most likely a Citroen importer would do this through an intermediary, most likely a Citroen importer.) This increased supply of dollars depresses the "price" of dollars, or the number of francs needed to buy a dollar. Similarly, the increased demand for francs *increases* the "price" of a franc, or the number of dollars needed to buy a franc. When this happens, the dollar depreciates (or decreases in value compared with the francs) and the franc appreciates (increases in value compared with the dollar). Note that the depreciation of any currency means other currencies must have appreciated (compared with the first currency).

Many factors affect exchange rates by influencing the demand for and the supply of currencies. Besides the currency exchanges needed for trading, currency exchanges are needed to grant foreign aid, for foreign travel, for military spending abroad, and by investors who buy land, stocks, and bonds or build factories or buy firms outside their own countries.

Table 6-1 shows the exchange rates between the U.S. dollar and the Japanese yen that existed at some point in three different years. In 1987, one dollar exchanged for 125 yen. Conversely, it took 125 yen to buy one dollar, so one yen could buy 0.80¢ (note that this is *less than* one cent). By 1990, the dollar bought 160 yen, so the dollar appreciated, or "got stronger" or "rose." Conversely, in 1990 each yen could buy 0.63¢, so the yen depreciated, or "got weaker," or "fell." The reverse happened between 1990 and 1996, when 105 yen exchanged for a dollar and a yen bought 0.95¢. Thus,

A **fixed exchange rate system** is where exchange rates between the currencies of two nations are established by government authorities.

A **floating exchange rate system** is where exchange rates between the currencies of two nations are established in foreign exchange markets by the supply of and the demand for currencies.

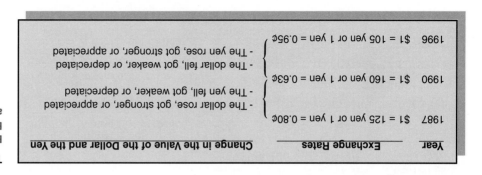

Table 6-1
Exchange Rates Between the U.S. Dollar and the Japanese Yen

Year	Exchange Rates	Change in the Value of the Dollar and the Yen
1987	\$1 = 125 yen or 1 yen = 0.80¢	
1990	\$1 = 160 yen or 1 yen = 0.63¢	- The dollar rose, got stronger, or appreciated - The yen fell, got weaker, or depreciated
1996	\$1 = 105 yen or 1 yen = 0.95¢	- The dollar fell, got weaker, or depreciated - The yen rose, got stronger, or appreciated

the value of the yen increased and the dollar "lost" some of its value. However, *within* each nation's borders, there is no effect on the "value" of each currency, or their purchasing power, so long as imported or exported goods or services are not involved.

Most people probably would prefer a strong dollar position over a weak one. "Strong" just *sounds* good—as in a "strong defense." However, the information in Table 6-2 would surprise a lot of these people.

The table shows that the Papermate Corporation sold a pen in the United States for a dollar in 1987, 1990, and 1996. It also sold the pen in Japan. Papermate still wanted a dollar for each pen it sold in Japan, but Japanese buyers had only yen. So Japanese stores charged the equivalent of a dollar—125 yen in 1987. In 1990, the Japanese needed 160 yen to buy the one-dollar pen because the dollar got stronger. Although U.S. buyers of the pen weren't affected by the stronger dollar, the Japanese were. Consequently, the Japanese bought fewer Papermate pens—and more Pilot pens (a Japanese brand). Thus, the strong dollar (and the weak yen) cost some Americans their jobs—those who produced pens (and other goods). But it *created* jobs for the Japanese, who sold more pens (and other goods) in the United States. The reverse happened between 1990 and 1996, leading Americans to buy fewer Pilots and more Papermates. That increased U.S. jobs—but reduced Japanese jobs.

The bottom half of Table 6-2 shows the mirror image of the pen situation for a Sony TV made in Japan. Sony wants 80,000 yen for each TV, whether sold in Osaka or Omaha. But Omaha buyers have dollars to spend, not yen, and in 1987 they needed $640 to buy Sony's 80,000-yen TV. However, by 1990 they needed only $500, as each dollar traded for 160 yen.

Table 6-2

Prices of American and Japanese Goods at Various Exchange Rates

Although prices of products could stay the same in the nation they were made in, they will change in other nations if exchange rates change.

	Exchange Rates and Year		
	$1 = 125 yen (1987)	$1 = 160 yen (1990)	$1 = 105 yen (1996)
American-Made Pen:			
a) Sold in the United States	$1	$1	$1
b) Sold in Japan	125 yen	160 yen	105 yen
Japanese-Made TV:			
a) Sold in Japan	80,000 yen	80,000 yen	80,000 yen
b) Sold in the United States	$640	$500	$762

Americans responded by buying more Sony TVs—and fewer TVs made in America at Zenith. Again, the stronger dollar hurt U.S. employment. Alternatively, the *weakening* dollar *helped* U.S. employment by 1996.

(Actually, there would be slight changes in the prices of the pen and the TV as a result of the purchasing shifts of the Japanese and the Americans. These purchasing shifts mean there would be slight changes in the demands for both products, which we could expect to cause slight price changes. We say slight because the share of the total demand for Papermate's pen represented by the Japanese market is quite small. Similarly, the world demand for Sony's TV set dwarfs the U.S. demand for Sony TVs.)

The most frequently discussed determinant of the strong dollar has been the growing federal budget deficit since the early 1980s. Budget deficits (which occur when government spending exceeds taxes) force the Treasury Department to borrow money by selling bonds. This forces up interest rates because more credit is being demanded from savers, creating a shortage of credit. Many foreign savers can then earn more interest in the United States than at home. To do that, they convert their currencies to dollars and buy American bonds. This increased demand for dollars makes the "price" of the dollar rise, meaning the dollar appreciates. In turn, American exports fall because foreigners must pay more for American-made goods. Americans also import more of the now cheaper foreign products. The reduced exports and increased imports lead to decreased U.S. employ-ment and output. This shows the intricate connections between economics and politics. If voters want more government spending and low taxes, and politicians oblige them, international economics creates some surprising losers.

America's Position in World Trade

A merchandise trade **deficit** is an excess of the value of a nation's imports of goods over its exports of goods.

The United States has had a **merchandise trade deficit** since 1976. This means in each of those years Americans imported more goods than they exported. A merchandise trade deficit is commonly called an unfavorable balance of trade. This is because most people believe the United States should import *less* than it exports. Conversely, a **merchan-dise trade surplus** (also called a favorable balance of trade) occurs when a nation exports more goods than it imports.

A merchandise trade **surplus** is an excess of the value of a nation's exports of goods over its imports of goods.

This exposes another misconception about international economics. The merchandise trade deficit doesn't "belong" to anybody or any govern-ment. Further, it isn't "bad" or "unfavorable," any more than a merchandise trade surplus is "good" or "favorable." A U.S. merchandise trade deficit merely means Americans have *voluntarily* decided to buy more from abroad than foreigners buy from Americans.

Many people experience a parallel situation in their personal finances. As noted earlier, purchases from others could be called "imports" and sales (of labor, for most people) to them "exports." The dollar value of a person's "imports" equals spending on consumer goods plus taxes (used mainly to pay for goods and services the government provides)—called "total outlays." The dollar value of that person's "exports" is the same as that individual's personal income from selling resources (working). But a person can have more total outlays than income.

How? By borrowing money. Is this "personal trade deficit" and borrowing "bad" or "unfavorable"? Apparently not, for people do so *voluntarily*.

A merchandise trade deficit means we are currently living "above our means," made possible by foreigners who send us more than we send them. That is neither bad nor good, so long as everyone involved makes decisions voluntarily in what they perceive to be their best interests.

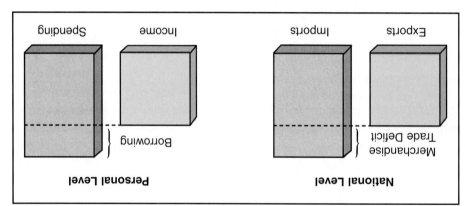

National Level

Exports   Imports   { Merchandise Trade Deficit

Personal Level

Income   Spending   { Borrowing

Figure 6-2

Comparing a Merchandise Trade Deficit to Borrowing by an Individual

Both nations and individuals can live "above their means" by borrowing. In effect, a nation borrows from foreigners when it has a merchandise trade deficit.

Eventually, people must pay off their personal debts. They do this when they have a "personal trade surplus"—when they spend *less* than they earn. Similarly, foreigners eventually will insist that we send them *more* than they send to us. Of course, that situation would be a merchandise trade surplus. Thus, Figure 6-3 shows these situations. Thus, a merchandise trade deficit will not go on forever, any more than a bank will allow someone to continue borrowing indefinitely.

The merchandise trade deficit is often incorrectly referred to as our trade deficit. The difference is that the merchandise trade deficit does not include the international sale of services, and the trade deficit does. Such services include accounting, engineering, and legal services, plus the sale of technologies that earn royalties and license fees. They also include spending by foreign visitors. The United States sells more services than its purchases (an excess of around $60 billion a year). This surplus in services is creating a lot of high-paying jobs in the United States.

From having a merchandise trade balance in the early 1970s, the United States developed deep deficits by the mid-1980s. Table 6-3 shows the U.S. record of exports and imports of goods (merchandise) since 1980.

Table 6-3

U.S. Merchandise Exports, Imports, and the Merchandise Trade Balance

The merchandise trade balance, shown in the last column, equals the exports of goods minus the imports of goods. It does not include the value of services sold abroad or purchased abroad.

Year	Exports (billions)	Imports (billions)	Surplus (+) or Deficit (−)
1980	$224.3	$249.7	− 25.4
1981	$237.1	$265.1	− 28.0
1982	$211.2	$247.6	− 36.4
1983	$201.8	$268.9	− 67.1
1984	$219.9	$332.4	− 112.5
1985	$215.9	$338.1	− 124.2
1986	$223.4	$368.4	− 145.0
1987	$250.3	$409.8	− 159.5
1988	$320.2	$447.2	− 127.0
1989	$361.7	$477.4	− 115.7
1990	$389.3	$498.3	− 109.0
1991	$416.9	$491.0	− 74.1
1992	$440.4	$536.5	− 96.1
1993	$456.8	$589.4	− 132.6
1994	$502.4	$668.6	− 166.2
1995	$575.8	$749.6	− 173.8
1996	$612.1	$803.3	− 191.2
1997	$679.7	$876.4	− 196.7
1998	$670.3	$917.2	− 246.9
1999	$684.4	$1046.9	− 345.6
2000	$785.6	$1244.9	− 459.3

Source: *The Economic Report of the President, 2002.*

Figure 6-3

Comparing a Merchandise Trade Surplus to Saving by an Individual

Both nations and individuals can save for the future. In effect, a nation lends to foreigners when it exports more than it imports.

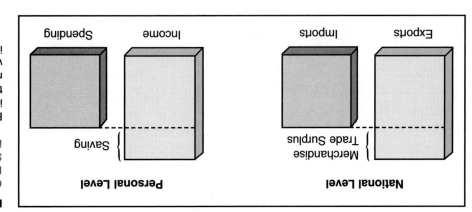

Table 6-4

U.S. Merchandise Exports and Imports by Area, 2000

The table shows that Canada is our largest trading partner, almost as important as all the nations of Western Europe combined.

Area	Exports		Imports	
	Amount (billions)	Percent of Total	Amount (billions)	Percent of Total
Canada	$179.0	23.2%	$233.7	19.1%
Japan	$63.6	8.2%	$146.5	12.0%
Western Europe	$178.8	23.1%	$243.4	19.9%
OPEC	$17.6	2.3%	$67.0	5.5%
Australia, New Zealand and South Africia	$17.2	2.2%	$12.7	1.0%
Eastern Europe	$5.9	0.8%	$16.1	1.3%
Other	$310.1	40.2%	$505.0	41.2%
Total	$772.2	100.0%	$1224.4	$100.0%

Source: *The Economic Report of the President,* 2002

Table 6-4 shows the countries and areas of the world where most U.S. trade occurs. Table 6-5 divides both exports and imports into product categories. A consistent bright spot for U.S. exports has been agricultural products, though even they suffered declines in recent years. As any American

Table 6-5

U.S. Exports and Imports by Category,2000

The table shows that capital goods is the largest category of both exports and imports for the United States.

Exports			Imports		
Item	Amount (billions)	Percent of Total	Item	Amount (billions)	Percent of Total
Agricultural Products	$47.5	6.1%	Petroleum	$120.2	9.7%
Industrial Supplies	$165.9	21.1%	Industrial Supplies	$173.6	13.9%
Capital Goods	$357.0	45.4%	Capital Goods	$269.6	27.9%
			ConsumerGoods	$281.6	22.6%
Automotive	$80.2	10.2%	Automotive	$149.1	15.7%
Other	$44.5	17.2%	Agricultural	$46.0	3.7%
			Other	$81.1	6.5%
Total	$785.6	100.0%	Total	$1244.9	100.0%

Source: *The Economic Report of the President,* 2002

driver knows, U.S. highways swarm with automotive imports. Ever since the increase in oil prices in the early 1970s, petroleum imports have also been a major foreign purchase. That's because the U.S. imports almost half of the oil it consumes. So, as oil prices rose, so did the number of dollars spent on oil. (Imports are measured in dollar amounts, not physical amounts, such as barrels of oil.)

Trade patterns have changed dramatically in this century. In 1900, the leading U.S. exports were: 1) raw cotton, $242 million; 2) wheat and wheat flour, $141 million; 3) iron and steel, $122 million; 4) hog products, $112 million; and 5) corn, $85 million. The leading imports were: 1) sugar, $100 million; 2) hides and skins, $58 million; 3) chemicals, dyes, and drugs, $54 million; 4) coffee, $52 million; and 5) silk, $45 million. Total exports were $1,499 million, and total imports were $928 million. You can be sure that the trade of the year 2100 will have about the same relation to our trade today as ours does to that of 1900.

OPPOSITION AND BARRIERS TO INTERNATIONAL TRADE

To be able to have high exports so it can have high imports, a nation does not require the best resources of every type. Natural-resource-poor Singapore, Hong Kong, and Switzerland prove that. Similarly, you need not have *every* asset that would help you get rich, such as intelligence, physical abilities, good looks and physique, creativity, and a pleasant personality.

Some people don't want others to have the right to buy and sell what-ever they want wherever they want. That is, they want to affect the amount of importing or exporting that people wish to do. This section considers why some people want to limit international trade and the ways of limiting it.

Arguments Against Free Trade

Free trade means no individual, group, institution, or government does anything to prevent any exchange of goods and services across inter-national borders. There are six common reasons for limiting foreign trade: 1) the low-wage argument; 2) the employment argument; 3) the infant-industry argument; 4) the strategic-industry argument; 5) the excessive-specialization argument; and 6) the unfair-competition argument.

Free trade refers to trade occurring between parties across international borders without any interference from governments.

THINKING CRITICALLY ABOUT
ECONOMIC QUESTIONS IN OUR LIVES

To Whom Do You Owe Allegiance—
Yourself or Your Neighbors?

Things to Consider

1. When you buy something, it is the second part of an exchange you make as a con-
    sequence of being a specialist. The first part of that exchange is when you make some
    good or service at your job.

2. Specialization raises society's living standards because the best-suited resources
    produce the goods and services. We all get involved in deciding which resources
    these "best-suited resources" are when we make our buying decisions. However, we
    don't make purchases with that goal in mind. Our goal is to maximize our own *indi-
    vidual* welfare levels. But our decisions end up accomplishing both goals simultane-
    ously. Therefore, each individual is as well off as possible, and society is as well off as
    possible because resources are used as efficiently as possible.

3. Think of why some people are reluctant to purchase products if they are not made
    locally (or in their own nation)—even if they cost more money. Why are they willing to
    sacrifice (in terms of higher prices)? Does the sacrifice make sense? Who is helped
    by buying only locally (or nationally) made products? Who is harmed by it? What is the
    effect on the economic welfare for society as a whole?

    See page 461 for the answer.

*Economically, what difference is there between restricting the importa-
tion of iron to benefit iron producers and restricting sanitary improvements to benefit undertakers?*   — Henry George

■ The low-wage argument suggests that if Americans buy goods from nations paying low wages, American workers will ultimately have to accept low wages as well in order to compete. But consider what happens when a well-paid attorney hires a teenager for yardwork at $5 per hour. Does the attorney become impoverished? No—just the opposite, for the attorney now has extra time to handle more cases. Similarly, if American workers concentrate on making high-value, sophisticated products that enable U.S. firms to pay high wages, U.S. living standards will be higher. Such a strategy depends upon a continuing high level of U.S. human capital in the form of well-educated and well-trained workers.

■ Bumper stickers that urge people to "Buy American" are rephrasing the employment argument that if Americans buy imports, there will be fewer U.S. jobs. For example, Americans buy 85 percent of their footwear from foreign firms, up dramatically since the 1950s. Consequently, over 800 U.S. shoe factories and suppliers closed down between 1972 and 1992. The federal government's Trade Adjustment Assistance Program assists workers who lost their jobs because of either: 1) imports that hurt their previous employer; or 2) products imported by their previous employer as a cost-cutting measure. It provides benefits for training and relocation.

But the *seemingly* sound employment argument is weak. First, suppose that instead of Americans importing roughly 10 percent of their goods and services, they import 80 percent. Most people would expect massive unemployment. Yet that is precisely the case in Hong Kong, Holland, Taiwan, and Switzerland—with unemployment rates no higher than in the United States. That is because the more a nation imports, the more it must export to pay for the imports. And more exports create jobs. (Incidentally, U.S. imports rose substantially from $43 billion in 1970 to $105 billion in 1995 with no sign that the unemployment rate was affected.)

The second way to attack the employment argument is to extend it. Suppose it's true that if Americans *can* make a product, it *should* be made in America. This provides U.S. employment, and U.S. employment is more important than foreign employment (to Americans, of course). But just as correctly, Californians could argue, "Why should we buy clothes made in North Carolina when California could employ people in its own garment industry?" So "Buy California" is promoted. Next, a San Diego resident says, "Because jobs in San Diego are more important than jobs in San Francisco, 'Buy San Diego' is my motto." Carried to its extreme, this argument would be no specialization and economies of scale. But at least everyone would be working—and long hours, too, just like pioneers and cavemen.

The point is, trade—whether between individuals living next door to each other or between individuals an ocean apart—doesn't affect *overall* employment very much. It primarily changes the *type of* employment. Take, for example, the aforementioned Mr. Kostner who wants to buy a Citroen. Suppose he decides to buy a Citroen that sells for 240,000 francs in France. The Citroen Corporation also will sell the car in the United States—if it receives 240,000 francs, plus shipping costs (which are ignored in the following calculations). Mr. Kostner's first step is to get the francs. Suppose the exchange rate is six francs to the dollar (so one franc "costs" 16.7¢). Mr. Kostner writes a $40,000 check to someone holding 240,000 francs. When he does this, he is actually demanding francs and supplying dollars in the market for foreign exchange. Next, assume that this action lowers the price of the dollar from 6.0 to 5.9 francs and raises the price of a franc from 16.7¢ to 16.9¢ (= 1 ÷ 5.9). (Actually, such a small purchase would not have this much of an effect, but this would happen if enough of such purchases were made.) The next Citroen buyer will have to pay $40,678—or $678 *more*. The price (240,000 francs) did not change in France, but, in effect, it rose in the United States. This price increase discourages further imports of Citroens and other French-made goods.

Next, observe what happens to the price of coal mined in the United States. Suppose that it originally cost 360 francs to buy a $60 ton of U.S. coal. But after the appreciation of the franc, it takes only 354 francs. Suppose France gets half its energy needs from U.S. coal and half from Saudi Arabian oil. Suppose further that Saudi Arabian oil sells for $15 (or 90 francs) per barrel and that four barrels of oil equal the energy in one ton of coal. Originally, the French didn't care whether they bought four barrels of oil or one ton of coal because each cost them 360 francs and provided equivalent energy. But now Mr. Kostner's action makes coal cheaper than oil—in francs only, as no energy prices change in the United States. Consequently, the French buy more coal from the United States, and employment rises at Peabody Coal Company and other U.S. mines. In turn, there is an increased demand for mining equipment made in the United States—draglines from Bucyrus-Erie, power shovels from Link Belt and Koehring, conveyor chains from Rexnord, and huge off-road trucks from Terex. And making these products requires laborers—*American* laborers.

It is obvious to everyone—especially the autoworkers—that Mr. Kostner "created" unemployment by not buying a car made by American laborers. It is not so obvious, however, that he "created" employment elsewhere in American industry. Few people make the connection between his car purchase and the new jobs at Peabody, Rexnord, Koehring, and Terex. And this is the effect of only one product—coal. All other American products become cheaper for the French as well and have similar employment-creating effects. These new jobholders all owe their jobs to people who are sometimes called traitors for not "buying American."

Figure 6-4 summarizes the chain of events following Americans' decisions to buy more foreign-made products.

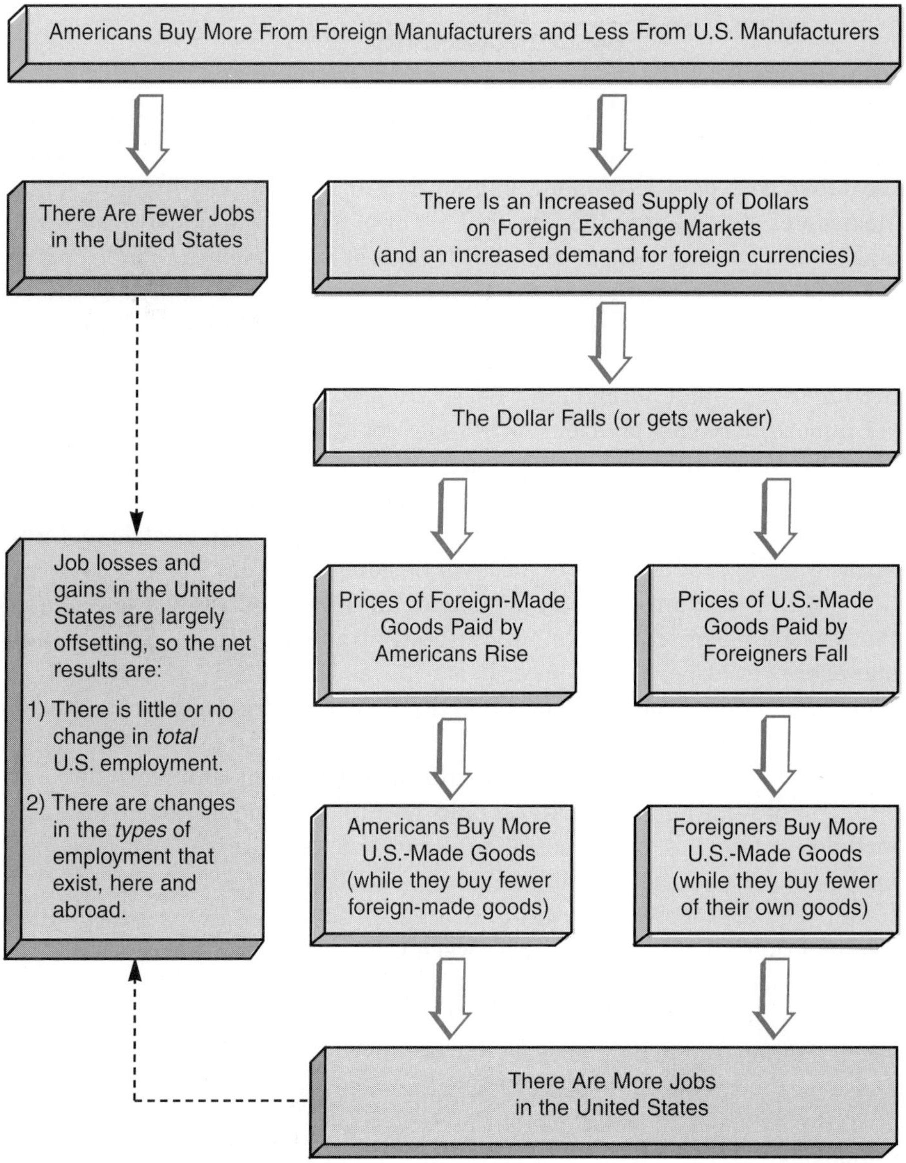

Figure 6-4

The Effect of an Increase in Imports on Employment

An increase in imports appears to reduce U.S. employment. But imports also lead to a falling dollar. In turn, that reduces imports and raises exports, both leading to more American jobs.

Another employment issue is the common belief that American labor-ers cannot compete against "cheap foreign labor." However, when referring to competition from foreign laborers, it is not the wage, but the **labor cost** that is most important. Labor cost refers to the amount of money a firm spends on labor for one unit of its product, an average. The formula shows that labor cost is not only affected by wages, but also by labor productivity.

> **Labor cost** is the amount of money a firm must spend on labor for one unit of its product, on average.

$$\text{Labor Cost} = \frac{\text{Wages}}{\text{Labor Productivity}}$$

Suppose an American worker making small engines receives $160 per day in wages and fringe benefits and produces 10 engines per day. Then the labor cost of a U.S.-made engine is $16 (= $160 ÷ 10). Suppose a Mexican engine maker pays the equivalent of $40 per day to a worker who makes only two engines per day. The labor cost of the Mexican-made engine is $20 (= $40 ÷ 2)—more than the U.S.-made one—in spite of the advantage of "cheap labor." Because they often have better machines, training, and work attitudes, American workers often do produce goods at lower costs than many low-paid foreigners. These are products the United States *can-not* import more cheaply from "low-wage" countries.

However, these advantages are not as important in producing other products, those which are difficult or impossible to effectively mechanize, such as shoes and products requiring much assembly (like electric motors). These are the products where jobs will be going abroad.

■ In the infant-industry argument, an "infant industry" is one so new that economies of scale have not yet been attained. Nor are workers and managers yet at peak efficiency. It is believed that if the industry is given some protection from foreign competition, it can eventually compete in international markets.

■ According to the strategic-industry argument, products that are vital for our national security should be produced here. Such products include armaments, steel, petroleum, and U.S. Navy ships. Many econo-mists say this is the best or the most justifiable argument against free trade. The argument was vital to passage of the Jones Act of 1920, which requires that all ocean shipping between U.S. ports be done with American-built, -owned, and -crewed ships.

■ The fifth argument against free trade is that it leads to excessive specialization and dependence on one or a few products. The loss of 30,000 Swiss jobs in the watch industry following the introduction of quartz watch-es in the 1970s is one example of the danger of concentrating in only a few industries.

■ The sixth objection to free trade is that it leads to predatory or unfair competition. Suppose Country A sells its refrigerators below cost in Country B, which also makes refrigerators. Eventually, the firms in Country B might be forced to shut down. Country A then has a monopoly and can charge much higher prices in Country B. Selling a product for a lower price abroad than at home or below production cost (which includes a 10 percent markup for overhead costs and 8 percent for profit) is called **dumping**. It is outlawed by the Tariff Act of 1930.

Dumping refers to selling a product abroad for less money than it sells for domestically.

THINKING CRITICALLY ABOUT ECONOMIC QUESTIONS IN OUR LIVES

If You Acted Like Bart Simpson in School, Why Are You Surprised When I Don't Buy What You Make?

Things to Consider

1. Many Americans try to avoid certain products if they are American made (cars, for example), seeking a foreign brand instead.

2. Many American companies are moving some or all of their operations abroad. One reason is that many American companies are having a difficult time finding skilled workers. They also respond with in-house education programs or by using equipment that is less complicated to operate (but usually less efficient as well).

3. Americans, on average, are less knowledgeable in math, science, and language skills than virtually all other industrialized nations. Can you use this fact to explain the behavior of consumers and firms stated above?

See page 462 for the answer.

Ways That Governments Can Interfere With Trade

Governments often interfere in the markets for internationally traded goods in various ways. This interference is called **protectionism** because its intent is to protect some elements of the economy from foreign competition. Thus, the policy of protectionism is the opposite of free trade. Six commonly used protectionist measures include: 1) tariffs; 2) quotas; 3) domestic content and mixing requirements; 4) bureaucratic control; 5) currency devaluation; and 6) export subsidies.

■ The most commonly used protectionist measure is a **tariff** or duty, which is a tax on an imported good. For example, a 20 percent tariff would increase the price of an imported $40 German clock to $48 (= $40 x 1.2). If a comparable American clock sells for $44, then sales of the American manufacturer would rise after such a tariff is levied. In the past, the United States commonly had tariffs above 50 percent. In recent decades, the concept of free trade has been increasingly accepted, and tariffs are much lower. Nations that are granted the lowest tariff rates for imports to the United States receive what is called most-favored-nation status.

■ The second obstacle to trade is a **quota**, which is a physical limit on the quantity of imports of a specific item. For example, the United States limits the quantity of sugar imports in order to aid American sugar cane and sugar beet growers and processors. When a country refuses to import any quantity of an item, it imposes a special kind of quota called a ban.

Voluntary restraint agreements are very similar to quotas, except that a foreign nation voluntarily agrees to limit how much it sends abroad. It does that to avoid an even stronger quota that the importing nation might impose. In 1982, the steel industry received protection from 29 foreign steel producers that agreed to reduce the import share of total U.S. steel usage from 26 percent to 20 percent.

■ **Domestic content and mixing requirements** constitute the third obstacle to trade. In this country, these require a U.S. industry to use a minimum percentage of U.S.-made parts in the final product. U.S. labor unions have long pushed for laws that would force automakers to use a minimum share of U.S.-made parts.

■ The fourth obstacle to trade is **bureaucratic control**, or "red tape" that makes importing of foreign goods into a country difficult. Such bureaucracy raises marketing costs and the price as well, so fewer foreign goods are purchased. For example, the Japanese have extraordinarily strict controls on food imports, so that only "perfect" fruits and other foods pass inspection.

Protectionism refers to government policies designed to protect firms and their employees from foreign competition.

A **tariff** is a tax on an import, designed to reduce the level of imports.

A **quota** is a physical limit on imports.

A **domestic content and mixing requirement** requires that a minimum percentage of a product's parts be made in that country.

Bureaucratic control is a method of reducing imports by establishing government "red tape" that importers must deal with.

Japan is also involved in another protectionist measure that is related to bureaucratic controls. Critics charge that the reason many major Japanese firms work closely with each other is to prevent foreign firms from doing business in Japan. For example, a Japanese auto maker would only buy parts from a Japanese firm in its "network" group of firms. These groups are called *keiretsu* and are resented by U.S. and other Western firms.

Currency devaluation is a government-sponsored reduction in the amount of a nation's currency that will exchange for other nations' currencies.

■ The fifth trade obstacle is **currency devaluation,** a government-sponsored depreciation of its currency. For example, if Spain devalues its peseta, Americans might receive 150 pesetas for a dollar rather than the current 120. Then, in effect, prices of Spanish goods sold here would fall to 80 percent of their original levels (= (120 ÷ 150) x 100). Consequently, Spain would export more to the United States. Also, Spaniards would pay 25 percent more for imports (= (150 - 120) ÷ 120 x 100), so their imports from the United States would fall.

An export subsidy is a payment by a government to an exporter to encourage exports by reducing the price of the item to be exported.

■ **Export subsidies,** the last interference in trade, are designed to boost exports by reducing the prices foreigners pay for a nation's exports. With a direct subsidy, the government makes up the difference between a producer's selling price and the lower purchase price paid by the importer. The United States subsidizes grain shipments that are sent to foreign countries through the Export Enhancement Program, which costs taxpayers about $1 billion a year.

There are also indirect subsidies that help firms sell their products abroad, including government-financed trade missions and fairs, help provided by embassy staff, and research support. For example, the U.S. Government gives industry, associations, and companies about $150 million a year to promote 66 U.S. foods and other farm products abroad through the Market Promotion Program.

Trade restrictions create winners and losers. Laborers and manufacturers in protected industries win from trade restrictions if the restrictions help them compete against foreign competition. However, consumers lose when denied the cheaper foreign goods, and taxpayers lose if they pay for export subsidies. The World Bank estimates that the combined protectionist measures of the United States, Western Europe, and Japan just for agricultural goods cost consumers and taxpayers $100 billion each year.

However, trade restriction is not a "zero-sum game"—that is, the winnings do not equal the losses. When there is less specialization and trade, the world as a whole has lower living standards because less efficient producers make the products. *Total* employment in each nation as well as in the world as a whole is probably about the same with or without international trade.

International Trade Agreements

In the past few decades, many nations made agreements to promote trade. Much of the impetus for such efforts came from the disastrous 1930s, when world trade virtually ceased, as each nation protected its own industries in the worldwide Great Depression. In fact, many economists believe that the trade wars of the late 1920s and 1930s among the industrialized nations was a major cause of the severity and duration of the Depression.

In 1944, the Bretton Woods Accord sought to promote a free flow of trade by establishing an orderly system of exchange rates. Its aim was to: 1) establish a set of rules to maintain fixed exchange rates; 2) ensure that any change in exchange rates would occur only if there were long-term balance-of-payments deficits or surpluses; and 3) guarantee that such changes would not lead to currency devaluation.   The International Monetary Fund (IMF) was established to carry out the Bretton Woods Accord. The IMF worked to ensure that nations maintained fixed exchange rates, and it consulted with nations if they wanted to change the rates. It also lent funds to nations with balance-of-payments deficits.

By the 1970s, various problems, including U.S. inflation and its balance-of-payments deficits, led to an abandonment of the Bretton Woods Accord and fixed exchange rates. This was partly precipitated by President Nixon's decision to stop guaranteeing payment of U.S. international transfers in gold, which ended the link between the dollar and gold. By the mid-1970s, most Western industrialized nations had adopted a floating exchange rate system.   The Jamaica Agreement of 1976 amended the IMF charter to ratify this move and to deemphasize gold as a basis for settling international accounts.

However, the strong fluctuations in exchange rates during the 1980s led to a disenchantment with floating exchange rates. Many nations began to order their central banks to buy and sell currencies in order to influence the exchange rates. Such a system of partly managed exchange rates is called a **managed float** (or a "dirty float"). Some people want to go further and return to a form of the gold standard. Then each nation would have its currency convertible into a fixed amount of gold, as determined by the government. Consequently, there would be no change in exchange rates.

A more direct approach to trade promotion was the postwar General Agreement on Tariffs and Trade (GATT). Under GATT, nations agree to meet periodically to negotiate reductions in tariffs. There were three periods of such reductions. The first was the Kennedy Round, extending from 1972 to 1977. The Tokyo Round began reducing tariffs in 1981. The Uruguay Round ended deliberations on further reductions in 1993.

A **managed float** is a system where exchange rates are influenced by supply and demand but are kept within certain bounds by government interference in foreign exchange markets.

The Uruguay Round was primarily intended to reduce trade restrictions on agricultural goods. The Uruguay Round also addressed trade restrictions on "intellectual property" (patents and copyrights), services (such as telecommunications), and textiles. Other issues addressed included foreign investment, export subsidies, and the role of less-developed nations in GATT. The Uruguay Round of trade liberalization is expected to increase world trade by $200 billion a year.

The World Trade Organization (WTO) recently replaced GATT. This multination body enforces the trade agreements of GATT and has the power to impose sanctions (penalties) on countries that do not abide by the agreements.

In 1987, the United States and Canada agreed to form a North American free-trade area. The agreement eliminated tariffs and reduced other trade barriers (quotas, subsidies, etc.) over a 10-year period, ending on January 1, 1999.

In August 1992, it was announced that Mexico was to be part of this North American free-trade area. The pact, known as the North American Free Trade Agreement (NAFTA), will eliminate tariffs and other barriers to trade and investment over a 15-year period, but many were scheduled to be eliminated much earlier, starting January 1, 1994. U.S. and Canadian banks, prior to this barred from Mexico, will be allowed to establish Mexican subsidiaries. Mexico will also allow foreigners to invest in its trucking firms, and foreign trucks and buses with international cargo will be allowed to travel in Mexico. It is likely that Mexican firms will be able to sell much more in the United States and Canada than they did before, and that is a major concern of American and Canadian firms and their employees. However, the reverse is also true. The trouble is, the firms and employees that stand to lose are not usually the ones that stand to gain.

In 1989, the United States established a new type of agreement, called a bilateral consensus agreement, with major foreign steel suppliers. Its purpose is to restrict subsidies of foreign steel industries, and it provides procedures for settling disputes that include arbitration (negotiations presided over by a nonpartisan nation).

Most European nations formed a free-trade pact that was implemented by the end of 1992. All forms of trade restrictions between the participants were eliminated. However, many Europeans hope they can go much further and form stronger economic and even political unions. Efforts are being made to replace all European currencies with a single new currency, called the euro. The Maastricht Treaty is to entail all these agreements. However, serious problems are faced by such unions, so perhaps only the free-trade aspect will come to fruition.

THE UNITED STATES IN THE GLOBAL ECONOMY

Americans must face the fact that old, as well as new, foreign competitors are economically stronger today. They must be aware of these competitors and how American workers and firms can deal with that competition. They must also be aware of how increasingly interdependent all nations of the world have become.

The Concept of a Global Economy

People who traveled abroad decades ago knew they were in a foreign country, for products and stores in other countries had unfamiliar names. However, if you travel today to England, India, Germany, the Philippines, or Japan, you will see factories with GM, GE, and Johnson & Johnson signs. One can buy a Big Mac in over 9,000 restaurants in 89 countries. Coke is available virtually anywhere in the world. (Almost 80 percent of Coca-Cola's earnings come from overseas.) Also, foreigners visiting here recognize their own firms' products, stores, and factories, such as Bic, Nestle, Shell, Nissan, Unilever, and Benetton. Sometimes it's hard to tell where a product comes from. Today a car may have French tires, a German engine, a Brazilian steering wheel, Canadian headlights, an American driveshaft, and Japanese paint.

Part of the reason for the blurring of national *economic* boundaries is the growth in the importance of the **multinational** (or multinational corporation). Although such a firm's headquarters might be in New York or Bonn or Tokyo, its stockholders live everywhere. It manufactures products in several nations—and it holds allegiance to no nation. It markets its products everywhere, and it might own a dozen subsidiaries in a dozen nations. Each subsidiary could be a multinational itself. Multinationals even act as quasi-governments because they engage in education (of their workforce), road construction and other types of infrastructure projects, and long-run planning of resource use.

Many people fear multinationals because of their size and to what that might lead. Their economic size gives them great political power to change whole cultures. For example, many people wonder if the world really should be "McWorlded," so that one can never really escape the United States by traveling abroad. Others fear the effects of multinationals on employment. They question whether a firm should be able to move production to plants abroad so readily, thereby disrupting the lives of those dependent upon the status quo.

A **multinational** is a firm with major operations and/or subsidiaries in several nations.

Competition in the Global Economy

By the 1960s, the United States was losing markets to firms in the rebuilt nations of war-torn Europe (Volkswagen of Germany, for example). Later competitors were the Pacific Rim nations of Japan, Korea, Taiwan, and Singapore. By the early to mid-1980s, increasing imports and trade deficits raised concerns about America's competitive strength. Studies everywhere examined why U.S. workers were (supposedly) less productive than foreign workers, why U.S. firms were so poorly managed, and why U.S. products were so shoddy. Even less-developed nations, including Argentina and Brazil in farm products, now give American firms competition in many areas. Finally, the formerly communist nations of Eastern Europe provide new challenges to American firms.

Many controversial ideas have been proposed to meet these challenges. One position is to regain the strong export position the United States once held in the manufacture of autos, steel, textiles, and so on—the so-called basic industries—through a policy known as reindustrialization. This requires massive investment in new facilities and manufacturing processes. It also involves new managerial structures, such as the Japanese approach to industrial organization. Many people believe that the United States can eventually regain its competitive advantage in these industries. Critics say this is folly, that America must allow these basic industries to wither away. They agree that these industries might have a slight *absolute* advantage in production. However, they argue that maintaining such industries prevents the United States from focusing on industries where America has a *very large* absolute advantage. Those are the industries where the United States has a *comparative* advantage. Compared with the Koreans, for example, U.S. engineers, machinists, and electronics specialists are much more plentiful and adept at making high-technology hospital equipment. An example of this concerns machines that make computerized axial tomographs, called CAT scanners, used in medical diagnosis. To use these same Americans to manufacture autos, a relatively simple task, would be wasteful because they could then *not* make CAT scanners. Critics of the basic industry approach maintain that future American exports will include many highly advanced products, such as medical equipment, lasers, synthetic materials to replace steel and other metals, computers, robots, holographic equipment, word processors and other communication/information-processing equipment, and high-speed transport equipment.

All of these products have something in common. They are all high-tech products. Promoters of these industries say it is no wiser for

Americans to produce all their own autos than it is for Jack Smith, chairman of General Motors, to repair his own car. Highly productive people have better things to do with their time and talents. In both cases, what is given up is the ability to produce more "complex" things that earn a very high income, which can be traded for "simple" things made by others. Let Smith manage General Motors—and let Americans produce high-technology products.

Whether the future will bring more or less trade and specialization—and more production of "basic" or high-tech goods in the United States—is not clear. As mentioned earlier, whether Americans can compete successfully in the markets for high-tech goods depends heavily on the skills of the American people. If the American education system does not improve, Americans won't be as successful in those markets. Then the more poorly educated workers will only be qualified to produce products that are relatively simple to make. Correspondingly, their incomes will be relatively lower. Americans will also help decide trade issues through their elected representatives. And how they decide depends largely upon how well they understand economics.

SUMMARY

Trade occurs primarily to gain the increased efficiency of resource use that comes from specialization. The principle works equally well whether the trade is between individuals in a country or between individuals in different nations. A nation should specialize in producing products in which it has a comparative advantage. The act of exporting reduces a nation's living standard, but exports give it the capability of importing, which raises its living standard.

Nations have the value of their currencies established against other currencies in either a fixed exchange system or a floating exchange rate system. If a nation's currency appreciates, its citizens will pay less for imports, and foreigners will pay more for its exports. Alternatively, if its currency depreciates, its citizens will pay more for imports and foreigners will pay less for its exports. Exchange rates fluctuate for many reasons, a primary one being a large budget deficit, which tends to make a currency appreciate. A nation has a merchandise trade deficit when it imports more goods than it exports, and vice versa for a merchandise trade surplus.

Some people object to free trade because they believe it: 1) brings lower wages; 2) causes unemployment; 3) doesn't allow new industries time to become efficient; 4) imperils the national security; 5) leads to overspecialization; and 6) leads to unfair competition. Obstacles to free trade include: tariffs, quotas, domestic content and mixing requirements, bureaucratic controls, currency devaluation, and export subsidies.

International trade was promoted by the Bretton Woods Accord of 1944 and the General Agreement on Tariffs and Trade (GATT). All of North America will become a free-trade zone when NAFTA is fully implemented. The structure of the global economy is changing so that the United States has new, strong competitors in many products. This has led to calls for protectionism, as well as for restructuring the economy so that the American firms can compete more effectively in the world economy.

QUESTIONS FOR DISCUSSION AND THOUGHT

1. An individual who decides to work longer hours and a nation that exports more goods and services are both giving up more (that is, they experience increasing costs). Why do you suppose most people do not see the similarity?

2. Find the exchange rate of the dollar for the German mark for today as well as a year ago. Can you explain any difference in the rates?

3. Ask some people if Americans should be in debt to foreigners. Do you agree with their positions? Why or why not?

4. Ask three people if they believe in completely free trade: 1) between nations; and 2) between the 50 states. Did anyone answer "yes" to one question and "no" to the other? What explains their inconsistency?

5. Suppose a group of people living in Italy buy a pasta firm owned by a family in your town, continuing to operate it in the same manner. Would you or anyone else in your town be upset? Now suppose the family that sold the firm buys a ski operation in Switzerland? They still live in your town, hiring local managers in Switzerland. Would you or anyone else in your town be upset by their action? If your answers are different to the two situations, can you reconcile the inconsistency?

6. A sugar corporation has 170 stockholders, each holding 100 shares, and each lives in a different country. Its office headquarters are in Nicaragua, where none of the stockholders lives. It grows sugar in 20 nations, has sugar refineries in 16 nations, and sells sugar in 180 nations. Do you call this a Nicaraguan firm? An American firm (as it was started here)? A British firm, who (as the founder, who is still a stock-holder, is a British citizen who lived in the United States when he founded the firm)? If all firms of the world ultimately get such diverse stock ownership, will it make sense to speak of American firms or British firms? What significant difference will it make to our economy?

PROBLEMS   See pages 484-485 for the answers.

1. Two nations, Abbaland and Bonoland, produce wine and brandy. The production possibilities of the nations are shown below, referring to their yearly output.

Point on the Production Possibilities Curve	Abbaland		Bonoland	
	Wine	Brandy	Wine	Brandy
A	200	0	160	0
B	150	30	120	100
C	100	60	80	200
D	50	90	40	300
E	0	120	0	400

a) What is the opportunity cost of wine in both nations?

b) What is the opportunity cost of brandy in both nations?

c) In which good does Abbaland have an absolute advantage?

d) In which good does Bonoland have an absolute advantage?

e) In which good does Abbaland have a comparative advantage?

f) In which good does Bonoland have a comparative advantage?

g) Draw production possibilities curves (straight lines, actually) for wine and brandy for both nations on separate graphs. Label A through E on both lines.

h) Suppose Abbaland is producing and consuming at point B on its curve and that Bonoland is producing and consuming at point D on its curve. Explain how both nations could benefit if they would specialize and trade.

2.   Following a fall in the dollar, Italian wine rises from $8 a liter to $10 a liter.   If the exchange rate used to be $1:3,200 lira, what is the new exchange rate?

3.   The Pakistani rupee rises so one dollar, which used to exchange for 20 rupees, now exchanges for 18 rupees. Pakistani cotton sells for 80,000 rupees a bale. How much did American importers have to pay (in dollars) before the fluctuations and how much after it?

4.   The British pound falls from one pound equaling $1.60 to $1.50. Top-quality London hotels cost 180 pounds a night. How much did Americans have to pay in dollars before and after the fluctuation?

5.   Suppose the United States exports goods valued at $450 billion in Year 1 and $550 billion in Year 2. Also, it imports $600 billion in Year 1 and $650 billion in Year 2. If Year 1 and Year 2 are consecutive years, how large is the merchandise trade balance in Year 2? Is it a surplus or a deficit? It is larger or smaller than in Year 1?

6.   A Japanese-made Toyota truck cost a U.S. importer $10,000 after the 25 percent tariff has been added. What did Toyota sell it for (ignoring shipping costs)?

APPENDIX
MEASURES OF INTERNATIONAL MONEY FLOWS

The merchandise trade balance covered earlier is only one measure of the flows of money across international borders. Money also crosses borders: when people travel, invest, or send money gifts abroad; when governments send foreign aid or carry on military operations abroad; and when individuals and firms purchase services abroad, such as insurance, banking services, and shipping. Therefore, the United States has four "balances" to consider: 1) the merchandise trade balance; 2) the balance of trade; 3) the balance on current account; and 4) the balance of payments. Figure A6-1

shows all these balances by comparing bar graphs of the various money flows into a country, called credits, and money flows out of a country, called debits.

■ The first credit is the value of exports of goods, which gives Americans money to spend. Offsetting this is the debit of imports of goods, and the difference between these is the merchandise trade balance (a surplus in this case).

■ Next are services Americans sell to foreigners, including: insurance, consulting services, banking and all other business services; the money foreign tourists spend in the United States; and the interest and dividends paid to Americans on U.S. loans and investments abroad. Offsetting this is a debit for the same kinds of services foreigners provide to Americans. The balance of trade refers to the difference between the addition of exports of goods and services and the addition of imports of goods and services (a deficit in this case).

■ The last credit involves any change in money that foreigners invest in American securities, land, stocks, factories, and the like. The purchase of New York's Rockefeller Center by Mitsubishi of Japan raised total foreign investment in the United States and amounted to money flowing here from abroad. Offsetting that are any similar flows of U.S. money abroad, such as Ford Motor Company's purchase of Britain's Jaguar Corporation. Finally, the balance of payments equals all these credits minus all these debits, or:

Balance of Payments = Total Flows Into the U.S.
– Total Flows Out of the U.S.

If there is any difference in these two flows, there is either a balance of payments deficit or a surplus (the situation in Figure A6-1). A deficit is financed in two ways. First, foreign central banks hold some of this amount as claims on official reserves (usually "sound" currencies, such as the dollar or British pound). If these banks do not demand payment, in effect they lend money to the United States. Second, holders of claims against the United States receive payment in gold, foreign exchange (currencies), or Special Drawing Rights (SDR). An SDR is a sort of "paper gold" because it is denominated in (or specified to be equal in value to) a fixed amount of gold. Nations can trade these rather than actual gold to settle international accounts.

The United States moved from a position of balance in the early 1970s to one of large deficits, which continue to the present. Essentially, these deficits mean that foreigners lend to Americans. Normally that would put Americans in debt to foreigners, unless foreigners were previously in

debt to Americans (in which case their debt to us would then be smaller). Indeed, foreigners were in debt to Americans until early 1985. Until that point, Americans held more assets abroad than foreigners owned assets in the United States. This means the United States was a creditor nation. But after 1985, the United States became a debtor nation, which means that, collectively speaking, Americans are now in debt to foreigners. However, that doesn't mean any American *personally* owes anything to any foreigner. (On the other hand, Americans *are* personally in debt because of the federal *budget* deficit, which is covered in more detail in Chapter 8.)

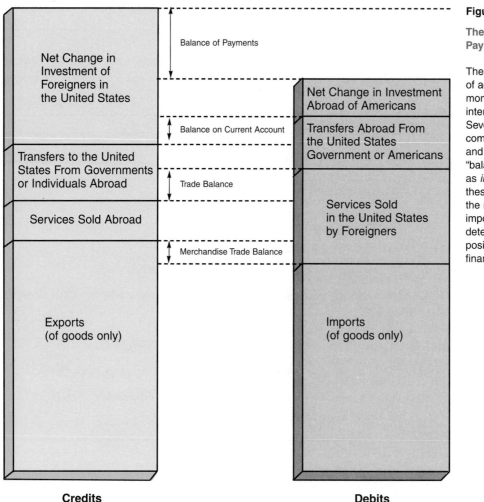

Credits   **Debits**

Figure A6-1

The Balance of Payments

There are several classes of activities that involve money flows across international borders. Several of these are compared in the figure and are shown as "balances" (more correctly, as *imbalances*). All of these balances appear in the news and are important figures for determining the U.S. position in international finance.

7 PROBLEMS IN A MARKET ECONOMY

CHAPTER PREVIEW

In using a purely capitalist economy to solve the economic problem caused by resource scarcity, some problems could be encountered. These involve externalities (where "bystanders" to economic decisions are involved), social goods, imperfect competition, and income inequality.

These problems sometimes get so large that society decides to get the government involved, either to try to prevent them or to deal with the consequences. This largely explains why we have governments in the first place.

CHAPTER OBJECTIVES

After completing this chapter, you should be able to:

◆ *Differentiate between private costs, external costs, private benefits, and external benefits.*

◆ *Outline the methods of preventing or reducing external costs.*

◆ *Outline the methods of dealing with the problem caused by external benefits.*

◆ *Outline the characteristics of social goods.*

◆ *Identify the causes and consequences of imperfect competition.*

◆ *Outline the methods the government uses to deal with imperfect competition.*

◆ *Explain why income inequality exists in a market economy.*

◆ *List the methods the government uses to redistribute income.*

Resources are scarce. Thus, to maximize economic welfare from them, we must use them only if the gain (benefit) exceeds what is given up (opportunity cost). People do this (and thus maximize their economic welfare) by correctly answering the three Basic Economic Questions: What to Produce?, How to Produce?, and For Whom to Produce? The purpose of an economic system is to answer these questions. The United States uses the capitalist economic system, where resources are privately owned and where economic decisions and exchanges are made in a system of free markets. Most Americans believe this system achieves the economic goals of efficiency, economic growth, and equity better than any other system.

However, these goals are not always met in a capitalist system because of four problems, sometimes called market failures: 1) externalities; 2) the failure to produce social goods; 3) imperfect competition between businesses; and 4) an unequal distribution of income. Most people believe that government should correct the damage caused by these problems or prevent them in the first place. This chapter explains these problems and gives examples of where they tend to occur.

USING RESOURCES THAT INVOLVE EXTERNALITIES

An **externality** is an activity that has an effect on someone else when a person acts out an economic decision that involves the use of resources or the consumption of a good or service. Externalities are sometimes called neighborhood effects because "those in the neighborhood" are affected when someone does something. Externalities are of two types: 1) when bystanders to the act suffer bad effects (or costs), there are **negative externalities**; and 2) when bystanders receive benefits, there are **positive externalities**.

Acts With Negative Externalities

An **external cost** is a cost of resource use that is not paid by the person who uses the resources (or the item they produce). For example, when a plane takes off, people near the airport give up some peace and quiet and some clean air. Yet, the passengers in the plane rarely notice the problems they cause for others. Candy wrappers on a sidewalk, unexpected noise from firecrackers, a traffic jam after an accident, chatter outside a classroom, a house with peeling paint, pets that roam the neighborhood, smoke from factories, nuclear fallout from bomb tests, and people in grubby clothes are other cases where negative externalities lead to external costs.

An **externality** is an activity that has an effect that some other party experiences when someone uses resources (or the goods or services produced with them).

A **negative externality** is an activity that has a negative effect on a second party when a first party uses resources.

A **positive externality** is an activity that has a positive effect on a second party when a first party uses resources.

An **external cost** is a cost of resource use that is not paid by the person who uses the resources.

The innocent bystanders are the losers. If you do something that creates an external cost and do nothing to compensate the one who suffers, the effect is the same as if you would insist that the stranger next to you at a restaurant pay part of your bill. The stranger gains nothing—but suffers some costs.

Why do those creating external costs commit these acts and expect others to pick up a share of the tab? It's because people often make decisions with only themselves in mind. People generally act when *their* benefits, known as **private benefits**, exceed *their* costs, known as **private costs**. Each of these decisions is considered to be a good private decision because it makes the *individual* better off.

A more technical reason for externalities stems from the fact that the property rights to the use of some resources are not well defined. Consider the air above Jim's yard. Is it his? If so, he can fill it with trees. But what if his towering trees block the sunlight needed to help his neighbor Joe's garden grow, or prevents a breeze from cooling Joe, or prevents Joe from ever seeing a sunset from his own yard? These "neighborhood effects," or externalities, are very clear here, and it is clear why they exist. It's either because: 1) Jim doesn't care about Joe's well-being; or 2) it was never made clear who owns the air above Jim's yard, so Jim acts as though *he* does.

For another example, suppose Lynn plays her boombox loudly in a park. If someone else is disturbed by it, external costs enter the picture. In Figure 7-1 the external costs are on top of the private costs. Adding together private and external costs equals the **social cost**—what everyone combined in society gives up when someone uses resources. The social cost

A **private benefit** is the benefit received by the person who uses resources.

A **private cost** is the cost experienced by the person who uses resources.

The **social cost** is the combination of private costs and external costs of using resources.

Figure 7-1

External Costs

In Case A, a good decision for an individual is a bad one for society, as society as a whole has more costs than benefits from the activity.

In Case B, external costs do *not* make the decision a bad one for society.

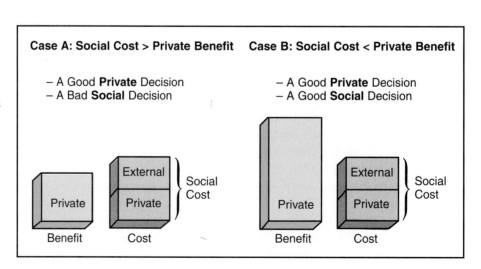

Case A: Social Cost > Private Benefit

– A Good **Private** Decision
– A Bad **Social** Decision

Private / Benefit

External / Private / Cost } Social Cost

Case B: Social Cost < Private Benefit

– A Good **Private** Decision
– A Good **Social** Decision

Private / Benefit

External / Private / Cost } Social Cost

exceeds the benefits Lynn receives, shown in Case A. Even though Lynn is better off playing the boombox, society as a whole is worse off. A good *private* decision is a bad *social* one. The word "bad" means members of society as a whole (including Lynn) have more to lose than they will gain from this decision. Realistically, it is impossible to measure the costs and benefits accurately, partly because they involve subjective value judgments.

Case B shows a situation where someone else, Cindy, enjoys music from a boombox much more than Lynn, as evidenced by the bigger private benefits. Now the private benefits *do* exceed the social cost, so playing the boombox in the park is a good private decision *and* a good social decision. Essentially, the rest of society should accept a little nuisance so that someone who truly loves music can hear it.

The major consequence of negative externalities is excessive production (or consumption) of products that produce external costs. Thus, resources are misallocated, which means too many resources are used to produce things that have external costs. For example, Lynn's boombox made the members of society collectively worse off, so What to Produce? is answered incorrectly. Society would be better off if her boombox didn't exist. However, producing the boombox for Cindy *is* a good decision. Thus, *some* boomboxes should be produced—but fewer than are produced in a free

THINKING CRITICALLY ABOUT ECONOMIC QUESTIONS IN OUR LIVES

Why Is Driving a Car a Privilege–Not a Right?

Things to Consider

1. You need a license to drive a car. Thus, we say that driving is a privilege, not a right.

2. You don't need a license to drive a bicycle. Or to eat a hot dog.

3. Cars, bicycles, and hot dogs are all goods. Why treat them differently?

   See page 462 for the answer.

market. In general, lesser amounts of products that have external costs should be produced.

Sometimes external costs are felt at a great distance or at some time in the future. Acid rain, caused mainly by burning coal in power plants, is a good example. The lakes of the Northeast and Canada are becoming more acidic, partly because of coal burned in the Midwest. In such cases, the association of the acts and the external costs are often difficult to make.

Another devastating (future) external cost might be the flooding of the world's coastal cities as a result of the destruction of tropical rain forests. These forests consume much carbon dioxide when their trees manufacture sugar, so after they are cut, the concentration of carbon dioxide in the atmosphere increases. It is increased still more by the burning of fossil fuels such as coal, oil, and natural gas. The problem is that carbon dioxide creates a "greenhouse effect." The earth, warmed by sunlight, gives off infrared (heat) rays that the carbon dioxide prevents from escaping into space. So the infrared rays heat the atmosphere. Consequently, global temperatures are expected to rise—perhaps eventually melting the polar ice caps and raising sea levels and turning the Midwest into a semi-desert.

Destroying tropical rain forests also robs us of potential medical discoveries in tropical plants. More than half of the world's plants live in these forests, and many have yet to be identified, much less studied for their usefulness. Unfortunately, many species will become extinct before identification. Thus, cures for cancer, heart disease, AIDS, or other diseases might be literally cut out from under us because of the economic decisions in the tropical countries.

Preventing or Reducing Acts With External Costs

How can such resource misallocation be limited or stopped by limiting or stopping the production of goods or services with external costs? There are several ways: 1) internalize external costs; 2) prohibit acts that cause external costs; and 3) reward good behavior.

■ Internalizing external costs means whoever causes the external costs must pay the equivalent of these costs (or at least part of them), usually to the government. Such payments usually take the form of special taxes. Examples include "sin taxes" on alcoholic beverages and tobacco products. (Alcohol consumption is involved in about 10,000 traffic deaths a year and causes many other external costs. Tobacco consumption is usually annoying to bystanders, and it also causes financial losses through medical expenses and property losses from fires.)

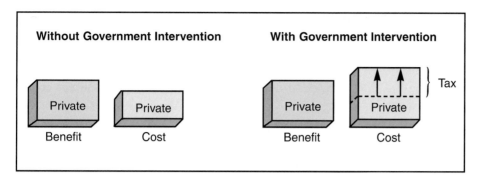

Figure 7-2

Altering Behavior
That Has External Costs

Taxes can discourage
individual behavior (such
as using a good or
service) that has external
costs by adding to the
private cost of the
individual.

Figure 7-2 shows that the tax increases the private costs to the point where there are more costs than benefits for the individual. This technique doesn't stop *all* acts that have external costs. For example, a steep tax on whiskey would stop someone from buying whiskey only if that person had costs and benefits as shown in the boxes. For another person, the benefits might still exceed the costs, so that person still buys the whiskey. But the intent is not to stop all acts that have external costs, only some.

THINKING CRITICALLY ABOUT ECONOMIC QUESTIONS IN OUR LIVES

Who Pays for Your Recycling Time?

Things to Consider

1. Consider how good decisions are made by using cost-benefit analysis.
2. What does it cost you to recycle household materials?
3. Why wouldn't most people recycle materials voluntarily?
4. Can you think of a method to ensure voluntary recycling?

   See page 463 for the answer.

In 1990, France became the first nation to tax air pollution when it imposed a 150-franc (about $27) tax per ton of sulfur dioxide. Another use of taxes to curb negative externalities is the application of Wisconsin's sales tax on disposable diapers, which are nonrecyclable and also create unsanitary landfills. However, cloth diapers are not taxed, as they do not create these problems.

■ The second way to curtail the problem of external costs is to prohibit the act itself. Examples include: the ban on the production and consumption of alcoholic beverages during Prohibition in the 1920s; anti-noise ordinances; laws prohibiting drunken driving, littering, and pollution; speed limits; and rules on yard and home maintenance.

A variant of prohibition was made part of the Clean Air Act of 1990. The act requires that emissions of sulfur dioxide (a contributor to acid rain) by public utilities be cut 50 percent by the end of the century. But plants that pollute less than their prescribed ceiling amounts can sell "pollution allowances" to other plants that exceed their amounts. This "market approach" provides a less expensive way for some utilities to meet pollution-reduction requirements as compared with investing in costly new equipment, while still resulting in the same amount of pollution reduction in total.

■ A third way to reduce external costs, although rarely used, discourages "bad" behavior by rewarding "good" behavior—much as a parent who pays a child for good grades. For example, governments could give awards for spotless driving records or pollution-free factories.

Acts With Positive Externalities

An **external benefit** is any benefit received by someone other than the person who uses resources.

An act involving a positive externality creates an **external benefit**. This occurs when some of the benefits of using resources go to someone other than the one who decides to use the resources (or the item they produce). Some examples: flowers in someone's *front* yard that please passers-by (*back* yard ones can't be seen); perfume or attractive clothing, which please people in contact with the wearer; and your education, which benefits those who touch your life. A rather unusual external benefit is the interest and excitement experienced by a fan of a sports team even though the fan doesn't buy a ticket to a game (experience a private cost). Merely watching a game on TV or reading about it provides benefits.

Usually someone who uses resources that benefit others doesn't care that others will receive any benefit. But such indifference can lead to a misallocation of resources. Thus, society fails to maximize its economic welfare because people answer What to Produce? incorrectly. Specifically, not enough resources are used to make goods and services that create positive externalities.

Suppose Dawn is deciding whether to attend her freshman year of college. Among the resources needed to educate her are some labor (teachers and staff) and some capital (desks, school equipment, and supplies). Suppose she must pay the full cost of these resources, $6,000 per year, which would be her private cost. She then considers how much she would benefit from the education, including her future income potential, the satisfaction of learning, and more social opportunities. Suppose she calculates this to be worth $4,000 per year, which means $4,000 is the most she would pay for the education. "It's not worth it," she says, and looks for a job instead. The diagram on the left side of Figure 7-3 illustrates this.

However, Dawn hasn't considered the *external* benefits the rest of society would get if she goes to college. These include cheaper and higher quality goods or services made by a better-trained worker (Dawn). She might become a better citizen because of her increased knowledge of government and economics and might be better company for her friends. The diagram on the right side of Figure 7-3 shows that these external benefits exceed Dawn's private benefits. The addition of these two benefits is called the **social benefit** of her education—what society *as a whole* gains.

Because the social benefit exceeds the cost of Dawn's education, it is best for society if she goes to college. If people would decide whether to go to school solely on the basis of *their* benefits and costs, many wouldn't go, and society would provide fewer educational services than it should.

The **social benefit** is the combination of private benefits and external benefits of using resources.

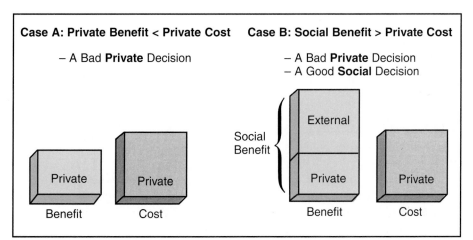

Case A: Private Benefit < Private Cost

    – A Bad **Private** Decision

Private Benefit   Private Cost

Case B: Social Benefit > Private Cost

    – A Bad **Private** Decision
    – A Good **Social** Decision

Social Benefit { External / Private } Benefit   Private Cost

Figure 7-3

External Benefits

In both cases, the decision is a bad one for the individual. But in Case B, it would be best for society if the decision is carried out.

Encouraging Acts With External Benefits

In order to make people do things that provide external benefits, governments occasionally become involved in people's lives. Governments do this by: 1) subsidizing people; and 2) forcing them to do things.

■ A subsidy can take the form of a payment one receives from the government for which nothing was done or given in return. It can also involve the government in paying some bill for a person. For example, the state might pay for 60 percent ($3,600) of Dawn's $6,000 education cost, leaving her to pay only $2,400. Consequently, she will go to school, for $2,400 is less than the $4,000 in benefits she receives. Figure 7-4 shows how subsidies change behavior, such as Dawn's. Education is subsidized primarily because everyone benefits from a better-educated public.

■ Another way to ensure that acts that have external benefits are carried out is to force people to do them. For example, children are forced to attend school until they are 16 or 18. Also, some governments require health inoculations, the use of seat belts (so everyone's insurance rates are lower), and snow removal from sidewalks. Such coercion bothers many people, who say, "I should have the freedom to decide if I want to wear a seat belt (get inoculated, wear a motorcycle helmet, have smoke alarms, and so on)." While these protests make sense, nobody lives unconnected to others. So long as most people want to be in insurance pools to cover their medical bills, there is at least some justification for restricting behavior that threatens the insurance "kitty."

This section dealt only with individuals' decisions that had external costs or benefits. The concept also applies to businesses and government agencies. For example, the Occupational Safety and Health Administration (OSHA) and the Federal Deposit Insurance Corporation (FDIC) were established to deal with problems caused by externalities of business (including accidents at work and losses of savings caused by bank failures).

Figure 7-4

Altering Behavior That Has External Benefits

Subsidies can encourage individual behavior (such as using a good or service) that has external benefits by reducing the private cost below the private benefit.

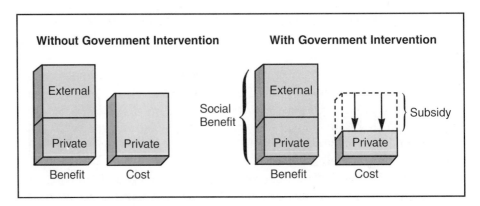

**THINKING CRITICALLY ABOUT
ECONOMIC QUESTIONS IN OUR LIVES**

Have You Ever Seen the West?

Things to Consider

1. People say we are running out of landfill space, so we set up recycling programs.

2. The American West has many areas that are unpopulated, desolate, and not physically attractive (at least to most people).

3. How can you reconcile the two points above?

See page 464 for the answer.

SOCIAL GOODS

The second problem of a market or capitalistic economy also leads to wrong answers to What to Produce? The problem is that social goods are not produced. **Social goods** (or public goods) have two characteristics that distinguish them from other goods (or private goods): 1) they are nonrival; and 2) they are nonexclusionary.

■ Nonrival means that even if you consume more of some good, there is not any less of it for others to enjoy. A lighthouse is nonrival. If the Thompsons go sailing and use a lighthouse for navigation, they do not interfere with anyone else who wants to use it. On the other hand, your notebook is *not* nonrival (it is rival). If your friend uses a sheet of paper from it, there is less for you to use.

■ To say a good is nonexclusionary means no one can be prevented from using it. The lighthouse is nonexclusionary, for no one can stop the Thompsons from seeing the light so long as everyone else can. Your notebook is *not* nonexclusionary. You don't have to let anyone use your paper. Other nonexclusionary goods include emergency weather sirens, civic holiday decorations, and road signs.

Thus, the lighthouse, the sirens, the decorations, and the signs are social goods, and the notebook is a private good. Other social goods (or ser-

A social good is a good which is nonrival and nonexclusionary, or one whose use can be shared by all and whose consumption does not leave less for others.

vices) include national defense and military equipment, street lights, highways, public fireworks displays, and city parks.

However, in a purely capitalist economy, few people would buy such goods, partly because of the "free-rider effect." This means if one person buys such a good—say, the lighthouse—everyone else can use it for free. If the Thompsons build it, they would resent such "free-riders" so much that they wouldn't build it in the first place. However, the main reason that social goods are not produced in a capitalist economy is that they are generally too expensive for one person to buy. Consequently, all members of society buy them collectively. Usually, governments purchase goods such as schools and roads from the private enterprises that actually produce them, although the governments often maintain these goods. However, there is a trend toward privatization, with more private businesses maintaining public goods under government contract.

IMPERFECT COMPETITION

Economists generally believe the ideal market structure is pure competition, where many small firms provide so much competition that firms make only normal profit and not "excessive" or economic profit. However, monopolistic competition, oligopoly, and monopoly are all types of imperfect competition that commonly exist in the economy. This is a problem because it reduces economic welfare by forcing the wrong answers to What to Produce? and For Whom to Produce?

Causes and Consequences of Imperfect Competition

In an industry with imperfect competition: 1) firms can determine the selling price to some extent; 2) competitors' products differ from each other; and 3) firms tend to be large and few. There are two major reasons for imperfect competition. First, the production processes of some goods and services are subject to economies of scale, meaning firms must become large in order to be efficient. Therefore, only a handful of firms are needed to meet market demand. Second, some industries have barriers to entry that restrict the number of competitors. These include patents, licenses, permits, copyrights, and control of an essential resource, such as a rare mineral ore. Another barrier is brand proliferation, which occurs when each firm has many brands of similar products, such as cigarettes and breakfast cereals. This forces a new competitor to spend a great deal of money to fight all these established brands of products.

A final barrier is government regulation that is intended to protect buyers of goods or services. Local, state, and federal regulatory boards are to determine which firms meet standards set by law. However, often these boards are dominated by members of the industry that is regulated, and they may reject firms that are potential new competitors—not to protect the public from bad products, but to protect the turf of established firms.

Imperfect competition has two primary negative consequences for society: 1) prices and profits are higher than in pure competition; and 2) less than the optimum level of output is produced.

■ Prices tend to be higher with imperfect competition than when firms are purely competitive. This creates somewhat higher profits for the imperfectly competitive firms. They even earn economic profits (income in excess of normal profit). However, these higher profits don't attract competing firms and resources as theory predicts (because of a barrier to entering the industry for new firms). In turn, stockholders receive higher dividends. Therefore, society incorrectly answers For Whom to Produce? (Recall that this question deals with how much income each person receives, thereby affecting how many goods and services each receives.) This is because the higher prices reduce the amount of goods and services consumers receive from their limited incomes. Also, the higher dividends increase the amount of goods and services stockholders can buy. So, the competitive market's answer to For Whom to Produce?—the answer assumed to be best—is not achieved.

■ A second negative consequence of imperfect competition is that the output level of each good and service is less than the optimum amount for society. What to Produce? refers to which of the goods and services that *could* be made with scarce resources *should* be made. Equally important, it refers to the quantity. There is only one "right amount" that maximizes the economic welfare of everyone combined. The reason this amount isn't always produced involves the law of demand. Because prices are higher in imperfectly competitive industries, buyers purchase less than the optimum amount of the goods and services of these firms. Consequently, the optimum amount is not produced.

Reducing Imperfect Competition and Its Effects

There are several ways to reduce the amount of imperfect competition or its negative consequences: 1) antitrust legislation; 2) higher tax rates for larger businesses; 3) special help for small businesses; and 4) price regulation.

■ Antitrust legislation was first aimed at trusts. These were firms that operated an industry of many firms as a monopoly because all firms placed their operations "in the trust" of the new firm. Standard Oil of Ohio, formed in 1870 by John D. Rockefeller, led to the first trust. By 1877, Rockefeller controlled 95 percent of all oil refineries. In 1879, he consolidated 27 firms into the Standard Oil Trust. In the next two decades, many other industries established trusts. The Sherman Antitrust Act of 1890 outlawed any "restraint of trade," meaning any effort to control any market to gain monopoly (price-setting) power. The Clayton Antitrust Act of 1914 and subsequent laws sought to promote competition between firms. The reasoning is that, with strong competition, prices reach equilibrium levels and profits are only high enough to keep businesses in operation.

■ The government taxes large firms (supposedly the imperfectly competitive ones) at higher rates than smaller firms. Corporations with higher incomes pay steeper federal corporate income taxes than small firms. Also, small firms can choose to do business under the Sub-Chapter S Corporation form ("S" stands for small). These corporations pay no corporate income tax, but the stockholders must pay personal income taxes on their earnings.

■ The federal government's Small Business Administration (SBA) provides loans to small businesses that can't get loans elsewhere. Many states offer workshops, seminars, and university extension programs to help people start and operate small businesses. Many governments also provide venture capital and "incubation centers" to help innovative entrepreneurs begin businesses. Finally, in the interest of competition, governments occasionally provide subsidies to keep some businesses alive. For example, for many years the federal government provided subsidies to air carriers. Another example is the SBA's set-aside program, which since 1968 has given (usually) small firms a break in bidding against (usually) large firms for federal government projects. Currently, about 4,000 companies are in the program, which is open to owners who are considered socially disadvantaged, especially minorities.

■ Recall from Chapter 4 that natural monopolies, including public utilities, have their prices regulated or approved by state public service commissions. The first major federal government regulation of prices of particular firms or industries involved railroads. The Interstate Commerce Act of 1887 created the Interstate Commerce Commission (ICC), partly to regulate shipping rates on traffic that crossed state borders. The most recent law was the cable television regulation law passed in 1992. It gives power to the Federal Communications Commission (FCC) to determine "reasonable rates" for basic cable services, as well as to set service standards. The FCC began to exercise that power in 1993.

UNEQUAL INCOME DISTRIBUTION

The last problem of a market economy, an unequal distribution of income, is probably the easiest to see. Although many Americans are well-off and some live in opulence, a short drive brings you face-to-face with poverty. One sees people living in shoddy houses, with worn clothing, and without adequate health care. Many people believe the country's income distribution is so unequal that it is unfair.

Income and Wealth Distribution

Income distribution—how many goods and services each person receives—is actually the answer to For Whom to Produce? Recall that a scarcity of resources means most people won't get all the goods and services they want. The goods and services produced in a nation can be distributed in an infinite number of ways, and only one way provides the maximum welfare for everyone combined. Finding that distribution is, therefore, an impossible task.

Two main financial measures are used to compare members of society: income distribution and wealth distribution. **Income** is the amount of goods and services one gets in some time period, such as a year. In modern societies, income is measured with money, which is used to trade for goods and services. Most people earn their income, which means they sell (trade) something of value—usually resources—for money. People can also receive income in the form of gifts, welfare payments, capital gains, or lottery winnings. Income distribution refers to how much income flows to each member of society in relation to what other members have. However, usually only earned income is considered.

Income refers to goods and services obtained for one's use. It can also refer to money earned or otherwise received which can be exchanged for such goods and services.

Wealth refers to how much power you have to purchase goods and services at any given moment—not over some period, as with income. Wealth is usually measured by equity or net worth, the difference between one's assets (what is owned) and liabilities (what is owed). Sometimes wealth is measured by assets alone. Wealth distribution refers to how much wealth different members of society have in relation to all the others.

Wealth refers to how much power a person has to purchase goods and services at any given moment.

Measuring wealth often involves the concept of **present value**, which is the value today of an asset or a flow of income that will be received in the future. Suppose someone is to pay you $1,080 one year from now and that the interest rate is eight percent. If the person offered to pay you $1,000 today instead, would you accept? In terms of money consideration (excluding tax considerations), you would be indifferent because you could put the $1,000 in the bank and earn $80 interest in a year and end up with $1,080 anyway. Thus, the present value of $1,080 to be received a year from

Present value is the value at the present of an asset or a flow of income that will be received at some point in the future.

now is $1,000. Consequently, a more realistic measure of wealth includes the value of property you have at the moment plus the present value of money and other things of value to be received in the future.

The most common way to measure both income and wealth distribution is to divide the nation into groups of equal numbers of people or families. Consider income distribution first. Suppose all American families are lined up, with the lowest-income family on one end and the family with the highest income on the other. Assume that there are 100 million families, split into five groups of 20 million families each. The poorest 20 percent of all families, or 20 million of them, all fit in the first group. The next poorest is the second group and so on until the fifth group, which has the 20 million families with the highest incomes. Next, add up the total income in each group. Finally, find what percent of the nation's total income each group earned. The difference in these percentages show the inequalities of income distribution. Table 7-1 gives such income distribution figures for the United States. (Incidentally, the top five percent of families generally receive between 17 and 18 percent of all income.) These figures, however, do not include welfare and other government payments, which primarily help the poor and make income distribution less unequal.

Table 7-1

The Distribution of Money Income by Income Class, 1998

The table splits all families into five income classes and shows the share of the nation's total income that each earned.

Income Class	Percent of Total Income Earned by Group
Lowest Fifth	4.2%
Second-Lowest Fifth	9.9%
Middle Fifth	15.7%
Second-Highest Fifth	23.0%
Highest Fifth	47.2%

Source: *The Statistical Abstract of the United States,* 2000

In the 1960s, the United States began defining poverty in terms of specific income levels. Take, for example, a family of two adults and two children. The government first finds what a family of four needs to spend on food at a "minimum diet level" for a year. It then multiplies that figure by three to get the official poverty level. Table 7-2 shows the official poverty levels for an urban family of four since 1960. The large increase in the poverty level is due primarily to inflation. The table also shows the percentage of all American families, as well as white and nonwhite families, that were below the poverty level since 1960. The figures include welfare and other government cash grants, but not in-kind incomes (goods and services given directly to people).

Similar procedures are used to measure wealth distribution, which is much more unequal than income distribution. In 1989, for example, the richest one percent of households held 37 percent of all assets. The richest 10 percent held 68 percent of the assets, while the remaining 90 percent held only 32 percent.

Table 7-2

Poverty Levels

The poverty level shown is for a family of four. The table also shows what percent of families fell below the proverty level.

Year	Poverty Level	Percent of Families in Poverty			
		All	White	Black	Hispanic
1960	$ 3,022	18.1%	14.9%	n.a.	n.a.
1970	$ 3,968	10.1%	8.0%	29.5%	n.a.
1980	$ 8,414	10.3%	8.0%	28.9%	23.2%
1985	$10,989	11.4%	9.1%	28.7%	25.5%
1990	$13,359	10.7%	8.1%	29.3%	25.0%
1991	$13,942	11.5%	8.8%	30.4%	26.5%
1992	$14,335	11.7%	8.9%	30.9%	26.2%
1993	$14,763	12.3%	9.4%	31.3%	27.3%
1994	$15,141	11.6%	9.1%	27.3%	27.8%
1995	$15,569	10.8%	8.5%	26.1%	27.0%
1996	$16,036	11.0%	8.6%	23.6%	26.4%
1997	$16,400	10.3%	8.4%	23.6%	24.7%
1998	$16,660	10.0%	8.0%	23.4%	22.7%
1999	$16,700	9.3%	7.3%	21.9%	
2000	$17,050				

Sources: *Economic Report of the President*, 2002; *Census Bureau Reports*

Why Incomes Are Unequal

Income is measured as the number of dollars flowing to a person during a year, and that depends mainly upon two things: 1) the price of the resource (or resources) sold; and 2) the amount of resources sold. Consider labor. The wage of any occupation (the "price" of labor) depends upon the demand for and the supply of that labor. This reflects the employers' need to hire such workers and how many qualified people want to do such work. Under competitive conditions, the wage paid will be the equilibrium wage. However, a laborer's income depends not only upon the wage, but also on how many hours that laborer works in a year—that is, the amount of resources sold. Similarly, you can find the income of the owner of a gravel pit by multiplying the price of gravel by the amount sold (and subtracting expenses).

Very few people accept what the free, competitive marketplace gives them when they have the opportunity to get more. People raise their incomes above competitive conditions by controlling labor demand and supply, colluding (price-fixing), collective bargaining, discriminating, and getting the government to help them in the markets they sell in through various techniques.

How the Government Seeks to Reduce Income Inequality

Does the American economic system give the best answer to For Whom to Produce? Even if the United States had pure capitalism, with highly competitive markets, would that system give the "best" answer? Few people would answer yes to either question (although libertarians and some others would answer yes). They believe that some people should have more income and some people less income than what they earn by selling resources at equilibrium prices.

Equity, one of society's economic goals, means everyone should have a fair share of the goods and services produced. However, defining "fair share" is difficult because it involves value judgments and personal philosophies. Many people believe that everyone has a *right* to the basic necessities of life—food, shelter, clothing, education, and medical care. Whether people *earn* any income to pay for them is not relevant in this philosophy. Nor is there much connection between the amount of goods and services they produce and the amount they consume—at least for basic needs.

An opposing philosophy holds that a person's consumption of goods and services should depend upon that person's production of goods and services. If you work much and produce a lot, then you will have a lot of goods and services as well. However, if you produce little, you will have few goods and services to consume. Followers of this philosophy say this promotes the greatest effort from individuals and maximum efficiency. They say people should have the right *to pursue* happiness (as stated in the Declaration of Independence), but not the right to happiness itself (in the form of goods and services). They would grant everyone the right to compete in the pursuit of income along with all others in all markets. Essential to that right is a "level playing field" for all market participants, which means the only thing that should matter in market transactions is productivity. That is, people who try to sell goods, services, and resources (their labor or other talents) *should be* discriminated against (meaning no one buys from them) if they are less productive than others. However, people should *not* be denied the opportunity to sell resources (be discriminated against) because of their

race, sex, creed, or any other reason.   Indeed, most Americans approve of
government intervention to prevent these other kinds of discrimination.

Most people support at least some government involvement in
answering For Whom to Produce? Governments can do this in three general ways: 1) direct intervention into markets; 2) raising productivity; and
3) direct payments.

■ First, governments sometimes intervene directly in resource or
product markets, generally to raise prices and the incomes of the sellers.
Examples include minimum wage legislation, the legalization of collective
bargaining and cartels in agriculture, farm price support programs, affir-
mative action programs, and minimum-markup laws for retailers.

■ Second, governments seek to raise the productivity of certain
resources. In turn, this causes the demand for these resources, as well as
their prices, to increase. One example is training or retraining programs for
the unemployed. The U.S. Government has about 150 such programs that
cost about $25 million a year. Another example is Head Start, a federal pro-
gram that provides up to two years of preschool for 800,000 poor children.
Small business management workshops and agricultural research seek to
boost productivity of business owners.

■ Third, governments raise some people's income directly with payments, either with cash or in-kind income (goods and services). Collectively,
such programs are called **income redistribution programs** because such
income payments come from someone else's income in the form of taxes.

These programs generally involve direct payments to individuals,
although occasionally business firms receive such payments. The most
widespread program is Medicaid, which covers almost 42 million people and
provides medical care to the poor. Child nutrition (free-lunch) programs in
public schools serve around 15 million children. Aid to Families with
Dependent Children (AFDC) provides assistance to low-income families
with children. About 13 million people are served by the program, which
costs the federal government about $13 billion a year. (In 1996, legislation
was passed to replace AFDC with federal grants to states, where recipients
would receive a maximum of five years of aid.) Supplemental Security
Income (SSI) provides benefits to almost seven million people who are old,
blind, or disabled. The Social Security Administration is responsible for
SSI. The Food Stamp Program, administered by the U.S. Department of
Agriculture, sells or gives away food stamps, which people use like cash to
purchase food. In 1998, 20 million people received food stamps, worth an
average of about $70 a person per month, with a family maximum of $426
for four people. The program, which costs over $25 billion a year, calculates
food stamp benefits according to a family's size and income (individuals also

**Income redistribution
programs** are
government programs to
make the income
distribution somewhat
closer to equality by
taking more taxes from
those with higher
incomes and/or giving
transfer payments to
those with lower
incomes.

can qualify). In 1999, a family of four was eligible for food stamps up to an annual net income of $16,704. Finally, many local communities provide what is commonly called General Assistance to those who receive an inadequate income and may not qualify for other programs. Such government relief programs were virtually unknown before the 1930s, and many had their start in the 1960s.

The Job Opportunities and Basic Skills (JOBS) program, part of the 1988 Family Support Act, requires AFDC recipients who are parents of children over age three (age one at state option) to participate in work, education, or training programs. Recipients receive child-care help and transportation. One adult in a two-parent AFDC household must look for a job. If none is found, 16 hours of community service work must be done each week. Young parents can work toward a high school degree instead. States must increase child support collection from absent parents.

The next chapter shows that "there is no such thing as a free lunch"—a favorite saying of economists. It means that any decision about scarce resources involves a cost. When the government is involved in such decisions, someone usually has to pay taxes to cover the costs. All four problems of capitalism covered in this chapter require government intervention—and thus require that citizens pay taxes to solve them.

SUMMARY

Four major problems appear in capitalistic economies: 1) externalities; 2) lack of social goods; 3) imperfect competition; and 4) an unequal distribution of income.

The first type of externality imposes external costs on people, and it results in excess production of products causing the externalities. Negative externalities can be reduced by: 1) internalizing the external cost; 2) prohibiting production of goods with external costs; and 3) rewarding people for "good behavior." Positive externalities provide external benefits to people. However, there is not enough production of goods and services that have external benefits. To encourage production of items with external benefits, the government: 1) provides subsidies; and 2) forces people to do things that provide external benefits.

Social goods have two characteristics. First, they cannot be denied to anyone. Second, if you increase the amount you use, there is not less for others. Because no individual will buy social goods, governments purchase and provide them. Social goods include such things as roads, police protection, and weather sirens.

Some industries are imperfectly competitive, which is due primarily to increasing returns to scale and barriers to entry. Prices and profits in such industries tend to be higher, and outputs are less than socially desirable. The government attempts to offset these negative aspects with antitrust laws, differential tax rates, and special aid to small businesses.

People sell resources at widely different prices, and some people don't sell many resources. Consequently, the income and wealth distribution in a capitalist economy is unequal. The government reduces such inequality by: 1) raising the prices of the resources sold by the poor; 2) raising the productivity of the poor; and 3) giving the poor money or goods and services.

QUESTIONS FOR DISCUSSION AND THOUGHT

1. Think of five things you have done that imposed external costs on others. Why did you do them?
2. Make a list of three things people do that produce positive externalities that, in your opinion, the government should subsidize. How do you justify such government expenditures?
3. Can you think of times when social goods, which are usually nonrival and nonexclusionary, are *not?* Why is that?
4. Do you think your local power company should face competition? Why or why not?
5. Is it true that "the rich get richer and the poor get poorer "? Why or why not?
6. The U.S. government has subsidized the arts for years. This results in lower ticket prices for plays, operas, ballet, and the like. A main reason for subsidies, in general, is to encourage consumption of items that provide external benefits. What are the external benefits for the arts that justify spending $120 million per year? As the arts are essentially entertainment, why doesn't the U.S. Government also subsidize professional sports? What are some external benefits of sporting events?
7. Use economic concepts to answer: Why do we have speed limits?
8. Residents of a city complained that their freeways were too crowded, so a new lane was added. Within months after reopening the freeway, it was just as crowded as before. How can this be explained? Where did all the "extra drivers" come from?
9. A city is considering replacing its aging storm sewer pipes with larger ones. These larger pipes cost $80 million more than the current smaller pipes would to replace. How should it decide whether to get the larger pipes? How can the extra benefits of the larger pipes vs. the smaller pipes be determined?

10. It is illegal for business firms to agree amongst themselves not to sell their products below a certain price. What is the justification for such legislation? Laborers *are* allowed to do the same thing (that is, agree not to "sell" their time below a certain wage). Can you reconcile or justify this inconsistency in treatment?

PROBLEMS   See page 485 for the answers.

1. Joe pays $2.30 for a pack of cigarettes. He would be willing to pay $2.80 a pack. Will a "sin tax" of 30 cents a pack change his behavior? Why or why not? Will a tax of 60 cents a pack change it? Why or why not?

2. Jane considers planting a rose bush next to her front porch. She decides not to when she sees the $12 price tag, as she was only willing to spend $8. If passersby were asked to contribute money to Jane to match their enjoyment of seeing the rose bush Jane planted, $6 would be collected in one summer. Other than collecting that $6, what can the City Council do to get Jane to buy the rose bush voluntarily?

3. In Time 1, the average income of the poorest fifth of Americans was $8,000 and $80,000 for the richest fifth. The poorest fifth earned four percent of the total income in Time 1 and the richest fifth earned 40 percent. By Time 2, the average income of *all* groups doubled. What happened to the income gap between these two groups? Therefore, what percent of the total income in Time 2 do both groups earn?

4. Betty won the lottery this year and will receive $100,000 this year, as well as in each of the next 9 years. What is the present value of the $100,000 she will get 10 years from now? Assume that the rate of interest will be five percent for the next 10 years. (Hint: You need to repeat the process explained in the chapter for each of the 10 years.)

APPENDIX: INTERNALIZING EXTERNAL COSTS

A supply curve for a product shows the relationship between the prices of the product and the amounts that firms find profitable to offer for sale. Because a product is profitable when the benefit of producing it (its price) exceeds its cost, the supply curve is also a reflection of production costs. However, supply curves reflect only the *private* costs paid by the firm. External costs are ignored.

Figure A7-1 shows a hypothetical supply curve for whiskey that reflects only private costs, labeled S_{PC}. Given the demand curve as shown, the price of a quart of whiskey is $10 and the quantity purchased is 900 quarts. Suppose the government estimates there is an external cost of $5 for each quart of whiskey consumed, on average. Also, suppose it imposes a tax of $5 per quart, to be paid by distillers. The distillers can view the effect in two ways. First, they might say they can now profitably produce only 370 quarts (rather than 900) at $10 per quart. The other 530 quarts earned low profits before the tax—so low that the tax now completely wipes out the profits. Thus, the supply curve appears to shift to the left by 530 quarts. Second, distillers might say they will continue to produce 900 quarts, but only if the amount of the tax is matched by a price increase. In this case, it appears that the supply curve shifted up by $5. Whatever viewpoint you choose, there is a new supply curve. It is labeled S_{SC} because it reflects all the costs of the whiskey, private plus external, which together equal social costs.

This shift in the supply curve, coupled with a constant demand, leads to a shortage of 530 quarts of whiskey at $10. As a result, the price rises to a new equilibrium price of $13. Thus, the consumer, not the distillers, pays most of the tax ($3 of the $5 tax or 60 percent). This is called tax shifting because firms shift (some of) the tax onto consumers. Many people believe this is the way it should be because the drinkers, not the producers, create external costs with their behavior.

Finally, notice that consumption fell from 900 quarts to 700 quarts after the price went up. That is the reason for internalizing external costs—to reduce the amount of the "problem good" that is produced and consumed.

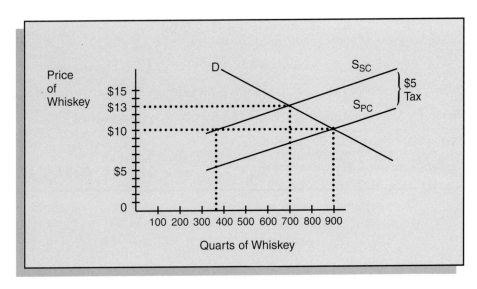

Figure A7-1

Internalizing External Costs

The external cost of whiskey is shown as the vertical distance between the two supply curves. S_{PC} reflects only the private costs of producing whiskey. S_{SC} reflects the private costs plus the external costs.

A $5 tax "covers" the external cost. Thus, the price rises and consumption falls by 200 quarts – one goal of the tax.

8 GOVERNMENT SPENDING, TAXATION, AND PUBLIC POLICY

CHAPTER PREVIEW

To solve the problems of a purely capitalist economy, we often turn to government solutions or involvement. But that, too, may lead to problems, as is pointed out by public choice theory.

This chapter introduces you to the many terms and concepts involved in government expenditure and revenue collection. Also covered is the concept of tax equity, or the fairness of the tax system.

Finally, the chapter covers the federal income tax system, from a brief history of it to the way in which tax assessments are determined.

CHAPTER OBJECTIVES

After completing this chapter, you should be able to:

◆ *Explain the main arguments of public choice theory.*

◆ *List the sources of government financing.*

◆ *Explain the relationship between a budget deficit and government debt.*

◆ *Differentiate between the benefits-received and the ability-to-pay principles.*

◆ *Determine whether a tax is regressive, proportional, or progressive.*

◆ *Sketch the history of the income tax.*

◆ *Explain how the IRS determines the amount of income tax one is to pay.*

The scarcity of resources forces societies to establish economic systems to answer the Basic Economic Questions. One of these systems is capitalism, the fundamental structure of our economy.

But recall the four classes of problems of a market economy that lead to government intervention: 1) externalities; 2) the failure of capitalism to provide social goods; 3) imperfect competition; and 4) an unequal distribution of income. To prevent these problems or to deal with their effects, governments spend money.

PUBLIC CHOICE THEORY

Everyone has heard some or all of the following comments:

The government spends too much money. Why can't Congress and the president balance the budget? The government wastes money on foolish projects. We don't need higher taxes to balance the budget—just have the government be more efficient. We're not preparing for the 21st century. If you don't vote, don't complain about the government. I hate those TV political-campaign ads that don't say anything about positions. The special-interest lobbies have the politicians in their back pockets. How can congressman John Smith call himself a conservative and then vote for that boondoggle?

All these comments are tied together in a relatively new body of economic thought. It is called **public choice theory**, which is a set of theories that seek to explain how voters and public officials make decisions to allocate resources to the public sector. Professor James Buchanan of George Mason University won the Nobel prize in economics in 1986 for his work on the theory.

Public choice theory refers to theories that seek to explain how voters and public officials allocate resources to the public sector.

How Resources Are Allocated by the Government

A significant share of our resources is collectively owned by citizens (or "the government"), including national forests, as well as most schools, dams, airports, and roads. Additionally, a significant share of the labor force is hired by governments to provide services.

Public choice theory explains how these resources get allocated to their roles in the economy. It states that the motives behind people's behavior in the public sector is little different than their behavior in the private sector. That is, people seek to maximize their own welfare, whether in buying an item in a store or being involved in a collective decision with fellow citizens. Such decision makers can be individuals voting in a referendum or in an election of representatives that offer their agenda for action. Alternatively, the decision makers can be elected officials or other nonelected officials who decide how much public money to spend and how to spend it.

A basic premise of public choice theory is that politicians maximize their own welfare by seeking to maximize their re-election chances. Public choice economists believe this often does *not* promote the maximization of welfare for society as a whole. Thus, public choice theorists have questioned how well or efficiently resources can be allocated in a democratic society.

Mistakes concerning resource use in private markets are often called "market failures." Mistakes concerning resource allocation that are made in the public sector are sometimes called "government failures." The next section outlines how these can occur.

Reasons for Public Sector Failure

Public choice theorists suggest that "government failures" explain why government budgets are so hard to balance and why government spending is as large as it is (seemingly "too high," according to many). There are five commonly mentioned reasons for government or public sector failure: 1) the majority-rule problem; 2) inefficient government bureaucracies; 3) the special-interest effect; 4) rational ignorance of voters; and 5) preference for short-run results.

■ Resources are used efficiently when they provide more benefits than (opportunity) costs. The majority-rule problem states that collective decisions made by voters can lead to resource use in the public sector where the benefits are *less than* the costs. Voters can also *reject* the use of resources where the benefits would have exceeded the costs. Either case results in a misallocation of resources.

For example, suppose a town of 19,000 voters/taxpayers is asked to approve the building of a $1.5 million swimming pool. If each taxpayer pays the same amount, each would have a cost of $78.95 (= $1.5 million ÷ 19,000). Suppose 10,000 voters each get $100 of benefits from the pool. Thus, each is willing to pay $100 and so votes yes. Also, suppose the other 9,000 voters don't swim or have children, so they get no benefits from the pool. They all vote no. The total benefit of the pool is $1.0 million (= $100 x 10,000). The total cost, at $1.5 million, exceeds that benefit. However, the pool is built because of majority rule—though it is a poor use of resources.

■ The second cause of government failure stems from inefficient government bureaucracies. Everyone has heard stories of how inefficient government enterprises are, from the post office to the military to the local public works department.

Public choice theory states that bureaucracies are not motivated by profits (and efficient, low-cost operations), but rather by power and prestige that is related to the size of their bureaucracies. Bureaucrats often resist "downsizing" of their departments, citing the loss of services to the public as a result. They occasionally deliberately spend all they can at the end of a fiscal period (if any money is left in the budget) so their budgets aren't cut in the future.

■ The special-interest group effect states that a small group can gain acceptance of a government program that is largely paid for by the rest of society. The decision is made primarily by the special-interest group, while the rest of society takes little notice. The reason is that those in the special-interest group have much to gain by the program and, so, are willing to incur great cost in lobbying for the program. They will travel to Washington or the state capital in person, *en masse*. Each member of the rest of society has little cost from any single program, perhaps a few dollars or cents a year. Thus, it is *not* in their best interest to spend much time and money to lobby against the program.

An example could be a flood-control dam benefiting a small town along a river in Missouri. If the federal government subsidizes 90 percent of the project, local residents would push hard for its passage, many traveling to Washington to do so. However, no individual from Maine or Oregon who opposes the dam would travel to Washington to lobby against it. However, perhaps after calculating all the benefits and costs to society as a whole, the dam would be a poor use of society's resources. The problem is akin to the "excessive use" of napkins by some patrons in restaurants who wouldn't dream of using four or five napkins at home when *they* have to pay for them directly.

The special-interest group effect is accentuated by the concept of "logrolling," where politicians representing special interests get legislative support from other politicians who want help in return on *their* special-interest projects. So, the dam might get built in Missouri with help from representatives from Texas if the Missouri representatives vote for a new air force training facility in Texas.

■ The next source of public-sector failure is called rational voter ignorance. It means voters often decide that the additional costs of obtaining information about candidates and issues in an election is less than the benefits of obtaining that information. Thus, voters often choose to remain ignorant, perhaps basing their voting on name recognition, physical appearance and speaking ability, or party affiliation.

One problem arising from this rational ignorance occurs when an elected official makes decisions that the citizens would *not* have made in a referendum. Thus, the wrong "package" of public goods could get purchased. This is similar to an uninformed consumer purchasing items almost at random in a supermarket, making decisions only on the basis of recognition of some of the brand names of the products. The consumer is certain to get less than the maximum economic welfare from the money spent.

■ The last public-sector failure predicted by public choice theory is the loss in long-run welfare because of a preoccupation with the present. Politicians find it easier to get re-elected when their programs have immediate payoffs but distant costs. They shy away from projects costing a lot of money upfront but that only offer a hope that benefits will be forthcoming in the distant future. Politicians know some voters are like children, who would rather be offered free candy bars than free math books.

Thus, public support of scientific and medical research, building of educational facilities, and early-intervention programs for troubled youths is perhaps less than is socially desirable. Further, spending for showy, quick-return projects (a sports stadium built to attract a pro-sports team, for example) tends to be higher than is socially desirable.

WHY THE GOVERNMENT SPENDS MONEY

For illustrative purposes, one can split government spending into two categories—first, purchases of goods and services, and second, spending on transfer payments.

The Government Purchases Goods and Services

In this first spending category, the government receives goods, services, or resources when it spends money. This is not the case with transfer payments, covered in the next section.

The largest share of government purchases of goods and services involves social or public goods. The federal government is involved in constructing highways, buying F-18 fighters for the Air Force, hiring toxic waste site inspectors, building flood-control dams, paying for trucks for the Forest Service, and buying land for new national parks. State and local governments purchase street lights and the electricity for them, school buildings, sanitation trucks, and flowers for boulevards. Governments also buy resources to produce private goods and services that many Americans prefer to have the government produce. These include mail service, Amtrak passenger train service, and unemployment insurance. Thus, governments buy trucks, trains, and buildings, and they hire administrators, clerks, secretaries, train conductors, park rangers, and many more employees.

Externalities also lead governments to buy goods and services. School buildings, teachers, and library books are resources used in providing education, and education provides external benefits. Similarly, public health services provide immunizations, which indirectly protect everyone. Negative externalities are more common and require much government spending for such uses as law enforcement staff and equipment, pollution-monitoring staff and health department equipment, and staff and facilities for municipal zoning departments.

Finally, market imperfections require government spending. The U.S. Department of Justice hires lawyers, economists, accountants, and secretaries to determine if proposed mergers would significantly reduce competition. The Small Business Administration provides resources and loans to aid small businesses. Federal and state agencies watch for cases of price-fixing, false advertising, and other "unfair competition" practices and illegal discrimination in markets.

The Government Processes Transfer Payments

The fourth problem of a market economy, an inequality of incomes, leads government to reduce the difference in the amount of goods and services poorer and richer people can buy in a purely market economy. A redistribution of income refers to efforts to reduce income inequality.

Governments use two broad ways to redistribute income: 1) with transfer payments; and 2) with differential tax payments.

■ In the first case, governments give certain people money, goods, or services—called **transfer payments**. People who receive transfer payments are not required to provide anything to the government or do anything for them in return. Essentially, the government transfers wealth from some people to other people with these payments.

A **transfer payment** is money given to someone by a government for which it receives nothing in return.

Generally, transfer payments involve paying money, called cash grants, to recipients. Some examples are unemployment compensation, subsidy payments to farmers, welfare payments, student grants, and Social Security payments. A second type of transfer payment is in-kind income, obtained when a person receives a good or a service rather than money. Such income includes free or partly free medical care (Medicaid, for example), food (such as surplus dairy products), as well as food stamps, housing (federal and local projects), and home repairs. Sooner or later virtually everyone receives a transfer payment, but poorer people generally receive more of them.

In recent years, the word entitlements has come to be virtually synonymous with transfer payments. It means that people are entitled to cer-

THINKING CRITICALLY ABOUT ECONOMIC QUESTIONS IN OUR LIVES

Why Don't Businesses Pay Taxes?

Things to Consider

1. In the long run, business owners will not produce an item unless all costs are covered by the firm's revenues. Costs include the explicit (cash) costs plus the implicit (opportunity) costs. If a business did *not* have enough revenues to cover all costs, the owner would have better opportunities in which to invest.

2. Corporations are assessed taxes. They *appear* to pay them. However, suppose no firm had paid taxes until now. Suppose all firms were earning only normal profit. Consider a firm with $10 million in revenues, $9 million in explicit costs, and $1 million in implicit costs. It earns an accounting profit of $1 million, but it has zero *economic* profit. The government now imposes a 20 percent profits tax, leaving the firm $800,000 in net income. However, now it has a $200,000 economic *loss*, as the tax payment is treated as just another explicit cost.

3. How will the firm respond? What will be the effect on other elements of the economy?

4. Do you still think that businesses pay taxes—or do they merely *collect* them (and who do they collect them from)? If so, what does that indicate about the government's efficiency in collecting taxes (or how much tax it collects with a given effort)?

    See page 464 for the answer.

tain benefits from the government as prescribed by law, including Social Security and welfare. However, other transfer payments, such as business subsidies, are not classified as entitlements.

■ The second way to redistribute income is to have poorer people pay less money in taxes than richer people. Consider defense spending. Dividing the total defense budget by the entire U.S. population gives a per capita figure of around $1,100 for 1997. Yet a poor person doesn't pay anywhere near that, and rich people usually pay much more. Thus, poorer people have a somewhat greater ability to buy goods and services for their own use with the money they "save" by not paying the full $1,100—and the rich have less.

Figure 8-1 uses two hypothetical people, Smith and Brown, to show how these two income redistribution programs work. Smith has more earned income (or gross pay) than Brown by a wide margin. First, note that Smith pays much more taxes than Brown. Second, note that part of Smith's taxes go to Brown in the form of transfer payments—both cash grants and in-kind income. (Although the diagram doesn't show it, some of Brown's taxes return to Brown as transfer payments, and some also go to Smith as transfer payments—yet these amounts are small when compared with the transfers shown.) At the end of this process, Smith still is better off than Brown. However, the difference is not nearly as large as it would be without income redistribution programs.

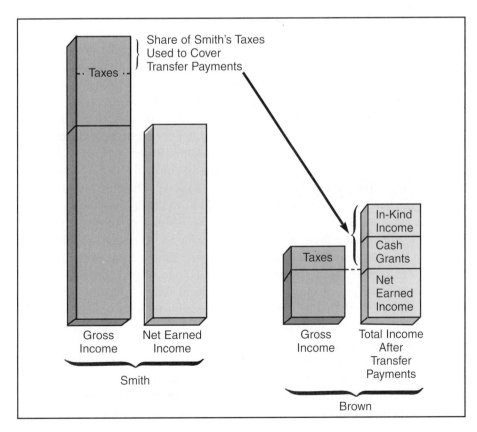

Figure 8-1

How Incomes Are Redistributed

One way to redistribute incomes is to take some income in the form of taxes from higher-income people, such as Smith, and transfer it to those with lower incomes, such as Brown. Such transfers can either be in cash form or in the form of goods and services, known as in-kind income.

Total Outlays of the Government

Total outlays refer to the total amount of money spent by a government, including spending for goods and services as well as transfer payments.

Adding government spending on goods and services to the amount of transfer payments equals **total outlays** of the government. Taken literally, this refers to the total amount of money "laid out" for all government programs combined. When one hears the term "government budget" on the news, it usually refers to total outlays.

THE FUNDING OF GOVERNMENT

If the government is to spend money, it must first get some. This section surveys major sources of its money and also addresses budget policy.

Sources of Money for Governments

Governments obtain money from dozens of sources, but most fit into four categories: 1) taxes; 2) earnings; 3) money received from other governments; and 4) borrowing.

■ Tax receipts are the largest source of revenue for most governments. There are taxes on income, real estate property, estates, imports (tariffs), the dollar amount of purchases (sales taxes), and the actual amount of a specific good purchased (excise taxes, such as taxes on tobacco products, alcoholic beverages, telephone service, and gasoline).

■ Governments earn money by charging for services they provide or for the use of their resources. For example, the federal government charges barge owners for using the locks on the Mississippi River, ranchers for grazing their cattle on federal lands, and patrons of the U.S. Postal Service for mail service. Also, publicly owned colleges charge tuition, state parks charge admission and camping fees, and state-owned liquor stores in some states profit from selling alcoholic beverages. Many of these sources of money are called **user fees**, as the users pay for the services provided.

A user fee is a charge assessed by the government for the use of its goods or services.

■ Only state and local governments get money from other governments. For example, most states provide funds to local governments. Often this is for "property tax relief," since much local financing comes from the property tax. Also, the federal government provides a wide variety of funding sources to local and state governments, such as block grants, which are given for specific uses.

Total receipts include all the money received by a government from taxes, earnings, and other governments.

■ The total of these first three revenue sources is called **total receipts**. Often that is enough to equal total outlays. However, like people, governments sometimes spend more money than they take in. Also like people, governments are able to do this by borrowing. *Unlike* people, governments borrow money when they sell bonds (also called securities). The federal government sells savings bonds, Treasury bills (or T-bills, which mature in less than a year), Treasury notes (with maturity dates from two years to 10 years), longer-term Treasury bonds (which mature anywhere from 10 to 30 years), and a few less common securities. State and local governments borrow by selling municipal bonds. Individuals buy government bonds, as do corporations, banks, insurance companies, mutual funds, foreigners, and even other governments. **Total funding** refers to the addition of all four sources of financing, and it equals total outlays, as shown in the box on the right side of Figure 8-2.

Total funding is the total amount of money a government has available to spend, including borrowed funds.

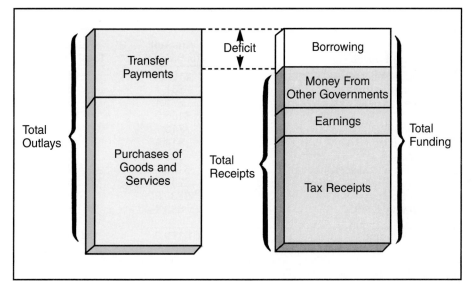

Figure 8-2

Government Spending and Funding

Governments spend money on transfer payments and goods and services.

Governments obtain money from taxes, earnings, other governments, and the sale of bonds (or borrowing).

The deficit refers to the amount of borrowing in a year.

The Financing Record of Governments

The following three tables show sources of money for various governments. Table 8-1 shows that the federal government receives the largest single amount of money from the individual income tax, followed by FICA taxes (Social Security taxes). The dollar amounts collected are shown in the second column and the share of total receipts in the third column. The last column shows the percentage that each funding source contributes to the federal budget.

Table 8-1

Federal Financing for
Fiscal Year 2001

The individual income tax
and social insurance
(FICA) taxes dominate
the sources of revenue for
the federal governent.

Funding Source	Amount (in billions)	Percent of Total Receipts
Individual Income Tax	$994.3	49.9%
Corporate Income Tax	$151.1	7.6%
Social Insurance	$693.9	34.9%
Excise Tax	$66.1	3.3%
Estate and Gift Tax	$28.4	1.4%
Customs Duties and Fees	$19.4	1.0%
Miscellaneous	$37.8	1.9%
Total Funding/Receipts	**$1,991.0**	**100.0%**

Source: *The Economic Report of the President, 2002*

Table 8-2

Financing of State
Governments in 1998

No single revenue source
dominates state finances
in the nation as a whole,
though that may be the
case in a specific state.

Funding Source	Amount (in billions)	Percent of Total Funding
Individual Income Tax	$160.7	13.6%
Corporate Income Tax	$31.4	2.6%
Excise Tax	$71.4	6.1%
Sales Tax	$156.0	13.2%
Property Tax	$10.7	0.9%
Other Taxes	$14.9	1.3%
Licenses	$29.7	2.5%
Charges and Miscellaneous	$149.7	12.7%
Revenue From Other Governments	$240.8	20.4%
Other Sources	$230.9	19.6%
Borrowing	$83.4	7.1%
Total Funding	**$1,179.3**	**100.0%**

Source: *The Statistical Abstract of the United States,* 2000

Table 8-3

Financing of Local
Governments in 1996

Like states, cities, as a
whole, have a rather
balanced source
of revenues.

Funding Source	Amount (in billions)	Percent of Total Funding
Property Tax	$198.5	24.7%
Sales Tax	$29.7	3.7%
Utility Income	$67.7	8.4%
Revenue From Federal Government	$26.9	3.3%
Revenue From State Governments	$243.6	30.4%
Charges and Miscellaneous	$237.3	29.5%
Total Funding	**$803.7**	**100.0%**

Source: *The Statistical Abstract of the United States,* 1999

Table 8-2 shows the sources of funding for all 50 states combined. Revenue from other governments, especially the federal government, contributes the largest single source of money. Sales taxes and individual income taxes are usually next in the order of importance. Several states have no income tax and some have no sales tax.

Table 8-3 lists the sources of revenue for all U.S. local governments combined, including cities, counties, villages, townships, and school districts. Money coming from other governments is the largest single source of funding for most cities. The largest single tax for cities is usually the property tax.

Combining Spending and Funding

In Figure 8-2 the amount of money borrowed equals the amount of the deficit, shown as the distance between the dotted lines connecting the two diagrams. A **budget deficit** equals the excess of total outlays over total receipts in a fiscal period (a year for most governments). A government finances a deficit by selling bonds (securities). Do not think the deficit is caused by transfer payments just because they are shown as the top part of the total outlays in the box on the left side of Figure 8-2. Spending for goods and services are equally important in creating the deficit.

> A **budget deficit** occurs when total outlays of a government exceed total receipts.

When total outlays equal total receipts, the government has a **balanced budget**. Laws require many local and state governments to balance their budgets, and there is much support for a constitutional amendment to force the federal government to do so.

> A **balanced budget** occurs when total outlays of a government equal total receipts.

If a government has more total receipts than total outlays, the difference is a **budget surplus**. The government can use this money to pay off any debt incurred in earlier years, or it can save it for the future.

> A **budget surplus** occurs when total receipts of a government exceed total outlays.

Deficits and Debt

Many people make the mistake of using the words deficit and debt as synonyms. Deficit refers to a shortfall of total receipts compared with total outlays over a *period of time,* usually a year. Debt refers to how much the government *owes* at some *point in time.* However, the federal government has several accounting methods that define debt differently. The most commonly used concept is the **public debt** (often called the national debt), which covers only the borrowing of the U.S. Treasury. It excludes borrowing by independent federal government agencies, such as the Tennessee Valley Authority and Farm Credit Services. Congress sets a maximum limit on the public debt, and it periodically raises the limit because of continuing deficits.

> The **public debt** is the money owed by citizens of the national government to those who purchase the government's securities.

Debt Instrument	Amount Outstanding (in billions)	Percent of Total Debt
Treasury Bills	$646.9	11.4%
Treasury Notes	$1,557.3	27.5%
Treasury Bonds	$626.5	11.1%
U.S. Savings Bonds	$176.9	3.1%
Other Nonmarketable Securities	$2,654.6	46.9%
Total Gross Public Debt	**$5,662.2**	**100.0%**

Source: *Federal Reserve Bulletin,* January 2002

The public debt equals the value of all outstanding government securities—all the Treasury bonds, bills, and notes not yet redeemed ("cashed in") or matured. Table 8-4 shows the amount of the various federal securities outstanding, as well as each one's share of the total.

The level of the public debt can be found by adding all the deficits of past years and then subtracting all past surpluses from that amount. Thus, the effect of a budget deficit is to increase the public debt, while a budget surplus decreases the debt.

The public debt can be viewed in two ways. First, the *gross* public debt is the total amount of money the federal government borrowed from all sources. However, around a fourth of such borrowing is from various government agencies and branches, such as the Federal Reserve Banks and the Social Security Administration. Second, economists focus on the *net* public debt, which counts only the debt held by private individuals and firms.

The public debt is largely an internal debt, which means Americans owe the debt largely to other Americans. However, two points must be made here. First, only some Americans own the debt (that is, they hold bonds), so paying it off would require a substantial adjustment in individual financial positions. Money would flow from those without bonds to those with bonds. Second, the debt is more of an external debt than it used to be. That means Americans owe a growing share of it to foreigners.

U.S. Deficits, Surpluses, and the Public Debt

Figure 8-3 shows U.S. budget deficits and surpluses since 1970. Figure 8-4 indicates that as deficits rose sharply since the mid-1970s, the public debt rose, too. If the U.S. budget surpluses, which started in 1998, continue throughout the first decade of the 21st century, the public debt could fall substantially. However, changes in the state of the economy and any tax cuts could alter the picture substantially.

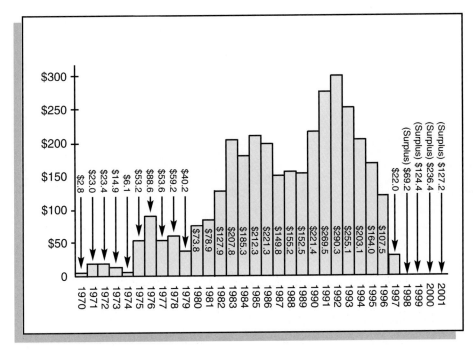

Figure 8-3

Federal Budget Deficits Since 1970

From very low levels extending from the 1950s to the early 1970s, deficits began to grow substantially in the mid-1970s. They began to decline in the 1990s, partly due to budget-reduction actions of increased taxes and reduced spending. In 1998 and after, the federal government experienced budget surpluses.

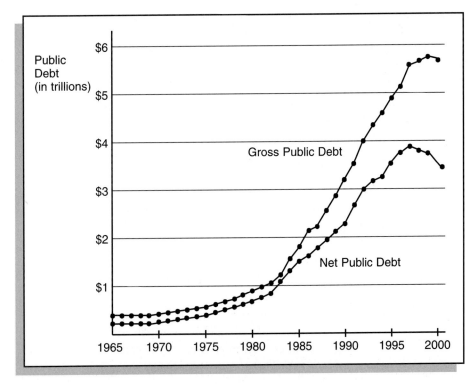

Figure 8-4

The Public Debt Since 1965

The top graph shows the gross federal (public) debt. Some of that debt is held by government agencies.

The bottom graph shows the net public debt.

Table 8-5

Ownership of the Gross
Public Debt, 2000

Holders of Securities	Amount (billions)	Percent of Total
U.S. Government Agencies and Trust Funds	$2,270.2	40.1%
Federal Reserve Banks	$511.7	9.0%
State and Local Governments	$246.2	4.3%
Savings Bond Holders	$184.8	3.3%
Depository Institutions	$197.8	3.5%
Mutual Funds	$339.0	6.0%
Insurance Companies	$116.6	2.1%
Pension Funds	$376.2	6.6%
Foreigners	$1,201.4	21.2%
Miscellaneous	$218.3	3.9%
Total	**$5,662.2**	**100.0%**

Source: *Federal Reserve Bulletin,* January 2002

Table 8-5 shows the status of the gross public debt in 1998 and who owned that debt—that is, who held those securities. It is now over $5 trillion, which means each U.S. citizen's share of it is over $20,000.

THE SIZE OF GOVERNMENT

No one doubts that government plays a major role in the economy. In this section, several ways to measure that role and then the actual data on government activity in recent periods will be presented.

How the Size of Government Is Measured

Three common measures of the size of government are: 1) the number of government employees; 2) the amount of spending the government does (this may include transfer payments); and 3) the amount of taxes the government collects.

However, such measures can be misleading if the size of government is compared over long periods. The population grows over time, along with living standards, prices, and several other important variables. Obviously, the various measures of government grow along with these other variables. This point tends to be misunderstood by people who complain that government has grown too much.

To avoid this misleading interpretation, the three measures of government are viewed in two ways: the absolute approach and the relative approach. Absolute measures of government include: 1) the *number* of government employees; and 2) the *dollar amounts* of either spending or taxes.

Year	Civilian Employees (in thousands)			Percent of Total Civilian Employment		
	Federal	State & Local	Combined	Federal	State & Local	Combined
1950	2,117	4,285	6,402	3.6%	7.3%	10.9%
1960	2,421	6,387	8,808	3.7%	9.7%	13.4%
1970	2,881	10,147	13,028	3.7%	12.9%	16.6%
1980	2,898	13,315	16,213	2.9%	13.4%	16.3%
1985	3,021	13,669	16,690	2.8%	12.8%	15.6%
1990	3,105	15,263	18,368	2.6%	12.9%	15.5%
1999	2,799	17,506	20,306	2.0%	12.6%	14.6%

Table 8-6

Government Employment

The number of employees is an absolute measure of the size of government.

The percent of total employment is a relative measure of the size of government.

Source: *The Statistical Abstract of the United States,* 2001

Relative measures of government include: 1) the *share* of the work force working for the government; and 2) government spending and taxes as a *share* of some measure of the nation's income, such as the GDP (gross domestic product). These relative measures help determine if the government is getting "out of balance" with other sectors of the economy.

Table 8-6 shows both absolute and relative measures of all civilian government employment. The number of employees (including part-timers) gives an absolute measure, and the percentage of total employment gives a relative measure.

Government Spending and Taxes

The next few tables and charts combine the other two methods of measuring government's size—spending and taxes. Figure 8-5 shows a trend of increased involvement in the economy by the federal government since 1960, when total outlays were around 18 percent of GDP. Total outlays increased to around 22 to 24 percent of GDP by the 1980s. In contrast, in the late 1920s the figure was only three percent.

The line for total receipts shows they have stayed between 18 and 20 percent since the early 1960s. Using this measure of government, one might conclude that the government has not grown since the 1960s. However, a better measure of the government's importance in the economy is what it is *spending* (basically, how much of society's resources it impacts). It can increase its spending with the same total receipts by borrowing. The divergence of the two lines on the chart indeed implies growing budget deficits, especially since the 1970s.

Figure 8-5

Federal Government
Outlays and Receipts as
a Percent of GDP

Receipts as a share of
GDP changed little in
the last four decades.
However, outlays grew
as a share of GDP.
Consequently,
federal deficits grew in
that period, as indicated
by a divergence of the two
graphs since 1960.

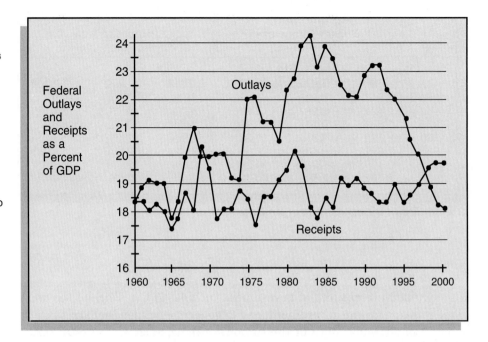

Table 8-7, showing total outlays, also considers state and local spending as well as federal spending since 1929. The left side of the table gives dollar amounts of spending—an absolute measure. The right side gives spending as percentages of GDP—a relative measure of government's size.

Table 8-7

Total Outlays of the
Federal, State and Local,
and All Governments
Combined

In addition to an absolute
growth in government
(dollars spent), all
governments are taking a
larger share of the nation's
income than earlier. That
is, the public sector has
grown relative to the rest
of the economy.

	Total Outlays (in billions)			Total Outlays as a Percent of GDP		
Year	Federal	State & Local	All Governments	Federal	State & Local	All Governments
1929	$2.7	$7.8	$10.3	2.6%	7.5%	9.9%
1940	$10.0	$9.3	$18.5	10.0%	9.3%	18.4%
1950	$41.2	$22.5	$61.4	14.3%	7.8%	21.3%
1960	$93.9	$49.9	$137.3	18.2%	9.7%	26.6%
1970	$207.8	$134.0	$317.4	20.6%	13.2%	31.3%
1980	$615.1	$432.3	$1047.4	22.6%	15.8%	38.3%
1985	$984.9	$656.2	$1641.1	24.0%	16.4%	41.0%
1990	$1270.1	$972.7	$2242.8	22.5%	17.6%	40.6%
1991	$1323.0	$1059.8	$2382.8	23.3%	18.5%	41.3%
1992	$1380.7	$1146.6	$2527.3	23.2%	19.1%	41.8%
1993	$1408.7	$1207.1	$2615.8	22.8%	18.4%	40.7%
1994	$1460.9	$1331.4	$2792.3	22.0%	18.9%	40.9%
1995	$1515.8	$1347.8	$2863.6	20.5%	18.2%	38.7%
1996	$1560.6	$1393.7	$2954.3	20.0%	17.8%	37.8%

Source: *The Statistical Abstract of the United States,* 1999

(The columns for all governments combined do not add up to the columns of the federal plus the state and local combination. This is because federal grants-in-aid money sent to states is excluded from total spending so that the money is not counted twice.)

The table shows some interesting points. Notice the figure for federal spending in 1929, $2.7 billion. That figure, which covered an entire *year* in 1929, was less than the amount that the United States spent *each day* in 1996. Of course, because of inflation's effect on the dollar's purchasing power, these dollars were not the same. Still, the increase is extraordinarily large. The United States now spends around $48,000 *every second*. In George Washington's administration, it took 12 *days* to spend the same amount.

Second, notice that until the 1930s the federal government spent less money than all state and local governments combined. The current federal dominance does not show any sign of reversing.

The second to the last column in Table 8-7 reveals the percentage of GDP spent by all governments combined. This figure rose from 9.9 percent in 1929 to more than 30 percent today. More than any other measure of government's size, this column shows why government takes a much larger "bite" from paychecks today than in the past.

The Federal Budget

Table 8-8 divides total outlays of the United States into 18 categories or "functions." Congress acts upon most of these functions separately when formulating the budget for the fiscal year, which extends from October 1 to September 30. For example, Congress acts on separate transportation and defense budget bills. There are 13 such bills in all. The president initially proposes the budget to Congress around February 1, giving Congress until October 1 to pass it for the president's signature. Occasionally this deadline is missed.

National defense recently surrendered its hold on first place in federal spending to Social Security/Medicare. The third largest item, interest on the national debt, grew rapidly in recent years. This was due to the rapid escalation in the public debt, coupled with relatively high interest rates in the 1970s and 1980s. The last major item in the budget is income security. This includes federal employee retirement programs, housing and food assistance for the poor, and unemployment compensation.

Table 8-8

Federal Budget,
Fiscal Year 2002

Social Security, Medicare,
income security, and
national defense, the
largest items in the
budget, comprise nearly
half of the federal budget.
As defense has declined
as a share of the budget
over recent years, interest
on the national debt has
taken a larger share.

Function	Amount (billions)	Percent of Total Outlays
National Defense	$348.0	17.1%
International Affairs	$23.5	1.2%
Income Security	$310.7	15.2%
Health	$195.2	9.6%
Social Security	$459.7	22.5%
Medicare	$226.4	11.0%
Veterans Benefits and Services	$51.5	2.6%
Education, Employment, and Social Services	$71.7	2.9%
Commerce and Housing Credit	$10.7	0.5%
Transportation	$61.2	3.0%
Natural Resources and Environment	$30.2	1.5%
Energy	(–)$0.6	0.0%
Community and Regional Development	$15.4	0.8%
Agriculture	$28.8	1.4%
Interest on the National Debt	$178.4	8.7%
Science, Space, and Technology	$21.8	1.1%
General Government	$18.3	0.9%
Administration of Justice	$34.4	1.7%
Offsetting Receipts	(–)$34.2	(–)1.7%
Total Outlays	**$2,052.3**	**100.0%**
Total Receipts	**$1,946.1**	
Deficit	**(–) $106.2**	

Table 8-9

Expenditures of State
Governments in 1998

Education dominates
spending by state
government, with public
welfare spending being
the next largest.

Function or Purpose	Amount (billions)	Percent of General Expenditures
Education	$294.8	35.6%
Public Welfare	$207.9	25.1%
Highways	$63.6	7.7%
Health and Hospitals	$64.0	7.7%
Corrections	$30.6	3.7%
Natural Resources	$13.5	1.6%
Police Protection	$8.0	1.0%
Housing & Community Development	$4.0	0.5%
Other	$141.1	17.1%
Total (General Expenditure)	**$827.7**	**100.0%**

Source: *The Statistical Abstract of the United States,* 2000

State and Local Government Budgets

Federal and state governments are involved in quite different areas of the economy. Generally, the major concern of states is education. Table 8-9 shows that over a third of state spending goes toward education, with public welfare holding second place at about a fifth of total outlays. Highways, health, and hospitals are other major areas of spending by states.

WHO SHOULD PAY THE TAXES?

After citizens decide that their government should spend money to solve economic problems, they must decide how much of the total outlays each person should pay. This section introduces some major factors in that decision.

Principles of Taxation

One way to decide each person's tax is to divide the budget by the population served by that government. That amount is what each person would owe, even children and retired people. For example, the roughly $1,800 billion federal budget would be spread evenly over roughly 270 million Americans—about $6,700 a person. Obviously, no one would suggest such a system, and governments actually charge each person a *different* level of taxes. To do this, a government must establish taxes that are based on specified ways that people differ from each other. Such a basis is called a taxing principle.

Characteristics in which people differ include age, income, value of real estate owned, amount of spending per year, number of children, how often they use government services, and the amount of money they give to charity. These characteristics are used in one or the other of the two most common taxing principles: 1) the benefits-received principle; and 2) the ability-to-pay principle.

■ The first taxing principle is the **benefits-received principle**. With this principle, the more services (benefits) one receives from the government, the more one must pay in taxes, regardless of income, wealth, or age. This is how people pay for goods and services purchased from private businesses. For example, everyone pays the same price for a loaf of bread, whether poor or rich, young or old.

The **benefits-received principle** is the taxing philosophy stating that if people receive more benefits from government services, they should pay more in taxes.

User fees are based on this principle, and some examples are: bridge tolls; tuition (the more classes one takes, the more one pays); stamps (the

THINKING CRITICALLY ABOUT
ECONOMIC QUESTIONS IN OUR LIVES

Why Not Tax People on Their Ability to *Earn*?

Things to Consider

1. The ability-to-pay taxing principle (used in the income tax, for example), has some strong disadvantages. What might they be?

2. These would be largely eliminated if we taxed people on their ability to *earn* (to earn income, that is). This ability could be indicated by their education, IQ scores, occupation, and so on.

3. What are some advantages and disadvantages of this proposed principle?

   See page 465 for the answer.

---

more letters one sends, the more postage one pays); and the gasoline tax (the more one uses the roads, the more gasoline one buys and taxes one pays).

■ Alternatively, taxes could be levied (charged) with the **ability-to-pay principle**. Then people who are more "able to pay" taxes would pay more than those who are less able. However, how is "ability to pay" determined?

It could be indicated by one's income. The more one earns, the more taxes one should be able to pay. Or wealth could indicate that ability, or some part of one's wealth, such as the value of real estate. Of course, governments use both of these—income in the income tax and wealth in the property tax. Governments also use other factors to determine ability to pay and, in turn, to adjust taxes of certain people. The number of one's dependents, for example, influences one's income tax payments.

> The **ability-to-pay principle** is the taxing philosophy stating that the more a person is able to pay taxes, as evidenced by income or wealth, the more taxes that person should pay.

Establishing an Equitable Tax System

Equity in taxation, meaning the fairness in the way taxes are levied, is an important objective of tax-bill writers. Their goal is a tax system that treats all taxpayers equally (equitably). A tax has horizontal equity when taxpayers in the same general economic situation (income, wealth, needs) pay about the same amount in taxes. A tax achieves vertical equity when taxpayers in higher economic positions pay more taxes.

But when a government tries to determine *what* to equalize, it runs into a problem. There are three major items or tax-payment criteria that tax-bill writers could equalize: 1) the number of dollars paid in taxes; 2) the percentage of income paid in taxes; and 3) the cost or burden of paying taxes. The problem is that it is impossible to equalize more than one of these at a time with any tax.

Figure 8-6 illustrates the impossibility of satisfying every taxpayer. One taxpayer earns $10,000 per year, while another earns $60,000 per year. Suppose the tax considered is the income tax. A different tax-payment criterion is equalized in each of three cases.

THINKING CRITICALLY ABOUT ECONOMIC QUESTIONS IN OUR LIVES

Why Aren't People Who Cheat on Their Taxes Money Ahead?

Things to Consider

1. People who underreport their incomes to the IRS (such as some small business owners or those receiving income from tips) show lower taxable incomes on their returns because they cheat, thereby reducing their income tax payments.

2. You would expect that their spendable income (or income after taxes) would be higher as a consequence. Over the long run, however, it is not. Theoretically, at least, their spendable incomes are about the same whether they cheat or not.

3. Explain this paradox, noting under what conditions this would occur.

   See page 467 for the answer.

■ In the first case, each taxpayer pays the same dollar amount, $2,000. The blue boxes beside the $2,000, connected by dotted lines, show this equality graphically. Such a tax system satisfies people who believe that if everyone gets the same amount of goods and services from the government, everyone should pay the same number of tax dollars (in other words, the benefits-received principle).

However, the poorer person pays 20 percent of income in taxes, while the other person pays only 3.3 percent, indicated by the difference in box sizes. Also, there is a difference in the cost or burden of paying taxes—the *opportunity* cost, that is. That burden is found by asking how each taxpayer *would have* spent the money if the taxes did *not* have to be paid. A poor person would obviously use the money to buy $2,000 worth of food, shelter, clothing, and the like—necessities. A typical person earning $60,000 would already have life's basic needs covered, so that person could spend the $2,000 on some luxuries, perhaps a summer vacation. According to the law of diminishing marginal utility of income, $2,000 of luxuries give less satisfaction than $2,000 of necessities. (This law is essentially an extension of the law of diminishing marginal utility covered in Chapter 14, page 408.) Thus, the box size for the taxpayer with a $60,000 income is smaller.

■ The second case satisfies those who believe that everyone should pay an equal percentage of income in taxes. Such a tax is commonly called a flat tax (because the *rate* is constant or "flat"). If the poorer taxpayer still pays $2,000 in taxes, or 20 percent of income, the $60,000-income taxpayer needs a tax bill of $12,000 to have a similar 20 percent rate. The dotted lines between the boxes, which signify equality, shift down to the middle set of boxes, shaded blue. But now the top set must be unequal. Now those people who want to equalize *taxes paid* will be unhappy. The bottom set also is still unequal. That's because although $12,000 involves more lost satisfaction than $2,000, it still comes from luxuries, and it still falls short of the benefits provided by $2,000 of necessities.

■ In the last case, these costs or burdens of paying taxes are finally equalized. The $18,000 in taxes cut so deeply into the middle-class taxpayer's "luxury budget" that this person finally gives up as much satisfaction as the poor person who gives up $2,000 of necessities. Thus, the last set of boxes, shaded blue, is equal. The $18,000 paid by the middle-class taxpayer results in a 30 percent tax rate. But now both the people who want an equal tax *rate* and those who want equal tax *payments* are unhappy. (In reality, finding such points of "equal burden" is impossibly difficult. Measuring the forgone benefits of each taxpayer cannot be done accurately, as such benefits are subjective. Yet, it is the source of much ill feeling between income classes and political groups.)

Tax-Payment Criteria	Taxpayer With an Income of $10,000	Taxpayer With an Income of $60,000
Taxes Paid	$2,000	$2,000
Percent of Income Paid in Taxes	20%	3.3%
The Cost or the Burden of Taxes	Necessities Forgone	Some Luxuries Forgone
Taxes Paid	$2,000	$12,000
Percent of Income Paid in Taxes	**20%**	**20%**
The Cost or the Burden of Taxes	Necessities Forgone	More Luxuries Forgone
Taxes Paid	$2,000	$18,000
Percent of Income Paid in Taxes	20%	30%
The Cost or the Burden of Taxes	**Necessities Forgone**	**Many Luxuries Forgone**

Figure 8-6

Equity in Taxation

Equity, (or fairness) in taxation is usually associated with the equal treatment of taxpayers. The problem is that there are several criteria with respect to taxes that we could equalize: 1) the dollar amounts paid in taxes; 2) the percent of income paid in taxes; and 3) the cost or burden of paying taxes.

Two taxpayers with different incomes, $10,000 and $60,000, are compared. Three tax-payment criteria that are used to establish tax equity or fairness are considered. In each case, the criterion that is equalized is shown in bold blue print.

In the first case, each pays the same dollar amount in taxes.

In the second case, the percentages of income paid by both are equal.

In the last case, each gives up the same benefits from other goods and services when paying their taxes. Thus, their costs (or "burdens") of paying taxes are the same.

In each case, measures of the two alternative criteria cannot be equalized, showing the difficulty of satisfying everyone on the issue of the fairness of taxes.

A **regressive tax** is one that takes a smaller percentage of the incomes of higher-income taxpayers than from those with lower incomes.

A **proportional tax** is one in which every taxpayer pays the same percentage of income into the tax.

A **progressive tax** is one that takes a higher percentage of the incomes of higher-income taxpayers than from those with lower incomes.

With such different viewpoints on what is fair, it's no wonder many people say taxes are "unfair." Further, because such viewpoints are value judgments, everyone is right—even though they disagree.

A common way of determining the fairness of a tax is to determine if it is regressive, proportional, or progressive. With a **regressive tax**, the percent of income paid in taxes decreases (regresses) as income rises. That is, poorer people pay a higher percentage of their incomes in taxes than richer people. A **proportional tax** takes the same percentage or proportion of everyone's income. A **progressive tax** takes a larger percentage of the incomes of higher-income taxpayers.

Figure 8-7 illustrates these three types of taxes. Consider two taxpayers, with incomes of $10,000 and $30,000. The figures below the diagrams give an example of each of the three types of taxes. In the first case,

Figure 8-7

Regressive, Proportional, and Progressive Taxes

Jones and Smith face a regressive, proportional, or progressive tax if Smith pays a smaller, an equal, or a greater percent of income in taxes than Jones, respectively.

	Regressive Tax		Proportional Tax		Progressive Tax	
	Jones	Smith	Jones	Smith	Jones	Smith
Income	$10,000	$30,000	$10,000	$30,000	$10,000	$30,000
Taxes Paid	$ 2,000	$ 3,000	$ 2,000	$ 6,000	$ 2,000	$ 9,000
Taxes as a Percent of Income	20%	10%	20%	20%	20%	30%

showing a regressive tax, the percentage of income paid in taxes drops from 20 percent for the poorer taxpayer, Jones, to 10 percent for Smith, who earns $30,000. In the case of a proportional tax, both Jones and Smith pay 20 percent of their income in taxes, but Smith pays triple the *amount* in taxes. With the progressive tax, Smith finally pays more in percentage of income paid in taxes as well as dollar amounts.

User fees and excise taxes are usually regressive because rich people generally don't pay much more in *dollar amounts* for such taxes than lower income groups. A general sales tax, which covers most items purchased, is also regressive. Even though everyone pays the same percentage of the *purchase price* in sales taxes, the percentage of *income* taken by the tax falls as income rises. That is because poor people usually spend all or most of their incomes, but people with higher incomes save some of theirs. Thus, they avoid sales taxes on that part of their incomes that is not spent. To deal with this regressiveness problem, many states have selective sales taxes, which do not tax food and other necessities. This makes the tax less regressive because now a large part of a poor person's income (the part used to buy necessities) is not taxed.

The only specific tax that is proportional is the FICA tax, which supports Social Security and Medicare. Yet it is only proportional up to a certain level of income—$84,900 for 2002. The tax rate for support of the retirement fund (which people know as "Social Security") plus the disability income fund is 6.20 percent. No one pays that tax on any income in excess of the maximum listed. However, the Medicare tax rate is 1.45 percent of wages, with no upper limit on income levels. Essentially, then, the FICA tax becomes regressive at income levels that are higher than these maximum taxed levels.

The federal income tax is the best example of a progressive tax. Table 8-10 shows some interesting income tax data. The first column divides taxpayers into various income categories, based on adjusted gross income (equal to gross income minus "adjustments to income," to be addressed below). The second column shows that the percent of income paid climbs as people get richer, indicating that the tax is progressive. The third column shows the dollar amount paid by the average taxpayer in each income group.

Although news stories abound about millionaires who don't pay any taxes, the *average* millionaire paid almost $800,000 in taxes in 1994. (Incidentally, the average millionaire earns much *more* than a million dollars—somewhere between two and three million.) The second-to-last column shows how much of the total taxes collected from all groups was paid by each group. Compare those figures with the last column, which shows the share of all tax returns (for returns on which taxes were actually paid) filed by each group. For example, taxpayers with incomes between $50,000 and $74,999 constituted 11.44 percent of all taxpayers, but they paid 18.30 percent of all income taxes collected. In 1994, the top five percent of taxpayers (who earn 27.8 percent of the nation's total adjusted gross income) paid 47.3 percent of all income taxes.

Table 8-10

Payment of Federal
Income Taxes by Income
Class, 1994

The second column shows
that the income tax is
progressive. The last two
columns show, for any
income class, the
percentage of all the
income taxes collected
that was paid by what
percent of the tax-paying
population.

Income Class (as measured by adjusted gross income)	Taxes as a Percent of Adjusted Gross Income	Average Taxes Paid per Taxpayer	Combined Taxes Paid by All Taxpayers in Income Class (billions)	Percent of Total Tax Receipts Paid by Income Class	Percent of All Tax Returns Filed by Income Class
Less than $1,000	3.3%	$27	$0.01	0.003%	2.06%
$1,000-$2,999	4.6%	$88	$0.1	0.03%	5.55%
$3,000-$4,999	2.9%	$118	$0.2	0.04%	5.11%
$5,000-$6,999	4.3%	$263	$0.4	0.08%	4.85%
$7,000-$8,999	3.7%	$298	$1.0	0.19%	5.07%
$9,000-$10,999	5.4%	$540	$1.7	0.31%	4.79%
$11,000-$12,999	6.2%	$743	$2.4	0.46%	4.71%
$13,000-$14,999	6.4%	$897	$3.2	0.61%	4.68%
$15,000-$16,999	7.5%	$1,201	$4.0	0.76%	4.32%
$17,000-$18,999	7.4%	$1,333	$4.3	0.81%	3.74%
$19,000-$21,999	7.6%	$1,559	$8.7	1.63%	5.47%
$22,000-$24,999	8.1%	$1,896	$10.1	1.90%	4.81%
$25,000-$29,999	8.8%	$2,423	$19.4	3.65%	7.06%
$30,000-$39,999	10.1%	$3,510	$41.9	7.88%	10.44%
$40,000-$49,999	10.8%	$4,849	$43.6	8.19%	7.84%
$50,000-$74,999	12.2%	$7,398	$97.4	18.30%	11.44%
$75,000-$99,999	15.1%	$12,916	$61.7	11.58%	4.15%
$100,000-$199,999	18.6%	$24,354	$82.8	15.55%	2.96%
$200,000-$499,999	25.8%	$72,214	$65.3	12.26%	0.76%
$500,000-$999,999	30.5%	$205,107	$30.3	5.70%	0.13%
$1,000,000 or more	31.7%	$787,994	$53.6	10.07%	0.06%
			$532.2	100.0%	100.0%

Source: *Statistics of Income Bulletin,* Summer 1996, Internal Revenue Service

THE FEDERAL INCOME TAX

The federal income tax is the largest single tax, and this section
briefly outlines its history and structure.

History of the Income Tax

The federal income tax first appeared with the Revenue Act of 1861,
when money was needed for the Civil War. Amended in 1862, it taxed
incomes between $600 and $10,000 at three percent, and higher incomes at
five percent. It ended in 1872 as revenue needs dropped.

Congress enacted another income tax in 1894, but the Supreme Court declared it unconstitutional because it was not apportioned according to the population in each state. However, the idea survived, and in 1913 the 16th amendment to the Constitution led to the enactment of the modern income tax, which began in 1916. However, its early effect was negligible, for by 1918 only five percent of income earners paid any income tax. The number of taxpayers rose from four million to 43 million during World War II. Withholding of taxes by employers began in 1943 to ensure payment of a growing tax liability.

The income tax, especially tax rates, changed significantly in the last several decades. The Economic Recovery Tax Act of 1981 was designed to stimulate economic growth through major cuts in tax rates. The Tax Reform Act of 1986 had two primary goals: 1) a tax that was much less complicated to calculate; and 2) substantial rate cuts that would encourage economic activity—especially entrepreneurial activity. The Tax Reform Act of 1993 substantially raised taxes on upper-income earners by creating two new income tax brackets (see below for an explanation of tax brackets). The Economic Growth and Tax Reconciliation Act of 2001 gave most taxpayers a rebate check in 2001 and also reduced tax rates on most taxpayers.

Structure of the Income Tax

Although our economy has an income tax, only a part of one's income is taxed, and that amount is called taxable income. To arrive at taxable income, one must first subtract from total income any "adjustments to income" (such as alimony payments, IRA contributions, moving expenses, and penalties for early withdrawal of savings from a CD) to get adjusted gross income. (See IRS Form 1040 for more specifics.)

Next, **deductions** are subtracted from this figure. Deductions can be determined in one of two ways: 1) using the standard deduction; or 2) itemizing deductions. Most people take the standard deduction, which for 2001 was $7,600 for a married couple and $4,550 for a single taxpayer. Other people itemize deductions if they can exceed the standard figure. This involves adding up a long series of items, including state and local taxes (excluding sales taxes), charitable contributions, medical expenses, casualty and theft losses, and interest on a home mortgage or home-equity loan.

A **deduction** is an amount of income on which you do not have to pay federal income taxes, often tied to a specific reason.

Finally, **exemptions** are subtracted. One exemption is given for each taxpayer and for each of the taxpayer's dependents. Exemptions rise each year, based upon the inflation rate. For 2001 they were $2,900. After the exemptions are subtracted, the remainder is taxable income.

An **exemption** is an amount of income for each dependent on which federal income taxes are not paid.

The **marginal tax rate** is the percent of federal income taxes paid on an extra dollar of earned income.

To ensure that the income tax is progressive, taxable income is not all taxed at the same rate. Taxable income is divided into categories, called brackets. Each bracket has its own tax rate, and higher brackets (those "holding" your higher levels of income) have higher rates. The **marginal tax rate** is the percent of an extra dollar earned that one would then pay in taxes. When people say they are "in" a certain tax bracket, they are referring to the marginal tax rate. Do not confuse this rate with the *average tax rate,* which is the percentage of *all* income earned, on average, that is paid in taxes. This is found by dividing income taxes paid by total income and expressing it as a percentage.

There are currently five income tax brackets. The tax rates on income in those brackets are 15, 27.5, 30.5, 35.5, and 39.1 percent. The two highest rates were added in 1993. The rates for the top four brackets were reduced in 2001. Table 8-11 shows how these brackets are applied to two of the four categories of income tax filers: 1) single; and 2) married filing jointly.

Table 8-11

Federal Income Tax Brackets for 2001

To find how much taxes one owed in 2001, first locate the filing status. Next, use the taxable income (from line 39, Form 1040) to come up with the tax bill.

Schedule X–Use if your filing status is **Single**

If the amount on Form 1040, line 39, is: Over–	But not over–	Enter on Form 1040, line 40	of the amount over–
$0	$27,050	_ _ _ _ 15%	$0
$27,050	$65,550	$4,057.50 + 27.5%	$27,050
$65,550	$136,750	$14,645.00 + 30.5%	$65,550
$136,750	$297,350	$36,361.00 + 35.5%	$136,750
$287.350	_ _ _ _	$93,374.00 + 39.1%	$297,350

Schedule Y-1–Use if your filing status is **Married filing jointly** or **Qualifying widow(er)**

If the amount on Form 1040, line 39, is: Over–	But not over–	Enter on Form 1040, line 40	of the amount over–
$0	$45,200	_ _ _ _ 15%	$0
$45,200	$109,250	$6,780.00 + 27.5%	$45,200
$109,250	$166,500	$24,393.75 + 30.5%	$109,250
$166,500	$297,350	$41,855.00 + 35.5%	$166,500
$297,350	_ _ _ _	$88,306.75 + 39.1%	$297,350

SUMMARY

In addition to resource misallocation in the private sector, governments sometimes use resources unwisely. Public choice theory explains how such resource misallocation occurs in the public sector. Much of the problem is that voters and government officals make decisions in the public sector that are in their self-interests, which doesn't necessarily coincide with the interests of society as a whole.

Governments spend money in order to purchase goods and services for their citizens, as well as to transfer wealth and income between their citizens. Governments get money from taxes, earnings, other governments, and borrowing. A budget deficit means that total outlays exceed total receipts, and vice versa for a budget surplus. A government goes into debt when it borrows money to finance a deficit. The U.S. Government ran very large deficits during much of the 1970s and 1980s.

The size of a government can be measured either: 1) absolutely, or in dollar terms; or 2) relatively, or in percentage terms when compared with another figure, such as the GDP. There has been substantial growth in both such measures for virtually all governments since the 1930s.

The benefits-received and the ability-to-pay principles are used to determine who should pay for government expenditures. A major goal in setting taxes is to achieve horizontal and vertical equity. Tax-bill writers attempt to achieve equity in taxation by equalizing: 1) the dollar amount of taxes paid; 2) the percentage of income paid in taxes; or 3) the burden of paying taxes. A progressive tax is one that taxes those with higher incomes at a higher tax rate than those with lower incomes. Alternatively, a regressive tax takes a larger share of a poor person's income. A proportional tax takes the same share of everyone's income.

The income tax is a progressive tax. After subtracting their exemptions and deductions, people pay different tax rates for different categories or brackets of their income. Income in higher brackets is taxed at higher rates. The 1986 Tax Reform Act was designed to introduce more fairness to the system by eliminating or reducing many tax breaks. Tax rates for taxpayers with higher incomes were raised in 1993.

QUESTIONS FOR DISCUSSION AND THOUGHT

1. List 10 things governments purchase today that they did not buy 50 years ago. Considering such purchases, were the "old days" better or worse?

2. What are five examples of user fees in your community?

3. What is your share of the national debt? If you have savings bonds in excess of that, are you still in debt to the other bondholders? Explain your answer.

4. Ask several people if taxpayers should: 1) pay equal amounts of taxes; 2) pay equal percentages of income paid in taxes; or 3) have equal burdens when paying taxes. If you note a connection with their answers and their economic position, can you explain the connection?

5. Is the income tax fairer since the two new brackets were added in 1993? Why or why not?

6. Why does the IRS give a tax exemption for children, but not for boats? After all, whether you choose to have a child or get a boat, you have less money left to buy other things. That is, your "ability to pay" taxes (or to pay for anything else) is lower. Because the government says your ability to pay (taxes) is lower for each child you have, you should have to pay less in income taxes. Why doesn't it do the same for people who choose to get satisfaction, not from children, but from boats? In essence, the government discriminates in favor of people who have children. Why? What makes children a "better way to use money" than boats? Is it to encourage items having external benefits, which is a main reason why governments subsidize things? Or is there some other reason?

7. Do you believe the government should give transfer payments to the poor? If you think so, why? And which poor people? Those living on the east side of the Pacific Ocean, or the west side? In general, the poor on the west side (in China, the Philippines, Laos) are poorer than on the east side. If you chose the east side (those living in California or Oregon), why do you discriminate in favor of the "rich" (or the not-as-poor)? Do you personally know any poor people in either of these two groups? If not, what justifies your discrimination?

PROBLEMS   See pages 486-487 for the answers.

1. The following information is for the federal government for a year's period. It purchases $860 billion of goods and services. It earns $58 billion from fees, and it collects $914 billion in taxes. It distributes $326 billion in transfer payments. How many bonds does it need it sell?

2. At the beginning of a certain year, the public debt was $4,760 billion. In that year, the federal govenment had $1,680 billion in total outlays and $1,520 billion in total receipts. Also, in that year, $88 billion of bonds were redeemed (cashed in). How many bonds did the Treasury have to sell by the end of the year?

3. Suppose the gross public debt is $4,920 billion. If the Federal Reserve System holds $480 billion of it, U.S. Government agencies hold $210 billion, and other governments hold $620 billion, how large is the net public debt?

4. Bill and Bob own houses in Darian. Bill's house is valued at $220,000 and Bob's at $110,000. Bill's income is $90,000 and Bob's is $42,000. Bill's property tax is $4,200 and Bob's is $2,100. On the basis of just these two taxpayers, is the property tax regressive, proportional, or progressive? Why would it be difficult to say for certain which it is for Darian as a whole?

5. A certain state has a selective sales tax of six percent. People who earn $10,000 of net income spend, on average, $9,500, of which 60 of their purchases are not subject to the sales tax. People who earn $60,000 spend, on average, $48,000, of which 40 percent is not subject to the sales tax. The intent of making a sales tax selective is to make it less regressive (or even progressive). Did this state succeed? How can you tell? Hint: Calculate the percent of net income that both groups pay in sales taxes under two assumptions: a) that some of their purchases are not taxed (which is the case above); b) that all of their purchases would be subject to the sales tax (in other words, it now a *general* sales tax).

9 INTRODUCTION TO THE MACROECONOMY

CHAPTER PREVIEW

The macroeconomy deals with the economy from a different perspective than has been used so far. It covers variables and concepts such as gross domestic product or total output, the labor force, the overall price level, and the inflation rate.

Essentially, macroeconomics allows us to see how successful we are in solving our economic problem that is caused by resource scarcity. We then seek to establish policies to improve the macroeconomy, usually through government action.

CHAPTER OBJECTIVES

After completing this chapter, you should be able to:

◆ *Explain how GDP is calculated and what factors influence its size.*

◆ *Calculate the inflation rate by using a price index.*

◆ *Differentiate between current GDP and real GDP.*

◆ *Calculate real GDP by using a price index.*

◆ *Calculate the unemployment rate.*

◆ *Compare and contrast the three categories of unemployment.*

No economy can provide its citizens with all the goods and services they want because resources are scarce. You learned concepts that explain how individual consumers, firms, or government agencies deal with scarcity. That part of economic theory, called microeconomics, concerns small sectors or individual units of the economy (firms, consumers, laborers, and so on). Microeconomics studies such things as how consumers maximize satisfaction, how firms maximize profits, how society should use public resources, how the price of a particular product is determined, and how worker productivity in a factory increases.

The next five chapters show how society deals with scarcity in a larger sense. This subject, called macroeconomics, studies large (macro) sectors of the economy and their relation to the nation's economic goals and the condition of resource scarcity.

MACROECONOMIC GOALS

There are three primary macroeconomic goals: 1) full employment; 2) price stability; and 3) economic growth.

■ If full employment is not achieved, it is as if labor resources were even more scarce than they already are (because some who want to work don't) or were used inefficiently. Thus, living standards would be lower. Full employment also leads to fewer social problems, such as crime and poverty.

■ Price stability means there is no or little inflation or deflation (where prices fall). When future prices are known, businesses are more willing to invest in capital equipment and innovations that will pay off in the future. Also, the purchasing power of incomes will not erode if prices are stable.

■ Economic growth, meaning an increase in the nation's total output of goods and services, allows living standards to grow. It occurs in various ways, including an increase in resource productivity and the development of new resources.

THE MEANING OF MACROECONOMICS

Much of the news about economics deals with macroeconomic topics: unemployment, recession, inflation, interest rates, economic growth, tax policy, fiscal policy, and monetary policy. These topics deal with macroeconomic variables. This chapter introduces most of these variables. Chapter 10 introduces others, which are associated with money. Chapters 11-13 focus on two aspects of such economic variables: 1) the relationships between the variables; and 2) how the government tries to influence these variables. As is always the purpose in economics, macroeconomics is studied to find out why the economy is not providing the greatest economic welfare, given the available resources—and then to make certain that it does.

An Introduction to Some Macroeconomic Variables

As a brief overview of this chapter, this section introduces some major macroeconomic variables (noted in italics). The *total output* of goods and services refers to the combined yearly output of all business firms and government enterprises. *Gross domestic product* is an indirect measure of that output. The *standard of living* refers to the output of goods and services available for each person, on average. The *economic growth rate* measures how fast the output of goods and services grows. *Total spending* or *aggregate demand* deals with the demand for output. The *inflation rate* measures price increases. Also covered are some labor statistics, such as the *labor force,* the *unemployment rate,* and *labor productivity*.

GROSS DOMESTIC PRODUCT

People always seem to be measuring things: their blood pressure, weight, income, and so on. People measure what is important to them, and they hope the measurements show they are closer to their goals.

Defining and Determining Gross Domestic Product

The ultimate economic goal of society is that all its members get all the goods and services they want. The scarcity of resources prevents that. However, the government does attempt to measure how much is produced to at least give us some indication of how successful we are in achieving that goal. How is that done? How is it possible to measure the output of trucks, strawberries, rock concerts, helium gas, and bread at one time? Because goods and services are different, their outputs can't be added—that is, they can't be measured directly.

However, it is possible to *indirectly* measure the combined output of unlike goods and services by using a common denominator for them. That common denominator is the dollar. Each year just so many toasters are produced, and firms sell them for a certain amount of money (or dollars). The same is true for haircuts, cars, and lawn mowers. Adding up the dollar amounts of every good and service gives an indirect measure of the physical amount of things produced. Thus, that dollar amount reflects the physical output of goods and services.

However, counting or measuring the same good twice must be avoided, for that would overstate output. Such a double-counting error would occur if the value of the steel used to produce a car were counted, and then that same steel were counted in the value of the car. The dollar value of a car includes the cost of all its components, including steel. The intent is to add up the dollar value of *final* goods, or goods that are ready for use. All other goods are called intermediate goods. All the goods in retail stores are final goods, as are concert tickets, computers, factory robots, insurance policies, and visits to the doctor. Intermediate goods include such items as coal, steel, sugar cane, lumber, and computer chips.

Gross domestic product (GDP) is the market value of all final goods and services produced in a year with resources located in the United States. It does not matter if the resources are owned by Americans or by foreigners. For example, the value of Honda cars produced in Ohio by Japanese-owned capital (the factory and the machines in it) is part of GDP of the United States. Also, the income earned working in the United States by Canadians is included in GDP because their income reflects the value of goods and services they produce in the United States.

One can think of GDP as the summation of each final good's price multiplied by its output. To illustrate, one could multiply the price of gasoline by the number of gallons produced, add that to the price of haircuts multiplied by the number of haircuts given, and so on. Figure 9-1 shows the relationship of GDP to output. Imagine that the box labeled GDP is filled with enough dollars to equal the value of all the final goods and services produced in a year. (That production is represented by the "pile" of output on the left.) It is impossible to measure that "pile" directly, for it is impossible to add up the pounds of potatoes, the number of cars, the barrels of beer, and all other output in a meaningful way. Therefore, it is measured indirectly by GDP, which *reflects* total output.

GDP does not include all of the nation's output, only the goods and services the government can measure. These include goods and services sold in legal transactions in marketplaces (stores, auto dealerships, and so on). However, GDP misses all output from the "underground economy." This includes work some people do for unreported cash to avoid income taxes (as when plumbers do work "on the side"), illegal drug production and sales, and underreporting of sales by retailers. Some economists believe such output is equal to a tenth of GDP or more. Often "underground" activity is legal, such as cutting a neighbor's grass or occasional babysitting.

In addition, production (work) people do for themselves doesn't appear in GDP. Those who paint their own houses, cook their own food, clean their own homes, build model airplanes, sew their own clothes, and

Gross domestic product is the dollar value of all final goods and services produced in a nation in a year with resources located in that nation.

Figure 9-1

The Meaning of GDP

GDP is an indirect measure of (or a reflection of) the amount of final goods and services produced.

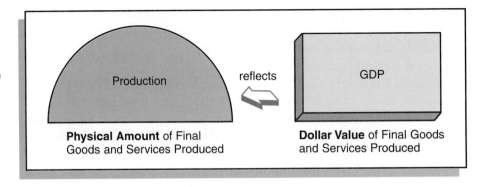

grow their own vegetables do not have this output included in GDP. This problem of understating output by using GDP is relatively large for poor nations, where many people produce much of their own food, shelter, and clothing.

Consequently, GDP only approximates the nation's total output. The Department of Commerce reports GDP for each quarter of a year and then again for the entire year. However, the quarterly report is stated at a yearly rate. For example, if the value of output was $1,600 billion in the third quarter, the report would state that "goods and services, as measured by GDP, were produced in the third quarter at a rate of $6,400 billion per year" (= $1,600 billion x 4).

GDP per capita is a monetary measure of the amount of final goods and services produced in a year for each person, on average, or the living standard.

GDP per capita refers to the value of goods and services produced in a year for each person, on average. It is found by dividing GDP by the population. This gives an indirect measure of the living standard, which is the *physical* amount of output available to the average person.

The economy often fails to produce as many goods and services as it could. **Potential GDP** refers to the dollar value of *potential* output, that is, the total output of goods and services when all the resources are fully used (commonly called full employment). Potential GDP might not be reached because, for example, many laborers could be out of work or many factories could be operating at less than full capacity.

Potential GDP is the value of final goods and services that would be produced at full employment.

Actual GDP is the value of final goods and services actually produced.

Actual GDP refers to the value of goods and services actually produced in a year. If less than the potential output is produced, potential GDP exceeds actual GDP, as illustrated in Figure 9-2. The *difference* between the two "piles" of output on the left or the two rectangles reflecting GDP on the right both indicate the degree of unused resources in the economy—unemployed laborers, factories with idle machines and inactive shipping departments, restaurant grills not being fully used, and idled coal and iron mines.

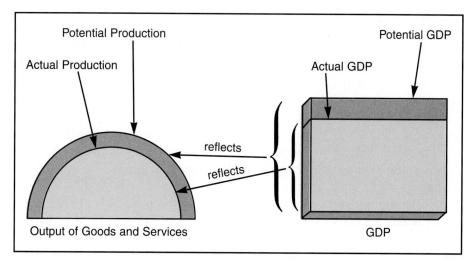

Figure 9-2

Potential GDP and Actual GDP

Often an economy produces less than it is capable of producing. Thus, its actual GDP is less than its potential GDP.

Problems in Using GDP When Prices Change

If the device used to measure output changes in some way, what happens? An analogy might help. Suppose that you dent a teaspoon so that it holds only two-thirds as much as it did before. If it's your only spoon, what do you do when a cake recipe calls for two teaspoons of baking powder? You must adjust your procedure to ensure an accurate measure, so you should now use *three* "teaspoons"—of the bent one, for 2 = 3 x 2/3.

A similar problem exists when measuring total output with GDP. The "measuring device" for output (the dollar) changes in "size" (what it can buy) every time prices in general rise or fall. If a change in GDP is to reflect only the change in the output of goods and services, there is a problem. Suppose total output does *not* increase from one year to the next but that prices *do* by 10 percent. Then GDP also rises by 10 percent.

How can GDP rise if output doesn't? This is possible because *two* factors determine GDP: 1) the output of goods and services; and 2) their prices. To solve this measurement distortion problem caused by changing prices, GDP must be adjusted—just like the baking powder measure had to be adjusted when the spoon was dented. It is necessary to "factor out" the price change or adjust GDP so that any change in GDP reflects changes in output alone. This is done with a simple mathematical equation. However, first it is necessary to construct a measure of the price level, just as it was necessary to determine how much the teaspoon was dented. Then we will know just how much to adjust GDP in order to eliminate the effects of price changes on GDP, leaving only the effects of output changes.

Constructing a Price Index

A **price index** is a
representation of all
prices.

The price level refers to *all* prices of *all* final goods and services, considered collectively. A **price index** is something that *represents* all prices in the economy (or the price level). The government uses numbers to represent prices because it is easy to increase or decrease numbers in response to changes in the price level. Since the purpose of the price index is to find out how much prices changed over time, a starting point in time—called the base year—is needed for the index. Then, if the price index rose by 23 percent from the base year to the present, it means that prices also rose by 23 percent.

The number 100 is always assigned to be the price index in the base year. It's harder to find the price index for the present year or any year in between because we need to know *how much* prices have risen since the base year. The government estimates this by noting the prices of a sample of all final goods and services, called a "market basket." In one price index, the Consumer Price Index (CPI), the Bureau of Labor Statistics makes a hypothetical purchase of some 400 items that typical urban wage earners buy. It checks 80,000 prices at 21,000 businesses in 85 urban areas. The "market basket" includes more of some things than others (perhaps five gallons of milk, but only two shirts) to better reflect true buying patterns of the public. The CPI is made up of the following categories, each followed by its importance or "weight" in the index, expressed in percentages: housing–41.4; food and beverage–17.4; transportation–17.0; medical care–7.0; apparel and upkeep–5.9; entertainment–4.4; all other goods and services–6.9.

Suppose this "market basket" costs $2,000 in the base year. (The government currently assigns the two-year period from 1982 to 1984 as the base "year.") If those same items cost $2,600 (30 percent more) today, then prices in general rose 30 percent since 1982-84. The price index would be 130 for this year.

The price index is used to determine the "cost of living." This refers to the amount of money people need to buy the things they typically buy. If the price index rises, you can assume it costs more to live—that is, to buy things in general. (Be careful not to equate the cost of living with the standard of living, which refers to the *amount* of goods and services available for each person, on average.)

The government has several other price indices: the implicit price deflator (or GDP deflator), which is used to adjust GDP for price changes; the producers' price index, which reflects prices that manufacturers charge to wholesalers; and various partial indices, such as the housing price index, which reflects only housing costs.

How the Inflation Rate Is Calculated

A price index can be used to calculate the inflation rate as well as to adjust GDP and other economic variables for price changes. Inflation is a condition of persistent increases in the price level. The **inflation rate** is the percentage increase in the price level from one year to the next. For example, the 2.5 percent inflation rate for 1995 means that, on average, prices were 2.5 percent higher on December 31, 1995, than they were on December 31, 1994.

The **inflation rate** is the percentage increase in the price level in a year, calculated by the percent increase in the price index.

The inflation rate is calculated between two consecutive years (called Year 1 and Year 2) with this formula:

$$\text{Inflation Rate} = \frac{\text{Price Index in Year 2} - \text{Price Index in Year 1}}{\text{Price Index in Year 1}} \times 100$$

THINKING CRITICALLY ABOUT ECONOMIC QUESTIONS IN OUR LIVES

What Has *Your* Price Index Done Recently?

Things to Consider

1. The Consumer Price Index (CPI) indicates the "cost of living" for a typical urban wage earner. It is used to calculate the inflation rate, which actually only pertains to such a person.

2. What if you are *not* typical? That is, what if you buy more—or less—of the items in the CPI market basket? If you sale shop or coupon clip more than most people? If you are a rural dweller? If you buy lots of oddball items? Or items whose prices either rise more sharply or less so than the items in the market basket?

3. How would you find the inflation rate that reflects *your* cost of living—so that you could really tell if your income is keeping up with *your* inflation rate?

See page 468 for the answer.

The government actually measures prices monthly and then reports the inflation rate for that month, but on a yearly basis. It assumes that prices will continue to increase in the 11 months that follow at the same rate they did in the month checked. For example, suppose the CPI was 120.0 in July 1990 and 120.6 in August 1990. Thus, the CPI rose 0.5 percent in one month, as 0.5 = (120.6 − 120.0) ÷ 120. Multiplying 0.5 percent by 12 (months) gives a six percent annual inflation rate on the basis of the July to August record (ignoring compounding effects).

It is also possible to look at price indices over many years and tell how long it took for prices to double, triple, quadruple, and so on. Suppose you want to know when prices were only a third of what they are today. First, you must find the price index for the present. Second, divide that price index by three. Finally, take the quotient you found in the second step and locate the year when it was the price index. For example, if today's price index is 180, then dividing it by three gives us 60. If the price index was 60 in 1971, then we can say that prices rose threefold since 1971 or that prices in 1971 were a third as high as today's prices. Then, when people say that today's dollar is only "worth 33¢," they're equating the purchasing power of today's dollar to that of 33¢ in 1971.

How GDP Is Adjusted for Price Changes

GDP reflects both the output of goods and services as well as the price level. If, over time, only the output changes, there is no measuring problem—any change in GDP came solely from the output change. But since prices usually *do* change, it is necessary to separate out the price changes from the GDP change. Once this is done, there is a special name for GDP—**real GDP**. (It is sometimes also called by two other names: constant-dollar GDP and GDP adjusted for inflation.) Real GDP is the most accurate measure of the production of goods and services. The GDP figure the government actually measures is **current GDP**, also called nominal GDP. Real GDP is calculated with the following formula:

Real GDP is the current (or nominal) GDP after adjusting for inflation, which gives the most accurate measure of production.

Current GDP is the value of final goods and services when using the prices existing at the time of production.

$$\text{Real GDP} = \frac{\text{Current GDP}}{\text{GDP Deflator}} \times 100$$

(Remember from earlier that the GDP deflator is a price index.) Suppose current GDP doubled during some period. Real GDP would also *tend* to double—but it wouldn't change at all if prices also doubled during the period.

Newspaper articles often refer to both current GDP and real GDP. Such articles also refer to the **economic growth rate**, which is the percentage increase in real GDP during the year (although it is also measured on a quarterly basis). Comparing outputs of two different years requires using real GDP because it avoids the distortion caused by price changes.

Such procedures that adjust for price changes also work for the measure of the living standard, GDP per capita. Because real GDP is the best measure of output, real GDP per capita is the best measure of the living standard because it reflects the amount of goods and services produced per person.

The economic growth rate is the percent increase in a year's time of the amount of goods and services produced in the economy.

Year	Current GDP	Real GDP (1996 dollars)	Real GDP per Capita (1996 dollars)
1960	$527	$2,357	$13,046
1970	$1,040	$3,549	$17,308
1980	$2,796	$4,872	$21,394
1985	$4,213	$5,690	$23,860
1986	$4,453	$5,886	$24,446
1987	$4,743	$6,093	$25,094
1988	$5,108	$6,349	$25,912
1989	$5,489	$6,569	$26,639
1990	$5,803	$6,584	$26,745
1991	$5,986	$6,669	$26,396
1992	$6,319	$6,891	$26,979
1993	$6,642	$7,054	$27,327
1994	$7,054	$7,338	$28,152
1995	$7,401	$7,537	$28,654
1996	$7,813	$7,813	$29,432
1997	$8,301	$8,160	$30,448
1998	$8,760	$8,509	$31,445
1999	$9,248	$8,857	$32,455
2000	$9,873	$9,224	$33,493

Table 9-1

GDP Figures for Selected Years (in billions, expect for the last column)

Sources: *The Economic Report of the President, 2002*
Survey of Current Business, January 2002

Table 9-1 shows actual GDP for selected years, shown in current dollars and in constant dollars (dollars with the purchasing power of 1996 dollars). It also indicates real GDP per capita. From these figures it is clear that the living standard has risen approximately two and one half times since 1960. Or, to look at it differently, to live today as people did in 1960, we'd have to give up 60 percent of the goods and services we have today.

The Expenditure Approach to GDP

There are several ways to measure GDP: 1) the production approach; 2) the expenditure approach; and 3) the income approach. The production approach, which was used earlier in the chapter to introduce GDP, adds the value of the production of all final goods and services to arrive at GDP. The expenditure approach assumes that total spending for goods and services must equal the value of goods and services produced—that is, GDP. (This is similar to saying that the money spent on getting a car repaired equals the amount of revenue the garage owner receives for the work. When all final goods and services are added together, we have GDP.) The income approach adds the income people earn while producing goods and services.

The reason all three approaches are acceptable is that money received by people (income) ultimately comes from sales (revenues) of items that people wish to consume (goods and services). In other words, each appeals to the idea that every purchase is a sale (money changes hands) and people give money to get some good or service in exchange.

Total spending (or expenditures), often called aggregate demand, can be divided into four components: 1) consumer spending; 2) investment spending; 3) government spending; and 4) net exports.

Consumer spending, or consumption, is the part of total spending that reflects the purchases of consumer goods and services.

■ **Consumer spending** (C), or consumption, includes all spending on consumer goods—those goods consumers buy to satisfy personal needs and wants, including food, clothing, cars, records, movies, and school supplies. It usually accounts for 60 to 70 percent of all the output produced.

Investment spending, or investment, is the part of total spending that involves spending on capital goods, construction, and a change in business inventories.

■ **Investment spending** (I), or investment, has three components: 1) expenditures by privately owned businesses for capital equipment, such as machinery, tools, and office computers; 2) spending on building construction in the private sector for homes and such business structures as offices, factories, warehouses, and pipelines; and 3) an adjustment for business inventories. An example might clarify this third component. Suppose Acme Shoe had a $60,000 inventory of finished shoes on January 1, 1997. On December 31, 1997, it had $80,000 worth of shoes, a difference of $20,000. However, that $20,000 of shoes was in the warehouse, so clearly no one had bought them. However, the Commerce Department acts as if the firm bought these shoes from itself. It uses this procedure to account for all the nation's production of goods and services. Alternatively, a firm could end a year with *fewer* inventories than it had at the beginning. To avoid the misleading assumption that spending exceeded output if the inventory is less at the end than at the beginning of the year, a negative figure is used for this third component of investment spending. Investment spending accounts for about 10 to 20 percent of total output.

■ **Government spending** (G) includes the part of government budgets used to purchase goods and services. This includes spending on military supplies, government buildings, and equipment for public schools. This government spending (federal, state, and local combined) accounts for between 20 and 30 percent of total production. It does *not* include spending on transfer payments because the government receives no goods or services whenever such payments are made.

> Government spending is part of total spending, including only spending for which governments receive goods and services in return.

■ **Net exports** (X - M) measure the difference between exports and imports. Exports (X) reflect spending by foreigners for (part of) our output, so it's similar in that respect to C, I, and G. However, some part of purchases by U.S. consumers, businesses, and governments are on foreign-made products. These are U.S. imports (M), and they must be subtracted from the spending on C, I, G, and X so that there is an accounting balance between the value of *domestic* output and total spending on that output. Compared with C, I, and G, net exports are usually small and will be ignored in the following chapters.

> Net exports refer to the difference in the value of exports and imports.

THINKING CRITICALLY ABOUT ECONOMIC QUESTIONS IN OUR LIVES

What Difference Will It Make to Your Great-Grandchildren if GDP per Capita Grows at Three Percent per Year Rather Than at Two Percent?

Things to Consider

1. A rise in GDP per capita means living standards rise.

2. A growth rate of two percent or three percent does not sound significantly different. What would be the difference between these two rates in how fast the living standard would rise in 70 years or so, or about the time your great-grandchildren will live?

3. What can you and others do to influence the living standards of your descendants?

   See page 469 for the answer.

Table 9-2

Total Spending
Components of GDP,
2000 (in billions)

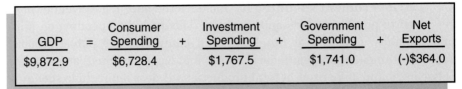

GDP	=	Consumer Spending	+	Investment Spending	+	Government Spending	+	Net Exports
$9,872.9		$6,728.4		$1,767.5		$1,741.0		(-)$364.0

Source: *Federal Reserve Bulletin,* January 2002

The following formula for GDP sums up everything. It shows that the value of total output (GDP) is equal to total spending on that output:

$$GDP = C + I + G + (X - M) = \text{Total Spending}$$

Table 9-2 shows these four components of GDP for 2000.

NATIONAL INCOME ACCOUNTS

Although GDP is a good first step in measuring the macroeconomy, there are other measures of elements of the macroeconomy besides GDP. In the 1930s, the economist Simon Kuznets established a way of connecting all these measures in what is known as the national income accounts. Table 9-3 shows the major elements of these accounts and their interrelationships. These accounts illustrate the third approach to GDP—the income approach.

The accounts start with GDP, the value of all final goods and services produced. Depreciation, also called capital consumption allowances, is subtracted from GDP to give **net domestic product** (NDP). Depreciation reflects the wearing out of capital. So the amount of capital produced each year to replace old capital is subtracted from GDP to give a more accurate view of the *additional* goods and services available as compared with the previous year.

Next, indirect business taxes, including sales, property, and excise taxes, are subtracted from NDP. The remainder is **national income** (NI), which equals the payments to the factors of production—wages and other employee contributions, interest, rent, and profits. GDP and NDP are fundamentally different concepts from NI in that they measure the value of production, while NI measures the amount of income earned. Because depreciation and indirect business taxes don't represent any person's income, they must be subtracted from GDP to arrive at NI.

Net domestic product
equals gross domestic
product minus
depreciation of capital
equipment.

National income
reflects the payments to
the factors of production.

	GDP (Gross Domestic Product)
	minus Depreciation
=	**NDP (Net Domestic Product)**
	minus Indirect Business Taxes
=	**NI (National Income)**
	minus Corporate Savings
	minus Corporate Income Taxes
	minus Social Security Taxes
	plus Transfer Payments
	plus Interest Paid by Governments
=	**PI (Personal Income)**
	minus Personal Taxes
=	**DI (Disposable Income)**
	minus Personal Consumption Expenditures (C)
=	**S (Personal Savings)**

Table 9-3

The National
Income Accounts

There are several
important macroeconomic
variables that appear in
the table, and their
relationships to each other
are shown.

However, NI does not include all the income people have available to them. Five adjustments must be made before arriving at that figure, which is known as **personal income** (PI). Three items are subtracted from NI and two are added to it. The first to be subtracted is corporate savings. Although owners of corporations earn profits, the part of profits that remain in the corporate accounts (savings, checking) is not available for spending by the firms' owners. The same thing holds for income taxes corporations pay. Finally, Social Security taxes also represent money that is not (immediately) available to people, even though the taxes are paid with income people earned from selling resources.

Personal income includes all income available to people before taxes.

Conversely, transfer payments add to the income people receive from selling resources, so they are added to NI. Interest earned on government bonds is also added to NI because it is income to people and was not counted in national income as interest income to resource owners.

Although personal income represents all the flows of money to people, it still does not indicate what they can spend. To find that amount, known as **disposable income** (DI) or disposable personal income, personal taxes must be subtracted. These are the various taxes paid by individuals for personal income taxes, property taxes, sales taxes, and the like. Finally, personal consumption expenditures (C) are subtracted from disposable income, leaving **personal savings** (S) as a residual. The consumption figure (C) includes interest payments on loans that individuals took out. Thus, it does not reflect a pure measure of the amount of goods and services purchased in the normal sense.

Disposable income equals personal income minus personal taxes.

Personal savings equals disposable income minus consumption.

LABOR RESOURCES AND MACROECONOMICS

In Chapter 5 you studied labor from a microeconomic perspective. The chapter explained wage determination, productivity of individual workers and occupations, and other aspects of labor. This chapter focuses on labor resources from a different, broader perspective.

The Labor Force

Figure 9-3 categorizes the entire population in various ways. At the top, the rectangle extending the whole width of the chart represents the entire population. The population is then divided into two groups, those in the labor force and those outside the labor force. The **labor force** includes everyone who has a job or is actively looking for a job. People not in the labor force include those not employed and not looking for work. This includes anyone under age 16, retired people, homemakers, most college students, and those in institutions, such as hospitals or prisons.

The labor force has two components: 1) the armed forces, including all military personnel; and 2) the civilian labor force. The civilian labor force is divided into the employed and the unemployed. Each month the government surveys 55,000 households and classifies someone as **employed** if that person is between the ages of 16 and 65 and worked one hour or more in the previous week. It classifies someone as **unemployed** if that person did not work the previous week but looked for work. "Looking" includes reading the employment ads, filling out an application, or stopping at an employment office. Someone does not have to collect unemployment compensation to be classified as unemployed.

The **labor force** includes all the people who are employed plus those that are unemployed.

An **employed** person is one who works at least one hour per week.

An **unemployed** person is one who is not working and who is actively seeking work.

Figure 9-3

The Labor Force

The population is split into various categories in the figure.

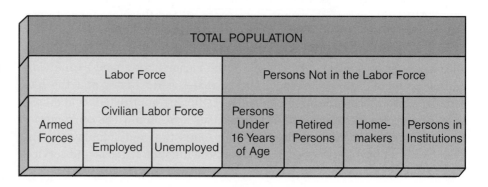

The **unemployment rate** is the percentage of the labor force that is unemployed. The government reports this figure monthly as well as yearly. The rate is determined with the formula:

$$\text{Unemployment Rate} = \frac{\text{Number of Unemployed}}{\text{Labor Force}} \times 100$$

Many people who want a job stop looking when they can't find one after a long search. The government calls the people who have stopped looking the discouraged unemployed. Officially, these people are not classified as unemployed. That's because the government can't always tell which people who are not working would actually work if offered a job. For

The **unemployment rate** is the percentage of the labor force that is unemployed.

THINKING CRITICALLY ABOUT ECONOMIC QUESTIONS IN OUR LIVES

Should Drug Dealers and Prostitutes Be in the Labor Force?

Things to Consider

1. Suppose that government statisticians who gather labor force data in their monthly interviews happen to contact drug dealers, prostitutes, and others who engage in illegal activities. If one of them were asked, "If you are not working, are you seeking work," and the answer is no, the person is not considered to be part of the labor force and is, thus, considered neither employed nor unemployed.

2. But the unemployment rate is supposed to tell what share of the labor force (the employed plus the unemployed) is out of work. But such people are productive (thus, employed) in the economic sense of the word. Productiveness is unrelated to legality. Therefore, shouldn't they be considered part of the labor force?

3. What effect, if any, does the government's omission of them have on the official unemployment rate?

   See page 469 for the answer.

Table 9-4

Selected Labor Statistics

Year	Population (millions)	Civilian Labor Force (millions)	Number of Unemployed (millions)	Civilian Unemployment Rate
1980	227.7	106.9	7.6	7.1%
1981	230.0	108.7	8.3	7.6%
1982	232.3	110.2	10.7	9.7%
1983	234.5	111.6	10.7	9.6%
1984	236.7	113.5	8.5	7.5%
1985	238.8	115.5	8.3	7.2%
1986	241.0	117.8	8.2	7.0%
1987	243.8	119.9	7.4	6.2%
1988	246.3	121.7	6.7	5.5%
1989	248.8	123.9	6.5	5.3%
1990	251.4	125.8	7.0	5.6%
1991	252.7	126.3	8.6	6.8%
1992	255.4	128.1	9.6	7.5%
1993	258.1	129.2	8.9	6.9%
1994	260.7	131.1	8.0	6.1%
1995	263.0	132.3	7.4	5.6%
1996	265.5	133.9	7.2	5.4%
1997	268.0	136.3	6.7	4.9%
1998	270.6	137.7	6.2	4.5%
1999	272.9	139.4	5.9	4.2%
2000	275.4	140.9	5.7	4.0%
2001	277.8	141.8	6.7	4.8%

Source: *The Economic Report of the President,* 2002

instance, some homemakers and retired people would work if offered nice jobs at high enough wages. Should these people also be classified as unemployed? No. Thus, the government says you must be looking for a job to be considered unemployed. Table 9-4 shows some labor statistics from 1968 to the present for the civilian labor force.

A problem with the unemployment rate is that it does not reflect the degree of *underemployment* that exists. This refers to people who are employed in positions below their job skills. It includes cab drivers with college degrees and laid-off machinists who flip hamburgers.

Types of Unemployment

Although there are many reasons for unemployment, economists fit unemployment into three categories: 1) frictional unemployment; 2) structural unemployment; and 3) cyclical unemployment.

■ Frictional unemployment means that "friction" in the economy prevents everyone from working all the time. There are several sources of this "friction." Some jobs are seasonal. Some people have just entered the work force and have not yet selected a job. Some workers have voluntarily changed jobs but haven't started their new ones yet. Finally, some workers aren't aware of available jobs for which they are qualified.

■ Structural unemployment refers to unemployment stemming from the changing structure of the economy. It occurs when jobhunters don't have the skills required for the available jobs. Some reasons for structural unemployment include: a new machine that is cheaper than using laborers ("technological unemployment"); a sharp drop in demand for a product (home movie cameras that use film, for example); or fewer jobs for the uneducated or extremely unskilled (the "hard-core unemployed").

■ Cyclical unemployment occurs during recessions or downturns in the economy that affect almost all industries. Such unemployment is potentially the largest of the three, and during the Great Depression of the 1930s it hit more than 20 percent of the labor force. In prosperous times it hardly exists because firms can't find workers to fill all job openings.

If the economy succeeds in creating jobs for everyone *except* the frictionally unemployed and the structurally unemployed, it is said to be at **full employment**. The economy will achieve potential GDP if it is at full employment. In the 1960s, this condition corresponded to an unemployment rate of about three or four percent. Today most economists say full employment means an unemployment rate of around five or six percent. Economists blame this increase on: an increase in required job skills while individual education levels decline (as reflected in lower SAT/ACT scores and achievement tests of today compared with those of several decades ago); a greater share of the labor force made up of women and teenagers, who have relatively fewer job skills (though women have closed much of the gap with men in the last two decades); and the growth of government-assistance programs, which provide sources of income other than employment.

Full employment is a condition of no cyclical unemployment, corresponding to approximately five to six percent of the labor force.

Another term, labor productivity, refers in macroeconomics to the efficiency of a very large group, sometimes even the entire labor force. In microeconomics it refers to a specific worker or a small group of workers. Recall from Chapter 3 that service workers generally have lower rates of productivity growth than workers producing goods.

The government reports the changes in productivity each quarter, especially for the nonagricultural private sector. These figures are indicators of the likelihood of U.S. success against foreign competition in the marketplace and against inflation.

SUMMARY

Macroeconomics studies large sectors of the economy, such as the labor force, total output, the price level, and interest rates. The major macroeconomic goals are full employment, price stability, and economic growth. When achieved, each of these goals reduces the problems caused by a scarcity of resources.

Gross domestic product indirectly measures the yearly output of final goods and services. Comparing GDP of two or more years is difficult because prices often rise over time. The problem is that price increases raise GDP just as increases in production do. Real GDP more accurately measures output because the inflationary effects are removed. Real GDP per capita is a measure of the living standard because it measures yearly output per capita.

The price level is measured or represented by a price index. A price index is calculated by comparing the cost of a given amount of goods and services in several time periods. The inflation rate is the percentage change in the price index in a year. The price index is also used along with current GDP to calculate real GDP.

GDP can be found by: 1) adding the value of all goods and services produced; 2) adding the incomes people get from selling their resources; and 3) adding the amount of purchases of all spenders. In the expenditure approach, GDP equals the amount of consumer, investment, and government spending plus the difference between exports and imports.

The labor force includes the employed and the unemployed. The unemployed include those out of work and those looking for it. The unemployment rate is the percentage of the labor force that is unemployed. The unemployed are often categorized as frictionally, structurally, or cyclically unemployed.

QUESTIONS FOR DISCUSSION AND THOUGHT

1. How much have living standards increased since you were born?
2. Did the "cost of living" ever increase 10,000 years ago, before there was money? In fact, *was there* a "cost of living" then?
3. How much have prices risen since you were born?
4. Why aren't homemakers and prisoners considered to be in the labor force?
5. Recalculate the real GDP for 1970, 1980, and 1990 if the GDP deflator index was: a) twice as high; and b) half as high as it really was. (Hint: You don't have to know the actual index number.)
6. Which do you believe is the most important—full employment, price stability, or economic growth? Did your own economic position influence your answer? How so?
7. All the food that people cook for themselves at home could be cooked in restaurants. If it was, that food preparation service would be included in the GDP. Therefore, if you were to get an accurate measure of total output (and GDP), you'd have to estimate how much home-cooked food would sell for in restaurants. What problems would you have in doing that?
8. What might be a reason why the unemployment insurance program would affect the unemployment rate? What would this effect be?
9. In the 1946 film, "It's a Wonderful Life," Mr. Potter cheated the Baileys (James Stewart and his uncle) out of $5,000. That doesn't seem like it should have been enough to break their business, a building and loan association (now known as a savings and loan), and cause all that despair to George Bailey. Can you explain why it did?

PROBLEMS   See pages 487-488 for the answers.

1. In the base year, a market basket of goods and services costs $3,260. Ten years prior to the base year, it cost $2,750. Ten years after the base year it cost $4,340. Find the price indices for all three years.

2. From the base year to the present, prices have risen 43.6 percent. What is the price index today?

3. In five years since the base year, the inflation rate was as follows: 3.6 percent, 4.1 percent, 1.3 percent, 2.2 percent, and 6.8 percent. What was the price index after the fifth year?

4. In three consecutive years, the price index was 160.6, 162.5, and 166.1. Find the inflation rate from the first to the second year, as well as from the second to the third year.

5. Find GDP, given the following information (all figures are in billions): construction–$120; exports–$65; consumption–$635; imports–$71; government spending–$362; inventory increase–$16; capital spending–$46.

6. Find real GDP if the GDP deflator is 160.9 and current GDP is $6,359 billion.

7. Find current GDP if real GDP is $5,250 billion and the GDP deflator is 90.6. What unusual thing happened in this economy?

8. Find current GDP if it was $3,280 billion a year earlier and, if during that period, the inflation rate was 6.3 percent and the total output of goods and services rose 1.7 percent.

9. Initially, real GDP was $4,157 billion. Over a three-year span, prices remained unchanged, and each year the economic growth rate was 1.8 percent. What was real GDP at the end of these three years? What can you say about the changes in current GDP over the same period? What more do you need to know to determine the dollar amount of current GDP?

10. If the economic growth rate between two years was 3.1 percent and real GDP was $6,750 billion in the second year, what was real GDP in the first year?

11. Find national income, given the following information (all figures are in billions): depreciation–$46; interest paid by governments–$18; GDP–$4,870; Social Security taxes–$856; personal savings–$83; indirect business taxes–$42; disposable income–$3,060.

12. With 6.3 million unemployed and an unemployment rate of 4.6 percent, how large is the labor force?

13. With a labor force of 131.6 million, 2.2 million structurally unemployed, and 1.3 million frictionally unemployed, how many people are out of work because of a downturn in the economy if 126.6 million have jobs?

Unemployed people who demanded work and financial assistance from the government in 1933. They had just attended a rally where several communist and other "radical" speakers were heard.
(Courtesy of the Milwaukee Public Library - Historical Photo Collection)

10 MONEY AND BANKING

CHAPTER PREVIEW

The use of money is the result of exchanges between specialists who are seeking to improve resource efficiency.

Before anything is used as money, it needs to fulfill several functions and to have several characteristics. Our money supply does that, and it is actually made up of several components. The commercial banking system is instrumental in determining the money supply through its ability to make loans.

The chapter introduces the Federal Reserve System, which controls our banking system and the money supply.

CHAPTER OBJECTIVES

After completing this chapter, you should be able to:

◆ *Describe the two alternative methods of exchange.*

◆ *Describe money.*

◆ *List the five characteristics something must have before it will be accepted as money.*

◆ *Describe the organization of the Federal Reserve System.*

◆ *Explain how banks create money.*

◆ *Explain how the Federal Reserve controls excess bank reserves and the money supply.*

For virtually all or most of the two million years that humans have faced the economic problem, people got along without using money. Although a primitive, subsistence economy can function without money, a modern economy can't. In this chapter you will learn what money is (you might be surprised) and how it helps to alleviate the economic problem caused by a scarcity of resources. You will also learn about the Federal Reserve System, the commercial banking system, and how both of these affect the money supply.

THE CONCEPT OF MONEY AND HOW WE MEASURE IT

What is money, the stuff people *say* they want so much—but then get rid of as fast as they can when they get it? It is a strange item indeed. Money is probably the only thing that is useless—*until you get rid of it.* (Think how useless a pocketful of money would be to someone shipwrecked on a deserted island where there is nothing to buy.)

The Concept of Money

Money plays an important role in achieving specialization and raising living standards. Each person specializes in producing some good or service in order to increase the efficiency of resource use, which, in turn, promotes higher living standards. However, this leads to individual specialists producing vastly more of a product than each needs or wants—but having little or nothing of whatever else is needed. Thus, specialization forces specialists to exchange their products.

There are two ways of trading: 1) by using the barter method; and 2) by using money. **Barter** is a system in which one person provides a good, service, or resource to another in exchange for some other good, service, or resource. Such trade requires that there be a **double coincidence of wants**, which means each person has what the other person wants and wants what the other person has. That would be a rare occurrence. For example, if someone tried to trade some surplus pencils for a bike, it could take years to make a trade. Economists call the time plus other things of value that are given up when making exchanges **transaction costs**. People who hate to spend time shopping and to endure crowds know about such costs. When people do comparison shopping to find the best deal, they deliberately increase their transaction costs. Whether that is a wise activity depends upon what they gain (in saved money) compared with the value of their time (the benefits it would have provided them if used differently).

Barter is a system of exchange or trade where some item is exchanged for some other item without the use of money.

A **double coincidence of wants** is a condition of barter exchanges, where each trader has what the other trader wants and wants what the other trader has.

Transaction costs are the costs involved in making an exchange, including money as well as costs of time and aggravation.

Throughout much of human existence, such high transaction costs discouraged people from specializing. Instead, they were self-sufficient, producing most of their own needs. Because they did not have the advantages of specialization, they generally were poor, living at a subsistence level. Frontier settlers were prime examples.

But thousands of years ago, an idea took hold that changed the world. A person who knew the value of specialization might have suggested: "Why not become a specialist and give your surplus to another specialist (say, John) in exchange for something you *don't* want, but which any other specialist (say, Bob) would in turn take from you in exchange for what Bob has? Then you would not have to spend time finding somebody who has what you want, *plus* who wants what you have. You merely give such people what they *don't* want—money." (We know people don't want money itself because they part with most of it as soon as they get it.) Thus, money eliminates the need to fulfill a double coincidence of wants.

Figure 10-1 illustrates the differences in these two systems of exchange. Suppose John produces nails and wants some cheese. In a barter system, he needs to find a cheese maker who needs some nails. Note that there are five cheese makers with whom John can trade—Mary, Bob, Chris, Shawn, and Elaine. But each of them wants different products. Only one (Elaine) wants nails. Thus, for John to make a trade, he needs to first find someone like Elaine and, second, they need to agree on how many nails to trade for each pound of cheese.

In the lower part of the figure, showing a money system, there are *five* possible trading situations, as John no longer has to find someone needing nails. Not only is it easier to find a trading partner, but John is also more likely to come up with a *better* trade because Elaine now has competition.

Money is a great invention because it makes exchanges so easy to make that they *are made*. By reducing transaction costs, money makes it more likely that people will be specialists, thereby reaping the rewards of greater efficiency and higher living standards.

Suppose that Jane, a beekeeper, could use some of the cloth produced by Steve. Before people used money, someone in Jane's situation could get Steve's cloth only if Steve wanted some honey.

Honey and cloth are useful (beneficial), so Jane and Steve are producing things of value to themselves or to others. Jane and Steve can use only a little of the honey and cloth they make. But they make more than they need because this increases their ability to trade for other items. By making more honey and cloth, Jane and Steve gain the power to purchase more of other things. That is, by increasing their production, they increase their purchasing power.

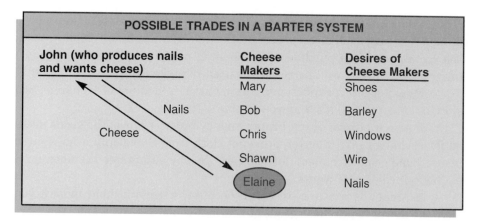

Figure 10-1

Trade in a Barter System and a Money System

John, a nail producer, wants some cheese. In a barter system, the only cheese maker he can trade with is Elaine, as only she wants nails. Only then is a double coincidence of wants achieved.

In a money system, John can trade with any of the five cheese makers, as each will accept his money, knowing that the money can be traded for any other good. Thus, money eliminates the necessity of achieving a double coincidence of wants before exchanges can occur.

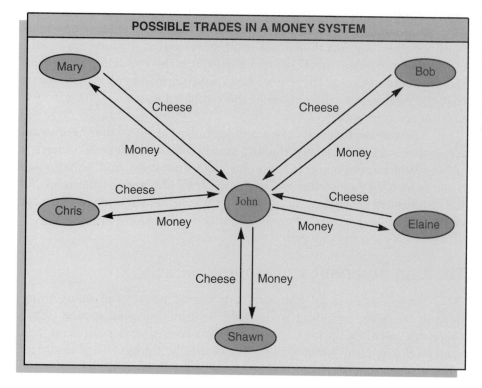

In a barter economy, people store purchasing power *in the things* they make. Jane and Steve would have had their purchasing power stored in the honey and cloth in their storage rooms. However, in a modern economy, people store purchasing power *in the money* they earn by producing things.

(They also store it in other assets that can be "denominated" or measured in money terms, such as corporate stocks and silver bullion.) Money, then, is a *representation* of purchasing power—the power people earn by producing things (really, by selling resources used to make things).

Money has three functions, serving as: 1) a medium of exchange; 2) a store of value; and 3) a standard of value.

■ As a **medium of exchange**, money replaces one of the goods needed for exchange. With barter, Jane got cloth from Steve only if he wanted honey. One good exchanged for another. Money eliminates the need for a double coincidence of wants.

■ Money is a **store of value** because, when you hold money, you have the power to purchase goods or services whenever you want. You store value in it, just like pioneers stored value in the grain they stored until the next harvest.

■ Money is a **standard of value**, allowing people to know how much more one thing is worth than another thing. A "unit of account" makes such comparisons possible. In the United States, it is the U.S. dollar; in Mexico, the peso; and in China, the yuan. Thus, a $70 price tag on a radio means that the radio has a value equal to the combined purchasing power of 70 units of account (dollars).

These three functions are not independent of each other. For example, if prices rise extremely rapidly, money will be useless as a store of value. People would resort to barter for many exchanges, and money would cease to be used as a medium of exchange. *Official* money (that issued by the government) may then be replaced by something else valued or accepted by the public, perhaps a foreign currency.

The Characteristics of Money

Many things could represent purchasing power, and many things have in the past, including gold, silver, bronze, and even stones. Early American colonists, lacking coined precious metals and significant local sources of ore, used commodity money—literally, things. They used rice, tobacco, sugar, beaver skins, and molasses as mediums of exchange.

Before people will accept something as money, it must meet several criteria that enable it to be a good medium of exchange. First, money should be portable. Carrying it around should be no problem (radioactive plutonium wouldn't work). Second, money must be durable (eggs wouldn't work). Third, money must be uniform—that is, all units (of a certain denomination) must have identical purchasing power (pumpkins fail this test). Fourth, money must be finely divisible so that it can buy things of

---

A medium of exchange is something that represents purchasing power and is used to obtain goods and services in market exchanges.

A store of value is something in which purchasing power is stored until the holder is ready to use it.

A standard of value is something that allows comparisons of value between goods and services, often called a unit of account.

THINKING CRITICALLY ABOUT ECONOMIC QUESTIONS IN OUR LIVES

Why Should You Care What Prices Are?

Things to Consider

1. Americans pay about 10 units of account to buy a nice lunch. Germans pay about 15, and Japanese pay about 1,200. (Units of account are dollars, marks, yen, pesos, pounds, etc.) Who pays the most for lunch? Does it matter? Why or why not?

2. People often complain about high prices. Or they ask how high prices can get (supposedly before causing some unknown problem).

3. Is there a "set of prices" (or price level) that is preferable to the rest? Thus, should you care if the actual set of prices is higher (or lower) than that "best set"?

   See page 470 for the answer.

small value, such as candy and safety pins (which explains why our unit of account is divided into 100 parts, or cents). Fifth, money must be scarce or rare. This ensures that it takes only a little of it to buy something. (Otherwise sand would have worked as well as gold did for so long. They were both uniform, durable, finely divisible, and portable—but sand wasn't rare and gold was. It might have taken a ton of sand to buy a dozen eggs.)

The Money Supply in the United States

What is (or should be considered) money in the United States? This might seem like an easy question, but at times even economists disagree on the answer. Remember, money is something that represents purchasing power (a store of value). This includes, of course, coins, paper money, and what is in our checking accounts. However, what about the bonds people hold or what is in their savings accounts—don't people call that money, too? Is it? Well, yes and no.

To understand that, it is important to realize that money is not only a representation of purchasing power (a store of value). It is also a medium of exchange. This means that before anything is used as money, businesses must readily accept it as an exchange for goods or services. Likewise, laborers and other sellers of resources must readily accept it. However, people can't make exchanges with assets such as bonds or savings account "money." Nor can they make trades with foreign currency, stocks, or their life insurance cash values, even though they store value in these assets. Economists call some of these assets "near money." They are assets that serve as a store of value, cannot buy things, but can easily be changed into a *spendable* asset—money. In general, economists use the concept of liquidity to judge how close something is to money. Cash and checking account money can be spent at any time, so they are fully liquid. However, you may have to visit your bank to get money from a savings account, so that money is less liquid. Further, land is very illiquid, as it might take months or years before it can be sold for money.

To deal with this money definition problem, the government has four classifications of money: M1, M2, M3, and L. Each of these money measures, called **monetary aggregates**, has its own purpose. Here the concentration will be on M1, the most liquid form of money, which consists of: 1) currency; 2) nonbank traveler's checks; and 3) checkable deposits.

A **monetary aggregate** is one of four classifications of the money supply.

■ All coins from pennies through the half-dollar coin constitute what is called fractional currency, which represents only two to three percent of M1. Fractional currency ensures that American money fulfills the divisibility characteristic of money.

Paper money is the second component of currency. A piece of U.S. paper money is called a Federal Reserve Note. The 12 Federal Reserve Banks (explained on page 292-293) distribute currency to the commercial banks. Each reserve bank has its "own" currency, as noted by the seal on the left front of each bill and the number on each corner. Every Federal Reserve District has its own letter and number. Paper currency accounts for 25 to 30 percent of M1.

However, M1 includes only currency held by people or businesses. Currency in banks is *not* money, strange as that seems. In fact, such currency has special names—vault cash or till money. Why is vault cash not money? Suppose you had $300 of money (purchasing power) in your checking account (which also is part of M1). You then write out a check for $100 for "cash" at your bank. After the teller gives you $100 in currency, you still have only $300 in money—$200 in checking plus $100 in currency. You merely *changed the form* of your money. So if $100 of checking account money disappeared when your balance dropped from $300 to $200, then

$100 in vault cash must have *become* money at the same instant. It does not change its physical appearance when the teller hands it to you, but what it *is does* change. It changes from ordinary green paper to a representation of purchasing power—money. (Remember, *that particular* hundred dollars of purchasing power of yours *used to be* represented by numbers in your checking account.) Consequently, no one can steal money from a bank—because it has none!

■ Nonbank traveler's checks also are money. Companies such as American Express issue such checks, which are usually just as easy to spend as cash. However, traveler's checks issued by banks such as the Bank of America are not included in M1, since the value of these checks is already included in the banks' own checking accounts. (Thus, if the checks *were* counted in M1, their value would be counted twice.)

■ Money in the form of checkable deposits is the largest component of money, usually comprising more than 70 percent of M1. A checkable account holds money that can be withdrawn or transferred to someone by writing a check. For large purchases or mail payment, a check is the most convenient and the safest way to pay. Deposits in checkable accounts are called demand deposits at commercial banks, negotiated orders of withdrawal at savings and loans, and share drafts at credit unions.

THINKING CRITICALLY ABOUT ECONOMIC QUESTIONS IN OUR LIVES

What Effect Does Counterfeiting Have on the Living Standard?

Things to Consider

1. Suppose a group of larcenous printers become counterfeiters and succeed in duplicating U.S. currency to perfection. After avoiding detection for a while, they decide to engage in counterfeiting on a full-time basis.

2. Assuming that they continue to avoid detection, what will happen to their real incomes? What will happen to the real incomes of the rest of the population? What will happen to the living standard?

See page 470 for the answer.

Checking account money is a bit abstract. *Where is* the money that is in the checking account? In your checkbook? The bank? Actually, it's *nowhere.* Remember, having money merely means you have *the power* to purchase things. You can't see or feel purchasing power—it's just "there." That's why paper money really isn't purchasing power *itself.* It merely *represents* this intangible thing called purchasing power. The purchasing power you have in your checking account is represented with numbers (rather than with metal or paper). Those numbers are not really in your checkbook—nor in the bank. They're just "there," for numbers are intangible. When Kristy writes a $20 check to Stacey, Kristy merely tells her bank to transfer 20 units of account of purchasing power ($20, that is) to Stacey. Then Stacey can place that purchasing power in currency form or in demand deposit form. Therefore, the check itself is not money. It is merely a form of communication between the check writer and the bank. To see this more clearly, note that the writing on a check is a sentence. If you wrote a $40 check to AT&T, it would read: Pay to the order of AT&T $40. Your signature, on record at the bank, proves that you ordered the bank to make the transfer.

Electronic funds transfer is the transfer of funds into and out of a checking account electronically without using paper checks.

Moving electrons (or electricity), a new form of communication between the depositor and the bank, have recently started to replace checks. With **electronic funds transfer** (EFT), you instruct your bank to transfer purchasing power (money) from your account to some store's or other account with electronic rather than written communication. This is more efficient in several ways. It saves a vast amount of paperwork (by store clerks, mail carriers, and bank employees). It allows you to "write electronic checks" everywhere (not just where people know you). Before the transaction is completed, the electronic system informs you if there is enough money in your account to cover the purchase. Such transactions are already being made by people who have **debit cards**. These look like credit cards but function as money. It might surprise you, but credit cards are not money because you can't buy anything with them. You can only *take possession* of goods by using credit cards. You actually buy the items you charged when you pay off your bill from the credit company.

A **debit card** transfers money from one's checking account to someone else's account in an electronic funds transfer.

An even newer device for buying things is a piece of plastic embedded with a microchip. Often called a smart card, a stored-value card, or an electronic cash card, it "holds" a certain amount of purchasing power. Every time it is used, its purchasing power is reduced by the amount of the transaction. In effect, the card is an electronic traveler's check. These cards are common in Europe and Asia. Some are used for a specific purpose, such as telephones. When smart cards are "used up," they are either "refilled" or, as with phone cards, they are simply thrown away.

M2 includes everything in M1 plus savings account deposits, time deposits (such as CDs, or certificates of deposit) up to $100,000, money market mutual fund shares and deposit accounts, plus overnight repurchase agreements. M3 differs in that it includes other near monies (government bonds, etc.) in addition to the components of M1 and M2. Note that the other measures of money include M1 and less liquid forms of money, such as savings accounts. Often, economists focus just on M1

Monetary Aggregate (or component of):	Amount in Billions (in December)	
	1990	2000
M1	$826.1	$1,088.2
Currency	$246.8	$529.9
Demand Deposits	$277.1	$311.3
Other Checkable Deposits	$293.9	$239.0
Traveler's Checks	$8.3	$8.0
M2	$3,339.0	$4,945.1
M3	$4,114.9	$7,108.4

Source: *Federal Reserve Bulletin,* January 2002

Table 10-1

Measures of the Money Supply

The government has three main measures of the money supply. They are called monetary aggregates, as each is composed of different financial instruments.

because the various measures move together. However, since the 1970s, financial innovations have caused the other measures of money to move far more quickly than M1. Thus, M2 has gained importance recently as a monetary aggregate.

Table 10-1 lists the actual amounts of each of these monetary aggregates. It also shows the share of M1 that each of its components represents.

THE FED, COMMERCIAL BANKS, AND THE MONEY SUPPLY

Money is vital to a well-functioning exchange economy. Commercial banks and central banks are the primary institutions that influence how much money exists in the economy.

The Federal Reserve System

In the 1800s and early 1900s, there were many serious monetary problems. One problem was the lack of a uniform national currency. In the early 1800s, each state-chartered bank printed its own currency.

Another problem was caused by the rapid increases and decreases in the availability of credit in the banking system, which led to frequent financial panics and depressions. Following one of these, the Panic of 1907, the National Monetary Commission was formed to study this problem.

The **Federal Reserve System** is the central bank of the United States, whose functions include regulating banks, providing financial services, and controlling the money supply.

A **central bank** is a "bankers' bank," which provides financial services for banks and which controls the availability and the cost of credit.

As a result, the **Federal Reserve System**, commonly called the Fed, was established by the Federal Reserve Act of 1913. It controls the banking system and provides an "elastic currency," or a money supply that changes with the needs of the economy. The Fed is a **central bank**, or a "bankers' bank," which provides commercial banks with financial services, just as individuals receive such services from commercial banks. Other nations also have central banks, such as the Bank of England, the Bank of Japan, and the Bundesbank (Germany).

The Fed consists of the Board of Governors, 12 Federal Reserve District Banks, the Federal Open Market Committee, and three advisory committees. The seven members of the Board of Governors are appointed by the president and confirmed by Congress for 14-year terms. One member is appointed to a four-year term as chairman. Alan Greenspan took over the position in 1987 and has been reappointed twice. The chairman is often called the second most powerful person in the country—and in terms of economic power, may be the *most* powerful.

The 12 Federal Reserve District Banks serve and control commercial banks in those districts. These banks (followed by their official district numbers) are in Boston (1), New York City (2), Philadelphia (3), Cleveland (4), Richmond (5), Atlanta (6), Chicago (7), St. Louis (8), Minneapolis (9), Kansas City (10), Dallas (11), and San Francisco (12). The commercial banks own these facilities. All federally chartered banks must belong to the Federal Reserve System, and state-chartered banks can join if they wish.

The Federal Open Market Committee consists of the seven Fed board members plus the presidents of five of the District Banks (the president of the New York district always serves on the committee). This committee directs the purchase and sale of government securities in order to control the money supply (addressed in more detail shortly).

The three advisory committees include: 1) the Federal Advisory Council, a 12-member body that advises the Board of Governors on economic and banking issues; 2) the Consumer Advisory Council that represents consumers and institutions that finance them; and 3) the Thrift Institutions Advisory Council, which provides information and views on the special needs and problems of thrift institutions. (See page 294 for an explanation of thifts.) It consists of one member from each of the 12 Federal Reserve districts.

The Fed has several roles. First, its most important role is controlling the money supply. If Fed members believe that the economy needs more (or less) total spending, they increase (or decrease) the money supply with three tools (examined in the next section). Its second role is to clear checks—to transfer funds between banks when one party writes a check to a second party who banks elsewhere. To keep better track of money and keep the banking system honest, the Fed was given the power during the 1980s to clear all checks (which it did not do before), even those at credit unions. Third, the Fed holds the reserves that commercial banks must keep on hand to meet any heavy withdrawals by depositors and to satisfy reserve requirements. Fourth, the U.S. Treasury deposits its money with the Fed (from tax collections and other activities) and also sells its securities through it. Fifth, the Fed regulates commercial banks through a series of rules on banking practices. Sixth, the Fed issues new currency to commercial banks and collects and destroys worn or "mutilated" money. Seventh, the Fed occasionally influences foreign exchange rates by buying or selling currencies of other nations. This is done in coordination with the U.S. Treasury, so it is not an independent function of the Fed.

The Fed doesn't control the money supply directly. Rather, it controls it indirectly by managing certain aspects of the banking system. Before considering how the Fed does this in detail, it is useful to understand more about the private commercial banking system.

The Commercial Banking System

In the past, when economies were smaller and less complex, a person who needed to borrow money generally did so directly from someone who had saved significant amounts of it earlier. The loan amounted to an exchange of purchasing power (money) between a saver and a borrower.

Today, only a tiny fraction of loans are made in this way. The complexity of our economy and the growth in the size of loans to finance large industrial and other projects require the pooling of the savings of thousands of people. This pooling and the subsequent granting of loans is carried out by **financial intermediaries**, businesses that act as middlemen between savers and borrowers.

Historically, financial intermediaries fell into two categories: commercial banks and thrifts. A **commercial bank** is defined by law as a firm that: 1) provides checking accounts; and 2) makes commercial (business) loans. There are about 9,000 commercial banks, and they are either nationally chartered by the Comptroller of the Currency (a U.S. Treasury agency) or state chartered. Banks that are Fed members are regulated by the Fed, and nonmember state banks are regulated by state banking boards. Bank deposits are insured up to $100,000 by the Federal Deposit Insurance Corporation (FDIC), an agency of the federal government.

There are three types of thrifts: 1) savings and loans; 2) mutual savings banks; and 3) credit unions. They are called thrifts because most of the savers are (thrifty) individuals with relatively small accounts. However, several acts of the federal government have blurred the distinctions between banks and thrifts.

■ A **savings and loan** (S&L), the first type of thrift, was originally designed to provide credit to home buyers. In fact, until recently savings and loans were limited by law to loans for homes (and small multifamily units). There are about 3,000 S&Ls, half federally and half state chartered. They are regulated by the Office of Thrift Supervision, a branch of the U.S. Treasury. Deposits up to $100,000 are insured by the Savings Association Insurance Fund.

■ The second type of thrift is the **savings bank**, also called a mutual savings bank. There are about 800 of these, concentrated in five eastern states. They are operated as cooperatives, which means the depositors are the owners. These banks are regulated by the Federal Reserve Board, and deposits up to $100,000 are insured by the FDIC. Recently, many S&Ls in the nation were converted into savings banks, partly to avoid regulation by the Office of Thrift Supervision and the associated examination fees.

■ The last type of thrift, the **credit union**, is a cooperative formed by members who work in the same firm or government agency or belong to the same union. The first was formed in 1909, and there are more than 14,000 today. Most are federally chartered, and these are regulated by the National Credit Union Association. Deposits up to $100,000 are insured by the National Credit Union Insurance Fund.

A **financial intermediary** is any institution that serves as a middleman between savers and borrowers when it accepts deposits and extends credit.

A **commercial bank** is a financial intermediary that provides checking accounts and makes commercial loans.

A **savings and loan** is a thrift institution that concentrates its loans in real estate.

A **savings bank** is a thrift institution that usually accepts small deposits and is owned by the depositors.

A **credit union** is a thrift institution associated with a place of employment or a union, operated as a cooperative.

THE HISTORY OF U.S. PAPER CURRENCY

Paper money has had a checkered past in the United States, but certainly an interesting one. It wasn't even clear for nearly a century if the Constitution authorized the United States government to issue paper money. It took the Supreme Court until 1871 to decide that it *was* constitutional.

Paper Money of the Revolutionary War

The seeds of the revolution were related to unpopular British taxes. Thus, the Continental Congresses of 1774 and 1775 were reluctant to impose taxes to support the fledgling confederation. So the printing of paper money was authorized, and the notes were called continentals.

Initially, continentals were denominated in terms of a Spanish coin, called a peso by the Spanish, but known as a Spanish milled dollar by the English. These dollars were commonly called pieces of eight, as they were worth or equal in value to eight *reales*, the *real* (or royal in English) being the smaller-value currency of Spain. Each "quarter dollar" was then worth two reales, or "two bits." A quarter dollar today still is often called "two bits." See the photo of both sides of this coin on page 299. Note the banners on the two columns on the reverse side of the coin. This was the basis for the dollar sign ($) of our own currency. (The word dollar stems from a coin minted in Bohemia in the 1500s by a prince named Jochaimsthaler. The coin was called a thaler.) For several decades, colonists had used these coins as the primary metallic medium of exchange.

By the end of 1775, there were $6 million of continentals in circulation, and by the end of 1779, $263 million. This rapid buildup led to the worst inflation in our history. Eventually, it took 170 continental dollars to trade for one gold dollar. The term, "not worth a continental," became a common phrase of scorn for anything of little value. Two of these continentals, one from 1775 and one from 1776, can be seen on page 299.

Currency of the State Banking Period

Article I, Section 8 of the Constitution authorized Congress, "To coin Money, regulate the Value thereof..." This was interpreted as denying the U.S. Government the right to issue paper currency.

However, the need for a medium of exchange led the Continental Congress to charter the first commercial bank in the United States in 1781, The Bank of North America. Soon after, states also began to charter commercial banks, and they were authorized to issue paper currency. By 1790, there were four commercial banks, and there were 26 by 1800, with $10 million of notes in circulation. Later, railroads, insurance companies, and private merchants were authorized to issue currency.

In 1791, Congress chartered the First Bank of the United States. It was authorized to issue currency up to the value of its capital stock. Its charter ended in 1811, and during its life, about $5 million of its notes circulated. That was about a fifth of the paper money of the nation, the rest provided by state-chartered banks.

The number of state banks grew throughout the first half of the 1800s, reaching 1,600 by 1860, with about $200 million in notes circulating. Each bank had its own design and size for its notes. There were over 30,000 varieties of color and design of them, which were easily and often counterfeited. Four of these can be seen on pages 299 and 300. Though each was denominated in dollars and was supposedly redeemable in gold, any two $5 notes would not necessarily have the same purchasing power. For example, to buy a wheelbarrow selling for $5 might have taken one $5 Citizens' Bank of Louisiana note, but *two* $5 Hagerstown notes.

The reason for this disparity in purchasing power was that a note's "worth" or purchasing power depended upon several main factors. The main one was how many of the notes were printed, particularly when compared with how much gold was on hand in the bank's vault to redeem the notes. Many banks "overissued" their currency, usually in the form of loans. Thus, these notes usually depreciated. Often banks went out of their way to avoid redemption of their notes by having offices in frontier hinterlands—so remote that it was said that "a wildcat couldn't find them." That was the basis for the term of the era, the "wildcat banking period."

United States Notes

As in the Revolutionary War, the government had trouble financing the Civil War. The political power to raise taxes was limited, and bond sales were disappointingly low. In August 1861, Congress authorized the first printing of U.S. paper currency. The notes were called demand notes, of which $50 million were printed. They were not made legal tender, which restricted their acceptability.

An even more desperate Congress passed the Legal Tender Act of 1862, which initially authorized the printing of $150 million of notes. Because these were made legal tender (for all debts except import duties and interest in the public debt), they initially were called legal tender notes. (See page 301 for an 1862 and an 1869 note.) However, because of their bright green backs, they soon obtained the name "greenbacks." Two more issues brought the total to $450 million by 1865. The large volume of their issue contributed to their loss of purchasing power. At one point, they only traded for as little as 38 cents (of a gold dollar).

Later, the notes became officially known as United States notes in order to give them more stature and acceptability. (See page 302 for two of these.) The last series was in 1963, and then only the $2 bill was issued (until 1971). Later notes all had red seals. (Note: The most recent $2 bills of today are actually Federal Reserve notes, with a green seal.)

Fractional Currency

The issuance of paper money during the Civil War quickly led to the cessation of the use of most coins of silver and gold. Most people believed paper money would lose its purchasing power over time, so they were not willing to exchange their coins for it.

Consequently, it became difficult to buy items selling for a few cents. To solve this problem, many businesses issued their own small-change notes, redeemed only at their offices. These were derisively called "shin-plasters." In July 1862, a law was passed calling for "postage and other stamps" to circulate as money. In March 1863, a new law authorized the printing of "fractional currency" (paper money of less than a dollar). (See an example on page 302.) These were printed until 1876. The notes were not legal tender (thus, not redeemable by the Treasury in coins). However, they *were* redeemable in postage stamps and U.S. notes.

National Bank Notes

The nuisance of thousands of state bank notes plus the federal notes in circulation, as well as the general discontent with the banking system, led to the National Currency Act of 1863 (and its replacement, the National Banking Act of 1864). The act also was designed to aid in financing the Civil War. It was "An act to provide a national currency secured by a pledge of United States bonds, and to provide for their circulation and redemption thereof." Related acts forced state bank notes out of existence with a 10 percent yearly tax on their circulation after July 1, 1866.

The act established a system of national banks (chartered by the U.S. Government). To issue notes, a bank had to purchase $30,000 of U.S. Government bonds (or a third of its capital, whichever was larger). Thus, the bonds "backed up" the notes, and their sales aided in financing the war. The notes of every bank were uniform in design and size, aiding in their acceptability. However, each bank (about 14,000 of them) had its own name printed on its currency. (See the examples on pages 305 and 306). The notes were also called national currency and circulated until about 1940.

Treasury Notes

Treasury notes, also called coin notes, were authorized by the Sherman Silver Purchase Act (also called the Legal Tender Act) of 1890. The act directed the treasury to buy 4^1/$_2$ million ounces of silver per month with the treasury notes. The intent was to offset the fall in silver prices. It was also intended to alleviate the problems caused by the deflation of the period, especially for farmers squeezed by falling prices who had fixed mortgage payments on their farms. The notes were given legal tender status and were redeemable in either silver or gold. They were only issued for two years. A photo of a treasury note appears on page 303.

Silver and Gold Certificates

Silver and gold certificates, issued until recent times, were a significant U.S. currency. Holders of these could take them to the U.S. Treasury (or its branches) and obtain silver or gold coin in exchange. (Read the wording on these notes shown on pages 303 and 304 that promise to do so.) Silver certificates were first authorized in 1878 (but did not circulate until 1886). Silver certificates were redeemable in coin until 1934 and bullion until 1968. Authorized in 1865, gold certificates were first released for public use in 1882 and were ordered out of circulation in 1933. In the 1800s, newly mined gold and silver could be exchanged for these certificates, and the government would then have coins minted to "back up" the certificates.

Federal Reserve Notes

Our current paper money, Federal Reserve notes, dates to 1914, following the establishment of the Federal Reserve System in 1913. The first series of these notes appears on page 306 (both front and back). The first notes were 25 percent larger than today's notes, though the photos don't show that due to photoreduction to comply with U.S. Treasury rules). They were redeemable in gold at any Federal Reserve bank until 1933. Federal Reserve notes had gold reserve backing until 1968 (though it had dropped to 25 percent by then, owing to the dwindling gold reserves of the United States and the growing supply of currency). The largest note issued was a $10,000 bill.

The fundamental design didn't change until 1996, beginning with the $100 bill. The change was needed to thwart counterfeiting, which had been made easier with new technology, especially color copiers. Counterfeiting is mainly a problem abroad, where the $100 bill is often the preferred bill.

A 1787 Spanish peso coin, commonly called a Spanish milled dollar or "pieces of eight," as it equaled eight Spanish reales, a lower-valued coin. Two reales, or a quarter of a dollar, was called "two bits." It was the main coin used in the late 1700s before the United States began to issue its own coins. The U.S.dollar sign ($) was derived from the banner around the pillars on the reverse side of the coin (on right).

Two examples of continentals (below, left and right). Generally, each state printed them, mainly to pay for the Revolutionary War. Supposedly, each was exchangeable for a certain number of Spanish milled dollars. So many of these were printed that a major inflation resulted. Consequently, the notes lost most of their purchasing power or value.

A state bank note of the "wildcat banking" period. It was issued by a state-chartered bank in Ohio in 1816.

Three state bank notes from the 1840s to the 1860s. The notes of each bank had a unique design, color, and shape. In 1860, there were about 5,000 different notes in circulation from all the banks in operation.

Some banks were more sound than others, due to better administrative practices. Consequently, the same denomination of any two banks (such as a $5 note) rarely had the same purchasing power. Thus, it could take more $5 notes of one bank than another bank to buy a certain item.

Such notes were supposedly exchangeable for gold or silver coin, which, thus, "backed up" the notes. But banks often issued much more currency than was allowed, leading to the devaluation of their notes.

An 1862 legal tender note, both front (above) and back (below) sides. They were commonly called greenbacks because of the dark green back. They were later called U.S. notes and were issued from 1862 until 1969. They were initially issued to pay for the Civil War, during which $450 million were issued. This note was called a "stoplight note" because the highlighted numeral in the center indicated which of the three issued denominations it was ($1, $2, or $3). The words legal tender meant they had to be accepted for payment of the debts listed on the back of the note.

An 1869 legal tender note. It was called a "rainbow note" because of its coloring. The words "Treasury Note" are not to be confused with the treasury notes of the 1890s (shown on page 303).

A United States note of 1917. This was a later version of the legal tender notes of the Civil War period. The actual size of this note was seven and three-eighths inches by three and one-eighth inches, or 43 percent larger than today's currency.

A United States note of the 1928 series, the first notes to be of the present smaller size of today's currency. All later U.S. notes (issued until 1969) had red seals. The last series (of 1963) were only issued in the $2 denomination.

A 10-cent fractional currency note of 1863. Such notes were issued because coins had disappeared from circulation following the issuance of legal tender notes in 1862. As legal tender notes rapidly depreciated in value during the Civil War inflation, gold and silver coins were hoarded because the notes were supposed to be exchangeable for coin. Thus, there was difficulty in making purchases of less than a dollar (very common in the 1860s) because the smallest legal tender note was $1.

A Treasury note of 1891. These were issued from 1890 until 1893 as stipulated by the Sherman Silver Purchase Act of 1890. They were exchangeable for either gold or silver coin.

An 1886 silver certificate with Martha Washington's portrait. These could be exchanged for silver coins at the U.S. treasury or its branches.

A silver certificate of the 1899 series. The actual size of these notes were seven and three-eighths inches by three and one-eighth inches.

A silver certificate, series of 1928. These notes were issued until the early 1960s. They were exchangeable at the U.S. treasury for silver coin until 1934 and bullion until 1968. That is the meaning of paper currency being "backed" by something of supposed "real value."

A gold certificate, series of 1902, both front and back sides. The earlier series of these notes had the nicknames of goldbacks or yellowbacks because of the color on the back. They were exchangeable for gold coin at the U.S. treasury. They were first issued in the 1880s and circulated until 1933, when the United States went off the gold standard. At that time, all gold coin and gold certificates were required to be turned into the U.S. treasury in exchange for other currency. Large denominations of gold certificates continued to be used for interbank transactions and by the Federal Reserve until recently.

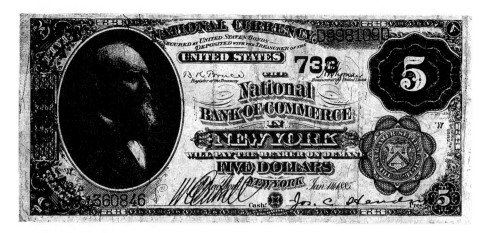

An 1885 national bank note, commonly called national currency. These notes were issued by nationally chartered banks that had purchased U.S. bonds. Each of over 14,000 banks printed its name on its notes, as well as its charter number. However, all notes were uniform in size and design. These notes were authorized by the National Banking Acts of 1863 and 1864. $17 billion were issued from 1863 to 1935. This note was called a brown-back note.

A 1908 national bank of the series of 1902. This series of notes honored President McKinley, who was assassinated in 1901.

A national bank note of the series of 1929, the last series of this type of currency. The notes were issued until 1935 and circulated until about 1940.

A Federal Reserve bank note of 1914. Although it stated "national currency" at the top, its issuance was based on the Federal Reserve Act of 1913. Thus, it was not the same kind of "national currency" as shown at the top of this page. Federal Reserve bank notes were issued from 1914 to 1918.

A Federal Reserve note of the series of 1914. This was the forerunner of U.S. currency of today. However, this note was seven and three-eighths inches by three and one-eighth inches, compared with six and one-eighth inches by two and five-eighths inches for notes today. The seal was also different. The 6-F means this note was issued by the Atlanta Federal Reserve District Bank. It was the sixth Federal Reserve district, and F is the sixth letter of the alphabet.

How Banks Create Money

One of the more baffling things about economics is how banks create money. To understand this, remember that coin and paper currency account for only about a fifth of our money and that the U.S. Treasury makes that form of money. Checkable deposits make up most of the rest. And such money is possible because of the banking system, especially because of the ability of banks to make loans.

Hundreds of years ago, there were no banks. Many people saved their money (often gold) at home. But goldsmiths commonly stored the gold of other people in their vaults for a fee. Over time, the receipts given by the goldsmiths to "depositors," rather than the gold itself, became the medium of exchange. It was said that the receipts were "as good as gold" because they were "backed by gold." Eventually, the goldsmiths realized they could lend out some of the gold, for it was unlikely that all "depositors" would want to draw out their gold simultaneously. (Today, as then, about the same amount is deposited each day as is withdrawn from a bank.) The borrowers of the gold could then use it to buy things. Now, did the total value of the savers' money (gold deposits) drop because of such loans? No, for their deposit statements still showed the same amounts (or balances) as earlier. Further, because the loans *added to* the purchasing power of the original money supply, the money supply increased. Eventually, instead of charging a fee to depositors, goldsmiths *paid* a fee—interest—in order to get more people to deposit (save) their money.

It isn't all that different today. Suppose you receive a check for $1,000 and open a checking account with it. Because of your deposit, your bank can now make a loan. However, the Fed requires banks to keep a certain share of such deposits as part of its **required reserves**, and they cannot make loans based on this share of those deposits. The **reserve requirement** is the percentage of such deposits the bank must keep on reserve, either in the bank vault or at the Fed. (It is called the reserve ratio when expressed in decimal form.) Suppose that it's 20 percent of your $1,000 deposit, or $200. Thus, the bank is free to lend an amount of money equal to the difference, or $800, to Susan, who wants a new stereo system. The bank either sets up a checking account for Susan, putting the $800 into it, or gives her a cashier's check. If she has a new checking account, she can write $800 worth of checks, so the $800 is money. She can also use the cashier's check to buy the stereo or anything else, so it, too, is money. Either way, where did the money come from? From *your* checking account? Well, how much is in your account now, assuming that you didn't spend any of it—$200 or $1,000? The answer is $1,000.

Required reserves refer to the amount of deposits upon which a commercial bank is not allowed to make loans.

The **reserve requirement** is the percentage of a commercial bank's deposits it must keep as required reserves.

So, where did Susan get the $800 for her stereo? After all, you still have all your $1,000 in your account. Almost magically, the bank "created it" from out of nowhere! Banks have such power. That's why it's important to grasp the concept that money is a *representation* of purchasing power. So, if Susan has more purchasing power (represented by money) and you don't have any less, then the bank must have created the money, thereby increasing the amount of purchasing power in the economy. This process repeats itself when Susan buys the stereo and the dealer deposits the $800 check. The dealer's bank can now lend 80 percent of $800, or $640. After many such "cycles," your original $1,000 deposit leads to a *multiple* increase in the money supply. The reason that coins and currency are only about a fifth of M1 is because they lead to the creation of demand deposits after they are deposited in banks. In turn, this leads to the creation of even more demand deposits after banks make more loans because of these deposits. This process occurs over and over until a very large amount of demand deposits have been created. (It's like two people who ultimately create a family of 100 people, but only make up two percent of the family themselves.)

Excess reserves refer to the difference between what a bank is allowed to lend and how much it has lent out.

The **deposit multiplier** refers to the number of times the money supply can expand if all excess reserves are lent.

Often banks make fewer loans than they are allowed to make on the basis of their depositors' money. This difference between what banks can lend and what they have already lent is called **excess reserves**, or the reserves banks have in excess of their required reserves. Because excess reserves are capable of creating new money, the Fed controls their amount in order to control the money supply. The **deposit multiplier** refers to the number of times the money supply could expand if all excess reserves were lent. It is found by using this formula:

$$\text{Deposit Multiplier} = \frac{1}{\text{Reserve Requirement}}$$

The Fed's Control of Bank Reserves and the Money Supply

The Fed controls these excess reserves and, in turn, the money supply, with three main techniques or tools: 1) the discount rate; 2) the reserve requirement; and 3) open market operations. Excess reserves give banks the ability to increase the money supply by using these reserves as the basis for additional loans. Thus, when excess reserves are increased, the money supply can grow faster. Conversely, when excess reserves are decreased, the money supply can't expand as fast.

■ The **discount rate** is the rate of interest the Fed charges its commercial bank members when it lends them additional reserves. When you put money in a checking or savings account, the bank can use your money (purchasing power) to create more purchasing power in the form of a loan. The Fed gives your bank another method of creating purchasing power through loans when it lends the bank these reserves. However, the Fed doesn't actually lend the bank any *money*—only what are called reserves. These reserves represent the ability to create purchasing power when your bank makes a loan to a business or a consumer. That purchasing power, in the form of a demand deposit, *is* money.

In reality, banks seldom borrow reserves from the Fed. When they do, it's usually because they find that they don't have sufficient deposits with the Fed plus vault cash (the two together are called legal reserves) to meet the reserve requirement. (Reserve requirements must be met with legal reserves.) This could occur if several major depositors at a bank withdrew their funds at a time when the bank had few or no excess reserves.

The reason the Fed changes the discount rate usually is not to change the amount of borrowing but to send a message to lending institutions. The message is that the Fed has either expanded or contracted bank reserves in alternative ways. Usually these actions coincide with moves in interest rates in financial markets.

■ Changing the reserve requirement is the second method the Fed uses to control bank reserves.   Figure 10-2 shows a bank that initially had $100 million in deposits from savings and checking account deposits. If the reserve requirement is 20 percent, then the bank must have $20 million in required reserves. Thus, it can make $80 million in loans. But if it has made only $60 million in loans so far, it has excess reserves of $20 million. Suppose the Fed reduces the reserve requirement to 15 percent. Then the bank needs only $15 million in required reserves, leaving $85 million that it can lend. Because it has lent only $60 million so far, it has $25 million in excess reserves, an increase of $5 million. This change appears in the diagram on the right. The middle diagram shows the reverse, where the Fed raises the reserve requirement to 25 percent. Since the bank now needs $25 million in required reserves, it is left with only $15 million in excess reserves.

■ The last method for changing excess bank reserves is **open market operations**, referring to the Fed's purchases and sales of federal government securities that the Treasury sells to finance the budget deficit. Often the initial buyers of these securities decide not to hold them to maturity, so their brokers find buyers for the securities (in the so-called secondary market for government securities). You can follow each of the steps

The **discount rate** is the rate of interest the Fed charges member banks that borrow reserves from it.

Open market operations refer to sales and purchases of securities by the Fed in order to control the level of excess reserves in the commercial banking system.

Figure 10-2

Changing the Reserve
Requirement

Following an increase in
the reserve requirement, a
bank needs more required
reserves, which reduces
its excess reserves by an
equal amount.

A decrease in the reserve
requirement reduces its
required reserves and
increases its excess
reserves.

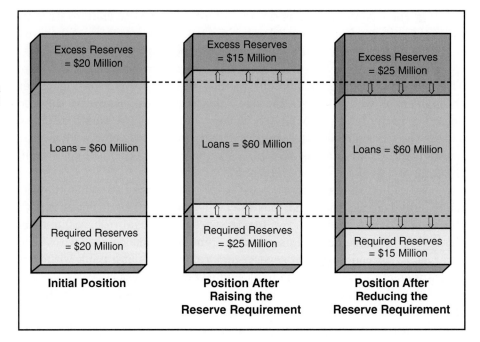

in this process in Figure 10-3. Suppose you buy a $10,000 T-bill from some individual through a broker. What happens to the total excess reserves in the entire banking system as a consequence? Nothing, for although your bank has $10,000 less in total reserves after you write a check to the broker, the seller's bank has $10,000 more after the seller deposited your check. These effects on reserves cancel each other.

However, suppose the Fed buys that T-bill instead. The Fed's $10,000 check is deposited in the original bondholder's bank, so reserves in the entire banking system rise by $10,000. Then isn't this increase offset by the $10,000 that the Fed no longer has in its checking account? No, for the Fed never really had the $10,000 to begin with. So where did it come from? From nowhere! If you wonder how that can be, just remember what money is—a representation of purchasing power. The Fed has the authority to grant such power, even to itself. That was mainly why the Federal Reserve System was established, that is, to establish an "elastic currency" or money that would expand (or contract) according to the needs of the economy.

Alternatively, suppose the Fed *sells* you a bond. If you write the Fed a check for $10,000, your bank's total reserves drop by that amount, leaving the bank less to lend. What does the Fed do with the $10,000? The Fed acts

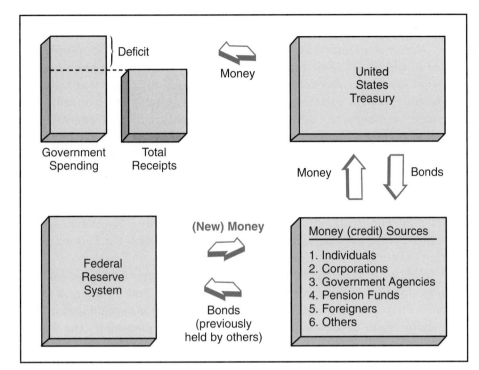

Figure 10-3

The Deficit and Money Creation by the Fed

The U.S. Treasury funds the budget deficit by selling bonds to various buyers. Occasionally the buyers sell these bonds to the Fed (before they mature). The Fed pays for them through its power to create new money when it issues checks to these bond sellers.

as if it never got the check. It neither spends it nor adds it to any savings or checking account. The money—$10,000 worth of purchasing power—simply vanishes. You surely couldn't do that with gold.

The Fed determines whether to expand or contract bank reserves by observing the **federal funds rate**. That is the interest rate on so-called federal funds, or excess reserves that commercial banks lend to each other. This rate gives the Fed an indication of the availability of credit in the entire economy and, consequently, of the likelihood of increased loans and spending. If there are few excess reserves, there is little credit available and the federal funds rate will be high. Alternatively, a low rate indicates ample excess reserves and availability of credit.

The **federal funds rate** is the rate of interest paid by a commercial bank for borrowing the excess reserves of another commercial bank.

Following this introduction to money, the next two chapters are concerned with problems of the macroeconomy. Often these problems have to do with the money supply. Finally, Chapter 13 explains, among other things, how the Fed uses changes in the money supply to deal with these problems.

SUMMARY

Money is an indirect consequence of specialization. When people specialize in the use of their resources to increase productivity, they need to exchange goods and services with each other. One way to exchange, though inefficiently, is with a barter system. Modern economies need a medium of exchange, or money, to make exchanges efficiently, which means with low transaction costs. Money is a representation of purchasing power, and it serves three functions, as: 1) a medium of exchange; 2) a store of value; and 3) a standard of value. Anything used as money needs to be portable, durable, uniform, finely divisible, and scarce.

The Federal Reserve System's primary functions involve regulating commercial banks and controlling the money supply. It consists of the Board of Governors, the District Banks, member banks, the Federal Open Market Committee, and three advisory boards.

Financial intermediaries, which connect savers and borrowers, include commercial banks, savings banks, savings and loans, and credit unions. They are either federally or state chartered, are regulated by federal and/or state agencies, and have their deposits insured by the federal government.

Commercial banks create money when they make loans that are made possible with bank deposits. They are required to keep a small share of deposits either at the Fed or in their vaults. Reserves held by banks in excess of their required reserves are called excess reserves. The Fed controls excess bank reserves and the money supply by changes in the discount rate and the reserve requirement and through open market operations. When excess reserves are increased by cuts in the discount rate and the reserve requirement or by the purchase of government securities, the money supply expands, and vice versa.

QUESTIONS FOR DISCUSSION AND THOUGHT

1. Try and make a hypothetical barter trade with some item you own, a trade you actually would be willing to make. Next, try and sell that same item for a price that is acceptable to you. Keep track of the total time each trade took. Was there any difference in time? Why?
2. Calculate the percentages of your "personal" M1 that are in the form of coin, paper currency, checking account money, and traveler's checks. How close are your figures to the actual M1? If they are much different, what explains the difference?
3. In what sense is counterfeit money actually money and in what sense is it not?
4. If you state that you "made more money" this year than last year, does that mean M1 is bigger this year than last year? Reconcile your answer with your statement.
5. For over a century, paper currency was "backed up" by gold. Why was this done? Why isn't it done now?
6. In what sense is a bond money? In what sense is it not?
7. Why can't the Fed control what share of our money is in the form of currency and demand deposits?

PROBLEMS   See page 488 for the answers.

1. How much money is there in coins, given the following figures (all in billions): traveler's checks–$40; paper currency–$863; M1–$3,599; and checkable deposits–$2,680?
2. Springfield National Bank has total deposits of $860 million and loans outstanding of $710 million. The reserve ratio is 0.11. What is the most amount of additional loans it is authorized to make?
3. Suppose that $10 billion of new currency suddenly appeared (and got into the hands of the general public). The reserve requirement is 16 percent and M1 is $460 billion. What is the highest level you would expect the money supply to rise to in a year or so, if nothing else happened to change it?
4. M1 rose from $620 billion to $660 billion over some period because $5 billion in new currency came into circulation. What was the reserve requirement? The reserve ratio?

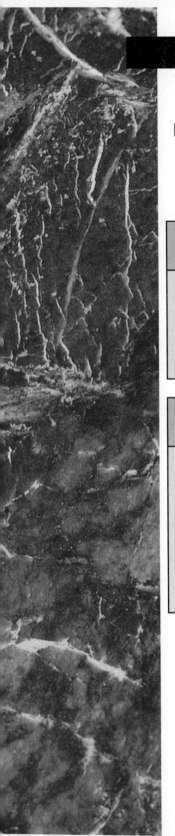

11

MACROECONOMIC EQUILIBRIUM AND RECESSION

CHAPTER PREVIEW

In a capitalist economy, the macroeconomy is subject to major swings in activity, called business cycles.

This chapter introduces the major factors determining the level of activity in the macroeconomy, as well as the reasons for a downturn in overall activity, known as recession.

CHAPTER OBJECTIVES

After completing this chapter, you should be able to:

◆ Compare and contrast the phases of the business cycle.

◆ Describe the conditions necessary for an economy to reach equilibrium.

◆ Explain why recession occurs.

◆ Indicate the causes of a decline in total spending.

◆ Explain why consumer, investment, and government spending decline.

One way people deal with the economic problem caused by the scarcity of resources is to specialize. Although specialization increases efficiency and, consequently, living standards, it also forces specialists to exchange with each other. However, sometimes people have trouble finding others with whom to trade. For instance, under such circumstances business owners don't sell as much as they would like. That is, they don't trade many goods or services for money. Further, many people who wish to sell their time for money (that is, they want to work) can't find anyone or any business to employ them. This inability to trade will result in idled resources and, thus, reduced living standards. This is what business cycles are all about.

ECONOMIC FLUCTUATION OR BUSINESS CYCLES

The subsistence economy of the distant past changed very slowly over time. Each year, all families produced about the same amount of whatever they needed the most and had time and ambition to produce. Consequently, the "gross domestic product" of these early economies changed little. Their "GDP" was the total output of goods and services of all families combined (measured in physical amounts, rather than in money terms as today). It increased mainly because the population grew and because occasional innovations increased the efficiency of resource use. However, because these people didn't specialize as much as we do, they remained poor by today's standards.

Specialization and exchange gradually became more common. When this happened, people produced goods and services for others rather than just for themselves. So long as people made exchanges by bartering, the economy remained similar to earlier times. People still needed about the same amount of the same things each year from the few people with whom they traded. Production didn't change much, except to the extent that weather affected agricultural output.

When the use of money made bartering obsolete, relationships between specialists changed. Instead of two specialists agreeing on an exchange and then making their respective products, specialists (either individuals or firms) began to make products *in anticipation of* exchanges (sales). Firms made brooms, stoves, and other products, storing them in warehouses of their own or their wholesalers until people bought them (or traded for them, but now with money). Today, when trading is very active for most people, the economy is said to be in prosperity. When trading slows down, the period is known as recession.

Figure 11-1

Phases of the
Business Cycle

Over a long period of time,
an economy repeatedly
experiences the business
cycle phases of peak,
recession, trough, and
recovery. These periods
can also be split into
expansions and
contractions.

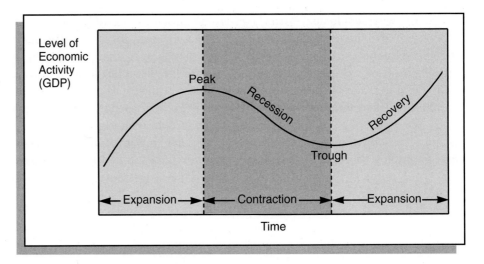

The Business Cycle

Business cycles
are changes in
macroeconomic
conditions, ranging from
prosperity to recession
and back to prosperity.

Peak refers to the
highest point in the
business cycle, where
economic activity is
the greatest.

A recession is the part
of the business cycle
when spending, output,
and employment are
falling, usually for a
period of two or more
quarters.

  Records from as long as 150 years ago tell about prosperity and recession. Because the good and bad times alternated, the economy experienced what economists call **business cycles**. However, although the word "cycles" sometimes implies *regularity* of change, business cycles are anything but regular. Prosperity can last a decade—or only a year—as can recession.

  The business cycle has four phases: 1) peak; 2) recession; 3) trough; and 4) recovery. Figure 11-1 illustrates these phases.

  ■ **Peak** means a high percentage of individuals and businesses succeed in selling (trading or exchanging) their resources and products. Jobs are easy to find. Most firms can sell any product or service they make, and it is relatively easy to become prosperous. If times are exceptionally good, the economy is said to be experiencing a boom.

  ■ Sooner or later the economy "cools off " or enters a **recession**, a time when many macroeconomic variables decline (recede). Businesses sell less and, in turn, cut production. Consequently, employment drops and job openings are rare. Years ago people called this a "bust" period. If conditions got bad very quickly, the frightened firm owners, investors, and employees panicked (partly because there were no government programs, such as unemployment compensation, to ease the burden). Such periods were known as panics, such as the Rich Man's Panic (1903) and the Panic of 1907. Finally, such a period was also called a contraction because the whole economy seemed to contract or grow smaller.

■ The next phase of the business cycle is the **trough**. As with an ocean wave, the trough refers to a low point—specifically, the worst point of the business cycle. Business sales and employment drop to their lowest point. Years ago people called this condition a depression. However, today the term depression refers to a severe and prolonged period of bad economic conditions. For instance, if the unemployment rate remained above 10 percent for several years, one would say the economy was in a depression. The last such depression was the Great Depression, lasting from 1929 through 1941.

> The **trough** is the worst part of the business cycle, which occurs just prior to the recovery phase.

■ When there is significant improvement in sales, employment, and other variables, the economy enters the **recovery** phase of the cycle. Like a patient recovering from surgery, an economy in recovery is still in relatively poor shape. However, sooner or later the economy returns to the prosperity phase. The period starting with the recovery and extending throughout the prosperity period to the next peak is called the expansion because the economy "expands" in size (more output, employment, and other positive trends).

> The **recovery** is the part of the business cycle when macroeconomic conditions have begun to improve, but before prosperity has been reached.

A MODEL OF THE MACROECONOMY

An economic model simplifies the way a certain part of the economy operates. All the variables, elements, and interrelationships don't appear in the model—just the main ones.

Figure 11-2 is a model of the macroeconomy that illustrates the connections between total spending, production, employment, income, taxes, savings, and spending by consumers, investors, and governments. When examining the model, keep in mind these assumptions: 1) there is no foreign trade; 2) there are no transfer payments—thus, people earn all their income; 3) the money supply remains constant; 4) the amount of resources and the level of resource efficiency remain constant; 5) all governments balance their budgets; 6) businesses pay no taxes—thus, all business income flows to the owners; and 7) financial institutions lend out all savings for investment spending, so consumers pay cash for their purchases. (These assumptions *can* be dropped, and the first one will be later on. This artificial simplicity makes it easier to understand the major relationships in the macroeconomy and how recession happens.)

Figure 11-2

A Model of the Macroeconomy

The major elements of the macroeconomy – spending, resources, output, and income – appear in the model. It shows the major relationships in the macroeconomy.

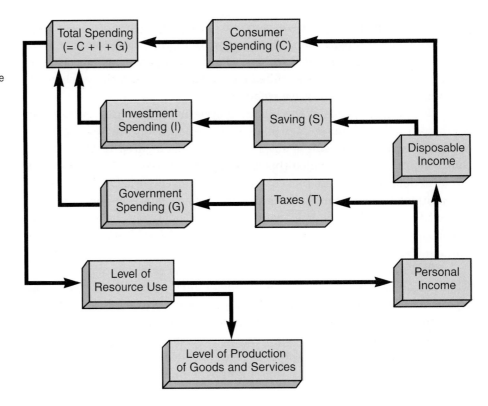

In examining the model, it's best to start at the top left, with total spending. (Total spending is often called aggregate demand—that is, the sum of the demands for all final goods.) Total spending is the GDP from the expenditure approach, composed of expenditures by consumers (C), investors (I), and governments (G). Net exports (X − M) do not appear because it is assumed there is no foreign trade. Total spending is the main influence on the next component in the model, the level of resource use. This "level" refers to how many workers businesses hire, how many supplies they buy, and how many factories they build. The higher total spending is, the more resources firms will buy. Firms want these resources in order to produce goods and services. As resource use increases, so does the level of production of goods and services.

People sell resources in order to earn income. Therefore, the more resources they sell, the greater their personal income is, including: 1) wages, salaries, and commissions paid to laborers; 2) interest paid to owners of capital; 3) rent paid to owners of natural resources; and 4) profits paid to entrepreneurs. (The government calculates personal income each month, but the government's figure differs from the model in that it includes transfer payments.)

In the model, personal income is divided into two parts—taxes and disposable income. Taxes allow governments to spend money on goods and services. Next, government spending (G) becomes part of total spending (the starting point). Disposable income refers to that part of personal income that people are free to "dispose of," the part they retain after paying taxes. People dispose of their income either: 1) by consumption, or spending on consumer goods (C); or 2) by saving (S), or not spending all or part of their income. Consumption provides the second leg of the total spending composite. The final leg is investment spending (I), including spending for capital goods, construction of buildings, and any change in inventories. It is assumed that firms borrow money for such spending or use their savings (such as retained earnings from their profits).

Now that you are familiar with the basic model (Figure 11-2), consider what else influences the three components of total spending.

■ First, consider consumer spending. Besides disposable income, consumer confidence in the economy's future is another major determinant of consumption. If people expect a recession, they will spend less now in order to have some money for the bad times ahead. Interest rates and the availability of credit also determine how much consumers spend. Lower interest rates and readily available credit encourage consumers to spend.

■ Second, interest rates, along with expectations of future sales and profit, determine investment spending. Predictions of good times ahead cause investment spending to rise because firms want to be ready with new capital equipment and factories when people start buying at a faster rate. Conversely, firms spend less on capital if they expect lower sales of their products in the future. Tax laws favoring business expansion stimulate investment spending. Finally, government regulation and "red tape" often discourage capital spending by businesses.

■ Third, government spending depends not only upon tax receipts, but also upon how much governments can borrow. In turn, borrowing by governments depends upon interest rates, the political acceptability of deficits, and legal or constitutional restrictions on such borrowing.

We can now use Figure 11-2 to show how an economy gets into recession or inflation. However, before using the model to illustrate recession or inflation possibilities, macroeconomic equilibrium, a condition where there is neither recession nor inflation, must first be considered.

THE MACROECONOMY IN EQUILIBRIUM

Equilibrium on the microeconomic level was covered in Chapter 2. The equilibrium price for a good is the price that balances consumers' desires for that good with the amount firms offer for sale, an amount called the equilibrium quantity. Now a similar situation is examined for the economy as a whole—the macroeconomy.

The Meaning of Macroeconomic Equilibrium

Macroeconomic equilibrium is a condition where there is no change in the major macroeconomic variables, occurring when total spending equals the value of total output.

Equilibrium GDP is the level of GDP at which the economy remains when all factors that influence it are balanced.

Macroeconomic equilibrium means certain macroeconomic variables don't change over time. The variables are those in the macroeconomic model, including total spending, the amount of production of goods and services (GDP), personal income, and employment. Several forces tend to increase or decrease each variable, but in equilibrium these forces balance each other. Thus, each variable does not change. So **equilibrium GDP** is the level of GDP that does not change over time because all the forces that influence it are balanced. (This view of equilibrium is called static equilibrium, where an economy does not grow. More sophisticated analysis involves the concept of dynamic equilibrium, where growth can occur. It is not the intent of this book to present such in-depth analysis.)

The beginning of this chapter focused on macroeconomic equilibrium in a subsistence, nonexchange economy, where almost everyone produced the same things each year and in the same amounts. Thus, the collective output of the members of society—their "GDP"—did not change either.

To keep things simple, we will proceed as if equilibrium occurs only when there is no inflation and no unemployment. This allows us to ask what changes would lead the economy into inflation or unemployment. However, as you will discover in Chapter 13, a group of economists called Keynesians believe that equilibrium can exist when there is unemployment or inflation and that government intervention is then required to solve these problems. The analysis is not much different in the Keynesian case, but you should be aware that equilibrium does not always mean there is no inflation or unemployment.

Conditions of Macroeconomic Equilibrium

Before proceeding, we must make another assumption about price levels in the model. "Price level" refers to the consideration of all prices simultaneously, as measured by a price index. It is assumed that in equilibrium there is only one price level. That is, prices in general don't rise (inflation) or fall (deflation).

GDP reflects the production of all businesses combined. Why would these firms produce the same amount each year, which they do in equilibrium? Think of why businesses produce anything at all—to sell their products and make a profit, of course. When customers buy more than previously, firms usually expand output. When customers buy less than previously, firms usually cut back on output.

Therefore, if a firm neither expands nor cuts back on output this year, apparently the managers think they can sell the same output as last year— no more and no less. This is because customers want to buy the same amount as last year. Now suppose that all firms are in this situation. Suppose further that the combined sales of all firms last year equaled the value of what they produced. Thus, their warehouse inventories neither increased nor decreased. Then the total output of the nation this year will not change from last year's level, for if total spending or aggregate demand doesn't change, firms will not change their outputs.

Look at what problems happen if that output level *does* change. First, if output expands and spending does not, firms store the extra output in warehouses—a costly procedure. Alternatively, if firms cut back on output while customers still want the same amount of goods and services, the firms must remove products from their warehouse inventories. Eventually, some customers won't get all they want to buy. Because this annoys customers and means profit opportunities are lost, firms try to avoid this situation. Thus, if total spending remains constant, firms neither expand nor contract output to avoid these problems.

Therefore, for an economy to reach macroeconomic equilibrium, it is necessary for total spending or aggregate demand to equal the total value of goods and services produced, given a particular price level.

An important question is: How does total spending or aggregate demand remain constant? A constant level of total spending is a part of macroeconomic equilibrium, along with a constant level of total production. Total spending equals the combined spending of consumers (C), investors (I), and governments (G). It's easy to imagine constant "spending" in a simple subsistence economy of the past. Of course, with no money and exchanging, those people didn't spend any money. However, they did spend *time and effort* to make things, the counterpart of today's consumer spending. Their efforts ("spending") didn't change yearly because their needs did not change.

Two main elements of today's economy, savings and taxes, pose potential problems for the stability of total spending. Economists refer to savings and taxes as **leakages** (that is, involving income or money that "leaks out" of the spending flow). That's because resource earners: 1) save

Leakages refer to the part of peoples' income that they do not immediately spend on goods and services, including taxes and savings.

some of the income they earn in order to buy goods and services *in the future;* and 2) use some of it to pay taxes to support the government. In other words, people don't spend all of *today's* income for goods and services received *today.*

Does the fact that people don't spend all their income mean that total spending drops each year? No, for someone else spends the part they don't spend. People usually don't save their money in cookie jars, but in banks and other financial institutions. In turn, these savings give financial institutions the ability to make loans so firms can purchase capital equipment and individuals can build homes. So long as *all* savings dollars find their way into investment spending, total spending will not fall just because some personal income "leaked" out of the normal spending stream.

Similarly, the taxes people pay don't just remain in government treasuries. Governments spend that money as fast as possible, it seems. Thus, *total* spending or aggregate demand can be the same as if people spent all their income themselves as soon as they earned it. What differs is that government spending is now part of total spending, making the consumer component smaller. So long as government spending equals taxes, the tax leakage won't cause total spending to fall.

Injections refer to additions to total spending in the macroeconomic circular flow, in the form of either investment or government spending.

A related term to leakages is **injections**, which refers to investment spending and government spending. It means "idle" money is "put to use" in purchasing goods and services—or money is "injected" into the "spending stream." (Note that this is not *new* money created by the Federal Reserve System. See pages 308-311 for review of how the Fed can change the money supply.)

Macroeconomic equilibrium is achieved if the combined injections equal the combined leakages—that is, if savings plus taxes equal investment spending plus government spending. In equilibrium, owners of resources use all the money they earn producing goods and services to purchase that same amount of goods and services. If total spending matches the value of production, firms will continue to produce the same amount, so there is equilibrium.

(A little clarification is in order here. In equilibrium, business firms sell exactly the same level of goods that they produce. Therefore, their warehouse stocks or inventories do not change. So the investment spending they carry out is only for capital equipment and construction. We call this their *intended* investment. Thus, we say the condition for equilibrium is when savings equal the *intended* investment, or where the leakages equal *intended* injections. However, as there are no inventory changes in equilibrium, the leakages equal the *actual* injections as well. Later, with recession, this similarity will disappear.)

Suppose the economy has a potential GDP of $8,000 billion. Suppose further that there is full employment, with 133 million people working out of a labor force of 140 million. (This means the balance, or seven million, are unemployed.) Thus, the unemployment rate is five percent (= 7 million ÷ 140 million x 100). Labor and the other resources produce $8,000 billion worth of output, which creates a similar $8,000 billion income for resource owners. They, in turn, must pay $2,000 billion of this in taxes, leaving a disposable income of $6,000 billion. If people save $1,000 billion of that, the remaining $5,000 billion is spent on consumer goods and services. Finally, suppose the government spends all the $2,000 billion it collects in taxes and investors spend an amount equal to the $1,000 billion of savings. Then total spending is $8,000 billion, for C ($5,000) plus I ($1,000) plus G ($2,000) equals total spending. The economy is in equilibrium, for firms again produce the same $8,000 billion of output they originally did. Figure 11-3 summarizes these events.

Incidentally, for equilibrium to occur, it is *not* necessary for investment spending to equal savings and for government spending to equal taxes—as it does in Figure 11-3. It is only necessary that investment and

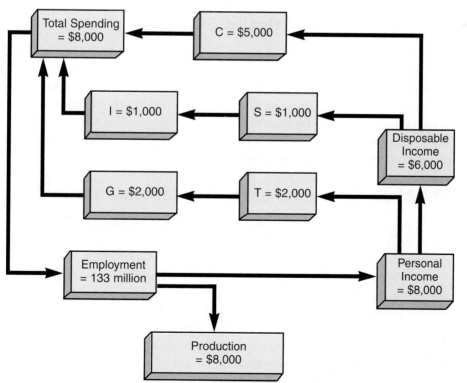

Figure 11-3

Equilibrium Conditions
(figures are in billions)

In equilibrium, the combined leakages, or savings plus taxes, equal the combined injections, or investment plus government spending. That ensures that all personal income is spent, thereby keeping employment and production at constant levels.

government spending *combined* (I + G) be equal to savings and taxes *combined* (S + T). This situation, when I + G = S + T, can also occur when investment spending exceeds savings—so long as taxes exceed government spending by the same amount. Using a numerical example, let I = $1,200, G = $1,800, S = $1,300, and T = $1,700—all expressed in billions of dollars. Then I + G = S + T, for $1,200 + $1,800 = $1,300 + $1,700—or $3,000 billion on both sides of the equation.

This example may seem irrelevant, but it helps illustrate an important phenomenon known as crowding out, where the government finances a deficit by taking savings that would otherwise have gone to private investment. We say "taking" savings because the government, unlike private investors, can pay *any* interest rate required to finance the deficit. Recall from earlier that the government borrows money to finance a deficit when it sells bonds. When the government competes with private investors for savings, it will increase the interest rate as high as is necessary to ensure that the government will be able to sell its bonds. Thereby, private investment spending financed with borrowed money will be reduced (there is more about this in Chapter 13). Of course, the government just runs up a bigger deficit in doing so.

INTRODUCTION TO RECESSION

The preceding section is mostly imaginary. Its assumptions and the equaling of injections and leakages rarely if ever happen. However, these pages weren't read in vain, for they will help to understand why recession occurs. Remember the purpose of models—to simplify the world so the primary relationships can be seen more clearly.

This section describes a recession, explains how economists predict recessions, and examines the causes of recessions.

The Major Characteristics of a Recession

Remember that certain economic variables "recede" in a recession. Three central events indicate that an economy is in a recession: 1) total spending falls; 2) production falls; and 3) employment falls.

■ First, total spending or aggregate demand decreases immediately preceding and during much of a recession. The drop can come from decreases in consumer spending, investment spending, government spending, or a combination of these. Each causes firms to lose sales.

■ Second, production of goods and services declines. Firms respond to lower sales by either cutting back on output or stopping production completely. This is reflected in a fall in real GDP. In a typical recession, real

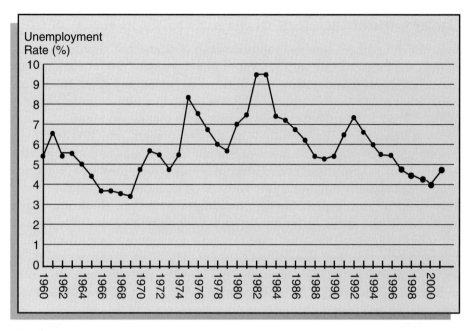

The unemployment rate has averaged about six percent since 1960. The rate rose during recessions.

GDP falls from one to three percent per year. In major depressions in the 1800s and in the 1930s, output often fell more than 10 percent. Generally, the economy is considered to be in a recession if real GDP falls for at least two consecutive quarters. However, real GDP could fall for only one quarter, then rebound for a quarter, only to fall again in the third quarter. If several other measures of the economy were unfavorable, this might still be called a recession. Most economists depend on the private National Bureau of Economic Research to determine when recessions start and end. Seven economists there examine many variables to make their judgements.

■ Third, employment falls and the unemployment rate increases during recession. However, because many people drop out of the labor force when jobs are scarce, the unemployment rate doesn't climb as high as one might expect. Jobs are much harder to find, layoffs are more common, and the "quit rate" drops (meaning people are less likely to quit their jobs).

Figure 11-4 shows the unemployment rate dating back to 1960. Since 1960, recessions occurred in 1960, 1970-71, 1974-75, 1980, 1982, 1990-91 and 2001-2002 as evidenced by the increases in unemployment rates. An increase in the unemployment rate can tip a presidential election away from the party in power. Such was the case in 1960 (which helped Kennedy against Nixon), 1976 (which helped Carter against Ford), 1980 (which helped Reagan against Carter), and 1992 (when a sluggish recovery was a major factor in Clinton's defeat of Bush).

Other Characteristics of an Economy in Recession

Several other economic conditions can indicate that there is a recession: 1) the inflation rate falls; 2) wages rise more slowly; 3) businesses cut costs sharply; 4) interest rates fall; 5) transfer payments rise; 6) tax collections fall; and 7) the budget deficit increases. Each of these is a consequence of one or more of the three major events considered above.

■ First, the inflation rate drops during a recession. (Be careful. A falling *inflation rate* doesn't mean *prices* fall. It just means they don't rise as rapidly as before. However, in steep recessions or depressions, the price level *might* actually fall, but this is rare. That situation is called *de*flation.) Very often in strong prosperities preceding a recession, there are sharp increases in the demand for many goods and services. If firms cannot expand rapidly enough to meet these increased demands, shortages appear. Consequently, prices of many items increase. However, in the recession following prosperity, demands for goods and services don't increase as much. In fact, they usually fall. Thus, there are fewer and smaller shortages (even many *surpluses*), leading to smaller price increases and less inflation.

■ Second, wages (and other resource prices) don't increase as much during a recession for similar reasons. In prosperous times, firms fight for the available workers by rapidly bidding up wages. In recession, with so many people seeking work, those who do hold jobs don't get such rapid wage increases as they did during periods of widespread labor shortages.

■ Third, businesses make sharp reductions in expenses during a recession. They do this to maintain their profit margins, which fall along with sales during recession. However, even reduced expenses can't save firms that have severe sales drops or were in financial difficulty before the recession. Thus, the number of business bankruptcies increases sharply during a recession.

■ Fourth, interest rates fall. An interest rate is a price—the price of credit. Recall that surpluses lead to falling prices and that surpluses are caused by either a decrease in demand or an increase in supply. During a recession, the demand for credit decreases because businesses and individuals take out fewer loans. Businesses see poor prospects for new ventures or for any new equipment paying for itself. Also, individuals fear they won't be able to repay their consumer loans if they lose their jobs.

■ Fifth, transfer payments rise sharply. The government receives more requests for assistance because of rising unemployment, reduced work hours, possibly reduced wages, and the like.

■ Sixth, the government takes in fewer tax receipts. Income tax collections are down because fewer people are working or getting overtime pay. Sales tax collections are down because sales are off during a recession.

THINKING CRITICALLY ABOUT ECONOMIC QUESTIONS IN OUR LIVES

Did Cavemen Have Recessions?

Things to Consider

1. Review the events of a recession. After all is said and done, what really is a recession? Review the material in Chapter 3 on specialization for a clue.

2. Then consider what is fundamentally the same or different about the economy today and that of one many thousands of years ago in "caveman times," especially with respect to what causes our recessions.

3. Given those similarities or differences, could cavemen have suffered a recession?

   See page 471 for the answer.

■ Seventh, rising transfer payments and falling tax receipts combine to create the last event of a recession—a growing budget deficit. For example, budget deficits rose in the 1930s in spite of Roosevelt's effort to balance the budget.

Attempts to Forecast Future Economic Conditions

Just as some try to predict the weather, others try to predict the future of the economy. The Department of Commerce calculates its Composite Index of Leading Indicators to do just that. For this index, it uses 11 economic variables, ones that "lead" the rest of the economy. This means the variables either move up or down *before* most other macroeconomic variables. They are: 1) stock prices; 2) building permits; 3) the length of the manufacturing workweek; 4) price changes for "sensitive" or key raw materials; 5) orders for new business equipment; 6) changes in the money supply; 7) the number of manufacturing layoffs; 8) length of delivery time for goods; 9) consumer confidence; 10) new orders for consumer goods; and 11) the number of unfilled orders for durable goods. (Durable goods, such as autos, furniture, and large appliances, usually last for a long time.

Nondurable goods, such as food, paper products, and toiletry articles, usually have shorter lives.)

Economists also try to predict the economic future by constructing mathematical models with equations that describe the relationships between major macroeconomic variables. The models are called **econometric models**. Using dozens and even hundreds of such equations, these model builders enter certain data (such as the money supply and tax rates) and let a computer predict the future of such variables as GDP, interest rates, and income growth.

An **econometric model** is a mathematical model of the macroeconomy used for forecasting.

CAUSES OF RECESSION— AN ELEMENTARY PRESENTATION

Suppose the economy has been at full employment for several years. In other words, actual GDP equals potential GDP. Firms produce all they can because consumers, investors, and governments want to buy all that output. So why would firms produce less—causing a recession?

This section introduces the major conditions and causes of a recession. It is a simplified model of the economy in which it is assumed there is a constant price level. Although this is not realistic, the model provides a fairly thorough explanation of how an economy can slip into recession. In the following section, that simplifying assumption is dropped. However, the increase in reality comes with the cost of increasing complexity.

General Conditions Leading to Recession

Remember that firms produce goods and services because somebody buys their output. So when customers decide to buy less than before, firms produce less. More precisely, aggregate demand or total spending on goods and services (C + I + G) declines. But why? Recall that when the economy was in equilibrium, total spending did *not* decline (or rise either). The reason was that leakages (savings and taxes) equaled injections (investment and government spending). (Remember, this investment was the *intended* spending on capital goods and private construction. It assumed there were no changes in business inventories.) Essentially, investors and governments spent all the "unspent" income.

However, now total spending *does* change—it falls. Apparently leakages no longer equal injections. In fact, leakages exceed injections. Simply put, the total of people's savings and taxes exceeds the amount of money businesses and people intend to use to buy capital goods and buildings plus the money governments intend to spend on goods and services. Thus, the difference between leakages and injections amounts to "unused money," which drags the economy down. The next section shows how such a condition can arise.

To summarize, there are two general conditions necessary for recession. First, total spending or aggregate demand must fall. Second, for total spending to fall, leakages must exceed intended injections.

Causes of a Decline in Total Spending

Look again at the circular flow model under equilibrium conditions in Figure 11-3 on page 323, where the economy is at potential GDP (as well as at full employment). The situation will now change as the economy in the model moves into recession. This can occur for two reasons: 1) leakages increase; and 2) injections decrease.

■ Suppose everyone decides to save more than before—say, collectively, $1,200 billion rather than $1,000 billion. Suppose that at the same time the government raises taxes from $2,000 billion to $2,400 billion, leading disposable income to fall to $5,600 billion. Then consumer spending will drop to $4,400 billion. Consequently, what happens to total spending? It depends upon what happens to investment and government spending. If they stay at $1,000 billion and $2,000 billion, respectively, then total spending drops to $7,400 billion (= $4,400 + $1,000 + $2,000). Figure 11-5 shows this, and the S and T boxes are shaded gray to indicate the cause of the recession.

(In reality, if the government would raise taxes by $400 billion, C would fall by less than $400 billion. That's because some of the $400 billion that was taken from people would have been saved and not spent. However, because it would be a small amount, it will be ignored here.)

Next, what happens to employment and production when savings and taxes increase? Probably nothing—initially. First, business owners may not be aware of the increase in savings (and the accompanying fall in consumer spending). Even if they are, they won't lay off workers immediately, since they do not know if the economic downturn is temporary or long term. If firms lay off experienced, productive workers, the workers might not be around to rehire when good times return. So firms wait as long as possible before cutting back on production and employment. After they do cut back, spending and production eventually might come into balance at a new equilibrium level, but lower than $8,000 billion.

Figure 11-5

Recession Caused by an Increase in Leakages

(figures are in billions)

Note that both savings and taxes rose from Figure 11-3. This led consumer spending to fall from $5,000 billion to $4,400 billion. Consequently, total spending fell by an equal amount. If production remains unchanged, inventories will build up in business warehouses.

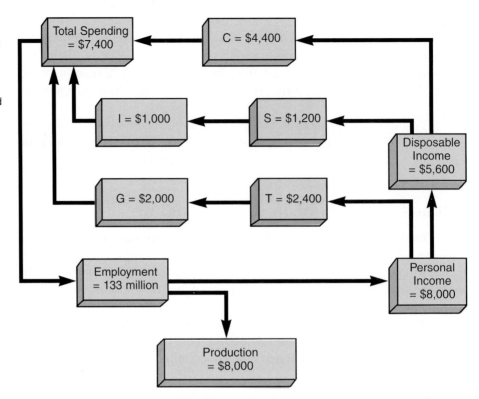

■ The economy can fall into a recession even when taxes and savings do *not* rise. This alternative route involves injections. Suppose investment falls to $800 billion and government spending falls to $1,600 billion. Again, total spending falls to $7,400 billion (= $5,000 + $800 + $1,600). Even though total spending falls for a different reason than increased leakages, the effect would be the same—production would fall, millions of people would be out of work, and total income would be down. The first stage of this scenario appears in Figure 11-6, where again the causes are shaded gray—but this time they're the I and G boxes.

Reasons Why Leakages Increase

Rising savings and taxes cause problems, but why should they rise? In other words, what ultimately causes the recession? This section deals with these two causes in turn.

■ First, consider the increase in savings. More than anything else, people's confidence in future economic conditions influences how much they save today. If most people expect economic hard times a year from now, they

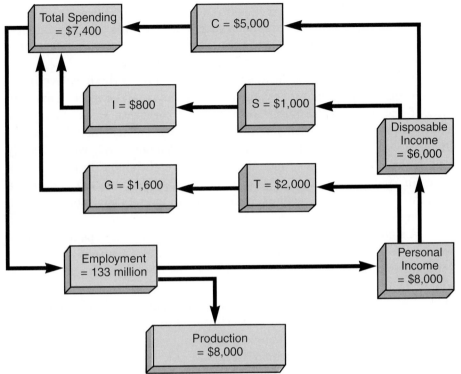

Figure 11-6

Recession Caused by a Decrease in Injections

(figures are in billions)

In this case, total spending fell from $8,000 billion to $7,400 billion because investment and government spending fell from Figure 11-3. Again, if production remains unchanged, inventories will build up in business warehouses.

will save more today than if they expect prosperity. Many won't buy expensive items they can delay, such as cars, large appliances, furniture, and other durable goods. Forecasters pay close attention to sales of durable goods to predict the future of the economy.

As can be seen, recessions often are caused by self-fulfilling prophecies. People expect bad times soon, so they make fewer purchases now. Eventually this can *create* bad times.

Many events can create a widespread fear of the future. One is a major stock market decline. The stock market crash of 1929 helped turn an ordinary recession into a major depression that lasted until 1941. People reasoned that because the market collapsed, the whole economy would go sour by 1930 or 1931. To protect themselves against the future, many people decided to fix their old Model T Fords rather than buying new Model A Fords. As a result, the Ford Motor Corporation and its employees suffered, as did thousands of other firms and millions of their employees.

The worse the Great Depression became, the more that people feared the future. In his inaugural address, President Roosevelt wisely warned,

"The only thing we have to fear is fear itself." A goal of his frequent "fireside chats" on the radio was to reduce such fears with his calming, fatherly manner. However, that fear was so intense that the economic behavior of some elderly people today still reflects that fear.

Severe stock market declines don't seem to have the negative influence on consumer spending any longer that many would expect. This is in spite of the much wider public ownership of corporate stock that exists today. (In the past, generally only upper-income earners bought stocks.) One example is the stock market crash of October 1987, which hardly caused a ripple in consumer spending. Another is the sharp decline in stock prices in 2000 and 2001. Little or no effect appeared in 2000 and only a moderate effect in 2001, perhaps contributing to the recession that began in that year.

A significantly larger effect on savings and consumer spending seems possible from terrorist attacks. The economy was already weak on September 11, 2001, but the terrorist attacks led to sharp reductions in consumer spending in the following months. The effect was not evenly distributed over the entire economy, as travel (especially air travel) and entertainment spending had precipitous declines. Only time can tell how important this new factor will be in our economy.

Another reason for an increase in the savings rate is an increase in interest rates. When interest rates rise, people tend to buy fewer products now so they can buy more later with their interest income. So there is an increase in the volume of deposits into savings accounts and other interest-earning accounts.

■ An increase in taxes is the second leakage that can cause a recession. The most likely reason for an increase in taxes without a corresponding increase in government spending is a drive to sharply reduce the federal budget deficit.

Reasons Why Injections Decrease

The other two causes of recession involve a decline in either investment spending or in government spending. Investment could fall for several reasons: 1) expectations of lower profits; 2) increased interest rates; and 3) irregularity of innovations.

■ First, if business owners believe profits will fall in the future, they will invest less in capital equipment. If they expect their sales will fall, they also will expect lower profits—and they will expect lower sales if they believe that the events just covered will happen.

■ Second, investment spending is likely to fall if interest rates rise. Many firms finance capital expenditures with loans. Thus, higher finance charges discourage such purchases—particularly the marginal ones (that is, the capital goods least likely to pay off). Construction, the other main component of investment spending, also falls as interest rates climb. That's because most people buy homes with credit and businesses rely on credit in order to build factories and offices.

■ Third, many economists believe that investment in capital goods comes in waves or is "lumpy" because of the irregularity of innovation. For example, the development of the auto led to massive investments in related plant and equipment that lasted into the late-1920s, when expansion and innovation slowed. Similarly, computer developments and applications led to mass purchases of equipment in the 1970s and 1980s—which will perhaps fizzle by the turn of the century. If such downturns in capital spending are large enough, other sectors of the economy, such as the suppliers of parts and raw materials, get caught up in it.

The last cause of recession, a decline in government spending, can occur for several reasons: 1) a budget-reduction package; 2) election of many conservatives; and 3) the end of a war.

■ First, a move to reduce a budget deficit could mean less government spending. If the United States decides to balance the budget, federal spending on roads, defense, and education could fall. This is one reason legislators fight closings of military bases in their districts. Shutting down even a small base can lead to a local "depression" due to snowballing effects. Fears accompanying a reduced deficit were very evident when Congress sought to reduce the deficit in 1993 and to a lesser extent in 1995-96.

■ Second, budgets could decline sharply even without a deficit. One reason could be the election of many conservatives, who would reduce government involvement in the economy for philosophical reasons and, consequently, reduce government spending. This occurred after the 1994 elections, when the Republicans gained control of both houses of Congress.

■ The end of a major war would also lead to a sharp decline in government spending. This happened after both world wars. Many people thought the Great Depression, which ended at the start of World War II, would resume after the war. The managers at Montgomery Ward, a leading retailer then, believed that, so they built few new stores. However, managers at Sears, a much smaller retailer at the time, thought the opposite. They believed that 10 million ex-servicemen wanted to buy houses—and fill those houses with items that Sears sold. The managers at Sears also believed there was a lot of "stored up" demand for goods because wartime rationing (used to deal with wartime shortages) prevented people

THINKING CRITICALLY ABOUT ECONOMIC QUESTIONS IN OUR LIVES

What Good Is a Recession?

Things to Consider

1. Recessions are considered to be bad news when they arrive, for obvious reasons.

2. Why might you consider them to be good news as well? That is, list some good effects of a recession, either for particular groups in society or for society as a whole. In doing this, think of economist Thorstein Veblen's comment of nearly a century ago: "A depression, far from being an unmitigated evil, acts as a good, cold douche (or shower) for the economic system."

    See page 471 for the answer.

from buying many items. So Sears greatly expanded its number of stores and leapfrogged its archrival.

End Notes on Recession

The simple macroeconomic model used in this chapter left out two other causes of recession—rising imports and falling exports. The sharp increase in oil prices following Iraq's invasion of Kuwait in August 1990 also led many people to expect recession in fall 1990. They expected the increases in spending on oil products to "leak out" of the economy. That would mean *less* spending on other goods and services made in the United States, thereby causing a recession. If the assumption of no foreign trade is relaxed, the model will have one more leakage and one more injection.

Some economists say the shift of the labor force to service jobs and away from the goods sector insulates the economy from recession because laborers who produce durables, such as appliances and cars, experience the worst employment fluctuations during recessions. As such labor shrinks in the labor force, the economy as a whole will fluctuate less. Also, many economists believe that the increasing diversity the economy is experiencing further protects it from major fluctuation if a few industries suffer decline.

AGGREGATE DEMAND AND SUPPLY ANALYSIS

The graphs in Figure 11-7 through 11-10 introduce concepts that allow a more rigorous discussion of recession. They are the aggregate demand function (or curve) and the aggregate supply function. It is assumed that: 1) there is a given level of technology and efficiency of resource use; 2) there is a given money supply; and 3) people earn a given level of money income. The four figures represent increasingly complex explanations of reality.

These graphs seem similar to demand and supply graphs for individual products. However, here the vertical axis measures not a *single* price, but rather the price level of all goods and services combined. As noted earlier, there is no actual way to measure that, but the price index is a representation of the price level. Likewise, here the horizontal axis doesn't measure the output of a *single* good or service, as with an ordinary demand or supply graph. Rather, it measures the entire collection of final goods and services produced, called real output. Again, this cannot be measured directly, but real GDP is a good "proxy" for this output.

The Aggregate Demand Curve

The aggregate demand curve, labeled AD, appears as a downward sloping line in Figure 11-7 (as well as in subsequent figures). Like a demand line for a single product, AD shows all the possible amounts that consumers, investors, and governments want and are able to buy with their given incomes at all possible price levels. This shows that people are able to buy more goods and services out of their incomes at lower price levels than at higher price levels.

It's important to note that the term total spending used until now is not precisely the same as aggregate demand in these graphs. Total spending refers to a specific *dollar* amount of spending on goods and services, assuming a *given* price level. However, in these graphs, aggregate demand reflects the *various* amounts of output—not any single amount—that are bought at *different* price levels. Just like the demand for a particular good or service, aggregate demand is a *relationship* between the price level of goods and services and the amounts of these goods and services that buyers seek to purchase.

Figure 11-7

Aggregate Demand and Aggregate Supply

The intersection of the aggregate demand and aggregate supply curves gives the price level and the equilibrium level of output in the economy.

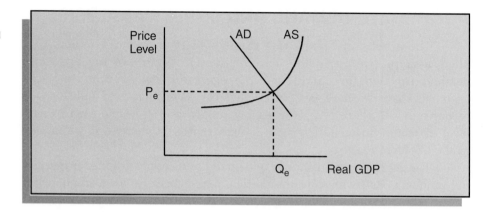

Why the Aggregate Demand Curve Slopes Downward

The demand curve for a single product and the aggregate demand curve slope downward for different reasons. The demand curve for a single product slopes downward because of the substitution effect and the income effect. The aggregate demand curve slopes downward because of: 1) the real balance effect; 2) the interest rate effect; and 3) the international trade effect.

■ The real balance effect means that a lower price level will lead to an increase in the quantity demanded of real output (or real GDP). This is because lower prices enable people to buy more with their stock of money and other financial assets. For example, if you had $200 in cash plus $1,000 in bonds, you could buy x amount of goods and services at a certain price level. If those prices suddenly were cut in half, your $1,200 in assets now enable you to buy twice as much.

■ The interest rate effect refers to an increase in the quantity demanded of real output as a consequence of a fall in the price level that causes interest rates to fall. To illustrate, suppose the price level fell by 10 percent. Suppose further that it would cost you $1,000 to buy x amount of goods and services before the price level drop. Following the drop, it would only cost $900 to buy them. If you put the $100 you saved in a bank, the supply of credit would increase in the economy. If enough people follow your behavior (as they, too, experience the price level drop), interest rates will fall (because excess reserves rose). In turn, businesses and individuals will borrow more money from financial institutions. This allows them to buy the extra real output shown by the downward-sloping aggregate demand curve.

■ The international trade effect refers to the increase in the quantity demanded of real output when a fall in the price level affects imports and exports. A falling U.S. price level (relative to the world price level) causes Americans to buy fewer foreign goods and services and more U.S.-made goods and services. Similarly, foreigners buy more U.S.-made goods and services and less of their own.

The Aggregate Supply Curve

Like the supply curve for an individual product, the upward slope of the aggregate supply curve (labeled AS) in Figure 11-7 shows that firms offer more output at higher price levels. They offer more for sale because, if prices rise but resource prices stay constant, they can afford to produce units of output that cost more to produce. (Remember, beyond a certain point, per-unit costs of products, or average costs, rise.) Thus, a higher price level makes it profitable to increase real output, which is shown by the upward slope of the aggregate supply curve. Bear in mind that the horizontal axis measures *total* output of *all* businesses—not just the output of a single firm or industry as in the case of a single product. Thus, the axis is labeled real output, which is measured by real GDP.

The steep part of the AS line shows that once output reaches a very high point, any extra output brings rapid increases in cost. This reflects such factors as factories on overtime, few skilled workers left to hire, and older, less efficient standby machines that are pressed into service. In other words, the economy is gradually nearing potential GDP.

Macroeconomic Equilibrium

Macroeconomic equilibrium is the condition where there is no change in total output (real GDP), total spending, employment, and so on. It occurs when the equality of leakages (savings, taxes) and injections (investment, government spending) leads to all the goods and services that are produced to be purchased by individuals, firms, and governments. In short, everything that is made is bought. Thus, firms have no reason to increase or decrease their outputs or, in turn, their employment levels.

This situation is shown in Figure 11-7. The equilibrium level of output is shown as Q_e on the horizontal axis. It is the result of the intersection of the aggregate demand curve and the aggregate supply curve. That intersection also is associated with the price level P_e. What this all means is that, if the price level is P_e, demanders (individuals, firms, and governments) wish to purchase the amount of goods and services equal to Q_e—which is also the level of output that firms offer for sale.

Figure 11-8

Aggregate Supply and Full Employment

The vertical part of the AS curve indicates that the economy can produce no more than Q^*_e because it has reached full employment or potential GDP.

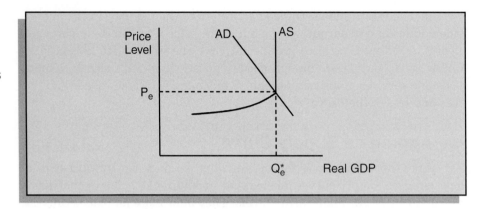

Figure 11-8 shows an aggregate supply curve where the economy *doesn't* gradually find production harder to increase, as in Figure 11-7. Rather, the economy abruptly reaches a limit to production at Q^*_e, which represents the level of output at full employment (its dollar value is potential GDP). Therefore, even if the price level rises above P_e, output will not increase because it *cannot* increase. This makes for a vertical AS line above P_e.

In Figure 11-8, the economy just happens to achieve equilibrium at potential GDP. However, suppose there is a shift in the AD curve. In Figure 11-9, AD_1 is in the same position as AD in Figure 11-8. AD_2 means there are now fewer goods and services purchased at any particular price level than previously. Specifically, only the quantity Q_2 of goods and services is bought at P_1. This is similar to a decrease in demand for a single product, when such a move creates a surplus. In this aggregate case, there is not a surplus of just one product, but for hundreds of thousands of goods and services. The size of this aggregate surplus can be measured by the horizontal distance between the AD_1 and AD_2 lines at P_1, the initial price level. This surplus measures the size of the "GDP gap" of a recession. Thus, the shift in aggregate demand is what the cause of a recession looks like graphically.

Prices fall in response to these surpluses, leading to two further responses. First, consumers, investors, and governments buy more goods and services at the bargain prices–Q_{e2} rather than Q_2. Second, because prices are lower, businesses can profitably produce only Q_{e2} amount of goods and services. Of course, this means that the economy reaches a new equilibrium position, with an output of Q_{e2} and a price level of P_2. Thus, there is no longer full employment, as output has fallen below its potential.

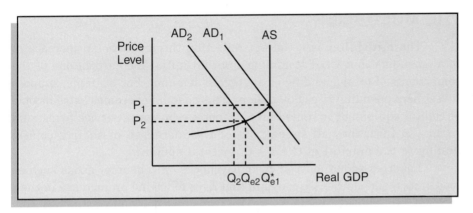

Figure 11-9

A Fall in Aggregate Demand

The fall in AD will lead to a lower price level (to P_2) and a lower output level (to Q_{e2}).

However, historical evidence shows that the general price level is not likely to fall significantly if a recession strikes. Thus, the reduction in aggregate demand would lead to an equivalent cutback in output—but with prices about the same. This means that the aggregate supply curve becomes a horizontal line below the full employment level of output. Figure 11-10 shows this situation. After a reduction in aggregate demand to AD_2, the economy again reaches a new equilibrium position, Q_{e2}, which is identical to Q_2 in Figure 11-9. Therefore, because prices do not fall, the GDP gap is larger than if they did fall. This can be seen graphically, where the GDP gap in Figure 11-10 (= $Q_{e1}^* - Q_{e2}$) exceeds the GDP gap in Figure 11-9 (= $Q_{e1}^* - Q_2$).

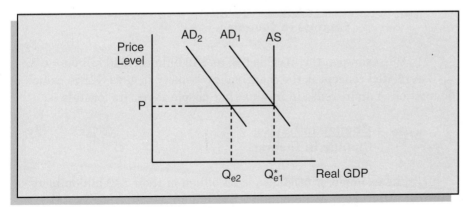

Figure 11-10

Declining Aggregate Demand, Recession, and Stable Prices

With a horizontal AS curve, a drop in AD will not cause a fall in prices, but output will fall (to Q_{e2}).

THE MULTIPLIER

The **multiplier** is the multiple increase in total spending and GDP that results from an initial increase in one of the components of total spending.

The **multiplier** is a concept reflecting the proportional increase in total spending and GDP stemming from an initial increase in one of the components of total spending or aggregate demand. For example, suppose investment spending rises $50 billion. This spending becomes extra income of capital equipment manufacturers, laborers, business service firms, and so on. In turn, they all spend part of the increases in their incomes, adding to the amount of C + I + G, or total spending.

Laborers spend most of their paychecks on consumer goods such as food, autos, and clothes, so consumption rises following an increase in their incomes. In addition, business service firms buy more office supplies, copiers, and desks, so investment rises again. In turn, the recipients of all this spending spend part of that money on a wide variety of items.

Suppose that after such "recycling of money" occurs many times over, total spending rises $250 billion. The multiplier value can be found by the formula:

$$\text{Multiplier} = \frac{\text{Change in GDP}}{\text{Initial Change in Total Spending}}$$

The multiplier is five in this example, as $250 billion ÷ $50 billion = 5.

The multiplier can be found in an alternative way, but first a new concept needs introduction. The marginal propensity to consume (MPC) is the fraction of an increase in income that people spend on consumption. Suppose everyone combined receives a $40 billion increase in income. If 80 percent of that increase in income is used to buy consumer goods and services, consumption rises by $32 billion, as 0.8 x $40 billion = $32 billion.

The formula for the marginal propensity to consume is:

$$\text{MPC} = \frac{\text{Change in Consumption}}{\text{Change in Income}}$$

In this example, the MPC is 0.8, as $32 billion ÷ $40 billion = 0.8.

A related concept is the marginal propensity to save (MPS), which is the fraction of an increase in income that people save. Its formula is:

$$\text{MPS} = \frac{\text{Change in Saving}}{\text{Change in Income}}$$

In the example, if people save $8 billion of their $40 billion increase in income, MPS = 0.2, as $8 billion ÷ $40 billion = 0.2.

Because people can either spend their income or save it, MPC plus MPS must equal one. This simply means that people will spend and save 100 percent of an increase in income—for there is nothing else they can do with it. As MPC + MPS = 1, then:

MPS = 1 – MPC

Finally, if either the MPC or the MPS is known, the multiplier can be found by using the formula:

$$\text{Multiplier} = \frac{1}{1 - \text{MPC}} = \frac{1}{\text{MPS}}$$

Returning to the example above, where the MPC = 0.8 and where the MPS = 0.2, the multiplier is:

$$\text{Multiplier} = \frac{1}{1 - 0.8} = \frac{1}{0.2} = 5$$

SUMMARY

The macroeconomy in capitalistic economies is subject to business cycles, during which the economy changes from prosperity to recession to recovery and back to prosperity. The macroeconomic model is useful in understanding these cycles because it provides a simplified view of the economy, with only the major macroeconomic variables included.

The macroeconomy is in equilibrium when none of the macroeconomic variables change over a period of time. Equilibrium occurs when the total spending on goods and services equals the total value of goods and services produced at a particular price level. This condition holds when savings and taxes combined equal the combination of investment and government spending. Essentially, all the income that people don't immediately spend will get spent by others, namely, investors and governments.

During a recession, there are decreases in total spending, production, and employment. Also, prices and wages rise less rapidly, businesses cut costs sharply, interest rates fall, and lower tax collections and higher transfer payments lead to budget deficits. Economists try to forecast recessions by building econometric models and by observing certain economic variables.

Recession occurs when total spending or aggregate demand falls below the amount needed to bring about full employment and potential GDP. This drop in total spending is caused by increases in savings or taxes and/or decreases in investment spending and government spending. Savings most likely will rise if consumers fear bad economic times are coming. Taxes will rise and/or government spending will fall if the government reduces the budget deficit. Investment spending is most likely to fall if businesses expect profits to fall in the future, generally because of bad times ahead. Any initial fall in spending leads to a drop in spending of a multiple amount.

QUESTIONS FOR DISCUSSION AND THOUGHT

1. Do you think there will be a recession next year? Why or why not?
2. As an ordinary individual, could you cause a recession? Why or why not?
3. Why wouldn't anyone in the economy know for certain if a recession was just beginning?
4. What if a recession lasted forever? What major changes would you see in the economy?
5. How could one tell if a recovery was over and a prosperity period had begun?
6. Would you expect people today to be more fearful of bad times in the future following a specific event (like a stock market crash) than people living in the 1800s? Would either group be more likely to react to expectations of a bad future? Why?
7. What could you do to promote macroeconomic equilibrium?
8. What, if anything, can you do to affect investment spending?

PROBLEMS   See page 489 for the answers.

1. If, between two periods, savings fall by $80 billion, investment spending falls by $60 billion, government spending falls by $30 billion, and taxes remain unchanged, what do you expect happened in the macroeconomy, and why?

2. If investment spending falls by $47 billion, government spending rises by $23 billion, and taxes rise by $2 billion, what will savings have to change by to create macroeconomic equilibrium?

3. If disposable income increases by $300 billion and people save five percent of it, how much will construction have to change to maintain equilibrium if capital purchases rise by $10 billion?

4. How would either the aggregate demand curve or the aggregate supply curve have to shift to cause each of the following conditions?
   a) real GDP falls and the price level rises
   b) real GDP rises and the price level falls
   c) the price level rises and real GDP rises
   d) the price level falls and real GDP falls

5. Assume that the aggregate demand curve and the aggregate supply curve (which continually rises to the right) intersect at a price level of 150. Starting at this position, how would the economy change if the price level fell to 100? Rose to 180?

6. During 1996, David Smith expected to earn $40,000 and had planned to save $4,000. He got an unexpected raise, boosting his income to $45,000. He ended up saving $6,000 in 1996. What was his personal MPS? His MPC?

7. Find the value of the multiplier in four different situations when:
   a) MPC = 0.7; b) MPS = 0.1; c) MPS = 0.2; d) MPC = 0.9

8. Suppose investment spending increases by $20 billion. If the economy was initially in equilibrium at $6,000 billion and the MPC is 0.8, what is the new equilibrium level?

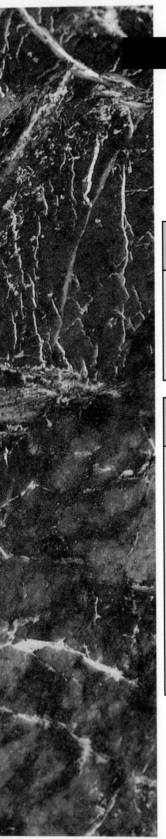

12 INFLATION

CHAPTER PREVIEW

Inflation refers to an increase in the overall price level. Although it seems like it is inevitable, we have not always experienced it in our nation.

This chapter explains how inflation comes about. It covers two main types of inflation, demand-pull inflation and cost-push inflation. It also covers some of the effects of inflation in an economy.

CHAPTER OBJECTIVES

After completing this chapter, you should be able to:

◆ *List some consequences of inflation.*

◆ *Explain how the general price level is determined.*

◆ *Explain how changes in total spending or aggregate demand influence changes in output, shortages, and inflation.*

◆ *Explain how demand-pull inflation occurs.*

◆ *Explain the relationship between the money supply and total spending.*

◆ *Explain how cost-push inflation occurs.*

◆ *List the main causes of a decline in production or in the rate of increase of production.*

To most Americans, it must seem that prices have been going up forever because they've faced inflation all their lives. But a 30-year old person living in 1895 would have thought just the opposite, for prices fell almost continually since 1865. So inflation isn't inevitable. It just seems so.

This chapter begins with a glance at some consequences of inflation and at some of the severe inflations in history. Then it explains why prices increase—in other words, why inflation happens. Two types of inflation are covered—demand-pull inflation and cost-push inflation.

As in the previous chapter, two approaches will be used to present the causes of inflation. First, a more elementary presentation will be made, using flow charts and diagrams. Second, a more sophisticated approach will use aggregate demand and supply curves. One can gain a very solid understanding of inflation without using the second approach.

ECONOMIES WITH INFLATION

Inflation is a condition in which the overall price level of an economy increases, generally over an extended period. The inflation rate refers to the percentage increase in the price level during a year.

Inflation is a condition in which the price level increases, generally over an extended period.

The Effects of Inflation

Some important effects of inflation include: 1) a decrease in the purchasing power of the dollar; 2) a redistribution of income and wealth; 3) a reduction in productive work; 4) a reduction in the savings rate; 5) a disruption of business plans; and 6) an increase in market interest rates.

■ First, during inflation the purchasing power of the dollar falls. Suppose that a pencil used to cost a nickel, so that you could buy 20 pencils for a dollar. If pencils now cost a dime, you can buy only 10 for a dollar, or half as many. If prices *in general* double, a given amount of income buys only half as much. Thus, real income, or the amount of goods and services that people can buy with a given level of **money income** (the number of dollars they earn), falls as prices rise.

Money income is the amount of money someone receives, usually from the sale of resources.

■ The second effect of inflation is a redistribution of income and wealth. Income is redistributed primarily because money incomes of people rise at different rates during inflation. Those whose money incomes rise at a lower rate than prices suffer a drop in real income. Historically, this has included minimum-wage earners, pensioners, welfare recipients, and many people not represented by unions. However, real income *increases* for those whose money incomes increase faster than prices, including many self-employed professionals, other business owners, and laborers in great demand. Occasionally people receiving a cost-of-living-adjustment (COLA), including many unionized workers and Social Security recipients, also have a gain in real income, even though COLAs are designed to keep recipients' money incomes rising at the same rate as prices. That occurs when the price index used to calculate inflation overstates the extent of inflation.

Inflation can also redistribute wealth. Speculative "investment objects" that often increase in value during inflation include precious metals, art, and rare stamps—bringing windfall gains to their owners. Likewise, real estate values commonly climb sharply during inflation. Thus, people who bought such items before their prices rose earn capital gains income. Another way to gain from inflation is with a long-term loan with a fixed, low interest rate. Because your income will likely climb sharply during inflation, the loan payment isn't as large a share of your paycheck. Also, you are paying back dollars that have less purchasing power than the ones you borrowed, amounting to a transfer of wealth to you. This assumes that there is no escalator clause, where a lender can increase the rate of interest on a loan during the payback period. (See the section on the effect on interest rates on the next page.) Of course, if there are winners from inflation, there must be losers—the same wealth is merely redistributed.

■ The third effect of inflation is a reduction in productive work. Entrepreneurs, innovators, and inventors are less productive when they take time from their work to look for tax shelters and other ways to cut their taxable income. The more time they spend seeking to avoid inflationary losses, the less they contribute to the economy.

■ The fourth effect of inflation is a reduced savings rate. Many people try to buy as much as possible before prices increase even further, thereby saving less of their incomes. Others spend more than otherwise on homes or other things they believe will increase in value during inflation. A lower savings rate means there are fewer funds to lend to businesses for innovations, capital equipment, and plant expansion. This could lead to a lower rate of economic growth and a slower growth in the living standard.

■ The fifth effect of inflation is disruption of business plans for the future. Because capital equipment and factories usually have long lives, firms want some certainty about future prices of what they buy and sell. Whether investments in capital pay off depends upon such prices. Without knowledge of future prices, firms tend to concentrate on more predictable projects that pay off in the short run, such as a new brand of soap. Revolutionary and innovative projects—such as extreme heat-tolerant ceramics, solar power, and electricity from nuclear fusion—often take expensive, long-term research. Long-term economic growth suffers when businesses shy away from such projects.

■ The last noteworthy effect of inflation is an increase in interest rates. (The interest rate here is the "market interest rate," explained in the paragraph after next.) The interest rate is the price of credit for the use of someone else's purchasing power (money) for a certain period. That price must cover the cost of extending credit before a financial institution grants a loan, including the cost of bank equipment, labor, and the interest the bank pays depositors (savers).

Suppose a bank considers lending you $1,000 for a year on January 1. That money could buy x amount of some good on that day. Also, suppose the bank needs $60 to cover the costs just mentioned—or six percent of $1,000. You will probably get the loan at six percent—*if* the bank expects that the $1,000 will still have the power to buy x amount of that same good on December 31. But what if the price of that good (and everything else) is expected to rise 10 percent (so that the $1,000 could buy only 0.9x)? Then the bank would have an *extra* cost—it would give up purchasing power when you gave back the $1,000. Therefore, it will charge you interest of $60 *plus* $100 (to cover this extra cost) or 16 percent (= $160 ÷ $1,000). That is why interest rates were high in the 1970s when inflation rates were high.

During inflation, knowledgeable people often distinguish between the market interest rate and the real interest rate. The **market interest rate** refers to the actual number of dollars of interest paid in a year for each $100 borrowed, expressed in percentage terms. It is what people usually mean by "the interest rate." The **real interest rate** gives a more accurate view of the true cost of borrowing. It recognizes that during inflation borrowers pay back loans with dollars that have less purchasing power than the dollars they borrowed. Thus, borrowers give up less for each dollar repaid than they received. Because this reduces their cost of borrowing, the following formula is used to find the real interest rate:

The **market interest rate** is the rate of interest as stated on the loan agreement, which is unadjusted for inflation.

The **real interest rate** is the rate of interest after adjusting for inflation, equal to the nominal rate of interest minus the inflation rate.

Real Interest Rate = Market Interest Rate – Inflation Rate   6%— inflation

9% market

For example, assuming an inflation rate of six percent, suppose a bank charges a market interest rate of nine percent—$90 for a $1,000 loan of one year. When the borrower pays back the $1,000 in principal, it *looks* the same as the $1,000 borrowed—but it's worth only $940 of the "old money" (= $1,000 – 0.06 x $1,000)—$60 less. Therefore, the loan cost only $30 (= $90 – $60), for a real rate of interest of three percent (= $30 ÷ $1,000 or 9% – 6%).

Inflation in the United States

The United States has faced five periods of significant inflation. The first occurred during the Revolutionary War. Prices rose more than several hundred percent because, rather than raising taxes, the states printed vast amounts of paper currency to pay for the war. Similarly, prices rose several hundred percent during the Civil War. The government had great difficulty raising sufficient taxes and borrowing enough to finance the war. In desperation, it printed paper money. The Confederate States printed much more paper money and, consequently, suffered ruinous inflation.

During World War I, prices doubled in just two years. Likewise, prices shot up during World War II, though not as much as they would have without price ceilings. However, after removal of these controls, prices zoomed upward in the late 1940s at rates of between 10 and 20 percent each year. The last period of major inflation began in the late 1960s and ended in the early 1980s. It accompanied the large spending increases on the Vietnam War and the social programs of the period. If these spending increases had been financed by tax increases, much of the inflation would have been avoided. However, politicians are usually reluctant to raise taxes.

Figure 12-1 shows the inflation record of the United States since 1960. The inflation rate was calculated using the Consumer Price Index.

Table 12-1

Inflation Rates
Since 1960

Inflation rates show the percentage increase in the overall price level between two consecutive years.

Year	Inflation Rate	Year	Inflation Rate	Year	Inflation Rate	Year	Inflation Rate
1960	1.7	1970	5.7	1980	13.5	1990	5.4
1961	1.0	1971	4.4	1981	10.3	1991	4.2
1962	1.0	1972	3.2	1982	6.2	1992	3.0
1963	1.3	1973	6.2	1983	3.2	1993	3.0
1964	1.3	1974	11.0	1984	4.3	1994	2.6
1965	1.6	1975	9.1	1985	3.6	1995	2.8
1966	2.9	1976	5.8	1986	1.9	1996	3.0
1967	3.1	1977	6.5	1987	3.6	1997	2.3
1968	4.2	1978	7.6	1988	4.1	1998	1.6
1969	5.5	1979	11.3	1989	4.8	1999	2.2
						2000	3.4
						2001	1.6

Some Notable Historical Inflations

Severe inflation is nothing new. The Roman Empire experienced it thousands of years ago. Prices in Europe doubled during the three years of the Black Death around 1350. In the 1500s, European prices more than tripled after the arrival of gold from Spanish plundering of the New World.

So far in the 20th century, there have been several notable hyperinflations, usually referring to inflation rates of a hundred percent or more. The largest was the Hungarian inflation of 1946. Estimates of price increases range as high as 800 octillionfold (800 plus 27 zeros). The disruptive effects made it easier for a communist takeover. Similarly, the Chinese inflation of the late 1940s, when prices rose as much as 10 billionfold over three years, contributed to the economic and political instability that led to the communist takeover in 1949. Prices in Greece rose over four billionfold from 1943 to 1944.

The most famous inflation occurred in Germany after World War I, from 1919 to 1923. After Germany lost the war, the victors (the United States, Britain, France, Italy, and Russia) imposed heavy money settlements, called reparations, on Germany. For necessary domestic spending and to pay the reparations, Germany printed large amounts of German marks. By 1923, the treasury kept 30 paper mills busy producing paper to make new money. The examples in Table 12-2 give an indication of how fast prices rose in the worst year, 1923. Overall, prices rose as high as six trillionfold during that period. To put that into perspective, imagine buying a hot dog today for $1—just before you leave for four years in France. Upon your return home, you order a hot dog, which you expect is still $1.

Table 12-2

Prices During the German Hyperinflation of 1919-1923

Prices rose most rapidly in the summer and fall of 1923.

Product	1923 Prices (in marks) in the Month of:			
	July	August	September	November
Liter of Milk	_____	38,000	8 million	_____
Kg. of Butter	26,000	2 million	220 million	6 trillion
Kg. of Bread	1,200	200,000	59 million	428 billion
Kg. of Bacon	_____	2.1 million	286 million	_____
Kg. of Beef	18,800	_____	_____	5.6 trillion
1 egg	5,000	_____	_____	80 billion

Source: William Guttman and Patricia Meehan, *The Great Inflation, Germany 1919-1923*, Westmead, Farnborough, Hants, England: Saxon House, D.C. Heath Ltd., 1975

Handing you the hot dog, the clerk asks for *six trillion dollars—or six million stacks* of *one million* dollars each! Would you be upset? The Germans were. So much so, in fact, that their government, the Weimar Republic, collapsed. That was followed by 10 years of economic and political turmoil until someone led them out of economic depression and political fighting— Adolf Hitler.

Hyperinflations still occur today. Bolivia's inflation rate reached 40,000 percent in 1985, and from 1986 to 1991, prices in Peru rose 2,200,000 percent. Following the breakup of the Soviet Union, the tumultuous economic problem in Russia were accompanied by *monthly* inflation rates of 25 percent in the early 1990s.

(See pages 351-354 for photos of some of the world's most serious inflations.)

THE PRICE LEVEL OF AN ECONOMY

The price level refers to a collective measure of all prices that exist at some point, and it is reflected by a price index. (The concept of a price index and its use in calculating the inflation rate was introduced in Chapter 9. So some of this section will be a review.)

What Determines the Price Level

The demand for and the supply of a particular product determine its price in an economic tug-of-war. Television sets could be an example. The demand for TV sets refers to the various numbers of TV sets that people are willing to buy (at all possible prices). The supply refers to the various numbers of TV sets that firms offer for sale. Buyers compete against one another for the available sets, and sellers are adversaries for the limited customers. Finally, buyers and sellers are adversaries when they haggle over the price.

Likewise, the price level of all goods and services *combined* depends upon demand and supply. However, the critical difference is that now demand refers to the total spending (or aggregate demand) for all products combined—C + I + G, or consumer, investment, and government spending added together. (Remember, this assumes a "closed economy," where there are no imports or exports.) One might think of total spending as the buyers' side of a giant auction where everything imaginable is sold. Imagine millions of consumers, business owners, and government purchasing agents with pockets full of money to spend.

Two notes of the worst of the German hyperinflation of 1919-1923. The top note is a 20-billion (milliarden) mark note, issued in October 1923. The bottom note is a one-trillion mark note, or a million million marks, of November 1923. (Billion in German translates to trillion in English.) In November 1923, it took five of these larger notes to buy a newspaper.

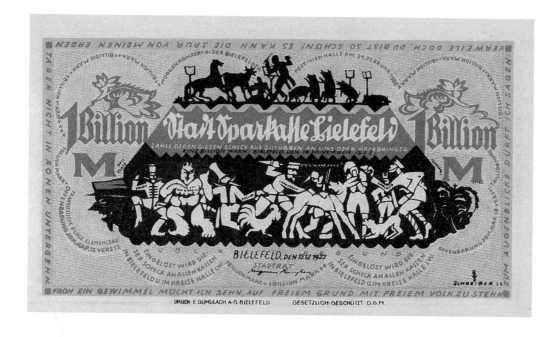

352

A 100-million pengo note of Hungary. This was the world's largest inflation, when prices rose over 800 octillion times (eight followed by 27 zeros) from 1945 to 1946.

Russian rubles. The one-ruble note was issued by the old Soviet Union. There was inflation of 25 percent a month for several years following the collapse of the Soviet Union in 1991. Whereas one ruble used to be more valuable than a dollar, by late 1996 one of these 5,000-ruble notes was worth about 80 cents.

A five-million drachma note of Greece in 1944. Prices rose over four million times because of World War II.

A 50-zloty note of Poland. Before the fall of communism, one of these notes was worth about 70 U.S. cents.

A 10,000-zloty Polish note, following the inflation associated with the fall of communism. This note was worth about 90 U.S. cents in the early 1990s.

354

This 1,000-peso note of Uruguay was overstamped with the notation N $1, standing for one new peso. Rather than print money of larger denominations, three zeros were dropped off all currency, as well as prices.

Like many European nations after World War I, Poland experienced severe inflation. Whereas a 1,000-marek note was "small change" in 1919 (see note at right), a 10,000-marek note of 1922 (below) was also worth very little three years later. The actual sizes of these notes were very large. The 1,000-marek note was eight and one-fourth inches by five and one-fourth inches.

Just as the "strength" of demand for an individual product influences its price, so, too, the "strength of aggregate demand" influences the price level. This "strength" means *how much* spending that C + I + G entails. High total spending tends to bring about higher price levels. Conversely, low total spending tends to cause lower price levels.

The "strength of aggregate supply" (essentially, how many goods and services are brought to the market by producers) plays an equal role in determining the price level. The more goods and services firms offer for sale, the lower the price level tends to be—partly because people buy large amounts only if prices are low. Conversely, lower levels of output tend to lead to higher price levels. The amount firms offer for sale at that auction, measured by GDP, refers to the total output of goods and services.

The word "tend" in the two preceding paragraphs emphasizes that there are two major factors determining price levels—total spending and the total amount of goods and services available or produced. (Or, in the more complex model used to explain inflation, these two factors are the aggregate demand and the aggregate supply.) Several concepts that were studied earlier in various chapters influence these two primary determinants of the price level. Total production (or aggregate supply) depends upon: 1) the amount of resources that are used; and 2) the output that producers get from them (resource efficiency).

Total spending (or aggregate demand) equals the addition of consumer spending, investment spending, and government spending on goods and services. The consumer part of total spending depends largely upon disposable income, which depends primarily upon how many people have jobs. Investment spending depends upon profit levels, the future expectations of the economy, and whether credit is cheap or expensive as well as available. Government spending depends upon the level of tax receipts and the desire of government officials and the public to have the government spend money.

How the Price Level Changes

To understand inflation (or what causes the price level to rise) it will help to review what causes the price of a particular product, such as shoes, to rise. Remember that whenever there is a shortage of shoes, shoe prices increase for two reasons. First, people who want shoes, but who can't find any to buy at the initial price, offer to pay more for the shoes available—bidding them away from other buyers who *can* get them. Second, shoe store owners realize that they can increase profits by boosting prices. The owners can replace customers they lose with people who want to buy shoes but can't find any to buy.   Finally, shortages appear whenever there is an increase in demand or a decrease in supply.

When prices *in general* increase, the situation for shoes occurs in thousands of markets at the same time.   There are widespread shortages brought on by either: 1) a *general* increase in spending (total spending or aggregate demand increases); or 2) a *general* decline in production (total output of goods and services or aggregate supply decreases).

In reality, production rarely falls—only during recession.   Both total spending and production usually increase each year.   Generally, widespread shortages and inflation occur whenever total spending rises at a *faster rate* than total production, or when aggregate demand rises faster than aggregate supply.   For example, if consumers, business firms, and governments try to buy eight percent more each year but output increases at merely five percent, shortages appear in thousands of markets.   Consequently, prices rise in thousands of markets.   There is inflation.

DEMAND-PULL INFLATION

Until this point, it hasn't been necessary to say *why* spending increases faster than output increases.   Perhaps spending is increasing too rapidly.   Alternatively, perhaps output is increasing too slowly.   In either case, the economy faces shortages and inflation.   Now you will learn that both cases are associated with a specific cause or a type of inflation.   The first cause, or the first type of inflation, is called demand-pull inflation.   The second, covered later, is called cost-push inflation.   Always keep in mind that both work by creating shortages and that, whatever their cause, all shortages look alike.   Thus, determining whether an inflation is one type or another is often difficult.

Conditions of Demand-Pull Inflation

Demand-pull inflation refers to an increase in the price level caused by an increase in total spending that exceeds the increase in available goods and services.

In its simplest form, **demand-pull inflation** occurs when total spending increases, but the total output of goods and services remains constant.   Suppose that at some point in the past C + I + G (total spending or aggregate demand) was $3,600 billion and that all buyers could buy all they wanted.   Suppose further that these buyers now want $4,000 billion worth of goods and services—but firms still produce the same $3,600 billion.   Buyers do not get the extra $400 billion worth of output they want, and there are widespread shortages to that extent.   Consequently, prices rise.

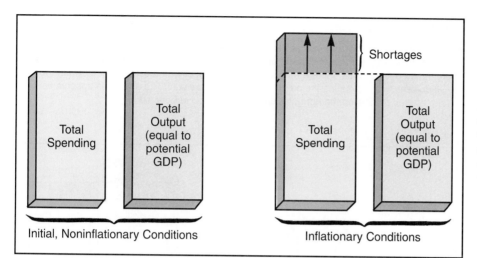

This is most likely to happen at full employment. (Remember that an economy at full employment has also reached its potential GDP.) Virtually all laborers have jobs, factories produce at full capacity, mines produce all the minerals possible, and so on. Firms *would like* to sell more output, but—for the moment—they can't make any more. However, firms that produce goods can temporarily reduce their inventories, thus boosting sales without an increase in output.

Figure 12-1 shows this situation. The columns on the left reflect the initial, noninflationary situation: the blue column represents total spending and the gray column total output. Because they are equal, it means the economy starts at macroeconomic equilibrium. The economy is assumed to be at full employment. The two columns on the right show an inflationary situation: total spending increases but total output does not—because it *cannot,* since the economy is still at full employment. The darker area at the top of the total spending column reflects the amount of shortages in the economy. The larger this area, the greater the inflation will be.

The above illustration assumes that only a few months elapse between the two time periods. That's because, as time goes on, new laborers enter the labor force, new factories are built, firms buy more productive capital equipment, technological advances occur, and countless innovations change the production processes. Suppose that, on average, such changes expand the economy's capacity (potential GDP) by 10 percent each year. (That's more than we can expect, but it makes the graphs easier to follow.) Then there can be an increase in total spending of 10 percent each year *without* creating widespread shortages.

Figure 12-2   A Demand-Pull Inflation Model

In each time period, the economy is at full employment (or potential GDP). However, the potential GDP grows 30 percent between each time period, due to a growth in resource availability and productivity. Aggregate demand (total spending) also rises by 30 percent between Period 1 and Period 2. Thus, there are no shortages and inflation there. However, between Periods 2 and 3, aggregate demand rises 50 percent, far outstripping the output increase of 30 percent. The difference appears as shortages (shown as the difference in column heights on the right), which lead to inflation in Period 3.

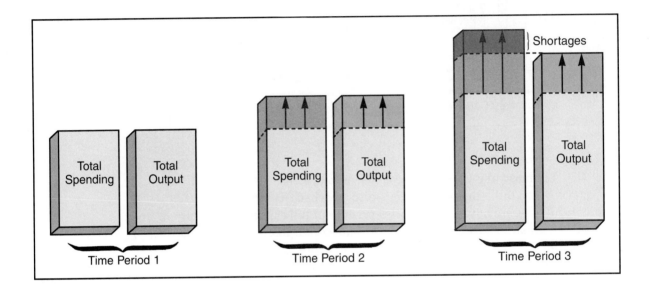

Figure 12-2 shows this situation over a span of several years—from Time Period 1 through Time Period 3. Assume that the economy starts at potential GDP in Period 1. Because total spending matches total output, there are no shortages, so there is no inflation. By Period 2, total spending rises 10 percent above Period 1. Since firms *can* produce 10 percent more and *want to*, total output also climbs 10 percent above the level in Period 1. Thus, the spending increase does *not* lead to inflation, as it did in the simpler case.

By Period 3, however, there *is* inflation because total spending escalates at 15 percent from Period 2 to Period 3. Firms cannot match this abnormal increase, since total output can increase at only 10 percent.

In general, the economy will experience demand-pull inflation if total spending increases faster than the total output of goods and services. And because the abnormal increase in spending is seen as the cause of the shortages and the price increases, it is labeled demand-pull inflation.

How Total Spending or C + I + G Increases

Why does total spending increase in the first place? Remember that total spending equals the sum of consumer, investment, and government spending. Since these three types of spending fluctuate, for the most part independently of each other, each one will be considered separately.

■ First, consumer spending. If it is assumed that the economy begins at conditions of full employment and no inflation, then personal income is at its maximum possible level. Remember from the circular flow diagram (Figure 11-2, page 316) that people can use personal income only for taxes, savings, and consumption. Thus, out of a given level of income, consumption will increase if taxes fall or if savings fall. Lower taxes mean disposable income is higher, allowing for higher consumption. Further, out of a given level of disposable income, lower savings also mean consumption rises. Since taxes and savings are both leakages, a decrease in leakages contributes to higher total spending. Furthermore, if leakages fall with the economy at full employment, such a fall is inflationary. See Figure 12-3, where the gray-shaded S and T boxes indicate the cause of the inflation.

Assume the economy begins with the full-employment-equilibrium conditions of Figure 11-3 (on page 323). Potential GDP is $8,000 billion, taxes are $2,000 billion, savings are $1,000 billion, consumer spending is $5,000 billion, investment is $1,000 billion, and government spending is $2,000 billion. Figure 12-3 shows conditions after a drop in leakages. Since $1,600 billion, rather than $2,000 billion, now go for taxes, disposable personal income rises from $6,000 billion to $6,400 billion (allowing consumption to increase by $400 billion). As savings drop to $800 billion (allowing for an additional increase in consumption of $200 billion), consumption jumps $600 billion (= $200 + $400) to $5,600 billion. Adding this to the $2,000 billion in government spending and the $1,000 billion in investment spending also pushes total spending up $600 billion to $8,600 billion. (*Why* this might happen is covered on the next page.)

Will employment be the next to climb—perhaps above 113 million? No, for the remaining seven million unemployed are the frictionally and structurally unemployed, the type extremely unlikely to find jobs. Consequently, production will not increase, so the extra spending merely creates shortages and inflation.

■ Another way for total spending to increase is for investment spending to increase. Remember, this includes spending for capital equipment, building construction, and increased inventories. Suppose it rises from $1,000 billion to $1,200 billion. Then total spending or C + I + G climbs by at least $200 billion.

Figure 12-3

Inflation Caused by a Decrease in Leakages

(figures are in billions)

Because saving and taxes fell from Figure 11-3, (on page 323) consumer spending rose from $5,000 billion to $5,600 billion. Consequently, total spending rose by $600 billion to $8,600 billion. As production cannot increase (because the economy is at potential GDP or full employment), this spending increase causes shortages and inflation.

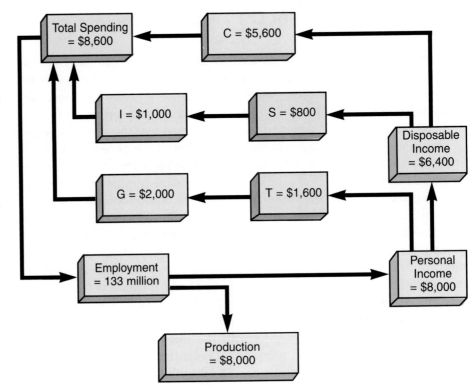

■ The final source of an increase in total spending is a growth in government expenditures. For example, although government expenditures began with a $2,000 billion level, suppose these expenditures climb to $2,400 billion. Again, total spending will rise, now by at least $400 billion. (Eventually, total spending could increase far more than that, following the multiplier effect that was introduced in Chapter 11.)

Both of these increases in injections (I and G) combine to boost total spending by $600 billion to $8,600 billion. These changes appear in the circular flow model in Figure 12-4, but now these are shaded gray to note the alternative causes of inflation that you saw in Figure 12-3. In Figure 12-4, leakages and consumption remain the same as Figure 11-3 on page 323. However, total spending rises by the same amount as in Figure 12-3. Consequently, the same amounts of shortages and inflation appear.

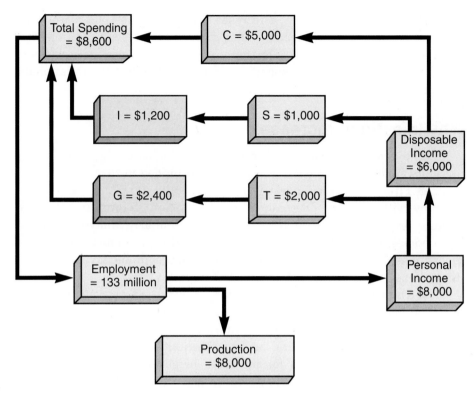

Figure 12-4

Inflation Caused by an
Increase in Injections

(figures are in billions)

In this case, total spending
rose from $8,000 billion to
$8,600 billion because of
increases in investment
and government spending.
Again, because the
economy is at potential
GDP or full employment,
these increase cause
shortages and inflation.

Why Leakages Decrease

It is now possible to probe more deeply into the causes of inflation.
The first two causes, lower taxes and lower savings, will be examined in this
section.

■ First, consider a drop in the savings rate. A primary factor affecting the savings rate is consumer expectations of the future. If consumers
believe that prosperity is on the way, they will probably spend more and
save less. They feel especially comfortable about buying durable goods.
Many things can promote consumer confidence in the future, such as
reports of improved employment, income, or GDP. Consumers also become
more confident when they see lots of help-wanted ads or read newspaper
stories about a healthy economy. Another reason for lower savings is a drop
in interest rates. Finally, the savings rate falls when consumers expect
prices to increase sharply in the near future. This, in turn, actually causes
prices to increase because, seeking to beat the price increases, consumers
buy more, thereby raising product demands.

■ Although it isn't likely, a decrease in taxes is the second reason why leakages decline. It is conceivable that a conservative sweep of Congress could lead to sharp tax cuts. On the other hand, conservatives probably would also slash government spending, which would offset the inflationary effect of tax cuts.

Why Injections Increase

The other two causes of inflation are increases in spending by investors and/or governments. Each will be examined in turn.

■ First, businesses invest in more capital goods if they believe the economy will improve. Second, they invest more if interest rates fall because projects are more likely to pay off. Similarly, individuals build more homes because of lower interest rates. Finally, a cluster of related innovations could lead to large investments in new equipment related to the innovations.

■ There are several reasons for steep increases in government spending. The most common reason is war. Inflation accompanied every major war in U.S. history. Wars take guns, aircraft, ships, uniforms, and the like, often increasing total spending beyond the limit of an economy's scarce resources. A second reason for increases in government spending is a spending increase on other public goods, such as the interstate highway system in the 1950s and 1960s and college expansion of the 1960s and 1970s. Finally, large increases in social welfare programs, such as the War on Poverty in the 1960s, lead to sharp increases in government spending.

EXPLAINING DEMAND–PULL INFLATION WITH AGGREGATE DEMAND AND SUPPLY CURVES

Demand-pull inflation can also be explained by using the aggregate demand and aggregate supply curves in the following figures. Figure 12-5 mirrors the more elementary explanation used in Figure 12-1 on page 357, where it is assumed that there is a fixed potential GDP. Consequently, the aggregate supply curve is fixed in position, shown as AS in the figure. At an initial aggregate demand AD_1, the economy is at full-employment equilibrium with a price level P_1. However, with an increase in aggregate demand to AD_2, consumers, investors, and governments now want to buy Q´ amount of goods and services at price level P_1. However, because firms cannot produce any more output at full employment, this extra demand merely turns into shortages of thousands of goods and services. Consequently, prices rise so that a new price level is reached at P_2.

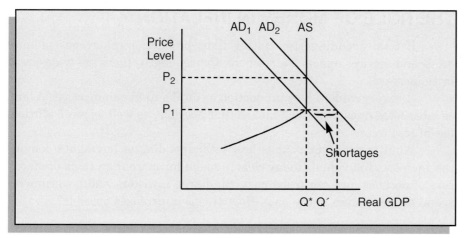

Figure 12-5

Demand-Pull Inflation

Because the economy is at full employment, the increase in aggregate demand only creates shortages. Consequently, the price level rises to P_2 (that is, there is inflation).

In Figure 12-6 the aggregate supply is allowed to shift out each year. This is made possible by economic growth. (This corresponds to the economy of Figure 12-2 on page 358.) Starting at a full-employment equilibrium level of output of Q_1^*, both aggregate demand and supply increase the same amount by Year 2—say, 10 percent. The price level is still P_1, as no shortages appear. The extra demand is met by the new extra capacity and output, which is the maximum possible expansion because of such technical factors as growth in the labor force. By Year 3, output and AS again increase by 10 percent. However, AD_3 is more than 10 percent higher than AD_2, perhaps 15 percent. The result is a shortage of goods and services—and inflation.

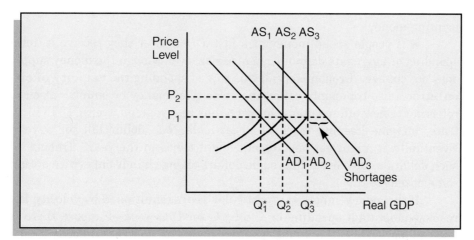

Figure 12-6

Demand-Pull Inflation With Increasing Aggregate Supply

An increase in aggregate demand out to D_2 is matched with output increases to AS_2. Thus, there is no increase in the price level above P_1. But the price level does rise to P_2 when the increase from AD_2 to AD_3 outstrips the rise from AS_2 to AS_3.

THE ROLE OF MONEY IN INFLATION

If total spending rises faster than production, shortages of most goods and services appear everywhere. Consequently, there are widespread price increases.

It is very evident how production or total output can increase. A larger labor force or capital stock makes that possible, as well as more efficient use of resources.

What is not so evident is how total spending or aggregate demand can increase. Individuals today clearly spend far more than their predecessors of decades and centuries past. Similarly, investors and governments spend far more than in the past. How are such increases possible?

How Total Spending Can Increase

An increase in total spending or aggregate demand is technically possible for either of two reasons: 1) there is an increase in the money supply; or 2) the money supply is used more often in a year.

■ The money supply (M1) includes coins, paper currency, checkable deposits, and traveler's checks. The public decides what *share* of each of these money forms it wishes to hold. However, the total money supply (or the *quantity* of money) is largely determined by the Federal Reserve System (the Fed). In this century (since 1913), the Fed has increased the quantity of money by a substantial amount. Last century, many factors affected how much the money supply increased, including the success of gold and silver miners and the willingness of politicians to pay the government's bills by printing money.

The velocity of circulation refers to how many times money is used in a year, on average.

■ If people spend money at a faster rate after they receive it, total spending or aggregate demand can also rise, even though the money supply does not change. Economists call this rate of spending the **velocity of circulation** (also commonly called the velocity of money or simply velocity), referring to how often dollars change hands in a year, on average. To illustrate, imagine keeping track of a particular one dollar bill for a year. Eventually, it might get used (spent) eight times in the year. Tracing all such dollars would reveal that some dollars change hands only twice a year, some dozens of times.

If the money supply of a particular year is multiplied by velocity, the result equals total spending or C + I + G for that year. Suppose there is $800 billion of M1 (the money supply) this year and that velocity is six.

Then total spending is $4,800 billion (= $800 x 6). Total spending could rise to $5,600 billion next year in two ways. First, the money supply could expand to $933.3 billion, for $5,600 = $933.3 x 6. Second, velocity could rise to seven, for $5,600 = $800 x 7.

Why would velocity increase? For one thing, EFT (electronic funds transfer) works faster than a paper check system in moving money around. Thus, widespread adoption of EFT will increase velocity. Various banking and business procedures and equipment also allow velocity to grow. Further, velocity increases during severe inflations, when people want to unload money before it loses purchasing power. However, there are limits to velocity. First, there is a physical limit to how fast people can spend money. Second, if inflation gets bad enough, people abandon money and resort to barter, at which point velocity falls.

The Equation of Exchange

As indicated above, total spending is found by multiplying the money supply by velocity, or:

Total Spending = Money Supply x Velocity
or
Total Spending = MV

Recall that total spending, or C + I + G, is one way of thinking about GDP. Thus, MV = Total Spending = GDP. Recall further that one can also think of GDP as the value of goods and services produced. This value could be found by multiplying the price of every item by the number of that item produced, then adding up all these "subtotals." An alternative approach uses the concept of the price level, represented by the letter P, and the total *quantity* of goods and services produced in a year, represented by the letter Q. Multiplying the price level (P) by the output level (Q) of the whole economy gives the *dollar value* of that output—namely, GDP. Thus, PQ = Total Value of Output = GDP.

As GDP = MV and as GDP = PQ, then MV = PQ, which is known as the **equation of exchange**. Essentially, the equation states the obvious, that total spending in the economy must equal the total value of goods and services produced. Yet this obvious statement, usually called an identity rather than an equation, gives insight into the importance of money in causing inflation.

The **equation of exchange** shows that the money supply (M), the velocity of money (V), the price level (P), and the level of output (Q) are related in the formula MV=PQ.

Velocity increases somewhat over time, but usually at a very low rate. The rate is so low that V is often assumed to be constant in the equation of exchange.

The quantity of total output of goods and services (Q) generally increases as well over time. Over the last century or so, our total output has been limited to yearly increases of about two percent. The limits on growth of the size or quantity of the labor force, capital stock, and natural resources, as well as their productivity, have limited our economic growth rate.

Thus, the magnitude of two of the four variables in the equation of exchange, V and Q, are known with some certainty. To *avoid* inflation, then, the requirement is quite clear: limit the increases in the money supply to about two percent per year.

Alternatively, an increase in the price level (P), or inflation, will occur if the money supply (M) increases faster than the level of output (Q). If M increases only slightly more than Q, the increase in P will be slight. That is, there will be only slight inflation. However, if the money supply is increased at very high rates, say, 40 or 400 percent per year, prices will rise substantially. That is the meaning behind the old saying, "Inflation is too much money chasing too few goods."

All of history's large inflations have this in common. In all U.S. wars, the money supply increased much faster than in peacetime. The tons of gold of the New World became coins of the Old World in the 1500s—and prices zoomed skyward. In 1923, Germany's 30 paper mills helped the money supply explode by *10 billionfold* from 1919. (See pages 351-354 for some of this money, taking notice how the denominations grew as time went on.)

There is a common fallacy about money and income. Money is a medium of exchange. People often say they want more money or that they "make money." What they really want is more *income*, and they earn income at their jobs. Income (actually, *real* income) is the *amount of goods and services* people receive in exchange for what they produce. However, income is invariably measured in dollar-value terms. So when you say your income is $20,000, you mean you can exchange that $20,000 for an equal dollar amount of goods and services. Or you can say that you have $20,000 worth of purchasing power.

Purchasing power for an individual is created by producing things of value—goods and services. Similarly, a nation *obtains* more collective purchasing power and real income only if more goods and services are produced in *total*. That is what is meant by economic growth.

If more money is printed, it will not increase national income. Only making more goods and services will do that.

THINKING CRITICALLY ABOUT ECONOMIC QUESTIONS IN OUR LIVES

What if Half of Everyone's Money Vaporized?

Things to Consider

1. Envision all the money in the United States today, including the coins, paper currency, checking deposits, and traveler's checks. Consider how much of this you currently possess.

2. Now consider cutting in half what money you have of each of these forms of money (imagine that it vaporized instantaneously). Likewise, imagine that every other person experienced a similar loss of half their funds.

3. Finally, consider that everyone's (money) income was cut in half as well.

4. What have you and others *really* lost? What is the only major macroeconomic variable that would change in the long run?

    See page 472 for the answer.

COST-PUSH INFLATION

To review, widespread shortages lead to inflation either if total spending increases or if production or total output decreases. (More technically, inflation occurs if there is: 1) an increase in aggregate demand when aggregate supply is constant; or 2) a decrease in aggregate supply when aggregate demand is constant.) However, because production usually *increases,* inflation usually occurs if total spending increases *faster than* production increases. Demand-pull inflation is associated with the problem of shortages resulting from abnormally large spending increases. This section shows that abnormally small increases in production also can cause shortages. As the price increases appear to come from increases in costs, it is called cost-push inflation. However, remember that slower increases in production will also lead to shortages, the immediate cause of price increases.

Conditions of Cost-Push Inflation

Cost-push inflation
refers to an increase in
prices caused by an
increase in the cost of
producing most goods
and services.

Cost-push inflation occurs when increases in average costs of production in many industries lead firms to increase prices, rather than to accept low profit margins. But why will costs escalate for so many firms? Although average cost is the amount of money needed to make one unit of something, it also reflects *the amount* of resources needed to make something. So if production costs are rising, then the amount of resources needed to make one unit of an item must be rising as well.

What could bring about such a situation? In the simplest case, it could happen if each business firm had a reduction in its output while using the same amount of resources. Each firm would have to spread its expenses over fewer units of output. Thus, each unit of output would have higher costs. On a strictly nonmonetary, physical basis, it means that each item made takes more resources to make it.

However, in a real economy, would production of all goods and services combined fall over an extended period? It's not likely—but it's possi-

THINKING CRITICALLY ABOUT ECONOMIC QUESTIONS IN OUR LIVES

Should We Blame Inflation on Business Owners Who Raise Prices and Union Leaders Who Push for Higher Wages?

Things to Consider

1. Businesses "set" prices. Therefore, if prices are rising, can't the blame for inflation be traced to business owners (or managers)?

2. Or perhaps we could blame leaders of labor unions and strikers. Aren't they to blame for pushing up wages and production costs, which force up prices?

3. Supposing the answer is yes in both 1 and 2, if both groups could simply "disappear," wouldn't that stop inflation?

See page 473 for the answer.

Figure 12-7 A Cost-Push Inflation Model

Conditions in the first two time periods are the same as in Figure 12-2. There is no inflation, as the rise in aggregate demand (total spending) can be matched with the 30 percent growth in capacity (potential GDP). Total spending also rises 30 percent by Period 3. However, total output increases at only 10 percent at the same time. Consequently, there are shortages and inflation. The restrictions on increases in output lead to higher production costs (*average* costs, that is). This, in turn, leads firms to raise prices, giving the name to cost-push inlfation.

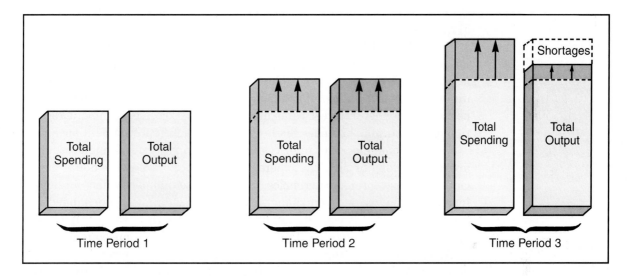

ble. That's why prices rose sharply during the Black Death in the 1300s. A third of the population died, so production fell sharply. Thus, the survivors (who inherited the victims' money) spent the same amount of money on fewer goods, creating shortages and inflation. Production could fall in wartime if factories, shipping facilities, and cropland were destroyed. This occurred during WWII, when many economies suffered severe inflations.

More commonly, cost-push inflation occurs not when production falls, but when production slows *its rate of expansion*. Suppose that total output usually rises at 10 percent each year. If total spending or C + I + G also climbs at 10 percent, there are no shortages or rising prices. But what if output merely grows at six percent during one of these years? Then there *will be* shortages—and inflation. People *try* to buy 10 percent more goods and services, but they can buy only six percent more.

Figure 12-7 shows both spending and output for each of three years. Between Periods 1 and 2, both spending and output rise at 10 percent per year, so no shortages or rising prices appear. But between Periods 2 and 3, spending keeps going up at 30 percent, while production rises at only six percent. The darker area on the top of the blue column for Period 3 represents the amount of shortages caused by these uneven increases.

Reasons Why Increases in Production Can Be Restricted

Average costs rise whenever total costs rise faster than output. This can happen for several reasons: 1) restricted expansion of capital; 2) an increase in foreign prices; 3) poor weather; 4) productivity restrictions; and 5) rising labor costs.

■ First, if the rate of increase in the capital stock slows and fewer innovations occur, production will rise more slowly. This can occur if there is a drop in the savings rate, so less money is available for purchasing capital equipment. Savings fall during high rates of inflation, during boom periods, and when interest rates are very low. Excess government regulation or unfavorable business tax laws also discourage investment spending.

■ Second, increases in prices that U.S. firms pay for foreign resources are passed along to their customers. This can occur when the dollar depreciates against foreign currencies. It can also happen when foreigners increase their prices, even though exchange rates remain unchanged. (A good example of this was the inflation of the 1970s that was partly blamed on the rapid rise in world oil prices caused by OPEC.) Consequently, sales of American firms drop when these increased foreign prices are passed along to American consumers. In turn, production falls in the United States.

■ Third, the primary effect of poor weather is on agricultural output because crop yields plunge and bad weather interferes with harvests. However, snow, hurricanes, and extreme cold or hot weather also curtail production in many manufacturing and service industries.

■ Fourth, a decline in labor productivity or even a reduction in the normal rate of advance in productivity restricts output. The slowing of advances in productivity during the last two decades or so has been attributed to such factors as: 1) new workers having low levels of education; 2) a decline in the work ethic; 3) poorer labor-management relations; 4) an increase in relatively less-skilled women (women, on average, have fewer years of experience than men, though the gap is closing) and teenagers in the workforce; 5) a shift toward labor-intensive service industries; and 6) an increase in drug and alcohol use by workers.

■ The fifth and last factor that causes cost-push inflation is closely connected to the fourth one. It involves the amount of money a business pays its employees for their labor in order to make one unit of output. In Chapter 6 you learned that this amount is called labor cost. It is calculated by the formula:

$$\text{Labor Cost} = \frac{\text{Wages/hour}}{\text{Labor Productivity}}$$

Labor productivity is the amount of a good or service a worker makes in one hour. It includes all workers, from those on the assembly line to the janitors and secretaries. Labor productivity is calculated by the formula:

$$\text{Labor Productivity} = \frac{\text{Total Output}}{\text{Total Hours Worked}}$$

Thus, combining these two formulas allows us to state that:

$$\text{Labor Cost} = \frac{\text{Wages/hour}}{\text{Output/hour}}$$

Average cost is the amount of money needed to buy the resources used to make one unit of a good or service, including supplies, utilities, machines, labor, and the like, on average. (The part of average cost used to pay employees is called labor cost.) If any one of the parts of average cost for a single good or service increases, its price will probably go up. However, that is *not* inflation because it is not widespread. However, if some part of average cost of a particular resource goes up for *most* firms in the whole economy and, consequently, prices rise for *most* products, that *will* cause cost-push inflation.

When the particular resource that rises in cost is labor, the resulting inflation is sometimes called wage-push inflation. It's merely one form of cost-push inflation. Another was the energy-push inflation of the 1970s.

If wages rise over a year in a particular firm or industry, one would expect the price of the good made by that firm or industry to rise as well. However, labor productivity is equally important in determining labor cost and prices. Like wages, productivity often changes over a year.

Economists disagree about the importance and even *the existence* of cost-push inflation. Some say cost-push inflation can exist only if there are increases in the money supply that exceed increases in total output. This means demand-pull inflation must occur to make it *appear* that there is cost-push inflation. This is what the Nobel Prize-economist Milton Friedman meant when he said, "Inflation is always and everywhere a monetary phenomenon." Chapter 13 further illustrates such differences of opinion among economists about macroeconomic problems and ways to solve them.

EXPLAINING COST-PUSH INFLATION WITH AGGREGATE DEMAND AND SUPPLY

Cost-push inflation is shown in the next two figures. Again, the simple case is shown first in Figure 12-8. Initially, the economy is at a full-employment equilibrium level of output of Q_1^* at price level P_1. Next, for various reasons, there is a reduction of the aggregate supply curve from AS_1 to AS_2. (Some reasons include the destruction of property and farmland during war or national disasters or sudden loss of population due to disease, famine, or war.) Thus, the level of output corresponding to potential GDP fell from Q_1^* to Q_2^*. Since there is no change in aggregate demand, this decline in output results in shortages. Consequently, the price level rises to P_2 at a new equilibrium level of output Q_2^*.

Figure 12-8

Cost-Push Inflation

If there is a drop in total output or aggregate supply and no change in aggregate demand, shortages will appear, leading to a higher price level.

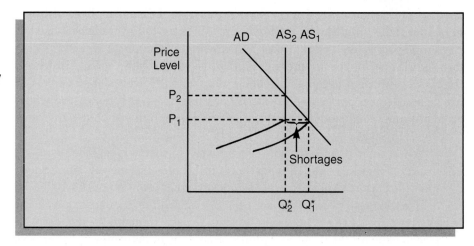

Figure 12-9 shows the more typical case of cost-push inflation, in which both aggregate demand and supply increase each year. This corresponds to Figure 12-7. There are no inflationary conditions between Period 1 and Period 2 because the extra output supplied of AS_2 over AS_1 matches the extra demand of AD_2 over AD_1—say, again, a 10 percent increase. However, in Period 3 the normal increase in aggregate demand of 10 percent to AD_3 is not matched by the normal 10 percent increase in output and aggregate supply (suppose it increases by only six percent). Consequently, shortages appear and the price level rises to P_2.

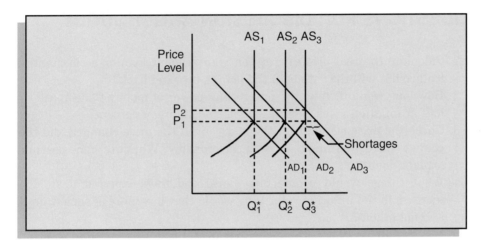

Figure 12-9

Cost-Push Inflation
When Output Increases

Inflation can result from increases in total output that fall short of increases in total spending. That is, the AS curve lags behind the AD curve, as occurs when AS_3 moves out less than AD_3, creating shortages. Consequently, the price level rises from P_1 to P_2.

SUMMARY

Inflation means the price level is rising. It leads to a fall in the purchasing power of money, a redistribution of wealth and income, a reduction in productive work, a lower rate of saving, a disruption in business planning, less investment, and higher interest rates. The United States had inflation in every major war.

The price level is primarily determined by: 1) the level of total spending or aggregate demand; and 2) the level of output of goods and services, or aggregate supply. The price level will increase because of: 1) widespread shortages after there is an increase in total spending; or 2) shortages following a decrease in the output of goods and services. Total spending can increase if there is an increase in consumer, investment, or government spending. Consumer spending will increase if savings or taxes fall.

Before total spending or aggregate demand can increase, either there must be more money in the economy or the existing money must be spent faster. Demand-pull inflation occurs if total spending rises faster than the output of goods and services (or if aggregate demand rises faster than aggregate supply). This generally occurs when the money supply increases faster than the output of goods and services.

Cost-push inflation occurs when production declines or when it does not increase as much as usual. This leads to higher production costs, which firms pass on to customers in the form of higher prices. Cost-push inflation can occur if war destroys capital, foreign resource prices increase, or when the weather is poor. The wage-push variant of cost-push inflation is most common if wages increase faster than labor productivity. This leads to higher labor costs, which firms again pass on in higher prices.

QUESTIONS FOR DISCUSSION AND THOUGHT

1. Calculate the real interest rate on your student loan or a classmate's loan. What will the rate be if the loan is not paid back?
2. How long would it take the purchasing power of money to decrease by half at inflation rates of three, eight, and eighteen percent?
3. Check the price of gold over the last year. If the price changed, did the changes have anything to do with the economy? What are some possible explanations?
4. What things would people buy more of if they expected a sudden increase in the inflation rate? Why would they buy more of some things and not others?
5. List five items that became cheaper in the last 10 years due to rapid increases in productivity. What do you think caused these large productivity increases?
6. Why are wartime economies so susceptible to inflation?
7. Why are prices for all goods and services what they are today, rather than 10 times as high or only a tenth as high?
8. If the inflation rate falls from eight percent to one percent, what will happen to the price level?

PROBLEMS   See page 490 for the answers.

1. For three consecutive years, the inflation rates were 6.1 percent, 3.7 percent, and 1.9 percent, while the market interest rates for car loans were 9.5 percent, 8.5 percent, and 7.5 percent. Which would have been the best year to take out a one-year car loan? The worst year? Show the calculations you used to answer the questions.

2. In Case 1, prices rise at one percent for each of the next three years. In Case 2, prices rise at 10 percent for each of the next three years. In Case 3, prices rise at 100 percent for each of the next three years. Calculate how many times higher prices are after three years in each case.

3. Taxes fall by $60 billion, savings rise by $20 billion, government spending falls by $10 billion, and investment spending falls by $10 billion. Initially, by how much will total spending change? Would you expect demand-pull inflation? Why or why not?

4. Suppose potential GDP is $6,000 billion and that an economy started out with the actual GDP (or equilibrium GDP) at $5,000 billion. The MPC is 0.6. If investment spending rises by $100 billion, calculate the new actual GDP (or equilibrium GDP). Would you expect demand-pull inflation? Explain your answer.

5. Using the equation of exchange, what would you expect the price level to do if the money supply rose by 1.6 percent, while the velocity fell by 0.2 percent and total output rose by 2.5 percent? Explain your answer.

6. If velocity rises by 0.3 percent and total output rises by 1.8 percent, what would the money supply have to change by to avoid changes in the price level?

7. Calculate the percentage change in labor productivity (to the nearest tenth of a percent) if a firm's total output rose from 1,630 to 2,260, while total hours worked rose from 216 to 280.

8. Calculate the labor cost in Year 1 and Year 2, given the following information: wages were $8.00 in Year 1 and $9.00 in Year 2; total output was 6,400 in Year 1 and 7,000 in Year 2; total hours worked were 480 in Year 1 and 520 in Year 2.

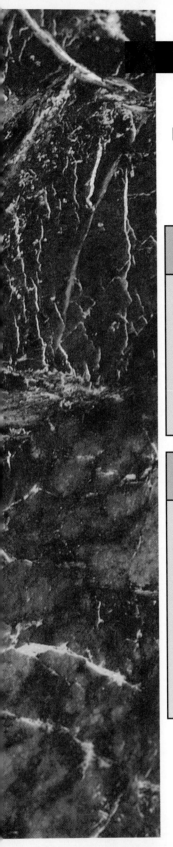

CHAPTER

13 MACROECONOMIC POLICIES

CHAPTER PREVIEW

Recession and inflation are the two major problems of the macroeconomy. Both are related to the level of total spending or aggregate demand.

Through government policies, we seek to prevent these problems from occurring. These include fiscal policy, carried out by the president and Congress. They also include monetary policy, carried out by the Federal Reserve System.

In addition, sometimes the government can control inflation by carrying out policies that boost total output. Such policies are called supply-side economics policies.

CHAPTER OBJECTIVES

After completing this chapter, you should be able to:

◆ *Outline the propositions of Classical Theory.*

◆ *Outline the propositions of Keynesian Theory.*

◆ *Describe the ways that fiscal policy can end recession.*

◆ *Explain the methods the Federal Reserve uses to end recession.*

◆ *Explain the ways fiscal policy is used to reduce total spending and inflation.*

◆ *Explain the methods the Federal Reserve uses to reduce inflation.*

◆ *Explain the methods available to end inflation by increasing production.*

Chapter 9 introduced the goals of macroeconomics—full employment, price stability, and economic growth. Chapters 11 and 12 presented some roadblocks to achieving those goals. This chapter outlines major policy tools the federal government uses to overcome these roadblocks. It introduces two theories of macroeconomics and notes the branches of government involved in the macroeconomy. The chapter also shows how the government tries to stop recession and inflation.

TWO THEORIES OF THE MACROECONOMY

Macroeconomic theories seek to explain how the macroeconomy works. Economists use them to explain changes in such variables as GDP, employment, production, interest rates, and price levels. Such theories also guide the government in making policies that affect the macroeconomy. In the last 200 years, two major macroeconomic theories have evolved: Classical Theory and Keynesian Theory.

Classical Theory

The oldest macroeconomic theory, **Classical Theory**, dovetailed with the developing models of the microeconomy that were based on a free market economy. Classical Theory was developed in the late 1700s and the 1800s. It has four major propositions: 1) Say's Law; 2) the normal state of the economy is to be at full employment; 3) recessions and inflations cure themselves; and 4) there is no need for government in the macroeconomy.

■ The major proposition is **Say's Law**, named for Jean Baptiste Say. It essentially states that "supply creates its own demand." Say noted that people sold resources (by working) and thus produced goods and services because they wanted to buy other goods and services. The money earned from creating a *supply* of goods and services created an ability to *demand* other goods and services.

■ Say's Law led to Classical Theory's second proposition that the normal state of the economy is full employment. Because people work in order to earn money to spend on goods and services, then everything people *produce* will create enough purchasing power to *buy* all the goods and services produced. In a way, the mass immigration to America from 1880 to 1920 proved this. Millions of people immigrated to America to find work—and found it. Many people believed that these immigrants "stole" jobs from people who were already here. However, the more immigrants available to work and to supply goods and services, the more people there were who demanded those goods and services.

Classical Theory is a body of economic thought developed in the late 1700s and 1800s, centering on the establishment of a free market economy.

Say's Law states that there will be an equivalent demand for goods and services for all the output people wish to produce.

■ The third proposition of Classical Theory is that any recession or inflation cures itself because of changes in prices, wages, and interest rates. Consider the problem of recession, caused by "insufficient spending" (or a drop in C + I + G). Remember that recession can begin with an increase in personal savings. However, doesn't Say's Law imply that people work to *spend*—and that they don't save? No, merely that people *eventually* spend their earnings before they die. Even though workers may not spend all the money they earn in the year they earn it, they will eventually spend it. In any particular year, there could be "unused" or unspent income. However, remember the role played by injections. The Classical economists, who said that all money flowing into leakages reappears as investment spending and government spending, said these injections compensate for leakages.

However, will there be *enough* injections to match leakages? The Classical theorists answered yes because any shortfall causing a recession also causes some events that compensate for leakages (see Figure 13-1).

THINKING CRITICALLY ABOUT ECONOMIC QUESTIONS IN OUR LIVES

Who Created More Jobs—President Reagan or President Washington?

Things to Consider

1. When up for re-election, presidents often point to the job growth over the last four years—if the growth is large.

2. From 1981 through 1988, the Reagan years, civilian employment rose from 100 million to 115 million. George Bush, running for president in 1988, implied that the Reagan-Bush administration did much to "create" 15 million jobs.

3. In George Washington's eight years, the entire *population* only rose by about a million, so he was much less "successful" in "creating jobs" than Ronald Reagan.

4. Consider Say's Law in evaluating the question posed above as well as George Bush's implication.

See page 475 for the answer.

Three of the main characteristics of a recession appear on the top of Figure 13-1.   They are: 1) there are surpluses of laborers (unemployment) because when total output is down firms need fewer workers; 2) firms have surpluses of goods and services because their sales have dropped; and 3) banks have "surplus" money because savers save more than borrowers borrow during a recession. The Classical economists said these three surpluses, like all surpluses, cause price decreases. These decreases are shaded in gray in Figure 13-1.

First, unemployment leads to reduced wages. Either: 1) firms cut wages, knowing they can hire replacements from the pool of the unemployed if some people quit; or 2) the unemployed offer to work at cut-rate wages, just to have a job. Because reduced wages make lower production costs possible, product prices fall, leading to higher sales that moderate the recession. Higher employment also contributes to higher consumer and total spending as the new workers spend their paychecks.

Second, prices of goods and services fall. Consumers, finding bargains, want to (and can) buy more with their paychecks. So firms meet these requests by hiring more workers to produce more. Even if the recession does not end as a result, at least it is not as bad as earlier.

Third, "surplus money" in banks prompts them to have a "sale on money." That is, interest rates fall, as the interest rate can be thought of as the "price" of credit. In response, people save less—and spend more. Also, as a result of cheaper credit, investment spending on capital equipment, factories, offices, and home construction climbs. Again, the recession moderates because of a flexible price.

Note that the government hasn't been mentioned yet. That's because adjustments in prices, wages, and interest rates are assumed to occur automatically in a free market economy in response to surpluses and shortages.

■ That leads to the final proposition of Classical Theory: the government has no role in ending a recession (or even inflation, since the events will reverse themselves). This complemented the Classical theorists' belief in a laissez-faire or "hands-off" policy in the microeconomy.

Keynesian Theory

These Classical Theory solutions to recession prevailed for more than a hundred years, until the 1930s. With some exceptions, recessions and depressions usually lasted only a year or two. However, the Great Depression lasted 12 years, was deeper than any previous one, and was worldwide. A British economist, John Maynard Keynes (pronounced "canes"), set out to determine why Classical Theory failed to explain the

Figure 13-1

Classical Theory Solutions to Recession

During recession, there are surpluses of products and resources, such as labor. These often stem from increases in savings or cuts in borrowing, contributing to a "surplus of credit."

Each surplus leads to price declines. In turn, this sets in motion events that increase total spending and overall activity in the economy, eventually ending the recession.

All these events occur without any government action. Thus, the Classical economists believed a recession would end even if the government did nothing.

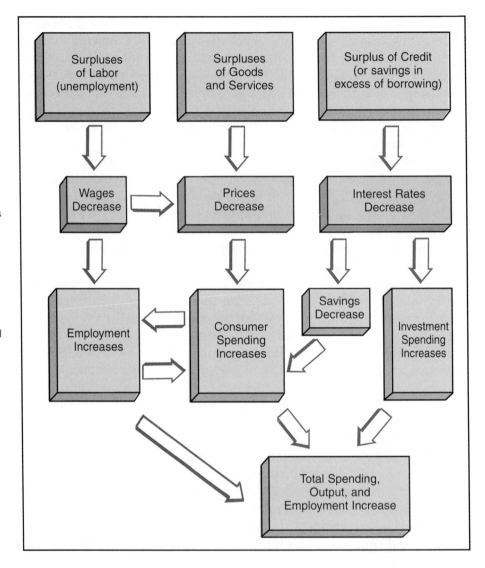

Great Depression. In 1936, he published his major arguments in *The General Theory of Employment, Prices, and Output.* It gave a different view of the world, given the changes in economic conditions. The world was never the same again—right up to the present.

Keynes proposed that: 1) the focus in macroeconomic study should be on total spending or aggregate demand; 2) there is no automatic cure for recession; 3) the economy might reach equilibrium at less than full employment; and 4) government action is necessary to ensure full employment.

■ Keynes' first proposition overturned Say's Law by focusing on total spending or aggregate demand, rather than total output, as the key to understanding macroeconomic activity. That is partly why economists today emphasize total spending—by consumers, investors, governments, and foreign traders—as the basis for explaining recession and inflation.

■ Keynes' second proposition was that falling prices, wages, and interest rates no longer provided an automatic escape from recession. First, prices no longer fell as often or as much as in previous depressions. This was due primarily to the growth of oligopolies—industries composed of big firms that preferred to reduce output, not prices, when recession hit. Second, wages fell less than earlier, partly because of the growing strength of labor unions. Also, cutting peoples' wages was increasingly considered to be socially unacceptable. Finally, Keynes believed that even if workers accepted wage cuts (as happened during the 1930s), product demand might fall even faster as workers, who now had lower incomes, reduced their spending. Thus, ironically, wage cuts might lead to even more unemployment, not less, as Classical Theory held.

A third attack by Keynes on automatic cures for recession suggested that even though interest rates still fell during a recession, the falling rates failed to end it for two reasons: 1) people didn't save less as rates had fallen, as expected; and 2) investment spending didn't increase much.

Keynes said people saved primarily for retirement and as a precaution against loss of income (from unemployment, for example). The interest rate was only a weak third factor determining savings. Therefore, during the Great Depression, when the thought of losing their jobs terrified workers—for there was no unemployment compensation and little welfare in the early 1930s—people saved *more,* not less.

Contrary to Classical Theory, Keynes also proposed that investment spending would not increase as predicted when interest rates fell. He noted that both interest rates and investment spending plunged in the 1930s. The explanation, according to Keynes, is that future profit expectations are far more important than interest rates in determining investment. During the Great Depression, expectations of profits from new factories or machines were generally very low to nonexistent. Thus, even if interest rates fell to zero, few firms would have borrowed much money. Such borrowing would have made as much sense as buying a fur coat just before moving to the tropics because it was on sale.

■ These failures of Classical Theory's automatic solutions to depression led to Keynes' third proposition: the economy might get bogged down in an unacceptably long and deep depression. That is, total spending, or C + I + G, might not be large enough to allow the economy to reach potential

GDP. Thus, it could reach equilibrium at less than full employment. Keynes thought the economy would eventually recover—but over an unacceptably long period.

■ Keynes believed that the government must act to boost spending high enough to allow the economy to achieve full employment. His proposal meant the government should have a budget deficit—thus driving the nation into debt during recessions or depressions. For the United States, this meant the days when the president and Congress sat idly by while the economy floundered were over. (His prescription was for a short period, not like the continuous deficits the United States has incurred since 1970.)

The solution to inflation would be just the opposite—to reduce total spending, partly by reducing budget deficits or even running a budget surplus.

GOVERNMENT AND THE MACROECONOMY

Although the Roosevelt administration provided much government assistance to the unemployed in the 1930s and early 1940s, it wasn't until the Employment Act of 1946 that the government committed itself to promoting full employment. Two branches or sectors of the federal government seek to achieve this and the other macroeconomic goals: the executive branch and the legislative branch. The Federal Reserve System also has a major role in this endeavor.

The Executive Branch

The president is the head of the executive branch. The president's primary control over the economy comes through White House influence on government spending and tax rates (both indirectly influence consumer and investment spending). Another executive branch participant is the budget director, who leads the Office of Management and Budget (OMB) and oversees government spending. The OMB proposes to the president how much the federal government should spend, and then the president makes the administration's budget proposal to Congress.

The Treasury Department is another vital part of the executive branch. The Secretary of the Treasury influences the president in determining tax rates, user fees, and the size of the budget deficit. The president also consults frequently with the Council of Economic Advisers (CEA). Each January, the Council provides the *Economic Report of the President,* a review of economic conditions and proposals for improving the economy. Finally, the president is also advised by officials from the Commerce

Department, the Labor Department, the International Trade Commission, and other agencies.

The Legislative Branch

Congress, the primary institution of the legislative branch, influences total spending in the economy through its power to authorize government spending and to collect taxes. The greatest economic power in Congress is wielded by the House Ways and Means Committee, the Senate Finance Committee, and the Joint Finance Committee. The Congressional Budget Office (CBO) is a counterpart of the OMB in the executive branch. The CBO has a staff of economists who provide members of Congress with information and advice. Often, the results are bills and laws which deal with taxes and government spending. They also do macroeconomic studies and economic forecasting.

The Federal Reserve System

Chapter 9 covered the Federal Reserve System (the Fed). It is headed by the seven-member Board of Governors, and the Federal Open Market Committee engages in open market operations. There are 12 Federal Reserve District Banks, which serve the thousands of commercial banks that are members of the Federal Reserve System.

Technically, the Federal Reserve System is not part of "the government." It is sometimes called a quasi-government organization, as it has elements of a private enterprise (its buildings and other facilities are owned by the member banks). However, its top staff is appointed by the president and confirmed by Congress, and its operating procedure is set by law.

The Fed has several functions, but controlling the availability and the price of credit (the interest rate) is the most important. It exercises this control primarily through: 1) changes in the discount rate; 2) changes in the reserve requirement; and 3) open market operations.

HOW THE GOVERNMENT DEALS WITH RECESSION

How do the various sectors of the government try to influence the macroeconomy? This section explains policies used to end recession. The next section shows how the government tackles inflation.

Recall that recession occurs when a drop in aggregate demand or total spending (C + I + G) leads firms to lay off workers, close plants, and

Expansionary policy is a government policy designed to end or to prevent recession, which is carried out through an increase in total spending or aggregate demand.

Fiscal policy refers to changes in taxes and/or government spending designed to influence the level of total spending or aggregate demand.

cut production. Total spending falls if: 1) savings and/or taxes increase; or 2) investment and/or government spending falls. In essence, recession is caused by "insufficient spending"—insufficient when compared with the (desired) level of spending needed to reach potential GDP. The solution to recession is to boost total spending to that desired level. Any policy to end (or to prevent) recession is called an **expansionary policy**, for the intent is to expand employment and output. Two broad sets of policies for achieving this are fiscal policy and monetary policy.

Expansionary Fiscal Policy

Fiscal policy refers to changes in government spending and/or taxes that are designed to change the level of total spending or aggregate demand. If the macroeconomic problem is recession, it is necessary to increase total spending or aggregate demand. Business owners will then want to hire more laborers and buy other resources so they can boost output. Implementation of fiscal policy is the responsibility of the president and Congress. Either can propose changes in taxes or government spending. However, generally both must agree on such policies, except when Congress overrides the president's veto. Usually such moves to change taxes and government spending occur during recession or inflation. Economists call such changes in policy discretionary fiscal policy because such movements in taxing and spending are at the discretion of the president and Congress.

There are two types of discretionary fiscal policy: 1) changes in taxes; and 2) changes in government spending.

■ The first expansionary fiscal policy action is to reduce taxes, either on individuals or businesses, or both. Cutting personal taxes gives people higher disposable incomes. Since this leads to more consumer spending, total spending rises, tending to moderate the recession. Reducing business taxes has a similar effect on businesses because the larger after-tax profits contribute to more investment spending on plant and equipment. Another fiscal policy option for business is an investment tax credit. This is a reduction in taxes for businesses equal to a certain percent of the money spent on capital goods. For example, with a 10 percent tax credit, a firm would save $900 in taxes if it bought a $9,000 machine.

■ The second expansionary fiscal policy action is to increase government spending on goods and services. As far as the expansionary effect is concerned, it usually doesn't matter how the money is spent, so long as it *is* spent. The government could buy more street lights or more trucks for the Postal Service—or start a war. Of course, war is an absurd suggestion, but it certainly brought prosperity during World Wars I and II, the Korean War, and the Vietnam War—but at a horrendous cost. However, the Great Depression ended in 1933 in Germany, eight years before it did here, largely because the Nazis were building up their war machine. The resulting employment was a major reason for Hitler's popularity.

Both expansionary fiscal policies—cutting taxes and raising government spending—result in a budget deficit, but Keynes thought this was an acceptable price for full employment. In the 1930s, however, few politicians accepted this. President Roosevelt believed that the government should have a balanced budget each year—even though the huge deficits of World War II helped bring America out of the Great Depression.

Total spending or aggregate demand also changes because of automatic fiscal policy. This involves **automatic stabilizers**, which are economic variables that change to moderate recession or inflation without anyone initiating any action. One such automatic stabilizer is unemployment compensation. When unemployment rises during recession, more people collect unemployment benefits. Because the recipients spend most of the money, such spending moderates the recession. Welfare payments, another automatic stabilizer, work similarly, as more people receive such benefits during recession. Farm subsidies represent a third class of stabilizers. Since farm prices and income often fall during recession, the subsequent increase in subsidies somewhat offsets a drop in total spending. The last major automatic stabilizer is the progressive income tax. When their wages or hours are cut during a recession, some people fall into lower tax brackets. Thus, they get to spend a larger share of their gross paychecks, again offsetting the spending drop that precipitated the recession. For example, suppose someone fell from the 28 percent tax bracket to the 15 percent bracket. Out of a given $1,000 of gross income (that had been taxed at 28 percent), they would pay $150 instead of $280, thereby having an extra $130 to spend.

> **Automatic stabilizers** are instruments that are used to carry out automatic fiscal policy, including transfer payments, farm subsidies, and the progressive income tax.

Some Problems of an Expansionary Fiscal Policy

Besides the deficit problem, an expansionary fiscal policy has some other problems, including: 1) political differences; 2) timing; 3) inflation from overstimulus; and 4) crowding out.

■ Democrats and Republicans often disagree on fiscal policies, a problem that is especially frustrating when one party controls Congress and the other party controls the presidency. However, even controlling both branches is often little better, as President Clinton found out when the minority Republicans derailed his economic stimulus package and jobs bill in early 1993 with a filibuster.

■ Ideally, a recession should be predicted a year or more in advance. It takes that long to change most tax laws and to initiate major spending projects. Often, however, a recession isn't recognized until *after* it starts because much government data collection is done quarterly and becomes available well after the measured economic activity occurs. Thus, the cure comes later than desired, possibly destabilizing the economy.

■ The third problem is overstimulus of the economy, which leads to inflation. Recession occurs when there is not enough total spending or aggregate demand to reach potential GDP. Determining the economy's shortfall of this "proper level" of spending might seem easy. Then the government could give the economy the appropriate shot of tax cuts and a government spending boost to close this "spending gap." However, it's not that simple, for it's hard to know just how big the gap is. After all, *how big* is potential GDP? The size of potential GDP depends partly on the meaning of full employment. Is it an unemployment rate of three, five, or seven percent—or even higher? There is much disagreement between economists and others on this matter.

Let's say authorities believe total spending should increase by four hundred billion dollars to provide full employment, however defined. Suppose Congress then cuts taxes by some amount and also begins some public works projects. However, what if these policies unexpectedly create *six* hundred billion dollars of extra spending? The two hundred billion dollars of "excess spending" will merely create shortages and inflation.

A difficulty in applying expansionary policy is that there is no precise level of spending that provides full employment without inflation. If the economy starts from a deep recession and expansionary fiscal policies cause total spending to increase, the unemployment rate steadily drops. At first, prices do not increase much, if at all. This is because most firms have competitors with excess productive capacity, so any price increase pushes buyers to a competitor who does *not* raise prices. Thus, prices stay fairly constant for a while. However, eventually, as the economy moves closer to full employment, some industries (the tire industry, for example) will reach their capacities before others. Additional expansionary fiscal policies begin to create shortages in *some* industries, even though the *overall* economy has excess productive capacity. Thus, *some* prices begin to climb (tire prices, in this case) while others stay firm. The closer the economy gets to full employment, the more common such price increases become. Or, the lower the unemployment rate becomes, the higher the inflation rate will be. As commonly stated, there is a tradeoff (at least a temporary one) between these two rates. Unfortunately, there is no point when both rates are at their ideal levels.

■ The last major problem of an expansionary fiscal policy centers on the budget deficit created by that policy. The government finances a deficit by selling bonds. However, if it wants to sell *many* more, it must raise the interest rate paid to the buyers of the additional bonds. This is necessary to draw the buyers' funds away from other forms of saving. In essence, such government borrowing raises the demand for credit, creating a shortage of credit at the original interest rate.

(Technically, what happens when larger deficits lead to higher interest rates is that purchasers of the additional government securities offer to pay less for them, just like you would be willing to pay less for additional units of any good you buy. For example, instead of paying the $10,000 face value on a bond, a buyer might offer to pay only $9,600. Suppose the bond pays $600 interest per year, or six percent of $10,000. Because the *number of dollars* of interest paid per year to the bondholder is the same whatever the price, the interest *rate* rises as bond prices fall. The interest rate on a bond, called the yield, is found by dividing the number of dollars of interest paid per year to the bondholder by the price of the bond. In this case, the yield would be 6.25 percent, or $600 ÷ $9,600 x 100.)

To compete against the government for credit, all borrowers, including chargecard users, home buyers, and businesses buying capital equipment and new factories, must pay higher interest rates. However, at higher interest rates, *some* spending that consumers and investors plan to do by using credit will not occur because interest rates are too high. This phenomenon is called **crowding out**, which means government spending "crowds out" private consumer and investment spending because of increased interest rates. Crowding out can occur in another way. The government could provide goods and services that individuals would otherwise have purchased. Thus, there is little or no net gain in total spending. Examples include: purchases of books by public libraries that lead to fewer books purchased by individuals; spending on government-owned mass transit systems that lead to fewer personal vehicles purchased; and spending on public education that leads to less private education.

Crowding out occurs when the increased deficit of an expansionary policy leads to higher interest rates and reduced consumer and investment spending.

Economists disagree about the extent of crowding out. Some say there is very little. Others say it is complete, which means fiscal policy actions can't raise total spending at all because any increase in government spending leads to an equal fall in private spending.

The top of Figure 13-2 summarizes expansionary fiscal policy. The goal is to increase production and employment by increasing total spending or aggregate demand. This is shown in the three unshaded boxes in the middle of the figure. In turn, total spending increases if consumer, investment, or government spending increases.

Figure 13-2

Expansionary Fiscal and
Monetary Policies

To prevent or end
recession, either fiscal or
monetary policies can be
used to boost aggregate
demand or total spending.

Three fiscal policy tools
appear in the more darkly
shaded blue boxes at the
top. A side effect of such
fiscal policies is a budget
deficit, along with higher
interest rates.

Three monetary policy
tools appear in the bottom
row of the figure in the
more darkly shaded
boxes. A side effect of
such monetary policies is
a faster rate of growth in
the money supply.

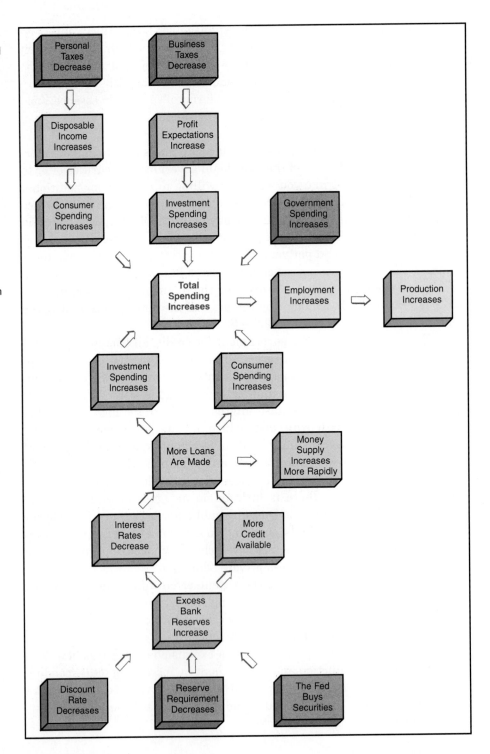

Expansionary Monetary Policy

The bottom section of Figure 13-2 deals with money or credit expansion, or monetary policy. The Fed always stands ready to help boost total spending if it is a little less than the "desired level." The Fed does not directly control consumer or investment spending. However, it makes it easier for consumers and investors to spend. The Fed accomplishes this through **monetary policy**, designed to control both interest rates and the availability of credit. During a recession, the Fed tries to increase excess reserves, which, in turn, leads to lower interest rates.

Excess reserves represent a bank's lending capacity that it has not yet used. So by increasing excess reserves, the Fed increases the availability of credit. In turn, that puts pressure on banks to reduce the interest rate they charge for loans (because banks must pay depositors interest in the funds that are, in effect, these excess reserves). This reduces the financing cost of purchases made with credit, thereby stimulating such purchases by consumers and businesses. An expansionary monetary policy is often referred to as an "easy money" policy—because credit is cheap and plentiful.

The Fed provides "easy money" in three primary ways: 1) it reduces the discount rate; 2) it reduces the reserve requirement; and 3) it buys government securities.

■ A commercial bank bases its decision to borrow reserves from the Fed partly on the cost of those reserves—the discount rate. Thus, if that rate declines, the bank is more likely to borrow more reserves. (That is, it follows the same law of demand consumers do when the price of a good falls—more credit is "bought.") In turn, the bank passes on these cost savings to its customers by reducing its loan rates. This encourages individuals and businesses to take out more loans to finance consumer and investment spending. Such loans increase the money supply, for the loans usually are deposited in demand deposit accounts. Thus, reducing the discount rate ultimately increases the money supply as well as total spending or aggregate demand.

■ When the Fed reduces the reserve requirement, commercial banks have their excess reserves increased without the banks taking any specific action. It occurs when some of the deposits the banks used to hold as required reserves now become excess reserves. The banks, eager to earn profits on those reserves, drop interest rates to coax consumers and businesses to take out more loans. Again, this increases the money supply and total spending.

■ The Fed can also fight recession by purchasing government securities from individuals, businesses, banks, and others. When an individual

Monetary policy refers to the control of interest rates and the availability of excess reserves and credit by the Federal Reserve System in order to influence total spending or aggregate demand.

sells the Fed a bond, the Fed replaces a nonspendable asset (a bond) with a spendable asset (money). When the money is placed in a demand deposit account, a bank can generate even more money out of the deposit through new loans. If a bank sells the Fed a bond, a nonlendable asset (a bond) is converted into lendable reserves. Thus, bond purchases by the Fed boost excess bank reserves, creating more and cheaper credit. Eventually, the money supply increases, as does total spending or aggregate demand, and the recession moderates or ends.

The Fed commonly reduces the discount rate during recession, but it rarely changes the reserve requirement because such a change has a huge impact. The Fed's most important tool is open market operations. Each day it trades billions of dollars in government securities with major commercial banks and brokerage houses. The trades are carried out by the Federal Reserve Bank of New York under the directives of the Federal Open Market Committee.

Like fiscal policy, monetary policy has problems. The Fed can over-react in trying to end a recession, creating too much credit and reducing interest rates too much, causing an inflationary spending boom. Probably the biggest problem occurs when economic forecasts are gloomy and it is vir-tually impossible to encourage spending with "cheap money." Often econo-mists liken the Fed's problem to pushing on a string. You can move one end of the string (like the Fed can boost excess reserves), but you can't move the other (make people borrow and spend more). This was partly why the recovery from the 1990-1991 recession was so sluggish and why the weak economy was an issue in the 1992 election. In early 1991, President Bush pleaded with Americans to take advantage of the low interest rates and borrow money to boost their spending. But he was unsuccessful and, conse-quently, unsuccessful in 1992 in the election.

CONTROLLING INFLATION BY RESTRICTING TOTAL SPENDING

The causes of recession and inflation are almost exact opposites. Too little spending causes recession. Too much spending causes shortages and inflation. So one might expect opposite solutions to these problems, and such anti-inflation policies will be explained now. Economists call these actions **contractionary policy**, for the intent is to contract the amount of total spending or aggregate demand and, in turn, the amount of shortages and price increases.

Contractionary policy is a policy designed to end inflation by reducing total spending or aggregate demand and, in turn, shortages.

The price level depends primarily upon the amount of total spending and the amount of goods and services produced (or the levels of aggregate demand and aggregate supply). Contractionary policy seeks to control increases in the price level by restricting total spending or aggregate demand. The next section shows how the same thing can be done by boosting production. While reading this section, refer to Figure 13-3, which summarizes contractionary policy.

Contractionary Fiscal Policy

The president and Congress can deal with inflation by: 1) imposing tax increases; and 2) cutting government spending. When they raise taxes on individuals, disposable income falls, as do consumer spending, total spending, shortages, and the inflation rate. (Similarly, if the government raised business taxes, businesses would cut their investment spending on new plant and capital equipment. However, this would lead to less output in the future and lower living standards. Thus, such a fiscal policy is not a good option if it is expected that investment will fall.) When the government cuts its budget, total spending or aggregate demand also drops. For example, the government could put highway projects on hold, reduce public services (such as job-finding services), close seldom used facilities in some national parks, cut back on projects to restore historical buildings, and close military bases.

The effect of contractionary fiscal policy on the federal budget is the opposite of an expansionary policy's effect. If there was a budget deficit prior to the tax increases or budget cuts, the deficit shrinks. If the tax increases and the budget cuts are strong enough, the budget becomes balanced or even ends up in surplus. (Keynes suggested budget surpluses during inflation, but he assumed a balanced budget prior to the inflation.)

In addition to these discretionary fiscal policy actions, automatic fiscal policy helps to moderate inflation. Unemployment compensation benefits and welfare payments fall as more people work during the prosperity of an inflationary period. Overtime pay, wage increases, and longer hours all push some people into higher tax brackets, so they get to spend a smaller share of their income. Farm subsidies fall as farm prices and incomes rise. All these events lead to reduced spending, which then moderates inflation.

Like expansionary policy, contractionary policies have some problems. Again, it's difficult to forecast inflation and the time needed to cure it. Politicians are reluctant to take unpopular actions (tax hikes or budget cuts) that can delay or prevent a necessary cure. An excellent example was the temporary income tax hike in 1968-1970, called a surtax (10 percent was added to each person's taxes). Taxes should have been raised in 1966 or 1967, when inflation began to get out of hand, but President Johnson was

Figure 13-3

Contractionary Fiscal and Monetary Policies

To reduce inflation, total spending or aggregate demand must be reduced so there are fewer shortages.

Two fiscal policies are shown in the top corners as a way to accomplish this. A side effect of such policies is a lower budget deficit or even a surplus budget.

Three monetary policies are shown at the bottom to bring about the same effect. A side effect of such policies is a reduction in the rate of growth of the money supply.

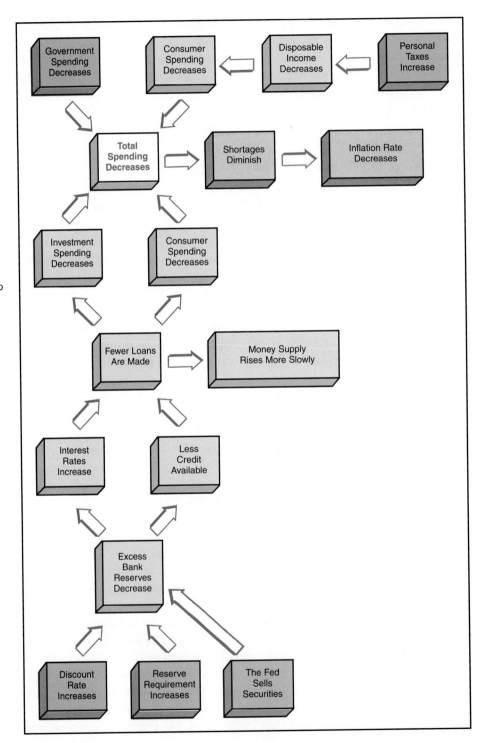

reluctant to increase taxes before his re-election campaign. He eventually accepted a tax hike, but it was too late. The severe inflation of the 1970s had been unleashed (though other factors contributed as well). Another problem was that everyone knew the surtax was temporary. So people saved less (and spent more). As a consequence, the effect on total spending was minimal.

Another serious problem of a contractionary policy is "overkill." It is possible to moderate the inflation with spending cuts, but excessive cuts create a recession. The last two budget surpluses that were associated with contractionary fiscal policies preceded recessions and occurred in 1960 and 1969. Thus, it is possible to overdo contractionary policy, just as it is possible to overdo expansionary policy. However, avoiding that overkill is a bit like avoiding an accident on a crowded highway. Pick up speed too fast (expansionary policy) and you hit the car ahead (inflation). Slow down too fast (contractionary policy) and you get rear-ended (recession).

Contractionary Monetary Policy

Suppose the economy experienced inflation in excess of seven percent and that M1 increased at nine percent each year for the last three years. If the Fed suspects that an excessive money supply expansion was the reason for the inflation, it might lower its M1 target to only a four percent increase. This might result in a spending increase equal to the rate of increase in the economy's productive capacity (potential GDP). Consequently, there would be fewer shortages and lower rates of inflation. Thus, contractionary monetary policy, called a "tight money" policy, occurs when the Fed slows up the money supply's rate of expansion.

The Fed carries out such a move in three ways: 1) it raises the discount rate; 2) it raises the reserve requirement; and 3) it sells government securities. When the discount rate is raised, banks are less likely to borrow from the Fed. Credit becomes a bit less available and more costly (higher interest rates) for consumers and businesses. They take out fewer loans, so the money supply climbs more slowly. Finally, total spending or aggregate demand rises at a slower rate. The same effect occurs when the Fed raises the reserve requirement, for banks now must convert some (lendable) excess reserves to (nonlendable) required reserves. Last, when people pay the Fed for the government securities sold by the Fed, their demand deposits fall. In turn, banks have less ability to extend loans.

As with fiscal policy, a major problem with monetary policy is the danger of "overkill." The Fed can easily cut back credit so much that it brings on a recession. Some people believe this happened in the early 1980s, a time of serious inflation that the Fed, under Chairman Paul

Volcker, wanted to end. The Fed successfully reduced inflation to less than three percent by the mid-1980s. However, that caused the recessions of 1980 and 1982. Yet other people believed that such drastic action was necessary to "break the back" of inflation and to end the expectations of continuous high inflation that virtually everyone had and which affected their economic behavior.

Another problem of monetary policy is that the timing might be off. If the Fed waits too long to contract credit, inflation can become much worse. By the time credit contraction does occur, the inflationary pressures may have evaporated, and the contraction could actually be harmful, causing an economic slowdown or even recession.

MACRO-POLICIES AND AGGREGATE DEMAND AND SUPPLY FUNCTIONS

In a recession, either expansionary fiscal or monetary policies can be used to increase aggregate demand. Figure 13-4 shows the economy to be in recession when aggregate demand is AD_1. The equilibrium level of output is Q_1, short of the full-employment output level of Q^*. By cutting taxes, raising government spending, or increasing bank reserves, aggregate demand shifts out to AD_2. The extra spending leads to extra output (out to Q^*) and employment (to full employment), which ends the recession. The price level rises somewhat to P_2. However, officials must be careful not to go overboard so that the new AD intersects the AS line on the vertical section, leading to a very rapidly rising price level.

Figure 13-4

Expansionary Policy

An increase in aggregate demand leads to the equilibrium output level rising from Q_1 to Q^*, the full-employment level of output. The price level also increases from P_1 to P_2.

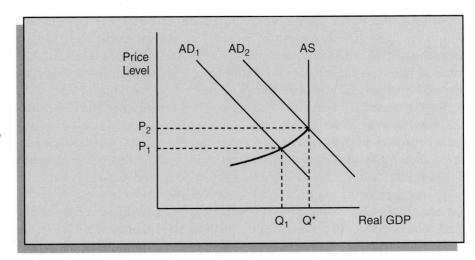

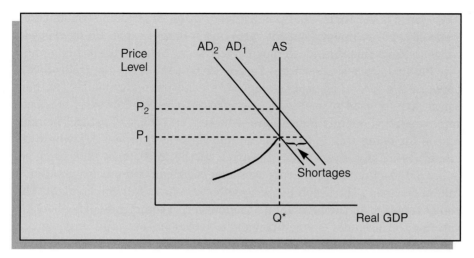

Figure 13-5

Contractionary Policy

To prevent the imminent rise in the price level to P_2 due to the shortages associated with AD_1, a contractionary policy shifts aggregate demand back to D_2, which eliminates the shortages.

Conversely, contractionary fiscal and monetary policies can be used to moderate or eliminate inflation, as shown in Figure 13-5. Initially, the economy has shortages at price level P_1, caused by excess demand compared with the economy's capacity to produce. If the government can act in time, it might be able to prevent all or most of the price increases (to P_2) these shortages will otherwise cause. If taxes are raised, government spending is cut, or if bank reserves fall, total spending or aggregate demand will fall to AD_2. If policy makers act with appropriate strength, no shortages will remain, and the inflationary pressures will disappear.

However, if they use too much strength and AD falls to the left of AD_2, output will fall below potential GDP (Q^*) and employment will fall below full employment. Policy makers aren't always as accurate, knowledgeable, or lucky as they would like to be, and expansionary and contractionary policies often are either overdone or underdone.

In reality, the AS curve is not vertical. Although more advanced economics explains its shape in more complex ways, a beginning way to understand its shape is to realize that there is no precise measure of full employment and potential GDP. Rather, there is a zone of unemployment rates where it becomes increasingly difficult to increase output in response to demand increases. Extra output is always possible, but at rapidly escalating costs. Thus, it is possible to expand output somewhat beyond Q^*.

Such a situation led to the discovery by an Australian economist of a tradeoff between unemployment rates and inflation rates. He developed a curve to show this relationship or tradeoff, and today it bears his name—the Phillips Curve, shown in Figure 13-6. (Actually, his tradeoff was between the rate of change in wage rates and unemployment.) The horizontal axis is used to measure unemployment rates. However, no actual rates are listed, merely indications of "lower" and "higher" rates. The main reason for doing this is that no one knows for certain exactly where the curve lies at any given time. (Research in the 1970s showed that it has appeared to shift rather sharply over time.) Instead of a precise notation of full employment, the graph notes a region or zone of full employment. This zone extends from the high end to the low end of common beliefs about the rate (or the percent) of unemployment that represents full employment. Nevertheless, it does include that area of unemployment rates where inflation does become a major problem if the economy faces increases in aggregate demand. Thus, the Phillips Curve is very steep in that zone, which means that "lower" unemployment rates will lead to "higher" inflation rates. Alternatively, at "higher" unemployment rates there is little likelihood of shortages. Thus, there should be "lower" inflation rates.

It is important to note that any tradeoff between unemployment and inflation rates is temporary. Laborers and other participants in the economy take various actions that "drive" the economy to a fairly narrow range of unemployment rates, no matter what the inflation rate.

Figure 13-6

The Phillips Curve

A short-term tradeoff often occurs between unemployment rates and inflation rates. High rates of one type are associated with low rates of the other. However, this relationship does not hold in the long run.

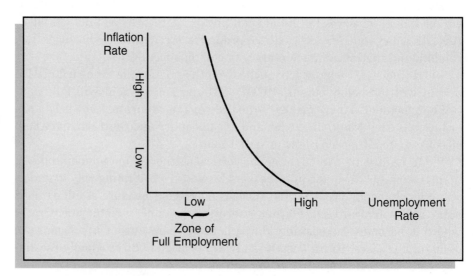

CONTROLLING INFLATION BY INCREASING PRODUCTION

Cutting demand (total spending) is one way to reduce shortages. Increasing supplies (total output) also reduces shortages. This second technique gained much popularity since the late 1970s, particularly during the early part of the Reagan administration. Such policies to boost production are often called **supply-side economics**.

The better-known supply-side economics policies of the Reagan administration generally fell into three categories: 1) altering the tax system; 2) reforming income redistribution programs; and 3) reducing business regulations. To the extent that they had merit in the 1980s, they will have merit any time in the future.

■ The economist Arthur Laffer popularized supply-side economics when he theorized that government might increase tax *rates* so much that tax *receipts* (collections) would fall. (For an extreme example, if the government took 95 percent of incomes, few people would work, at least in jobs where the government could get at their incomes, so the government would collect almost no taxes.) He suggested sharp cuts in tax rates in order to increase tax collections. This is the main policy move favored by supply-siders—to cut taxes in order to spur more work and production. Supply-siders favor three tax reforms. The first is a lower tax rate for everyone. According to supply-side theory, lower taxes encourage people to work longer hours, get second jobs, start businesses, and so on. They do so because the government no longer takes such a big bite out of paychecks. Thus, the 1981-1983 tax cut reduced tax rates over a three-year period so that everyone paid about 25 percent less in federal income taxes. Second, supply-siders support a less progressive income tax, again to encourage working, but also because a less progressive tax provides more after-tax income for upper-income people. Because these people save relatively more of their incomes, more money becomes available for investment spending on capital equipment, new plants, and research and development. This boosts the economy's productive capacity. Third, supply-siders want lower business tax rates, again to encourage investment spending.

■ Another part of the supply-side economics program seeks to reduce or reform various income redistribution programs so there is more incentive for people to seek employment. Supply-siders believe that welfare and unemployment compensation programs reduce people's willingness to work. They maintain that the budgets for these programs should be cut. Similarly, they believe minimum wage laws reduce the willingness of firms to hire workers and increase production, so these laws should be repealed.

Supply-side economics refers to government policies designed to increase total output or aggregate supply for the purposes of increasing economic growth and moderating inflation.

THINKING CRITICALLY ABOUT ECONOMIC QUESTIONS IN OUR LIVES

Who Shot Liberty Valence?

Things to Consider

1. In the 1960s Western film, "The Man Who Shot Liberty Valence," no one in the film knew who killed the town bully, Liberty Valence (Lee Marvin), in an evening gunfight (except the killer in the dark— played by John Wayne). Everyone thought that Jimmy Stewart's character did, a mild-mannered, peace-loving lawyer (even he thought so). His political star rose as a result of the ignorance, becoming a popular senator.

2. "Who Killed the Inflation" could be a sequel, having to do with the taming of the inflation of the 1970s by the early 1980s. President Reagan got much of the credit, and his star rose partly because of that.

3. Who would play the part of John Wayne's character—the *real* "inflation killer"? That is, who and what *really* dealt with the inflation? Why would most in the movie cast not have known how the "killing" was done and who did it?

See page 476 for the answer.

■ Last, supply-side economists want to reduce government regulation of businesses. They believe that less regulation encourages more risk-taking to find more efficient production methods. It also leads to more investment spending, another boost to the nation's productive capacity.

Without any other action, a tax cut leads to a budget deficit. However, according to supply-side theory, the deficit will not last long, since the economic growth created by supply-side policies will yield more tax revenues from the additional people who work and from higher incomes in general.

Throughout the 1980s, economists disagreed about the effectiveness of these programs. The major criticism was that the ballooning deficits of the Reagan years did not shrink as predicted. Another criticism related to "trickle-down theory." This proposed that the tax savings and other benefits of the policies, though initially benefiting high-income people the most, would eventually be passed on (or "trickle down") to everyone else. This would take the form of higher real incomes following innovations by (rich?) entrepreneurs and higher employment as part of an expanding economy. However, these benefits were difficult to see and measure. Therefore, many believed they didn't occur. Also, many thought they would take too long to materialize. Thus, "the rich get richer" adage harmed the prospects for the policies. By the 1990s, fewer people were championing supply-side economics as our salvation.

   Figure 13-7 shows how supply-side economics is used to moderate inflation. Suppose the price level is initially at P_1. However, with the positions of AD and the initial aggregate supply at AS_1, the resulting shortages will soon cause the price level to rise to P_2. However, if various government actions lead to a higher aggregate supply at AS_2, the shortages will disappear (or will not appear in the first place if the actions occur fast enough)—as will the inflation threat. There also will be a higher level of output, an increase from Q_1^* to Q_2^*. Thus, two macroeconomic goals are achieved—low inflation and a higher economic growth rate.

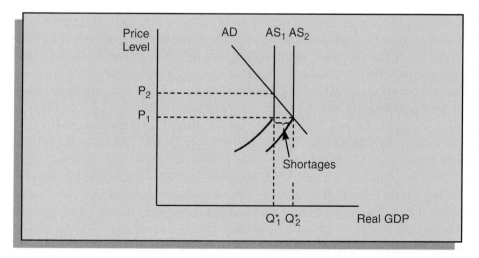

Figure 13-7

Supply-Side Economics

Supply-side policies have two goals: first, to prevent price increases that would otherwise occur (to P_2); second, to boost total output (to Q_2^*) and to raise living standards.

RECENT MACROECONOMIC ISSUES AND DEVELOPMENTS

In the last few decades, much attention has focused on several macroeconomic issues and theoretical developments in macroeconomics. This section introduces some of them.

The Budget Deficit Problem

Keynes, who proposed budget deficits during recessions, never suggested that we have them *every* year. (He proposed budget *surpluses* in years when an "overheated" economy was threatened with inflation.) However, there have been deficits every year except two since 1960—and every year since 1970. In the 1980s, the United States usually had deficits of between $100 and $200 billion. Many critics blamed Reagan's tax cut and the huge military buildup for these deficits. His supporters blamed them on the widespread increase in spending initiated by Congress. These large deficits continued into the mid-1990s. Whatever the cause, interest on the growing debt eats up about a sixth of the current federal budget.

In July 1993, Congress passed a budget-reduction bill, largely on President Clinton's proposals. It was a five-year package that was expected to reduce the deficit by $496 billion over that period. Of that, $255 billion would come from spending cuts and $268 billion would come from increased taxes, partly offset by $27 billion in tax breaks. The top income tax rate was raised to 36 percent (up from 31 percent). Also, a 10 percent surtax was added on people earning more than $250,000—in effect, creating a new bracket of 39.6 percent.

These measures, plus the tax-generating effect of a booming economy of the late 90s, led to budget surpluses for fiscal years 1998 through 2001. In January 2001, projections were made for cumulative surpluses of $5,610 billion by 2011. However, deficits returned by 2002, primarily due to the recession of 2001-2002, a large increase in federal spending (partly due to the 9/11 attacks), and the 2001 tax cut and rebates. By January 2002, that 10-year projection of surpluses dropped to $1,600 billion.

It should be noted that many people, including some economists, do not worry much about the deficit and see substantial benefit in it. First, they believe that its size in comparison with GDP is not large. The net public debt is about 54 percent of GDP, so we can easily manage to pay the interest on it. Second, they point to other healthy economies that have even larger deficits (as a percent of total outlays), such as Japan. Third, they believe that the government can do very productive things with the funds that are borrowed (the deficit). If the funds pay for construction and improvement of the infrastructure, that increases resource efficiency. Similarly, improved schools can increase labor productivity. Finally, government-sponsored research can lead to cures for diseases and technological breakthroughs that raise productivity.

The Emergence of Monetary Policy

Virtually ignored from the 1930s through the 1960s, monetary policy gained stature again in the 1970s and 1980s. People started to watch the weekly reports of the changes in M1 or M2 as a signal of what the Fed was up to and what the economy would do next.

This was partly due to the failure of fiscal policy. People wanted *some* handle on the macroeconomy. More important, the increased stature of monetary policy today is due to a group of economists who are known as **monetarists**. They believe that, more than anything else, changes in the money supply explain changes in current GDP and prices.

They also believe that virtually all business fluctuations are due to erratic and excessive changes in the money supply. That is, a 12 percent increase one year, followed by a four percent increase the next, and so on, lead to periods of recession and inflation. Therefore, because the Fed often *causes* what it attempts to prevent, monetarists say the Fed should not even *attempt* to counteract recession and inflation.

However, monetarists do believe it is possible to have an economy without significant inflation or recession. They say that this could happen if the Fed increased the money supply by the same percentage each year, equal to the rate of increase in the productive capacity of the economy—potential GDP. In that way, all extra output could and would be produced and sold, so there would be no shortages or inflation. Such a policy is called a monetary rule, and it would entail selecting some particular monetary aggregate (M1, M2, etc.) to increase at the same percent, year in and year out.

The New Classical Economics

Another body of economic thought, **new classical economics**, was developed in the 1970s and 1980s and initially seemed to support the monetarists. Robert Lucas of the University of Chicago won the Nobel prize in 1995 for his work on the subject.

The major proposition of the followers of this school is **rational expectations theory**. It maintains that fiscal and monetary policies to end recession or inflation will fail because people have learned what to expect from such policies in the past. For example, they have learned that

A **monetarist** believes the money supply is a primary factor explaining macroeconomic activity and that recession and inflation can be avoided with an increase in the money supply equal to the rate of increase in total output.

New classical economics is a school of thought centering on rational expectations theory, which discounts the government's ability to succeed in macroeconomic policy due to people making adjustments in their behavior following such policy.

Rational expectations theory is the belief that any macroeconomic policy will be offset by actions of the private sector due to anticipated problems following those policies.

expansionary policy often leads to inflation and, consequently, higher inter- est rates. Thus, if Congress cuts taxes or the Fed expands the money sup- ply, lenders demand higher interest rates to compensate for the expected inflation. These higher rates then prevent any increase in spending the authorities had in mind.

New classical economists also believe that the Fed cannot control *real* interest rates. They maintain that these rates depend on technological con- siderations (such as banking technology) and practical considerations (such as present vs. future consumption). They believe the only interest rates the Fed can control are *market* interest rates. Further, as it is real interest rates that primarily determine economic behavior, they believe the Fed has little effect on economic behavior. Again, this viewpoint coincides with that of the monetarists.

Some say the new classical economists have displaced the mone- tarists. Others say monetarism is on the decline because it was never capa- ble of accomplishing what it was expected to do. Critics of monetarism say it is impossible to control the money supply well enough for a monetary rule to work. Still others, who still believe in monetarism, say the Fed never gave it a chance to work.

No wonder critics say that if all economists were laid end to end, they would never reach a conclusion. This is hardly true, but perhaps their dis- agreements prove that, contrary to what the dismal Thomas Carlyle said, economics is *not* a dismal science, after all. A bit confusing maybe, but not dismal.

SUMMARY

Classical Theory was the first body of macroeconomic theory. It was based upon Say's Law, which held that people would always be able to produce and sell as much as they wanted. Thus, there would be no unemployment, at least in the long run. Because recessions and inflations would be automatically cured by flexible prices, wages, and interest rates, there was no need for government to solve these macroeconomic problems.

Keynesian Theory is based upon the role played by total spending. Keynes believed that total spending would not be large enough to provide full employment all the time. Therefore, he proposed that the government make up for this lack of spending with increases in government spending and/or cuts in taxes. Thus, deficit spending was to be used to end recession.

The executive branch of the federal government, Congress, and the Federal Reserve System all attempt to manipulate the economy to promote full employment and stable prices. The president and Congress do this mainly by controlling total spending through tax and budget changes. The Fed controls total spending by influencing the cost and the availability of credit.

Expansionary policy to end recession is carried out by the fiscal policy actions of tax cuts and increases in government spending. It also includes the Fed's monetary policy actions of reducing the discount rate, reducing the reserve requirement, and buying securities. Each of these actions by the Fed increases excess reserves, increases the availability of credit, and reduces interest rates.

Contractionary policy to end inflation uses the fiscal policy actions of raising personal taxes and cutting government spending. Also, the Fed raises the discount rate, raises the reserve requirement, and sells securities. These actions by the Fed decrease excess reserves and the availability of credit, leading to higher interest rates. Inflation can also be reduced through supply-side economics programs that increase the output of goods and services.

In recent years, fiscal policy has fallen in popularity, partly because of the growing deficits and the crowding out of private spending by government spending. The role of monetary policy has grown, and more people are paying attention to the role of money in the macroeconomy. The new classical economists point out that people learn from past experiences with government policies and take actions to offset these policies.

QUESTIONS FOR DISCUSSION AND THOUGHT

1. Look up the Democratic and Republican party platforms of 1936 and 1940. What is the evidence of a belief or a disbelief in Keynesian Theory?
2. Would there be any change in the excess reserves of the entire banking system if you found a lot of gold and sold it to a gold merchant? Why or why not?
3. Check discount rates since 1990. What explains any changes in the rates?
4. What would you propose for today's fiscal policy? Why?
5. If a recession was just about to occur, would it be a good policy for the Fed to cut the discount rate and sell bonds? Why or why not?
6. If the budget deficit had been rising for several years and the inflation rate was rising as well, what connection, if any, could you make between the two events?
7. If the inflation rate was very high and the nation was entering a war, what would be the rationale for raising taxes?
8. What connection might be made between the rate of increase in the money supply and the size of the budget deficit?
9. If you are secure in your job, what effect could Fed policy have on you?

PROBLEMS   See page 491 for the answers.

1. Suppose that 30-year U.S. Government bonds, paying $600 interest per year, had been selling for $9,700 for some time. The Fed then acts to change total spending or aggregate demand. This results in a bond price of $9,500. Calculate the bond yield (to the nearest tenth of a percent) for both periods. What was the Fed trying to do and why?
2. The yield on $10,000 Treasury bills paying $800 interest per year drops from 8.6 percent to 8.2 percent following a Fed action. What were T-bill prices before and after the Fed's action?
3. Potential GDP is $7,000, but actual GDP is only $6,500. So government spending is increased by $100 billion to get the economy to full employment. Calculate the multiplier and the MPC.
4. Before a tax cut, the government collected $2,000 billion in taxes, where the average tax rate was 20 percent. After the cut to 18 percent, it collected $2,700 billion. Calculate the level of national income before and after the tax cut. (Tax Collections = Tax Rate x National Income)

14 CONSUMER ECONOMICS

CHAPTER PREVIEW

Consumers deal with their own economic problem by using cost-benefit analysis and marginal analysis. This chapter explains how consumers make decisions in the marketplace.

The chapter also covers the concepts of advertising, insurance, and credit, all vital to consumer behavior and welfare. Finally, it ends with an analysis of the various forms of savings and investments open to individuals.

CHAPTER OBJECTIVES

After completing this chapter, you should be able to:

◆ *Explain how consumers use marginal analysis in deciding how much to buy of an item.*

◆ *Describe the various financial records and instruments used by consumers.*

◆ *List the purposes and possible consequences of advertising.*

◆ *Explain the purpose and concept of insurance.*

◆ *Outline the pros and cons of consumer credit.*

◆ *Compare and contrast the various types of credit available to consumers.*

◆ *Outline the various laws and other government efforts to aid the consumer.*

◆ *Compare and contrast the various savings forms and investment instruments.*

One of the first things covered in this book is that the scarcity of resources forces us to choose which things will be made and which will not be made. It also must be decided how much of each good and service to make. The equilibrium quantity in the market in Chapter 2 answered the "how much?" question for steak. Every good or service has a similar equilibrium quantity.

This chapter explains the source of product demands—that is, the reasons why people buy what they do and in what amounts. In short, this is a closer look at consumer decision making, first explained in Chapter 1. Additionally, this chapter covers the many aids available to consumers, the role of advertising and insurance, the role of consumer credit, and the various forms of personal investing and saving.

DECISION MAKING BY CONSUMERS

Society has scarce resources (labor, capital, entrepreneurship, and natural resources) from which it strives to get as much benefit as possible. Your personal counterparts of these resources are your time and money, since you don't have enough of either to buy and do all you want.

Rational people use scarce time and money so their welfare is maximized. This occurs when the benefit of using any time or money exceeds the opportunity cost. Decision making requires careful thought about the use of your time and money because time and money are not like air—which is *not* scarce. (However, *clean* air may indeed be scarce.) Because you can always find all the air you need, you never have to think about your next breath. However, should you climb a high mountain, careful use of the available air (forced, deep breaths, perhaps) will increase your welfare.

Economic welfare from scarce dollars is maximized when the benefits received from the last dollar spent on each good and service are equal. This situation is called **consumer equilibrium**. It is a condition when no changes in purchases can increase economic welfare.

For example, say you buy $10 worth of soda in a month and that you spend $9 by the 26th. On the 30th, you spend your 10th and "last dollar," and the benefits you get are the "benefits received from the last dollar spent on soda." Also, say you buy $12 worth of gasoline at $1 per gallon. The last gallon you put in the tank, the 12th one, takes your "last dollar" spent on gasoline. You maximize economic welfare when the "last dollar" spent on soda provides benefit equal to that of the "last dollar" spent on gasoline, as well as on records, steak, shirts, and so on.

Consumer equilibrium is a condition where a consumer receives the same amount of satisfaction from the last dollar spent on each item and where it is impossible to improve economic welfare by changing buying patterns.

Marginal utility is the additional satisfaction received from consuming one more unit of a good or service.

Marginal utility is the amount of satisfaction or benefits received from the last unit of some good or service consumed. In the gasoline example, this "last unit" is the 12th gallon. The marginal utility is the enjoyment (benefit) you receive from going wherever that 12th gallon takes you. Or consider the soda example, where you spend $30 on, let's say, 60 sodas at 50 cents each. The enjoyment from drinking the last soda—the 60th one—is your marginal utility from soda.

The **law of diminishing marginal utility** states that each additional unit of a good or service consumed by an individual provides less satisfaction than the previous unit.

The **law of diminishing marginal utility** states that the marginal utility falls as you consume additional units of any good or service. For example, although you might drink several sodas in succession on a hot day, none satisfies you more than the first. For another, a fourth bedroom is less useful than the third, the third less than the second, and so on.

Suppose you want to buy both soda *and* gasoline. How much of each should you buy? You should buy that quantity for which the "last dollar" spent on each gives equal satisfaction. Because gas is $1 per gallon and a soda is 50 cents a can, the gas from your "last dollar" (the 12th gallon) should give satisfaction equal to the "last dollar" spent on soda (the 59th and 60th sodas combined).

Figure 14-1 helps you determine how much soda and gas to buy. The marginal utility, represented by different sized boxes, falls for both soda and gas as you consume more. If you buy only 12 gallons of gas, you get a lot of satisfaction from your 12th and "last dollar." Also, if you buy 60 sodas at 50 cents each, the satisfaction from your 30th and "last dollar" is the combination of the utility from the 59th and 60th cans of soda. Because these two small boxes combined are far smaller than the box for the 12th gallon of gas, it means you get "more bang for the buck" from the last dollar spent on gas than the last dollar spent on soda. This means you incorrectly answered your personal What-to-Produce (or Buy)? question. You either bought too much soda, too little gas, or both. The diagrams show that: 1) if you increase gas purchases to, say, 14 gallons, the marginal utility of gas falls; 2) if you decrease soda purchases to, say, 56 cans, the marginal utility of soda rises. Finally, note that the marginal utility of the 14th gallon of gas is exactly double that of the 60th soda. Because the price of gas is double that of soda, you arrived at the point where the "last dollar" (or *half*-dollar in this case) spent on both items gives the same marginal utility.

This analysis can help you in two ways. The first involves what economists call peak demand. Many things come in different sizes or capacities, and you need to decide which size or capacity best suits you. Examples include cars (seating and engine size), houses, VCRs (taping and programming capacity), and luggage. Larger sizes are usually more beneficial

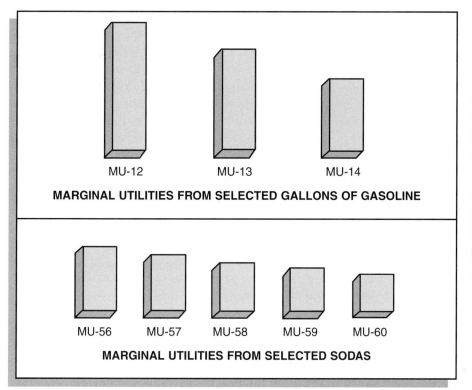

MARGINAL UTILITIES FROM SELECTED GALLONS OF GASOLINE

MU-12   MU-13   MU-14

MU-56   MU-57   MU-58   MU-59   MU-60

MARGINAL UTILITIES FROM SELECTED SODAS

Figure 14-1

Marginal Utilities of Gasoline and Soda

The marginal utilities fall for both gasoline and soda. The marginal utility of the 14th gallon of gasoline is twice that of the 56th soda. Prices are $1 per gallon for gasoline and 50¢ for soda.

Consequently, the utility received per dollar is equal when the consumer buys 14 gallons of gasoline and 56 sodas, the point of consumer equilibrium.

because they can accommodate you at your time of greatest need—the point of peak demand. However, larger sizes cost more, so you should buy for your peak demand only if the *extra* benefits you receive from the larger size exceed the *extra* cost. For example, an optional eight-cylinder engine provides more power (and benefit) than a six-cylinder engine. However, the larger engine costs more to buy and operate. If you could use the extra money to buy something else that would provide more satisfaction than the extra power, then you should get the six-cylinder engine.

The second way this analysis can help you involves your job. A prospective employer might ask, "Which is more important to you, the salary or the satisfaction from getting a job done?" One response might be, "It depends upon *which* dollar of my salary you mean. The *first* few thousand dollars in salary, which I will use to keep me alive, will be far more important than any enjoyment I will get from work itself. However, after you pay me $20,000, I will use an *extra* $1,000 to buy luxuries, which will provide less satisfaction than $1,000 worth of necessities. So perhaps a raise of $1,000 to $21,000 will not mean as much as the job itself."

Often people buy things partly to impress others. Examples include: buying a Rolex watch, a BMW, or a two-carat diamond; eating caviar; and vacationing at Club Med. Thorstein Veblen, a plain farm boy who became a famous and controversial economist in the late 1800s, called such purchases conspicuous consumption—that is, buying things that make you stand out. Many people say such purchases are irrational and a waste of money. Yet, if someone craves prestige and truly gets happiness from the attention that conspicuous spending attracts, who are we to presume that we know a better way to spend that person's income?

Societies can use different economic systems to answer What to Produce? One purpose of using a market system is to ensure **consumer sovereignty**. This means the consumer is sovereign (has supreme power) in the marketplace and should dictate what products are made, as well as their style and quality. Many people say the reverse is true, that firms control our material lives through their vast economic power. They believe consumers are powerless when confronting business practices that result in less than maximum economic welfare.

Consumer sovereignty refers to a condition in which the consumer ultimately directs which goods and services get produced.

THINKING CRITICALLY ABOUT ECONOMIC QUESTIONS IN OUR LIVES

What if the Marginal Utility of Everything Were Zero for Everyone?

Things to Consider

1. Suppose that the law of diminishing marginal utility were so "strong" that, if you consumed the second unit of any good or service, the marginal utility would drop to zero. Only the first unit of anything would provide you utility or benefit. Also, suppose that everyone else in society experiences the same situation. Thus, additional *quantities* of goods and services would yield no extra benefits.

2. Further, suppose that better *qualities* of goods and services would also yield no one any extra satisfaction or benefit.

3. Compared with reality, what would be the effect on society's economic welfare? On the living standard? On the economic problem?

   See page 476 for the answer.

AIDS IN MANAGING YOUR MONEY

Whether your income is $5,000 or $500,000 a year, you can make thousands of *un*wise decisions about how to spend your money. This section provides a general framework on money management and suggests specific aids to help you manage your finances more wisely.

Ways to Use Income

The previous section proposed a framework for the wise spending of money on goods and services. However, that section focused on money that is spent *in the present*. However, *all* income need not be spent today. Some can be saved to spend in the future. To find the proper share of income to save, you must follow the same marginal analysis used earlier. Simply put, you should spend a given amount of dollars in the period when the benefits are the highest. Undoubtedly, some dollars of everyone's income will be spent in the present. However, after the basic necessities are bought, usually some of any remaining income is more beneficially spent in the future.

Another way to use income is to swap some of it for an assurance that you will always have a certain amount of income and/or wealth. This is what people do when they buy insurance.

A final way to dispose of income is to give it away. Because money is scarce, giving it away might seem irrational. However, the act of giving money, goods, services, or time usually benefits the giver as well as the receiver. People simply feel good (get benefits) when they give to others. People give money to charity or provide estates when they receive more benefits from giving money than from buying goods and services themselves with the money. (Also, people often give money away, not to get any benefit, but to avoid guilt, shame, or embarassment when society expects everyone to contribute money for some "worthy" cause. In such cases, the "benefit" of giving is the avoidance of cost. Thus, the giving is still done to maximize one's welfare.)

General Financial Management

After good cost-benefit analysis, record keeping is the next step in converting your income into economic welfare. Specifically, it means: What did you do in the past, what is your present situation, and where do you *want* to be in the future? To help you in this matter, you need at least two financial instruments: 1) a cash flow statement; and 2) a net worth statement.

■ The cash flow statement first lists all sources of income and cash, including that from employment, investments, and businesses, as well as alimony, government assistance, tax refunds, insurance settlements, items you sold, gifts, and gambling winnings. Next, the total of all these cash sources is adjusted by savings (cash put into a form that you do not intend to spend on any good or service in the near future). Savings reduces your available cash figure. On the other hand, you might have some dissavings, the term used for assets such as savings accounts or a stock portfolio that are turned into cash and used for spending. This dissavings adds to your total cash flow. Next, subtract any money you gave up that did not directly provide you with goods and services in return. This includes taxes, gifts you gave, union dues, charity, and fines. The remainder is what you spent for goods and services.

If you're in financial difficulty, checking over these records can suggest where you might be able to cut spending, especially if you compare yourself to the national average. You might want to set up a budget, a type of cash flow statement for the *next year,* which will help you make ends meet.

■ The second useful financial instrument is the net worth statement. Unlike a cash flow statement, which shows what went on *during some period,* this shows your financial condition *at some point.* You first list all your assets—whatever is yours that you can measure in dollar terms. This includes savings and checking accounts, bonds, stocks, real estate holdings, insurance cash value, and auto value. Next, list your liabilities—whatever you owe. This includes charge accounts, loans, taxes to be paid, and unpaid bills. The difference between your assets and liabilities is called your net worth or equity. It shows what you could spend at that moment if you took everything you owned and paid off everything you owed. If, however, your liabilities exceed your assets, you have a negative net worth. A lender probably will not lend you anything, fearing that you will declare bankruptcy, a process through which you can be legally absolved of paying your debts.

Table 14-1 shows a hypothetical (but not necessarily typical) balance sheet or net worth statement for an individual. Because all the combined assets ($220,000) exceed the sum of the liabilities ($80,000), this person is "worth" $140,000.

A **financial plan** is a financial instrument designed to ensure that one's retirement goals will be met by considering the earnings, spending, and savings of the working years.

Many professionals can help you when you're in financial difficulty or simply want help. A relatively new financial specialist provides a **financial plan**, designed to ensure that your current and future income, spending, savings, and personal investment patterns will allow you to achieve some specified retirement goals. Professionals who offer such help are called financial planners.

Assets		Liabilities	
Checking Account	$300	House Mortgage	$64,000
Savings Account	$14,000	Unpaid Bills	$200
Bonds	$2,600	Taxes Due	$1,600
Life Insurance Cash Value	$1,100	Auto Loans	$6,800
Autos	$13,600	Installment Loans	$7,400
House Value	$113,000	**Total Liabilities**	**$80,000**
Stocks	$16,400		
Pension Value	$59,000		
Total Assets	**$220,000**	**Net Worth**	**$140,000**

Table 14-1

A Net Worth Statement

Assets are items that are owned. Liabilities are items that are owed.

Net worth is the difference between assets and liabilities.

Consumer Publications and Aids

Hundreds of aids are available for consumers. Probably the best known is *Consumer Reports,* a magazine of Consumer's Union, a nonprofit organization that compares various brands of products. *Changing Times* is a magazine that covers a wide range of topics, from product evaluation to home ownership to retirement planning. *Consumer Information,* a U.S. Government listing of more than 500 publications for the consumer, is available from congressional representatives. *Consumer News* is a bimonthly publication of the U.S. Office of Consumer Affairs. The Better Business Bureau publishes a series of booklets to help consumers, and its local offices monitor business practices of local firms. Local and national media provide information to help consumers make better purchases and investment decisions.

Various grades and standards establish a measure of a product's benefits. Private firms or organizations provide some of them. Some examples are: Underwriters Laboratories (UL); Good Housekeeping (Seal of Approval); and the Society of Auto Engineers (SAE), which sets standards for oil and other lubricants.

Several federal agencies establish grades and regulate product standards. Some examples are: the FDA (Food and Drug Administration), which regulates food and drug safety; the USDA (U.S. Department of Agriculture), which sets grades for meat, milk, and other foods; and the Consumer Product Safety Commission, which tries to reduce product danger (for example, it forced lawn mower manufacturers to add devices that automatically turn off the engine when you leave the mower).

In 1962, President Kennedy declared that consumers should have four "freedoms": 1) to be informed about products; 2) to have safe products; 3) to have product choices; and 4) to have a voice in consumer issues. Consequently, if there was ever a "Decade of the Consumer," it was from the mid-1960s to the mid-1970s. It might be said that the decade began with Ralph Nader and his book, *Unsafe at Any Speed,* in which he attacked the Corvair automobile as extremely dangerous. Many other groups arose to represent consumers, and laws were passed to establish consumer rights. It was the beginning of the end of the philosophy of *caveat emptor,* or "Let the buyer beware," which means that it is the consumer's responsibility to guard against faulty or unsafe products. By the 1970s, this responsibility was shifting to the government. The government's role changed, not so much because legislators mistrusted business owners, but because they believed that consumer decisions are so difficult in our complex world that consumers need help.

However, not everyone is happy with this new role of government as well as the anti-business attitude that often accompanied the consumer movement. Regulations and product redesign always add new costs, and these must be passed on to consumers if the firms are to remain profitable. However, some firms, especially those that are weaker or are in highly competitive situations, often find it difficult to absorb these costs and/or to raise their prices. Some, therefore, are forced out of business.

ADVERTISING

Advertising has always been a controversial aspect of capitalism. Its primary purpose is to influence the demand for a good or service. A firm uses advertising to: 1) increase demand; and 2) make it more inelastic (or less elastic). When the demand for something increases, more will be purchased at whatever price is charged. That ensures higher sales and, most likely, higher profits. The second goal of advertisers, to increase inelasticity, ensures that if one firm that makes a product raises its price, few buyers will flee to the competition. Thus, advertising tries to establish brand loyalty.

Advertising is not productive in the normal sense (that is, it doesn't produce an enjoyable or useful item for people so society *as a whole* is better off). Although it *is* useful for the advertiser (for increasing sales receipts), collectively, people are no better off because of advertising. Its primary effect is to shift the way people spend their money. While one firm is better off, its competitors are equally worse off. It appears to be a zero-sum game, where the winnings equal the losses and, collectively, society as a whole is no better off because of advertising. Thus, when viewed from society's perspective, all the labor and other resources used by advertisers are wasted.

Yet, perhaps society as a whole *does* benefit from advertising. After all, it could help consumers make better decisions by providing information about a product, including technical data and a general description of the advertised item. Therefore, the resources used in advertising *are* productive. Moreover, advertising helps firms achieve economies of scale (when they sell more), so resource efficiency increases. Advertising can also increase competition between business firms, which helps keep prices down (although this is somewhat offset by the higher costs of the advertising itself).

However, advertising can have an *unfavorable* consequence if the consumer receives the *wrong* information. One might not receive as much satisfaction from smoking cigarettes, wearing designer jeans, or driving the flashiest car as advertisers promise. So ads may distort the consumer's cost-benefit analysis. This is one reason for the ban on liquor and cigarette advertising on television and radio (another reason is to minimize the external costs from those products).

Many people believe that a related unfavorable consequence of advertising is "excessive" materialism, which means society's values are "distorted." Rather than deriving their primary satisfaction from family, friends, nature, spiritual well-being, and the like, these critics say too many people seek "the almighty dollar" and what it can buy. This leads to sociological problems, including crime, class conflict, and drug abuse, all related to the stress of the "rat race." However, economists would argue that it is impossible to determine if materialism is excessive. Again, as when someone buys a showy item, only those who make such "materialistic" decisions know if they are correct.

A final unfavorable consequence of advertising is a preference for spending now rather than in the future. Bombarded with advertising, some people can't seem to stop spending until all their income is gone. If such spending is widespread, total savings in the nation will be too low to finance heavy spending on capital goods and on the research and development needed for innovation. In turn, efficiency of resource use will grow more slowly, as will living standards. People in the United States, on average, save relatively small shares of their income when compared with other industrialized nations.

INSURANCE

In an economy that is largely capitalistic, people have little protection against property losses caused by accidents, thefts, fires, and storms, or against loss of income when they can no longer work. Such losses are financially painful or even catastrophic. Fortunately, they are infrequent. People who consider such potential losses unacceptable join together in a "pool" and agree to share the losses of all those in the pool. The premium is the amount each pool member puts into the "kitty," used to compensate loss-sufferers. Thus, the purpose of insurance is to protect against *unacceptably large* financial losses.

Many years ago, individuals organized and operated the first pools by themselves. Fraternal organizations such as the Elks, the Eagles, and the Moose are remnants of such times. Today, private enterprises create pools that people join when they buy insurance. However, many such enterprises are mutual companies, which technically are owned by the policyholders, so in a way they are similar to the earlier fraternal organizations.

Recent years have brought a rash of extremely large insurance awards, which insurance firms blame for rapidly rising insurance premiums. Higher insurance costs have led to the growth of self-insurance. A self-insured firm or government unit (such as a city park and recreation department) sets money aside in a budget each year to cover expected *average* losses over several years. If the expectations of losses prove correct, there will be enough money set aside to cover the losses. The "insured" will find this beneficial whenever premiums of a private insurer exceed the self-insured "premiums" or budget set-aside.

Virtually all losses that people insure against fall into four categories: 1) property losses; 2) loss of income; 3) liability losses; and 4) medical expenses.

■ Most people own property that would be very expensive to replace, such as autos, homes, and jewelry. Comprehensive and collision auto insurance and homeowner's insurance guard against losses of property.

■ People lose the opportunity to earn income in three main ways. The first is illness and/or injury. "Sick pay" prevents income loss during short-term illness. Of course, firms can pay people for producing things only when they are well. Thus, "sick pay" is a special type of "insurance settlement" provided by the employer.

Disability insurance gives protection against income loss due to long-term injury or illness. Although it replaces only part of the disabled person's income, no income tax is paid on it. Some employers provide such insurance, and individuals can purchase it for themselves. The Social Security Administration also provides payments to the disabled. Workers' compensation provides protection against income loss resulting from job-related injury or illness. State laws require employers to provide such insurance, which they purchase from private companies.

The second main way people lose the ability to earn income is by losing their jobs. State and federal laws require employers to pay a tax to finance a government-operated unemployment compensation program. If you lose your job through no fault of your own, you can collect a certain share of your working income, usually for up to 26 weeks, but occasionally up to 39 weeks or more.

Death is the last major cause of loss of income. Life insurance provides payment to someone surviving the deceased, called the **beneficiary**. Although people generally buy their own life insurance, many employers provide a modest amount as a fringe benefit. The Social Security Administration also provides a small death benefit.

A **beneficiary** is the person receiving the payment in the event of the death of someone having life insurance.

Life insurance comes in three major forms. The first is term insurance, which one buys to provide protection against income loss for a specified term. Whole life insurance, in addition to providing protection against income loss (for your beneficiary, actually) for the length of the policy, provides a method of saving. Part of the premium goes to an account that earns interest over the life of the policy. The amount in this account, called the cash value, is paid to a beneficiary upon death. However, if one does *not* die during the life of the policy, this cash value is received at the end of the policy. One also can borrow against this cash value. Finally, endowment insurance pays the policyholder a sum of money if the holder is alive after a certain period. The beneficiary receives a death benefit if death occurs before that point.

■ People also insure against the loss they would suffer if they caused someone else to lose something of value, such as property, health, or income. Such people are **liable** for these losses, which means that they must repay the person who suffered the loss. Liability insurance for autos or homes provides protection against such losses. Doctors, lawyers, and other professionals buy liability insurance to insure against malpractice suits.

Liable refers to being responsible for a loss suffered by another person.

■ Medical expense is the last major loss that people cover with insurance. Everyone knows how expensive modern health care can be. Such costs are high partly because widespread economies of scale are not as feasible in producing medical services as in, say, making pencils and shoes. It is simply impossible to mass produce most medical services, largely because the services provided are unique for each patient. Medical services now comprise 14 percent of GDP, and that percentage is steadily climbing.

To prevent large personal losses from medical bills, people buy accident and medical insurance. However, one person in seven has no such protection. Most people get protection from their employer as a fringe benefit and pay little directly. Medicare, which is part of the Social Security system, is a federal program of medical insurance for the elderly. While many medical insurance policies have limits on payments, the sharp increase in extremely expensive services has led to the popularity of catastrophic insurance, which pays up to several million dollars in bills. In the past few decades, escalating medical costs have spurred a movement supporting federally mandated insurance for everyone. Called national health insurance (or "socialized medicine"), such coverage is common in most other industrialized countries and universal in socialist nations. Because the government is already involved in the payment of medical bills, the United States is more than halfway to such a system.

CREDIT

One way to deal with a financial problem is to use credit. It increases the power to purchase goods and services beyond the limits set by one's income. When one uses credit, part of other people's incomes (their savings) is used.

The Benefits of Credit

Credit provides several benefits. First, it allows consumers to buy items when prices are abnormally low, so the price savings exceed the interest charges. Second, when in the form of chargecard credit, it provides convenience. You don't have to carry much cash when traveling to places where no one accepts your checks. Last, credit lets you enjoy the things purchased with credit earlier in life than your scarce income allows.   Such things can be enjoyed for a longer period, so you get more satisfaction from them. A home is the best example. Most people would have to save money until they were at least 40 before they could buy a home with cash. People buy homes with credit when they receive loans in exchange for mortgages. A **mortgage**, a borrower's promise to repay a loan, gives the lender the right to foreclose on the property (take it back) if the borrower doesn't repay the loan. (Incidentally, people often mistakenly equate their loan to their mortgage when they say they are "paying off their mortgage.")

A **mortgage** is a document given to a lender by a borrower, stating that the lender can take possession of the property in the event of default.

Since lenders charge interest for the use of money, is it wise (rational) to buy with credit? If the satisfaction from the extra time you enjoy an item exceeds the satisfaction you would get from the other goods and services you could have bought with the interest money, then it is. Because you have to pay interest when you buy with credit, you can buy *fewer* goods and services *in total* over your lifetime. However, most people accept this in order to have some things for a longer time.

The Costs of Credit

Credit has a downside as well. For individuals, the major problem is difficulty in repaying the credit, often because of an unexpected decrease in income or an excess use of credit. Many people blame the latter on the ease of obtaining credit cards from firms that are eager to extend credit, regardless of cardholders' ability to repay such loans.

For society as a whole, excess use of credit causes slower economic growth. As with advertising, easy credit might distort the proper balance of spending and saving. A decline in total savings in the nation could lead to less spending on capital goods and research and development, thereby reducing economic growth.

Types of Consumer Credit

Consumer credit usually falls into three categories: 1) open account credit; 2) automatic overdraft service; and 3) loans.

■ The first is revolving or **open account credit**. A credit card account is the best example. The lender extends a prearranged amount of credit. As the loan is paid back, the credit again becomes available—it "revolves." Although interest rates are quite high (occasionally more than 20 percent), many people pay off their bills before the next month's statements, avoiding any finance charges. Firms where you use your credit card pay the credit firms a fee in order to be associated with the credit system. In order to reduce such fees, some firms (especially gasoline stations) give discounts for paying in cash.

Open account credit, or revolving credit, refers to where one receives a certain amount of credit to be used, a kind which can be used again after the loan is repaid.

■ The second form of credit is **automatic overdraft service**, which allows you to write "bad" checks without having to pay for returned ("bounced") checks. Whenever you overdraw your checking account, your bank covers the amount you overdrew with a loan. Although you must pay interest on this credit, it is less than the fee for a bounced check.

Automatic overdraft service is a form of credit received when a financial institution covers an overdrawn demand deposit account with a loan.

■ A loan is the third form of credit. Actually, all credit amounts to a loan, but here a loan means that the borrower asks to borrow a specified amount of money for a specified period. Such loans fall into two broad categories. The first is a secured loan. With such a loan, the lender receives security against financial loss if the borrower defaults (fails to repay the loan). The lender does this by requiring the borrower to provide **collateral**, which is an asset the lender will acquire upon default. In the cases of houses, cars, and large appliances, the item bought with credit is itself the

Collateral is some asset a borrower agrees to give to a lender if a loan is not repaid.

collateral. Usually the lender can't sell such assets at the full purchase price, and there are administrative costs in default that lenders must cover. Consequently, lenders require a down payment, which means that they lend only part of the amount needed for the purchase.

If the lender knows the borrower is an extremely good credit risk, the borrower might be granted an unsecured loan, also called a signature loan. Here the lender requires no collateral, only a signature.

Laws Regarding Consumer Credit

Complaints of excessive finance charges, discrimination in obtaining credit, harassment of borrowers who fell behind in payments, and other problems led to several credit laws: 1) the Consumer Credit Protection Act; 2) the Fair Credit Billing Act; 3) the Equal Credit Opportunity Act; and 4) the Fair Debt Collection Practices Act.

■ The first was the Consumer Credit Protection Act of 1969. More commonly known as the Truth in Lending Act, it requires lenders to clearly state all finance charges as simply as possible. It also limits the losses a credit card holder can suffer when some unauthorized person uses the card.

■ The second credit law, the Fair Credit Billing Act of 1969, focuses on applications for credit cards and billing. Related to it is the Fair Credit Billing Act of 1971, which regulates the use of information by credit bureaus. It gives people legal access to their credit files and the right to prohibit specific people from access to their files. It also requires that credit files be monitored for accuracy.

■ The Equal Credit Opportunity Act of 1974 prohibits discrimination in credit application on the basis of color, religion, national origin, race, sex, age, marital status, and whether the applicant receives welfare.

■ The Fair Debt Collection Practices Act of 1979 prohibits lenders from using certain practices to collect from borrowers who are behind on their payments. Such practices include threats of violence, contact at odd hours, and complaints to a borrower's employer.

SAVINGS AND PERSONAL INVESTING

Although people consume (spend) much of their income soon after they earn it, most people save some money, primarily for a "rainy day" or retirement. Saving is after-tax income that is not spent. However, saving differs from **personal investment**, which is the use of savings plus additional borrowed funds for the purpose of earning additional income. (Take care not to equate this investment with the investment in macroeconomics.

Personal investment refers to the use of savings and/or borrowed funds for the purpose of earning more money.

That refers to spending on privately owned capital, private construction, and inventory buildup.) Following is a brief introduction to the most common ways of saving and investing.

Ordinary Savings Plans

The passbook account is the most common way to save. Known simply as a savings account, it pays relatively low interest, but it is perfectly safe. If an insured bank fails (goes broke), the Federal Deposit Insurance Corporation (FDIC), a federal agency, will cover up to $100,000 of each depositor's savings. Similar insured accounts are available at savings and loans and credit unions.

Another common savings form is a certificate of deposit (CD), usually set up for a larger amount for a specified period (six months, two years, and so on). Interest rates are higher than on passbook accounts and increase both with the amount deposited and the period length. CDs also have government protection.

A trust is a savings account at a trust company (often affiliated with a bank) for a minor or one who is not capable of handling funds. Such accounts often are provided by parents or insurance benefits. The trust company invests these funds and dispenses them to the individual according to the wishes of the one who set up the trust.

As noted earlier in this chapter, some people also save when they buy life insurance policies (other than term insurance).

Money market funds, which gained popularity in the 1970s, are set up by (nonbank) firms that collect savings from many people and invest the money in various places (often in large CDs). Although savers have no protection (insurance) for their money because the firms are not banks, the funds often earn higher interest rates. Most banks now have "money market accounts," but they are not true money market plans because they have less risk and are insured.

Retirement Savings Plans

Although they started in the 1960s, Keogh accounts and individual retirement accounts (IRAs) came into their own in the late 1970s. They are strictly for retirement purposes. Keoghs are for self-employed (nonincorporated) people and IRAs for employees. Their great advantage is that the interest earned is not taxable until the money is drawn out after age 59½. Such income is called tax-deferred income. Also, if an employee does not have a pension plan at work, or if the employee has a pension plan but is at a lower-income level ($25,000 for individuals and $40,000 for couples), the

IRA contribution reduces taxable income by the same amount. The contribution is entered on IRS Form 1040 as an "adjustment to income." This means the person defers paying income taxes on that amount until after retirement. There are two major advantages to this. First, interest income is earned on the deferred taxes until the money is drawn out. Second, people are often in a lower tax bracket when they retire, so they end up paying less taxes on the amount of income they contributed than if they had paid taxes in the year they earned the money. However, IRA deposits are limited to $2,000 per year for a single person, $2,500 for a married couple when only one person works, and $4,000 if both spouses work.

Another relatively new savings instrument for retirement that allows contributions and interest earned to be tax-deferred is a 401(k) plan, available only through some private enterprise employers. In 1996, up to $6,000 could be contributed in a 401(k) plan (or up to 20 percent of one's income up to $30,000). That figure increases each year, and in 1998, 25 percent can be contributed. A similar plan, a 403(b) account, often is available for government employees.

THINKING CRITICALLY ABOUT ECONOMIC QUESTIONS IN OUR LIVES

When Should You Start an IRA or 401(k)?

Things to Consider

1. Suppose you plan to save some money for retirement in a tax-deferred account.

2. If you earned six percent interest per year, what difference will it make if you save a particular dollar at age 29, 41, or 53? Specifically, how much more will you have by age 65 of you saved at 29 or 41 or age 53? (Hint: Notice that the ages are 12 years apart. You can use the "Rule of 72" to answer the question.)

3. In terms of money accumulated by age 65, clearly it's better to save a dollar as soon as possible. But what are some other factors you must consider when deciding when to save that dollar?

See page 477 for the answer.

Most larger employers offer their employees a pension, essentially income received after retirement. It shows up neither in gross pay nor take-home pay. Consequently, they pay taxes on the pension benefits only when they receive them after retiring. Most pension funds have two parts. One part is financed by the employer, the other by the employee (which should be considered savings rather than income). Sometimes the employer also pays the employee's part as a fringe benefit. To qualify, or be "vested" for a pension, a person generally must be an employee for five years. Usually the benefits become better the longer one works at one job, so frequent job-switching can prove costly when you retire. In 1974, The Pension Benefit Guarantee Corporation was established. It is a federal agency that insures the pensions of over 40 million workers in 85,000 private firms.

Stocks and Bonds

Ownership of a stock by a stockholder means ownership of a share of a corporation. People buy stocks to earn income in two ways: 1) from capital gains, which means they sell stock for more than they paid for it; and 2) from dividends, which is how corporations distribute profits. Stocks can be purchased in many firms, generally through a stockbroker. (See Appendix B for more on the stock market.)

A bond is a promissory note that the seller of the bond gives to the buyer. The bond seller promises to pay back the amount stated in the note when it matures (reaches the end of the loan period). Thus, a bond seller borrows money and a bond buyer lends it. The bond states the amount of interest to be paid, as well as the maturity date. There are three primary issuers (sellers) of bonds: 1) the federal government, which sells savings bonds, Treasury bills (T-bills), Treasury notes, and Treasury bonds; 2) state and local governments, which issue municipal bonds; and 3) corporations, which sell corporate bonds.

Other Methods of Saving and Investing

One of the most common forms of personal investing is in real estate, especially in homes. Paying off a home loan is actually a form of saving for retirement. Because homeowners have paid for their homes, they can enjoy them during retirement, while using their retirement income for something else. A home can be an investment if its value escalates faster than prices in general and if the owner sells it and spends those capital gains. Many people also buy income property, which is bought strictly to earn income, whether from the excess of rents over expenses or from capital gains. Such property includes apartments and other dwellings, commercial property (such as stores, factories, and offices), and undeveloped land.

Some people try to strike it rich by investing in commodities, which generally are raw (unprocessed) agricultural goods. Because commodities have wide price swings, caused by changes in weather and yields, people can make a lot of money (or *lose* a lot) in buying and selling them. Commodities are traded in the futures market, so called because a buyer agrees to pay a certain price at a specified future date for a given amount of the commodity. This agreement is called a futures contract. Such buyers, called speculators, bet that the actual market price on that future date will be higher than the price they agreed to pay. The difference in these prices is the speculators' profit (or loss) when they sell the contract to a user of that commodity.

Commodities traded include corn, oats, wheat, pork bellies (for bacon), flaxseed, hogs, cotton, sugar, coffee, cocoa, and orange juice. The primary locations of such trading are the Chicago Board of Trade and the Chicago Mercantile Exchange.

People save or invest in dozens of other ways. They trade in foreign exchange (foreign currency). They also buy gold, silver, platinum, and other precious metals, and they invest in stamps, art, and antiques. Of course, some of these savings methods are safer than others.

SUMMARY

The overall goal of consumers is to maximize satisfaction from their scarce money. This is accomplished when the last dollar a person spends on any good or service gives the same benefit as the last dollar spent on every other good and service. Under these conditions, the person has achieved consumer equilibrium. The benefit from additional units of any good or service consumed is always less than from earlier units. Besides having to decide what to buy, each person must also decide: 1) how much to spend in the present and how much in the future; and 2) how much money to give to others.

Cash flow statements, budgets, net worth statements, and financial plans are designed to ensure that people will maximize their economic welfare from their scarce wealth and income. Many publications are available to help consumers make better choices.

Although advertising is designed to aid the seller, it can serve the consumer by providing information for good decision making. However, advertising could also provide wrong information and might lead to a lower economic growth rate.

Insurance spreads financial risks among many people so that individuals are not financially ruined. People insure themselves against loss of property value, loss of income, loss if liable for another's loss, and loss from medical bills.

Credit allows people to buy more things in the present than they could with their own purchasing power. However, buying on credit means that a person can buy fewer things in total over a lifetime because of the interest paid. Credit usually takes three forms: open account credit, automatic overdraft service, and secured loans. In the last few decades, the federal government passed several laws to protect consumers in credit matters.

Besides saving money for the future, many people use their savings as well as borrowed money to earn more money in personal investments. These include stocks, bonds, real estate, commodities, and precious metals. Because these investments are somewhat risky, people should also have some assets in regular savings accounts, pensions, and special retirement plans.

QUESTIONS FOR DISCUSSION AND THOUGHT

1. Suppose you buy a pair of sunglasses for $20 and do not regret it. Also, suppose you do *not* experience diminishing marginal utility with sunglasses. How many pairs of sunglasses would you buy if: 1) your net income is $10,000 per year? 2) your net income is $10 million per year? 3) you have an unlimited income?

2. Find five examples of people who, you suspect, bought things for the sake of conspicuous consumption. Ask them why they bought the items. Did they lie?

3. Ask five people who work full time if they have both auto and disability insurance. If they don't have both, ask them why. Do you think they are rational?

4. Under what conditions would it make sense to borrow money at 20 percent interest in order to get into the stock market?

5. Keeping records of your spending takes time, which itself is a valuable resource. What good can possibly come out of it, especially if you take care that each of your purchases provides you with more benefits than any other way of spending your money?

6. On a per-pound basis, raw potatoes are much less expensive than frozen french fries or other processed potatoes. What sense does it make to buy anything other than raw potatoes?

7. When you see three cans of corn selling for a dollar in store, how many are you likely to buy? How did you arrive at your decision?

8. Americans, on average, save between three and six percent of their take-home pay. Koreans, on average, have much less than half the real incomes of Americans, but they save nearly 20 percent of their take-home pay. If anything, you would think the savings rates would be reversed, so how can you explain the great difference in savings rates? (Note: It has nothing to do with price levels or what things cost, as those differences are taken into consideration when real incomes are compared.)

PROBLEMS   See page 492 for the answers.

1. Becky likes hot dogs and pizza slices, eating several of each per month. The table shows her marginal utilities for each of six hot dogs and pizza slices for the next month. The price of hot dogs is $1 and the price of pizza slices is $2. If Becky is to achieve consumer equilibrium, how many hot dogs and how many pizza slices should she buy? You need to calculate the marginal utility she gets per dollar spent on each item. Which does she like more, hot dogs or pizza slices, and how can you tell? Which does she tire of more quickly, and how can you tell?

	Number Eaten					
	1	2	3	4	5	6
MU of Hot Dogs	120	100	90	70	40	20
MU of Pizza Slices	280	180	100	60	20	10
MU / dollar Spent on Hot Dogs	___	___	___	___	___	___
MU / dollar Spent on Pizza Slices	___	___	___	___	___	___

2. Calculate the net worth of the Sampson family if it has the following information: tax refund due–$200; bills to pay–$620; house value–$117,400; clecking-account balance–$400; auto value–$18,400; house mortgage–$80,300; savings bonds–$6,700; auto loans–$7,600; savings account–$20,500; stocks held–$8,200; pension value–$21,100.

APPENDIX A: CONSUMER EQUILIBRIUM

To maximize their economic welfare, consumers need to be aware of the satisfaction received from the last dollar spent on each specific item bought. That amount of satisfaction for a specific item is found by dividing the marginal utility by the price. A consumer is considered to be in equilibrium when this amount is identical for every item bought. Then there is no reason for the consumer to change spending patterns, for the maximum amount of economic welfare has been achieved. Such an equilibrium condition for a consumer who buys n number of items is shown by:

$$MU_1/P_1 = MU_2/P_2 = ... = MU_n/P_n$$

Thus, for any two goods X and Y, the following also holds:

$$MU_x/P_x = MU_y/P_y$$

This condition can be used to show why consumers follow the law of demand. If the price of X rises, then:

$$MU_x/P_x \text{ falls and, consequently, } MU_x/P_x < MU_y/P_y$$

The consumer now gets less satisfaction from the last dollar spent on X than from the last dollar spent on Y. Now the consumer's welfare is not maximized. One way to correct this is to reduce the quantity of X consumed, which raises MU_x (because of the law of diminishing marginal utility). In turn, this raises:

$$MU_x/P_x \text{ and the consumer buys less of X until } MU_x/P_x = MU_y/P_y$$

Therefore, the consumer again is at equilibrium—though facing a higher price at a lower consumption level. This is exactly what you expect when looking at a demand curve.

A second response to an increase in the price of X is an increase in the purchase of a substitute good. If Y is a substitute for X, then as more of Y is consumed, MU_y declines. In turn, there is a decrease in:

$$MU_y/P_y \text{ and the consumer buys more of Y until } MU_x/P_x = MU_y/P_y$$

Once again the consumer is at equilibrium, and this consumer response explains shifts in demand caused by price changes of substitutes.

APPENDIX B: THE STOCK MARKET

Personal investment in corporate stocks has always been a popular, though more risky, form of investment. Stocks are purchased for two primary reasons: 1) to earn dividends; and 2) to reap capital gains, obtained when the stock rises in value.

"The stock market" is actually divided into two sectors. In the first, known as the primary market, corporations issue new stock in order to raise funds for operations and expansion. If the corporation is offering stocks to the general public for the first time (that is, it is "going public"), this is called an initial public offering (IPO).

However, many people will buy stocks only if they can sell them any time they wish. They do so in the secondary market, which is what most people consider to be "the stock market." In this market, people buy and sell stocks through stockbrokers, who function as middlemen in connecting their clients with other people who want to buy or sell stocks. These are not newly issued stocks, but were initially bought by someone else from corporations in the primary market. Thus, the corporations do not get to use the money that new buyers use to buy the stocks.

The oldest and largest secondary market is the New York Stock Exchange (NYSE), commonly called the Big Board, located on Wall Street in New York City. Around 2,000 stocks of America's major corporations are traded there. Other secondary markets are the American Stock Exchange (AMEX), the Nasdaq Stock Market, 14 regional markets, and many foreign markets (such as the Japanese Nikkei and the London Exchange).

Most newspapers' financial sections publish the following information on individual stocks: 1) the highest price and the lowest price the stock traded at in the past 52 weeks; 2) the company name (followed by its symbol or abbreviation); 3) the dividend per share; 4) the percent yield, calculated by dividing the dividend per share by the current stock price; 5) the price-to-earnings (P/E) ratio, found by dividing the stock's price by the (per share) corporate earnings in the previous four quarters; 6) the trading volume for the day, reported in amounts of hundreds of shares; 7) the high and low prices the stock traded at on the previous day; 8) the closing price on the previous day; and 9) the net change in price, or the difference in the closing price for the day and the closing price for the previous day. (See the following sample stock listing from a newspaper.)

People interested in the stock market watch several indicators that measure the price movements of many stocks simultaneously. Dow Jones and Company publishes the best-known indicators, including the Dow Jones Industrial Average (DJIA), the most closely watched one.

52 Weeks High	Low	Stock	Div.	Yld %	P-E Ratio	Sales 100s	High	low	Close	Net Chg.
		– A–A–A –								
17¾	5¾	AAR	.44	2.6	25	50	17¼	16¾	16¾	- ¼
37¾	27½	ACF	1.40	4.1	15	205	34¾	34	34½	+ ½
20	12¼	AMF	.50	3.1	..	380	16⅜	16	16⅛	- ⅜
38¼	13¼	AMR Cp		..	..	2872	34¾	33⅜	33⅝	-1
24½	4	AMR wt		..	..	228	20½	19½	19½	-1⅛
18⅜	13¼	AMR	pf2.18	12.	..	25	18⅛	18	18	.....
39⅜	24⅞	AMR	pf2.13	6.2	..	54	35⅜	34½	34½	-1⅜
10⅝	2½	APL		..	..	58	10¼	10	10	- ⅛
55	26	ARA	2.05	4.1	14	326	49¾	49½	49¾	+ ¼
79⅞	29	ASA	3a	4.6	..	458	67¾	65⅝	65⅞	- ⅜
50	14½	AVX	.32	.8	63	5	39½	39¼	39¼	- ½
48¾	28½	AbtLab	1	2.1	18	1310	47¾	46¼	47¼	+ ¾
30⅛	25¾	AccoW n	.50	1.9	22	93	27⅜	26⅞	26⅞	- ⅜
27½	15⅝	AcmeC	.40	1.6	..	13	24⅝	24¼	24⅜	- ¼
14⅜	5¾	AcmeE	.32b	2.5	42	7	12⅞	12¾	12⅞	.....
19⅞	5½	AdmDg	.04	.2	15	17	17⅞	17⅝	17⅞	.....
17⅞	12½	AdaEx	1.73e	10.	..	35	17⅛	16⅞	17	....
15¼	6⅝	AdmMI	.24	1.6	14	51	15	14½	14¾	- ⅛
28	12⅝	Advest s	.16	.7	13	86	24½	24	24⅜	- ¼
66⅝	13	AMD s		..	63	1043	59¼	57	57¾	-1¼
44⅜	32⅞	AetnLf	2.64	6.9	7	1079	38⅝	38	38⅛	- ¾
65	52⅜	AetL	pf4.94e	8.4	..	7	58¾	58¾	58¾	+ ¾
40½	8¼	Ahmns	.60	1.8	..	1235	33	31⅞	33	+ ⅜
7	2⅜	Aileen		..	..	66	6	5¾	6	+ ¼
50⅞	23⅝	AirPrd	1	2.2	15	215	47¼	46⅛	46⅜	- ⅝
27¼	10	AirbFrt	.60	2.6	24	35	23¼	22⅞	23	+ ⅛
3⅜	2	AlMoa n		..	6	129	2⅞	2¾	2¾	.....
33½	24¾	AlaP	pfA3.92	13.	..	10	29¾	29⅜	29¾	+ ⅜
7⅝	5¾	AlaP	dpf.87	12.	..	26	7⅛	7	7⅛	- ⅛
74½	56	AlaP pf	9	13.	..	z650	69	68	68	-1
99	74	AlaP pf	11	11.	..	z70	98½	98½	98½	+1
81½	58	AlaP pf	9.44	13.	..	z350	71½	71	71	-1¾
70	51	AlaP pf	8.28	13.	..	z100	64½	64½	64½	+1¼
20¼	13	Alagsco	1.76	9.0	7	6	19¾	19⅝	19⅝	.....
18⅝	4⅞	AlskAir	.12	.7	14	452	18⅛	17½	17½	.....
39⅝	23¾	Albany	1.40	3.5	20	116	39⅝	39⅝	39⅝	.....
24⅛	10¾	Alberto	.54	3.2	14	6	16¾	16¾	16¾	- ¼
29	16	Albtsn s	.60	2.2	14	70	27⅞	26¾	26¾	-1⅛
35¼	17⅞	Alcan	.90	2.8	..	785	32½	31⅞	32	- ½
36⅛	18	AlcoStd	1.12	3.2	13	88	35⅜	34⅞	34⅞	- ⅜
27⅝	18⅝	AlexAlx	1	3.9	259	8278	26¾	24¼	25⅞	+1¾

52 Weeks High	Low	Stock	Div.	Yld %	P-E Ratio	Sales 100s	High	low	Close	Net Chg.
24⅝	19⅞	ACan	pf2.80	12.	..	1	23½	23½	23½	.....
19½	7½	ACntC n		..	29	82	u19⅞	19⅜	19⅞	+ ½
50¼	27	ACyan	1.75	3.7	19	876	47⅝	46½	47½	+ ⅝
32⅝	28½	ADT s	.92	3.2	13	73	29	28⅝	28⅞	+ ⅛
20	15⅞	AEIPw	2.26	12.	10	4154	18⅝	18¼	18½	+ ⅛
74⅜	26⅜	AExp s	1.92	2.9	14	3920	68	65⅞	66½	- ¾
49⅝	17⅝	AExp wi		..	..	78	46	44⅝	45	-1
24⅛	9⅜	AFamil	.60	2.8	13	55	21¼	21⅛	21¼	.....
24⅛	10½	AGnCp s	.80	3.5	9	188	23	22⅝	22⅞	- ⅛
58¾	49⅜	AGnl	pfA3.67e	6.8	..	103	53⅞	53⅝	53⅝	- ¼
67	50⅝	AGnl	pfB3.43e	5.5	..	26	63	62¾	62¾	+ ⅜
52¾	31	AGn	Ipf3.25	6.6	..	3	49½	49½	49½	.....
20⅞	15⅝	AGIBd	2.16	12.	..	56	18⅜	17⅞	18⅛	+ ⅜
35½	21¼	AGnCv	5.07e	16.	..	10	32⅛	31¼	31¼	- ½
23⅞	17¼	AHerit	.96	4.4	10	4	22⅛	22	22	- ¼
16⅛	8¾	AHoist		..	..	68	15¼	14½	14⅞	- ¼
52¼	35⅝	AHome	2.40	5.3	12	2592	45⅝	44⅞	45⅛	- ½
49	28	AHosp s	1	2.2	15	1277	45⅜	44⅞	45	.....
37¼	14½	AMI s	.48	1.5	17	618	33½	32⅝	32⅞	- ⅝
11¼	3	AmMot		..	..	1008	9⅜	9⅛	9¼	.....
40	25¼	ANatRs	3.16	8.6	6	143	38⅛	36¼	36¾	-1⅝
26⅜	3½	ASLFI s		..	..	387	20¼	19¼	20	- ¼
13¾	8⅜	AShip	.80	6.4	14	35	12½	12¼	12½	+ ¼
38⅛	17	AmStd	1.60	5.0	21	223	32⅛	31¾	31¾	- ⅜
24¼	11¼	ASteril	.40	2.0	13	309	19⅝	18⅞	19⅝	+ ¼
105½	42¾	AmStr	1.44	1.4	12	35	100¾	98⅝	99¾	- ⅞
35½	14¼	AmStr wi		..	..	1	34	34	34	-1
52⅝	39⅛	AStr pf	5.51	11.	..	3	50⅞	50⅞	50⅞	- ⅛
70¼	50	ATT	5.40a	8.6	8	7211	63⅛	62¾	62¾	- ¼
73¼	52½	ATT pf	4	6.1	..	71	66	65¾	65¾	- ⅛
38½	30¼	ATT pf	3.64	9.8	..	115	37¼	36¾	37	+ ¼
39¾	31⅝	ATT pf	3.74	9.8	..	627	38	37¾	38	+ ⅜
29¼	14	AWatr	1.40	5.2	6	45	27⅛	26⅞	27⅛	+ ¼
11¾	8⅝	AWat	pf1.25	11.	..	z50	11	11	11	+ ¼
26⅝	19⅞	AHotl n	.59e	2.5	..	204	23⅜	23	23¼	- ⅛
36¼	19⅜	Ameron	1.60	4.8	9	15	33¾	33¼	33½	- ½
65¼	21½	AmesD	.40	.6	20	152	62⅛	61½	61⅝	+ ¾
50	25⅛	Ametk	1.20	2.7	17	88	44¼	44	44¼	.....
24¾	12½	Ametk wi		..	..	5	22½	22½	22½	.....
30¼	17⅛	Amfac	1.44	5.5	14	115	27	26⅜	26⅜	- ⅜
26⅝	15¾	Amfes	n2.12t	11.	7	413	19½	18½	19⅛	- ½
106¼	45½	AMPIn	1.60	1.7	29	527	97¾	95⅞	96	-2¼

The DJIA, instituted in 1896, is an outgrowth of a method used by Charles Henry Dow in 1884 to reflect the level of all stock prices. Dow used the arithmetic average of 11 stocks as a representative of all stocks. Today the DJIA use the stocks of 30 corporations, each a major figure in its industry. Calculation of the DJIA no longer uses a simple average of these 30 representative stocks, as it did earlier. That is, it doesn't just add the prices of all 30 stocks and divide by 30 (the "divisor"). Partly due to stock splits over the years, the "divisor" was reduced from 30 to less than one today. A stock split means a corporation offers two or more new (and lower-priced) shares of stock for one share of original stock. This often occurs when a stock's price rises too high for it to be an attractive purchase. Thus, the DJIA average is much higher than the price of any particular stock. For example, if the "divisor" was 0.9 and the 30 stocks sold for an average of \$96, the DJIA would be 3200, or (\$96 x 30) ÷ 0.9.

The Securities and Exchange Commission (SEC) is a federal agency that regulates the stock market. One of its regulations prohibits "inside trading," where someone trades stocks because of information received from an "insider." If someone (such as an accountant or an attorney) has advance knowledge of mergers, stock splits, and so on, that knowledge cannot be passed on to stockbrokers or those wishing to purchase stocks.

Mutual Funds

In recent decades, a new way of investing in stocks led to many people getting into the stock market who otherwise would not have. They invest in mutual funds, composed of stocks of many corporations. When investors put money in these funds, they are said to have purchased shares in the mutual fund. The value (or price) of a share is essentially found by dividing the total value of all the stocks in the fund by the number of shares in the fund. The great advantage to investors (thus, their popularity) is that much time in selecting a wide range of stocks to put in their portfolios. It is wise to have many stocks to avoid having "all your eggs in one basket" in case one of the stocks falls sharply in price.

In effect, investors hire the managers of mutual funds to select stocks that achieve their goals. One goal might be stocks that are likely to rise in value very quickly. Another is to have stocks that pay high dividends. Finally, investors might want stocks that are the least likely to fall in value. No particular stock is likely to achieve all of these goals. Further, because there are thousands of stocks on the market, it would take enormous amounts of time to analyze them all so a portfolio can be built around a particular goal. Thus, the advantage of buying mutual funds. Each fund specializes in a particular strategy, such as aggressive growth, which includes stocks most likely to rise in value very rapidly. Other funds specialize in income stocks, which include stocks most likely to pay high, steady dividends.

Many daily newspapers have listings of all or some of the more than three thousand mutual funds. Like listings for individual stocks, these listings have information that investors "read" to see how each fund is performing. The *net asset value* (NAV) is the price at which the fund's shares are sold. The abbreviation (Chg) refers to the *change in net asset value* from the previous day's closing price. The *expense ratio* refers to the amount the fund charges for its operating expenses, expressed as a percentage of assets. The abbreviation (YTD % return) refers to the fund's *total returns for year to date*. It is equal to the percentage change in net asset value over the period, assuming all dividends (from the stocks) and other distributions were reinvested in the fund. The *three-year risk* indicates how well the fund is doing vs. three-month U.S. Treasury bills, relative to other funds in the same investment class. The *maximum load*, expressed as a percentage, is the amount that investors pay to invest in the fund. (Funds can have "front-end loads," where payment is made upon investing, or "back-end loads," where payments are deducted when the account is closed. "No-load funds" require no cash payments to be in the fund—only operating expenses.)

GLOSSARY

ability-to-pay principle   The taxing philosophy stating that the more a person is able to pay taxes, as evidenced by income or wealth, the more taxes that person should pay

absolute advantage   Occurs when a particular resource of a class of resources is the most efficient or productive at a task of all resources of that class

absolute price   The amount of money that is paid for one unit of an item

actual GDP   The value of final goods and services actually produced

allocative efficiency   Refers to the situation where firms produce the goods and services most preferred by consumers

arbitration   A process of settling differences between labor and management, where the terms of a third party must be accepted

authoritarian capitalism   An economic system where most resources are privately owned and where heavy use is made of the command economic system

authoritarian socialism   An economic system where most resources are publicly owned and where government authorities answer most economic questions

automatic overdraft service   A form of credit received when a financial institution covers an overdrawn demand deposit account with a loan

automatic stabilizers   Instruments that are used to carry out automatic fiscal policy, including transfer payments, farm subsidies, and the progressive income tax

average cost   The amount of expenses in producing one unit of a good or service, on average

average fixed cost   The amount of overhead or fixed expenses in producing one unit of a good or service, on average

average variable cost   The amount of operating or variable expenses in producing one unit of a good or service, on average

balanced budget   Occurs when total outlays of a government equal total receipts

balance sheet   A business statement showing the condition of a business at a point in time, listing the firm's assets and liabilities

barrier to entry   Anything which prevents a new firm from entering an industry, including patents, copyrights, licenses, permits, franchising requirements, and high capital costs

barter   A system of exchange or trade where some item is exchanged for some other item without the use of money

Basic Economic Questions   The sets of questions to be considered in allocating resources, including What to Produce? How to Produce? and For Whom to Produce?

Basic Economic Systems   The systems upon which the structure of all economies are based, including the traditional, the command, and the market systems

beneficiary   The person receiving the payment in the event of the death of someone having life insurance

benefit   Any satisfaction received from an economic activity

benefits-received principle   The taxing philosophy stating that if people receive more benefits from government services, they should pay more in taxes

budget deficit   Occurs when total outlays of a government exceed total receipts

budget surplus   Occurs when total receipts of a government exceed total outlays

bureaucratic control   A method of reducing imports by establishing government "red tape" that importers must deal with

business cycle   Changes in macroeconomic conditions, ranging from prosperity to recession and back to prosperity

capital   Any good used to produce another good or service

capital-intensive   A production process where the largest share of the costs involve capital resources

capitalism   An economic system whose main characteristics include individuals making decisions about their privately owned resources in a system of competitive, free markets

cartel   An organization of sellers that seek to control a market, which usually involves raising the price in that market above equilibrium, accompanied by a restriction in output to avoid an unsold surplus

central bank   A "bankers' bank," which provides financial services for banks and which controls the availability and the cost of credit

centrally directed   Refers to an economic system where economic decisions are largely made by government authorities

change in demand   A change in the amount buyers are willing to purchase at each price, even though there is no change in price

change in supply   A change in the amount sellers wish to sell at each price

Classical Theory   A body of economic thought developed in the late 1700s and 1800s, centering on the establishment of a free-market economy

closed shop   A workplace in which a person must be a member of a labor union before beginning to work

collateral   Some asset a borrower agrees to give to a lender if a loan is not repaid

collective bargaining   Refers to the actions of a group of laborers operating in unison to improve their wages, fringe benefits, and working conditions

command economic system   A Basic Economic System in which economic decisions are made by government authorities

commercial bank   A financial intermediary that provides checking accounts and makes commercial loans

communism   A form of authoritarian socialism popularized by Marx and Engels, where eventually the state would disappear, with all production carried out in the best interest of the community

comparative advantage   Occurs when a particular resource has the lowest opportunity cost in producing something of all resources of that type

competition   Refers to the struggles of market participants for the purpose of maximizing their economic welfare

constant returns to scale   Describes a production process in which an increase in inputs of x percent results in output increasing by x percent

consumer equilibrium   A condition where a consumer receives the same amount of satisfaction from the last dollar spent on each item and where it is impossible to improve economic welfare by changing buying patterns

consumer sovereignty   A condition in which the consumer ultimately directs which goods and services get produced

consumer spending   The part of total spending, also called consumption, that reflects the purchases of consumer goods and services

continuous production process   The breakdown of a product's manufacture into a series of steps, where specialized machines do a large share of the production, and where raw materials continually enter the production process and finished products continually exit the process

contractionary policy   Government policy designed to end inflation by reducing total spending or aggregate demand and, in turn, shortages

cooperative   A form of business where those who are served by the business are the owners and where control of the business is shared by all equally

corporation   A form of business owned by stockholders, each having limited liability, and where the business is considered to be a person in legal matters

cost-benefit analysis   A method of comparing costs and benefits to determine whether resources should be used in a certain way

cost-push inflation   An increase in prices caused by an increase in the cost of producing most goods and services

craft union   A labor union composed of workers working in the same craft or job description

credit union   A thrift institution associated with a place of employment or a union, operated as a cooperative

crowding out   Occurs when the increased deficit of an expansionary policy leads to higher interest rates and reduced consumer and investment spending

currency devaluation   A government-sponsored reduction in the amount of a nation's currency that will exchange for other nations' currencies

current GDP   The value of final goods and services when using the prices existing at the time of production

debit card   It is used to transfer money from one's checking account to someone else's account in an electronic funds transfer

decrease in demand   A decrease in the amount buyers are willing to purchase at each price

decrease in supply   A decrease in the amount sellers offer for sale at each price

decreasing returns to scale   Describes a production process in which an increase in inputs of x percent results in output increasing by less than x percent

deduction   An amount of income on which you do not have to pay federal income taxes, often tied to a specific reason

demand   The relationship between the various amounts that buyers are willing to purchase of some item and all possible prices of that item

demand-pull inflation   An increase in the price level caused by an increase in total spending that exceeds the increase in available goods and services

deposit multiplier   The number of times the money supply can expand if all excess reserves are lent

derived demand   The demand for a resource which stems from the demand for the good or service which that resource produces

discount rate   The rate of interest the Fed charges member banks that borrow reserves from it

disposable income   Equals personal income minus personal taxes

division of labor   Where each laborer carries out only one task in the production process of a single product

domestic content and mixing requirement   It requires that a minimum percentage of a product's parts be made in that country

double coincidence of wants   A condition of barter exchanges, where each trader has what the other trader wants and who wants what the other trader has

dumping   Selling a product abroad for less money than it sells for domestically

econometric model   A mathematical model of the macroeconomy used for forecasting

economic growth   An increase in the output of goods and services

economic growth rate   The percent increase in a year's time of the amount of goods and services produced in the economy

economic loss   The shortfall of a firm's total revenue compared with the sum of its explicit plus implicit costs

economic profit   The excess of a firm's total revenue over its explicit plus implicit costs

economic system   The institutions, concepts, and procedures a society uses to deal with the problem created by a scarcity of resources

economics   The study of how members of society choose to use scarce resources in order to maximize economic welfare

efficiency   Refers to the ratio of inputs to outputs, or how well resources are used, either in a specific production process or in an entire nation

elastic   Refers to a demand relationship where a given price change results in a proportionately greater change in purchases

elasticity of demand   Refers to the responsiveness of buyers to changes in price with respect to the amount purchased

electronic funds transfer   The transfer of funds into and out of a checking account electronically without using paper checks

employed   Someone who works at least one hour per week

entrepreneurship   Refers to the characteristics of an enterprising person, one who provides financial backing and management for a business and who often has an innovative idea

equation of exchange   It shows that the money supply (M), the velocity of money (V), the price level (P), and the level of output (Q) are related in the formula MV = PQ

equilibrium GDP   The level of GDP at which the economy remains when all factors that influence it are balanced

equilibrium price   The price where the amount buyers are willing to purchase equals the amount sellers offer for sale

equilibrium quantity   The amount of an item that is exchanged (sold or purchased) at the equilibrium price

equilibrium wage   The wage where the number of workers employers wish to hire equals the number of qualified people looking for work

equity   The difference between total assets and total liabilities, also known as net worth

excess reserves   The difference between what a bank is allowed to lend and how much it has lent out

exchange rate   The rate of exchange between the currencies of two nations, or the price of one currency in terms of another currency

exemption   An amount of income for each dependent on which federal income taxes are not paid

expansionary policy   Government policy designed to end or to prevent recession, which is carried out through an increase in total spending or aggregate demand

explicit cost   A business cost that involves payment of money to a seller of a resource

export subsidy   A payment by a government to an exporter to encourage exports by reducing the price of the item to be exported

external benefit   Any benefit received by someone other than the person who uses resources

external cost   A cost of resource use that is not paid by the person who uses the resources

externality   An activity that has an effect that some other party experiences when someone uses resources (or the goods and services produced with them)

factor market   A market in which a resource is traded or exchanged

federal funds rate   The rate of interest paid by a commercial bank for borrowing the excess reserves of another commercial bank

Federal Reserve System   The central bank of the United States, whose functions include regulating banks, providing financial services, and controlling the money supply

financial intermediary   Any institution that serves as a middleman between savers and borrowers when it accepts deposits and extends credit

financial plan   A financial instrument designed to ensure that one's retirement goals will be met by considering the earnings, spending, and savings of the working years

fiscal policy   Changes in taxes and/or government spending designed to influence the level of total spending or aggregate demand

fixed exchange rate system   Where exchange rates between the currencies of two nations are established by government authorities

floating exchange rate system   Where exchange rates between the currencies of two nations are established in foreign exchange markets by the supply of and the demand for currencies

free trade   Trade occurring between parties across international borders without any interference from governments

French Utopians   A group of early socialists of the 1700s who were concentrated in France

full employment   A condition of no cyclical unemployment, corresponding to approximately five to six percent of the labor force

GDP per capita   A monetary measure of the amount of final goods and services produced in a year for each person, on average, or the living standard

good   Anything that has physical substance that is produced by humans with resources

government spending   Part of total spending, including only spending for which governments receive goods and services in return

gross domestic product   The dollar value of all final goods and services produced in a nation in a year with resources located in that nation

growth recession   A state of economic growth so slight that the unemployment rate rises

implicit cost   A business cost that does not involve any payment of money to a seller of a resource

income   Goods and services obtained for one's use. It can also refer to money earned or otherwise received which can be exchanged for such goods and services

income effect   The decrease in purchases as the result of an increase in an item's price, as one's income can buy fewer items, and vice versa

income redistribution program   A government program to make the income distribution somewhat closer to equality by taking more taxes from those with higher incomes and/or giving transfer payments to those with lower incomes

income statement   A business statement showing the condition of the business over a period of time, containing information on revenues, costs, and profits or losses

increase in demand   An increase in the amount buyers are willing to purchase at each price

increase in supply   An increase in the amount sellers offer for sale at each price

increasing returns to scale   Describes a production process in which an increase in inputs of x percent results in output increasing by more than x percent

industrial union   A labor union composed of people who work in the same industry at many different crafts or jobs

industry   Refers to all the firms that produce a particular good or service

inelastic   Refers to a demand relationship when a given price change results in a proportionately smaller change in purchases

inflation   A condition in which the price level increases, generally over an extended period

inflation rate   The percentage increase in the price level in a year, calculated by the percent increase in the price index

injections   Additions to total spending in the macroeconomic circular flow, in the form of either investment or government spending

innovation   A change in the way resources are used

institutionalists   A group of economists of the early 1900s who believed that institutions, customs, and values explained economic behavior better than the traditional principles

interchangeable parts   Refers to a situation where each of part of one unit of a firm's product is identical to the respective parts of all other units

investment spending   That part of total spending that involves spending on capital goods, construction, and a change in business inventories

labor   Nonorganizational human effort needed to produce a good or service

labor cost   The amount of money a firm must spend on labor for one unit of its product, on average

labor demand   The relationship between wages and the number of people employers wish to hire

labor force   All the people who are employed plus those that are unemployed

labor-intensive   A production process where the largest share of the costs involve labor resources

labor productivity   The output produced by a laborer working one hour

labor shortage   A condition in a labor market when employers want to hire more workers at a specific wage than there are people willing to work

labor supply   The relationship between the wage and the number of people willing and qualified to work

labor surplus   A condition in a labor market when there are more people willing to work at a specific wage than employers are willing to hire

laissez faire   A government policy of minimum interference with the economic affairs of businesses and into all markets

law of comparative advantage   It states that a resource should specialize in producing a product in which it has the lowest opportunity cost of all other resources

law of demand   At higher prices for an item, buyers want to purchase less of it, and at lower prices, they want to purchase more of it

law of diminishing marginal returns   As additional amounts of a single resource are added to a production process, the marginal product eventually declines

law of diminishing marginal utility   Each additional unit of a good or service consumed by an individual provides less satisfaction than the previous unit

law of supply   At higher prices for an item, sellers will offer more of it for sale, and at lower prices, they will offer less for sale

leakages   A part of peoples' income that they do not immediately spend on goods and services, including taxes and savings

liable   Being responsible for a loss suffered by another person

limited liability   Where stockholders in corporations are only liable for the firm's debts to the extent of their investment in the firm

living standard   The amount of goods and services produced in a nation in a year for each person, on average

long run   A period of time long enough for a firm to increase or decrease its capital stock

macroeconomic equilibrium   A condition where there is no change in the major macroeconomic variables, occurring when total spending equals the value of total output

macroeconomics   The branch of economics that studies the behavior of large sectors of the economy and their related variables and relationships

managed float   A system where exchange rates are influenced by supply and demand but are kept within certain bounds by government interference in foreign exchange markets

marginal cost   The additional cost in producing an additional unit of output of a good or service

marginal product   The additional output of a good or service that results from the addition of one more unit of a particular resource to a production process

marginal revenue   The additional sales or total revenue for a seller as a consequence of producing and selling one more unit of output of a good or service

marginal revenue product   The value of the output of a good or service produced by adding one additional unit of a resource, such as a laborer

marginal tax rate   The percent of federal income taxes paid on an extra dollar of earned income

marginal utility   The additional satisfaction received from consuming one more unit of a good or service

market   A place where people meet to exchange things of value

market interest rate   The rate of interest as stated on the loan agreement, which is unadjusted for inflation

market socialism   An economic system that combines the public ownership of resources with a system of markets that largely directs resource use

mass markets   Markets for goods and services where there are very many buyers, made possible by a large population and efficient transportation and communication systems

mediation   A process of settling differences between labor and management, where a third party's opinion is requested by both sides but does not have to be accepted

medium of exchange   Something that represents purchasing power and is used to obtain goods and services in market exchanges

mercantilism A system where governmental policies were established to promote exports and discourage imports for the purpose of accumulating gold and silver

merchandise trade deficit The excess of the value of a nation's imports of goods over its exports of goods

merchandise trade surplus The excess of the value of a nation's exports of goods over its imports of goods

merger A combination of two or more corporations into one

microeconomics The branch of economics that studies the economic behavior of individuals, including consumers, firms, and resource sellers, and the variables and relationships relating to them

monetarist Someone who believes the amount of the money supply is a primary factor explaining macroeconomic activity and that recession and inflation can be avoided with a steady increase in the money supply equal to the rate of increase in total output

monetary aggregate One of four classifications of the money supply

monetary policy The control of interest rates and the availability of excess reserves and credit by the Federal Reserve System in order to influence total spending or aggregate demand

money income The amount of money someone receives, usually from the sale of resources

monopolistic competition A market structure where there are very many firms, each having a slightly different product that is sold at slightly different prices, and where usually is ease of entry into and exit from the industry

monopoly A market structure where there is only one firm and where there is a barrier to entering the industry

mortgage A document given to a lender by a borrower, stating that the lender can take possession of the property in the event of default

multinational A firm with major operations and/or subsidiaries in several nations

multiplier The multiple increase in total spending and the GDP that results from an initial increase in one of the components of total spending

national income Reflects the payments to the factors of production

national union An organization of all the local unions of one type in the nation

natural resource Anything necessary in a production process that appears in nature

negative externality An activity that has a negative effect on a second party when a first party uses resources

net domestic product Equals gross domestic product minus depreciation of capital equipment

net exports The difference in the value of exports and imports

new classical economics A school of economic thought centering on rational expectations theory, which discounts the government's ability to succeed in macroeconomic policy due to people making adjustments in their behavior of allowing such policy

normal profit The total of a typical firm's implicit costs in an industry

oligopoly A market structure characterized by a few large firms with significant price-setting power and unique products and where there are significant barriers to entry

open account credit Also known as revolving credit, where one receives a certain amount of credit to be used and which can be used again after the loan is repaid

open market operations Sales and purchases of securities by the Fed in order to control the level of excess reserves in the commercial banking system

opportunity cost The benefit given up from the best of the remaining alternative ways of using resources when they are used in a specific way

optimum scale of plant The size of a firm's capital stock that allows it to produce with the lowest average cost

partnership A type of business structure with more than one owner, each sharing responsibilities and being liable for the debts of the firm

peak The highest point in the business cycle, where economic activity is the greatest

personal income Includes all income available to people before taxes

personal investment The use of savings and/or borrowed funds for the purpose of earning more money

personal savings Equals disposable income minus consumption

Physiocrats The first true economists, who believed in natural law and that all wealth came from the land or working it

positive externality An activity that has a positive effect when a first party uses resources

potential GDP The value of final goods and services that would be produced at full employment

present value The value at the present of an asset or a flow of income that will be received at some point in the future

price The rate of exchange of money for one unit of what is sold

price ceiling The maximum price allowed by law in some market

price floor The minimum price allowed by law in some market

price index A representation of all prices

private benefit The benefit received by the person who uses resources

private cost The cost experienced by the person who uses resources

private enterprise An organization that produces a good or service and is owned by one or more individuals

private property Resources owned by one or more individuals

product market A market in which a good or service is exchanged

production possibilities curve A graph showing all possible combinations of two goods that it is possible to produce with a set of resources

progressive tax A tax that takes a higher percentage of the incomes of higher-income taxpayers than from those with lower incomes

proportional tax A tax in which every taxpayer pays the same percentage of income into the tax

protectionism Government policies designed to protect firms and their employees from foreign competition

public choice theory Theories that seek to explain how voters and public officials allocate resources to the public sector

public debt The money owed by citizens of the national government to those who purchase the government's securities

public enterprise A government enterprise that produces a good or service

public property Resources owned by all the citizens of a government

pure competition   A market structure characterized by many small firms, each having identical products sold at a single market price, and where there is easy entry into and exit from the industry

quota   A physical limit on imports

quantity demanded   The amount of an item buyers wish to purchase at a specific price

quantity supplied   The amount of an item sellers wish to sell at a specific price

rational expectations theory   The belief that any macroeconomic policy will be offset by actions of the private sector due to anticipated problems following those policies

real GDP   The current or nominal GDP after adjusting for inflation, which gives the most accurate measure of production

real income   The amount of goods and services that can be purchased with a given money income

real interest rate   The rate of interest after adjusting for inflation, equal to the nominal rate of interest minus the inflation rate

recession   The part of the business cycle when spending, output, and employment are falling, usually for a period of two or more quarters

recovery   The part of the business cycle when macroeconomic conditions have begun to improve, but before prosperity has been reached

regressive tax   A tax that takes a smaller percentage of the incomes of higher-income taxpayers than from those with lower incomes

relative price   The amount of some other good or service that can be exchanged for one unit of some particular good

required reserves   The amount of deposits upon which a commercial bank is not allowed to make loans

reserve requirement   The percentage of a commercial bank's deposit it must keep as required reserves

resource   Anything necessary to produce a good or service

resource allocation   Refers to how resources are directed to specific uses

right-to-work law   A state law, authorized by the Taft-Hartley Act, outlawing union shops in that state

savings and loan   A thrift institution that concentrates its loans in real estate

savings bank   A thrift institution that usually accepts small deposits and is owned by the depositors

Say's Law   It states that there will be an equivalent demand for goods and services for all the output people wish to produce

scarce   Something available in limited amounts and which provides utility or benefit

service   Anything that has no physical substance that is produced by humans with resources

short run   A period of time when a business is not able to change the amount of its capital stock

shortage   The excess of what buyers wish to purchase over what sellers offer for sale at some given price. It is found as the excess of the quantity demanded over the quantity supplied.

single proprietorship   A type of business where there is only one owner, who faces unlimited liability and earns all the profits

social benefit   The combination of private benefits and external benefits using resources

social cost   The combination of private costs and external costs of using resources

social good   A good which is nonrival and nonexclusionary, or one whose use can be shared by all and whose consumption does not leave less for others

social overhead capital   Capital goods which provide the foundation for all production by supplying such services as electricity, transportation, communication, education, and public safety

specialization   The use of a resource to produce only one item, or perhaps to produce only part of an item

standard of value   Something that allows comparisons of value between goods and services, often called a unit of account

standardization   Refers to the matching size, shape, and pattern of parts of products of different firms

store of value   Something in which purchasing power is stored until the holder is ready to use it

subsidiary   A corporation that is owned by another corporation

substitution effect   The act of buyers purchasing less of an item whose price rises because a substitute good becomes a better purchase, and vice versa

supply   The relationship between the amount that sellers offer for sale of some item and all possible prices of that item

supply-side economics   Government policies designed to increase total output or aggregate supply for the purposes of increasing economic growth and moderating inflation

surplus   The excess of how much sellers offer for sale over what buyers are willing to purchase. It is equal to the excess of the quantity supplied over the quantity demanded

tariff   A tax on an import, designed to reduce the level of imports

the economic problem   The difficulty caused by the combination of an unlimited desire for goods and services and limited resources

total cost   Includes all the costs of producing a specific amount of output of a good or service

total fixed cost   Includes all the overhead or fixed costs of producing a specific amount of output of a good or service

total funding   The total amount of money a government has available to spend, including borrowed funds

total outlays   The total amount of money spent by a government, including spending for goods and services as well as transfer payments

total receipts   Includes all the money received by a government from taxes, earnings, and other governments

total revenue   The total sales received by a firm from producing and selling a specific amount of output a good or service. It is found by multiplying the price by the amount sold.

total variable cost   The sum of all the operating or variable costs of producing a specific amount of output of a good or service

traditional economic system   A Basic Economic System where all economic decisions are made the way they were made in the past

transaction costs   The costs involved in making an exchange, including money costs as well as the costs of time and aggravation

transfer payment   Money given to someone by a government for which it receives nothing in return

trough   The worst part of the business cycle, which occurs just prior to the recovery phase

unemployed   A person who is not working and who is actively seeking work

unemployment rate   The percentage of the labor force that is unemployed

union shop   A workplace in which a person is required to join a union following a brief period

unlimited liability   The condition where an individual is responsible for all the debts incurred by a business

user fee   A charge assessed by the government for the use of its goods or services

velocity of circulation   How many times money is used in a year, on average

wealth   How much power a person has to purchase goods and services at any given moment

work rule   A worker-influenced guideline on how to perform a certain job

SOME MATHEMATICS NEEDED IN ECONOMICS

The material on the next four pages covers mathematical concepts frequently used in this book, including percentages, factor changes, rates, and graphs.

MEASURES OF VARIABLES

A variable is any unit of measure that can range from a smaller amount to a larger amount. Land area, a person's weight, and income are variables. The purposes here are: 1) to show how to calculate changes in variables; and 2) to show how to compare the magnitudes of two variables.

Percentage

The most elementary use of percentages is simple percentage, where, essentially, one seeks the ratio of one variable to another. It is found by:

$$\text{Percentage} = \frac{\text{(Amount of A)}}{\text{(Amount of B)}} \times 100$$

For example, if B is a 32-gallon barrel of crude oil and A is the amount of gasoline that can be refined from the oil—say 20 gallons—then 62.5% of a barrel of crude oil is gasoline, or 20/32 x 100 = 62.5%

Percentage changes are usually expressed in one of two ways. Most common is a percentage increase or decrease in a variable, found by:

$$\text{Percent Change in A} = \frac{\text{(Change in A)}}{\text{(A in Time 1)}} \times 100$$

$$= \frac{\text{(A in Time 2 – A in Time 1)}}{\text{(A in Time 1)}} \times 100$$

For example, if a child's weight increases from 80 to 87 pounds between two birthdays, the child's weight increased by 8.75%, as:

(87 – 80)/80 x 100 = 7/80 x 100 = 0.0875 x 100 = 8.75%

For another example, if a firm has costs of $460,000 in Year 1 and $500,000 in Year 2, its costs rose by 86.95%, as:

(500,000 – 460,000)/460,000 x 100 = 40,000/460,000 x 100 = 86.95%

Occasionally a variable is expressed as a "percent of" what it used to be. This is found by:

$$\text{A in Time 2 as a Percent of A in Time 1} = \frac{\text{(A in Time 2)}}{\text{(A in Time 1)}} \times 100$$

For example, if your income rose from $10,000 last year to $12,000 this year, your income this year is 120 percent of last year's income, or:

$12,000/$10,000 x 100 = 1.2 x 100 = 120%

Factor Changes

Another way to measure the changes in variables is through factor changes, given by the formula:

$$\textbf{Factor Change in X} = \frac{\textbf{(Level of X in Time 2)}}{\textbf{(Level of X in Time 1)}}$$

For example, if the value of a firm's capital rises from $4 million to $12.8 million, it experiences a factor increase of 3.2 times or a "3.2 fold" increase in its capital stock, as:

$12.8/$4 = 3.2x factor increase

Factor changes and percentage changes in variables often are given simultaneously. The formula connecting the two is:

Percentage Change in X = 100(Factor Change in X – 1)

For example, a threefold increase or a tripling of a firm's debt is equivalent to saying its debt rose by 200 percent, for:

200 = 100(3 – 1)

The following columns for factor changes and percentage changes show equivalent changes on any given line.

Factor Change in X	Percentage Change in X
1.2x	20%
1.5x	50%
2.0x	100%
2.5x	150%
3.0x	200%
4.0x	300%

Rates

"Rate" is used to indicate several different measures of variables. First, it could mean a percentage change in a variable over time. For example, "wages were rising at a five percent yearly rate in the 1980s" means that wages were five percent higher each year than the previous year. Second, rate could mean the "flow" of one variable as compared with another. For example, the "wage rate" is the amount of money paid (variable one) or "flowing to" a worker for each hour of time worked (the amount of time is variable two). A secretary's typing rate might be 90 words (variable one) per minute (time being variable two). And the unemployment rate is the number of unemployed laborers (variable one) as a share or percent of the labor force (variable two). As a final example, the interest rate refers to the amount of interest paid (variable one) as a percent of the money borrowed (variable two).

GRAPHING

Generally a graph shows the relationship between two variables. Table A1-1 shows a relationship between two variables, x and y. This is a "direct relationship," which means both variables change in the same direction. Note that as x increases, so does y. Conversely, in an "inverse relationship," as one variable increases, the other decreases.

Two types of graphs are commonly used to display such relationships. The first is the bar graph or histogram, where variable x is measured along the horizontal line, called the x-axis. The vertical line, called the y-axis, is used to measure the magnitude or the size of y. The height of each of the bar graphs can be measured on the y-axis by extending a horizontal line from the top of a bar graph over to the y-axis. Often bar graphs also have this magnitude stated within or next to the graph, as does the one in Figure A1-1. The same data in Table A1-1 are shown in Figure A1-1. The variable that does the causation, called the independent variable, is usually placed on the x-axis. The dependent variable, the one that is influenced by the independent variable, is placed on the y-axis.

The other type of graph, the line graph, is similar in concept. Again, there are two axes, called x and y, except now a point is located where the top of the bar graph would be in that form of graph, as is shown in Figure A1-2. The pair of numbers beside each point indicates the magnitudes of variable x and variable y, respectively. Finally, Figure A1-3 shows these points connected with a line—a graph. Any such point on a line graph always gives two "pieces" of information, found by dropping straight down to the x-axis to measure the amount of x and then by moving horizontally to the y-axis to find the magnitude of y.

Table A1-1   A Direct Relationship

Variable x	Variable y
1	16
2	20
3	24
4	28
5	34

Figure A1-1   A Bar Graph or Histogram

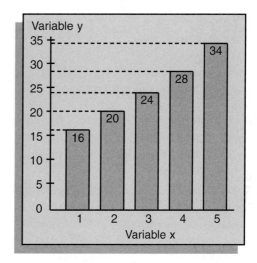

Figure A1-2   A Two-Variable System of Coordinates

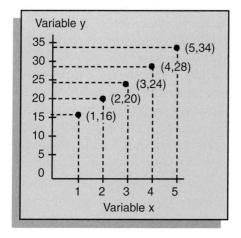

Figure A1-3   A Line Graph

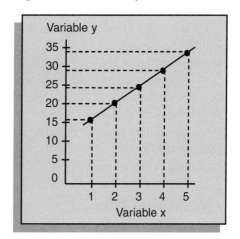

ANSWERS TO CRITICAL–THINKING QUESTIONS

How Much Does It Cost to See a Concert for Which You Purchased a $20 Ticket—If Tickets Are Being Scalped for $80?

The *price* of Item X is the amount of money you give up to get one unit of X. The *cost* of Item X is the amount of Item Y you give up when you buy a unit of X. More precisely, the cost is the *benefit* that amount of Item Y would have provided you. That is, the cost of X is the lost opportunity from Y.

Suppose you paid $20 for a music concert ticket and there was no scalping activity. Then the concert cost you the benefit of $20 spent on the best alternative use of your money, say, two $10-CDs of the same group performing at the concert.

However, suppose you paid $20 for a ticket and someone offered to pay you $80 for it. But you refused the offer and went to the concert. You could have purchased eight CDs for the passed-up $80. Thus, it cost you the benefits provided by eight $10–CDs to attend the concert. That is, it *cost* you what it would take $80 to buy. So, you could say the concert cost you $80 to attend, even though you only *paid* $20. Thus, there are no "cheap seats" at concerts where scalping occurs.

What would the concert cost you if you bought a (face-value) $20 ticket from a scalper for $80? Again, it cost you the benefit from eight CDs. Thus, the *cost* is the same for people who pay face-value prices for tickets as for those who pay higher scalper prices. Only the *price* is different.

Therefore, does it make any difference what you pay? Yes, for getting a "cheap" face-value ticket of $20 provides you a (tax-free) windfall income of $60. If you attend the concert, you essentially spend that windfall income on the concert ticket *plus* the $20 you paid with cash. Alternatively, if you accept the offer of $80 and stay home, you use $20 of that $80 to "pay back" yourself for the ticket price, leaving you with a net gain of $60—your windfall income.

Why Do You Follow Other Cars as Closely as You Do?

There is a rule of thumb promoted by safety officials for safe driving: Keep at least one car length of distance behind another car for every 10 miles per hour of speed—six lengths at 60 MPH and so on. A high percentage of drivers do not follow that rule. Who is right—the officials or the drivers? Most economists would say the drivers, for the drivers are all constantly practicing cost-benefit analysis.

A rational person does something only if the benefit of the act exceeds the (opportunity) cost. However, deeper analysis of many decisions will show that there are varying *degrees* of carrying out decisions. Consider, for example, buying a soft drink. Quite often you can order small, medium, or large sizes. So your decision is not simply: Should I buy a soft drink? Rather, it is: If I buy a soft drink, how much should I buy? You approach this more difficult question by breaking up the act into segments or degrees. You then consider the benefit of each segment and compare it to the cost.

So long as the benefits exceed the costs for additional segments, you keep "getting deeper into the act." In the soft-drink case, if a 50-cent, 10-ounce small size provides more benefit than any other way of spending 50 cents, you will buy *at least* a small drink. If a 70-cent medium is 16 ounces, you will buy *at least* that size if the benefit from the extra six ounces provides more benefit than any other way of spending the extra 20 cents. Finally, you will buy at least one 90-cent large 24-ounce drink if the extra eight ounces provide more benefit than any other way of spending the *extra* 20 cents. Of course, you can also buy two (or more) large drinks.

You face a similar decision on a road: How close should you follow the car ahead? Let's say you decide that the "segments" of the decision are car lengths of distance. So, for instance, at 60 MPH your question is: Should you be one car length back? or three? or six? or ten? and so on.

To answer this, first consider the extra benefit of moving one car length closer. It is primarily the time saved because you are that much closer to your destination. But it could also be the additional ease of passing (if that is what you intend). Finally, it could be the extra gas mileage gained when you are following in the "draft" of the driver ahead—the area of lower air resistance immediately following a vehicle. Overall, each additional car length provides about the same additional benefit as all other car lengths.

Second, you must consider the extra cost of each car length that you move closer. It primarily consists of two elements: the extra danger of an accident and the extra stress of driving closer. Unlike the extra benefits, these extra costs are virtually zero for most car lengths (the 100th, the 80th, the 40th, and so on). That is, you are just as safe and stress free at 100 lengths as you are at 40. However, these extra costs rise very sharply as you get very close to the car ahead. At 60 MPH, moving from ten to nine car lengths is very different than moving from four to three. And moving from two car lengths to one becomes very exciting—and dangerous (costly). Because the benefits of moving up are constant for each car length and because the costs rise sharply, eventually you stop closing the gap before coming to within a fraction of an inch from the car ahead.

Observe the many thousands of "close encounters" you see on roads before you actually see an accident. One would think there would be more. But left to their own cost-benefit analyses, drivers maximize their welfare, considering both their time and safety. No one needs safety officials or police officers to regulate distances between cars. Also, no one needs to regulate speeds. In fact, if legislators, safety officials, and the police *do* succeed in reducing speeds, society's *overall* welfare is *diminished*—not raised, as these well-meaning but misguided people believe. Thus, they *increase* the problem caused by a scarcity of resources (including time). However, police *do* become productive when they remove *irrational* people from the road: drunks, nonobservant drivers, etc. But for the rest of the drivers, let them seek their own level of speed, distance followed, etc. They almost invariably know what they're doing.

Do You Eat the Right Animals?

Do you eat the right animals? And just how do you decide to eat the ones you do? These are not the most pleasant thoughts, but the answers are vital to maximizing your economic welfare and to understanding what you do at the dinner table.

The proper way to answer this question is to gauge the benefits of eating the meat of every animal there is (with the possible exception of humans, but cannibalistic tribes even included *them*, as did a few who faced starvation, such as the famous 1846 Donner party on the California Trail and those whose plane crashed in the Andes mountains in the 1970s). Benefits usually take the form of the taste and the nutrition provided by the meat of each animal.

The hangup people have with certain animals is the *cost* of eating them. Besides the monetary costs, the costs of eating include the effort and time in chewing (cattle steak is more difficult to chew than chicken) and the damage to your heart from animal fat (whale blubber is about the worst, with bear meat a close second). But often the most significant cost of eating meat is psychological. Some people can't bear the guilt of being associated with the death of a dog (although Koreans have no hangups with this). Or a horse. But the Belgians and French aren't queasy about eating horse meat. In fact, many people in St. Louis benefit from this because a meat-packing plant there butchers horses and exports the meat to Europe. Vegetarians differ from meat-eaters in that they refuse to have *any* animal killed so they can eat it. The rest of us think only *some* animals should be spared. But, I wonder, have vegetarians considered this: almost all of the animals that die to feed us would never have had any life *at all* if we didn't eat them. We humans would never allow tens of millions of cattle, sheep, pigs, and chickens to live for any other reason. We wouldn't tolerate them wandering around the streets and in our yards. So, although their lives rarely end naturally, at least the animals (the ones we eat) get to have *some* life. So, vegetarians, *help* an animal live. Eat one!

The main point to be made is that we often refuse to eat an animal because it is not in our tradition to do so. We bypass the market economic system in such decisions and use the traditional economic system. Why else would most of us refuse to eat one of the cleanest and most fastidious animals, that washes its own food (the raccoon), and relish one of the dirtiest (the pig)?

If You Had to Set the Price of Everything, How Would You Do It?

Most people never realize that they seldom see significant surpluses or shortages of goods, services, or resources. Situations such as the shortage of Cabbage Patch dolls one Christmas, water in California in recent years, and parking spaces in certain areas are rare. So are surpluses such as certain agricultural commodities, (unemployed) unskilled workers, and unpopular goods. Further, people rarely realize that such surpluses and shortages would be commonplace if the "right" prices did not exist. If you or any other person had to set the price of everything without any idea of what the "right" market-clearing prices were, our world would be full of shortages and surpluses.

The price of an item reflects its relative scarcity. The relative scarcity refers to a rather abstract comparison of how much buyers wish to purchase of an item as compared with how much of it is offered for sale. In turn, offers to buy and offers to sell depend upon a multitude of other factors.

First of all, consider offers to purchase. At $20, say, there will be many more people willing to purchase television sets than books on economics because of the difference in satisfaction or benefit each provides. In addition, for each item there are a multitude of markets, each with its own demand. Geography, for example, has a major influence on the demand for certain foods. People in the Boston area demand brown eggs more than white eggs. People in eastern Wisconsin are crazy about frozen custard, a product virtually unknown elsewhere. It's a form of soft, high-fat ice cream with eggs added and which is served fresh (that is, immediately upon being made). And grits are a staple of people in the South. Seasonal changes and many other factors lead to varying demands between items.

Second, consider offers to sell. Again, geography plays a role in explaining differences between items, especially in the case of agricultural crops. Peaches will rarely grow in Vermont, but they will be abundant in Georgia. The content of the ground is occasionally another factor explaining supply differences. Iron ore is more abundant than aluminum ore, and platinum ore is one of the least abundant ones. So at, say, one dollar per pound of pure metal, more iron will be produced than aluminum, and perhaps no platinum will be produced at all. The availability of labor is another factor affecting supply. People who can clean houses are far more abundant than those who can repair computers. Thus, you would find that you could get far more firms to clean your house at $10 per hour than will repair your computer at $10 per hour.

If your job is to set the price of everything, you have to set at least several million prices because there are at least that many items sold, from cars to the thousands of components in a car, such as the posts on the spark plugs. In addition, you would have to set the price in every labor market. There are thousands of different jobs, and each geographical area has a different labor demand and supply. Then you have to set the price of land in every part of the country, from rich farmland to poor, from small town lots to choice Manhattan real estate. Also, you need to price each building in the nation. And don't forget all the prices of each stock, bond, and other financial instrument. And all the used items and antiques.

Your task is a bewildering one. And remember, make certain you set each price so it isn't set too high, leading to a surplus, or too low, leading to a shortage. Good luck!

Are Cookie Prices Higher in Malls Because the Rents Are So High— Or Is It the Other Way Around?

You've probably noticed that the prices you pay for fresh-baked cookies are significantly higher in a mall. You also might have noticed that prices in general are higher in downtown New York, Chicago, and other large cities. The clothes, jewelry, and many other items can usually be purchased in suburbs or smaller towns for less. Prepared food is an especially good example. Sandwiches, fresh-baked cookies, and the like are often ridiculously high-priced in those places.

If you ask a clerk or manager why they charge so much, you will probably be told the main reason is that they have to pay much higher rents than stores do in small towns and the suburbs. Thus, they must pass on these higher costs to you in the form of higher prices if they are to make a profit.

That sounds reasonable, but it is wrong because everybody has it backwards. David Ricardo exposed a similar myth in the early 1800s. The prices of bread and wheat had been high for some time, causing hardship for the poor. People then believed that the price of wheat was so high because farmers had to pay very high rents on land used to grow wheat. Ricardo stated that wheat commanded a high price because of its great benefit in the form of bread. Remember, the greater the benefit, the greater the demand and, very likely, the greater the price. The Industrial Revolution, which led to higher living standards, was a major source of this high demand for bread.

The high price of wheat led many farmers to grow wheat. But as the demand for land grew, the supply of it did not increase accordingly because there was only so much land. Thus, land eventually began to command very high rents from those who wished to grow this valuable commodity. Ultimately, the profits of the sellers of this valuable commodity (wheat) earned no greater profits (for their time and investment) than the sellers of most other items. But the landowners were much better off for the growth in popularity of wheat.

Very often people derive more benefit from eating a cookie in a mall than at home. It may taste the same, but there are other benefits to eating than the taste. It's like drinking. Most people are much less likely to drink a beer or a mixed drink at home alone than they are in a bar with friends. Chocolate chip cookies in malls, especially if eaten in the presence of other chocaholics, produce a "high" that's hard to beat. Hot dogs and peanuts at ball games are similar, almost being part of a ritual. And jewelry spotted in a fancy window display in a classy big city is often very tempting—more tempting than in Podunk Junction.

With such large benefits from these items in these locations, people are willing to pay higher prices than elsewhere. Shop owners know that, so prices are very high. You would think that would lead to fat profits for the shop owners. However, the people who lease the space to the shop owners also know what's going on. So property owners charge a fortune to rent those shops. Ultimately, then, it is the property owners who are the beneficiaries of your willingness to pay more in these locations.

Disasters: Do They Cause Disastrous Prices?

In 1992, a hurricane devastated Homestead, Florida. Houses and businesses were very much in need of repair or replacement. Thus, there were abnormally high demands for plywood sheets, lumber, and other building materials. There was no immediate matching increase in the supply of these items of the magnitude of the demand increase. Consequently, prices increased several fold for many construction items. The same thing happened to ice, chain saws, food, and other items.

The residents of Homestead were outraged, and a city ordinance was passed limiting price increases. That response would be understandable—from those who do not understand how the market system operates, such as people in communist countries. (Suppose the same people who favored the ordinance owned property where several competing developers wished to build a mall or theme park or golf course. What would be their response? Demand for their land suddenly increased sharply but the supply remained constant. Would they sell the land for what they paid for it? Or would they demand a much higher price?)

If the prices had *not* gone up sharply in Homestead, vast shortages would have quickly developed. It would have taken considerable time to end these shortages. Allowing prices to rise sharply would have led suppliers hundreds of miles from Homestead to send products to Homestead and still earn a profit. Nobody would force anyone to pay very high prices for, say, plywood sheets, so a purchase of such a sheet would imply that the benefit of the sheet exceeded the cost, in spite of the high price. True, the price would be high, but decision making is still rational and people would be getting all they wanted at those prices.

Another point needs to be made that is often missed in these situations. Flexible prices serve to ration items to those deriving the most benefit from them. If ice sold for the same price after the hurricane as before, someone who did not suffer any damage or had not lost electricity might buy ice for a picnic. Someone else, who was *not* fortunate enough to find ice because of the shortage, might lose hundreds of dollars of food in a defrosted, nonoperating freezer. Therefore, higher prices usually lead to the cessation of less valuable uses of items that are extremely scarce.

Aren't We Happier Than Our Great-Grandparents Were?

Originally, treadmills were meant to be deceptive—the ones on which animals were placed to produce power, that is. Horses, sheep, and dogs were placed on them, and they were enclosed to prevent escape. The inclined platform upon which they stood slid backwards (because, like modern treadmills, the platform was an endless apron that revolved around two shafts). So, as they walked up the incline—or *tried* to, they failed because the track slipped back faster when they tried to climb faster. A pulley connected to one of the shafts over which the apron revolved provided power on farms before the days of electricity and internal combustion engines.

Similarly, the *intent* of increased living standards is to move up our level of satisfaction or to increase our happiness or welfare. Such a direct relationship between the consumption of goods and services and happiness would be expected, but some studies have found some disturbing anomalies.

Some studies have found that, for individuals, the more effort that is exerted at producing things, the greater the economic welfare and the greater the level of happiness. It is also generally found that the higher the economic class people are in, the greater the satisfaction people feel about their (economic) lives. This second finding is essentially an aggregation of individuals in the first finding.

However, with due respect to the difficulty of comparing generations, it has been found that people do *not* perceive themselves as happier than earlier generations. This is in spite of the fact that living standards can easily double over a span of two generations or less. Thus, today we "run faster" (produce and consume more) than earlier generations, but we are no further ahead than our ancestors in what *counts*—happiness. We're on a treadmill. Thus, much of our success in raising living standards has been for nothing.

Two plausible explanations can be offered for this anomaly. First, we are the victims of rising expectations. People expect economic conditions to significantly improve over the condition of their parents and sometimes believe they have a *right* to such improvement. However, when they arrive at that higher plateau, it provides no big boost in contentment. It's like people would like to say, "OK, we made it. Now what?" Perhaps much of the joy of the higher living standard was in the *anticipation* of that boost—not the boost itself. Oftentimes people experience this with a long-awaited good or service. Looking forward to the day of delivery is virtually everything, and possession is almost anti-climactic.

A second explanation of the "treadmill effect" is that each generation has little realization of the position of its economic welfare compared with that of previous generations. Simply stated, people don't know how good they have it. They don't appreciate what they have, so they derive no more satisfaction from their abundance than their great-grandparents did from their paltry means. Perhaps only a small percentage of 20-year-olds could accurately describe the material world when their grandparents were young, or at least the *average* person of their grandparents' generation.

The solution? Perhaps it simply lies in sitting back more often and *counting*—actually counting—what you have that earlier generations didn't. And that amounts to counting your blessings.

Would Your Great-Great-Great-Great-Grandparents Have Expected You to Have a Job?

If you are in your 20s now and could take a trip back in time to visit your great, great, great, great-grandparents when they were in *their* 20s, you would probably be in the years from 1800 to 1820 or so. You would likely be on their very small farm.

If it was early in the morning, between five and seven, they would be feeding their cattle, poultry, hogs, and horses. During this time they would also milk their cows and gather eggs for breakfast. If they hadn't already done so, they would chop wood to cook breakfast. All the food would be produced on the farm, including cheese and butter. The house would be lit with candles they made of beeswax from their own beehives. Perhaps the house itself was built by them, as were many of the furnishings in it. Mornings and afternoons would be filled with a myriad of activities likely unknown to you: spinning wool, knitting sweaters, making pillows or quilts, making soap, whitewashing the barn, digging a well (with a pick and shovel), making shoes, flailing grain (using two clubs connected with a chain to remove seeds from the stalks), and a hundred other tasks. You wouldn't have to ask them a silly 1990s question: "What do you do for a living?" You can see that they do *everything* "to live." They are "fully employed" from dawn to dusk and beyond, never once worrying about not having a job.

Suppose you tell them how things will change throughout the 1800s. People will cease certain tasks, one by one. Wool spinning is one of the first tasks to go, as the spinning jenny does a better job. Candles will be replaced by kerosene lamps by the 1870s. Threshing machines will replace the flail by the 1890s. And on and on. Your ancestors are thinking, "Wait a minute, what are we going to do with our time? We're industrious and *like* to work. And you're telling us we're going to be working less. Therefore, we will be unemployed *more*. And you, you visitors from the 1990s, how much of what we have here do you still make yourself?" You inform them that you only make soap. They respond, "Oh, you poor dear! How hungry, ill-clothed, and ill-housed you must be. You can't eat soap, wear it, or build a house out of it. But at least you're clean! May God and your friends and relatives be charitable to you so you don't starve and freeze to death!"

You tell them not to worry, for you make soap, *every* day *all* day in a soap factory. When they ask what you do with all that soap, you ask them how their (yet-to-be-born) grandchildren of 1900 were going to obtain their spun wool, kerosene lamps, and so on. It would be possible because the products they *did* produce in 1900 would be made in larger volume so that an excess of their personal needs would be produced. If one of those items was honey, then eventually someone who spun wool would wish to have some honey. A trade could then take place called a barter exchange. Eventually, money would be used more commonly so the cumbersome barter system could be largely abandoned by the end of the 1800s.

When all this happens over several centuries, there will be time enough so the employment shifts will hardly be noticed, and painful periods of unemployment almost unknown. Unless you experienced two periods separated by hundreds of years and observed the increased specialization and trade over time, it's not very clear how we changed and, perhaps, how we are still changing.

Are You Rich? Why—or Why Not?

Achieving economic success is often a matter of locating a great amount of scarcity and then reducing that scarcity. And that often entails "seeing" or realizing what isn't there. This is perhaps quite vague, but the following elucidation should make the capitalistic economic system much easier to understand for you.

The price of anything—a good, a service, land, capital, labor (or time), stocks, etc.—is usually an indication of its relative scarcity. Essentially, relative scarcity refers to how much something is wanted as compared with how much of it people are willing to provide. Something that people want in vast amounts and which is extremely rare will usually have a very high price. If that same very popular item is everywhere to be found, such as water in the Great Lakes region, it won't command a very high price.

To have a high income, you need to sell something (including time) that has a high price. Thus, you will be on the road to a high income if you can find something that: 1) isn't around or, at least, is extremely rare; and 2) people want very much or *would* want very much if they only knew it existed. The last step to a high income is to reduce the relative scarcity of that very high-priced item by selling lots of it. Usually such an item is a good or a service (although it could also be a rare and very productive labor skill).

The trouble is, success at this task usually requires one to imagine something that could exist but that doesn't yet exist. Yet the patent office has had millions of ideas presented to it that fulfill this criterion. However, most never sold for a high price and in large quantities—if at all—proving the difficulty of scoring big in a capitalist economy.

Nevertheless, there are many examples of almost ridiculously easy success stories. The safety pin was developed in just a few hours. The inventor sold the idea for the equivalent of about one thousand of today's dollars because he thought that was pretty good pay for a few hours work. He never got rich. But a later inventor of a fastener did when he saw how difficult it was to remove burrs from his pants that he got in a weed patch—and Velcro was born. The inventor of the nylon-string "weedeater" doesn't have to work anymore. While in a fast-food restaurant, he noticed the weeds and grass underneath a fence which the lawn mower couldn't reach. Besides using shears or sickles, he wondered how the weeds could be cut easily. It didn't take him long to "see" what wasn't there—a high-speed, rotating nylon string. Finally, why didn't *you* think of putting a carved-pumpkin face on a trash bag? No one did until around 1980.

One of the most obvious inventions, one might think, should have been the wheel. But its invention was a two-step process, the second step being the hardest and the longest in coming. The first step was realizing that round things could be pushed more easily than other shapes, such as cubes. Most early societies moved heavy objects, such as large stone blocks, on a series of cylinders, usually logs. The Incas of South America, for example, moved stones up to 10 feet high many miles in this way. They had a highly organized, efficient empire and a well-developed system of accounting and mathematics. Yet, they never got to the second step of wheel invention. That step actually involves four substeps. First, the cylinder needs to be made so that it has a very low height. That is, it has to be squat, like a tuna can. Second, a round hole must be made in the center of the cylinder. Third, the same must be done with another identical cylinder. Fourth, another long cylinder with a diameter slightly smaller than the holes that were made must be placed through the two large cylinders. This, of course, is an axle. The rest is easy. Combine two sets of wheels and axles, add a box, and the wagon is born. Add an engine and pretty soon you've got a Ford. And Henry Ford got very rich selling them.

Why Don't They Build Bigger Train Locomotives?

Almost invariably, you will find that the powerplant on a land-transport vehicle will have one powerplant or engine to power it. And the larger the vehicle to be moved, the larger the powerplant. Cars, trucks, and buses all fit that situation.

However, not freight trains. Although you often see one locomotive pulling a train, usually you will see multiple locomotives, often three or four. This anomaly should lead people to make one of two statements. First, someone might say that locomotives are made too small. Some manufacturers would be able to sell much larger locomotives because it would be easier (and cheaper) to hook up one locomotive to a train than three or four. Further, the fuel efficiency should grow as the size rises, so the average cost of pulling a train should fall. Thus, railroad companies would be very willing to purchase larger locomotives. However, if such a locomotive were possible and so efficient, it certainly would have been made by now. So something must be wrong with this explanation.

The second (and the most plausible) explanation is that there are decreasing returns to scale beyond the current largest size locomotive available. That means that, if a locomotive's engine had 50 percent more cylinders or cylinders with a 50 percent larger bore and was larger and heavier, the cost of pulling a ton of weight would be higher than with current locomotives. That is, the average cost of hauling freight would rise. This is because even though a larger locomotive could pull, say, 100 percent more weight, it might cost 150 percent more to purchase and operate such a locomotive. In that case, it is better to double the pulling capacity by connecting two smaller engines. The total cost would only rise 100 percent, not 150 percent, so the average cost would remain about the same.

Will We End Up Taking in Each Other's Laundry?

Sooner or later you will hear that question. Someone will tell you that so many jobs involving the manufacture of goods are being lost through mechanization that only service jobs will be left, such as laundry service. What's more, people worry that because some service jobs pay relatively little, most jobs of the future will pay less than those lost because of mechanization. But that is a myth which has its source in anecdotal evidence (observing a few cases here and there) and in not seeing the whole picture.

While the loss of a job through innovation is usually bad *for the individual* who lost the job, that job loss is good for *society as a whole*. It means that fewer resources overall are needed to produce the same level of output as before. (You may think that, although fewer labor resources are used, more capital resources are used, so perhaps *overall* resource use is greater. But that is not true because then the cost of production would be higher.)

The ultimate (but unrealistic) goal is to have just one person working in each industry. One person would make all the cars, another all the television sets, and so on. That would cut the cost of production so much from the present so that the prices of cars, television sets, and everything else would be a small fraction of what they are now. Then we each could enjoy the many things we now can't afford, and those things would be produced by the present "excess" auto and TV-makers.

However, that won't happen, at least with services, because most services can't be mechanized very well. This doesn't mean our living standards will be low just because services will increasingly dominate the future job picture. If *overall* productivity is high, including the goods sectors, then the living standard will be high, no matter what laborers produce. It's a simple matter of dividing (a high) total output by the population.

In a world where there are few jobs producing goods and where virtually all of us produce services, indeed *some* of us will take in the laundry of others. That has been happening already. Some services will be relatively easy to produce with unskilled laborers. Therefore, such labor markets will be flooded with such applicants because they don't have the skills to work elsewhere. Such services include food services (especially fast-food operations), cleaning services, and car-wash operations. These workers will be paid relatively low wages for the foreseeable future.

But also in that world, some people will be providing other services that require relatively more skills. These include airline personnel, repairers of sophisticated machines, environmental engineers and technicians, and workers in finance, such as stockbrokers, loan officers, and financial planners. Fewer people will qualify for such positions, so they will earn much more income than other service workers.

Above all, remember that the goal in economics is to reduce the impact of a scarcity of resources. Thus, we should laud any success in reducing labor needs in a production process, even in the service industry. However, because it is less likely to occur there, we *will* be trading services ("doing each other's laundry").

Should There Be Stores Downtown?

As societies became more urban, primarily in the 1800s, residential areas developed around a central business district in every town. By the late 1900s, a large share of the downtown business districts were mere shadows of their pasts. There are fewer businesses in downtowns today, and many that remain face hard times, victims of major malls and strip malls in outlying shopping areas, as well as the expansion of the Wal-Mart empire. Many cities have spent and continue to spend vast amounts of money to renovate and beautify their downtowns to entice shoppers. But such expenditures might be wasteful if downtowns are not the places stores should be.

To better understand this issue, it is useful to review the concept of trade. Specialization leads people to trade, and the concept of comparative advantage is used to determine *what* each person should trade. The concepts of supply and demand, considered simultaneously, determine *how much* of one thing needs to be given up when trading for something else. This is what prices reflect. The last thing to determine is *where* trading should take place.

Merchants generally don't care where they sell things, *per se*. They just want to make certain it is the location where they can sell very much and where their costs are low. In turn, low cost partly depends upon the cost of land and access to transportation facilities. It is possible that these criteria could be met either in downtown areas or in the outskirts of town. But things that are important to consumers are much more likely to be fulfilled in the outskirts. Buyers want to drive to stores on wide streets, and they want easy access to parking and lots of parking space. They want protection from the elements when they go from store to store, so the stores (or the storefronts) should be under a roof. Finally, they don't want to drive very far to shop, so the stores should be near their homes.

These consumers' criteria are fulfilled much better by large, enclosed malls. The smaller, more numerous strip malls better fulfill the proximity-to-residential-areas criterion. But both do better than downtowns, which *did* provide close proximity to residences of the 1800s. Also, in the 1800s, parking was not a problem because people usually walked to markets or took public transportation.

So what should be done with downtowns? They could be converted to parks, to new residential areas, or to government offices. Such transitions or partial transitions are already being made for very many cities. But the efforts of downtown boosters are impeding such transition with questionable tax and subsidy policies.

Should Some Towns in the Great Plains Become Ghost Towns?

Things aren't the same in Nebraska and the rest of the Great Plains as the old days. Farms established in the 1800s were usually less than 200 acres, whereas now one and two thousand-acre farms are the norm. Therefore, there are fewer farmers living in the Great Plains. When farms developed, grocers, implement dealers, department stores, doctors, and dozens of other specialists and enterprises soon followed to serve the farmers. They congregated in villages and small towns, perhaps 10 miles apart, on average. By and large, business owners earned reasonable incomes for those periods. Many towns had several firms of each type so there was significant competition as well as enough business for each firm to prosper. A sort of balance developed between the total farm population and the number of towns and businesses to serve them.

Gradually, this balance was lost. Farm machinery became larger, allowing a farmer to till more acreage. Those farmers with more financial strength and expertise eventually absorbed the lands of their less successful, small-operation neighbors. Consequently, the farm population steadily dropped and still continues to drop.

However, the number of towns has changed little since the early 1900s. So merchants in these towns gradually fought increasingly pitched battles for a dwindling market. It was like a small pond of fish fighting to survive in a drought as the pond shrinks to a puddle. Almost everyone suffered in every town. If only towns (and all their inhabitants) would have "disappeared" at the same rate as the farm population, this suffering would not have occurred. But towns rarely do that. Nevertheless, if many small towns in the Great Plains today would disappear, those remaining would look healthier. You would not see the sights you often see in towns today: boarded up businesses, vacant houses, poor streets and roads, and rusting hulks of vehicles.

Should You Have the Right to Quit Your Job?

A contract is essentially an agreement on the terms of trade when a buyer and seller exchange something, whether it is a good, a service, a house, land, or time (labor). Contracts can be made to cover any length of time, including a one-time transaction of a few seconds in a store to one-year teacher contracts to multiyear service contracts on appliances. After the contract has expired, neither the buyer nor the seller has any further obligation to the other trader.

That lack of further obligation means that once you have been a buyer, you don't have to buy the same thing again. For example, if you buy a taco from Juan at Juan's Tacos, you are not required to buy another. Your reasons for not buying any more might be the silliest in the world, but that is your right. Alternatively, you can and might buy thousands of Juan's tacos over a period of years if it suits you. However, if you stop buying his tacos after 10 years, Juan's income and economic welfare will fall, but you have the right to hurt him in that way.

But Juan doesn't have to sell you a second taco if he doesn't want to. (However, civil rights acts prevent him from refusing to sell to you because of your race, religion, and a few other characteristics.) His reasons might sound silly to you, like closing precisely at 8:00 and refusing to sell you a taco at 8:01 because he wants to go home. He has the right to hurt you in that way—that is, preventing you from spending your money in the best possible way at 8:01.

Virtually all of us accept these conditions of trading in a market system—until it comes to labor. The seller's side of a labor market, however, does work pretty much the same way as it does for goods. If you sell eight hours of your time to someone who buys it (known as an employer), you don't have to sell another hour of your time (that is, work another hour) if you don't care to. (There are some exceptions, such as a two-week notice or workers under contract. But even these contracts are often readily broken.) Your reason can be as silly as you'd like. It could be because you've become lazy or you don't like to take orders. Or because you don't like a co-worker. Or because you've won the lottery and don't need the money. The 13th amendment to the Constitution prohibits involuntary servitude, so you can turn down any offer to sell your time (except in a military draft). And this is a wonderful part of our society, part of the freedom we cherish.

Would you grant the buyer of your time (your employer) the same freedom that you have—that is, to stop trading your time? Would you grant your employer the right to stop buying your time, whatever the reason, at any time—that is, to lay you off or to fire you? Most people would probably say no because it could hurt them. Their income would fall. Of course it would. Just like Juan's would if you stopped buying his tacos, perhaps because you bought Sally's tacos instead (because Sally's were better, or "more productive").

Sometimes employers would also like to buy a "better-tasting taco" (a new, more productive employee). After all, what's good for the goose is good for the gander. But the buyers in labor markets (employers) often don't have the same rights as the sellers (employees).

How Can Shaquille O'Neal Be Worth $17 Million a Year?

Shaquille O'Neal and a few other lucky stiffs have a higher yearly income than you could ever expect to earn in several lifetimes. How, you might ask, could anyone be so stupid as to pay them that much? Can anybody be worth that much?

First of all, O'Neal didn't get that salary primarily by being lucky. And neither are other highly paid people, from entertainers to corporate executives, usually paid a lot primarily because of luck.

In a competitive market, no single person dictates the price, including the price of labor services provided. The higher the benefit a buyer expects to derive from an item, the more the buyer is willing to pay to obtain it. But if there are many sources of such valuable items, usually the buyer need not pay too much, as competition holds down the price.

Shaquille O'Neal is expected to produce an enormous amount of benefits for the owner of a basketball team and the fans. So teams could be expected to be willing to pay a lot to O'Neal. Would they have to if 33,000 other people could play like he can? No. But only an extremely small number can, so O'Neal *does* get a lot of money—less, the Los Angeles Lakers hope, than he is expected to earn them in extra net revenues. If they bring in $17 million a year more because of O'Neal, he was a steal at $17 million.

Nobody forced the Lakers to fork over so much money. So the expected benefits of signing O'Neal must have exceeded the expected costs.

Why Is a Wheat Farmer More Deserving of Help Than a Potato Farmer?

Pity potato farmers. They are at the mercy of the fickle consumer and the elements. If we suddenly cease eating french fries to cut down on fat consumption, a large surplus of potatoes would lead to plunging potato prices. The same thing would happen if the weather improved for growing potatoes.

Growers of most other crops and owners of other agricultural enterprises face similar vagaries of the market. Growers of beans, flax, carrots, and peppermint, as well as producers of pork, beef, and chicken, all put up with such market uncertainty. Outside of federal crop insurance in some cases and occasional access to subsidized credit, these farmers are on their own in a competitive world.

But why did Congress, the president, and the Department of Agriculture decide to help out farmers of a few dozen types of commodities, most notably wheat, corn, cotton, dairy products, and peanuts? Perhaps it's akin to the government's "too-big-to-fail" policy in the banking industry. It is believed that the entire economy cannot absorb the failure of some companies, like big banks and manufacturers such as Chrysler Corporation. Similarly, we can afford to lose the carrot farmers, but not the wheat farmers. There are simply too many wheat farmers. Or perhaps it's because there are more voters on wheat farms than on carrot farms. But then, what's that got to do with the price of eggs?

To Whom Do You Hold Allegiance—Yourself or Your Neighbors?

Television commercials, bumper stickers, newspaper ads, and occasionally friends and acquaintances exhort you to buy American-made products rather than foreign-made ones. Or you might be encouraged to shop in your local areas so your money "stays home and helps out your neighbors." Once you decide to limit your purchases to a geographical area smaller than the entire planet, you have a major problem deciding which border at which to stop. Your nation's border? The state border? The county border? The city limits? A 10-block radius from your home? Or five blocks?

You can avoid that problem by seeking to maximize your own economic welfare and forgetting about that of some producer, laborer, or merchant somewhere. You accomplish that by purchasing items anywhere in the world that maximize the benefits from your income. You owe that to yourself. You do *not* owe any favor to your local, state, or national merchants, manufacturers, or laborers. If they want your business, it's up to *them* to satisfy you better than someone else. If we all did that, total world-wide economic welfare would be higher than now, where many of us get less than maximum welfare because we arbitrarily favor some local, regional, or national seller who is less than top-notch.

One criticism of this policy is that we will hurt the employment prospects of our neighbors—whoever we decide is our neighbor. But look around you and see the very high percentage of people you know who are employed. That percentage is not much different than it was in the 1800s when people were much more likely to buy locally made products. Buggies, beer, clothes, and building materials almost always came from their *nearby* neighbors. Now we are much more likely to buy our cars, beer, clothes, and building materials from more distant "neighbors." What is different is that we specialize more than people did in the past. Your local community likely produces fewer goods than it did a hundred years ago. But it produces *far more* of each good. So *total* employment in most commodities is little affected—only the *kind* of employment has changed.

If You Acted Like Bart Simpson in School, Why Are You Upset When I Don't Want to Buy What You Make?

Bart Simpson is an underachiever—and proud of it. Once someone like Bart starts working, do you think he'd be proud of the product he made? Would it hold up or do what it is supposed to? If it was a car, would you feel safe driving it at 65 MPH?

There are a lot of Bart Simpsons in school today, students who do not wish to learn much. Two-thirds of eighth graders watch three hours or more of TV daily. Half of all these same eighth graders can do only fifth-grade math work, according to a 1991 prototype of the American Achievement Tests, which the Bush administration wanted given to all fourth-, eighth-, and twelfth-grade students by the mid-1990s. The prototype also found that only 54 percent of high school seniors could do seventh-grade math. Math is not the only problem. Reading and comprehension levels have been dropping for decades. The average high school student has a vocabulary of over 10,000 words less than a student of the 1950s. Knowledge of history and geography is so skimpy it's almost laughable, if it weren't so sad and ominous.

Part of the problem is that American students usually spend 180 days in school. European children usually spend 210 days, and Japanese children spend 240 days. Besides, foreign children spend more hours per day in school and usually have more homework. Thus, foreign expectations and standards are higher. When asked in a poll taken in 1990 if "poor curriculum/poor standards" was a major problem at schools in America, only eight percent of Americans said it was. Underachievers—and proud of it!

We can clearly expect that employers will have a more difficult time with a workforce having fewer skills. Directions will be flubbed more often, chemicals will get mixed incorrectly, invoices will have more errors, and dangerous flaws will appear in products. Countless interviews and polls indicate that firms already have faced these problems. That is the reason that in-house education is being offered at a rapidly growing number of American corporations. Until these corporate programs and a better overall educational system succeed in bringing the U.S. workforce up to world-class standards, why should that workforce be upset if their compatriots favor foreign-made products so often?

Why Is Driving a Car a Privilege—Not a Right?

You rarely, if ever, need anyone's permission to eat an apple or to ride a bicycle. Also, you don't need any government license or permit to eat an apple. You might have to get a license for your bicycle, but you don't need a license to *ride* it. That is, you don't need a bicycle driver's license, like you need a car driver's license. Your bicycle license is, then, comparable to your car registration—a source of revenue for your local or state government.

Thus, you have a right to eat apples or ride your bicycle just about any place and any time you wish. However, you often hear that you don't have a right to drive a car. You must earn the *privilege* to do that.

What's the difference? They are all goods, like any other that we can freely use. Why treat cars differently? The reason is that cars often result in significantly greater external costs than apples or bicycles. The only trouble you might cause others when eating an apple is the core you leave lying on the table or that you throw on the ground. Riding your bicycle might occasionally bother others you come close to.

However, you can easily kill others while driving a car, or at least injure them. Also, you can cause them serious property loss. These are all external costs. Therefore, to prevent these costs, like some other external costs, society prohibits the acts having negative externalities. That is, society prohibits those acts that are expected to cause external costs. These include cars driven by children, incapacitated people, those using drugs or alcohol excessively, or those who drive recklessly.

Who Pays for Your Recycling Time?

This appears to be the decade in which the concept of recycling materials becomes as common as it was a century ago, when things were rarely thrown away until they were repaired a few times or used for other purposes. The rapidly rising living standards in the 20th century led to our growing landfill problem for two reasons. First, the sheer volume of the goods we purchased increased. Two, our growing incomes led us to be able to afford to throw things away rather than return them (e.g., bottles) or repair or mend them (e.g., clothes). In short, we bought time with our increased incomes.

However, we also discovered that we bought a lot of trouble—smelly, unsightly landfills, some which leaked toxic contaminants into our water supplies. Thus, an increasing number of states and local governments are mandating recycling of various materials. By the year 2000, it may even be illegal to throw out a soup can.

Good, a lot of people say. And it *is* good, at least in that there will be fewer piles of garbage. But think of a major reason why we were throwing things away in the first place. It bought us time, as it was often faster to buy a new item than to repair or mend old items. Turning that around, we believed our time was valuable enough to pay extra money to save some of it.

Soon you will be required (or already are required) to spend some of your time recycling. So far no one has calculated what this will cost the average person or all of us collectively in a year. Surely it will be in excess of 10 hours a year, maybe as high as 30 hours. Would you give up 30 hours a year without pay to help out people you don't know and will perhaps never see? Not many would. But that's what you're being forced to do with mandatory recycling.

How can we avoid that? Perhaps some of it can't be avoided. But many items could have "recovery-price incentives" built into their prices to guarantee recycling. For example, every metal can could have a 20-cent charge added to it. Anyone who returns it in a flattened state to a recycling center would get 20 cents. *You* may not want to bother to clean the can, remove its paper, and carry it to a recycling point. But *someone* will gladly come to your house to get 100 or 200 of your cans every month or so for the $20 to $40 it is possible to get. In that way, you don't spend time recycling that you don't care to, the returner gets paid for his time spent, and you don't add to the nation's landfills as much as before. Of course, some states already do that with aluminum beverage cans. It works quite well, so why not extend it to *everything* we don't want in landfills—instead of introducing involuntary servitude for no pay?

Have You Ever Seen the West?

Landfills, when they're being constructed and filled, aren't pretty. But when they are filled to capacity, they could actually be made to look as attractive as many natural scenes, especially a countryside of rolling hills. They can be forested, used as parklands, or made into golf courses. They could become ski hills in an area of level land.

However, one major problem is that we usually construct landfills close to the sources of the refuse—near metropolitan areas. Consequently, that maximizes the likelihood of the NIMBY (Not in *My* Back Yard!) syndrome. That is why you hear that we are running out of room for landfills. We're not. There's plenty of space. What really is the case is that virtually no one is willing to have one's own property or a neighbor's property used for a landfill—so long as there is no compensation. But if each neighbor within a mile of a proposed landfill were offered $10 million, very few would protest its construction. People would fight to *have* landfills near them.

On the other hand, many parts of the West have virtually no people, vegetation, and wildlife, and don't really qualify as great-looking property. Parts of eastern Wyoming and Montana, Nevada, and significant parts of New Mexico, Arizona, and western Texas fit this description. But two major difficulties stand in the way of western landfills. First, costs of transporting the refuse would certainly be higher than now. However, if specialized unit trains were used, much like trains now hauling coal from Wyoming to powerplants in the Midwest and the East, costs could be kept reasonable. (Actually, trains now traveling *to* Wyoming travel with empty cars, so the *extra cost* of hauling refuse would not be that large.) The second problem is a special NIMBY case. People in one state usually vehemently object to refuse coming in from another state. This may be especially true with these western states, which all have some truly spectacular scenery. People there might believe that all parts of their state are beautiful and wouldn't want to sully any part of it.

Why Don't Businesses Pay Taxes?

Whenever any government has a fiscal crisis, someone will always say, "Raise taxes on businesses. We working people pay more than our fair share already!" In fact, perhaps we should have businesses pay *all* the taxes that are needed to cover any government budget. Then "working people" would have *no* taxes to pay.

If it only were that easy! Many (but not all) economists believe that businesses only *appear* to pay income, property, and other types of taxes. In fact, they only serve as collection agents for governments. They "collect taxes" (that is, they obtain revenue for the government) either by building the business taxes into their prices or by paying their employees less. Remember that a business, like an individual, will do something only if its benefit exceeds its cost. Its benefit is primarily the revenue it gets when it sells a good or service. Its cost involves both its explicit (cash) costs as well as its implicit (opportunity) costs.

Suppose that until now no business ever paid any kind of tax. Assuming a significant amount of competition in all industries, in the long run each firm would earn at least its normal profit. That means every firm manages to pay its expenses and has funds left over to cover all implicit (opportunity) costs. The competition would ensure that few, if any, firms would earn any economic profit, at least not in the long run.

Now suppose that all state governments suddenly impose an income tax of 10 percent on all business profits. There will be no immediate change in revenue because of the taxes. There are also no changes in the explicit expenses or implicit costs of firms. However, the effect of the taxes is the same as if explicit costs rose. What the firm owners have left to spend has been reduced. So their returns (or benefits) from operating their businesses have fallen. But because their returns were previously just high enough to keep them in business, now they earn less than that. That is, they fail to earn normal profits and suffer economic losses (but likely no accounting losses).

Businesses, most of them being in the same boat (with economic losses), have three choices. First, they could begin to close down their operations. Eventually, supplies of all products would fall. Because demands would not fall, shortages would appear. Next, prices would rise. Prices would rise so long as it took for all the tax collections from businesses to be returned to businesses in the form of higher revenues.

Second, the first step above might be skipped because each business owner or manager realizes that all other businesses face the same problem. They also realize that some firms will soon go out of business and that prices will rise. So as soon as taxes are imposed, firms immediately raise prices so that no firm is forced out of business by inadequate returns.

Third, instead of raising prices, firms could cut the wages of their workers. When all firms combined cut wages enough so the total drop in wages equals the total taxes they pay, the wage cuts would stop.

Any way you look at it, people who don't own businesses are in the same position. After businesses are forced to pay taxes and nonowners get a tax cut, the nonowners pay the equivalent of their tax cut in higher expenditures on goods and services, or they earn an equivalent amount less of income.

To make it worse, collectively, people are not really in the same position. When businesses are forced to pay taxes, the IRS and other tax agencies must hire large numbers of employees to process all the paperwork. Extra building space, computers and other equipment, vehicles, and other resources also must be purchased to support the larger tax collection system. And these purchases require more tax revenue. Thus, by trying to pay less in taxes we end up paying *more*.

Finally, note who is *really* helped by business tax laws. Firms hire experts to ensure that the minimum amount of business taxes are paid. The IRS hires experts to prosecute business tax evaders. Both of these groups of experts are called lawyers.

Why Not Tax People on Their Ability to Earn?

The ability-to-pay principle, used in the income, property, and sales taxes, states that the higher your income and/or wealth, the more you should pay in taxes. But there are some problems with that principle that could be alleviated by using a new taxing principle, one based on the ability to earn (to earn income, that is).

With this principle, the greater the likelihood of you earning more income, the more you would pay in taxes. There are many factors affecting how much income you earn, but several major ones include how many years of education you had, how well you did in school (as, perhaps, indicated by your GPA), your IQ, your age, and the occupation you chose. These factors, and perhaps a few more, could be combined into a formula that could be used to determine your earning capacity.

There are certain advantages to using this principle. First, it would eliminate the current problem of a reduced incentive to work longer hours or harder. Under the current system, the percentage of your income taxed increases as you earn more. Many people would like to work more than they do now, but they are discouraged by the high amount of extra taxes they would pay. This includes people who are offered overtime work, those who might wish to take a second job, those who are considering a promotion, and those who might like to start a part-time business. Some of these people now believe they are punished for being ambitious. They often pay many times more for any specific government program, such as national defense, than someone who voluntarily chooses to work less. They feel suckered by the bulk of taxpayers. But with the ability-to-earn principle, you would pay just so much in taxes, no matter how much you actually earned. Income from moonlighting and the like would not be taxed.

The second advantage is that people would be encouraged to make full use of the abilities and education they have. They would also have second thoughts about going to college with no real goal in mind, which often wastes the resources of society.

The third advantage is that tax liabilities would be easier to determine. The problems of unreported income would cease to exist because what your actual income is doesn't matter.

There are also some disadvantages to the ability-to-earn principle, probably enough to doom its introduction. First, it would discourage people from getting educated. Both the length of their education and how well they did in classes would be reduced in many cases.

Second, a GPA earned in one school doesn't indicate the same earning capacity of a GPA from another school. A 3.5 GPA at Harvard indicates a much higher likelihood of earning a high income that does, say, a 3.5 GPA at Podunk U.

Third, if IQ scores were factored into the formula to determine taxes, there would be several problems in using them. They are not always accurate because of various testing problems, including a cultural bias against certain minorities.

But above all, the main value in considering a different kind of taxing principle is that it encourages us to think about our currently used taxing principles. We then learn about the weaknesses and strengths of those principles, and we might be led to work out some of the problems with them.

Why Aren't People Who Cheat on Their Taxes Money Ahead?

Some people do not report all of their income to the IRS. They include most people working in the "underground economy," some waiters and waitresses, and some taxi drivers and others who receive tips. Also, some business owners who receive cash for their products, such as bar owners, underreport their sales. All of these people pay less in income taxes because of their cheating.

But in terms of money in their pockets after all is said and done, the average person in these groups is no better off. Further, some might actually be *worse* off, while some indeed do gain somewhat, but always less than they save in taxes.

The analysis of this situation depends upon the law of equimarginal returns and the free flow of resources into occupations and industries. The law essentially states that the total net package of an occupation tends toward equality with that of all other occupations. For example, people in occupations having a lot of "psychic income" (pleasant, interesting, and challenging work) tend to earn less money than people in other occupations. The same thing holds for "psychic costs," where more of these costs lead to a higher money income. Thus, the "net gain" of working, equal to the money income plus the psychic income minus the money cost (uniforms, commuting expenses, etc.) and the psychic costs tend toward equality for all occupations. Essentially, this means when *all things* are considered, one occupation is about as "good" as any other.

Suppose none of these people has yet ever underreported their income. Then suddenly they all start to do it. Initially, they will perceive no change in wages, psychic income, or the cost of working. But their saved taxes could be interpreted as a form of money income, or at least it has the same effect as an increase in wages. With no change in the job itself or in any aspect of other occupations, some people working in other occupations now consider changing jobs. When everyone *did* pay their taxes, and when everyone continued working in the same field, it meant that everyone's opportunity cost of working was covered (otherwise they would want to switch jobs).

Some honest people now find that their opportunity costs are no longer covered because these costs rose. That is, some of the jobs they gave up earlier (taxi driving, etc.) now "pay" more because less taxes are paid when working at them. So gradually people begin to seek employment where they, too, can cheat on their taxes. However, because there is no change in demand in any occupation, these job switchers cause labor surpluses to develop in the occupations they move into. There is now a lower equilibrium wage in each of these occupations, and eventually wages will fall to that lower equilibrium. It will continue to fall so long as new entrants into the "dishonest" occupations perceive advantages there. Thus, ultimately the tax cheaters are in the same boat financially after taxes have been considered. It was all for nothing.

Bar owners face a similar situation. If everyone knows you can get away with underreporting sales so that net income can be higher, the profit rate will be higher than it is for an industry requiring similar skills and capital requirements where cheating cannot be done. Eventually there will be a net inflow of resources into the bar industry in the form of people and the bars they own. But customers don't wish to drink any more because of such inflows. Consequently, a surplus of drink-selling capacity occurs, and drink prices fall. Thus, the ultimate gainers are not the bar *owners*, but the bar *customers*. However, if licenses are limited so new bars cannot be established, the real estate prices of existing bars rise because the demand for taverns rises but the supply remains constant. New owners then may cheat all they want, and they *have to* cheat just to come out even after paying the inflated price of the tavern.

On top of all this, many tax cheaters often have a guilt trip to bear as well. And as all their attempts to come out ahead financially were for nothing, they have a *net loss* after all is said and done. Economics is so cruel!

What Has *Your* Price Index Done Recently?

A price index is a representation of all prices. In the case of the Consumer Price Index, 400 representative items of everything we buy are used to represent the price level of all goods and services. If this price index rose by x percent in a year, then we know that all prices rose by x percent, on average. In turn, you know that you will have to spend x percent more each year in that year just to buy the same items you bought in earlier years.

This is all true if you are "typical urban wage earner," meaning that you have the same spending habits as the hypothetical urban wage earner that the Bureau of Labor Statistics assumes exists. However, there are at least three ways that you could differ from this "typical person." That will, in turn, limit the usefulness of the price index for you. First, you could have a different product mix than typical buyers. For example, you might purchase significantly more pinto beans, kerosene, nylon windbreakers, and concert tickets than a typical person. If these items aren't in the 400 sampled, and if the prices of these items rise very little or very much compared with the 400 items selected, the price index will give a distorted indication of what you personally will experience with respect to price increases. Your product mix can be significantly different from the typical person for several reasons, among them being differences in culture, age, income, and tastes.

The second reason why the price index might give you a distorted view of your relevant prices could be that you could be a "sale shopper" and a coupon-clipper far more than most people. Thus, the prices you pay aren't the same as those surveyed by the Bureau. A final reason would be if you pay cash for everything and have no loans on your car or house. Then the interest component of the Consumer Price Index has no relevance to you.

To have a more accurate price index and to calculate your "personal inflation rate," you need to do some calculations. First, you need to calculate a cash flow statement for a year. That statement will show how much money you spend on food, housing, and all other major categories in a year. Second, find the share or percentage each category was of your total expenditure on goods and services. (Such expenditures do not include taxes, charity, union dues, fines, etc.) Third, find how much the prices of these categories of items rose in a year. You could use the government's index for such categories or you could calculate the price increases of your own special categories of goods and services.

Finally, you need to calculate a weighted average of the price increases of all these categories. This takes into consideration how important each category of items was compared with the others as well as the price increase of each category. This weighted average is found by multiplying the share of total expenditures of the first category by the percent increase in prices of that category, then adding that to the share of total expenditures of each of the other categories by the percent increase in prices of each of the other categories.

When you have a weighted index for two consecutive years, you can calculate your "personal inflation rate" by finding what percent your index rose over that two-year period.

What Difference Will It Make to Your Great-Grandchildren if GDP Grows at Three Percent Rather Than Two Percent?

One percent of anything doesn't sound like much, so it is something that will concern few people. But if the people are your great-grandchildren and you are now very young, they would be concerned.

The convenient Rule of 72 gives us quick insight into the effect of economic growth. This rule allows us to see how many years it takes something to double. That number of years is found by dividing 72 by the percent increase in some variable. Take population growth, for example. If it grows at 2.4 percent per year, the population will double in 30 years (= 72/2.4).

Real GDP per capita, a measure of the living standard, usually grows each year. If it grows at one percent per year, it will take 72 years for the living standard to double. A growth rate of two percent per year will double our living standard in 36 years (= 72/2), and it will take 24 years to double if we grow at three percent per year (= 72/3).

Suppose you wanted to know your great-grandchildren's living standard 72 years from now as compared with yours. If our economy grows at two percent, the living standard will be four times as high as today. That's because it will double in 36 years and double again in the next 36 years, or twice in 72 years, and 2 x 2 = 4. If the economy grows at three percent, however, the living standard will rise eight times because it will double every 24 years, or three times in 72 years, and 2 x 2 x 2 = 8. Thus, the living standard will rise by twice as much (eight times compared with four times) if the growth rate is only half again as much (three percent compared with two). That's the power of compounding.

You may ask, "What do I have to do with all of this?" A lot, as the growth rate depends upon what we do today. If we would save more of our income, eventually much of it would be used for investment in new and improved plant and equipment in businesses. That would boost our efficiency and productive capacity. Other things that we can do to increase the growth rate include: improve the education system, improve the infrastructure, and shift our economic focus from the short-run view to the longer-run view. Your great-grandchildren would be thankful.

Should Drug Dealers and Prostitutes Be in the Labor Force?

The U.S. Government counts people as unemployed only if they are: 1) not earning a paycheck from a private business or a government enterprise; and 2) actively seeking employment by reading the want ads, filling out job applications, etc.

Generally, drug dealers, prostitutes, and others who engage in illegal economic transactions do not fulfill either of these criteria. Therefore, the government does not include them among the unemployed. Consequently, they are also not included in the labor force.

But should they be? After all, they are engaging in economic activities, however objectionable to many. So they are productive in the purely economic sense and are, therefore, expending labor (time). If they weren't productive, they couldn't sell anything for very long. Thus, the government's unemployment figures are not quite accurate for this reason. Specifically, official unemployment rates are higher than they should be. For example, suppose the government says the labor force is 120 million. If it finds six million people who are unemployed, the unemployment rate is five percent (= 6 ÷ 120 x 100). If there are four million "other employed," as discussed above, the "true" labor force is now 124 million. There are still six million unemployed, so the unemployment rate falls to 4.84 percent (= 6 ÷ 124 x 100).

Why Should You Care What Prices Are?

People are very often concerned about how much money they pay for things. After many years of expressing such concerns and after comparing current prices with past prices, many people believe that the level of prices itself is a problem. They make the mistake of thinking that one *level* of prices, in and of itself, is better than another, without thinking of anything else that is related to those price levels.

Italians and Japanese "pay much more" for items than we do, such as several thousand of their units of account (lira and yen) for a lunch. We usually pay less than 10 of ours (dollars). But that doesn't bother them to pay so much more than we do, and it shouldn't. It's not the price, *per se*, that is important. It's the price as compared with one's income that counts. Take a car, for example. Say its price is $20,000. If your net income is $5,000 per year, you will probably never buy it. It would take you 48 months to pay for it without having any money with which to buy anything else. If, however, you earn $40,000, you could pay for it with six month's salary and could easily purchase it.

As the years go by, then, the thing to be concerned with is how long you have to work to buy various items. Then, even if lunches eventually cost you $10,000, you couldn't care less because you would only have to work five minutes to pay for them if you earned $120,000 per hour.

What Effect Does Counterfeiting Have on the Living Standard?

The living standard reflects the amount of goods and services produced in a nation in a year for each person, on average. It is found by dividing the total output of goods and services by the population.

Therefore, it is clear that the amount of money in circulation will have no influence on the living standard, at least not directly. You may find some who will argue that the living standard is affected indirectly by the influence that money has on total output. But that effect would be very slight and of short duration. If it were possible to increase the living standard by having more money in circulation, all the government would have to do is print it and pass it around. But that wouldn't work, so the government doesn't bother.

Even if some people successfully engage in counterfeiting, the living standard would not increase because their actions would neither increase total output nor reduce the population. However, their *incomes* would increase, as they could now have more goods and services "coming in" to them. But then less is available for everyone else, so it's pretty much of a wash nationwide.

But not quite, for if they do consistently get away with counterfeiting, they may eventually quit working. And if they don't work, they can't produce goods and services. Thus, total output would fall (though very slightly) and so would the living standard.

Did Cavemen Have Recessions?

It is easy for people to see the outward signs of a recession: reductions in spending, production, profits, employment, and income. However, it is more difficult to see the more elementary thing that occurs during a recession. Therefore, people often can't answer whether or not cavemen faced recessions, too. They didn't.

It is vital to realize that the spending we do on goods and services is the modern counterpart to the trading in economies of the past. Those trades were done because specialists had excesses of the items they made after producing for their own needs. They *had* to trade these excesses because it was the only way for them to get the items they did *not* make. Charity would not have been up to the task.

Employees in today's factories, offices, labs, and shops aren't really all that different than earlier specialists. People make tires, bubble gum, repairs, vinyl, and other items that others get to use. But people today don't directly trade these items for what they want. Their employers give them the value of what they produced in the form of paychecks.

In today's recessions, some people are simply less willing to make trades than they were earlier. That is, they buy fewer goods and services. Of course, the obverse of that is that merchants and manufacturers are also trading fewer goods and services away. In turn, they have less reason or less ability to trade for resources. That is, they cancel plans to buy capital equipment or to expand their buildings, and they hire fewer laborers.

Cavemen didn't trade like we do or even as people did a couple of hundred years ago, when barter was much more common. And trade of the self-sufficient, agrarian economies of the 1700s and early 1800s was very limited compared with today. But it was certainly more voluminous than tens of thousands of years ago.

Therefore, if cavemen didn't trade, they couldn't *reduce* the amount of trading they did. And if recession is essentially a reduction in trading, they could not have experienced recessions.

What Good Is a Recession?

There is an old saying that is probably supposed to give comfort to those in dire straits: There is good and bad in everything. Recessions can be pretty nasty situations, so what good could we expect out of one?

Actually, there are at least six major ways that some or all participants in an economy can benefit from a recession. It doesn't mean that all these benefits combined exceed the cost of a recession. It merely shows that there is good and bad in at least *one* thing.

First, recessions encourage firms to become more efficient in order to reduce their costs. If they don't, they are more likely to go bankrupt. Managers of firms facing recession are more likely to alter jobs, the use of machinery, management techniques, and anything else that might squeeze costs out of an operation. The 1980-82 recession was especially effective in changing many firms into leaner operations so they could better withstand the 1990-91 recession.

Second, in a similar way, governments are forced to become more efficient during a recession because revenues fall and requests for government aid rise at that time.

Third, the inflation rate invariably falls during a recession because falling demands for goods and services reduce the opportunity for firms to raise prices as much. In fact, you may hear some people say that at times we need a recession to bring down the inflation rate. That's the same sort of logic that states that because we need a fire to roast a pig that we should burn down the house. It works, but what a cost!

Fourth, the savings rate increases during a recession. Actually, that may *cause* a recession. But in the long run, a higher rate of savings will lead to a higher rate of investment in capital goods. This occurs because increased savings will lead to reduced interest rates. In turn, the increased capital stock will increase our living standard at a faster rate in the future. Thus, assuming that the increased savings rate becomes permanent, a recession could eventually lead to a higher economic growth rate.

Fifth, some industries actually do better during a recession. These include repair businesses because people are less likely to buy new appliances, cars, and so on in a recession. Resale shops and sellers of lower-quality merchandise also do better in bad times. Consumer credit companies and pawnshops also have a larger volume of business during hard times.

Sixth, for a more philosophical argument for recession, bad times lead many of us to be more aware of how good the good times were (and will be when they return). Many people who remember the Great Depression and witnessed the occasional extravagance, decadence, avarice, and greed of the 1970s and 1980s can be heard to say, "What we need is another depression."

What if Half of Everyone's Money Vaporized?

Suppose the economy has been in an equilibrium state for some time, with no recession and no inflation. There also has been full employment. There has been no economic growth, and there has been a constant money supply and a velocity of circulation. The prices of all items would be at equilibrium and would not change in this equilibrium state.

Now suppose that half the money supply suddenly vaporized. Half the currency and coins you (and everyone else) hold would disappear. If you had two $20 bills, you'd have only one. Half of all checking account deposits would disappear (for example, a $216 balance would shrink to $108). In addition, suppose everyone's income was cut in half. Would it make much of a difference in the things that really count in the economy? No, not much, if anything.

The most important thing to note is that there would be no change in our productive capacity. All our machines, buildings, and working skills would be left intact. But if our incomes were cut in half, the demand for every good and service would fall very sharply. Thus, soon after the money vaporized and our incomes fell, manufacturers and merchants would face huge surpluses of their goods and services. Consequently, prices would soon fall. Bear in mind that the firms' expenses already had fallen because of the wage cuts, so they would have plenty of room to cut their prices and still earn their normal profits. Eventually, prices of all goods and services would fall to about half of what they were initially. Because our *money* incomes were cut in half, as were prices, our real incomes (or the living standard) would be unchanged. And that's what really counts.

In essence, this is what happens when a country introduces a new currency. Countries generally do this when hyperinflations lead to ridiculously high prices for everything. The currency people have carries many zeros, and perhaps a 100 or 1,000 peso or mark or whatever unit-of-account note would be the smallest used. Wallets and handbags bulge with currency needed for minor shopping trips. The new currency is often 1,000 or more times "smaller" than the old currency, but it is worth that many times more. For example, people may receive one unit of the new currency for 10,000 of the old currency.

Uruguay did an unusual thing in the 1970s, which essentially amounted to 99.9 percent of its money vaporizing. It called in all its paper notes of denomination 1,000 pesos and larger. It then rubber stamped each with a number one thousandth as large. All "old" 1,000-peso notes became a "new" one-peso note. All 10,000-peso notes became 10-peso notes, and so on. It was cheaper to do that than print up an entire new currency, and the effect was the same. Prices quickly became only one thousandth of what they were originally.

Should We Blame Inflation on Business Owners Who Raise Prices and Union Leaders Who Push for Higher Wages?

It seems pretty simple. Inflation means prices are going higher. Business owners like it when prices are higher. They make more money that way. And who put the price tags on all those items you see in stores? You—or the owners of the firms? The owners, of course. So, stopping inflation is a simple matter of "eliminating" any business owner who raises prices too much. But economic issues are not always as simple as they seem. Let's take a look at just two flaws in the analysis above.

First, there are a lot of goods and services being sold for much less than we are *willing* to pay. Think of all the flavoring you get from a box of salt, which might last a single person a whole year. If you've ever eaten unsalted vegetables or meat, you know the value of that salt. You would perhaps pay several hundred dollars a box if you had to. That or eat bland food all the time. Yet, you've never even paid one dollar for a box, and you usually pay much less than that. There are countless items like that, including life-saving medicines, pencils, gasoline (Europeans pay three to four times what Americans do), and potatoes. Why don't the "money-hungry" manufacturers and merchants charge the prices they would *like* to—much higher ones? It's not because they are stupid, ignorant, or nice. It's because *they* don't set the prices. Those prices are determined in a complex interplay of many forces, all working through the concepts of supply and demand. Owners of firms don't generally "set prices." They are merely the ones with the most knowledge of the markets they deal in, including where *supply and demand* "set the prices." Owners of firms merely note what the prices are, but they are set elsewhere.

The second point to make is that there is often confusion between high prices and rising prices. When people think prices are high, they could mean that they are higher than you would expect them to be. Perhaps a lower expected price stems from the belief that the item cost relatively little to produce. People could also believe that high prices are the result of complex or otherwise expensive production processes. This sort of a reason is more readily accepted, as in the case of a tailor-made suit.

But *high* prices are not the same as *rising* prices. Therefore, even if owners of firms are to blame for high prices because they have the power to set them, it doesn't mean they have the power to move them up at the rate they do. That rate is, of course, the inflation rate. Perhaps it would be useful to make a comparison. Suppose you held a pot against a ceiling with a long pole. Also suppose the ceiling can move vertically, like an elevator in its shaft. Perhaps someone shorter than you couldn't reach the ceiling with the pot. Perhaps another person could but couldn't hold it too long because of a lack of strength. Only you can keep the pot ("prices") high. But if the ceiling rises, can you control how fast the pot will *rise*? No, because someone else controls where the ceiling will be and how fast it will rise, if indeed it does. If the ceiling rises at eight percent per minute and you are tall enough and strong enough, you can push up the pot higher at a rate of eight percent per minute. You, of course, do not determine the eight percent rise in the pot's height, but people might think you have that power. The power is in the hands of whoever is on the controls of the elevating mechanism.

In economics, the power to affect how fast prices rise does not reside in the hands of business owners, any more than you had the power to determine the rate at which the pot rose. The power to establish the rate of price increases is possessed by those who control the Federal Reserve System. But business owners often take the rap.

Union leaders and the rank-and-file also often get blamed for inflation. Employee wages are part of the expenses of firms. These expenses, when added to the necessary profit margin needed to remain in business, determine the prices of the goods and services we buy. Therefore, when striking union members succeed in increasing their wages, they make the expenses of their employers rise. In turn, prices must rise, putting us in an inflationary state.

When employees receive an increase in wages, they receive more money in a year. That money must come from somewhere, but where? From their employers, you might say. But doesn't that mean that, after paying all their expenses (which are now higher), that there is less left over for profits? True, you respond, but they raise prices to generate enough extra revenues to cover their extra expenses. All right, but aren't buyers now able to purchase less because of higher prices? That will cause a recession. But because recessions are relatively rare and wage increases are not, apparently the wage increases *don't* cause recessions. So what prevents recessions? The buyers must be able to compensate their cut in purchasing power (when prices rise) with an increase in purchasing power in the form of higher incomes. After all, wages *did* increase.

This all seems to neatly explain the cost-price spiral you occasionally hear about. *Seems* is right, as the explanation misses an important point. Notice that the total volume (or dollar amount) both of expenditures on goods and services as well as the payment for labor services is higher after these increases in wages and prices. There are only two ways to get such an increase in the volume of transactions. First, the same amount of money must be getting spent more quickly. This, of course, means the velocity of circulation must increase. Second, there must be more money in the economy. This is what actually explains the increase in the volume of transactions most of the time.

Is there any employee who can increase the money supply? No, for only the Fed can do that. So union members and their leaders are no more to blame for inflation than business owners.

Who Created More Jobs—President Reagan or President Washington?

Not to be outdone by George Bush, Bill Clinton, running for re-election in 1996, boasted about the millions of jobs that were created during his first four years in office. The implication was that he was largely responsible for this growth. The implication of neither man was truthful. But perhaps both Bush and Clinton actually believed they had such powers, so it can't be said that they were lying to get votes.

What if there were no president? Or no government, for that matter? Would there be any jobs? Or any job growth over any eight-year period? If the word "jobs" means people are working, then yes, there would be jobs and job growth. This is not an unreasonable scenario, for there have only been governments (and presidents or other leaders) for a tiny fraction of human history. Thus, if people did *not* have jobs (worked, that is), they could not have survived. And given that the population grew over the past several million years of human existence, then the number of jobs must have grown as well.

How was this possible without a president? Remember that Say's Law states that "supply creates its own demand." Over a period of time, it implies that the more output that is produced (supplied) in an economy, the more power there is to purchase (demand) goods and services. One way that is possible to produce more output is to have a larger population. So, the more people there are, the more output there is, the more that is demanded, the more that is sold–and *the more jobs there are*. Thus, job creation can occur with or without presidents. If it occurs when there are presidents, it doesn't mean they create the jobs any more than they create the rainfall that occurred during their terms in office.

A president might be able to make a reasonable claim to have created jobs by pointing to some specific acts. These could include public works projects, education programs, export-promotion programs, and dozens of others. However, there are two possible flaws in this reasoning. First, these actions could lead to offsetting job *losses* for any number of reasons (which are too lengthy and complex to be covered here). But few people would either recognize such job losses or would associate them with these government actions. Thus, the president would *seem* to have a case. Second, had these actions *not been taken*, some other actions might have occurred in the economy to create the same number of jobs. Like what? Like all the things that happened before the 1780s when presidents first appeared.

Who Shot Liberty Valence?

In the 1960s film epic, "The Man Who Shot Liberty Valence," Jimmy Stewart rode to fame in a western town, which led to a seat in the U.S. Senate, on the popular belief that he shot and killed the town bully, Liberty Valence, played by Lee Marvin. Stewart played an idealistic young lawyer from the East, who shunned force and the use of guns to settle disputes. But he was finally goaded into a gunfight with the bully, in which Valence was killed. John Wayne played his normal role, a tough, no-nonsense man who wasn't afraid of Valence. But of course, he also scorned the lawyer's meekness. Hiding out in the dark during the gunfight, Wayne killed the villain in the same instant the lawyer fired (and missed). However, only Wayne knew that, so the wrong man got the credit for the death of Liberty Valence. But it didn't matter. Only the outcome did.

In economics, however, it does matter who gets the credit. In October 1979, Paul Volcker, chairman of the Federal Reserve Board, along with the other board members, sought to reduce the inflation rate by cutting back sharply on the growth of the money supply. This policy was intensified throughout 1980. Eventually, the policy was successful in reducing the inflation rate from over 12 percent down to three percent through much of the early 1980s.

A large share of the American public was unaware of who Volcker was and what he did. So a former actor got the same credit that Jimmy Stewart did. The public believed that he was the person who tamed inflation. That former actor's name: Ronald Reagan. That myth was very handy in his 1984 re-election bid against Walter Mondale. People love inflation-slayers.

The curtailment of the money supply growth had another effect, this one not so salutary. It produced the recession of 1980, which actually extended into 1982 after a brief lull. It was the worst recession since the Great Depression. When many Democrats, who knew very well who caused the recession, tried to lay the blame on the Reagan administration, Reagan coolly responded, "Who, me?"

Democrats and Republicans alike will often let you believe economic myths if you don't have the ambition to sort out fact from fiction. Anyhow, it was a great "remake" of "The Man Who Shot Liberty Valence."

What if the Marginal Utility of Everything Were Zero for Everyone?

The marginal utility (MU) refers to the extra satisfaction received when consuming one more unit of something. If your MU exceeds zero for Good X, it means you would find it useful to have one more unit of Good X. If the MU is zero, it means that an extra unit of Good X provides you no satisfaction. It would have no value.

There are many things you would like to have now because they would provide more satisfaction than you currently receive. You could likely find use for a new car, or a second or third car, or a sportier or more luxurious car. A larger or more luxurious house or apartment would also likely please you more than your current one. Therefore, the marginal utilities of many items are positive for you and everyone else (except, perhaps, billionaires).

But if all your marginal utilities were zero, it means that no matter how many additional goods and services you get or how much additional quality you receive, you will be no happier. If everyone was in the same situation, society as a whole could be no better off in terms of its economic welfare. Thus, we would no longer face a scarcity of resources. If we can't make use of any additional good or service, then we have no use for any additional resources with which to make them. We would have solved the economic problem.

When Should You Start an IRA or a 401(k)?

Some people believe they will be able to retire on their Social Security checks. Others believe that Social Security, plus their employer-provided pensions, will get them through. But many others are not counting on either to be large enough (or to be there to begin with). They put money away each year into an Individual Retirement Account (IRA) or an employer-associated 401(k) or 403(b) plan. Each allows you to avoid income taxes on an amount of income equivalent to what you have saved until you draw out that money upon retirement.

These are superb ways to save money, if, indeed, you believe saving is wise for yourself (it doesn't necessarily have to be). The question is, when should you begin such programs? Only you can answer that because only you can tell when it is best to exercise your purchasing power (spend your money): soon after you earn it or in the future. Again, only you can best determine that. However, you will find very many people saying the best time to save is the present. That is, start as soon as possible, perhaps right after college. Those are the sort of people who tell you what to order in a restaurant, as though they know your tastes better than you do.

Whenever you start, you should be very aware of the effects of compounding. Let's say that you are able to earn a six percent return on money placed in some tax-deferred retirement plan. Left untouched, each of the dollars you salt away will grow to two dollars in 12 years. They will double again every 12 years. If you retire at age 65, a dollar saved at age 53 will be worth two at 65. But if you save a dollar at age 41, it will turn into *four* dollars at 65. And if you save a dollar at age 29, that dollar will become *eight* dollars at 65.

Of course, the period of time for your nest egg to double will vary with the interest earned. Higher rates will shorten the period, and lower rates will lengthen it. Nevertheless, the earlier you save a dollar, the longer it can work for you and the more it will grow to by the time you retire.

ANSWERS TO PROBLEMS

CHAPTER 1

1. a) **Bob**, who cuts 10,571 square feet per hour (= (9,000 + 5,000 + 12,000 + 11,000) /3.5), is more efficient than Jason, who cuts 8,500 square feet per hour (= (8,000 + 4,000 + 12,000 + 10,000) /4).

   b) **Sara** is more efficient, as she can make 15.45 crusts per hour (= 85/5.5), while Julie can make 15.0 crusts per hour (= 90/6).

   Julie can make a crust in exactly **four minutes** (= 60/15). Sara can make a crust in 3.883 minutes or **three minutes and 52 seconds** (= 60/15.45).

   c) **Kristin** is more efficient, as she cleans as much area per hour as Ken (= 180 square feet = 7,200/40 = 5,760/32) but has to work with smaller windows. Thus, she has to work with more edges and corners, which take much time, for the same area.

2. a) i-**815** (best of 815, 466, and 720)
   ii-**720** (best of 652, 466, and 720)
   iii-**815** (best of 652, 815, and 720)
   iv-**815** (best of 652, 815, and 466)

   b) **She will buy the CD player**, as the 815 "satisfaction units" she receives exceed her opportunity cost of the 720 "satisfaction units" she could have had by having her car tuned up.

   c) Given that the numbers listed represent her actual benefits, **she should still get the CD player,** as it provides more benefits (815) than she gets from the tuneup (720).

3. a)

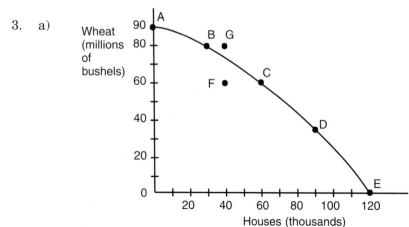

b) First: **10 million bushels of wheat** (= 90 - 80); second: **20 million bushels** (= 80 - 60); third: **25 million bushels** (= 60 - 35); and fourth: **35 million bushels** (= 35 - 0).

c) The first 30,000 houses are built with carpenters who are very poor farmers, as society has little to lose when they *don't* produce wheat. The second 30,000 houses are built with *former* wheat farmers. However, as they are better farmers than the first group that became house builders, more wheat must be given up to get the second set of houses as compared with the first. This shows that the law of increasing costs is in operation.

d) The **zone of inefficiency**   e) The **zone of impossibility**

CHAPTER 2

1. a) **demand falls** (as grapefruit juice is a substitute source of vitamin C), **supply is unchanged, price falls,** and **quantity falls**
    b) **demand rises** (benefits of oranges rises), **supply is unchanged, price rises,** and **quantity rises**
    c) **demand is unchanged, supply falls** (production costs rise), **price rises, and quantity rises**
    d) **demand rises** (prices of complement falls), **supply unchanged, price rises, and quantity rises**
    e) **demand is unchanged, supply rises** (an innovation lowers cost), **price falls, and quantity rises**
    f) **demand falls** (buyers wait for lower prices), **supply is unchanged, price falls,** and **quantity falls**

2.

Price	Q-Demanded	Q-Supplied
$12	24	16
$13	23	17
$14	22	18
$15	21	19
$16	**20**	**20**
$17	19	21
$18	18	22
$19	17	23
$20	16	24
$21	15	25
$22	14	26

Equilibrium price is $16, and the **equilibrium quantity is 20 million.** With a price ceiling of $14, there will be a **shortage of 4 million CDs** (= 22 - 18). With a price floor of $21, there will be a **surplus of 10 million CDs** (= 25 - 15).

CHAPTER 3

1. With one shift, the **labor productivity is 4.18 shirts/hour** (= 48,620/11,640).
   With two shifts, the **labor productivity is 4.35 shirts/hour** (= 95,460/21,960).

   The first shift has 11,640 hours of labor (= 260 + 16) x 40 + 12 x 50).
   The second shift adds 10,320 hours of labor (= 240 + 14) x 40 + 4 x 40) for a total of 21,960 hours on two shifts.

   It takes **14 minutes and 21 seconds** to make a shirt on the first shift (= 60 minutes/4.18 shirts per hour), and it takes **13 minutes and 48 seconds** to make a shirt when there are two shifts (= 60 minutes/4.35).

   The average cost will tend to fall after adding a second shift because it takes less time to make a shirt (and "time is money").

2.

	Output Level		Opportunity Cost	
Person	Bagging	Stacking	Bagging	Stacking
Debra	12	36	3.00 cartons	0.33 customers
Jim	14	31	2.21 cartons	0.45 customers

Debra has a comparative advantage in stacking (as 0.33 is less than 0.45).
Jim has a comparative advantage in bagging (as 2.21 is less than 3.00).
Debra has an absolute advantage in stacking (as 36 is more than 31).
Jim has an absolute advantage in bagging (as 14 is more than 12).

3. The point of diminishing marginal returns occurs with the **third clerk** as the marginal product falls to $1,200 from $1,400.

4. **The single, larger building is more efficient** because the same amount of building materials is used for the floor and the ceiling, even though the walls are twice as high. With the two smaller buildings, twice as much floor and ceiling materials are needed for same storage capacity as a single, large building. Thus, the single building should be built, as the storage cost per box is lower. This indicates that there are increasing returns to scale as the building becomes larger. (See the following figures for proof.)

Building Section	Building Size and Square Footage for Building Section	
	100 x 100 x 10	100 x 100 x 20
Walls	4 x 100 x 10 = 4,000 sq. ft.	4 x 100 x 20 = 8,000 sq. ft.
Floor	100 x 100 = 10,000 sq. ft.	100 x 100 = 10,000 sq. ft.
Ceiling	100 x 100 = 10,000 sq. ft.	100 x 100 = 10,000 sq. ft.
Total	24,000 sq. ft.	28,000 sq. ft.

Building materials needed for 200,000 boxes are 48,000 square feet for the two smaller buildings (2 x 24,000) and 28,000 square feet for the single building. The total cost of building materials for the two smaller buildings is $240,000 (= 48,000 x $5) and $140,000 for the single building (= 28,000 x $5). The average cost of storing a cubic foot of boxes is $1.20 for the two smaller buildings (= $240,000/200,000) and $0.70 for the single building (= $140,000/200,000).

5. The relative price for a refrigerator fell from **0.2 appendectomies** (= $400/$2,000) to **0.15 appendectomies** (= $600/$4,000). The relative price for an appendectomy rose from **5.0 refrigerators** (= $2,000/$400) to **6.7 refrigerators** (= $4,000/$600).

The relative prices changed this way because it was more possible to find innovations (mechanization, most likely) in the manufacture of refrigerators than in doing an appendectomy (because each patient is different, thereby demanding human involvement).

CHAPTER 4

1. Just the design and prototype cost for the Cadillac is $800 per car (= $80 million/100,000). This cost is only $100 per car for the Chevrolet (= $70 million/700,000). These costs are part of the average fixed cost (AFC) of car manufacturing. As average cost (AC) includes AFC, the larger volume of Chevrolets made allows the average cost to be lower than for the Cadillac. Consequently, the price for the Chevrolet tends to be lower for this reason alone.

2.

Firm	Total Revenue	Total Cost	Gross Profit	Net Income	Assets	Liabilities	Net Worth	Net Margin	Rate of Return on Equity
A	$800,000	$600,000	**$200,000**	**$160,000**	$4.0 mil.	$2.4 mil.	**$1.6 mil.**	**20%**	**10%**
B	$40 mil.	$38 mil.	**$2 mil.**	**$1.6 mil.**	$60 mil.	$40 mil.	**$20 mil.**	**4%**	**8%**

3.

Assets		Liabilities	
Accounts Receivable	$16,000	Loans	$44,000
Bonds	$3,000	Accrued Wages	$2,000
Cash on Hand	$11,000	Accounts Payable	$2,000
Capital Equipment	$15,000	Accrued Taxes	$8,000
Land and Buildings	$210,000	Total Liabilities	$56,000
Total Assets	$255,000	**Net Worth**	**$199,000**

4.

Output	Total Fixed Cost	Total Variable Cost	Total Cost	Total Revenue	Profit (Loss)
0	$100	$0	$100	$0	($100)
1	$100	$220	$320	$220	($100)
2	$100	$300	$400	$440	$40
3	$100	$390	$490	$660	$170
4	$100	$530	$630	$880	$250
5	$100	$690	$790	$1100	$310
6	$100	$910	$1010	$1320	$310
7	$100	$1160	$1260	$1540	$280

The output level (Q) to maximize profit is **5 or 6,** where the level of **profit is $310.**

The break-even point is **between the first and second unit.**

CHAPTER 5

1:

Wage	Demand	Supply
$16	10	110
$15	20	100
$14	30	90
$13	40	80
$12	50	70
$11	**60**	**60**
$10	70	50
$9	80	40
$8	90	30

a) **$11 per hour**
b) **60**
c) **Shortage of 60 workers** (= 90 - 30)
d) **Surplus of 100 workers** (= 110 - 10)

2.   Of Professor Robert's suggestions:
   a) will cause a labor surplus and falling wages (bad suggestion)
   b) will cause a labor shortage and rising wages (good suggestion)

   Of Professor Green's suggestions:
   a) will cause a labor surplus and falling wages (bad suggestion)
   b) will cause a labor surplus and falling wages (bad suggestion)

   Of Professor Hanson's suggestions:
   a) will cause a labor shortage and rising wages (good suggestion)
   b) will cause a labor shortage and rising wages (good suggestion)

   Of Professor Rollin's suggestions:
   a) will cause a labor shortage and rising wages (good suggestion)
   b) will cause a labor surplus and falling wages (bad suggestion)

   Professor Hanson's suggestions are the best, as both are likely to succeed.

CHAPTER 6

1. a) **Abbaland–0.6 brandy   Bonoland–2.5 brandy**

    In Abbaland, as producing 200 wine forces it to forgo 120 of brandy, each unit of wine forces it to give up 0.6 brandy (=120/200). In Bonoland, as producing 160 wine forces it to forgo 400 brandy, each unit of wine forces it to give up 2.5 brandy (=400/160).

    b) **Abbaland–1.67 wine** (=200/120)   **Bonoland–0.40 brandy** (160/400)
    c) **Wine** (as 200 is larger than 160)
    d) **Brandy** (as 400 is larger than 120)
    e) **Wine** (as 0.6 is less than 2.5 – see answer a)
    f) **Brandy** (As 0.4 is less than 1.67 – see answer b)
    g)

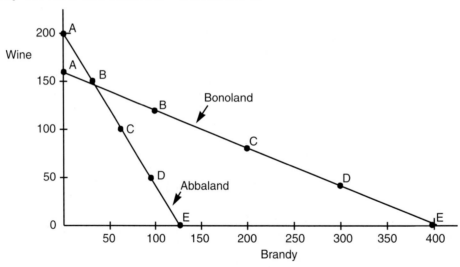

    h) Now there are 190 wine produced (=150 + 40) and 330 brandy (= 30 + 300) in both countries combined. If Abbaland specializes in wine, there will be 200 wine produced (a gain of 10), and if Bonoland specializes in brandy, there will be 400 brandy produced (a gain of 70).

2.   It takes 25 percent more ($10/$8 x 100) to buy a liter of wine. Thus, it now takes $1.25 to exchange for 3,200 lira, rather than $1.00 as earlier. Therefore, the new exchange rate is **$1:2,560 lira** (= 3,200/1.25).

3.   **Before: $4,000.00** (= 80,000/20)
       After: $4,444.44 (= 80,000/18)

4.   **Before: $288** (= 180 x $1.60)
     After: $270 (= 180 x $1.50)

5.   There is a **deficit** in Year 2 of $100 billion (= $650 - $550). It is **smaller** than in Year 1, when it was $150 billion (= $600 - $450).

6.   Toyota's selling price is **$8,000** (= $10,000/1.25). The U.S. Customs Department charges 25 percent of $8,000 (or $2,000) upon entry into the United States, bringing the total cost to $10,000.

CHAPTER 7

1.   **No,** for a tax of 30 cents forces him to pay $2.60 (= $2.30 + $0.30), which is still below the $2.80 he is willing to pay. **A tax of 60 cents will cause him to stop smoking**, as his benefit (= $2.80) is less than his cost of $2.90 (= $2.30 + $0.60).

2.   **It could subsidize rose bushes by more than $4.** For example, the city could pay rose bush dealers a rebate of $5 for every bush they sold if they agree to reduce the price by an equal amount. Then the price would be $7 (= $12 - $5), leading Jane to buy the rose bush.

3.

	Income Level		Percent of Total Income		
Time	Poorest Fifth	Richest Fifth	Poorest Fifth	Richest Fifth	Total Income
1	$8,000	$80,000	4.0%	40.0%	$200,000
2	$16,000	$160,000	4.0%	40.0%	$400,000

The income gap grew from $72,000 in Time 1 (= $80,000 - $8,000) to $144,000 in Time 2 (=$160,000 - $16,000). Total income in Time 1 is $200,000 (= 1/0.4 x $80,000 or = 1/0.04 x $8,000). As the average of all groups doubled by Year 2, so does the total income, to $400,000. Thus, **the poorest fifth still earns four percent of the total income** (= $16,000/$400,000 x 100), **and the richest fifth still earns 40 percent of the total income** (= $160,000/$400,000 x 100).

4.   The present value of $100,000 received 10 years from the present is **$61,357** (= $100,000/$1.05^9 = $100,000/1.6298).

Incidentally, if the money was received one year in the future (or in Year 2), the present value equals $100,000/1.05; if received two years out (or in Year 3), the present value equals $100,000/(1.05 x 1.05); etc.

CHAPTER 8

1. **$214 billion**, which equals the size of the deficit, found by subtracting total receipts of $972 billion (= $58 + $914) from total outlays of $1,186 billion (= $860 + $326).

2. **$248 billion.** The budget deficit was $160 billion that year (= $1,680 - $1,520), so it had to sell at least $160 billion in bonds. But some of the previous debt was paid off ($88 billion) as well during the year. As that could only have come from borrowed money (obtained through bond sales), the total bond sales for the year were $248 billion (= $160 + $88).

3. **$3,610 billion** (= $4,920 - $480 - $210 - $620)

4.

Taxpayer	House Value	Income	Taxes	Percent of Income Paid in Taxes
Bob	$110,000	$42,000	$2,100	5.00%
Bill	$220,000	$90,000	$4,200	4.67%

It is **regressive,** as a lower-income earner (Bob) pays a higher percent of his income (5.00%) in property taxes than a higher-income earner (Bill, who pays 4.67%).

One cannot say if Darian's property tax is regressive overall because it is necessary to know the average property tax bill of *all people* earning $42,000 as well as for all people earning $90,000. It could be that Bill has a much less valuable home than most people who earn $90,000 (or vice versa for Bob). Thus, the tax could actually be progressive, the opposite of what it appears to be here.

5. **Yes, it did.** Actually, the tax is progressive, as the percent of income paid in sales taxes rises from 2.28% to 2.88% as income levels rise from $10,000 to $60,000. (See the following to see where these percentages came from.)

Type of Tax	Income Level	Sales Taxes Paid	Percent of Income Paid in Taxes
Selective Sales Tax	$10,000	$228 (= 0.06 x 9,500 x 0.4)	2.28% (= 228/10,000)
	$60,000	$1,728 (= 0.06 x 48,000 x 0.6)	2.88% (= 1,728/60,000)
General Sales Tax	$10,000	$570 (= 0.06 x 9,500)	5.7% (= 570/10,000)
	$60,000	$2,880 (= 0.06 x 48,000)	4.8% (= 2,880/60,000)

A general sales tax is regressive, as the percent of income paid in taxes falls from 5.7% for the taxpayer earning $10,000 to 4.8% for the taxpayer earning $10,000.

CHAPTER 9

1. The price index 10 years prior to the base year was **84.4** (= 2,750/3,260 x 100).
   The price index in the base year was **100.**
   The price index 10 years past the base year was **133.1** (= 4,340/3,260 x 100).

2. **143.6** (= 100 x 0.436 + 100)

3. **119.2** (see the table)

Year	Price Index
Base Year	100.0
2	103.6 (= 100 x 0.036 + 100)
3	107.8 (= 103.6 x 0.041 + 103.6)
4	109.2 (= 107.8 x 0.013 + 107.8)
5	111.6 (= 109.2 x 0.022 + 109.2)
6	**119.2** (= 111.6 x 0.068 + 111.6)

4. **1.18%** (= (162.5 - 160.6)/160.6 x 100)
    2.22% (= (166.1 - 162.5)/162.5 x 100)

5. **$1,173 billion** (= 635 + 120 + 16 + 46 + 362 + 65 - 71)

6. **$3,952 billion** (= 6,359/160.9 x 100)

7. **$4,757 billion** (= 5,250 x 90.6 x 100)
    The price level fell since the base year.

8. **$3,546 billion** (= 3,280 x 1.063 x 1.017)

9. **$4,308 billion** (= 4,157 x 1.018 x 1.018)
    As prices did not change, **current GDP rose at the same yearly rate of 1.8%.** In order to know the dollar amount of current GDP, **the size of the price index needs to be known.**

10. **$6,547 billion** (= 6,750/1.031)

11. **$4,782 billion** (= 4,870 - 46 - 42)

12. **137 million** (= 6.3/4.6 x 100)

13. **1.5 million.** 5.0 million are out of work in total (= 131.6 - 126.6).
    Thus, the amount of cyclical unemployment is 1.5 million (= 5.0 - 2.2 - 1.3).

CHAPTER 10

1. **$16 billion** (= 3,539 - 863 - 2,680 - 40)

2. **$55.4 million** (= 860 x 0.89 - 710)

3. **$522.5 billion** (= 460 + 10/0.16)

4. **12.5%** and **0.125** (= $5/$40)

CHAPTER 11

1. **A recession would occur** because total spending would fall by $10 billion, as the increase in consumer spending of $80 billion made possible by a drop in $80 billion in savings is more than offset by a drop of $90 billion in injections (I and G).

2. **Savings must fall by $26 billion.** There is a net fall in injections of $24 billion (= $23 up from G minus $47 down from I). Taxes rise by $2 billion, thereby forcing C to fall by $2 billion. Therefore, total spending falls by $26 billion (= 24 + 2). To offset that, savings must fall by the same amount ($26 billion).

3. **Construction must rise by $5 billion.** Savings rise by $15 billion (= 0.05 x 300). To maintain equilibrium, investment must rise by $15 billion. As capital expenditures rise by $10 billion, construction must rise by $5 billion (= 15 - 10).

4. a) **aggregate supply falls**
    b) **aggregate supply rises**
    c) **aggregate demand rises**
    d) **aggregate demand falls**

5. The price level could fall to 100 if either:
    a) **aggregate demand falls while aggregate supply is unchanged**
    b) **aggregate supply rises while aggregate demand is unchanged.**

    The price level could rise to 180 if either:
    a) **aggregate demand rises while aggregate supply is unchanged**
    b) **aggregate supply falls while aggregate demand is unchanged.**

6. His personal MPS is **0.4** (= ($6,000 - $4,000)/$5,000). His MPC = **0.6** (= $30,000/$5,000).

7. a) **3.3** (= 1/(1 - 0.7))
    b) **10.0** (= 1/0.1)
    c) **5.0** (= 1/0.2)
    d) **10.0** (= 1/(1 - 0.9))

8. **$6,100.** The multiplier equals 1/(1 - 0.8) or 5. Total spending rises $100 billion (= 20 x 5). Thus, the new equilibrium rises by $100 as well, from $6,000 billion to $6,100 billion.

490

CHAPTER 12

1.   **Year 1**, where the real interest rate was the lowest. The real interest rate for each of the years were:
   a) Year 1: 3.4% (= 9.5 - 6.1)
   b) Year 2: 4.8% (= 8.5 - 3.7)
   c) Year 3: 5.6% (= 7.5 - 1.9)

2.   Case 1: **1.03 times** (= 1.01 x 1.01 x 1.01)
        Case 2: **1.33 times** (= 1.1 x 1.1 x 1.1)
        Case 3: **8 times** (= 2 x 2 x 2)

3.   Total spending rises by **$20 billion** (= 60 - 20 - 10 - 10), as:
   a) T fell $60 billion, leading to C rising by $60 billion (assuming that MPC = 1.0)
   b) S rose $20 billion, leading to C falling by $20 billion
   c) I fell $10 billion
   d) G fell $10 billion

   One cannot tell whether there will be inflation or not until it is known what the levels of potential GDP and actual GDP are.

4.   **$5,250 billion.** The multiplier is 2.5 (=1/(1 - 0.6)). Thus, as I rises by $100 billion, the equilibrium GDP rises by $250 billion (= 100 x 2.5) to $5,250 billion. One would not expect demand-pull inflation, as the potential GDP is $6,000 billion. Therefore, the extra spending would lead to extra output, rather than shortages.

5.   **The price level would fall by 1.1%.** Total spending (MV) would rise by 1.4% (= 1.6 - 0.2). But as total output rises by 2.5%, surpluses develop, leading to price decreases.

6.   **The money supply would have to rise by 1.5%**, equal to the difference between the 1.8% rise in output and the 0.3% rise in velocity.

7.   **Labor productivity rose 6.9%.** Labor productivity was initially 7.55 (=1,630/216) but rose to 8.07 (=2,260/280). Thus, it rose 6.9% (= (8.07 -7.55)/7.55 x 100).

8.   Labor cost in Year 1: **60.0¢** (= $8.00/(6,400/480) = 8/13.3)
        Labor cost in Year 2: **66.7¢** (= $9.00/(7,000/520) = 9/13.5)

CHAPTER 13

1. Bond yield in Period 1: **6.2%** (= 600/9,700 x 100)
    Bond yield in Period 2: **6.3%** (= 600/9,500 x 100)

    The higher bond yield means the Fed raised interest rates. It did so to reduce spending or aggregate demand, most likely to prevent inflation.

2. Before: **$9,302** (= 800/0.086)
    After: **$9,756** (= 800/0.082)

3. **The multiplier is 5** (= 500/100), as total spending and GDP must rise by $500 billion to reach potential GDP. Thus, **MPC = 0.8,** for 5 = 1/(1 - 0.8)

4. Before: **$10,000 billion** (= $2,000/0.20)
    After: **$15,000 billion** (= $2,700/0.18)

Note: Tax Collections = Tax Rate x National Income

CHAPTER 14

1.

	Number Eaten					
	1	2	3	4	5	6
MU of Hot Dogs	120	100	90	70	40	20
MU of Pizza Slices	280	180	100	60	20	10
MU / dollar Spent on Hot Dogs	**120**	**100**	**90**	**70**	**40**	**20**
MU / dollar Spent on Pizza Slices	**140**	**90**	**50**	**30**	**10**	**5**

Becky should eat **three hot dogs and two pizza slices** per month, as the third hot dog and the second pizza slice each provide her 90 "satisfaction units per dollar."

If she had eaten none or few of each, **she likes pizza slices more.** For instance, the first slice provides 280 "units," greater than the 120 for the first hot dog. The same holds for the second and third unit of each. However, the *fourth* slice satisfies her less (60) than the fourth hot dog (70). as do the fifth and sixth. That implies that **she tires of pizza slices more quickly than hot dogs** (also implied by the faster decline in the marginal utilities for pizza than for hot dogs).

2. **Net worth: $104,380**

Assets		Liabilities	
Tax refund due	$200	Bills to pay	$620
House value	$117,400	House mortgage	$80,300
Checking balance	$400	Auto loans	$7,600
Auto value	$18,400	TOTAL LIABILITIES	$88,520
Savings bonds	$6,700		
Savings account	$20,500		
Stocks held	$8,200		
Pension value	$21,100		
TOTAL ASSETS	$192,900	NET WORTH (= A. - L.)	**$104,380**

INDEX